MODERN CANADA

MODERN CANADA

1945 TO PRESENT | EDITED BY Catherine Briggs

OXFORD
UNIVERSITY PRESS

OXFORD
UNIVERSITY PRESS

Oxford University Press is a department of the University of Oxford.
It furthers the University's objective of excellence in research, scholarship,
and education by publishing worldwide. Oxford is a registered trade mark of
Oxford University Press in the UK and in certain other countries.

Published in Canada by
Oxford University Press
8 Sampson Mews, Suite 204,
Don Mills, Ontario M3C 0H5 Canada

www.oupcanada.com

Library and Archives Canada Cataloguing in Publication
Modern Canada : 1945 to present / edited by Catherine Briggs.

Includes bibliographical references and index.
ISBN 978-0-19-543240-4 (pbk.)

1. Canada—History—1945-. I. Briggs, Catherine, 1965-, author,
editor of compilation

FC600.B75 2014   971.064   C2013-907160-1

Cover images: *Top row*: Hockey: Richard Lautens/GetStock.com; Charter signing: © Government of Canada.
Reproduced with the permission of the Minister of Public Works and Government Services Canada (2013). Source:
Library and Archives Canada/Credit: Robert Cooper/Canada. Office of the Prime Minister collection/e008300499;
Middle row: Pride flag/Canadian Flag: ©iStockPhoto.com/carterdayne; Peacekeepers: UN Photo/Eskiner Debebe;
Expo 67: © Government of Canada. Reproduced with the permission of the Minister of Public Works and Government
Services Canada (2013). Source: Library and Archives Canada/Expo 67 (Montréal, Quebec) collection/e000988793;
Bottom row: Girl holding flag: © iStockPhoto.com/phi2; Elijah Harper: John Hryniuk/GetStock.com;
Parliament: ©iStockPhoto.com/AK2

Printed and bound in the United States of America

1 2 3 4 — 17 16 15 14

Contents

Contributors

Stephen Azzi
  Carleton University
Stephanie Bangarth
  King's University College, University of
  Western Ontario (Western University)
Michael D. Behiels
  University of Ottawa
Raymond Blake
  University of Regina
Catherine Briggs
  St Jerome's University, University of Waterloo
Ruth Compton Brouwer
  King's University College, University of
  Western Ontario (Western University)
Dominique Clément
  University of Alberta
Ryan Edwardson
  Trent University and independent researcher
Alvin Finkel
  Athabasca University
Augie Fleras
  University of Waterloo
Barbara Freeman
  Carleton University
Michael Goldfield
  Wayne State University
Matthew Hayday
  University of Guelph
Matthew Hennigar
  Brock University
Robert Huebert
  University of Calgary
Brooke Jeffrey
  Concordia University

Małgorzata Kieryło
  Canadian Museum for Human Rights
Tina Loo
  University of British Columbia
Hector Mackenzie
  Department of Foreign Affairs and International
  Trade (Canada) and Carlton University
Mark J. McLaughlin
  University of New Brunswick
David Newhouse
  Trent University
Bryan D. Palmer
  Trent University
Carmela Patrias
  Brock University
Andrew Preston
  Cambridge University
Sean Purdy
  University of São Paulo
Matthew Roth
  University of Waterloo
Robert Rutherdale
  Algoma University
Christabelle Sethna
  University of Ottawa
Corey Slumkoski
  Mount Saint Vincent University
Miriam Smith
  York University
Chance Minnett Watchel
  University of Calgary
David Webster
  University of Regina

Acknowledgements

I would like to thank Caroline Starr and Tanuja Weerasooriya at Oxford for their commitment to this project and Judith Turnbull for her excellent copyediting. Special thanks to Tanuja for her ongoing encouragement during the various stages of this book and for her invaluable assistance in determining and compiling content and dealing with the many obstacles along the way.

I would also like to thank all the contributors to this collection, particularly those authors who prepared new, previously unpublished articles thereby bringing interesting and exciting new insights to this study of the post 1945 period. Many of the contributing authors deserve extra acknowledgement for their collegial support and warm humour and for their willingness to make suggestions and aid on other components of the book.

Special thanks to my colleague at St Jerome's, Ryan Touhey, for giving me a "crash" course on the state of scholarship in Canadian international relations which greatly aided in the development of that part.

Finally, warm thoughts are due to my partner, Susan Smarda, for her patience and invaluable support during the many days and weeks that this project commanded my attention.

The author and publisher would like to thank the many reviewers whose thoughtful comments and suggestions have helped to shape this book.

Introduction

The period from 1945 to the present was one of fundamental change in the nation, socially, politically, economically, and culturally. In many ways, it can be construed as a revolutionary era, as the Canada that existed before 1945 bears little resemblance to the country and people that evolved in the decades following the Second World War. Still, the term "revolution" may seem too extreme, as this fundamental transformation in Canada did proceed, for the most part, in a peaceful and orderly manner (perhaps in keeping with the Canadian national character). The articles in this book seek to reveal the fundamental change that has transformed and redefined Canada as a nation. While change has most certainly characterized Canada since 1945, there is no doubt that in many areas this change is not complete. As well, there is no doubt that the nation continues to face challenges and issues that cause uncertainty, division, and conflict. However, along with their exploration of this uncertainty, division, and conflict, these articles will also reveal the evolution of Canada in the direction of tolerance, diversity, and greater social justice.

Economic and Demographic Context

To understand the developments of the postwar years, we need to examine the economic and demographic trends of the period. While the state of the economy (and the related population factors) did not directly cause the changes and challenges faced by postwar Canadians, it certainly facilitated change and the pace of change. Two major trends have been noted for Canada's economy since 1945. First, the economy experienced structural changes that significantly altered the sectors in which Canadians were employed. Most of these changes had begun in the late 1800s, such as the decline in agricultural and resource-based employment. The increase in service-sector employment, while also evident before 1945, accelerated dramatically in the postwar years owing to overall growth in the economic prosperity of Canadians, which increased their demand for services and led to the vast expansion of health, education, and social services. The other major feature of the economy since 1945 is growth. As Norrie *et al.* state, "[T]he economy today is larger, richer, and much altered compared to that of 1945." In 1950, the gross domestic product (GDP) was $127 billion compared with $908 billion in 2004. If one were to account for population growth, it is noteworthy that GDP per capita still more than tripled (Norrie *et al.* 2008, 362).

To examine the economic developments of the postwar period beyond the above two common characteristics, it is useful to divide the period into two time frames, 1945 to 1973 and 1973 to the present. While Canadians have experienced a much larger, wealthier, and diverse economy, the approximately 25 years following the Second World War were a "golden age" of economic prosperity, security, and stability, characterized by high employment levels, rising wages, and an improved standard of living. Economic prosperity facilitated even greater security and opportunity through the expansion of health, education, and social services. These "boom" years witnessed massive population growth and greater ethnocultural diversity as a result of the postwar baby boom (the large generation of children born between 1945 and 1965) and large-scale immigration. By the mid-1970s, however, the economic boom came to an end, leaving the nation to face debt, recession, and insecurity. Governments at all levels began to question government intervention in the economy and implemented cutbacks to social spending while Canadians grappled with higher unemployment and inflation. While the population boom would also slow down by the 1970s, the impact of the postwar cohort would continue to influence the nation's direction fundamentally, while the transition to diversity would continue, and even accelerate, after 1970 because of changes in immigration laws. All of these issues need to be explained because they affected or influenced the other political, economic, and social transformations examined in the chapters of this book.

1945–1973: Prosperity and Growth

On a number of macroeconomic indicators, the years from 1945 to 1973 were characterized by growth and prosperity. Average growth rates, measured in terms of real GDP, saw an impressive 6.4 per cent increase each year between 1950 and 1973. Unemployment rates also reveal the general economic security and stability of most Canadians, fluctuating but for the most part remaining below 3.6 per cent from the late 1940s until 1958. An economic downturn from 1958 to 1962 resulted in unemployment rates going above 6 per cent, but overall the average unemployment rate for the entire period from 1950 to 1973 stayed in the 4 to 6 per cent range. Between 1944 and 1978, the average income of Canadians more than doubled, a substantive improvement in standard of living even when inflation is taken into consideration. While the inflation rate did soar during the Korean War, it remained in the healthy range of 1 to 2 per cent per year until the mid-1960s (Norrie *et al.* 2008, 362; Bothwell *et al.* 1981, 10–13). In general, these were good years, giving Canadians, for perhaps for the first and only time, a long period of sustained economic health and security.

A number of factors contributed to this 25-year economic boom, a few of which are discussed below, as they pertain to other challenges and changes experienced in these years. One important factor—the international environment—provided a number of opportunities for expanded markets and greater demand for Canadian products. Canada emerged from the war undamaged physically and structurally and with greatly expanded economic productivity and capacity as a result of its wartime production. Canadian exports thus found markets among European countries devastated by war, particularly given the American decision to allow monetary credits under the Marshall Plan to be spent in Canada. American demand and markets for Canadian products also increased steadily through this period, spurring growth in a number of economic sectors but significantly in resources. Americans continued to purchase prewar products, such as pulp and paper, but also demanded new ones, such as potash, uranium, iron-ore, and, importantly, oil and natural gas. US demand for western oil, accompanied by rising international prices and driven primarily by American corporations, precipitated a massive expansion in productivity and investment in the exploration, extraction, and distribution of Alberta oil, leading to Alberta's own 30-year boom (Taylor 2009, 158–60). US demand for Canadian products was driven by an overall expansion of the American economy, in part resulting from the United States' economic leadership in the postwar Western world, but also from the US military-industrial complex. As the United States assumed the role of a superpower and leader of the Western world, the threat and at times reality of military engagement with the Soviet Union led to a constant state of preparedness, facilitating a vast expansion of defence production that required many of Canada's products. Finally, trade between Canada and the United States (and other countries) grew significantly because of the general liberalization of trade and capital flows in the years after 1945, the result of multilateral negotiations through measures like the General Agreement on Tariffs and Trade (GATT) and of a number of Canada-US agreements for preferential treatment. The impact of these combined factors was a fundamental reorientation in Canada-US trade patterns. Canadian exports to the United States were 38 per cent of all Canada's exports in 1946 (Britain and Western Europe, 47 per cent), but had already risen to 65 per cent by 1950 and would continue to rise (Norrie *et al.* 2008, 374). The United States had become Canada's major trade partner, a reality that by the late 1950s led some Canadians to raise nationalist concerns about Canada's ability to make autonomous decisions on international matters, given this high level of integration and, potentially, dependence.

Consumer spending and demand similarly spurred economic growth. It is generally agreed that there was considerable pent-up consumer demand among postwar Canadians. For average Canadians in the immediate postwar period, the experience of deprivation during the Depression and of shortages in basic goods during wartime rationing created both a real and a psychological need for basic goods and consumer extras. It could be argued that in 1945 the psychological insecurity of the preceding 15 years had created a need for security and stability, which postwar Canadians sought to gratify, partially, through the acquisition of better homes, cars, appliances, and a wide range of consumer goods. Postwar Canadians achieved high levels of consumption because of the excellent employment rates, rising incomes, and relatively stable inflation rates noted above. As well, as Canadians received steadily higher levels of education and as more of them, including married women and mothers, entered professional and service-sector occupations, the household income of average Canadians steadily increased. The baby boom further expanded consumption. Postwar parents had to purchase new and larger homes, as well as more toys, clothes, and consumer goods, to give the desired material security to their children (see Owram 1996). As Norrie *et al.* point out, housing starts in 1962 went from a "healthy 150,000" to an "amazing 268,000" in 1972. Houses, in general, were also larger in size and supplied with more up-to-date appliances and heating (Norrie *et al.* 2008, 380).

Economic growth and prosperity was also the result of a high level of government spending that expanded demand and employment. In the immediate postwar years, the federal government directed spending towards easing the transition to peacetime, to avoid the economic and social dislocation that had occurred after the First World War. Under a range of programs that came to be referred to as the Veteran's Charter, the federal government facilitated veteran re-establishment through demobilization grants, medical care and pensions for the disabled, credits and loans for the expansion or starting up of small businesses, and vocational training through free university or technical education (accompanied with a living allowance). Such measures were widely credited with easing the veterans' transition to employment and economic security; indirectly they also jump-started the economy through millions of dollars of spending (Bothwell *et al.* 1981, 99). Infrastructure development also encouraged economic growth and market development, particularly in industries related to the US economy. The joint Canada–US St Lawrence Seaway project, which deepened and improved the canal system to permit larger ocean vessels to pass, allowed for improved shipping of resources such as iron-ore to the United States. The Trans-Canada Pipeline brought natural gas from Alberta to the demand centres of central Canada, furthering the expansive production of this new resource.

Perhaps the most significant increase in government spending related to economic growth and the overall economic prosperity of Canadians resulting from the development of the welfare state. By war's end, a consensus existed among average Canadians, policy analysts, social scientists, and politicians regarding the need to develop policies and programs, paid for through public money, to provide universal health care, accessible and expanded higher education, and economic security programs to shield Canadians from poverty and destitution. In fact, an evolving concept of "social citizenship" held that these initiatives were not only desirable so as to promote greater equality in the conditions of Canadians but in fact were entitlements held by Canadians. Freedom from want became a new right of citizenship in Canada as in many other countries. Previous to 1945, Canada had developed few social welfare measures; the main programs that did exist were veterans' benefits and an old age pension, both of which were based on means testing and provided meagre assistance. In the years 1945 to approximately 1973, however, the structure and main components of the welfare state were put in place—for example, the Old Age Security Act and the Old Age Assistance Act (1951); the Canada Pension Plan/Quebec Pension Plan (1966); the Hospital Insurance and Diagnostic Services Act (1957); the Medical Care Act (1966); and the Canada Assistance Plan (1966) (see Finkel 2006). Many of these programs required federal-provincial cooperation, as these areas fell under provincial jurisdiction even though the federal government had greater access to financial resources. The need for federal assistance owing to the substantial cost involved resulted in the greater centralization of power and increasing cooperation during this first period, but gradually it precipitated an increase in federal-provincial tension and regionalism. There is no doubt that the welfare state developed in these first years as a result of the economic prosperity and growth of this era; economic prosperity provided the revenue to fund the programs, and in turn the welfare state facilitated economic growth through the provision of a minimum level of economic security (thus maintaining people's ability to consume), an expansion of jobs in the service sector, and infrastructure development, such as hospital and postsecondary education buildings to house these services. Budget surpluses, together with wide public support, led governments at all levels and of all political parties to support welfare state expansion, even as these programs quickly came to dominate government spending.

The wide public support of welfare programs stemmed from what has been termed "postwar liberalism." Politicians and average Canadians emerged from the Second World War with vivid memories of the devastating poverty and economic instability of the Depression and the limited and ineffective government efforts to ameliorate these conditions. In contrast, government economic management during the war years provided an alternative model, one that had facilitated the full employment, stable prices and wages, and economic growth and productivity that had allowed for a total mobilization. Anxiety about a return to depression and a desire for economic security and stability led policymakers and average Canadians to believe that government could and should continue to intervene in the marketplace to stabilize or even out what many had come to believe were natural boom-and-bust periods in a free-market, capitalist economy. Keynesian economics, first developed in the 1930s, argued that the goals of full employment and an end to poverty could be achieved by contra-cyclical government policies by which governments would increase and encourage spending during times of economic downturn and decrease spending during unhealthy inflationary spirals. Through the 1945–73 period, politics and public policy utilized Keynesian concepts to achieve the main goals of postwar liberalism—a minimum level of economic security and equality of opportunity for all citizens. Universal medicare, expanded access to education, and social security were principle policies towards achieving these goals. While public policy at times violated pure Keynesian concepts, as evidenced by the massive infrastructure spending during times of economic growth, politics was nonetheless characterized by a great increase in government intervention in the economy and in the lives of citizens.

Related to the economic growth of this period was a similar boom in the population. During these years, the Canadian population rose from around 11.5 million in 1941 to 18.5 million by 1962 and 22.5 million by 1973. Most of this population growth in the period up to 1962 was the result of the postwar baby boom. Social planners had expected an increase in the birth rate following the war, as couples reunited and society returned to normal, but not one that would last 20 years! Yet, the experience of the Depression, followed by six years of war, meant that young Canadians had delayed marriage and family formation and experienced sustained insecurity and instability. The combined impact was a postwar generation of young adults who craved security and stability, measured in part through materialism, as noted, but also through an idealized notion of "traditional" family life. Postwar couples married at higher rates and settled down to a family life based on the traditional gender norms of the homemaker, the stay-at-home mother, and the breadwinning father (see Owram 1996). As a result, the fertility rate rose dramatically starting in 1946. The average number of children per woman aged 15 years to 49 was 3.1 to 3.5 during the 1920s, but dropped below 3 for most of the Depression. By 1945, the fertility rate began to skyrocket, reaching a high of 3.9 in 1957 and 1961, and then began a gradual decline, dropping to 1.8 in 1974 and remaining below that level ever since (HRSDC, n.d.). The result would be a large increase in population and a significant generation that would have a great impact on the social, political, and economic history of the postwar years. Owing to the size of the baby boom generation, their concerns and needs would shape public policy, leading, for example, to an expansion in educational facilities once they entered school and influencing the direction of social movements once they reached their teenage and young adult years. Part of the familism of postwar Canadians was their strong focus on giving their children all the material goods and opportunities they had lacked. Thus, the baby boom would also drive the high levels of consumption that characterized the years from 1945 to 1973.

An additional factor in population growth during these years was immigration. The economic boom of the postwar years led to a demand for more workers, both skilled and unskilled; the increase in jobs was also fuelled by the shortage of workers because of the low birth rates during the Depression and the war. Economic demand, combined with international pressure on Canada to open its doors to displaced persons and refugees in response to a number of refugee crises, led Canada to relax its admissions criteria. From 1946 to 1962 (one of the highest periods of immigration in the nation's history), 2,151,505 immigrants entered Canada, along with a 250,000 refugees (Kelley and Trebilcock 1998,

311–13). Labour-market needs generally influenced the selection of immigrants, even including refugees to some extent, with an emphasis on agricultural workers and labourers in the earlier postwar period shifting to a greater emphasis on skilled-trades people and professionals over time. While economic criteria were primary in immigrant selection, officials generally preferred immigrants from north and western Europe. However, by the early 1950s, applications from these preferred countries began to decline as their own economies recovered. With the influx of refugees, primarily from eastern European countries such as Poland and Hungary, the ethnic composition of immigrants and, thus, of Canada slowly began to diversify by the 1960s.

While economic growth and labour-market demands would lead Canada to open its doors during these years, additional factors would propel fundamental changes in immigration policy, resulting in greater cultural and ethnic diversity. In 1945, Canada's immigration policy was largely exclusionary; criteria focused primarily on who would *not* be admitted as opposed to outlining the principles and objectives of immigration for Canada (Knowles 2007, 203–4). Exclusionary criteria included race and ethnicity, which—combined with the substantial discretionary power exercised by immigration officials—left Canada with an openly racist and discriminatory immigration policy. However, early in the postwar years, social movements emerged to challenge racism and discrimination and to fight for the protection of the rights and freedoms of all Canadians. Internationally, events such as the Holocaust in the Second World War, the refugee crises, and decolonization movements in the developing world increasingly raised awareness of racism, discrimination, and the oppression of minorities among average Canadians. Further, Canada's active participation in world affairs through the United Nations and the multi-racial Commonwealth, as well as the idealistic image held by many of Canada as a peacekeeper and objective middle-power, soon led to opposition to racist and discriminatory policies and laws by a wide range of Canadians. The first major revision of immigration policy was in 1962 when race, colour, and country of origin were removed as criteria for consideration of immigrant applications. Instead, unsponsored immigrants were to be evaluated on the basis of new criteria concerned mainly with skills, education, and training. The emphasis on economic criteria, primarily labour-market suitability, was further codified in 1966 when the points system was introduced as an objective means to assess these economic criteria (Knowles 2007, 195). Overall, these changes resulted from a combination of the human rights discourse with a changing view of immigration as a positive factor in economic growth (Kelley and Trebilcock 1998, 315).

1973–Present: Economic Stagnation and Change

In the early 1970s, Canada's economy, along with that of other western industrialized countries, began to display some disturbing signs of stagnation and even decline in terms of macro-economic performance. In terms of percentage change in real GDP, Canada experienced significantly slower and unstable economic growth in the years from 1973 to 1982 with an actual decline of 3 per cent with the 1982 recession. Economic growth strengthened through the rest of the 1980s but began to decline in the early 1990s, with another real decline of 2 per cent in 1991. Following this second serious recession, growth rates stabilized, with an average annual growth rate of 2.6 per cent from 1993 to 2005 (Norrie *et al.* 2008, 402). While these GDP rates were healthy, they were still below the economic growth seen in the boom years.

More troubling for Canadians than unstable and slower growth rates were the combined problems of high unemployment and inflation that characterized the 1970s and 1980s. The unemployment rate began to rise around 1973, reaching 7.1 per cent in 1975, having gone above 6 per cent for the first time in the postwar years except for the brief economic downturn of 1958 to 1962. The unemployment rate continued to rise, reaching a high of 11.3 per cent in 1984, after which it first declined until 1989 but rose again to reach double digits—11.4 per cent—in 1993. Unemployment then began another decline, stabilizing around 6 to 7 per cent from 2000 to the present, except for the 2009 recession. Although the unemployment rate has stabilized, Canadians have not seen a return to the excellent rates below 6 per cent that characterized the 25-year period after 1945. These troubling unemployment patterns coincided with similar patterns in the rate of inflation. Together, high inflation accompanied by high unemployment was referred to as "stagflation." Inflation rose from 3 per cent in 1971 to over 7 per cent in 1973, and would remain relatively high, reaching rates between 10 and 12 per cent from 1980 to 1982. Inflation declined for the remainder of the 1980s but skyrocketed up to the double digits again from 1989 to 1991. Since 1991, the inflation rate has declined and stabilized at around 2 per cent per year (Norrie *et al.* 2008, 402). While high unemployment combined with a rising cost of living was problematic for individual Canadians, it presented real challenges to government in terms of developing fiscal or monetary responses. Keynesian concepts of contra-cyclical spending presented a conflict. High unemployment should be addressed by increasing spending directed at job creation, but high inflation demanded a contraction of the money supply. Not surprisingly, this contradiction left policy-makers uncertain about how to respond and that led them to examine the internal and external economic factors behind these economic problems.

A number of complex and interconnected factors caused Canada's decline in economic performance, some of which were the result of changes in Canada since 1945. Rising unemployment was partially due to an increase in the numbers of those desiring employment, notably through the 1970s and early 1980s, as the large baby boom cohort began to enter the labour force. The boomers' demand for jobs was even more pronounced because this generation included women as well; women's labour force participation had increased substantially by the early 1970s because of women's obtaining higher levels of education and job training and the impact of the women's movement. Ultimately, the natural rate of unemployment had risen by the 1970s because, thanks to the influx of large numbers of young people, including women, the overall labour force was larger relative to the demand. As well, technological and structural changes in the economy sometimes called for skills that Canadians lacked. In addition, with Canada's relatively good employment insurance benefits, Canadians may have been reluctant to retrain or to relocate in pursuit of employment (Norrie *et al.* 2008, 404).

More troublesome were problems relating to the international competition facing certain sectors of the Canadian economy. By the 1970s, Japan had recovered from the devastation of the Second World War and had developed an efficient industrial sector, effectively competing for North American markets in key products, such as cars, electronics, and, increasingly, computers. Over the period, Japan would be joined by other emerging economies, such as Korea, Taiwan, and China. In addition, Canadian manufacturing (and other sectors) faced additional costs and disadvantages relating to such competition, as it had to comply with more stringent environmental and labour standards, higher wages, and the expense of supporting social security programs and employee benefit plans. The presence of foreign, primarily US, multinationals in key economic sectors led to profits potentially going out of the country, a lack of re-investment in Canadian subsidiaries, and decisions made in the best interests of the parent country. While politicians and policy-makers struggled throughout the 1970s to develop policy responses to these issues, by the early 1980s a fundamental reorientation occurred in concepts about government "management" of the economy.

By the early 1980s, politicians and policy-makers in Canada (and elsewhere) began to advocate neo-liberalism, both as a theory to explain economic problems and as a way to respond to them. Neo-liberal theorists argued that the economic problems since the 1970s were the result of the barriers or distortions in the capitalist marketplace caused by government intervention since 1945. In particular, they charged that government regulations and subsidies, as well as Crown corporations, were measures that distorted the marketplace or impeded competition and initiative. While neo-liberals were not specifically opposed to government provision of social programs, such as health care, they did point to the extensive cost of these programs and called for reduced social spending to address growing government deficits, both provincially and federally. Ever-increasing levels of government debt could not be sustained and were causing high inflation. With the election of Brian Mulroney's Progressive Conservatives in 1984, neo-liberalism replaced postwar liberalism as the dominant ideology guiding public policy. As a result, governments since 1984 (regardless of party affiliation) have pursued neo-liberal policies directed towards reduced government intervention in the economy and facilitating greater marketplace control. Deregulation occurred in many areas, such as the removal of government-set grain rates to allow railways to compete with the trucking industry and the decision to allow more private competitors into the airline and phone service industries. Another notable example is offered by the oil industry. After 1984, the Mulroney government moved quickly to dismantle most of the taxes and regulatory measures of the National Energy Program (NEP), ostensibly placing the energy sector under the control of the international marketplace. This measure was viewed positively by Alberta (and the other oil-producing provinces), as the NEP had been a source of considerable federal-provincial tension in that it seemed to favour the interests of consumers in central Canada to the disadvantage of the producers (Taylor 2009, 187–9, 240–2). In the 1970s, provincial governments began to challenge the centralization of federal power that had evolved since 1945, arguing against federal encroachment in areas of provincial jurisdiction. By reducing federal intervention in the economy, neo-liberalism indirectly promoted a decentralized model of federalism that recognized the relative autonomy and power of the provinces and focused specifically on "national" matters such as foreign policy and international trade.

Decentralized federalism has become a central tenet of most federal governments since 1984, in part due to the ideology of neo-liberalism and in part to the challenges posed by Quebec nationalism and to some extent by the demands of the First Nations. However, federal withdrawal from areas of provincial jurisdiction has had negative ramifications for the welfare state. Although Canadian politicians and policy-makers have consistently voiced support for the main components and principles of the welfare state, particularly universal health care, governments have sought to cut government spending, balance budgets, and lower taxes as part of the neo-liberal agenda. The implications for social spending have been significant. Since the 1970s, no major new social programs have been introduced and federal governments have gradually reduced their financial commitment to fund the programs that existed. From a commitment of 50 per cent federal funding for health care under the 1966 Medical Care Act, the federal role has steadily declined. Faced with a large deficit in 1996, the Liberals merged the transfer payments for health and those for social assistance programs (formerly under the Canada Assistance Plan, 1966) into a single transfer, with a drastic cut in funding levels. With cuts to transfers such as these, consecutive federal governments have weakened much of their influence (through regulations or provisions as to how the money can be spent), strengthening provincial authority but potentially diminishing national uniformity and increasing regional inequity.

A second component of neo-liberal ideology, and an important change in the economic direction for Canada since 1980, has been trade liberalization. Faith in a self-regulating free-enterprise economy applied also to international trade; barriers to trade such as tariffs were to be removed to allow open and free competition and the easy trade of goods among nations. In 1989, Canada signed a free-trade agreement with the United States by which all barriers to the free exchange of goods and services were to be removed within 10 years. Proponents of the agreement argued that it would give Canadian business and exports secure access to the vast American market. Similarly, they pointed to the fact that globalization was already underway. Trade liberalization was proceeding with measures such as the GATT negotiations, albeit slowly, and trading blocs such as the European Economic Union had begun to form. The expansion of world trade with the addition of countries like Japan was also a reality. As well, many Canadian politicians and business people were aware of protectionist tendencies within the United States, having experienced the "Nixon shocks" of the 1970s, which strengthened their conviction that Canada needed to secure access to US markets or face even greater economic distress (Taylor 2009, 235–40; see also Muirhead 2004). Trade liberalization proceeded with the free-trade bloc expanded to include Mexico in 1993 (North American Free Trade Agreement [NAFTA]) and with Canada agreeing to enter the World Trade Organization (WTO) in 1995, a body empowered to make and adjudicate trade disputes. While free trade has brought many economic benefits to Canadian business, it has also led to renewed concerns about Canadian sovereignty and about control of decision-making in economic policy. Mechanisms for resolving trade disputes, whether through NAFTA or the WTO, potentially could diminish Canadian control over matters such as resource conservation and environmental regulations if these were to be viewed as trade barriers. Economic nationalism—the concern that because of Canadian economic "dependence" on US markets the United States might exercise control over Canadian policy-making, including foreign policy-making—has also emerged significantly.

Along with the challenges to federalism, national unity, and sovereignty resulting from these problems and developments of the post-1973 era, there were also some continuities from the previous period. Immigration rates slowed down significantly, often as a result of lower quotas set by immigration officials in response to poor economic conditions or decreased labour-market demand. However, immigration policy remained objective and non-discriminatory, with economic criteria still the primary considerations for the admission of independent immigrants. Consequently, Canada's ethnic and cultural composition continued to diversify in the period after 1973, particularly as immigrants increasingly came from countries or regions previously deemed undesirable. As fewer immigrants came from the traditional source countries in north and western Europe, more came from parts of Asia, the Caribbean, Africa, and South America (Knowles 2007, 230). In 1971, the federal government introduced official multiculturalism; in addition, the human rights movements continued to fight for the protection of the rights and freedoms of Canadians as well as for their equality of opportunity. All these goals were significantly strengthened by the Charter of Rights of Freedoms (1982). Despite the challenges of this period, Canadians were steadily moving towards a culture and national identity based on diversity, tolerance, and equality and rights for all.

Outline of the Book

To present an examination of the major changes and challenges of the postwar years, this book is divided into five parts, with each having three topic chapters that, in turn, contain two separate articles, or readings.

The first part of the book explores changes and challenges surrounding national identity and nationalism. Chapter 1 examines immigration and multiculturalism. While multiculturalism has become both a demographic reality and a source of Canadian identity, both articles reveal that the reception and experience of immigrants have varied significantly over the postwar years owing to a number of social and political factors, and that multiculturalism as a policy still faces a number of challenges. Chapter 2 explores the evolution of English Canadian identity from one based on the British ethnocultural heritage to one based on more distinctively "Canadian" attributes and symbols. Uncertainty surrounding the existence of a Canadian identity is revealed in the debates and government policies relating to culture. The final chapter in Part I examines the distinct and increasingly separate national identity of Quebec and of the First Nations, both of which pose serious challenges to the concept of a Canadian identity and to national unity as a whole.

Part II, "Federalism, Liberalism, and Regionalism," examines the nature of federal-provincial relations, concepts of and challenges to federalism, and the evolution of and challenges to the welfare of Canadians. Chapter 4 examines the growth of regionalism in both the West and Atlantic Canada, but reveals very distinct differences in regional identity and unity. In the postwar years, western Canada continued to generate regional political parties as a result of opposition to federal intervention in provincial affairs; however, this opposition was not necessarily unified, as Alberta's provincialism manifested differently from that of Saskatchewan and Manitoba. While Atlantic Canadian politicians similarly felt neglected by federal policy-makers, this region was not able to sustain a strong regional unity, even after the entrance of Newfoundland increased its relative weight in the union. Chapter 5 examines the nature of the welfare state and its relationship to postwar liberalism. While the expansion of the welfare state was certainly the result of the postwar commitment to social justice, increasing federal-provincial tension also acted to stimulate social policy reform. Similarly, despite the improvements to social and economic well-being resulting from the expansion of the welfare state, low-income families continued to struggle to achieve a decent standard of living. Finally, chapter 6 examines the development of a more decentralized federalism with the change from liberalism to neo-liberalism in the postwar era and the implications for a range of policies and programs, as well as the role, conflicts, and contradictions faced by the labour movement in trying to protect and promote the interests of working Canadians.

Part III, "Canada and the World," begins with a chapter on Canada's role as a middle power from 1945 to the mid-1960s. The first article in chapter 7 examines Canada's "golden age of diplomacy" and considers whether this was more myth than reality, while the second provides an example of the difficulties Canadian diplomats faced in the Vietnam War era in balancing Canada's commitment to multilateralism with its allegiance to the United States. The question of the extent to which Canada could act as an objective middle power and in the interests of international security and humanitarianism is further explored in chapter 8, which focuses on the role of Canadians in the developing world. The first article examines Canadian foreign policy on Indonesia and determines that it was driven primarily by economic goals and alliance politics. The second article focuses on non-governmental organizations involved in development aid and the challenges faced by the

Protestant churches in the transition of their mission organizations from a commitment to evangelization in the developing world to the provision of secular social and economic development aid. Canada's relations with the United States are further explored in chapter 9 through an examination of two concerns held by Canadians. The first article explores nationalist debates relating to Canadian sovereignty and economic development due to the significant integration of Canada's economy with that of the United States. The second discusses Canada's concerns over and responses to the potential threats by the United States to Canadian sovereignty over the Arctic.

Part IV, "The Rights Revolution," highlights the achievements and controversies of Canada's "rights revolution" since 1945. Chapter 10 examines the human and civil rights movements that began in the immediate postwar years and sought to eradicate racial and religious discrimination, in part through the achievement of anti-discrimination legislation. Although these movements were primarily focused on racial and religious discrimination, women began to voice the concept of sex discrimination even before the women's liberation movement took hold in the late 1960s. Chapter 11 discusses the expansion of the human rights movements from the 1960s to the early 1980s. Human rights movements grew in membership and in the methods and concepts of rights and equality they espoused. Particularly important for the development of the human rights discourse of this time was recognition of the systemic and institutional racism that evaded solution through anti-discrimination laws and public education. Chapter 12 looks at the significant impact of the Charter of Rights and Freedoms on individual and group rights in Canada since 1982, in particular its influence on what has been termed "judicial empowerment."

Part V, "Changing Values and Norms," considers the massive changes in the lifestyles, values, and norms of Canadian society. Chapter 13 focuses on the rise of environmental activism and consciousness, but also highlights the difficulties involved in balancing economic development with environmental protection and environmental justice. Chapter 14 explores the culture of youth and resistance that characterized the late 1960s as the baby boom generation came to young adulthood. Focusing on the examples of aid to war resisters and demand for access to birth control, both articles reveal how youth challenged the values and norms of mainstream Canadian society. Chapter 15, the final chapter of the book, discusses changes in family, work, and gender roles. The first article reveals the challenges and successes of women in the male-dominated occupation of news journalism in the years from 1945 to 1975, while the second examines the conceptualization of fatherhood and its relationship to masculinity in the immediate postwar years.

In addition to its six articles, each part of the book includes further elements that aid student understanding of the major debates, themes, and issues of the period. Each part begins with a timeline and an introduction explaining the historical context and placing the articles within the developments and debates of this context, and concludes with a list of suggested readings, a list of key terms, a series of questions to further encourage understanding of how the arguments and content of each article relates to the major themes and debates of the section, and a list of relevant websites. As well, text boxes prepared by the editor have been inserted in some of the articles. These text boxes explain the terms, themes, or concepts mentioned in one or more of the articles or that are integral to the larger themes of that section. Finally, to help students more fully appreciate how Canada developed since 1945, the book ends with a conclusion that explores some of the interconnections between the different parts of the book as well as additional themes or issues that were omitted from or explored only briefly in the articles.

Works Cited

Bothwell, Robert, Ian Drummond, and John English. 1981. *Canada Since 1945: Power, Politics, and Provincialism.* Toronto: University of Toronto Press.

Finkel, Alvin. 2006. *Social Policy and Practice in Canada: A History.* Waterloo, ON: Wilfrid Laurier University Press.

HRSDC (Human Resources and Skills Development Canada). *Canadians in Context—Population Size and Growth.* Web: www4.hrsdc.gc.ca.

Kelley, Ninette, and Michael J. Trebilcock. 1998. *The Making of the Mosaic: A History of Canadian Immigration Policy.* Toronto: University of Toronto Press.

Knowles, Valerie. 2007. *Strangers at Our Gates: Canadian Immigration and Immigration Policy, 1540–2006.* Rev. edn. Toronto: Dundurn Press.

Muirhead, Bruce. 2004. "From Special Relationship to Third Option: Canada, the U.S. and the Nixon Shock." *American Review of Canadian Studies* 34:439–62.

Norrie, Kenneth, Douglas Owram, and J.C. Herbert Emery. 2008. *A History of the Canadian Economy.* 4th edn. Toronto: Thomson Canada.

Owram, Doug. 1996. *Born at the Right Time: A History of the Baby Boom Generation.* Toronto: University of Toronto Press.

Taylor, Graham D. 2009. *The Rise of Canadian Business.* Don Mills, ON: Oxford University Press.

PART I

National Identity and Nationalism

TIMELINE

1945	Canadian Arts Council established
1947	Revocation of Chinese Exclusion Act
1949	Massey Commission appointed (reports 1951)
1951	Amendments to the Indian Act (removal of ban on sun dance and potlatch)
1952	CBC Television begins broadcasting
1956–7	Arrival of Hungarian refugees
1957	Canada Council established
1958	Board of Broadcast Governors set up to license radio and television
1958	Beginning of Dominion Day/Canada Day celebrations
1960	Passage of federal Bill of Rights by Conservative government of John Diefenbaker
1960	Enfranchisement of Status Indians
1960–6	Jean Lesage and Liberals form government in Quebec
1960s	"Quiet Revolution" in Quebec
1962	Immigration Act reformed to remove ethnicity and race as criteria
1963	Creation of the Royal Commission on Bilingualism and Biculturalism
1965	Canada's new flag implemented
1965	George Grant's *Lament for a Nation* published
1967	Canada's centennial year with celebrations at Expo 67
1967	Further reform of the Immigration Act with the points system introduced
1968	Separatist Parti Québécois formed
1968	Canadian Radio-television Commission established
1968	Social Sciences and Humanities Research Council created from the Canada Council
1969	National Indian Brotherhood formed
1969	White Paper on Indian Policy introduced
1969	Official Languages Act implemented
1970	Indian chiefs of Alberta issue response to the White Paper
1970	October Crisis in Quebec; War Measures Act implemented by Trudeau government
1970	CRTC imposes regulation requiring 30 per cent Canadian content in radio programming
1971	Introduction of multiculturalism as official government policy
1972	Canada wins the first Canada-Soviet hockey series
1973	Creation of a Multiculturalism Directorate in office of the Secretary of State

continued

1973	Supreme Court decision in Nisga'a case recognizes Aboriginal land title	**1988**	Enactment of Multiculturalism Act
1973–6	Arrival of Chilean refugees	**1990**	Oka Crisis near Oka, Quebec
1974	Berger Commission appointed	**1990**	Meech Lake Accord expires owing to opposition in Manitoba
1976	Immigration Act amended to define who could come to Canada	**1990**	Bloc Québécois formed
1976	Parti Québécois wins provincial election	**1991**	Manitoba inquiry into treatment of Aboriginal people in justice system
1977	Task Force on Canadian Unity appointed (Pépin-Robarts)	**1992**	Charlottetown Accord is negotiated but is rejected in a national referendum
1980	First Quebec referendum on sovereignty-association	**1994**	Parti Québécois wins provincial election
1981	Federal government and the provinces (except Quebec) reach a deal on Constitution	**1995**	Second Quebec referendum rejects sovereignty-association
1982	Constitution Act, including Charter of Rights and Freedoms, proclaimed	**1996**	Report of Royal Commission on Aboriginal Peoples released
1982	National Indian Brotherhood becomes the Assembly of First Nations	**1998**	Federal government apologizes for its treatment of Aboriginal peoples
1985	Indian Act amended to remove clause that discriminated against women	**1999**	Supreme Court upholds fishing rights of Donald Marshall
1987	Federal government and the provinces negotiate the Meech Lake Accord	**2002**	Immigration Act replaced by the Immigration and Refugee Protection Act
		2003	Quebec Liberals defeat Parti Québécois in provincial election

Introduction

Nationalism and national identity underwent significant change in the post–Second World War years and became prominent issues of contention, dominating politics and policy-making and challenging national unity. While a uniform, collective Canadian identity may never exist, the postwar years changed the national characteristics that defined Canadians.

The question of nationalism, particularly in relation to national sovereignty and autonomy, arose following the war's end. The pride many Canadians took their wartime accomplishments provided the basis for patriotism. Yet the decimation of Britain and its decline as a world power, together with a growing awareness of and aversion to racism and to ethnic nationalism (as discussed in Part IV) weakened British imperialism and the long-held belief in British superiority that had provided the basis of nationalism for many English Canadians. At the same time, economic and military integration with the United States continued to grow, facilitated by trade agreements and cooperation in defence production and participation in defence organizations such as NATO (North Atlantic Treaty Organization) and NORAD (North American Aerospace Defense Command). By the 1950s, politicians and academics had begun to express concern about Canadian independence in economic and military decision-making, such as in the Gordon Commission report of 1958 and John Diefenbaker's contradictory but decidedly nationalist stance on the BOMARC missiles (discussed in more detail in Part III). Concerns about American cultural domination had arisen as well, particularly by the late 1950s, as American popular culture flooded Canadian radio and television and Hollywood dominated the production and distribution of movies. As Ryan Edwardson demonstrates, these concerns about national unity and sovereignty shaped the direction of cultural policy in the postwar years, as government intervention in culture increased dramatically owing to the idea that culture can be used to identify and potentially create a "Canadian national sense of self."

By the 1960s, additional postwar trends brought the issue of nationalism and national identity to the forefront of politics and public concern. High rates of immigration, including several waves of refugees, had begun to change the demographic and ethnic composition of the country from its traditional French and English cultural and ancestral heritage. Between 1962 and 1976, the federal government drastically altered immigration policy, removing racial, ethnic, and religious discrimination from the immigrant selection process, a policy that would place Canada firmly on the road to multiculturalism. In addition, Quebec and its French-Canadian population emerged from the Quiet Revolution with a new national identity, one that included defining *les québécois* as a "nation" and demanding fundamental changes to federalism so as to place the Quebec government (as the government of the French) on an equal footing with the federal government. Recognizing the potential of this nationalist ideology and the alienation of many in Quebec owing to the signing of the 1982 Constitution Act without Quebec, Brian Mulroney (leader of the federal Progressive Conservative Party) determined to undertake constitutional negotiations with Quebec, championing two major constitutional reform packages—first, the Meech Lake Accord 1987 and then the Charlottetown Accord 1992, both encompassing the concept of a federation of two equal nation-states, Quebec and Canada. Michael Behiel's study of these events reveals why both attempts at constitutional reform would fail, leaving Quebec nationalists further alienated, the Progressive Conservative Party politically decimated, and the nation further fractured by regional and group divisions.

By the mid-1960s, in a surge of organization and activism, Canada's First Nations joined Quebec in asserting a new cultural nationalism, demanding redress for past injustices and eventually fighting for recognition of Aboriginal and treaty rights. The definitive spur to Native activism came in 1969 following the Trudeau government's White Paper on Indian Policy. The main proposals of the White Paper were to eliminate Indian status, repeal the Indian Act, and give ownership of land to individual Natives. In theory, this proposal sought to make Native Canadians equal to all other Canadians, with the same rights and status as citizens. Opposition to the proposal by the First Nations was immediate and forced the government to withdraw the proposal; Native peoples were not interested in integration and assimilation into Canadian society. As David Newhouse argues, the period since the release of the White Paper has seen profound change in the level of Aboriginal political activism and in the Native peoples' ability to get Aboriginal issues onto the political agenda, as well as accomplishments in other areas such as the arts and education. Newhouse points in particular to a fundamental change in government policy, with a shift from favouring the assimilation of Aboriginal peoples to increasingly accepting an Aboriginal right to self-government. While positive in his assessment of these accomplishments, Newhouse also speaks of the challenges ahead for all Canadians as they seek to determine "how to accommodate Aboriginal self-government into the governing structure of Canada so that Aboriginal governments can govern effectively." Similar to Quebec, the First Nations have also posited themselves as a "nation within a nation."

In response to these challenges to nationalism and national identity, federal governments since the 1960s have increasingly emphasized national symbols and events as a means of encouraging national identity and creating an "imagined community." For example, in 1964, the Pearson government introduced a new flag for Canada, a measure intended to replace the British symbolism of the Red Ensign with the distinctively "Canadian" maple leaf, a national symbol theoretically inclusive of both English and French and the many immigrant and ethnic groups that increasingly made up "Canadians." In his study of 1st of July (Canada Day) celebrations, Matthew Hayday examines how the federal government sought to encourage a national identity and national unity through this annual event and how the concepts of identity changed through the postwar years. Hayday reveals that, from the beginning of July 1st commemorations in 1958 to the 1990s, concepts of Canadian identity evolved from an emphasis on the nation's British and military heritage to an emphasis on multiculturalism and diversity, tolerance and individual rights, the inclusion and importance of Aboriginal peoples and cultures, and individual achievements in sports, science, and other areas.

As Hayday's article suggests, by the early 1970s, Canada underwent a shift from ethnic nationalism to civic nationalism, both at the political and policy level and in the collective identity of many Canadians (although ethnic nationalism remained). In 1971, the Trudeau government enacted official multiculturalism, and multiculturalism was further strengthened as a core Canadian characteristic with its inclusion in section 27 of the Charter of Rights and Freedoms. The shift towards civic nationalism intensified with the 1982 charter as social equality and human rights and freedoms became defining characteristics of Canadians. As Canadians increasingly absorbed the idea of multiculturalism with its concomitant characteristic of tolerance, the racial, ethnic, and religious diversity of the country continued to increase. Although tolerance and inclusivity for immigrants have improved dramatically since 1945, studies have repeatedly shown indirect prejudice, discrimination, and "otherization," particularly during times of international, national, or economic turmoil, and particularly for groups that deviate significantly (or appear to) from the ideological, normative, and institutional characteristics of Canada. In a case study that examined Canada's reception of two refugee groups, the Hungarians in 1956–7 and the Chileans in 1973–6, Stephanie Bangarth notes the humanitarian and human rights ideals that propelled numerous voluntary agencies to lobby government and to provide resettlement aid; yet she finds that the Canadian government's response was much more accommodating in the case of Hungarians fleeing a Communist regime than it was in the case of the later Chileans, who, although fleeing an oppressive fascist dictatorship, nonetheless were viewed suspiciously because of potential socialist-communist sympathies. In his study of the history and nature of Canada's multiculturalism policy, Augie Fleras argues that Canadians still support multiculturalism to a significant degree for many reasons, including its importance to national identity. However, Fleras also contends that multiculturalism is a "project in progress," as its basic objective of facilitating unity through integration and inclusivity of all people regardless of country of origin is challenged by the increasingly complex and multiple identities that many people hold. Multiculturalism will have to evolve to become a policy based on inclusivity of these "multiversal" conceptions/identities.

CHAPTER 1

Immigration and Multiculturalism

◎ **1.1: "Under Repair," "Work in Progress": Trajectories of Canadian Multiculturalism**

Augie Fleras

Introduction: The Politics of Mapping Multiculturalism in a Diversifying World

The age of international migration has made it abundantly clear: immigrant-receiving societies must realign their governance patterns to innovatively accommodate the politics of diversity (Castles and Miller 2009; Conference Notes 2011a; Biles and Frideres 2012). Conventional frameworks for living together along integration lines are increasingly contested by the principles of inclusivity as governance models. Canada is no exception to this inclusivity challenge in securing a living together in/with/through diversities. Its commitment to an official multiculturalism as an integrative governance model is widely admired and generally supported for linking cultural accommodation with anti-racism, social justice, human rights, and citizenization (Environics Institute 2010; Kymlicka 2011a, 2011b; Hyman *et al.* 2011; ACS/Mosaic Institute 2012; Murphy 2012). Admittedly, Canada's multicultural commitments are less than what they seem. Reference to multiculturalism can conceal a bewildering assortment of ideological positions and theoretical models (Nagle 2009); as a result, it can mean everything

yet nothing depending on context or intent. For some, multiculturalism is largely a blank screen for projecting a range of fears and fantasies; for others, a lightening rod for capturing public discontent over issues of immigration, national unity, and government policy (Oliver 2006). That the principles of an official multiculturalism remain largely hidden from the general public is not without consequences (Reitz and Banerjee 2007; Kymlicka 2008). Multiculturalism as policy and project is either differently understood by most Canadians (Yan *et al.* 2009/10) or subject to sometimes withering if often unwarranted criticism (Kay 2008; Paquet 2008; Mansur 2011).

Canada's state multiculturalism is coming under siege from within and without. The emergent dynamics of transmigration and multiversality are contesting the constitutive principle of a place-based governance, including the Westphalian assumption of nation and state as mutually constituent and spatially congruent (Conference Notes 2011b). The logic behind multiculturalism as a society-based governance is proving inadequate for addressing transnational frames of otherness articulated by the complexities of transmigration that transcend the nation-state and corresponding notions of a singular identity and belonging. Or as Raka Shome (2012, 145) contends in criticizing conceptual frameworks that ignore the limits of multiculturalism for engaging with modes of otherness that exceed the nation-state, "in a world of connecting and colliding cultures, where what happens elsewhere impacts the here, although the elsewhere and the here are not always geographically where we think they are." Not surprisingly, metaphorical references to multiculturalism as a mosaic of bounded ethnic communities are increasingly discredited as experientially obsolete and politically questionable. Proposed instead are more fluid and interactional governance models that capitalize on the dynamics of negotiating cultural differences on a daily basis with folk who differ from each other (everyday multiculturalism) (Wise and Velayutham 2009; Ho 2011).

Its status as an unfinished project in progress notwithstanding, multiculturalism remains the governance of choice in Canada (ACS/Mosaic Institute 2012). Surveys indicate that most Canadians remain supportive of multiculturalism, even if this support comes with strings attached (Environics Institute 2010). Several theories have been offered in defence of its popularity and success. Canadian political philosopher Will Kymlicka argues that the principle of multiculturalism enjoys support because it offers a low-risk option for managing diversity (Kymlicka 2004/7; Kymlicka 2005; also Reitz 2011). In contrast to the situation in many European jurisdictions, immigrants to Canada tend to be here legally, most profess liberal values, and many possess educational and skill levels that resonate with twenty-first-century economic realities. Canada's geographic remoteness from migrant/refugee-producing countries (unlike the United States with its Mexican border) allows it to select immigrants based on labour-market needs and national priorities, thereby further diminishing the risk factor when responding multiculturally to uninvited newcomers. The legitimacy of multiculturalism is also bolstered by the following factors: its status in statute (Multiculturalism Act, 1988) and constitution (Constitution Act, 1982); its pervasiveness as a whole-of-government responsiveness to minority needs; its centrality in informing Canada's national identity and institutional entrenchment in the everyday lives of Canadians; and its role in enhancing minority rights, including the Charter of Rights and Freedoms and the Citizenship Act. The fact that Canada commemorates each June 27th as Multiculturalism Day speaks volumes about its symbolic salience in a country bereft of unifying symbols.

Alternative explanations (including that proposed by the author [Fleras 2009]) suggest that multiculturalism's popularity and success reflect Canada's sociological status as an immigration society. An immigration society is anchored along five normative lines: (1) regulations are in place to control the flow of newcomers; (2) immigrants are valued as assets for society-building; (3) they are expected to settle permanently by acquiring citizenship; (4) entitlement to essentially the same rights as the native-born is a given; and (5) programs such as multiculturalism facilitate their settlement and integration. Canada's immigration program is not just about getting in; it's also aimed at assisting newcomers to settle down, fit in, and move up, with multiculturalism playing a key role in facilitating the transitioning. Canadian attachment to the multiculturalism-immigration nexus reflects and reinforces a perception of immigration and immigrants as "under control" rather than "out of control," as is the case elsewhere. The conclusion appears inescapable: multiculturalism in Canada is about constructing an integrated immigration society that balances a commitment to redistribution ("equality") with recognition ("respect") in advancing a collective "us." This commitment to inclusivity may explain why Canada remains a global outlier in the multicultural sweepstakes while other countries are discarding multiculturalism as an immigrant governance model—either a good idea gone bad or, alternatively, a bad idea performing precisely to specifications (Fleras 2009; Kymlicka 2011a, 2011b).

In this article, I want to argue the obvious yet the counter-intuitive in explaining the success and popularity of Canada's state multiculturalism. Multiculturalism works as a model of immigrant governance in Canada because of an underlying rationale that eschews the divisiveness of a "we/they" dichotomy. The logic of an inclusive "us" is endorsed in which the mainstream "we" accommodates the minority "they" by collapsing "their" concerns into "our" collective commitments (also Hyman *et al.* 2011; Winter 2011; Forum of Concerned Citizens of Europe 2012). According to this model of belonging and accommodation, Canada's federal multiculturalism goes beyond micro-managing the "other" per se. It's about managing the mainstream to move over and mutually adjust through removal of discriminatory barriers and prejudicial attitudes. The words of the federal department of Citizenship and Immigration Canada are apropos: "Canada's approach to diversity has traditionally balanced two objectives: to encourage integration, and to ensure that the broader society is welcoming and that it accommodates diversity" (CIC 2012, 2).

However progressive this integrative commitment, dilemmas abound in defining the limits of multiculturalism as diversity governance in a globalizing context (Shome 2012). Can multiculturalism be reframed along inclusivity lines as a governance model for living together in a twenty-first-century world of dizzying changes and demanding diversities (Brydon and Dvorak 2012)? In a world in/trans/formed by the forces of transmigration, what's the point in subscribing to a place-based multiculturalism as governance model when immigrant notions of belonging and identity are no longer tethered to conventional notions of territory or ethnicity (Fleras 2011)? Can a new multiculturalism 2.0 engage with the globally connected, transnationally interspersed, and increasingly multiverse citizens without spiralling into irrelevance (Habacon 2007)? The article argues in the affirmative for each of these questions. A commitment to a multiculturalism 2.0 may prove its worth in the twenty-first-century world of transmigration and multiversality by realigning Canada's governance model to accommodate the differential accommodation of differentiated differences (i.e., to accommodate different ways of accommodating differences-within-differences). Forging a multiversal framework for living together in/with/through a diversity of diversities will prove a formidable undertaking, particularly in light of recent government moves to retrench and curtail along neo-assimilationist lines. To put

these arguments to the test, this article (a) begins by deconstructing Canada's official multiculturalism, including its evolutionary trajectory from past to present; (b) continues by demonstrating how this multicultural model is about transforming the "we" to forge a more inclusive "us"; (c) conceptualizes the emergence of multiversality as the basis for an inclusivity governance; and (d) concludes by exploring how the reframing of Canada's multicultural governance model along multiversal lines may be progressive but is also likely to generate a conflict of interest.

Official Multiculturalism: Policy, Statute, Program

That Canada is officially multicultural is stating the obvious. Yet the irony is improbable: from its inception in 1971 when it barely merited a single paragraph in Canada's national newspaper (*The Globe and Mail*), official multiculturalism has evolved to the point where it encapsulates how Canadians think about themselves and their relationship to the world while orchestrating a national consensus over the principle of living together in/with/through diversity (Lupul 2005). Multiculturalism originated in the quest for Canada-building by establishing an integrative model for respecting differences, engaging mainstream institutions, promoting integration, and learning an official language (Kunz and Sykes 2008; *Globe and Mail* 2011b). It persists for precisely the same reasons, namely, to accommodate immigrants and minorities by modifying the rules of integration (Kymlicka 2012). The goal of multiculturalism as governance has never wavered from its underlying rationale—the possibility of living together with differences without differences getting in the way or spiralling out of control. Only the means for achieving this goal have changed because of demographic changes and political developments. Ethnicity-based solutions have given way to equity-grounded reforms followed, in turn, by the promotion of civic belonging and participation and, more recently, by a commitment to integration and social cohesion (CIC 2012). In other words, four

TABLE 1.1 | Policy Shifts in Canada's Official Multiculturalism: An Unfinished Work in Progress

	Ethnicity Multiculturalism (1970s)	Equity Multiculturalism (1980s–early 1990s)	Civic Multiculturalism (1995–2005)	Integrative Multiculturalism (2006–present)
Dimension	Cultural	Structural	Social	Societal
Focus	Respecting differences	Fostering equality	Living together	Social cohesion
Mandate	Ethnicity	Race relations	Civic culture	Citizenship
Magnitude	Individual adjustment	Inst. accommodation	Full engagement	National safety/security
Problem	Prejudice	Racism/discrimination	Exclusion	Segregation/extremism
Solution	Cultural sensitivity	Remove barriers	Inclusion	Shared Canadian values
Outcomes	Cultural capital	Human capital	Social capital	National (comm)unity
Key Metaphor	"Mosaic"	"Level playing field"	"Bridging the bonds"	"Strangers becoming neighbours"

overlapping policy stages in focus and mandate can be discerned in the evolutionary trajectory of an official multiculturalism—*ethnicity*, *equity*, *civic*, *integration* (Fleras 2012a).

Multiculturalism as Policy

Canada's official multiculturalism drew inspiration from publication of the *Report of the Royal Commission on Bilingualism and Biculturalism* in 1969 (see Haque 2012). The findings of the royal commission concluded that Canada comprised a multicultural commonwealth of many nationalities, albeit within the bicultural (or binational) framework of two founding peoples. But various ethnic minority groups, especially Ukrainians and Germans, lobbied vigorously for inclusion and recognition, arguing that their language, culture, and contributions were as vital as Quebec's to Canada-building (Jaworsky 1979). Ethnic lobby groups rejected the two founding nations concept, with its implication that some Canadians were more deserving than others. Endorsed instead was a descriptive ideal that captured the contribution of the "other ethnics" in advancing the cultural enrichment of a multicultural Canada. Pressure to create a new symbolic order was further heightened by the forces of Quebec's increasingly militant nationalism in the aftermath of the Quiet Revolution.

The multicultural nod to ethnic minorities was envisaged as a potential counterbalance to neutralize (or depoliticize) Canada's bi-nationalism focus (Forbes 2007). Finally, with British values losing their saliency in defining Canada's identity (see Jakubowicz 2005), multiculturalism emerged as an ideological moral glue for binding Canadians together into an interactive mosaic. A new national unity strategy evolved, one based on a vision of Canada not only as a bi-national covenant between French and English but also as a multicultural contract among equality-seeking individuals from diverse ethnocultural communities (McRoberts 1997).

The origins of multiculturalism proved political. As a political bargain to address a national unity crisis, multiculturalism originated to counteract Quebec nationalism, to defuse growing Aboriginal activism following Trudeau's White Paper, to thwart American cultural annexation, to cater to the growing number of racialized immigrants in urban regions, and to appease the concerns of long-established European ethnicities (Kymlicka 2011a, 2011b). Nonetheless, Canada is an exception when it comes to the multicultural management of diversity. Unlike most countries, Canada's approach to diversity management reflects a broader legislative framework, supported by policies, programs, and initiatives

MULTICULTURALISM AS IDENTITY

Although multiculturalism as a policy, in terms of its objectives and impacts, continues to be a subject of debate among academics, policy planners, and interested citizens, there is less contention over the idea that multiculturalism has become part of the Canadian identity. In this construct, multiculturalism contributes to a common sense of identity for Canadians, as it speaks to the reality that "Canadians" are composed of diverse and multiple cultures/ethnicities, but also because it encompasses the associated civic ideals of tolerance and equality.

The introduction of official multiculturalism in 1971 resulted from several factors; important among them were objectives related to identity and unity. By 1971, Canada was already a multicultural society, although diversity would increase dramatically in the succeeding decades as a result of reforms to immigration policy. In addition, the traditional British identity held by many Anglo-Canadians was receding in importance, while Quebecois nationalism presented as an increasingly separate and disunifying force. Thus, multiculturalism was seen as one means to provide a common basis of identity while encouraging both the integration and the full participation of all groups within the national life. In this sense, it was intended to encourage greater national cohesiveness and unity.

While multiculturalism and the associated ideals of equality and tolerance do appear to have become part of the Canadian identity, many commentators contend that multiculturalism actually creates more division than unity. It is contended that by emphasizing difference and potentially encouraging groups to identify with external countries/groups, multiculturalism discourages the development of an identification as "Canadian" and encourages division. In addition, multiculturalism is a reality much more so for some regions of the country than others. In parts of the West or the North, multiculturalism holds less identifying value, as these areas are far less diverse. Consequently, multiculturalism potentially encourages regionalism, as it addresses more the reality of the southern parts of central Canada.

developed and delivered across the whole of federal government (Bloemraad 2011; CIC 2012). A policy commitment to multiculturalism within a bilingual framework was proclaimed in 1971 when Prime Minister Pierre Elliott Trudeau declared his Liberal government's intent to embrace "multiculturalism within a bilingual framework." In the words of Trudeau, the linking of individual rights with equal status under multiculturalism would "strengthen the solidarity of the Canadian people by enabling all Canadians to participate fully and without discrimination in defining and building the nation's future." Four major principles secured the original multicultural model:

- *Equality of status:* Canada does not have an official culture; all cultures are equal

(yes, Canada would continue to privilege mainstream laws, rules, conventions, etc., but it would not explicitly favour any particular culture, while consciously supporting an individual's freedom of choice) (Forbes 2007).

- *Canadian identity:* Diversity defines who/what is Canadian.

- *Personal choice:* The right for individuals to freely identify with the cultural tradition of their choice without incurring a penalty for doing so or refusing to do so.

- *Protection of individual rights:* Freedom from discrimination and removal of discriminatory barriers and cultural jealousies.

To implement these principles, the government proposed initiatives to (1) help those cultural groups with a willingness to develop, share, and contribute to Canada; (2) assist the members of all cultural groups to overcome cultural barriers to full participation in Canadian society; (3) promote creative encounters and exchanges among all Canadian cultural groups in advancing national unity; and (4) equip immigrants with the means to acquire one of Canada's official languages so that they might fully participate in Canadian society.

An ethnicity commitment to multiculturalism initially focused on the protection and promotion of Canada as an ethnic mosaic. Initially, official multiculturalism was not targeted at immigrants or racialized minorities (McAndrew *et al.* 2008). It was aimed instead at established European minorities such as the Ukrainians to assist them in protecting their languages and ethnic customs from the Russification policies of the Cold War era (Lupul 2005). But a commitment to cultural preservation was not high on the multicultural agenda—at least not beyond an initial commitment when powerful ethnic lobbyists prevailed (Jaworsky 1979). If anything, the goals of official multiculturalism were integrative in two ways. First, official multiculturalism eliminated those discriminations rooted in cultural prejudices while improving minority and migrant participation and integration. This commitment was predicated on the assumption that migrants and minorities were more likely to embrace Canada and Canadians emotionally if they were secure ("non-defensive") in their own cultural skin (Adams 2007; CIC 2011). Second, official multiculturalism created a new symbolic order in which ethno-nationalism would disappear as a marker of identity or dispenser of rewards. A multiculturalist Canada would no longer rank ethnic groups vis-à-vis their relational status in bi-national society. Nor would it exclude them because they lacked founding-settler status (French and English). A contrastive view of unified Canada was proposed instead, one that envisaged Canada as a community of communities (as later described by Prime Minister Joe Clark)

rather than as a two-nation state (Hutcheon 1998; Forbes 2007). In short, the basic tenet of multiculturalism reinforced the then counter-intuitive: that balancing national unity with social integration and cultural diversity was not a contradiction in terms. To the contrary, this trifecta of goals—diversity, integration, and unity—could prove mutually reciprocating in advancing Canada's interests, provided the appropriate architecture was in place (see also Reitz 2011). Of paramount importance in crafting a balancing act was the logic of making the mainstream move over and construct space through removal of prejudicial attitudes and discriminatory barriers. Clearly, then, multiculturalism was never intended to celebrate immigrant differences per se, although the policy was increasingly twisted in that direction. As Trudeau explained later in life, the introduction of multiculturalism was aimed at celebrating people's right to become full members of Canadian society regardless of their country of origin—not to retreat into their ethnic corners but to participate fully through creative encounters (Cobb 1995). With multiculturalism, people could identify with and belong in Canada through their ethnicity if they so chose, but always in a restrictive sense: that is, one could be Lithuanian, but always a Lithuanian in Canada.

Multiculturalism as Statute

Canada's multiculturalism agenda was revised in the early 1980s (Fleras 2009). A commitment to equity multiculturalism sought to address the more pragmatic concerns of recently established racialized immigrants whose visibility complicated the prospect of integration. The need to dismantle discriminatory barriers superseded concerns over cultural preservation and ethnic identity as keys to integration. A focus on the principles of equity, social justice, and institutional inclusiveness followed accordingly (Fleras 2003). Funding allocations shifted to incorporate spending on the more equity-oriented goals of anti-racism, race relations, and institutional accommodation rather than simply doling out money to ethnocultural organizations or events as had been the case. The political profile of official multiculturalism was further consolidated with the Constitution Act and the Charter of Rights and Freedoms, which came into effect in 1985. In that the "Charter would be interpreted in a manner consistent with the preservation and enhancement of the multicultural heritage of Canadians" (section 27), multiculturalism was constitutionally entrenched as a distinguishing feature of Canada at the highest levels of political decision-making.

Canada's status as the world's first statutory multiculturalism (see below) was further secured with passage of the Multiculturalism Act in 1988. Passage of the Multiculturalism Act confirmed the displacement of biculturalism for multiculturalism as Canada's defining feature in the psyche of English-speaking Canadians (Hutcheon 1998). The Act also secured a legal framework to guide federal responsibilities and activities, in addition to establishing a set of principles for achieving the equality of all Canadians (CIC 2012). More specifically, it sought to foster a respect for cultures, promote participation, acknowledge the contribution of minorities to Canada, ensure equality before the law, foster inter-group interaction, encourage in-group bonding as a precondition for out-group bridging, preserve minority languages while strengthening the status and use of official languages, and accelerate institutional inclusiveness at the federal level through removal of discriminatory barriers.

Despite ambiguities and logical contradictions (Hutcheon 1998), provisions of the Multiculturalism Act advocated an inclusionary framework for living together in diversity, in part by privileging integration over separation, interaction over isolation, equal opportunity over ethnic deficit/penalty, and participation over withdrawal (Adams 2007). A commitment to removing discriminatory barriers and respecting cultural differences put the onus on the mainstream to move over and mutually adjust, even as newcomers are expected to integrate into the existing system (Fleras 2012b). A textual analysis of the Multiculturalism Act by Fries and Gingrich (2009) confirmed the pervasiveness of these recurrent themes—diversity,

harmony, equality, resource, and barrier removal. Admittedly, the Multiculturalism Act remains a largely aspirational policy framework instead of an obligatory statute with specific goals, measurable targets, enforceable timetables, and penalties for noncompliance (Reitz and Banerjee 2007). Nevertheless, aspirational or not, the Act completed the Canada-building project associated with passage of the Official Languages Act in 1969, the Statement on Multiculturalism in 1971, and its enshrinement in the Constitution Act of 1982. Each of these initiatives converged in the hope of creating a unified and inclusive Canada so that no one would be excluded for reasons beyond his or her control (Kymlicka 2004/7; Sibley 2006; Haque 2012).

Multiculturalism as Program

The history of multiculturalism as a program can be drawn from the *Annual Report on the Operation of the Canadian Multiculturalism Act*. A series of annual reports since 1988 have highlighted initiatives undertaken by Citizenship and Immigration Canada and other government departments (CIC 2012). These reports are helpful in demonstrating a transitioning in the focus and mandate of Canada's multicultural program. For example, consider the renewal of the multiculturalism program in 1996 in reaction to the 1995 referendum on Quebec's sovereignty-association project. The near-death experience of almost losing the "plot" in Quebec prompted the federal government to bolster national unity, identity, and belonging through promotion of Canadian symbols (Winter 2011). Three strategic goals prevailed: civic participation (full and equal involvement), social justice (equitable treatment), and identity (foster a Canada in which all Canadians identify and belong regardless of their cultural background). The renewed program prioritized the following commitments: (a) facilitate the active participation of ethnic minorities; (b) support community initiatives to reduce ethnic conflict and hate crimes; (c) make public institutions respectful of, reflective upon, and responsive to difference; (d) foster more inclusive federal departments and agencies;

(e) foster the integration of newcomers instead of creating a plural society; and (f) increase public awareness of multiculturalism and cross-cultural understanding of difference. Over time, priority objectives reinforced a commitment to institutional change (inclusivity through removal of discriminatory barriers), federal institutional change (integration of diversity into policies, programs, and services), combat racism (including removal of discriminatory barriers, anti-racism programs, and cross-cultural understanding), and civic engagement (promotion of an inclusive citizenship via participation in public decision-making) (CIC 2011). Kymlicka (2011, 17) writes:

> Multiculturalism has never been seen in Canada as an alternative to citizenship, or as a transitional phase that immigrants pass through on the road to becoming "real" Canadians who no longer need multiculturalism. Multiculturalism is a right in Canada, but it is seen as a right that one possesses *as a Canadian:* it is about how we conceptualize the role of ethnic identities and ethnic organizations in our ongoing civic and political lives, and not just about techniques of newcomer integration.

A recent shift in the multicultural agenda can be discerned. An explicit integration-focused multiculturalism has emerged in reaction to global security concerns, from the trauma of "9/11" to the Toronto terror scare in June 2006 (when 18 males were apprehended on suspicion of fomenting terror). This integrative focus is aimed at neutralizing the threat of ethno-religious extremism (Kunz and Sykes 2008; CIC 2009), thereby ensuring a safe and cohesive Canada based on shared values and common identity. The key objectives of the new multiculturalism program focus on constructing an integrated and socially cohesive society while promoting intercultural and interfaith dialogue and understanding, fostering citizenship and civic pride, improving institutional responses to the needs of minorities, and respecting Canada's core democratic values (CIC 2012). An integrative approach to multiculturalism articulates three main policy objectives: (1) build an integrated and socially cohesive society by promoting civic engagement among all Canadians; (2) make federal institutions more responsive to Canada's diverse populations through removal of discriminatory barriers and fostering intercultural understanding; and (3) promote Canadian values abroad by participating in international discussions on multiculturalism and diversity (CIC 2011). The ethos of an integrative agenda is captured in this statement delivered on Multiculturalism Day (27 June) by Jason Kenney, the minister of citizenship, immigration, and multiculturalism (CIC 2011):

> Canada is one of the most ethnically, culturally, and religiously diverse countries in the world . . . formed by citizens from many cultural backgrounds who have come to live together in harmony in this free land . . . Canadian Multiculturalism Day is an opportunity to reflect on both the contributions of Canada's various cultural communities and the *values that we all share*: freedom, democracy, individual rights, and rule of law. Canada's future depends on us growing together. *That is why our multiculturalism programs continue to encourage all Canadians to embrace our shared values, history, and institutions and to build a strong, integrated society.* (Emphasis, mine)

To sum up: references to Canada's official multiculturalism as an "unfinished project" and a "work in progress" are not without merit. Multiculturalism as a complex and contested governance policy has evolved over time from ethnicity to equity to civic to integration as reflected in the 1971 policy statement, the 1988 Multiculturalism Act, and the annual reports from 1988 onwards. But changes in points of emphasis notwithstanding, a commitment to Canada-building through institutional inclusivity and minority integration remains a constant (Fleras 2009; Kymlicka 2012). To be sure, constructing a model of Canadian multiculturalism is a tricky affair. Any proposed model must address a host of complexities, including

(a) different levels of meaning associated with multiculturalism (as fact, ideology, policy, practice, critique); (b) both the 1971 policy statement and the 1988 Multiculturalism Act; (c) a reading of official statements such as the annual reports; (d) constants that weave throughout the different policy stages; and (e) government refusal to define the substance of an official multiculturalism.

Towards a Multiculturalism 2.0: Balancing the Mosaic with Multiversality?

> Ours is a messy world where established institutions are struggling with new, fluid realities but where new, more flexible modes of governance are yet to be found. (Ang 2011, 31)

Diversity and difference are not what they once were (Vertovec 2007). In these turbulent times of unforeseen fractures, unlikely hybrids, and unregulated entanglements, Canada's diversity is becoming increasingly diverse (Latham 2007/08). A new multiversal reality has emerged that transcends a mosaic model of multiculturalism that once prevailed, one in which Canada was metaphorically organized around fixed and homogeneous (essentialized) ethnic cultures whose coercive powers could mould or motivate. Canada is now reconfigured around a diversity of diversities—a multiversal dynamic comparable in status to Britain, where the term "superdiversity" provides a description and a proposed model of/for British society beyond the multiculturally based ethnic minorities paradigm (Vertovec 2006, 2010; Blommaert and Rampton 2011). Both multiversality and superdiversity conjure an intensely diversifying reality involving a dynamic and complex interplay of individuals with multiple origins who are transnationally connected, socio-economically differentiated, racialized, and discriminated against; internally diverse communities because of gender, class, age (intergenerational differences), and sexuality; international students, foreign migrant workers, and faith-based communities; and immigrants who are struggling to establish identities that bridge their traditional past with their transnational present (Latham 2008; Conference Notes 2011a). Not surprisingly, identities and demands are more fluid, nuanced, and multidimensional than they used to be because of (a) shifting interests, (b) conflicting allegiances and loyalties beyond predefined groups, and (c) collective aspirations in search of public affirmation (Florby et al. 2009; Fanshawe and Sriskandarajah 2010).

Awareness is growing that diversity itself is becoming more diversified ("multiverse") thanks to the diffusion of categorical identity politics (Government of Canada 2011; Conference Notes 2012; also Faist 2010). According to the Robert Latham (2007/08), the word "multiverse" conveys the idea of multiple social universes. Differences in a multiverse universe persist across many overlapping and intersecting universes, resulting in a limitless array of transcendent belongings, fractured affiliations, and splintered identities (Wong 2007). The experiences, aspirations, and realities of second- and third-generation descendants of immigrants have outgrown those mosaic metaphors with their connotations of static and essentialized cultural differences (Habacon 2007). To date, however, efforts to reconceptualize this diversification of differences have faltered, as Castles (2011, 26) concedes:

> Multiculturalism was a great step forward, but the term at least—if not the content—is beyond rescue. We need a new politics of diversity and new ideas about building social relations in open and fast-changing societies. Such ideas are not likely to come from theoretical reflection, but may perhaps emerge from the everyday praxis of living together in multicultural cities.

Mosaic models of multiculturalism as a lens for expressing multiversality cannot address the increasing fragmentation of differences along multidimensional lines and multiple vectors (Vertovec 2007; Modood et al. 2010). State initiatives for framing and responding to multiple identities and transnational belongings tend to default into a relatively narrow spectrum and static expression of a sticky ("essentialized") ethnicity. A tick box approach to ethnic identity not only excludes those who fall outside standard classifications but also privileges a person's or group's ethnicity as a core value that continues to determine people's behaviour or to box them in, in defining who they are (Habacon 2007). In the end, the framing of differences along mosaic lines creates a tendency to apply simple—even simplistic—responses and solutions to complex realities. But multiversal multiculturalism proposes to correct this mono-myopia through the differential accommodation of a diversified diversity (Vertovec 2007; Fanshawe and Sriskandarajah 2010). A commitment to the multiversality of the everyday focuses on the lived realities of differentiated differences with respect to how they are encountered, experienced, and negotiated in the ebb and flow of daily situations and ordinary spaces (Wise and Velayutham 2009).

A reluctance to rethink the politics of hyper-diversity exposes the limits of an official multiculturalism as a governance model in a globalizing and diversifying world (Latham 2009; also Mawani 2008; Shome 2012). And yet reference to a multiversal multiculturalism as inclusivity governance is proving a challenge in its own right. Is a commitment to a multiversal governance a case of society-in-differences or differences-in-society (Sandercock 2003; Parekh 2005)? A differences-in-society perspective commits itself to a particular political doctrine or vision of the good society, then asks how much diversity can be incorporated within the limits set by society or vision. This integrative multicultural framework reflects and reinforces a mosaic governance model of making society safe from differences as well as making it safe for differences. By contrast, a society-in-difference approach begins by accepting the primacy, reality, and desirability of diversities and differentiated differences, then adjusts its political, social, and culture life accordingly. The mandate for an inclusivity multiculturalism is not just about making society safe

from, and safe for, society. More to the point, it entails constructing an inclusivity governance that acknowledges the reality of multiversality by making a diversity-of-diversities safe from society yet safe for society. Several corollaries follow: a multiversal multiculturalism rejects a top-down mindset in which central authorities define what differences count and what counts as difference; it also rejects a multicultural governance model that endorses a people's right to be different; and yet it insists that everyone must be different in the same way instead of allowing them to be the same (as in similar) in fundamentally different ways (Ang 2011).

A pending conflict of interest may disrupt this trajectory towards multiversal inclusivity as multicultural governance. Canada's current multiculturalism agenda embraces a new phase whose operative logic conforms to the neo-assimilationist principles of integration and cohesiveness (CIC 2012). Endorsement of an integrative multiculturalism may resonate with modernist notions of Canada-building that align diversities along mosaic lines. But an articulated commitment to cohesiveness, civic engagement, and integration as governance blueprint is incommensurate with the governance principles of a multiversal multiculturalism. Instead of encouraging Canadians to engage with differences in a deep and meaningful way, an integrative multiculturalism implicitly depoliticizes diversity in the hope of blunting the emergence of ethnic enclaves perceived as incubators of criminality or instigators of extremism (Joshee et al. 2010). Still, there is hope in balancing an integrative multiculturalism (diversity in unity) with a multiversal multiculturalism of more complex patterns inhabiting a differentiation of differences (unity in diversity), for in the final analysis Canada is much more than a mosaic (juxtaposition) of diverse ethnocultural groups, as initially implied by an official multiculturalism. It constitutes a complex and kaleidoscopic site of hybridized fusions and differentiated fissions involving the interpenetration of differences-with-differences—or to paraphrase John Ralston Saul (2009), a mixed Métis nation of settler-indigeneity hybridity.

Time will tell if the inclusivity principles of a multiversal multiculturalism can move beyond the neo-assimilationist framework of an integrative multiculturalism. Moves towards such a multiversal commitment to differentiated differences and differential accommodation are mildly encouraging at best, challenging at worst. As Latham observes (2009), it's one thing to support policies that build on the singular notion of accommodating multiple cultures. It's quite another to open the floodgates to the multiversal challenge of accommodating different ways of accommodating differentiated differences, especially when the many universes come into noisy contact with each other without a roadmap to show the way. Consider only the challenge of crafting an inclusive citizenship when individuals and communities are globally connected yet astonishingly diverse in culture, religion, language, and identity (PRI 2009). Nevertheless, there is much to commend in endorsing a multiversal multiculturalism in a postnational Canada. While not a perfect governance model in a transmigratory and diversifying world by any stretch of the imagination, it is perhaps one of the lesser imperfect models in the art of living together in/with/through diversities, equitably and in dignity.

References

ACS/Mosaic Institute. 2012. *Younger Canadians Believe Multiculturalism Works; Older Canadians, Not So Sure*. Toronto, 24 April.

Adams, Michael. 2007. *Unlikely Utopia: The Surprising Triumph of Canadian Pluralism*. Toronto: Viking.

Ang, Ien. 2011. "Ethnicities and Our Precarious Future." *Ethnicities* 11:27–31.

Biles, John, and James Frideres. 2012. Introduction to *International Perspectives: Integration and Inclusion*, ed. J. Frideres and J. Biles, 1–16. Montreal and Kingston: McGill-Queen's University Press.

Bloemraad, Irene. 2011. *The Debate Over Multiculturalism: Philosophy, Politics, and Policy*. *Migration Information Source*. Retrieved from www.migrationinformation.org.

Blommaert, Jan, and Ben Rampton. 2011. "Language and Superdiversity." *Diversities* 13 (2). Retrieved from www.unesco.org.

Brydon, Diana, and Marta Dvorak. 2012. "Negotiating Meanings in Changing Times." In *Crosstalk: Canadian and Global Imaginaries in Dialogue*, ed. D. Brydon and M. Dvorak, 1–20. Waterloo, ON: Wilfrid Laurier Press.

Castles, Stephen. 2011. "Globalization, Ethnic Identity, and the Integration Crisis." *Ethnicities* 11 (1): 24–6.

Castles, Stephen, and Mark Miller. 2009. *The Age of Migration*. 4th edn. New York: Guildford Press.

CIC (Citizenship and Immigration Canada). 2011. *Canadian Multiculturalism: An Inclusive Citizenship*. Ottawa.

———. 2012. *Annual Report on the Operation of the Canadian Multiculturalism Act, 2010–2011*. Ottawa.

Cobb, Chris. 1995. "Multiculturalism Policy May Be Outdated, Say MPs." *Ottawa Citizen*, 4 July.

Conference Notes. 2009. *Beyond Multiculturalism? Envisioning the Immigration Society*. Berlin, 4–6 June.

———. 2011a. *Reframing Multiculturalism for the 21st Century Reality*. International Symposium on Multiculturalism, University of Ottawa, 21–2 November.

———. 2011b. *Living Together in Diversity*. Central European University, Budapest, 21–2 May.

———. 2012. *Language and Superdiversity*. Sociolinguistics Symposium 19, Freie Universitat Berlin, 22–4 August.

Environics Institute. 2010. *Focus Canada 2010: Survey of Canadian Attitudes toward Social Issues*. Toronto.

Faist, Thomas. 2010. "Towards Transnational Studies: World Theories, Transnationalism, and Changing Institutions." *Journal of Ethnic and Migration Studies* 36 (10): 1665–87.

Fanshawe, Simon, and D. Sriskandarajah. 2010. "Beyond Box-Ticking: Super-Diversity and the End of Ethnicity Politics in Britain." *Confluence: South Asian Perspectives*, 7 August. Retrieved from www.confluence.org.uk/.

Fleras, Augie. 2003 *Engaging Diversity. Multiculturalism in Canada*. Toronto: Nelson.

———. 2009. *The Politics of Multiculturalism: Cross-National Perspectives in Multicultural Governance*. New York: Palgrave Macmillan.

———. 2011. "Doing It Differently: 40 Years of Official Multiculturalism." Paper presented to the 40 Years of Multiculturalism Conference, Ottawa, September.

———. 2012a. *Unequal Relations: The Politics of Race, Ethnic, and Aboriginal Relations in Canada*. 7th edn. Toronto: Pearson.

———. 2012b. "Policing the Kaleidoscope: Inclusivity as Bridge Building." Paper presented to the Association for New Canadians, St John's, NL, 20 March.

———. 2012c. "Living Together with/in/through Diversities." Paper presented to the Living Together in Diversity Conference at the Central European University, Budapest, 21 May.

———. 2012d "From Mosaic to Multiversality: Repriming Multicultural Governance in a Postnational Canada." *Canadian Ethnic Studies* 43 (1/2): 17–39.

Florby, Gunilla, Mark Shackleton, and Katri Suhonen. 2009. *Canada: Images of a Post/National Society*. New York: Peter Lang.

Forbes, Hugh Donald. 2007. "Trudeau as the First Theorist of Canadian Multiculturalism." In *Multiculturalism and the Canadian Constitution*, ed. S. Tierney, 27–42. Vancouver: UBC Press.

Forum of Concerned Citizens of Europe. 2012. *Living with Diversity: For a Politics of Hope without Fear*. An open letter from the Forum of Concerned Citizens of Europe. Retrieved from www.eurozine.com.

Fries, Christopher J., and Paul Gingrich. 2009. "A 'Great' Large Family: Understanding of Multiculturalism among Newcomers to Canada." *Refuge* 27 (1): 36–51.

Globe and Mail. 2011a. "Super-Diversity." 12 March.

——— 2011b. "Canadians Show Ambiguity towards Multiculturalism," 7 October. Retrieved from www.getintheknow.ca/.

Government of Canada. 2011. "Super-Diversity in Canada," by Nicola Gaye. *Policy Horizons Canada*, June. Available online at www.horizons.gc.ca/.

Habacon, Alden E. 2007. "Beyond the Mosaic: Canada's Multiculturalism 2.0." Paper to the Annual Summer Conference, The Stranger Next Door: Making Diversity Work.

Haque, Eva. 2012. *Multiculturalism within a Bilingual Framework*. Toronto: University of Toronto Press.

Ho, Christine. 2011. "Respecting the Presence of Others: School Micropublics and Everyday Multiculturalism." *Journal of Intercultural Studies* 32 (6): 603–19.

Hutcheon, Pat Duffy. 1998. "Multiculturalism in Canada." Paper presented to the World Congress of International Sociological Association, Montreal, July.

Hyman, Ilene, Agnes Meinhard, and John Shields. 2011. "The Role of Multiculturalism Policy in Addressing Social Inclusion Process in Canada." Prepared for the Canadian Multicultural Education Foundation, 1 June.

Jakubowicz, Andrew. 2005. "Multiculturalism in Australia: Apogee or Nadir?" *Canadian Diversity* 4 (1): 15–18.

Jaworsky, John. 1979. "A Case Study of Canadian Federal Government's Multicultural Policies." MA thesis, Department of Political Science, Carleton University, Ottawa.

Joshee, Reva, Carla Peck, Laura A. Thompson, Ottilia Chareka, and Alan Sears. 2010. "Multicultural Education, Diversity, and Citizenship." Working

paper for the IALEI Workshop on Multicultural Education, Seoul, Korea, 17–19 February.

Justice Department. 2002. *The Politics of Multiculturalism—Cultural Diversity in Canada: The Social Construction of Racial Differences*. Retrieved from www.justice.gc.ca/.

Kay, Barbara. 2008. "Multiculturalism Was Canada's Biggest Mistake." *National Post*, 8 April.

Kunz, Jean Lock, and Stuart Sykes. 2008. *From Mosaic to Harmony: Multicultural Canada in the 21st Century*. PRI Project: Cultural Diversity. Government of Canada.

Kymlicka, Will. 2004/7. "The Global Diffusion of Multiculturalism: Trends, Causes, and Consequences." Paper originally delivered to the International Conference on Leadership, Education, and Multiculturalism in the Armed Forces, La Paz, Bolivia, 2004. Reprinted in *Accommodating Cultural Diversity*, ed. S. Tierney, 17–34. Aldershot: Ashgate. Also in *Governing Diversity*, ed. R. Panossian *et al*., 11–18. EDG Kingston, 2007.

———. 2005. "The Uncertain Futures of Multiculturalism." *Canadian Diversity* 4 (1): 82–5.

———. 2007. "The Canadian Model of Diversity in Comparative Perspective." In *Multiculturalism and the Canadian Constitution*, ed. S. Tierney, 61–90. Vancouver: UBC Press.

———. 2008. "The Current State of Multiculturalism in Canada." Prepared for the Multiculturalism and Human Rights Branch, Government of Canada.

———. 2011a. Invited Symposium: New Direction and Issues for the Study of Ethnicity, Nationalism, and Multiculturalism. "Multiculturalism in Normative Theory and in Social Science." *Ethnicities* 11 (1): 5–31.

———. 2011b. "The Evolving Canadian Experiment with Multiculturalism." Symposium International, Dialogue Quebec-Europe, Montreal, 25–7 May.

———. 2012. *Multiculturalism: Success, Failure, and the Future*. Washington, DC: Migration Policy Institute.

Latham, Robert. 2007/8. "What Are We? From a Multicultural to a Multiversal Canada." *International Journal* 63 (1): 23–42.

———. 2008. "Canadian Society Is Not Just Multicultural; It is Multiversal." ResearchSnapShot. York University, Toronto.

———. 2009. "After Multiculturalism: Canada and Its Multiversal Future." *Canada Watch*, Fall, 28–30.

Lupul, Manoly. 2005. *The Politics of Multiculturalism: A Ukrainian-Canadian Memoir*. Toronto: Canadian Institute of Ukrainian Studies Press.

Mansur, Salim. 2011. *Delectable Lie: A Liberal Repudiation of Multiculturalism*. Mantua Books.

Mawani, Aysha. 2008. "Transnationalism: A Modern Day Challenge to Canadian Multiculturalism." Paper presented to the Annual Meeting of the International

Communication Association, Montreal, 22 May. Retrieved from www.allacademic.com.

McAndrew, Marie, Denise Helly, Caroline Tessier, and Judy Young. 2008. "From Heritage Languages to Institutional Change: An Analysis of the Nature of Organizations and Projects Funded by the Canadian Multiculturalism Program (1983–2002)." *Canadian Ethnic Studies* 40 (3): 149–69

McRoberts, Kenneth. 1997. *Misconceiving Canada: The Struggle for National Unity*. Toronto: Oxford University Press.

Modood, Tariq, Jan Dobbernack, and Nasar Meer. 2010. "Tolerance and Cultural Diversity Discourses in Britain." Centre for the Study of Ethnicity and Citizenship, European University Institute, Florence.

Murphy, Michael. 2012. *Multiculturalism: A Critical Introduction*. New York: Routledge.

Nagle, John. 2009. *Multiculturalism's Double-Bind: Creating Inclusivity, Cosmopolitanism, and Difference*. Aldershot, UK: Ashgate.

Oliver, Donald. 2006. "Canadian Multiculturalism in Theory and Practice: Individual and Group Rights." Presentation to the University of Aarhus, 13 October.

Paquet, Gilles. 2008. *Deep Cultural Diversity: A Governance Challenge*. Ottawa: University of Ottawa Press.

Parekh, Bhikhu. 2005. *Rethinking Multiculturalism: Cultural Diversity and Political Theory*. 2nd edn. New York: Palgrave Macmillan.

PRI (Policy Research Initiative). 2009. *Understanding Canada's "3M" (Multicultural, Multi-Lingual, and Multi-Religious) Reality in the 21st Century*. Final report, June. Ottawa: Government of Canada.

Reitz, Jeffrey. 2011. "Pro-immigration Canada: Social and Economic Roots of Popular Views." Institute for Research on Public Policy, no. 20 (October).

Reitz, Jeffrey, and Rupa Banerjee. 2007. "Racial Inequality, Social Cohesion, and Policy Issues." In *Belonging?*, ed. K. Banting *et al.*, 489–546. Montreal: Institute for Research on Public Policy.

Ryan, Phil. 2010. *Multicultiphobia*. Toronto: University of Toronto Press.

Sandercock, Leonie. 2003. "Rethinking Multiculturalism for the 21st Century." Working Paper No. 03-14. Research on immigration and integration in the metropolis. Vancouver: Vancouver Centre of Excellence.

Saul, John Ralston. 2009. *A Fair Country: Telling Truths about Canada*. Toronto: Viking/Penguin.

Shome, Raka. 2012. "Mapping the Limits of Multiculturalism in the Context of Globalization." *International Journal of Communication* 6:144–65.

Sibley, Robert. 2006. "Trudeau Reconstructed." *Ottawa Citizen*, 4 June.

Simmons, Alan. 2010. *Immigration and Canada*. Toronto: Canadian Scholars Press.

Vertovec, Steven. 2006. "The Emergence of Super Diversity in Britain. Centre for Migration, Policy, and Society." Working Paper No. 25. Oxford, UK.

———. 2007. "Super-diversity and Its Implications." *Ethnic and Racial Studies* 30 (6): 1024–54.

———. 2010. "Toward Post-multiculturalism? Changing Communities, Conditions, and Contexts of Diversity." *International Social Science Journal* 61 (199): 83–95.

Winter, Elke. 2011. *Us, Them, and Others: Pluralism and National Identity in Diverse Societies*. Toronto: University of Toronto Press.

Wise, A., and S. Velayutham, eds. 2009. *Everyday Multiculturalism*. New York: Macmillan.

Wong, Milton. 2007. "Introduction: Origins of Multiculturalism in Canada." Paper to the Annual Summer Conference, The Stranger Next Door: Making Diversity Work, Couchiching Institute on Public Affairs, 9–12 August.

Yan, Miu Chung, Shirley Chau, and Dave Sangha. 2009/10. "An Exploratory Study of How Multiculturalism Policies Are Implemented at the Grassroots Level." *Canadian Ethnic Studies* 41 (3): 49–67.

◎ 1.2: Citizen Activism, Refugees, and the State: Two Case Studies in Canadian Immigration History

Stephanie Bangarth

Of all the elements of Canada's immigration policy, those relating to the admission of refugees have been the most controversial and the most criticized. But for much of Canadian immigration history, neither politicians nor public officials made any distinction between immigrants and refugees. It was not until the passage of the 1976 Immigration Act that refugees constituted an admissible class for resettlement. Until that time, special refugee admission schemes were made possible only with the passage of orders in council that suspended normal immigration regulations and permitted relaxed criteria for screening. Ministerial permits achieved the same thing. As a result, in the post–World War II period, Canada would see refugees arrive from around the world, such as 165,000 Eastern European displaced persons, 38,000 Hungarian refugees in 1956, 11,000 Czechs and Slovaks in 1968, 7,000 Ugandan Asians in the early 1970s, and over 6,000 Chileans in the period from 1973 to 1976.

This article explores the reception of Hungarian refugees over the course of late 1956 and 1957 and that of Chilean refugees from 1973 to 1976. It will highlight how concerned Canadians lobbied the state to live up to human rights ideals and modify discriminatory immigration policy in post–Second World War Canada. In both cases, success was realized in light of current-day views on inclusion and political ideology. While the Hungarian refugees were fleeing a Communist state and welcomed as democratic refugees, Chilean refugees fleeing a fascist state were viewed with suspicion by government officials. To varying degrees both cases highlight how citizen activism around immigration issues evolved over the course of the mid-twentieth century and how the state and social justice ideals clashed then as they do now.

My interest in refugee reception stems from my family history, particularly that of my father and my great aunt and great uncle, who were refugees from Hungary but at different points in time. My father came to Canada from Hungary as part of the massive post–World War II exodus of "Displaced Persons" (the official term used by the Canadian government), 165,000 of whom Canada accepted out of the devastation of postwar Europe. Having been a "DP," and particularly one from an enemy nation, my father certainly had negative early memories about his reception by Canadians. DPs were shunned by Canadians, and the term "DP" itself was hurled at them in a fashion not unlike a racial epithet. Only a few years later, in 1956, my great aunt and uncle would be treated to a much warmer reception from Canadians as part of the incredible

wave of Hungarian refugees in the aftermath of the failed Hungarian Revolution. Hearing their stories, I was struck by how much their experience was marked by assistance from voluntary organizations, both in the refugee camps and later in Canada. This article, then, reflects a long-time interest in the politics of refugee policy and refugee reception.

Enter the Hungarians

In late October 1956, pro-democracy, anti-Soviet demonstrations directed at the Soviet-backed government of Matyas Rakosi broke out in Budapest. Fearing that its control of the Warsaw Pact was unravelling, the Kremlin ordered the Red Army to put down the uprising on 4 November 1956. Events quickly turned violent. Soviet forces clashed with protestors, killing roughly 20,000 and imprisoning many more.[1] To escape a similar fate, tens of thousands of Hungarians crossed the border into neighbouring Austria. While NATO (North Atlantic Treaty Organization) was unable to intervene militarily—conflict over control of the Suez Canal divided its members—it was able to relieve the pressure placed on Austria. Days after the invasion, Canadian immigration officials reinforced the number of immigration officers at the Canadian embassy in Vienna, loosened the normal requirements concerning proper travel documentation, medical exams, and security clearances, and enlisted commercial airplanes to transport the refugees out of Austria. The effort produced impressive results: by the end of 1957 more than 37,000 Hungarians had been accepted into Canada. But government actors were not the only ones responsible for this shift in policy; indeed, the response was truly country-wide and would not have been possible without the support and assistance of a wide range of voluntary Canadian organizations that lobbied the federal government for a more humane response to the mass movement of refugees from Hungary. Throughout the crisis, the federal government relied heavily on groups such as the Canadian Council of Churches (CCC), the Canadian Catholic Conference, the Canadian Rural Settlement Society, the Canadian Jewish Congress

(CJC), the Canadian Red Cross (CRC), the Canadian Hungarian Relief Committee, the Canadian Hungarian Protestant Ministerial Association, the Canadian Christian Council for the Rehabilitation of Refugees, the Canadian Welfare Council, and the Jewish Immigrant Aid Society (JIAS) to assist with the resettlement and integration of the Hungarian refugees who arrived in Canada.[2]

In early November, Prime Minister Louis St Laurent and his cabinet met to determine the nature of Canadian relief efforts. According to one of many memoranda on the subject, it was clear that cabinet members were aware that "unless the West gives some expression of its solidarity with and sympathy for the Hungarians, we will have lost the last remnants of our prestige in all of Eastern Europe."[3] To that end, they considered their options, chief among which was the idea of giving monetary aid that would be administered by the Canadian Red Cross for aid to refugees outside of Hungary. A grant of $100,000 to the CRC was subsequently approved at the meeting, representing one of the first transnational links in the early stages of the Hungarian refugee crisis. Later, Lester B. Pearson, secretary of state for external affairs, recommended that an additional offer of $800,000 be made available to the CRC to provide relief, including, "to the extent practical and economical, of appropriate supplies of Canadian origin." In his lengthy memo to cabinet, Pearson justified the increase in monetary aid to the CRC by observing the importance of aid from Western countries "on humanitarian as well as political grounds," and noted that providing substantial emergency relief would serve as a replacement for military intervention.[4]

On 13 November the minister of immigration, J.W. Pickersgill, met with ethnic organizations representing not only Hungarian groups but also representatives from other Eastern European countries. At that time, Pickersgill resolved that the Canadian government would take steps to alleviate the suffering of refugees in Europe and to allow for their entry into Canada. Days later at a meeting hosted by the International Institute of Metropolitan Toronto, officials of the Department of Citizenship and Immigration (DCI) met again with the Canadian-Hungarian

Federation (the national umbrella organization of Hungarians in Canada) and also with church, voluntary, and social groups, including the Canadian Council of Churches and the Canadian Red Cross. What emerged from these meetings was a clear indication of the shared goals of the federal government and the voluntary organizations, initially that adequate reception for Hungarian refugees be secured. It was also clear that the government and the voluntary agencies did not yet appreciate issues of concern at this early stage to the Hungarian representatives, whose knowledge stemmed from their contacts in the refugee camps in Austria: money for refugee arrivals; refugee sponsorship, including for children as well as older and sick refugees; and the clarification and increased leniency in the granting of visas under current regulations.[5] The measured responses on the part of both government and voluntary officials can be explained by the relatively small numbers of Hungarian refugees making their way to Canada by this point.

Nonetheless, offers of employment, sponsorship, and other assistance for Hungarian refugees were flooding DCI headquarters and its offices throughout Canada as its director, C.E. Smith, noted in a memo to Col. Laval Fortier (deputy minister of immigration) dated 22 November. At the same time, applications from refugees without direct sponsors were being refused, with the rate of refusal being one out of every three applications. The contradiction between the large pool of assistance from voluntary agencies and the tangible desire of refugees to come to Canada, as well as the possibility of adverse publicity if applications continued to be refused at the present rate, resulted in government officials turning to voluntary agencies for help. Historically, such cooperation between voluntary agencies and the state on matters relating to refugee and immigration reception was not uncommon. In the immediate postwar period, the CCC and the JIAS, among other groups, established an amicable relationship with the departments of Citizenship and Immigration and of Labour. It was, for all intents and purposes, a mutually beneficial relationship: the federal government obtained reliable partners that were able to relieve it of much

IMMIGRATION POLICY REFORMS (1962–76)

In the years following 1945, Canada implemented significant reforms to immigration policy through which the criteria for assessing immigrant applications transitioned from subjective and overt racism to objective criteria without regard to race, ethnicity, national origin, or religion.

Immigration became a policy issue in the years following the war as Canada witnessed increased demand for entry into the country from displaced persons in Europe and refugee claimants from troubled areas (such as the Hungarians in 1956). In the early years, however, Canada maintained its historical and overtly racist immigration policy, a policy that gave preference to peoples from western and northern European countries. Change began with the Conservative government of John Diefenbaker in 1957. The general shift towards the promotion of equality and protection of human rights (the topic of Part IV), as evidenced by Diefenbaker's introduction of the federal Bill of Rights in 1960, meant that such blatant racism in immigration selection could no longer by justified. As a result, in 1962 new regulations with regard to unsponsored immigrants were introduced, removing race, ethnicity, national origin, and religion as criteria for determining admittance. Henceforth, immigration levels and individual applications would be assessed on the basis of economic and labour-market demands of the country and thus on criteria such as education and job skills. While economic need had always been a major factor in immigration policy, the 1962 reforms also reflected the recognition that Canada's maturing and more technological economy increasingly demanded skilled workers as opposed to general labourers. These reforms were solidified in 1967 with the introduction of the points system. Intended to remove subjectivity in determining admission owing to the wide discretion held by immigration officials, the new system allotted points based on criteria such as education and the economic demand for certain skills. Applications since 1967 have been based on the achievement of the required number of points.

By the 1970s, the federal government decided to amend the Immigration Act to reflect the above reforms, as the previous changes had been introduced as regulations. In addition to the need for a new immigration act to reflect the principles and processes introduced in 1962 and 1967, there was also a belief that the Act should outline the purposes of immigration for Canada rather than continue to focus on who should be excluded from Canada. The 1976 Immigration Act achieved these goals, outlining four categories of immigrants, including the independent class based on the points system. The Act also outlined the fundamental purpose of immigration for Canada, describing immigration as a positive means to achieve the nation's demographic, economic, cultural, and social goals.

of the burden of refugee resettlement; the CCC and the JIAS were provided with opportunities to fulfil their obligations to their international contacts while at the same time satisfying their humanitarian and spiritual impulses. The Rural Settlement Society of Canada, the CJC (with the JIAS), the Canadian Christian Council for the Rehabilitation of Refugees, and the CCC were singled out in a memo as "national voluntary agencies with which we [the Immigration Branch of the Department of Citizenship and Immigration] have dealt for

some time." Moreover, the memo indicated that government officials were well aware of the international contacts of these agencies, suggesting that voluntary agencies could contact "their affiliates or representatives in Europe" to find refugees suitable for sponsorship and that these agencies would essentially serve as another arm of refugee recruitment for the government.[6]

The Canadian Red Cross, via its affiliation with the International Committee of the Red Cross and in cooperation in Europe with the Intergovernmental Committee for European Migration, played a valuable transnational role in the refugee crisis and could be counted among the major organizations regularly present at official meetings held between federal government departments, the Ontario government, the Unemployment Insurance Commission, and other voluntary agencies. Additionally, the CRC worked closely with the Canadian Hungarian Relief Committee in dispersing the funds collected by way of the Hungarian Relief Fund. In many ways, the activities of the CRC in the Hungarian refugee crisis represented an extension of its work among refugees and orphans in the post–Second World War period and earlier during the that war when the society contributed volunteer services and $80 million in goods and money.

In the early days of the refugee crisis, the CRC engaged in its customary fundraising initiatives when faced with a humanitarian emergency. In early November, it initiated the Canadian Red Cross Hungarian Relief Fund, launched in cooperation with the Canadian-Hungarian Federation. The fund would be used to purchase medical and hospital supplies, bulk food, and clothing for distribution by the International Red Cross in Hungary. It was only when the Soviet Army had quelled the Hungarian Revolution two weeks after its outbreak that envoys from the Red Cross were allowed to enter Hungary. As an aside, by mid-February 1957, the CRC Hungarian Relief Fund exceeded the national objective of $500,000.[7]

The CRC frequently made use of information politics as a strategy to obtain a desired outcome, presenting certain information to the public to encourage government action. For example, in January of 1957, Marguerite Wilson, director of public relations for the CRC Society in Quebec toured the refugee camps in Austria, noting in her report to Red Cross headquarters in Toronto the courage of the refugees and the high regard for the CRC in Europe. According to Wilson, "the camps maintained by the Canadian Red Cross in Austria were cleaner, with better facilities than the other camps." Such information about the nature of the relief process and about the burgeoning needs of refugees in the early stages of

the crisis was important in highlighting the value of the CRC Hungarian Relief Fund.[8]

Furthermore, the available primary evidence reveals that the CRC was influential in the early period in persuading the federal government to offer a more generous and liberal response regarding the admittance of Hungarian refugees. Dr W.S. Stanbury, national director of the CRC, played an important intermediary role with the Canadian-Hungarian Federation in relaying information about the specifics of Canada's immigration policy pertaining to the Hungarian refugees. Ominously, Stanbury expressed to R.A.D. Ford, head of the European Division of the Department of External Affairs, his worry about the "reaction of the Hungarian-Canadians when it became entirely clear to them that in fact Canada was not proposing to give any assistance to refugees in the way of admitting them to this country except in cases which would be obviously profitable to Canada."[9]

In response to pressure from within and without government circles, on 26 November in the House of Commons, Pickersgill went much further in committing his government to the reception of Hungarian refugees. In a speech that Col. Laval Fortier referred to as the "Magna Carta for the movement of Hungarian refugees," Pickersgill reiterated his government's commitment to giving priority to applications from Hungarian refugees, stating that any responsible individual or organization in Canada was free to sponsor immigrants, that arrangements would be made for those refugees requiring medical treatment, and that refugees would be given assisted passage to Canada.[10]

In addition to cooperating with organizations such as the CRC, the CCC, and other voluntary immigrant settlement groups, the federal government, by way of the DCI, mined assistance from a variety of sources. Toronto's Board of Education approved sending up to 10 teachers to Holland to teach English to Hungarians in refugee camps in that country.[11] Other indications of the link between international organizations and localized Canadian efforts include the efforts of the Canadian YMCA groups to provide recreational activities in Hungarian refugee camps in Austria. The Canadian response was prompted by an urgent appeal for recreational, social, and educational facilities from World YMCA-YWCA representatives. Additionally, Canadian students and professors were asked by the World University Service (WUS), an international student relief and exchange organization, to contribute to an international fund for the rehabilitation of their counterparts who had fled from Hungary. At a meeting of the Canadian branch of the WUS in late November, its executive secretary told of more than 1,300 Hungarian students and professors in refugee camps in Austria and Yugoslavia. Funds raised in Canada would be used to provide temporary housing for them and to effect their transfer to other countries. The response was impressive. While operating under their own financial strain, Canadian universities pledged $100,000 to the fund and 14 universities pledged to accept students, waive tuition fees, and offer free housing. They were aided by the CRC, which assisted in identifying appropriate recipients.[12]

Further nods to the centrality of volunteer organizations in the Hungarian refugee crisis are evidenced by government officials' requests that such groups orchestrate local aid, housing, and employment for refugees and enforce the government's wishes to settle refugees in specific regional areas. To assist voluntary agencies in their work, the federal government produced educational and guidance materials on refugee reception. These materials, along with other related primary sources, reveal the myriad ways in which the reception of Hungarian refugees was framed. These framing devices include, but not limited to, humanitarian concerns, anti-communist rhetoric, assimilationist language, and "otherization."

A "Special Hungarian Issue" of the *Citizen*, a publication of the Canadian Citizenship Branch of the Department of Citizenship and Immigration, was one such tool made available to agencies assisting in the reception of Hungarian refugees.[13] Drawing on available current scholarly literature in the section on "Understanding the Refugee Immigrant," the author likened the refugee to a transplanted flower that needs to set down roots and be cared for in order to survive, flourish, and remain in its new environs. Another section

related a story of "English through Gestures," an account from a young couple in Ottawa who opened their home to "Joseph _____, Age 25, General Labourer, R.C.," as he was described on the file card given to them by an immigration officer. Without a knowledge of Hungarian, the young couple "tried to insist that Joseph use English words." In the interim, however, they became "masters of the sweeping gesture, the dramatic shrug, and the expressive face." The story goes on to relate the trials and tribulations of refugee reception and refugee adjustment, involving such issues as language barriers, food differences, and frustrations arising out of joblessness, and concludes that "Joseph still has a long way to go and many things to learn before he will become the good Canadian citizen he is capable of being."[14]

In some ways, the *Citizen* special edition reflects the Cold War anti-communist international environment and, thus, the federal government's motivation for becoming involved in the refugee crisis. In its analysis of Hungarian Canadian organizations, the writer notes that most Hungarians tended to participate in mutual benefit societies. The more recent associations concerned with Hungarian political matters "differ widely in their ideals but they are united in their anti-communism and nationalism. Their orientation is towards Hungary rather than towards Canada but observers believe that this type of organization will gradually lose its strength."[15]

The *Citizen* special edition is interesting for the nature of the information it supplied to prospective and current volunteer agencies assisting in refugee reception. A brief section on the contribution of earlier Hungarian immigrants to Canadian life indicated that Hungarians were noted in Canada for their pioneering farm activities in Saskatchewan and, later, for developing the tobacco industry in Ontario. In urban centres, Hungarians were renowned for their restaurants, "justly famous for their splendid cooking and special Hungarian dishes." Factory work, the arts, and medicine were other areas of employment singled out by the writer, who also noted that "Hungarians . . . appear to excel at figure skating and are now devoting their talents to teaching this sport in Canada."

The pamphlet also included information on available dictionaries, word lists, and other aids, such as the Hungarian versions of the *Handbook for Newcomers* and *How to Become a Canadian Citizen*, both published by the Canadian Citizenship Branch. Also included in the list of resources were two National Film Board documentaries, both featuring a Hungarian soundtrack: *Canadian Notebook* (1953), which highlighted the experiences of newly arrived immigrants in various regions of Canada to give an impression of the living and working conditions in Canada, community life, and educational facilities; and *Physical Regions of Canada* (1953), a film that described the physical and economic geography of Canada on the basis of the six natural divisions. A brief (and colourless) one-page synopsis of Hungarian history was provided on page 23 of the *Citizen* special edition, along with a reading list of publications about Hungary so that, presumably, volunteers and Canadians could choose to inform themselves about the newcomers in their midst. Lastly, an action plan titled "Suggestions for Local Committees" offered potential and existing volunteers ideas on how to organize, what types of representatives to include, and how to make arrangements for such necessities as accommodation, refugee reception, interpreters, language classes, counselling, financial advice/assistance, social activities, and, importantly, liaising with the Canadian Citizenship Branch.[16] The latter would be especially important in maintaining an effective advocacy network, both domestically and internationally, with the relevant federal departments relying on coordination to determine the nature of the Canadian response to the crisis while interacting with international organizations to obtain information.

While it is not possible in the confines of this article to discuss the many ways that volunteer organizations and local groups provided refugee reception across Canada, a representative sampling may be obtained via the *Citizen* special edition and in the pages of the *Globe and Mail*. When the first group of Hungarian refugees arrived by sea at the port of Quebec on 9 December 1956, they were met by over 3,000 people at the docks,

there to bid them welcome. The crowd threw bags of candy and packages of cigarettes to the newcomers while a military band played the national anthems of Canada and Hungary. Government and religious officials then bade the refugees welcome. The reception committee of the Bien-Être des Immigrants, the coordinating body for refugees in Quebec City, was responsible for the event. When my great aunt and uncle arrived on 7 January 1957 at Pier 21 in Halifax by way of the Spanish steamship *Venezuela*, they were greeted by many Haligonians, one of whom gave them tickets to a concert by the Halifax Philharmonic. Such generosity is still fondly recalled to this day.[17]

Generally speaking, accommodation for the Hungarian refugees was offered in nearly every centre of Canada at which they arrived, usually as a result of church coordination. Such hospitality was normally in the form of hostels, private homes, and church accommodation, although larger centres, such as Ottawa, established larger temporary residences in government buildings and barracks. A counselling service provided by the International Institute of Metropolitan Toronto was made available to refugees in Toronto who moved out of the hostels.

Across the country, Canadians organized entertainment for the refugees, which often doubled as fundraising opportunities. The staff of the Conservatory of Music in Regina, Saskatchewan, organized a public concert, with recent Hungarian refugees as the guests of honour. Proceeds from the concert went to the Hungarian Relief Fund. Nathan Phillips, mayor of Toronto, declared Saturday, 15 December 1956, to be "Toronto Hungarian Relief Day," with the funds to be directed towards the relief of Hungarian refugees in Europe.[18] In Brantford, Ontario, in mid-November, women lined up for almost two hours for a tea service at the local YMCA-YWCA, which raised $1,079. At an interdenominational rally on 18 November in Mount Brydges, Ontario, more than 100 families offered to open their homes to refugees. On 9 January 1957, a Hungarian festival was held at the Royal Ontario Museum in Toronto, the proceeds of which helped Hungarian students to continue their studies in Canada. A program of Hungarian

Galt Museum. Used with permission.

A group of Hungarian refugees at the Lethbridge train station in Alberta, 10 December 1956.

folk music and folk dancing, exhibitions of old and new Hungarian arts and crafts, and a lecture on Hungarian rug design were among the attractions of the festival. Even the Hungarian ethnic media contributed to refugee reception. Free, short-term subscriptions to two Hungarian Canadian newspapers, *Kanadai Magyarsag* (published out of Toronto) and *Kanadai Magyar Ujsag* (published out of Winnipeg), were offered to refugees with mailing addresses.[19] Additionally, Hungarian and other ethnic organizations donated money to the Hungarian Relief Fund and expressed their support for the Hungarian struggle. It was estimated that 10,000 Canadians from 16 ethnic groups participated in a march in downtown Toronto on 3 November 1956 to focus attention on the situation in Hungary.

From the early days of the revolution, when Hungarians were raising money for the CRC to send food, clothes, and medical supplies to Hungary, to some months later, when a series of cheques from various Italian groups in Toronto were donated to the Hungarian Relief Fund, it was clear that already-established immigrant communities were as eager as any in Canada to offer assistance.[20] But the crisis had the unanticipated effect of heightening the expectations of such groups, unrealistically so in fact; for some groups, the Hungarian crisis was, not a "one-off," but rather the standard to which future national responses to humanitarian crises should aspire. Indeed, Gerald Dirks aptly notes that "the unqualified success of the Hungarian resettlement program for Canada acted as a useful precedent when in subsequent years, individuals and groups urged the Government to embark upon other humanitarian schemes aimed at relieving the plight of a portion of the world's refugees."[21]

Enter the Chileans

In 1973, over 7,000 Chilean and other Latin American refugees were admitted to Canada following the violent overthrow of Salvador Allende's democratically elected Socialist-Communist government. Chilean and non-Chilean supporters of the old regime had fled the oppression directed against them by Chile's new military ruler, General Augusto Pinochet, in the wake of the coup. Although Canada took the refugees in, it did so grudgingly—at least initially. Despite pressure from Amnesty International and church, labour, and Latin American groups, the government was slow to react, not wanting to antagonize Chile's new administration and the United States government, which had criticized Chile's slide into economic disarray under Allende. When Argentina faced a military coup d'état in March 1976, an event that marked the beginning of Argentina's now famous "Dirty Wars" of 1976 to 1983, a second wave of Chilean refugees sought to come to Canada.

In the aftermath of the 1973 coup, Canadians, especially members of the Protestant and Roman Catholic churches of Canada, called on the Canadian government to denounce the human rights abuses and grant asylum to Chilean refugees located both inside Chile and in neighbouring Argentina. Robert Andras, the minister of immigration, and Mitchell Sharp, the minister of external affairs, remained reluctant to do so. On the advice of Canadian Ambassador to Chile Andrew Ross, the Canadian government had recognized the Pinochet junta on 29 September 1973 on the ground that it was the only authority in the country. This decision was not well received by refugee advocates, as Andrew Thompson notes.[22] Many questioned whether the Canadian government was displeased to see the Allende government fall. Andras and Sharp, however, feared that among the refugees were terrorists, communists,

and other subversives. Only after a chorus of disapproval from various social justice groups did they re-evaluate their position and begin the process by which Canada would take in more than 4,500 Chilean refugees by the end of 1976.

But political advocates were also integral to the efforts to expand refugee rights. Conversations about a fact-finding mission to Chile began in the spring of 1976. Increasingly disturbing reports regarding imprisonment and exile for political reasons, harassment of refugees, and repression of human rights in Argentina and Uruguay were heard alongside the continuing news of oppression in Chile. The Inter-Church Committee on Chile agreed to sponsor a visit by three Canadian members of Parliament to the three countries of the so-called southern cone of Latin America. Several other Canadian organizations, including Amnesty International, Oxfam Canada, and the Canadian Catholic Organization for Development and Peace, supported the effort. The purpose of their mission was twofold: to observe and evaluate the refugees' situation and the Canadian response to their needs; and to observe the general situation of human rights in the countries visited.

Each of the three MPs involved in the mission were noted for having taken a special interest throughout their careers in issues of human rights and in the Chilean situation in particular. Andrew Brewin, a member of the New Democratic Party, represented the Toronto riding of Greenwood from 1962 to 1983. His legal experience, advocacy of civil liberties, and knowledge of immigration policies were well known, as was his adherence to the tenets of the Anglican faith. David MacDonald, a Progressive Conservative and United Church minister, represented the Prince Edward Island constituency of Egmont from 1965 to 1979. His interest in human rights and issues of world development had led him to undertake several previous fact-finding missions, many together with Brewin.[23] Louis Duclos was a Roman Catholic Liberal MP who represented the Quebec riding of Montmorency. In addition to his years as a civil servant, Duclos spent several years in the Canadian embassy in Bogota, Colombia. The three members thus represented the three major Canadian political parties, three diverse geographical backgrounds, and three major Canadian religious denominations. They embodied a variety of previous international roles and a long experience with discussions of external affairs and immigration in the House of Commons.

The three MPs set out for Santiago, Chile, on 27 September, only to learn that owing to a high-level junta decision they would not be permitted to enter Chile. Instead, they arrived in Buenos Aires, Argentina, on 30 September and would spend much of their 10-day visit in Buenos Aires and Montevideo, Uruguay. They arrived back in Canada on the 11 October 1976. The issue of General Pinochet not allowing the Canadian politicians into the country was of great concern because Canada had had diplomatic relations with Chile for many years and the country had sought out Canada for both private and public financial investment, including investment by way of mining and nuclear reactors.

During their time in Argentina, they met with various government and United Nations officials, the Canadian ambassador to Argentina, human rights organizations, and a number of refugees from Chile. Beyond learning that conditions in Chile, Uruguay, and Argentina were dismal in regard to human rights violations and persecutions at the hands of right-wing death squads, they also learned of the plight of refugees from Chile and Uruguay. These refugees had been given access to Argentina, but their status had never been regularized. When in September 1976 the Argentinean government decreed that all refugees in the country must register with the authorities by October's end, many refugees became fearful that with registration their information would become known to those who composed the death squads. They also dreaded returning to their country of origin where their political views and activities might make them victims of repression. These concerns were not unfounded, as the three MPs found many refugees living in terror.

As part of their mission the MPs also examined Canada's refugee assistance program. As no refugee policy was specifically in place, assistance measures were done on a group by group basis. As of July 1976, the Canadian government pledged to accept 6,000 refugees from Chile, with 4,500 already in Canada leaving a surplus of 1,500. The main concern that Brewin, MacDonald, and Duclos had with the acceptance of refugees by Canadian officials was that of delay. The processing of refugee applications from Chile took an average of four weeks, during which time applicants would be in danger of seizure by the Chilean police. No similar delays were encountered in bringing in Hungarian refugees in 1956, Ugandan Asians in 1972, or Vietnamese in 1975. In fact, the Canadian government was able to grant refugee status to 6,000 Ugandans in two months in 1972, yet took 18 months to admit the first 1,500 Chileans after the Allende government fell. Moreover, the Canadian government also did not suspend prior medical, security, and immigration procedures to speed the removal of Latin American refugees, and RCMP officers in Santiago turned down a high proportion of the initial wave of refugee applications in 1973–4 on the basis that they composed security threats for Canada. Immigration officers were also found to be treating refugees much as they treated ordinary immigrants (e.g., using similar forms and questions based on the points system), allowing very few special considerations in view of the emergency situation.[24] What Brewin, MacDonald, and Duclos did not yet know, and what would come out in the report of the McDonald Commission on RCMP Wrongdoing in 1981, was that the Mounties unfairly branded many would-be refugees from Chile as subversives, accepting without question American CIA (Central Intelligence Agency) assessments of Chileans as communist troublemakers.[25]

The government painted the Chilean refugees as subversives and dangerous to Canada. It was certainly out of step with the Canadians, many of whom by way of various organizations were urging the government to accept the refugees, just as they had done in past crises. As one Canadian wrote, "I hate to think that the lives of Chileans innocent of any wrong-doing may be jeopardized by a fear of what the United States might think or by an exaggerated and groundless fear that Chilean refugees might 'subvert' our democracy."[26] Supportive correspondence from Canadians across the country flowed to the three MPs; many urged that the same accord be given to Chilean refugees as had been accorded to Hungarian, Czech, and Ugandan refugees.[27] A member of the Manitoba Legislative Assembly wrote Minister of Manpower and Immigration Bud Cullen, informing the minister that he had

> met some of the present Chilean refugees, both in northern Manitoba and in Winnipeg and they include skilled adult educators, a miner, a former chief of police, a customs agent and a secretary, etc. All those I have met so far will, I feel, make good citizens. I will do my best to help my constituents understand this problem and to support you in action that will alleviate the severe hardships and distress of those people who's [sic] only crime has been to be politically active.[28]

The government was also out of step with the efforts of other nations, including Holland and Sweden, which were treating the Chilean refugees outside the normal flow of immigrants. In their report, the three MPs recommended that standards for the definition and admission of refugees be set out clearly in legislation or at least in explicit regulations. Along with their recommendation that a separate and suitable application form for refugees be prepared, Brewin, MacDonald, and Duclos suggested that all UN-accredited refugees be considered as refugees for the purposes of Canadian immigration. As of the report's publication in November 1976, while Canada accepted the United Nation's definition of a refugee, it did not accept the UN determination or assessment of who is a bona fide refugee. Indeed, Canadian immigration officers were known to reject a high number of refugees registered by the UNHCR (United Nations High Commissioner for Refugees).

That there was considerable friction between NGOs (non-governmental organizations), church groups, and refugee organizations and the federal government is clear in the case of the Chilean refugees. As Thompson notes, church groups were increasingly aware over

the course of the 1970s that their relationship with Pierre Trudeau's Liberal government had become strained. Many believed that instead of being motivated by humanitarian obligations, the federal government was influenced more by domestic politics and Cold War machinations.[29] Numerous agencies called for the UN Protocol definition of refugees to be incorporated into the new Act. Many hoped that this would prevent a repetition of Canada's unresponsive attitude towards the Chilean refugee crisis. The year 1978 marked the first time an immigration act included a humanitarian category for refugees needing protection and resettlement. The Act also established the Private Sponsorship of Refugees Program, which allowed Canadians to be involved in the resettlement of refugees. To that end, in 1979, Canadians enthusiastically sponsored the Vietnamese "Boat People" under these new rules. On 21 January 1979, three designated classes of refugees were created in accordance with subsection 6(2) of the 1976 Immigration Act. These classes were the Indochinese, the Latin American Political Prisoners and Oppressed Persons, and the Eastern European Self-Exiled Persons. All persons in these classes had to demonstrate their ability to become successfully established in Canada, a requirement that reflected the continuing importance of economic considerations in Canadian refugee policy. Both Indochinese and Eastern European refugees faced more relaxed standards than did the Latin American refugees. While the two former groups were fleeing Communist regimes, the latter was constituted primarily of victims of right-wing regimes who had to demonstrate that they had a well-founded fear of persecution or that they had been detained for legitimately expressing free thought or exercising civil liberties, in addition to proving their ability to become established in Canada. A noted improvement, reflective of the report written by Brewin, MacDonald, and Duclos, was that they were not required to be outside the country when making their claim.

At the same time as the refugee crisis was being investigated, Brewin, MacDonald, and

Duclos detailed the human rights violations in Chile, among them activities of the death squads. Provocatively, they linked the restoration of human rights as a precondition for the granting of loans and capital from Canada or from the rest of the international investing community. In the 1970s, the issue was with Noranda Mines in Chile and Canadian bank loans to that country, which Canadian churches, via the Taskforce on the Churches and Corporate Responsibility and Amnesty International, continued to protest.[30] Over the course of the MPs' visit to South America, President Pinochet made some derogatory remarks about the nature of their trip. In the words of David MacDonald, "I think if the President of Chile can take that kind of abusive and offensive attitude to Canadian parliamentarians . . . I think the reflection on our country as such . . . I think that we are in an impossible situation in seeing any kind of Canadian investment and in particular any kind of public investment being advanced."[31] Here he was speaking directly to the potential for Canadian mining investment in Chile, something that today has enriched the pockets of individuals such as Peter Munk of Barrick Gold.[32] Incidentally, at a shareholders' meeting in Toronto on 9 May 1996, Munk, chair of Barrick Gold Corporation, praised General Augusto Pinochet for "transforming Chile from a wealth-destroying socialist state to a capital-friendly model that is being copied around the world." Regarding Pinochet's human rights record, Munk said, "[T]hey can put people in jail, I have no comment on that, I think that may be true. . . . I think [the end justifies the means] because it brought wealth to an enormous number of people. If you ask somebody who is in jail, he'll say no. But that's the wonderful thing about our world; we can have the freedom to disagree."[33]

Change or Continuity?

Perhaps not surprisingly the relationship between the voluntary agencies and the federal government was never quite the same after the Hungarian crisis. In the decades that followed, many of the organizations cited herein have remained heavily involved in the resettlement process; however, they have increasingly taken on the role of opponent rather than of partner. For this reason alone, the Hungarian refugee crisis and the response that followed remain pinnacle events in terms of transnational cooperation. If nothing else, they proved that the combination of political and advocacy group pressure and coordination could lead, at least under certain circumstances, to more humane refugee reception, even if only momentarily.

On the other hand, advocates of the Chilean refugees were dissatisfied with Ottawa's handling of the crisis. The slow response led many to become increasingly suspicious of the federal government's commitment to refugees. As several scholars of Canadian immigration and refugee policy have noted, the response to the crisis helped to foster the perception that Ottawa was far more willing to accommodate refugees fleeing Communist regimes on the left than those escaping fascist regimes on the right. This was made abundantly clear by the late 1970s, as Canada's response to the boat people of Vietnam fleeing a leftist government was in marked contrast to that which was extended, and continued to be extended, to victims of right-wing regimes such as that in Chile.

Today, refugees continue to be problematized. The year 2011 marked the sixtieth anniversary of the UN Convention on Refugees, but instead of marking this in a positive way, the Canadian government reintroduced Bill C-4 (the Preventing Human Smugglers from Abusing Canada's Immigration System Act, formerly Bill C-49) in June 2011. Among other measures, the bill proposed the mandatory detention of some refugees, including children, without independent review. The Canadian Bar Association has pointed out in a formal brief that this contravenes the Canadian Charter of Rights and Freedoms as well as international law.[34] When Bill C-49 was originally introduced in October 2010 (introduced, not by the immigration minister, but by the public safety minister), it drew criticism from the opposition parties and other critics, who said it punishes the victims of human smuggling, not the criminals. Reintroduced in 2012 as Bill C-31, the Protecting Canada's Immigration System Act was passed in Parliament on 28 June. It remains to be seen what effect the new legislation will have and especially whether future refugees will continue to be viewed with suspicion, as in the case of the Chilean refugees in the 1970s, instead of with acceptance, as in the case of the 1956 Hungarian refugees.

Author's Note: My appreciation goes to conference attendees at MANECCS 2010 and CARFMS 2011 for their comments on earlier forms of this research and to my research assistants, Caitlin McCuaig and Matthew Brown, who embody the very best that King's history students have to offer.

Endnotes

1   Anna Porter, "It Still Haunts Us All," *Globe and Mail*, 14 October 2006, F1, F6.

2   See Gerald E. Dirks, "Canada and Immigration: International and Domestic Considerations in the Decade Preceding the 1956 Hungarian Exodus," in Robert H. Keyserlingk, ed., *Breaking Ground: The 1956 Hungarian Refugee Movement to Canada* (Toronto: York Lanes Press, 1993), 5–11; Library and Archives Canada (hereafter LAC), DCI, vol. 117, "Minutes of the Meeting Respecting Hungarian Refugees," Toronto, 27 November 1956; Andrew Thompson and Stephanie Bangarth, "Transnational Christian Charity: The Canadian Council of Churches, the World Council of Churches and the Hungarian Refugee Crisis, 1956–1957," *American Review of Canadian Studies* 38, no. 3 (Autumn 2008): 295–6.

3   Michael D. Stevenson, ed., *Documents on Canadian External Relations*, vol. 23: *1955–1956, Part II* (Ottawa: Minister of Public Works and Government Services, 2004), 461.

4   Ibid., 474, 477.

5   LAC, DCI, vol. 117, file 3-24-34-1, vol. 1, Report of Meeting Convened with the Hon. J.W. Pickersgill and Ethnic Representatives from Countries behind the Iron Curtain, 13 November 1956; International Institute of Metropolitan Toronto, Minutes of Meeting, 19 November 1956; Minutes of an Informal Meeting Held at the Office of the Citizenship Branch, Department of Citizenship and Immigration, 22 November 1956.

6   LAC, DCI, vol. 117, file 3-24-34-1, vol. 1, Department of Citizenship and Immigration, Immigration Branch memo, from the director to the deputy minister, 22 November 1956; Thompson and Bangarth, "Transnational Christian Charity," 297–302.

7   "Red Cross Directs Drive to Provide Aid to Hungary," *Globe and Mail*, 6 November 1956; "All Her Savings," *Globe and Mail*, 9 November 1956; "Russians Let Red Cross Aid Enter Hungary," *Globe and Mail*, 12 November 1956; "Hungarian Fund Goes Over Top; Total at $512,071," *Globe and Mail*, 11 February 1957. It should be noted that, at about this same time, Pearson was expressing his disappointment in subscriptions from the public to the Red Cross fund in a confidential memo to the minister of finance. While he called for more money to be released from the government purse, he also commented that the government should have taken a stronger lead in the public eye to ensure more private contributions. Memo, Secretary of State for External Affairs to the Minister of Finance, 11 January 1957, in Stevenson, ed., *Documents on Canadian External Relations*, 492.

8   *Globe and Mail*, 19 November 1956, 11 January 1957.

9   Confidential memorandum from Head, European Division, to Under-Secretary of State for External Affairs, 14 November 1956, in Stevenson, ed., *Documents on Canadian External Relations*, 473. Concern over the stinginess of Canadian policy was not restricted to the above-mentioned groups, however. See LAC, DCI, vol. 117, file 3-24-34-1, vol. 1, "Minutes of an Informal Meeting Held at the Office of the Citizenship Branch, Department of Citizenship and Immigration, Toronto, Ont.," 22 November 1956.

10   Canada, House of Commons, *Debates*, 26 November 1956, 36–40.

11   *Globe and Mail*, 18 January 1957.

12   Ibid., 21 and 22 November 1956, 21 December 1956.

13   LAC, DCI, vol. 117, file 3-24-34-3, vol. 1, "Special Hungarian Issue," *Citizen* 3, no. 1 (February 1957): 1.

14   Ibid., 8–11. The author of the piece noted that when Joseph left for work in the Gatineau Hills, he took with him books on "Learning the English Language" and was also supplied with half a dozen bottles of Tabasco sauce to make "anaemic Canadian meals more palatable to his Hungarian taste. Included also in his luggage were several cans of paprika, which is a seasoning more familiar to him than our salt and pepper."

15   Ibid., 17.

16   Ibid., 17–19, 21–4.

17   Maria Toth and Imre Toth, interview, 2006.

18   *Globe and Mail*, 15 December 1956.

19   LAC, DCI, vol. 117, file 3-24-34-3, vol. 1, "Special Hungarian Issue," *Citizen* 3, no. 1 (February 1957): 19–20; *Globe and Mail*, 11 January 1957, 13 and 19 November 1956.

20   *Globe and Mail*, 3 November 1956, 30 January 1957.

21   Dirks, "Canada and Immigration," 11.

22   Andrew S. Thompson, *In Defence of Principles: NGOs and Human Rights in Canada* (Vancouver: UBC Press, 2010), 22.

23   David MacDonald, interview, 2011.

24   Andrew Brewin, Louis Duclos, and David MacDonald, *One Gigantic Prison: Report of the Fact-Finding Mission to Chile, Argentina and Uruguay* (Toronto: Inter-Church Committee on Chile, November 1976), 12–15.

25   Bill Johnston, "Cautious Kindness: Canada's Refugee Law," *Refuge: Canada's Periodical on Refugees* 1, no. 2 (1981): 5.

26   LAC, GFF, letter, Perry Jr to Fairweather, 4 January 1974.

27   LAC, ABF, vol. 22, file 3, II.

28   LAC, ABF, vol. 74, file 3.

29   Thompson, *In Defence of Principles*, 22–3.

30   LAC, ABF, vol. 42, files 2 and 3.

31   Brewin, Duclos, and MacDonald, *One Gigantic Prison*, 19.

32   Peter Munk, born in Budapest, Hungary, to a well-off Jewish family, was in his teens when Hungary was invaded by Nazi Germany in 1944. His family managed to escape via the Kasztner Train, which carried 1,684 Jews to safety in Switzerland, and Munk came to Canada in the early 1950s as a refugee. His story, and that of the Kasztner Train, is detailed in Anna Porter's award-winning work *Kasztner's Train: The True Story of Reszo Kasztner, Unknown Hero of the Holocaust* (2007).

33   Asad Ismi, "Pinochet's Profiteers: Canadian Business in Chile." *Peace Magazine*, July/August 1997, www.asadismi.ws/pinochet.html.

34   Canadian Bar Association brief, November 2010, www.cba.org/CBA/submissions/pdf/10-78-eng.pdf.

Works Cited

Brewin, Andrew, Louis Duclos, and David MacDonald, *One Gigantic Prison: Report of the Fact-Finding Mission to Chile, Argentina and Uruguay.* Toronto: Inter-Church Committee on Chile, November 1976.

Canada. House of Commons, *Debates*, 1973–9.

Canadian Bar Association brief, www.cba.org/CBA/submissions/pdf/10-78-eng.pdf.

Dirks, Gerald. *Canada's Refugee Policy: Indifference or Opportunism?* Montreal and Kingston: McGill-Queen's University Press, 1977.

Globe and Mail, 1956–7.

Hawkins, Freda. *Canada and Immigration: Public Policy and Public Concern.* 2nd edn. Montreal and Kingston: McGill-Queen's University Press, 1988.

Ismi, Asad. "Pinochet's Profiteers: Canadian Business in Chile." *Peace Magazine*, July/August 1997, www.asadismi.ws/pinochet.html.

Johnston, Bill. "Cautious Kindness: Canada's Refugee Law." *Refuge: Canada's Periodical on Refugees* 1, no. 2 (1981).

Keyserlingk, Robert, ed. *Breaking Ground: The 1956 Hungarian Refugee Movement to Canada.* Toronto: York Lanes Press, 1993.

Library and Archives Canada (LAC), RG 26, vol. 117, file 3-24-34-3, vol. 1, "Special Hungarian Issue," *Citizen*, February 1957, vol. 3, no. 1.

———, MG 32, C72. Gordon Fairweather Fonds (GFF).

———, MG 32 C26. F. Andrew Brewin Fonds (ABF).

———, RG 26. Department of Citizenship and Immigration Fonds (DCI).

MacDonald, Rev. David. Interview. 4 August 2011.

Porter, Anna. "It Still Haunts Us All." *Globe and Mail*, 14 October 2006, F1, F6.

Stevenson, Michael D., ed. *Documents on Canadian External Relations.* Vol. 23: *1955–1956, Part II.* Ottawa: Minister of Public Works and Government Services, 2004.

Thompson, Andrew S. *In Defence of Principles: NGOs and Human Rights in Canada.* Vancouver: UBC Press, 2010.

Thompson, Andrew S., and Stephanie Bangarth. "Transnational Christian Charity: The Canadian Council of Churches, the World Council of Churches, and the Hungarian Refugee Crisis, 1956–1957." *American Review of Canadian Studies* 38, no. 3 (Autumn 2008).

Toth, Maria, and Imre Toth. Interview. 31 August 2006.

CHAPTER 2

"Canadian" Identity and Culture

◎ 2.1: FIREWORKS, FOLK-DANCING, AND FOSTERING A NATIONAL IDENTITY: THE POLITICS OF CANADA DAY

Matthew Hayday

On 1 July 1958, viewers of the Canadian Broadcasting Corporation (CBC) witnessed the first nationally simulcast television broadcast in Canadian history. Governor General Vincent Massey's Dominion Day address emphasized the "two great streams" that had influenced Canadian history—the English and the French. He observed that through confusion and compromise, a great country had arisen, developing free and great institutions around the central pillar of the Crown, a symbol of both heritage and duty. Seven years later, viewers of CBC Television and Radio-Canada observed Dominion Day festivities taking place on Parliament Hill. Bilingual hosts Alex Trebek and Henri Bergeron welcomed them to Canada's ninety-eighth birthday celebrations, featuring a succession of performers who had come from across the land "bearing gifts." The opening act from British Columbia was the Cariboo Indian Girls Pipe Band, a dozen tartan-clad teenaged girls from the Shuswap First Nation who performed traditional bagpipe music. Twenty-six years later, Canadians who tuned in to the Canada Day special saw a very different face of Aboriginal Canada in the folk-rock group Kashtin, who opened and closed the 1991 festivities with their Montagnais-language rock music.

All three events were arranged by the federal government in honour of the anniversary of Confederation. The contrasts among them are striking, even on the sole basis of the role played by Aboriginal people in the televised celebration. Massey's speech ignored Canada's First Nations. The 1965 celebration presented an image of Aboriginal girls assimilating to white Canadian culture, whereas the Aboriginal Canadians of 1991 were maintaining the language of their ancestors and fusing Western rock music with First Nations' themes and language. Massey was the queen's representative to Canada, the teenagers from 1965 were amateur performers, and the rockers from 1991 were Juno Award–nominated professional singers. Massey and the Cariboo Girls were part of Dominion Day celebrations; Kashtin was part of a Canada Day event. Much had changed in the federal government's celebration of a landmark anniversary of Canada's political evolution.

For Canadians, 1 July marks the anniversary of the creation of the Dominion of Canada with its four original provinces in 1867. Of the six provinces that joined later, only Prince Edward Island did so on 1 July. In Newfoundland, it is a day of mourning for soldiers killed in the First World War Battle of Beaumont-Hamel.

The first of July is thus not necessarily an obvious rallying point for all Canadians—but then, so few things are in a country marked more by slow evolution and compromise than by violent change or revolution. By the mid-1950s, both Empire Day (23 May) and Victoria Day (24 May) had declined in importance to Canadians, as had the empire and monarch they honoured. Parades for St-Jean-Baptiste Day (24 June), honouring French Canada's patron saint, drew huge crowds in Montreal and Ottawa in the early 1950s but held little appeal for English speakers. Thus, in 1958 federal officials selected the holiday of Dominion Day as a component of its public policy agenda to foster certain conceptions of Canadian identity. In subsequent years, politicians considered and tested a succession of other possible names (Canada's Birthday, Canada Week) before renaming the holiday "Canada Day" in 1982. Tracing changes in the content and form of the day's celebrations and examining the political considerations that drove these experiments help us to understand the development of federal national identity policies in post–Second World War Canada. . . .

For the past 30 years, historians, political scientists, and other scholars have devoted considerable attention to the study of nationalism and its intersection with cultural practices, examining the manner in which the socially constructed "imagined communities"[1] we refer to as nations often rely on invented traditions to foster national solidarity and pride.[2] Social psychologist Michael Billig argues that the reinforcement of national identities is an ongoing process. Elements of "banal nationalism," such as languages, displayed flags, and the media's use of a rhetorical "us," continually naturalize and reinforce feelings of nationalism.[3] . . .

Less has been written with the aim of understanding commemoration as part of a public policy agenda. Graeme Turner contends that the 1988 Australian Bicentenary should be examined as a cultural policy initiative by the Australian government to "teach" its people how to celebrate their national identity, even if the

promoted hybrid identity failed to receive full acceptance.[4] To what extent was this the case in Canada? Canadian politicians and bureaucrats viewed Canada Day as a tool to reinforce government policies related to national identity and unity. Politicians and bureaucrats worked with their partners in the media and civil society to attempt to craft holiday celebrations that supported their conceptions about what Canadian identity *should* be, in the hope that this vision would be accepted by Canadians.

How were these policies crafted? Pluralist models of public policy formation posit that governments act as brokers between interest groups competing to influence policy. Conversely, elite-driven models emphasize the ideological viewpoints of politicians. While citizen groups were sometimes consulted by the government, and politicians had specific visions of Canada they sought to advance, the following analysis will demonstrate that interest groups were rarely central to the considerations of Canada Day organizers. Moreover, transitions between ideologically opposed governments did not always lead to radical policy shifts regarding Canadian national identity. For this reason, the historical institutionalist approach to policymaking must be considered. This approach focuses on the autonomous roles and power of the state and bureaucratic actors and on the ongoing impact of previously enacted public policies.[5] While political leaders sometimes intervened in the overall messages and format of Canada Day, the bureaucrats who worked for the Secretary of State Department (now Canadian Heritage) provided the institutional memory and backbone of these celebrations. They normally took the initiative to develop new programming ideas or attempted to maintain certain elements in the face of apathetic or even antagonistic political climates. While public response to these events, gauged through evaluations, polling, and newspaper coverage, can be found, the internal documentation of the Secretary of State Department suggests that officials often maintained policies despite lukewarm or critical public and media reactions.

Understanding this interplay of politics, bureaucracy, and the public provides a fuller picture of the history of public policy development.

What was this Canadian identity that was being fostered? José Igartua argues that in the 1960s English Canadians turned away from their previous British-centric identity models and adopted one rooted in bilingualism and multiculturalism.[6] Bryan Palmer agrees with Igartua that the British-centric identity was abandoned in the 1960s but argues that no new model of identity emerged to replace it.[7] Conversely, Eva Mackey contends that a multicultural, tolerant, heterogeneous identity has been fostered by the Canadian government since the 1970s. This process ironically reasserted the central role of white, undifferentiated Canadians as the arbiters of national identity, while also making them feel left out of an identity politics centred on difference. Moreover, Mackey contends that the Canadian state has fostered a discourse of the "crisis" of Canadian identity to allow it to play a central role in regulating the politics of identity.[8] In response to Mackey, one might say that the history of Canada Day policy suggests that, prior to the 1970s, crises did not affect the government's celebration policies. While political and constitutional crises did play a role after 1976, these were hardly invented by the federal government; rather, they were major challenges to circumvent, particularly since Canadians trusted their governments less in these decades. Dominion Day and Canada Day celebrations were considered an element in a broader strategy of national unity and identity formation, although successive governments struggled to come up with a structure for the holiday that would be both popular with Canadians and lead to more spontaneous community-based celebrations. As the following analysis will demonstrate, while ambivalent attitudes about Canadian identity persisted in the 1990s, new identity models were definitely being promoted by the government and gaining greater popular acceptance (at least in English-speaking Canada) by the 1980s. Igartua, thus, is perhaps premature in contending that this new identity had gelled by the 1960s, but

Palmer overstates his case about the complete drift of Canadian identity after this decade. By 1992—Canada's 125th anniversary—a tradition and public policy of celebrating Canada Day had solidified. It stressed a Canadian identity that was centred on diversity, individual rights, and achievement, and it was attracting significant public support.

Are National Holidays Consistent with British Tradition? Diefenbaker's Dominion Day Conundrum

Federal government involvement in the organization of 1 July celebrations was instigated by the Progressive Conservative government of John Diefenbaker, first elected in 1957, mere days before the ninetieth anniversary of Confederation. Firm believers in the virtues of Canada's British heritage, the Conservatives, while in the opposition, had frequently criticized the Liberal government's gradual phaseout of the term "Dominion" from national institutions.[9] The *Ottawa Journal* observed that restoring this term was one of Diefenbaker's pet causes and that Canadians could expect "Dominion" to return to prominence under his watch.[10] The following May, his cabinet authorized Secretary of State Ellen Fairclough's proposal for a formal Dominion Day event on Parliament Hill.[11]

Fairclough's staff had been discussing a Dominion Day celebration, and many reasons had been advanced against one. William Measures, director of Special Division, noted that 1 July was normally a day of exodus from Ottawa. He did not consider Canada to be a retrospective country, but rather a forward-looking one that was confident in its future. Symbolic elements would be problematic, because both the flag and anthem questions were unresolved. Perhaps more damning, he argued, government ceremonies to celebrate a national day were "unusual in British countries. Some people regard them as an evidence of national immaturity. . . . Annual government ceremonies are contrary to Canadian and Commonwealth tradition." He also cautioned that if the event was begun, it must continue every year without interruption, because starting and stopping the event due to weather or fatigue or lack of public interest "would create uncertainty, perhaps derision."[12]

Why, then, did Fairclough press forward? Duty was certainly a consideration. Measures pointed out that the governor general had called for these celebrations back in 1868, even if successive governments had ignored that request. There was also the centennial of 1967 to consider; Dominion Day celebrations could build excitement and enthusiasm. More important was the consideration of two key target groups: children and immigrants. Measures observed that "perhaps the organization of an annual public festival on July 1 would establish in the memories of present day children the happy memories which their parents and grandparents have of May 24." He further noted that "new Canadians . . . should be made aware of the heritage of their adopted country, and should join in the celebration of the chief Canadian anniversary."[13]

Fairclough requested $14,000 from cabinet, including $10,000 for fireworks. Most other costs were minimized by using military and government personnel for key features of the ceremony—a 21-gun salute, trooping of the colour, and a carillon concert. Although Fairclough envisioned the governor general's presence for the trooping of the colour, she explicitly did not request the presence of the prime minister or cabinet. Measures had cautioned against beginning a tradition that required that the prime minister be in Ottawa every 1 July. She did suggest that the customary sittings of the House of Commons be cancelled in order to allow parliamentarians to attend.[14] Cabinet authorized her request on 20 May 1958.

The early celebrations of Dominion Day were formal and militaristic. Each year featured the governor general's address, which was broadcast on CBC Television and Radio-Canada in 1958 and 1960. There was no official celebration in 1959, but it is probably safe to say that most Canadians did not notice, in light of the visit of Queen Elizabeth II, which coincided with the day. The events also included concerts by the Peace Tower's carilloneur, a trooping of the colour ceremony, and, in 1960, the naval sunset ceremonies. Fireworks were cancelled in 1960 because of noise complaints from the Ottawa General Hospital.[15] (In most subsequent years, fireworks were both the most popular and most expensive element of the festivities.) On the whole, these early attempts to institute a tradition of Dominion Day observance stressed the formal, tradition-oriented aspects of the day that linked Canada to its British past and were very much reflective of the Diefenbaker government's attempts to shore up Canada's relations with Britain and the commonwealth.

"A Colourful Folk Element"

Television had been a significant, although limited, aspect of the first Dominion Day events of the Diefenbaker years, which had featured addresses to the nation by the governor general and the queen. In 1960, the CBC broadcast "Dominion Day: A Day to Remember," a program that profiled six new Canadians taking the oath of citizenship on Parliament Hill. By February 1961, federal government officials were thinking of ways to broaden the appeal of Dominion Day ceremonies both within and beyond Ottawa. Ellen Fairclough, then minister of citizenship and immigration, wrote to Secretary of State Noël Dorion, suggesting ways to modify the festivities, such as adding more popular features to the program that would draw on Ottawa's folk festivals. . . .

Folk performances were extremely popular with mid-century audiences, a fact exploited by Nova Scotian tourist promoters.

Ellen Fairclough noted that a variety of well-trained groups performing musical interludes would be "quite colourful and worthy of the location and occasion. The dances should be particularly good television material." Although the television audience was the priority, Fairclough stressed that "the professional quality should not be so dominant that, when seen by the television audience across the country, the performance would discourage rather than encourage emulation."[16] This challenge of providing televised entertainment without discouraging local attendance and organization of community celebrations would prove to be a constant conundrum for federal organizers.

The program for Ottawa's Dominion Day celebrations was thus expanded to include high-calibre folk music and dance performances, starting with the Feux-Follets dance troupe from Montreal in 1961 and then broadening to include more acts in subsequent years. Segments from the folk performances aired on the CBC and Radio-Canada from 1961 to 1963, as did the naval sunset ceremony.[17] They proved to be a popular draw for the local audience, with estimates ranging from 10,000 to 35,000 spectators in attendance.[18] These folk performances demonstrated a shift in the government's portrayal of Canada. With an eye to the citizenship function of Dominion Days, folk groups were encouraged to perform material from a variety of national, indigenous, and ethnic traditions, including French-Canadian, Ukrainian, Israeli, Italian, and Abenaki. However, Fairclough's vision was clear in 1961: "The program should be so composed as to enable Canadians generally to identify themselves with it. It should have strong appeal to them as an expression of the historical evolution of our country. This principle should govern the extent to which the program would include New Canadian participants."[19] British-Canadian and French-Canadian songs and dances were to occupy the central place. Nonetheless, the scope of the activities and their audience was expanded in the early 1960s. In this respect, . . . folk elements supported a modernizing, multicultural vision of Canada, rather than an idealized British past. Moreover, multi-ethnic folk dances reflected an urban diversity, which was less evident in rural Canada.

The 1963 election of Lester Pearson's Liberals did not substantially alter Dominion Day festivities, which built upon the foundations already laid by Secretary of State officials.

Continuity was evident in the selection of performers for the centrepiece variety show. C.M. Isbister, deputy minister of citizenship and immigration, observed that "the three ethnic groups which shared the early history of our nation, namely the Indians, French and the Anglo-Saxons, could be featured annually, while the remaining numbers would be presented by as many different ethnic groups as the program can accommodate." Sensitive to the televised format, he noted that the Ottawa event must be well attended, as the crowds would be visible on television.[20] The Department of Citizenship and Immigration and the CBC expanded the variety show component, phasing out military pageantry in favour of the more popular folk performances. These were extended in length to fill a 60- to 90-minute broadcast, and in the range of performers, who were flown in to represent each province.[21] The massed armed forces bands performed for the live audience but were dropped from television coverage.

The Pearson government also introduced significant new themes for the Dominion Day ceremonies, starting with a bilingual and bicultural focus. Bilingual masters of ceremonies hosted the 1965 and 1966 televised specials. This change was important, as the events were simulcast on the CBC television network and Radio-Canada. Program organizers were always careful to include francophone performers, not only from Quebec, but also from other French-Canadian or Acadian communities. The focus on this theme is not surprising. Pearson had launched the Royal Commission on Bilingualism and Biculturalism in 1963; its reports began appearing in the mid-1960s. Multiple ethnic groups were featured in these shows on a rotating basis from year to year, allowing for the inclusion of a variety of displays of traditional ethnic dances, songs, and martial arts. The selection of "Indian" performers reflected the assimilationist discourse of the Department of Indian Affairs up to the 1960s. Aboriginal performers tended to be presented in Euro-Canadian guise, whether as tartan-clad Shuswap girls from British Columbia playing the bagpipes or a Cree baton-twirling champion from Manitoba. While these performers had a variety of reasons for participating, the incorporation of the pipe band, which formed in 1958 at the St Joseph's Mission residential school run by the Oblates of William Lake, BC, explicitly reflects political motives (they also performed at Expo 67). Father H. O'Connor, principal of the school,[22] wrote to the Secretary of State Department: "We would like the people of Canada to see the better side of our Indian people and we feel sure that there is no better means of educating our Canadian people to see this better side than to have such a fine group of Ambassadors representing the Indian people."[23] The cost of transporting the band to Ottawa for the Dominion Day event was prohibitive, so the extra costs were defrayed by special funding from the Centennial Commission and the Department of Indian Affairs.

Reinvention Breeds Contempt

The centennial celebrations of 1967 were, by all accounts, a great success. In addition to the eye-popping summer-long spectacle of Montreal's Expo 67, a full slate of events took place on Parliament Hill. Secretary of State Judy LaMarsh hosted the birthday "Hullabaloo," which included a massive birthday cake and a variety show with performers from all regions of Canada. After so much effort had been placed into building up 1 July as a day of celebration, federal bureaucrats believed that these centennial celebrations would naturally lead to continued strong enthusiasm for Dominion Day. In this, they were mistaken. The decade that followed was marked by efforts to overhaul the nature of 1 July celebrations, with deleterious effects.

Planning for 1968 began with an ambitious agenda for an even larger Ottawa event, including an interdenominational religious service and a Rideau Canal flotilla.[24] But organizers ran into massive roadblocks from cabinet, which refused to approve funds, and the CBC, which cited financial concerns and decided not to broadcast the show.[25] Organizers scrambled to pull together $35,000—far less than the $57,000 allocated

for 1966 or the $150,000 for 1967. Canadians outside of Ottawa were not able to watch the 140 performers who had been brought in from across the country.

The resulting event was a disaster. J. André Ouellette, executive assistant to Secretary of State Gérard Pelletier, sent a blistering memo to Undersecretary of State G.G.E. Steele criticizing the complete lack of Indian or Eskimo performers, the failure to play the national anthem, the weak French in the religious service, and the Show on the Hill, which he characterized as being "une de très mauvaise goût."[26] . . .

The federal government was willing to try again. Ouellette noted that planning for future events needed to start earlier and involve more people. He called for a "Canadianization" of the event, which would entail a smaller role for the governor general, a larger role for the prime minister, and a more central place for Canadian symbols such as the omitted anthem.[27] In this, one detects a reframing of what the Trudeau government thought of as "Canadian," since the Diefenbaker government certainly thought it was putting on a Canadian event!

The next seven years featured a hodge-podge of largely unsuccessful attempts to rework Dominion Day. The variety show was moved indoors to the National Arts Centre from 1969 to 1971. Although the new setting was less vulnerable to being rained out, the new "Bonjour Canada" programming suffered numerous flaws. Envisioned as Canada's version of Royal Command performances in Britain, the event largely failed to inspire.[28] Attempting to downplay the "ethnic" components of the past in an effort to "focus on Canadians"[29] such as singer-songwriter Gordon Lightfoot and classical pianist André Gagnon, the performances received a lukewarm reception, attracting press coverage mostly for the poor quality of the hosts' bilingualism.[30] It did not help that the focus was diverted from Ottawa in 1970 and 1971 towards Manitoba's and British Columbia's centennial events. Public relations consultant Paul Break had felt this would create a greater focus on Canadian people, and less on Ottawa, while CBC producers

Wilfred Fielding and Thom Benson argued that a standard program every year, featuring stars, lacked enough public appeal to compete with other programming.[31] The prime minister and cabinet were thus flown off to Winnipeg and Victoria after their brief attendance at morning festivities in Ottawa, despite warnings from Secretary of State officials against shifting the focus from the national capital.[32]

The centrepiece events returned to Parliament Hill in 1972 in a celebration marred by the unilingual French hosting of pianist André Gagnon (English dubbing was provided for the television audience).[33] In subsequent years, the headline performers failed to attract excitement, other than fiddler Ti-Jean Carignan. Eugene Forsey complained to Secretary of State Hugh Faulkner that there was "nothing to remind people of the breadth and diversity of the country" and that there were few songs and dances from the country's ethnic groups.[34] Forsey's observation draws our attention to the fact that although bilingualism was heavily promoted in the Trudeau-era Dominion Day events, multiculturalism was largely sidelined. The CBC again declined to cover the 1974 show, and although the 1975 slate of performers included ethnic folk performances and was viewed by 60,000 spectators on Parliament Hill, it failed to generate enthusiasm among politicians.[35] The Ottawa media reported favourably on the concerts, which attracted between 25,000 and 70,000 spectators,[36] but other Canadian papers only gave cursory attention to the events. After the hoopla surrounding the centennial, the festivities of subsequent years paled by comparison.

Given the uncertainty and ever-changing forms of the 1 July events on Parliament Hill and the fiscal pressures facing the government, it was not a shock when the federal government eliminated funding for Dominion Day events for 1976. . . . It would take the national unity–shattering election of the Parti Québécois (PQ) in November to lead to a revival—and yet another reconception—of the government's approach to celebrating 1 July.

The "National Love-Feast"

The election of the PQ created a crisis in Ottawa that extended through the Secretary of State Department.[37] Senior civil servant Bernard Ostry was seconded to oversee a large ad hoc staff running a $4-million Canada Day program. The "Great Canadian Birthday Party" had two major components. The first was a coast-to-coast gala televised variety show, linking stages in every region of the country, featuring the biggest name Canadian stars willing to perform (most high-profile Quebecois artists declined and were instead part of the $6-million Fête nationale celebrations in Quebec on 24 June). The show ran live for over three hours on all but two (both in Quebec) of Canada's radio and television stations. Planning for 1978 envisioned a repeat performance, with festivities "coordinated as a national love-feast, giving the people of each Province, or Territory, the feeling that on their particular day their fellow Canadians were thinking of them and wishing them well."[38] In 1979, the central event was scaled back to the Ottawa stage, but with top-level professional performers.

These shows featured a spectrum of big-name Canadian stars, including Ginette Reno, Bruce Cockburn, Anne Murray, and Buffy Sainte-Marie, francophone artists from diverse regions of the country, and First Nations, Inuit, and Métis performers. Less evident was the multi-ethnic face of Canada, although Ukrainian Shumka dancers and soul singer Salome Bey were both featured twice. Half of all Canadians watched the 1977 show.[39] Radio-Canada's French Services Division suggested that the show was not well received in Quebec,[40] but an evaluation by Complan Research Associates showed that Quebecers watched the program in numbers comparable to those in English Canada. Fifty-four per cent believed that the celebrations would make it more likely that Canada would stay united, versus 18 per cent who thought they made separation more likely.[41] In subsequent years, the audience for the television show shrank but still pulled in numbers comparable to those for the Grey Cup.

Starting in 1977, the federal government also began direct seed funding for community-based celebrations. The Canadian Folk Arts Council and the Council on Canadian Unity were authorized to allocate $2 million as start-up grants to community-based groups that wanted to organize picnics, fireworks, festivals, or other activities in honour of Canada's birthday. The program's goal was "to remind people of their history, to provide a perspective of the current difficulties and to encourage a re-commitment to the country."[42] Thirty per cent of the funding was earmarked for Quebec events. Evaluations concluded that these events were well attended, but that more could be done to link them with other events across the country, in order to foster a greater sense of national unity.[43]

External evaluations carried out by Byward Consultants also suggested that themes be developed that de-emphasized regional and linguistic differences and were grounded in emotional appeal, that "[strove] to respect and reflect the regional and cultural diversity of Canada but which . . . transcend[ed] provincialism."[44] Although there was intense debate over whether the Canada's birthday programming was accomplishing its implicit goal of combating separatism, this crisis of national unity had prompted the federal government to change its approach to the national holiday and focus on sponsoring local activities in addition to its activities in Ottawa. By the late-1970s, it was clear that the targeted audience was no longer limited to new Canadians and children, but extended to the entire population of Canada, particularly francophone Quebec.

Local Celebrations, National Symbols, and Canadian Achievement

The 1979 election of Joe Clark's Conservatives had consequences for Dominion Day. Clark's government opted to scale down the scope of the 1980 events dramatically, cancelling the large-scale evening variety show.[45] External evaluators suggested a low-key, local, and participatory approach, observing that "no other approach would work, in part because there is now a great deal of cynicism towards Canada Day."[46] In keeping with Clark's "Community of Communities" approach to Canada, $1.2 million was maintained to sponsor community-based events.[47]

Clark's government did not survive to implement this policy shift, falling on a budget vote in December 1979. Trudeau's returning government thus had to decide whether to reinstate the slashed funding and organize a celebratory bash that would take place six weeks after Quebec's sovereignty-association referendum. Secretary of State Francis Fox urged caution, noting that a huge nationalistic party might be "psychologically harmful if it's not perfectly in tune with the post-referendum atmosphere."[48] A mix of party politics and public policy considerations carried a decision not to reinstate the funding. Any criticism related to cutting the Parliament Hill show could be blamed on the Clark government, whereas reintroducing the funding would open the Trudeau government to criticism of its extravagance—a particular worry, given the size of the federal deficit. Policy considerations also played a role. Organizers defended shifting from an "overly structured, professional entertainment-type" event to one featuring "more informal, popular participatory activities providing scope and opportunity for spontaneous manifestations by Canadians . . . of their pride of nationhood and of the significance they attach to Canada's birthday."[49]

The National Committee for Canada's Birthday was established to coordinate the local celebrations for 1 July 1980. Committee Chair Yvon Des Rochers stressed that "Canada's birthday should belong to Canadians, not to governments." He observed that the government was moving away from direct involvement in festivities, wanting Canadians to participate in these events rather than "sit[ting] back and be[ing] entertained by professionals."[50] Although most of the government funding was distributed to communities, a sizeable grant was allocated to the National Capital Region (NCR) for a substantial event on Parliament Hill and in surrounding parks.[51] One common element linked these otherwise decentralized activities: in 1980, "O Canada" became the official national anthem. Groups across the country were strongly encouraged to organize noonday singings of the anthem, with the Ottawa group led by Prime Minister Trudeau—linking Canadians coast to coast as an imagined community singing together. The National Committee felt that events went well and that the day should continue to be "apolitical, non-partisan and decentralized."[52] *Ottawa Citizen* journalists Tim Harper and Andrew Cohen agreed, noting the "homegrown" nature of the festivities on the Hill.[53] The NCR committee was less sure of this direction, calling for the revival of the CBC-produced *Show on the Hill*.[54]

The federal government maintained the same approach to 1 July for the next seven years. The anniversary of Confederation fell under a new social policy directive, adopted in the fall of 1980, which sought the "development of a cultural thrust related to the understanding and enhancement of national identity and symbols."[55] The name "Dominion Day" itself had been something that the Liberals sought to change. Although colloquial use of the term "Canada Day" had been prevalent since the 1960s, a long succession of cabinet-sponsored and private member's bills to make this official had failed to pass since the 1940s, and it took a private member's bill sponsored by Vaudreuil MP Hal Herbert to officially change the name to Canada Day. The bill passed a virtually deserted House of Commons on 9 July 1982 and cleared the Senate on 25 October. The celebrations of 1983 were centred on the "Canada Day" name, and the National Canada Day Committee was restructured as a body federating the Canada Day committees for each province and territory and the NCR, replacing the Council for Canadian Unity and the Canadian Folk Arts Council as granting bodies.[56]

The celebrations of the early 1980s sought to solidify Canadian recognition of major new symbols such as the anthem, flag, and the renamed "Canada Day." The new constitution and Charter of Rights of 1982, however, were not emphasized that year, perhaps because of the controversy

surrounding their adoption. In the mid-1980s, organizers developed additional themes. The first, "Explorers of Canada," was tied to the major anniversary celebrations taking place in 1984, including the 450th anniversary of Jacques Cartier's arrival in Canada. Secretary of State Serge Joyal hoped that the events would unite the country in a national celebration of the "sense of adventure" that had led to Canada's exploration.[57] This theme was incorporated into key events and speeches related to Canada Day, including the formal midday celebrations on Parliament Hill, which were carried on CBC and the Radio-Canada network.[58] A number of theme-based activities were developed by the Canada Day committees in conjunction with the Secretary of State to foster shared experiences among Canadians, such as national poster contests and activity books for children.[59] Clearly, organizers sought to create common experiences for Canadians on their national day, even while continuing to stress the local celebrations.

Several Canada Day committee members and civil servants were uncertain about having a theme beyond simply "Canada."[60] Nevertheless, themes were maintained in Canada Day events organized under Brian Mulroney's Progressive Conservative government, which was concerned that even the modified format of Canada Day was too centralized and that there was "now a need to return it to the grass roots."[61] But the approach of holding federally coordinated local celebrations with common themes and symbols had proven popular. A 1984 Gallup Poll indicated that 73.2 per cent of Canadians approved of federal financial support for Canada Day celebrations.[62] Thus, Secretary of State Walter McLean's staff continued to develop new themes, which included "A Salute to Canada's Youth" in 1985, a tie-in to the International Youth Year; "Canada: In Motion, in Touch" in 1986, which was linked to the "Transportation and Communications" theme of Vancouver's Expo; and "Citizenship" in 1987, the fortieth anniversary of the passage of the Citizenship Act. Attendance at the Ottawa-based events continued to grow, from 170,000 in 1984 to 325,000 in 1985, and passing 400,000 in 1988.[63] The live crowd for the Parliament Hill evening variety show alone was estimated at 50,000 to 70,000 in the late-1980s.

Returning to the Centre While Maintaining the Grassroots

Although community celebrations of Canada Day were considered successful by many government organizers, by 1986 both the Nielsen Task Force on Culture and Communications and the National Capital Region Canada Day Committee were arguing in favour of a return to a higher national profile for Ottawa-based events.[64] Early in 1987, Secretary of State officials proposed moving the formal ceremony on Parliament Hill to the early evening, hoping the CBC would cover both this ceremony and the more festive variety show that followed.[65] In 1988, the CBC aired the professionally produced variety show on Parliament Hill. The broadcast also featured clips from events earlier in the day in Ottawa, St John's, Vancouver, and Canada's Expo pavilion in Brisbane, Australia. Canadian achievement was a dominant theme. Three Olympic-medal-winning figure skaters (Elizabeth Manley, Tracy Wilson, and Rob McCall) and Paralympic medallist Rick Hansen, Canada's "Man in Motion" and ambassador to the Canadian pavilion in Australia, were featured prominently.[66]

After what they considered a successful broadcast in 1988, CBC executives agreed to a longer-term commitment to a national Canada Day variety show, with content from both Ottawa and other sites. Secretary of State officials decided to hold two separate events each Canada Day. The first was a more formal official affair, controlled directly by the Department of the Secretary of State, featuring speeches by the governor general and the prime minister that were interspersed with musical performances. The evening variety show was coordinated largely by the National Capital Commission, but with input from CBC, the Secretary of State, and other involved parties. Corporate sponsors were also sought out for the variety show and for other events, such as the poster contest, starting

in the mid-1980s.[67] Most years also featured attempts to link the theme of Canada Day to historic anniversaries—1989 being the 125th anniversary of the Charlottetown Constitutional Conference—or to internationally sponsored years,[68] such as 1993's International Year of Indigenous Peoples. Audiences for these broadcasts grew steadily, with a viewership of 700,000 in 1990 doubling to 1.5 million in 1991.[69]

Organizers were attempting to broaden the scope of how Canada was conceptualized, moving beyond the limitations of the variety show format. Building on the anthem, the flag, and "Canada Day," a symbols kit was developed in the mid-1980s for schoolchildren, and anniversaries of the adoption of these symbols were highlighted in festivities. Organizers also attempted to develop new Canada Day songs, including "This Is My Home," which they hoped would repeat the success of Bobby Gimby's 1967 anthem "Ca-Na-Da."[70] Activity books of the 1980s launched a new focus on Canadian achievers beyond the performing arts. The young achievers book of 1985, for example, profiled Canadians under age 30 who were accomplished in athletics, the arts, and the military. In later years, a "Canadian Achievers" segment was added to the official ceremonies.[71] Whenever possible, organizers highlighted international accomplishments, such as those of astronaut Roberta Bondar in 1992. Throughout the late 1990s, Prime Minister Jean Chrétien routinely trumpeted Canada's United Nations ranking as the best country in the world in which to live.

One can detect both continuity and substantial change in these presentations of Canadian identity in the Canada Day events of the late 1980s and early 1990s. As organizers of Canada 125 began to prepare for the 1992 spectacle, they identified the need for messages that would target youth, Natives, and multicultural organizations. Such messages would focus on citizenship, official languages, the environment, and symbols of Canada.[72] In the fervour surrounding the Meech Lake and Charlottetown constitutional negotiations, Quebec nationalism and separatism certainly had not dissipated as a concern; the organizing committee for Canada Day 1992 included a representative of the Federal-Provincial Relations Office to oversee these issues. Politicians' speeches often focused on unity and Canada's capacity for flexibility. A strong contingent of Quebecois performers, including Michel Pagliaro, Diane Tell, Marie-Denise Pelletier, and Nanette Workman, was incorporated into the variety shows leading up to this anniversary. The presence of the performers implicitly suggested unity,[73] but Céline Dion went even further in her participation in the Canada 125 celebrations. Dion delivered a short speech expressing her hope that politicians of all stripes would help Canada through the difficult times of the constitutional crisis. Although she was criticized for her efforts by Quebec media such as *Le Journal de Montréal*, Dion's message was precisely what organizers hoped for. Moreover, organizers always ensured that non-Quebecois francophones were included in the variety shows, in order to present a pan-Canadian image of the Canadian *francophonie*.

The Aboriginal peoples' component of Canada Day had also changed dramatically. In striking contrast to the 1960s assimilationist presentations, First Nations performers were central to the 1990s variety shows, and their contributions to Canada were routinely mentioned in the official speeches. First Nations performances often incorporated indigenous languages, including Kashtin's 1991 performance in Montagnais and Susan Aglukark's 1992 performance in Inuktitut. The year 1993 was proclaimed the International Year of Indigenous People and featured high-profile celebrities from Canada's Aboriginal communities, including composer John Kim Bell, a Mohawk, as master of ceremonies, and numerous performers, including Graham Greene, Tom Jackson, and Susan Aglukark.

Multiculturalism had been a central element of the "new Canadian"–targeted Dominion days of the 1960s. However, with the decision to move away from ethnic folk performances, multicultural diversity was less overtly showcased in the variety shows. The theme remained present in planning documents for these spectacles, but the more visible manifestations of Canadian diversity were the achievers in sports, sciences, and other fields featured in the non-performance aspects of Canada Day in the 1980s and 1990s.

By 1992, the organization of Canada Day had become institutionalized, coordinated by an experienced staff who worked in a permanent directorate with ongoing stable funding. Yet even after a successful celebration of the 125th anniversary of Confederation, debriefing meetings featured recurrent concerns about how to make participation more active, whether to invoke additional themes beyond pride in Canada, and whether the current format should be completely revamped.[74] These doubts about a successful event lead one to contemplate the broader significance of the Canadian government's policy of commemoration and how it relates to national identity.

Conclusions

Certain elements of the Canada Day festivities of the early 1990s would have pleased John Diefenbaker. The formal, militaristic elements of the 1958 commemoration were echoed in the 21-gun salute and inspection of the guard rituals of the midday formal ceremonies. Canada's British ties continued to be embodied in the governor general, the central political figure at the midday events. Although the intended audience had broadened to include all Canadians, the priority audiences of the Diefenbaker-era organizers—new immigrants and youth—continued to be major target groups for planners.

However, political and bureaucratic considerations had led to significant changes in the 1 July events. A new symbolic order was crafted and deliberately reinforced around a central idea of a "Canadian" celebration of a renamed "Canada Day"—a term that had greater resonance among francophones and new Canadians. A new anthem and maple leaf flag served as distinctly Canadian symbols featured in promotional materials.

One can also trace the development of a more populist approach to the ceremonies.

Highly formal structured events gave way first to the inclusion of folk performances, then to a massive variety show with popular entertainers and a deliberately crafted party atmosphere in the nation's capital, echoed by federally sponsored picnics and other events coast to coast. As federal organizers discovered which celebratory elements were popular with Canadians, they incorporated them into their official plans for Canada Day—and into the vision of Canadian identity they were promoting.

The government's image of Canadian identity underwent key—although sometimes subtle—transformations. In the 1960s, a more bilingual, ethnically diverse image of the country that explicitly recognized Aboriginal peoples and regional allegiances became part of the events. Pan-Canadian linguistic duality was a constant thread in the festivities from the 1960s onward. Over the decades, there was a shift in depictions of Aboriginal people; they were no longer portrayed as having adopted Euro-Canadian values, but instead as maintaining First Nations indigenous languages and traditions or as creating a new fusion of Aboriginal and Euro-Canadian practices. Ethnic diversity passed from an explicit and foregrounded "folk"-oriented portrayal of the performers' cultures of origin to a presentation of Canadians from many different backgrounds as achievers in a culture that valued scientific and athletic accomplishment. Canada Day ceremonies thus served as a vehicle for promoting the government's liberal, civic conception of a Canada rooted in individual achievement and diversity. The entire thrust of these celebrations also shifted from a performance and entertainment-based event to one that increasingly attempted to deliver messages about Canadian achievement on an international scale in science, athletics, and international peacekeeping. Attendance at these events and program evaluations demonstrated the increased awareness and popularity of 1 July as Canada's national holiday.

From a policy perspective, the structure of Canada Day celebrations was an ongoing source for debate. Canada Day implied a nationwide celebration in its name; as employees of the federal government, Secretary of State organizers wanted the day to be celebrated nationally in a way that would foster a sense of national community. It was not easy to promote a common celebration with thousands of kilometres separating Canadians from each other. Television could show Canadians celebrating in many communities, linking these events in a single broadcast. It could also focus attention on the central celebration in Ottawa and show that Canadians (both performers and audience members) from many provinces had gathered together to celebrate on Parliament Hill. But as organizers and politicians alike lamented, television spectatorship alone did not constitute the active, dynamic celebration they had hoped to foster.

Despite these concerns, the combination of funding local and Ottawa-centred celebrations, coupled with common symbols, activities, and themes in local events, advanced a popular tradition of celebrating Canada Day. Even if some Canadians opted for the passive option of the television special, they were still being exposed to the messages presented by Canada Day. One may debate whether Canadians accepted the organizers' conception of Canada, but strong attendance and audience figures suggest that these messages were reaching Canadians. Now hundreds of thousands of people flood Ottawa's streets every 1 July, while in communities across Canada families attend local picnics and flock to fireworks displays. The CBC continues to cover the formal midday ceremonies from Parliament Hill and in most years covers at least part of Ottawa's evening festivities. Despite format changes and near cancellations, the tradition of celebrating the anniversary of Confederation took root in the decades following the first such event on Parliament Hill, and the federal government continues to be an active sponsor of these events. . . .

After decades of supporting the observance of Canada Day, the federal government has managed to reinforce certain conceptions of Canada. A discourse of Canada as a land of ethnolinguistic diversity, with two official languages and many cultures, has been repeatedly stressed.

This discourse has also fostered the theme of Canada as a land of individual rights, tolerance, and opportunities for achievement. In these respects, the new symbolic order and commemorative policies encouraged by the Canadian government have reinforced policies of bilingualism, multiculturalism, liberal individualism, and the Charter of Rights. Although this national identity did not fit easily into models of ethnic nationalism and was often resisted, particularly in Quebec, it did match the broader policies of national identity that the government had been developing since the 1960s and provided a flexible identity that was adaptable to the changing demographics of the country.

Author's Note: Many thanks to my colleagues in the University of Guelph History Writing Group and the anonymous *Canadian Historical Review* (*CHR*) reviewers for their helpful comments on earlier versions of this article. The Social Sciences and Humanities Research Council (SSHRC) Postdoctoral Fellowship Program provided early financial support for this research. Reproduced with permission from *Canadian Historical Review*.

Endnotes

1   Benedict Anderson, *Imagined Communities* (London, UK: Verso, 1983).

2   Eric Hobsbawm and Terence Ranger, eds., *The Invention of Tradition* (Cambridge, UK: Cambridge University Press, 1983).

3   Michael Billig, *Banal Nationalism* (London, UK: Sage, 1995).

4   Graeme Turner, *Making It National: Nationalism and Australian Popular Culture* (St Leonards, NSW: Allen & Unwin, 1994), 68–9.

5   On public policy models, see Miriam Smith, *A Civil Society? Collective Actors in Canadian Political Life* (Peterborough, ON: Broadview, 2005).

6   José Igartua, *The Other Quiet Revolution: National Identities in English Canada, 1945–71* (Vancouver: UBC Press, 2006).

7   Bryan D. Palmer, *Canada's 1960s: The Ironies of Identity in a Rebellious Era* (Toronto: University of Toronto Press, 2009).

8   Eva Mackey, *The House of Difference: Cultural Politics and National Identity in Canada* (Toronto: University of Toronto Press, 2001), 5–13.

9   This made it unlikely that Liberals would use "Dominion Day" for nationalist purposes in the 1950s.

10 Richard Jackson, "Diefenbaker to Stop 'Tinkering,' Word 'Dominion' on the Way Back," *Ottawa Journal*, 29 June 1957.

11 Cabinet Conclusions, 20 May 1958, vol. 1898, series A-5-a, RG 2 Privy Council Office, Library and Archives Canada (hereafter LAC).

12 W.H. Measures to Undersecretary of State, 11 March 1958, file 7215-1, pt 1, box 24, BAN 2002-01308-X, RG 6 Secretary of State, LAC.

13 Ibid.

14 Memorandum to Cabinet, 9 May 1958, file 7215-1, pt 1, box 24, BAN 2002-01308-X, RG 6, LAC.

15 Noël Dorion to Ellen Fairclough, 24 January 1961, file 7215-1, pt 1, box 24, BAN 2002-01308-X, RG 6, LAC.

16 Ellen Fairclough to Noël Dorion, 8 February 1961, file 7215-1, pt 1, box 24, BAN 2002-01308-X, RG 6, LAC.

17 Doug Nixon to H.G. Walker, 27 June 1961; M. Sadlier to H.G. Walker, 29 May 1962, file PG 18-21, vol. 917, series A-V-2, RG 41 CBC, LAC.

18 "16,000 Defy Heat to Watch Hill Celebrations," *Ottawa Journal*, 2 July 1963. (This article estimates 10,000 at the main festivities.) Eric Bender, "35,000 Thrill to Glorious 95th Birthday Party Show," *Ottawa Journal*, 3 July 1962.

19 Ellen Fairclough to Noël Dorion, 8 February 1961, file 7215-1, pt 1, box 24, BAN 2002-01308-X, RG 6, LAC.

20 C.M. Isbister to minister, 14 August 1964, file 7215-67, pt 1, box 26, BAN 2002-01308-X, RG 6, LAC.

21 Memo from W. Martin, 19 May 1965, file PG 18–21, vol. 917, series A-V-2, RG 41, LAC.

22 Elizabeth Furniss, *Victims of Benevolence: The Dark Legacy of the Williams Lake Residential School* (Vancouver: Arsenal Pulp, 1992), 110–11; Irene Stangoe, "Scottish-Indian Pipers from the Cariboo," in *Looking Back at Cariboo-Chilcotin with Irene Stangoe* (Surrey: Heritage House, 1997), 136–8.

23 H. O'Connor to Miquelon, 8 March 1965, file 1-7-4/1-1, pt 1965, box 15, acc. 1986–7/419, RG 6, LAC.

24 G.G.E. Steele to Secretary of State, 31 May 1968, file 7215-68-2, pt 1, box 26, BAN 2002-01308-X, RG 6, LAC. On public religion in the 1960s, see Gary Miedema, *For Canada's Sake: Public Religion, Centennial Celebrations and the Re-making of Canada in the 1960s* (Montreal and Kingston: McGill-Queen's University Press, 2005).

25 G.G.E. Steele to George Davidson, 14 June 1968; C.J. Lochnan to G.G.E. Steele, 24 June 1968, file

7215-68-4, pt 1, box 27, BAN 2002-01308-X, RG 6, LAC.

26   J. André Ouellette to G.G.E. Steele, 18 July 1968, file 7215-68, pt 1, box 26, BAN 2002-01308-X, RG 6, LAC.

27   J. André Ouellette to G.G.E. Steele, 18 July 1968, file 7215-68, pt 1, box 26, BAN 2002-01308-X, RG 6, LAC.

28   Memo from C.J. Lochnan, 28 March 1969, file 7215-69-8, box 27, BAN 2002-01308-X, RG 6, LAC; P.M. Tellier to Michael Pitfield, 29 December 1970, file 7215-70, box 28, BAN 2002-01308-X, RG 6, LAC.

29   Minutes, 20 May 1969, file 7215-69-2, box 27, BAN 2002-01308-X, RG 6, LAC.

30   Blaik Kirby, "CBC's Holiday Concert Marred by Its Clumsy Bi-bi Flaws," *Globe and Mail*, 2 July 1970.

31   Minutes, 11 February 1969, file 7215-69, box 27, BAN 2002-01308-X, RG 6, LAC.

32   Michael Pitfield to Jules Léger, 12 August 1969, file 7215-70, box 28, BAN 2002-01308-X, RG 6, LAC.

33   "A Hurt to a Good Cause," *Ottawa Journal*, 5 July 1972.

34   Eugene Forsey to Hugh Faulkner, 3 July 1973, file 7215-73, box 28, BAN 2002-01308-X, RG 6, LAC.

35   Graham Glockling to Pierre Forget, 21 April 1975, file 7215-75, box 28, BAN 2002-01308-X, RG 6, LAC.

36   Audience estimates varied widely. Sheila Copps, "Free Family Fun Fiery," *Ottawa Citizen*, 2 July 1974; Maureen Peterson, "Thank You, Canada for a Great Party," *Ottawa Journal*, 2 July 1975.

37   Matthew Hayday, "La francophonie canadienne, le bilinguisme et l'identité canadienne dans les célébrations de la fête du Canada," in *Entre lieux et mémoire: L'inscription de la francophonie canadienne dans la durée*, ed. Anne Gilbert, Michel Bock, and Joseph Yvon Thériault (Ottawa: Presses de l'Université d'Ottawa, 2009), 103–4.

38   Festival Canada 1978, 5th revision, 24 October 1977, file PG 18-21-3, vol. 917, series A-V-2, RG 41, LAC.

39   "Canada Day 1977: A Report and Recommendations, 8 Sept. 1977, Ottawa," file 32, vol. 32, MG 31 D230, G. Hamilton Southam, LAC.

40   Memo, 21 May 1978; memo from Peter Meggs, 24 August 1977, file PG 18-21-3, vol. 917, series A-V-2, RG 41, LAC.

41   Twelve hundred and seventy interviews were conducted, including 290 in Quebec: file 7215-77, pt 4, box 29, BAN 2002-01308-X, RG 6, LAC.

42   National Museums of Canada submission to Treasury Board, 11 May 1977, file 7215-77, vol. 1, box 29, BAN 2002-01308-X, RG 6, LAC.

43   André Fortier to Secretary of State, 4 August 1977, file 7215-77, pt 4, box 29, BAN 2002-01308-X, RG 6, LAC.

44   Byward Consultants, "Recommendations for a Federal Government July 1st Program 1978—Summary," 14 October 1977, file 7215-78, pt 1, box 29, BAN 2002-01308-X, RG 6, LAC.

45   Ann Chudleigh, "Proposals for a Medium-Profile Celebration of Canada's Birthday in 1980," 24 September 1979, file 7215-80, pt 1, box 30, BAN 2002-01308-X, RG 6, LAC.

46   Canada Day Report, 30 October 1979, file 7215-1, pt 4, box 25, BAN 2002-01308-X, RG 6, LAC.

47   Secretary of State Memorandum to Cabinet, 22 January 1980, file 7215-80, pt 1, box 30, BAN 2002-01308-X, RG 6, LAC.

48   Secretary of State Memorandum to Cabinet, 9 April 1980, file 7215-80, pt 1, vol. 1, box 30, BAN 2002-01308-X, RG 6, LAC.

49   Secretary of State submission to Treasury Board, 17 April 1980, file 7215-80, pt 2, box 30, BAN 2002-01308-X, RG 6, LAC.

50   Yvon Des Rochers to community newspapers, 9 June 1980, file 7215-80, pt 2, box 30, BAN 2002-01308-X, RG 6, LAC.

51   Citizens' Committee, National Capital Region, Report to the National Committee—Canada's Birthday, file 7215-80, pt 2, box 30, BAN 2002-01308-X, RG 6, LAC.

52   National Committee Report to the Secretary of State on Canada's Birthday Celebrations 1980, 15 August 1980, file 7215-80, pt 3, box 30, BAN 2002-01308-X, RG 6, LAC.

53   Tim Harper and Andrew Cohen, "Flag Waving on the Hill," *Ottawa Citizen*, 2 July 1980.

54   Citizens' Committee, National Capital Region, Report to the National Committee—Canada's Birthday, file 7215-80, pt 2, box 30, BAN 2002-01308-X, RG 6, LAC.

55   Secretary of State Memorandum to Cabinet, 15 January 1981, file 7215-81, pt 1, box 31, BAN 2002-01308-X, RG 6, LAC.

56   Celebration of Canada Day 1983, file 7215-83, pt 2, box 37, BAN 2002-01308-X, RG 6, LAC.

57   Serge Joyal to MPs and senators, 28 February 1984, file 7215-84, pt 2, box 41, BAN 2002-01308-X, RG 6, LAC.

58   Notes for remarks by the Secretary of State of Canada, 1 July 1984; prime minister's 1984 Canada Day address; speech to mark Canada Day by Jeanne Sauvé, file 7215-84, pt 6, box 41, BAN 2002-01308-X, RG 6, LAC.

59   *Great Canadian Adventures Colouring and Activity Book* (1984), file 7215-88-6, pt 1, box 23, BAN 2002-01223-7, RG 6, LAC.

60   Minutes of Canada Day meeting, 3 December 1986, file 7215-87-11, pt 1, box 20, BAN 2002-01223-7, RG 6, LAC.

61   Walter McLean to Brian Mulroney, 21 December 1984, file 7215-85-1, pt 1, box 13, BAN 2002-01223-7, RG 6, LAC.

62   Ministerial briefing for Canada Day 1985, file 7215-85-1, pt 2, box 13, BAN 2002-01223-7, RG 6, LAC.

63   1 December 1988 agenda, "Notes for Your Consideration, Canada Day 1989," file 7215-88-11, pt 1, box 23, BAN 2002-01223-7, RG 6, LAC.

64 Thérèse St-Onge and Guy Tanguay, 1986 Canada Day
    Celebrations Final Report, file 7215-86-5, pt 5, box
    31, BAN 2002-01308-X, RG 6, LAC; minutes of Canada
    Day meeting, 3 December 1986, file 7215-87-11,
    pt 1, box 20, BAN 2002-01223-7, RG 6, LAC.

65 Harris Boyd to Bonnie Clingen, 7 January 1987, file
    7215-87-1, pt 2, box 18, BAN 2002-01223-7, RG 6, LAC.

66 Harris Boyd to undersecretary of state, 23 December
    1988, file 7215-88-8-1, pt 1, box 23, BAN 2002-01223-7,
    RG 6, LAC.

67 Canada Day Program—Backgrounder for Meeting, file
    7215-88-11, pt 1, box 23, BAN 2002-01223-7, RG 6, LAC.

68 Sometimes the "International Year" theme was
    deliberately avoided. In 1986, the International
    Year of Peace theme was explicitly downplayed
    by the Department of External Affairs because
    of its involvement with the Star Wars project and
    US-USSR summitry.

69 21 January 1992 Inter-departmental Meeting, Canada
    Day 1992 minutes, file 07215-92-2, pt 2, box 1, BAN
    2003-02126-4, RG 6, LAC.

70 Theme Show Guidelines, file 07215-90-8-2, pt 2, box
    10, BAN 2003-00093-3, RG 6, LAC.

71 Floralove Katz to Bruce Devine, 7 February 1990, file
    07215-90-8-2, pt 1, box 10, BAN 2003-00093-3, RG 6,
    LAC.

72 Inter-departmental Steering Committee minutes,
    4 February 1992, file 07215-92-2, pt 2, box 1, BAN
    2003-02126-4, RG 6, LAC.

73 Canada Day Draft Program, file 07215-92-2, pt 3,
    box 1, BAN 2003-02126-4, RG 6, LAC. This ration-
    ale for performer selection is explicit in the planning
    documents.

74 Minutes of Inter-departmental Committee Meeting,
    Canada Day 1993, 7 December 1992, file 07215-92-2-
    1, pt 3, box 1, BAN 2003-02126-4, RG 6, LAC.

◎ 2.2: CANADIANIZATION: CULTURE AND NATIONHOOD IN THE POSTWAR YEARS

Ryan Edwardson

That the Canada of today is not the Canada of 50 years ago (or of 50 years before that) is obvious. Yet there is an overwhelming sense of "one" Canada, something essentialistic, its existence given, natural, and unquestioned. This sentiment testifies to the power of nation-building. Elie Kedourie pulls back the curtain of nationalism in noting how populations have come to believe inherently that "humanity is naturally divided into nations, that nations are known by certain characteristics which can be ascertained, and that the only legitimate type of government is national self-government."[1] But as Kedourie and other scholars of nationalism are quick to point out, nations are a relatively recent phenomenon, emerging largely during the eighteenth and nineteenth centuries as the age of empires and colonies gave way to a time in which countries became consolidated into nations, each assigned a distinct flag and its citizenry bought into the task of constructing a distinct national narrative. Whereas countries are built through political, economic, and industrial infrastructures,

nations are not so much built as they are conceptualized into existence; they are ideological constructs seemingly real and concrete yet in actuality a shifting and contested collection of signs and symbols. Countries exist in stone and mortar, whereas nations are an "imagined community," as Benedict Anderson has called them, existing amongst the stone and mortar.[2] As ideological constructs, nations require periodic adaptation. Canada has not escaped this need. During the twentieth century, Canadian nationhood has been adapted to the rise of domestic and foreign mass media; to changes in immigration and ethnic demographics; to a growing continentalization accompanied by the threat of American imperialism; to an increasingly politicized Quebecois nationalism; and to a shift from an ethnic nationalism that emphasized a "two races" Dominion of Canada to a civic nationalism of multiculturalism and socio-liberal values.

Culture, or more specifically the ways in which it has been used, has made possible both the imagining as well as the reimagining of the nation, promoting an essentialistic reality while also adapting the nation to changing demographics. It makes possible a communalism in which one feels an inherent connection with fellow citizens not simply on the basis of sharing citizenship but on the basis of a sense of shared experience and an essentialistic sense of self. This nation-building requires securing access to systems of communication that have fallen under the umbrella of culture, whether publishing, the arts, broadcasting, film, or related areas, in order to exert control over content and disseminate national identifiers. Now, it is important to note that the concept of culture itself has not been static and thus that what has been identified as cultural and used for nation-building has changed over the decades. Culture, as Raymond Williams has famously phrased, is "one of the two or three most complicated words in the English language," its meaning ranging from farming and agriculture to social refinement and enlightenment.[3] During the twentieth century, that meaning has shifted from associations with spiritual refinement and moral elevation to, later in the century, any form of activity, association, grouping, or other such phenomenon that was fully capable of being identified within commercial terms anathematic to earlier conceptions.

Canadianization can be thought of as a paradigm in which culture is used to identify and popularize a Canadian national sense of self. Characteristic of this is how the identification of culture, and the model of nationhood for which it was being rallied, dramatically changed. In the post–Second World War period, one finds no less than three waves of Canadianization, overlapping and contested, but nonetheless present and possessing distinct characteristics: (1) an early to mid-century cultured nationalism that rallied the arts in an attempt to ensure a spiritually enhanced Dominion of Canada during the colony-to-nation transition; (2) a new nationalism in the 1960s that turned to multi-brow cultural outlets and called upon the state to ensure domestic discourse in times of immense continentalism and a shift from ethnic to civic national identity; and (3) a cultural industrialism advanced by Pierre Trudeau

and the Liberal Party as of 1968 and continuing today under the leadership of the Department of Canadian Heritage, which bureaucratized the relationship between culture and national identity for the sake of federalism and economic growth. The change has been significant, from the Dominion of Canada, with its high-cultured nationalists who decried the socially corrosive commercialism of the mass media and shunned anything more than arm's-length state involvement in the arts, giving way to a multi-ethnic nation in which culture has become structured by the state as a commercial resource, much like lumber or mining. The qualitative assessments of cultural good and the promotion of national identifiers so important in early uses of culture in nation-building were in large part replaced by quantitative tallies using sales and economic growth as the measure of cultural strength.

At the start of the post–Second World War period, Canada was still very much within a Canadianization movement that had taken shape decades earlier within a wave of nationalism linking the arts and learned areas to the health and success of the colony-to-nation transition. The turn of the century had brought with it a modernity of industrialization, urbanization, and mass media, complete with tremendous social ills, poverty, and commercialization. Canada was growing economically, but many people worried about the toll being taken on spirituality and morality. An enlightened nation required a cultured spirit, it was believed, and thus the arts and learned areas were key to ensuring that Canada did not simply become a soulless industrial monolith. Influential nationalistic socio-political elites (a "nationalist network" as identified by historian Mary Vipond), popular artists, and concerned Canadians saw the arts and learned activities as means of ensuring that Canada was nurtured during what was viewed as a crucial period of growth.[4] Mobilizing new learned periodicals such as *Canadian Forum*, *Queen's Quarterly*, and *Canadian Bookman*, helped them to chart the course of nation-building by engaging in political, social, and cultural issues and events. "No country has reached its full stature, which makes its goods at home, but not its faith and its philosophy," *Canadian Forum* argued in its October 1920 inaugural issue. The periodical pontificated on its desire to "to trace and value those developments of arts and letters which are distinctly Canadian."[5] This mobilization of culture offered a means of offsetting the allure of commercial mass media. Racy American pulp periodicals, lowbrow radio programs with their copious advertisements, and escapist Hollywood films became the bane of a sociocultural elite who feared that the moral foundation necessary for a healthy nation would go undeveloped. From this perspective, mass entertainments promoted mass debauchery and lowered the nation into the spiritual gutter, whereas the arts allowed people, and in turn the nation, to be lifted towards the summit. This cultural specificity existed as an almost paradoxical combination of transplanting and replicating international (but, in this time of strong British heritage, not necessarily "foreign") successes in the Canadian context while at the same time encouraging a proliferation of domestically rooted identifiers.

Although culture was idealized as something separate from the corrosiveness of commerce, the division was never a reality. Many craftspeople operated within a cultural economy that required the commoditization of their work and led to the founding of such organizations as the Canadian Handicrafts Guild, the Canadian Authors Association, the Sculptors Society of Canada, and the Canadian Society of Graphic Art. Yet, with an underdeveloped economic infrastructure and no viable source of state support, artists relied to a large degree on patronage from the likes of the Massey family, Lord Strathcona, and Sir Edmund Walker (their patronage in turn further cementing their positions as influential social figures). Patronage, which allows for a selective support of cultural activity based on the interests of the patrons themselves, was crucial because the state had little role in supporting cultural activities. Other than a few concessions, most notably the National Gallery of Canada, there was little in the way of cultural facilities. There was no national ballet, theatre,

or orchestral venues, all of which many argued were fundamental to the cultural life of a nation. The federal government had little interest in developing the arts, viewing state involvement as politically perilous. After all, spending money on the arts came with the risk of being seen as shaping public tastes, limiting freedom of thought, and wasting taxpayer dollars on subsidizing the entertainments of the "long hairs" at the expense of broader infrastructural improvements.

Government intervention into the mass media was easier to justify, since broadcasting waves were limited in quantity and radio programming had proven itself to be an incredibly powerful means of informing and influencing the masses. With broadcasting growing from a small-scale activity into a burgeoning commercial enterprise, complete with foreign-produced programming and abundant advertising criticized for targeting the baser human interests, concerned Canadians, notably Graham Spry and the Canadian Radio League, called upon the state to create a publicly owned broadcasting network that could regulate private-sector entrepreneurs and ensure domestic content. The federal government bore witness to the power of broadcasting in 1927 with the temporary linking of stations, from coast to coast, as a means of disseminating the Canadian Diamond Jubilee celebrations held in Ottawa.[6] Establishing the Canadian Radio Broadcasting Commission in 1932, the precursor to the Canadian Broadcasting Corporation (CBC, 1936), was a pragmatic decision by a state that understood the importance of the airwaves as a natural resource, limited in number and able to sway the masses. Likewise, although film was by no means a limited natural resource along the lines of broadcasting, the desire to mobilize it for educational and industrial needs led to the creation of the National Film Board of Canada (NFB) in 1939. Under the guidance of John Grierson, a Scottish-born documentary filmmaker who had helped Britain to develop its state film production agency, the NFB quickly established itself as an important provider of educational and entertaining films serving a wide audience.[7]

The post–Second World War period initially continued according to this earlier paradigm of

CIVIC NATIONALISM AND ETHNIC NATIONALISM

In Canada, both civic nationalism and ethnic nationalism can be found to shape the sense of nationhood and identity, as evident in the topics explored in Part I.

Ethnic nationalism refers to a sense of belonging to a nation (either a distinct geo-political entity or a group inhabiting a common area) based on a common ethnicity. With this common ethnicity, this form of nationalism is based on having a common culture, such as language or religion, and a common heritage. Ethnic nationalism, thus, is a factor in the identity and objectives shaping the Quebecois and First Nations in Canada since 1945 and informs the individual identity of many other cultural groups within the nation.

Civic nationalism refers to a sense of belonging to a nation based on the people holding and having shared political values and political rights. It originates in the premise that power rests in the people, and thus governance is democratic and responsible and guarantees rights and equality to all citizens. In Canada, the promotion of civic nationalism has increased since 1945, positing a distinct and inclusive "Canadian" identity based on the civic virtues of multiculturalism and tolerance, the protection of human rights and freedoms, and equality of opportunity.

The promotion of civic nationalism since 1945 results from the belief of many Canadians (such as former prime minister Pierre Trudeau) that it is the best way to derive a common sense of belonging and pride as Canadians, and thus encourages and maintains national unity. Conversely, it is recognized that ethnic nationalism is not a possible means of achieving identity and nationalism for Canadians given the multicultural nature of the country and the challenges posed by Quebecois nationalism and the First Nations. In fact, a nationalism based in ethnicity is not only impossible but would potentially lead to further division and a retreat from the substantive gains towards the protection and promotion of equality since 1945. Thus, civic nationalism, through the promotion of common civic virtues such as tolerance and equality, presents the possibility of developing a common Canadian identity that can bind Canadians while promoting inclusivity and opportunity. Civic nationalism as identity is evident particularly in "national" symbols such as the Charter of Rights and Freedoms and multiculturalism policy.

Canadianization, with its ongoing struggle for greater support of the arts and culture of the nation. Fortunately for culturalists, the end of the war brought with it state postwar planning and reconstruction, complete with the assigning of federal funds to areas requiring investment and development. Seizing upon the idea of a federal commission surveying the arts and learned areas, Liberal Party Minister of Defence Brooke Claxton, backed by Vincent Massey and others, exerted pressure upon Prime Minister William Lyon Mackenzie King. Despite his earlier decrying of the "mad desire to bring about state control and interference beyond all bounds," King begrudgingly formed the Royal Commission on National Development in the Arts, Letters and Sciences in 1949.[8] With Massey taking the helm, the commission undertook the first major survey of cultured and learned activities in Canada and served as an opportunity to articulate and bureaucratize the relationship between national identity and culture in Canada. The so-called Massey Commission offered Canadians a platform for voicing economic and ideological interests that had been building for decades. Representatives throughout the arts, academia, mass media, and even citizen organizations, church groups, and other "concerned onlookers," as described by historian L.B. Kuffert, sent letters to ensure their positions were heard.[9] Complaints focused on the anemic straits of the arts and learned communities, the lack of resources, the dilapidated facilities (if they existed at all), and the shameful way Canadians had to rely on external resources (the American Rockefeller family was a major contributor to Canadian arts) owing to the Canadian state's neglect of cultural activities. This anemia was compounded by the vast growth of commercial mass media and plentiful American imports that, in the view of many culturalists, eroded national life. The problems were not new, of course, but the opportunity to voice the complaints and bureaucratize recommendations for change led to an unparalleled rallying of the arts and learned communities.

Like-minded allies were found in the Canadian Broadcasting Corporation and National Film Board of Canada, two bodies that offered content of significant public good and had long employed members of the arts community and other skilled cultural workers. For their part, the CBC and NFB viewed the Massey Commission as an opportunity to strengthen their position (and access to federal monies) at a time when their private-sector competition called for an end to public-sector dominance and for greater access to state funding and advertising dollars. The CBC was at this time the only broadcast network and consisted of publicly and privately owned stations that were required to provide CBC programming while also having non-network hours on which to broadcast independent and often commercially driven American programming. In defending its position as the sole broadcast network, one in which the CBC both regulated and competed with the private sector, the CBC explained that despite budgetary difficulties it nonetheless managed to provide approximately 80 per cent Canadian content and have 80 per cent of its offerings be commercial free.[10] With television broadcasting on the horizon—and, for some Canadians located across the border from American transmitters, already a reality as of 1948—consolidating the strength of the public broadcasting system was as important an issue as ever.

Composed in significant part by the same people who had fought for its creation, the Massey Commission not surprisingly supported the cultural and academic communities. Its report included recommendations that, looked at broadly, called upon the federal government to fund the production of artistic and learned goods and experiences while at the same time limiting the proliferation of private-sector mass media (and its large amount of American content). Establishing a commission was one thing, but acting on its recommendations was something else entirely; and the federal government chose to avoid involving itself in any cultural controversies, including the controversy surrounding the recommendation for an arm's-length body to fund the arts. Historian Paul Litt has colourfully noted how "throughout the early 1950s the Liberal government tossed the Council proposal around like a hot potato, but could never bring itself to serve it up to the public."[11] This was despite international precedence. The Arts Council of Great Britain had been in place since 1945, and given that it was a British institution, it offered an important example for Canada to follow. A Canadian arts council did not become a reality until 1957, and even then it was due in large part to the political pressure exerted by the Liberal Party's own John Deutsch, Jack Pickersgill, and Maurice Lamontagne in convincing the government to make a unique use of over $100 million in tax revenue that came with the deaths of Izaak Walton Killam and Sir James Hamet Dunn. Given the source of the revenue, advocates argued that the government finally had a way to establish an arts-funding council without being seen as taking money out of the coffers of the working class. Keeping an arm's-length relationship between the Canada Council for the Arts and the state served everyone's interests. For artists, the council would relieve their worry about political meddling, while for the federal government, in the words of Bernard Ostry, it would help to placate "the politicians' fear of having to answer for the high-jinks of artists."[12]

All in all, the commission offered a formidable platform for the articulation of culture as a refining force in a dominion still identifying with and treasuring its British inheritance. Yet the audience for the commission's recommendations had always been inherently limited in terms both of participants and of the disinterest of the federal government. The debates and activities were of little concern to the Canadians who enjoyed the mass entertainment increasingly available in the 1950s. As of 1952, television signals, both from over the border and within Canada, permeated homes with exciting and fascinating content. Radios and record players continued to sell in large quantities as advances in technology and production made them increasingly cheaper, and by the mid-1950s, their sales went hand-in-hand with the rise of "rock and roll" and its roster of American stars, idolized around the world. Bill Haley and his Comets hit the scene in 1954, the first to popularize rock and roll. Two years later he would be eclipsed by the more youthful, and controversial, Elvis Presley. In 1957, the formative year of the Canada Council for the Arts, audiences flocked to such Hollywood blockbusters as *Gunfight at the O.K. Corral* (Burt Lancaster and Kirk Douglas) and *The Bridge on the River Kwai* (William Holden and Alec Guinness). Pulp fiction offered action, adventure, mystery, and erotica with the likes of *Black Mask*, *Famous Detectives*, *Two-Gun Western*, and *Spicy Adventure Stories*. And established photo magazines, led by *Time* and *Life*, continued to offer windows into the lives of entertainers, politicians, socialites, and people from exotic lands.

With this mass media gold rush in full swing, domestic mass media producers and disseminators did not give up on their quest for larger audiences, access to advertising dollars, and an end to the privileged position of their public-sector competition. The electoral victory of the private-sector friendly (and public-sector criticizing) Conservative Party in 1958 marked the end of decades of Liberal Party rule and provided a tremendous opportunity for private-sector broadcasters. Prime Minister Diefenbaker made no secret of his belief that the CBC was, as Knowlton Nash has phrased it, a "propaganda mouthpiece for the Liberals."[13] A year later, convinced by the promise of increased tax monies if advertising

dollars were kept in Canada rather than being allowed to go to over-the-border American stations, Diefenbaker supported the request of the Canadian Association of Broadcasters (CAB) for new freedoms from the CBC network and the ability to compete directly with the CBC and American stations. If Canadians were going to watch American programming, the CAB argued, they might as well watch it from Canadian stations so that advertising monies remained in the country. In exchange for having a second television network (which eventually took shape as CTV), the CAB was to abide by Canadian content regulations requiring a minimum amount of domestic programming, as airwaves were a limited natural resource regulated by the government on behalf of all Canadians.

Private-sector film producers, struggling for exposure in theatres loaded with cheap (and market proven) American imports and unable to access government contracts that were funnelled to the NFB, joined in on the call for state support and new opportunities. The Association of Motion Picture Producers and Laboratories of Canada urged the federal government to examine the economic possibilities of a domestic feature film industry, going so far as to request a quota that would ensure screen time for Canadian films. The move was not unprecedented. Britain had formed the National Film Finance Corporation and established a box-office quota back in 1949. And Britain was not alone, as many other governments had enacted similar means of support. Yet the NFB, likely worried about an American backlash to a Canadian quota system that would in turn hurt its exports to the United States, persuaded the federal government not to institute a quota.[14]

Finally, periodical publishers struggled against cheaply available and economically proven American imports, particularly "split-run" editions of *Time* and *Reader's Digest*, which used foreign-produced content but attracted domestic advertising. Industry figures argued that periodicals, often cast as simple entertainment and tainted by their commercialism and abundant advertisements, actually made a significant contribution to the national community by facilitating discourse between Canadians. *Maclean's* and *Mayfair* offered valuable insights into social and political affairs, *Chatelaine* was a voice for Canadian women, and even the likes of *Canadian Homes and Gardens* were an essential means of sharing the ways in which Canadians lived. The struggles of the industry were significant enough to prompt the federal government to form the Royal Commission on Publications in 1960 to examine the way in which Canadian advertisers could deduct the expense of advertising in American (and other foreign) periodicals, rather than only in domestic ones. The complaint was much like that of private-sector television broadcasters who saw advertising monies as the vital blood of the industry (and complained about the loss of it to American competitors). The commission came to the conclusion that by simply not allowing advertisers to receive a tax credit for advertising in a foreign magazine, the government could take an action that "involves no 'tax on ideas or information,' no actual interference with readership preference, and, with no tax or customs duty, would have the merit of administrative simplicity."[15] Although the government acted upon the recommendation in part with the Paperback and Periodical Distributors Act of 1964, it was in essence a concessionary measure, limiting the tax-exemption incentive to advertisers purchasing space in Canadian periodicals but, and significantly, exempting the *Time* and *Reader's Digest* split-run editions. Pearson decided that maintaining good relations with the US government on the eve of ratifying the Auto Pact (a ratification that the US State Department warned might not go forward if the periodical legislation went through without concessions) meant curtailing the publication industry legislation.[16] It was yet another disappointing setback for domestic mass media producers struggling against the exports of a more sizable market.

Concerns over American saturation of the Canadian mass media marketplace increased throughout the 1960s. Although private-sector broadcasters had been given greater access to the airwaves in exchange for promises to support domestic producers (backed by legislation designed to ensure its fulfilment), they resorted to cheap generic game shows and musical variety programs.[17] In some cases, as Secretary of State Judy LaMarsh complained in the House of Commons, the broadcaster spent even less by filling airtime with "some individual playing an organ in an empty studio."[18] Programs could be aired multiple times a day, particularly in the audience-absent night-time hours, in order to more easily fill the Canadian content requirement without any added expense, as there was no minimum expenditure criteria or non-repetition clauses within the Canadian content regulation. This reliance upon imports continued throughout the various industries. Neither radio nor movie theatres had any reason to offer content other than that which was imported from abroad, relying on foreign songs and Hollywood offerings for sure-fire profits. In the arts and learned areas, there were similar difficulties. Established theatrical and musical venues, the pride and joy of earlier cultural nationalists, continued to rely upon foreign works that had been proven to attract audiences with little concession made to domestic playwrights and composers. Shakespeare and Bach were well-established seat sellers. Even universities seemed to give preference to foreign offerings, often hiring non-Canadian academics to teach foreign-focused curricula and snubbing domestic academics as being less qualified for having been educated in Canada.[19] One finds the national origin of cultural content coming to mean more than the distinctions between cultural brows, and both indigenous highbrow and new ideas of "popular culture" as middlebrow extracted, from the offerings of mass society and as such a valid space of expression, understanding, and identity, coming to mean more than simply culture as equated with refinement and taste. From this evolving point of view, a comic book like *Captain Canuck* (with its national signs and symbols key to entrenching a national sense of self) made a greater cultural contribution to the nation than did the Shakespearean performances put on by the Stratford Festival, so strongly supported by an earlier generation of cultural nationalists.

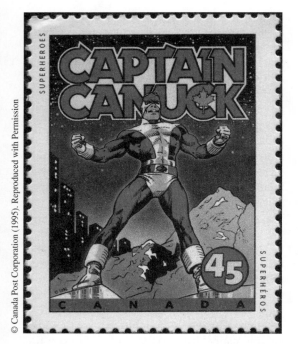

A Canadian postage stamp featuring Captain Canuck.

Concerns about American cultural influence were amplified by changes in the international standing of the United States. Continentalism during the 1950s, undertaken by a Liberal Party government seeking the economic benefits of closer relations with the United States, and a consumer industry clamouring for mass imports had brought great prosperity and consumer selection to many Canadians. Yet by the 1960s there was a growing sense of unease over just how close the Canada-US relationship had become, a feeling made all the more immediate by the decline of John F. Kennedy's "Camelot" in favour of Lyndon B. Johnson and a country torn apart by race riots, violent civil protests, and the Vietnam conflict. The rise of a "new nationalism," as it commonly came to be described, and the influential figures at its helm sought to limit the influence of the United States and characterized the country as a threat to Canada's stability. Unlike earlier generations of nationalists, who had sought to protect the country during its colony-to-nation

transition, this new nationalistic paradigm sought to prevent Canada from slipping back into colonial status—this time as a colony within the American empire. "During the last fifty years we have freed ourselves of traces of colonial status insofar as Britain is concerned," economist Walter Gordon argued in a 1967 interview, "but having achieved our independence from Britain, we seem to have slipped, almost without knowing it, into a semi-dependent position in relation to the United States."[20]

Unlike cultural nationalism during the first half of the century, which was largely the reserve of the artistic and learned community, their patrons, and like-minded citizenry, this new generation of influential nationalists and cultural intelligentsia emerged largely from the middle class and spanned a breadth of occupations and areas of interest. From the economic and business sectors came Walter Gordon and Melville Watkins with warnings that Canada's increasing economic dependence on the United States meant a loss of domestic control; academics Robin Mathews and James Steele drew public attention to the proliferation of American academics and the problems associated with having a generation of university and college students taught foreign course material at the expense of domestic content; Margaret Atwood and Farley Mowat penned treatises on the need for a national literature; and publishers, notably Mel Hurtig and Jack McClelland, rallied support for the printed word as a key device in ensuring national sovereignty. Although this new wave of cultural nationalism shared with its earlier counterpart a concern about the United States, it was based not on a desire to protect the nation from lowbrow commercial imports and moral degradation but rather on concerns about American imperialism and Canadian sovereignty.

This new nationalism fit well within the larger debates about Canadian identity in the 1960s. Together, the weakening relationship between Canada and Britain (symbolized in large part by Canada taking on a new national flag, the Maple Leaf, to replace the colonial Red Ensign, in 1965), an increasingly North American–focused economy and consumer culture, changes in immigration demographics, and a fading of ethnic nationalism in favour of civic nationalism meant that the Dominion of Canada and the "two founding nations" archetypes were no longer compatible with the social, economic, and ethnic demographics. A broader, state-based recognition of the country's increasingly multicultural composition emerged with the 1963–7 Royal Commission on Bilingualism and Biculturalism, initially designed to affirm the dualistic Anglo-Celtic and French-Canadian "two nations" approach to Canadian identity but, in offering a forum for publicly discussing ethnicity and nationhood, making it possible for assertions of multiculturalism to be made by other ethnic communities seeking to affirm their place within the national framework. The commission ended up shifting from biculturalism to multiculturalism while affirming the bilingual character of the country. This multiculturalism contributed to a growing sense that Canadian identity involved a significant degree of tolerance, open-mindedness, and social equality. Canada as a "Peaceable Kingdom," an idea that continues to resonate today, was a core concept of this inwardly focused reimagining of the national self that took place during the 1960s. The new nationalism picked up on this sentiment. "What we hoped for in this movement was the growth in this country of a new mood or new political climate," Abraham Rotstein has remarked. "Not only did we have in mind the self-awareness of cultural and economic domination, but the release of other forces as well—those of mutual concern for our regional, class and personal inequalities, as well as a greater extension of social justice and genuine democracy."[21]

Culture had a prime position in this reconfiguration of nationhood, in what many felt to be a struggle for national sovereignty and survival. Journalist Peter C. Newman, in correspondence with Rotstein in the summer of 1965, noted that "surely the most important aspect of nationalism is to build up a purely Canadian cultural barrier to preserve this society against American cultural intrusion, which is the more dangerous form of imperialism."[22] This position was certainly

one with which Rotstein agreed. *Getting It Back: A Program for Canadian Independence*, co-authored by Rotstein and Gary Lax, argues that "the issue of an independent creative cultural life in this country may be the ultimate determinant of our prospect of survival."[23] Cultural solutions to the crisis were often as radical in tone as the discourse itself (radical discourse being a staple of the 1960s). Demands included restricting key positions in sites of identity construction (art gallery directorships, heads of university departments, etc.) to Canadian citizens; the diverting of state funding from "internationalist" orchestras and theatres to those performing domestic pieces and productions; and implementing a bevy of federal investments, subsidies, tax-deduction incentives, and quota systems in the mass media and arts institutions to support the production and, just as crucially, dissemination of domestic cultural experiences across cultural brows. To push for quotas was certainly more controversial (if not more of an anathema) than requesting funding and subsidies, yet quotas were deemed essential to ensure that production actually made it past the bulwark of profit-minded distributors who were proven to have given little support for domestic production. Only then could one be guaranteed to have more Canadian content on art gallery walls, in university syllabuses, on theatrical and orchestral stages, on television and radio airwaves, and on the screens of movie theatres. In the words of the persuasive Committee for an Independent Canada, its leadership involving such respected national figures as Walter Gordon, Abraham Rotstein, Peter Newman, Jack McClelland, and Claude Ryan, a quota "is simply a device to cause some segment of society to do some currently unpopular or unfashionable thing which has been deemed to be in the best interests of society in general."[24]

This approach not only frustrated American-friendly mass media distributors but also revealed divisions within cultural communities. Many established venues relied upon drawing audiences with established plays and musical performances, while many culturalists, holding on to the earlier cultural paradigm, feared that tying the arts to something so parochial could be seen as nationalism. Author and literary critic John Metcalf describes it as a situation in which "the cultural nationalists have attempted to influence the government into Culture by Decree; they have lobbied for subsidy, regulation, and quota. It does not seem to have penetrated with them that culture cannot be imposed."[25] For many with this mindset, art was to be for art's sake, not art for nation's sake, as art could only flourish in an open atmosphere free from national considerations. What some nationalists argued was simply a measure for ensuring domestic opportunities, opponents saw as infringing on the very essence and internationalism of the arts. No longer was it enough to have support for the arts and recognition of their contribution to the socio-morality of the nation. Now the question centred on "Canada" within the arts.

Whereas the federal government had long avoided engaging with arts and culture in Canada, it dramatically changed its position with the electoral victory of the Liberal Party and Pierre Elliott Trudeau in 1968. Trudeau displayed great interest in mobilizing cultural resources for the sake of the nation—or, more precisely, doing so for the sake of federalism. Trudeau was a critic of nationalism, as were many people. After all, the world wars had seemingly discredited nationalism as a functional and healthy tool for social construction, having reduced it to an antiquated, anti-progressive, and negative social force. Yet such associations arose from equating "imperialist nationalism" with "defensive nationalism," as academic Robin Mathews argues, a form of socio-political expression misconstrued by those who did not care to understand the difference.[26] For Trudeau, the threat to the nation came not from the United States, but from an increasingly sovereignist Quebecois nationalism and, on a smaller scale and as a more direct threat to the Liberal Party itself, from the growing popularity of the New Democratic Party (NDP) and its new nationalist allies. Liberal self-preservation and federal stability both stood to benefit from a move in which the government would simply

seem to be responding to demands for reform in the arts and mass media.

A strong federal Canada required nothing less than that use be made of existing cultural frameworks while new federally friendly ones were introduced. To this end, the state relationship with culture underwent a landmark change with the Arts and Cultural Policy of 1968 earmarking federal funds for artistic endeavours that would support national unity, thereby severing the state's previous and long-standing arm's-length relationship with the arts. The goals were "to forge national unity," "to develop and promote bilingualism," and "to give a cultural dimension to our political and economic democracy and a more democratic dimension to our cultural activities."[27] Under the supervision of the Department of the Secretary of State, the policy went hand in hand with an enlarged cultural bureaucracy designed to organize federal cultural activities, administer the dispersal of funds, quantify their economic success, and, more generally, appease cultural nationalists while further solidifying the position of the Liberal Party and federal leadership. Not surprisingly, such an unprecedented move was controversial. Famed literary figure George Woodcock complained that "Trudeau's view was basically that the control of the nation's cultural life, especially of its arts, is essential for the consolidation of political power, and cultural policies should be directed towards supporting a government's principal aims."[28]

Federal restructuring of cultural life involved regulatory changes where jurisdiction permitted and providing economic incentives where federal involvement was otherwise controversial or outside of federal control. Federal monies were earmarked for arts groups that promised pro-federal results; existing Canadian content regulations for television broadcasters were strengthened and a similar set introduced for radio broadcasters; domestically owned publishing companies received new subsidies; the notorious *Time* and *Reader's Digest* exemption was removed in the hope of promoting advertisers' use of domestic periodicals; the Canadian Film Development Corporation (CFDC) invested in domestic production; an increase to the Capital Cost Allowance (CCA) encouraged private-sector investment; a voluntary quota was established with several film distributors; changes to immigration law were made, requiring universities to assess Canadian candidates for academic positions (in contrast to a systemic discrimination favouring foreign academics); and federal funding was provided for the development Canadian Studies programs in domestic and foreign universities.[29]

The results and responses were certainly mixed. Federal earmarking of funds harmed the lauded arm's-length relationship, while the reduction of monies to the Canada Council forced it to reprioritize its funding criteria. "The willingness to fund 'national unity' through the arts," criticized Gertrude Lang, chair of the Canada Council, "but not adequately to fund the arts themselves, is evidence of an attitude to cultural policy which gives me great concern."[30] Yet the Canada Council, particularly as of 1978 under the guidance of Mavor Moore, took a strong turn towards domestic works. For the television sector, Canadian content regulations continued to lead to little more than cheaply made time-fillers, certainly not a surprise given that, according to CTV figures in the mid-1970s, an hour of American programming cost approximately $4,000 (about a quarter of the cost of domestic programming) yet brought in $30,000 to $50,000 advertising revenue.[31] Success in radio was more evident, with some performers able to use local airplay to rally domestic attention and establish a limited career for themselves without first relocating abroad, although for the most part stations continued to rely upon domestic performers who were already popular in the United States. The voluntary quota quickly crumbled owing to a lack of reinforcement; the CCA became a tax shelter for low-budget films that often went unscreened, and, under the guidance of the Canadian Film Development Corporation, subsidies attracted Hollywood productions that accessed grants by employing Canadians in menial positions and that then added American flags, automobile licence plates, US mailboxes, and other signifiers of Canadian cities being made over into American ones. The irony of taxpayers thus further subsidizing Hollywood's hegemony over the Canadian feature film market has been one of the CFDC's legacies. *Porky's*, a teenage sex-romp comedy, was perhaps most symbolic of what was achieved in the early years, bringing in $150 million (US) in international sales in its first few years.[32] Federal support for the publishing industry helped keep businesses afloat and even ward off bankruptcy, while ending the *Time* and *Reader's Digest* exemption gave domestic periodicals a better chance at success. Canadian authors had the fortune of being publicly thought of as talented, something that could not be said for the mass media sector as a whole. Paul Audley, in *Canada's Cultural Industries*, notes how "public attitudes toward television are totally different from public attitudes towards Canadian books. The public think of Canadian writers as bloody good, as good as anybody has, but when it comes to television, they think about it as, first of all, coming from central Canada and second, being low budget."[33] Finally, as for academia, economic support for Canadian Studies programs and associations at home and abroad—from the Association for Canadian Studies in the United States to the Japanese Association for Canadian Studies—provided students with the opportunity to engage with Canada as a topic of study, while aspiring academics had better, albeit still limited, opportunities than before to teach in venues of higher education.

The actions of the federal government eroded the autonomy of the high arts so fundamental to the Massey generation and earlier Canadianization efforts, while in the reliance of the arts upon bureaucratic qualitative measures of success, these actions diminished the qualitative national identifiers that had been at the core of the new nationalist approach to culture and national identity. Yet the results served the interests of bureaucrats and those of many in the cultural economy. It is telling that between 1968 and 1977 royalties to members of the Composers, Authors and Publishers Association of Canada increased from $364,000 to $2,256,000.[34] Culture came to be treated as an industry to be developed—a provider of jobs, of economic growth, and of tax monies. Economic growth allowed the state to justify its intervention in cultural life, statistics becoming the mantra for displaying national cultural vitality. Whether or not the content served nation-building interests, the concerns of those in the cultural community who advocated an increased availability of content that spoke to fellow Canadians—without consideration for sales in the international marketplace—faded into the background as culture came to be identified as an industry requiring development and exportation along lines similar to lumber, agriculture, and manufacturing. "We are not just talking about a quaint Canadian culture," a member of the Standing Committee on Broadcasting, Films and Assistance to the Arts argued back in 1973, "but about developing a business which we can then export and compete with in the marketplace, in exactly the same way that the Americans and others have done so successfully here."[35] The success achieved in using culture to strengthen national identity was now, strangely enough, founded upon the very elements that culture had earlier been used to combat. The situation would have confused and horrified Vincent Massey and his colleagues.

Only three decades earlier the Massey generation had identified Canadian content in high-cultural terms and sought to foster a domestic form of international artistic achievement as a means of elevating the masses and the Dominion of Canada itself. And it had only been during the past two decades that a new period of nationalism had rallied a multi-brow cultural paradigm, backed by a push for access to the outlets of cultural dissemination, during a transition from ethnic to civic nationalism and shaped by concerns about American imperialism. Now the federal government was at the forefront of fostering culture and its connection to a national sense of self, having come to believe that funding productions based on their economic viability and sales—achievements evidenced by financial and employment gains—and equating cultural vitality with market success would contribute to a Canadian identity. Stepping forward to the turn of the century, one finds Minister of Canadian Heritage Shelia Copps linking the success of national cultural life with Canada's economic vitality and declaring how "the cultural sector contributes over 22 billion dollars to our Gross Domestic Product. It employs over 640,000 Canadians. . . . I am proud to be a member of a government that recognizes the critical role that arts and culture plays in our lives, and in our society, and that realizes that if our own culture is to flourish, it must be cultivated."[36]

The paradigm continues today with a bevy of tax incentives and subsidy programs (Canadian Broadcast Program Development Fund, Feature Film Fund, Book Publishing Industry Development Program, Cultural industries Development Fund, the Canadian Film and Video Tax Credit, among many others) spanning across the cultural industries. Whereas qualitative assessments are slippery in their subjectivity, industrialism offers hard numbers with supposedly concrete evidence of cultural health and national vitality. And, despite the glaring problems, cultural bureaucrats find themselves able to point to industry activity as evidence of success despite the fact that quantitative gains are no measure of qualitative achievements. Until this core strength of the current Canadianization paradigm is somehow eroded, this paradigm seems destined to be the status quo for at least a while longer.

Endnotes

1   Elie Kedourie, *Nationalism* (New York: Praeger, 1960), 9.
2   Benedict Anderson, *Imagined Communities: Reflections on the Origin and Spread of Nationalism* (London, UK: Verso), 1991.
3   Raymond Williams, *Keywords* (Glasgow: William Collins Sons and Co., 1976), 76–9.
4   Mary Vipond, "The Nationalist Network: English Canada's Intellectuals and Artists in the 1920s," *Canadian Review of Studies in Nationalism* 7 (Spring 1980): 32–52.
5   "Introduction," *Canadian Forum* 1 (October 1920): 3.
6   Robert Cupido, "Sixty Years of Canadian Progress: The Diamond Jubilee and the Politics of

Commemoration," in *Canadian Identity: Region, Country, Nation*, ed. Caroline Andrew, Will Straw, and J.-Yvon Thériault (Montreal: Association for Canadian Studies, 1988), 19–33.

7 Andrew Rodger, "Some Factors Contributing to the Formation of the National Film Board of Canada," *Historical Journal of Film, Radio, and Television* 9, no. 3 (1989): 259–68.

8 Maria Tippet, *Making Culture: English-Canadian Institutions and the Arts before the Massey Commission* (Toronto: University of Toronto Press, 1990), 73.

9 L.B. Kuffert, *A Great Duty: Canadian Responses to Modern Life and Mass Culture, 1939–1967* (Montreal and Kingston: McGill-Queen's University Press, 2003), 4.

10 Canadian Broadcasting Corporation (CBC), *Submission to the Royal Commission on Development in the Arts, Letters and Sciences* (Ottawa: Canadian Broadcasting Corporation, 1949), 40.

11 Paul Litt, *The Muses, the Masses, and the Massey Commission* (Toronto: University of Toronto Press, 1992), 238.

12 Bernard Ostry, *Cultural Connection* (Toronto: McClelland and Stewart, 1978), 99.

13 Knowlton Nash, *Swashbucklers: The Story of Canada's Battling Broadcasters* (Toronto: McClelland and Stewart, 2001), 178.

14 Ryan Edwardson, *Canadian Content: Culture and the Quest for Nationhood* (Toronto: University of Toronto Press, 2008), 93.

15 Royal Commission on Publications, *Report of the Royal Commission on Publications* (Ottawa: Queen's Printer, 1961), 79.

16 Edwardson, *Canadian Content*, 106–7.

17 Susan Gittins, *CTV: The Television Wars* (Toronto: Stoddart, 1999), 73.

18 Judy LaMarsh, House of Commons, *Debates* (1 November 1967), 3748.

19 Edwardson, *Canadian Content*, chaps 4–5.

20 Walter Gordon, quoted in Kari Levitt, *Silent Surrender: The Multinational Corporation in Canada* (Toronto: Macmillan of Canada, 1970), 1–2.

21 Abraham Rotstein, "Is There an English-Canadian Nationalism?," in *The Walter L. Gordon Lecture Series, 1977–78*, vol. 2 (Toronto: Omnigraphics, Inc., 1978), 16.

22 Peter C. Newman to Abraham Rotstein, 7 July 1965, Library and Archives of Canada (LAC), MG 31-D73, Abraham Rotstein Fonds, vol. 4, file 78.

23 Abraham Rotstein and Gary Lax, *Getting It Back: A Program for Canadian Independence* (Toronto: Clarke, Irwin, 1974), xii.

24 Committee for an Independent Canada, "Theatre in Canada: A Reluctant Citizen," prepared for the Edmonton Policy Conference, September 1972, 12.

25 John Metcalf, *What Is a Canadian Literature?* (Guelph, ON: Red Kite, 1988), 102.

26 Robin Mathews and James Steele, *The Struggle for Canadian Universities* (Toronto: New Press, 1969), 40–1.

27 LAC, RG 97, box 359, file 5400-0, pt 2, from September 2/69 to November 17/69, "Summary of the Brief on the Government's Cultural Policy," n.p.

28 George Woodcock, *Strange Bedfellows: The State and the Arts in Canada* (Vancouver: Douglas & McIntyre, 1985), 107.

29 Edwardson, *Canadian Content*, chap. 7.

30 Canada Council, *Annual Report* (1977–8), 7.

31 Robert Babe, *Canadian Television Broadcasting Structure* (Ottawa: Minister of Supply and Services Canada, 1979), 65.

32 Telefilm Canada, *Annual Report* (1982–3), 6.

33 Paul Audley, *Canada's Cultural Industries: Broadcasting, Publishing, Records and Film* (Toronto: James Lorimer, 1983), 21.

34 Graeme Gibson, "Waiting for Blondin," *Journal of Canadian Studies* 10, no. 2 (May 1975): 31; Canadian Radio-television and Telecommunications Commission (CRTC), *Special Report on Broadcasting in Canada, 1968–78*, vol. 1 (Ottawa: CRTC, 1978), 74.

35 Standing Committee on Broadcasting, Films and Assistance to the Arts, *Minutes* (13 May 1973), 4.

36 Department of Canadian Heritage, "Speaking Notes for the Honourable Shelia Copps, Minister of Canadian Heritage, on the Occasion of the Announcement of a Major Investment in Canadian Culture," *Tomorrow Starts Today* (Toronto), 2 May 2001, n.p.

Bibliography

Anderson, Benedict. *Imagined Communities: Reflections on the Origin and Spread of Nationalism*. London, UK: Verso, 1991.

Babe, Robert. *Canadian Television Broadcasting Structure*. Ottawa: Minister of Supply and Services Canada, 1979.

Canada. Canadian Broadcasting Corporation (CBC). *Submission to the Royal Commission on Development in the Arts, Letters and Sciences*. Ottawa: Canadian Broadcasting Corporation, 1949.

Canada. Canada Council. *Annual Report*. 1977–8.

Canada. Canadian Radio-television and Telecommunications Commission (CRTC). *Special Report on Broadcasting in Canada, 1968–78*. Vol. 1. Ottawa: CRTC, 1978.

Canada. Department of Canadian Heritage. "Speaking Notes for the Honourable Shelia Copps, Minister of Canadian Heritage, on the Occasion of the Announcement of a Major Investment in Canadian Culture." *Tomorrow Starts Today* (Toronto), 2 May 2001.

Canada. House of Commons. *Debates*. 1 November 1967, 3748.

Canada. Library and Archives of Canada (LAC). MG 31-D73, Abraham Rotstein Fonds, vol. 4, file 78, P.C. Newman to A. Rotstein, 7 July 1965.

———. RG 97, box 359, file 5400-0, pt 2, from September 2/69 to November 17/69. "Summary of the Brief on the Government's Cultural Policy," n.p.

Canada. Royal Commission on Publications. *Report of the Royal Commission on Publications*. Ottawa: Queen's Printer, 1961.

Canada. Standing Committee on Broadcasting, Films and Assistance to the Arts. *Minutes*. 13 May 1973.

Canada. Telefilm Canada. *Annual Report*. 1982–3.

Committee for an Independent Canada. "Theatre in Canada: A Reluctant Citizen." Prepared for the Edmonton Policy Conference, September 1972.

Cupido, Robert. "Sixty Years of Canadian Progress: The Diamond Jubilee and the Politics of Commemoration." In *Canadian Identity: Region, Country, Nation*, ed. Caroline Andrew, Will Straw, and J.-Yvon Thériault, 19–33. Montreal: Association for Canadian Studies, 1988.

Edwardson, Ryan. *Canadian Content: Culture and the Quest for Nationhood*. Toronto: University of Toronto Press, 2008.

Gibson, Graeme. "Waiting for Blondin." *Journal of Canadian Studies* 10, no. 2 (May 1975): 30–2.

Gittins, Susan. *CTV: The Television Wars*. Toronto: Stoddart, 1999.

"Introduction." *Canadian Forum*, no. 1 (October 1920).

Kedourie, Elie. *Nationalism*. New York: Praeger, 1960.

Kuffert, L.B. *A Great Duty: Canadian Responses to Modern Life and Mass Culture, 1939–1967*. Montreal and Kingston: McGill-Queen's University Press, 2003.

Levitt, Kari. *Silent Surrender: The Multinational Corporation in Canada*. Toronto: Macmillan of Canada, 1970.

Litt, Paul. *The Muses, the Masses, and the Massey Commission*. Toronto: University of Toronto Press, 1992.

Metcalf, John. *What Is a Canadian Literature?* Guelph, ON: Red Kite, 1988.

Nash, Knowlton. *Swashbucklers: The Story of Canada's Battling Broadcasters*. Toronto: McClelland & Stewart, 2001.

Ostry, Bernard. *Cultural Connection*. Toronto: McClelland & Stewart, 1978.

Rodger, Andrew. "Some Factors Contributing to the Formation of the National Film Board of Canada." *Historical Journal of Film, Radio, and Television* 9, no. 3 (1989): 259–68.

Rotstein, Abraham. "Is There an English-Canadian Nationalism?" *The Walter L. Gordon Lecture Series, 1977–78*. Vol. 2. Toronto: Omnigraphics Inc., 1978.

Rotstein, Abraham, and Gary Lax. *Getting It Back: A Program for Canadian Independence*. Toronto: Clarke, Irwin, 1974.

Tippet, Maria. *Making Culture: English-Canadian Institutions and the Arts before the Massey Commission*. Toronto: University of Toronto Press, 1990.

Vipond, Mary. "The Nationalist Network: English Canada's Intellectuals and Artists in the 1920s." *Canadian Review of Studies in Nationalism* 7 (Spring 1980): 32–52.

Williams, Raymond. *Keywords*. Glasgow: William Collins Sons and Co., 1976.

Woodcock, George. *Strange Bedfellows: The State and the Arts in Canada*. Vancouver and Toronto: Douglas & McIntyre, 1985.

CHAPTER 3

Nation within a Nation

◎ 3.1: MULRONEY AND A NATIONALIST QUEBEC: KEY TO POLITICAL REALIGNMENT IN CANADA?

Michael D. Behiels

From the moment Brian Mulroney became leader of the Progressive Conservative Party in 1983 he was determined to create a political realignment in Canadian politics. He was obsessed with obliterating the Liberal Party as Canada's "government party." . . . Mulroney was confident that he could use Quebecois nationalist and secessionist movements to transform Quebec into the bastion of his Progressive Conservative Party. With the support of Conservative parties and governments from the Atlantic provinces, Ontario, and the West, Mulroney believed that a disciplined Progressive Conservative Party would become, after two or perhaps three successful elections, the new "government party" of Canada. . . .

Since joining the Conservative Party in the mid-1950s, Mulroney had been an ardent Red Tory and a John Diefenbaker Canadian nationalist who proudly promoted "One Canada" and an interventionist federal government. Mulroney applauded, supported, and then agonized over Diefenbaker's determined but ultimately unsuccessful attempt to rebuild the Conservative Party's long-vanished base in Quebec.[1] Once Trudeau re-established the Liberal Party's dominance over Quebec from 1968 to1979, with his policy of official bilingualism and a tough stance on separatism, Mulroney knew

that a divided Conservative Party—torn over the issue of "two nations"—could not achieve power let alone fulfil Diefenbaker's dream of a momentous political realignment in Canada.

On the question of Quebec and its place in Confederation, Mulroney, an inordinately ambitious and well-connected Quebec businessman and politician, became a supporter of Trudeau's vision of Canada and national unity. This ideological shift, as well as his high-rolling aggressive campaign, contributed to his defeat in the 1976 Conservative Party leadership race.[2]

After he witnessed the political dominance of the Parti Québécois (PQ) following its election in November 1976, the clash of Canadian and Quebecois nationalisms during the 1980 referendum on secession, and Trudeau's attainment of the Constitution Act, 1982 with its popular yet controversial Canadian Charter of Rights and Freedoms, Mulroney altered his political strategy and tactics. He came to understand the potent political force of Quebecois nationalism, the ideological driving force behind Quebec's ongoing economic, social, cultural, linguistic, and political "Quiet Revolutions" since the 1950s.[3] Once he decided to seek the party leadership again in the early 1980s, his political

Premier Robert Bourassa and Prime Minister Mulroney congratulate each other on 3 June 1987 during the Meech Lake Accord meetings.

strategy and tactics were heavily influenced by Quebec's impassioned nationalist environment. The re-emergence in Quebec of nationalistic discourse leading up to and during the 1984 federal election provided Mulroney with the illusive key required to make a breakthrough. That key was the Constitution Act, 1982, with its Charter, which Trudeau had put into place following more than a decade of divisive mega-constitutional politics. For nationalist and class reasons, Quebec's political and intellectual circles would not or could not give their consent to the Constitution Act, 1982. Having broken ties with the francophone and Acadian minority communities outside Quebec in the 1960s, they rejected the charter's section 23—education rights for Canada's official-language minorities—because it eroded exclusive provincial control over education.[4] Led by Claude Morin, they concocted a powerful and disturbing myth whereby the Quebecois "people" had been betrayed by Canadian politicians during the "night of the long knives."[5]

Leading Quebecois nationalist politicians, journalists, and academics, exemplified best by Lucien Bouchard, convinced Mulroney that the

key to winning the hearts and minds—and the political support—of *les québécois* was to remove or override the offending clauses of the Constitution Act, 1982 and its Charter so that these would conform to the modern constitutional vision of the Quebecois francophone majority. Quebecois nationalists and separatists of all stripes had been striving since the 1960s to achieve their far more radical and comprehensive conception of political realignment. They were determined to transform the long-established reality of pan-Canadian cultural and linguistic duality—French Canada and British Canada—into a new conception of a territorial duality of Quebec and Canada, reconfigured into a decentralized confederation of two equal nation-states. The challenge for Mulroney, who was seeking a more modest form of political realignment, was to make this Quebecois nationalist territorial conception of an equal Quebec/Canada duality co-exist with the conception of the equality of the provinces already entrenched in the Constitution Act, 1982, as exemplified in the general amending formula of 7/50, whereby seven provinces comprising 50 per cent of the population and Parliament can alter most provisions of the Constitution.

Convinced that the road to Canada's political realignment came via Quebec's signature on an amended Constitution Act, 1982, Mulroney opened mega-constitutional negotiations with Premier Robert Bourassa's Liberal government, re-elected to office in 1985, thanks in part to his five-point constitutional agenda. Between 1986 and 1992, Canadians witnessed not one but two destabilizing rounds of mega-constitutional politics. The Quebec round, quickly transformed into the provincial round, culminated in the Meech Lake Constitutional Accord of 30 April 1987.

When the accord failed to be ratified within the three-year deadline, a second, more comprehensive constitutional-reform package, dubbed the Charlottetown Consensus Report, was negotiated by Joe Clark, the premiers, and four national Aboriginal organizations, but this deal was rejected by Canadians in their first-ever national constitutional referendum on 26 October 1992. Mulroney's and Bourassa's failed attempts to achieve their respective political realignments via mega-constitutional politics ended both of their political careers. What Prime Minister Mulroney had conceived as a straightforward process of displacing the Liberal Party as Canada's governing party had a much different outcome from the one he had intended, encompassing both the rise of new parties in the West and Quebec and the virtual destruction of the Conservative Party. The purpose of this chapter is to explain this remarkable turn of events.

Canada, Quebec, and the Constitutional Conundrum

. . . To the dismay and chagrin of the national and provincial Conservative parties and the Parti Québécois, the Liberal Party regained office in the 1980 election under the leadership of a chastened yet reinvigorated and formidable Pierre Elliott Trudeau. As promised repeatedly in the 1979 campaign but played down in 1980, Trudeau fully intended to settle the national-unity crisis. He began by defeating the Quebecois separatists in the 20 May 1980 referendum by a resounding margin of 20 percentage points, 60 to 40.[6] True to his word, Trudeau announced in the House of Commons on 21 May 1980 his government's decision to proceed unilaterally with a constitutional resolution to patriate the British North America Act, 1867, with an amending formula and a Charter of Rights. Following negotiations and a failed September 1980 constitutional conference with the premiers, lengthy public hearings on a constitutional resolution before a joint committee of the Senate and the House that

garnered strong public support for the charter, three provincial court rulings—one against the resolution—followed by a reference to the Supreme Court of Canada (which ruled that the resolution was legal but politically unconstitutional) and several appeals to the British crown, courts, and Parliament. Trudeau achieved his goal. On 5 November 1981 Trudeau and all the premiers except René Lévesque approved an amended constitutional package.[7]

Mulroney, Quebec, and the Constitutional Imperative

The PQ government's decision to reject the Constitution Act, 1982 provided the Conservative Party with the political opening it had been seeking for nearly two decades. . . .

The national Liberal Party's monopoly over Quebec had to be broken at all costs if an ambitious Mulroney hoped to become prime minister. Mulroney and his Quebec team, Michel Cogger, Peter White, Jean Bazin, Bernard Roy, and Rodrique Pageau, built a political base in Quebec by obtaining public endorsements from well-known Liberals like Paul Desrochers and PQ supporters like Lucien Bouchard; gaining control of the provincial Conservative Party executive; creating nearly forty riding organizations where they did not exist; and increasing the party membership, which in 1983 stood at a dismal 10,000. Mulroney, who supported Trudeau's Constitution Act, 1982 and Charter of Rights, denounced Clark's constitutional proposal for full financial compensation to any province opting out of shared-cost programs under provincial Jurisdiction.[8] The amending formula could not be altered without unanimous consent, and, Mulroney argued, if it was altered it would end up putting federal funds at the service of the PQ's drive to dismantle Canada.[9] Thanks to a spirited and determined leadership campaign which he carried into the Conservative leadership convention in mid-June 1983 at the Ottawa Civic Centre, Mulroney narrowly defeated Joe Clark on the fourth ballot. He did so in large measure by garnering the votes of 60 per cent of the 726 registered Quebec delegates and nearly 70 per cent of John Crosbie's votes when he was knocked out after the third ballot.[10]

The year 1984 was a tumultuous one on the national political scene. It began with Prime Minister Trudeau abruptly announcing his resignation on 29 February, after a walk in a blinding snowstorm. John Turner, returning from his sojourn in the private sector, defeated Jean Chrétien for the leadership of the Liberal Party in a bitter struggle and assumed the office of prime minister. His stint in office was brief. Badly misjudging a momentary surge in the polls for the Liberals, Turner called a fateful snap election for 4 September. Mulroney and his strategists were ecstatic with both developments. They preferred to face Turner rather than Chrétien, especially in the battle for the hearts and minds of Quebecois. . . . Turner appeared distinctly uncomfortable with minority-language issues, both inside and outside Quebec, and he displayed little or no rapport with his Quebec caucus and constituency militants, many of whom remained profoundly loyal to Trudeau and Chrétien.[11]

Mulroney, realizing that the Liberal Party remained deeply divided between its Turner and Chrétien wings, set out to exploit these divisions in order to destroy the Liberal bastion in Quebec. . . .

From the moment Mulroney entered federal politics in 1976, he had consistently portrayed himself as an ardent supporter of a bilingual and multicultural Canada. He was opposed to the theory of "two nations" entrenched via a constitutional special status for Quebec because, in his view, it threatened national unity. In fact, on this issue his vision of the country was similar to Trudeau's. . . .[12]

Yet, by the time the summer 1984 federal election was underway, Mulroney was already shifting his constitutional position dramatically. The reason was simple. He was convinced that, for struggling Progressive Conservative candidates . . . to defeat incumbent Liberals, they would have to be able to win the hearts and minds of Quebecois conditional federalists, Liberal neo-nationalists, and disillusioned PQ supporters.

If they failed, Mulroney would not make the breakthrough in Quebec that he had promised Conservatives, a prerequisite to becoming prime minister with a majority Tory government. He did not relish the thought of repeating Joe Clark's humiliating experience of 1979.[13]

Appealing to Quebecois nationalists of all stripes, especially the intellectuals and journalists who influenced public opinion, was not going to be an easy task for a well-known partisan Tory federalist like Mulroney. Always the superb opportunist, he decided that the most effective way to signal his dramatic shift on the constitutional question was to convince a longtime friend and PQ militant, Lucien Bouchard, to join his Quebec Conservative team. Dismayed at the collapse of the Parti Québécois and the imminent departure of René Lévesque, Lucien Bouchard agreed to join the Tory campaign as a speechwriter. In undertaking his version of what Lévesque dubbed the federalist "beau risqué," Bouchard most assuredly had his own Quebecois nationalist agenda. Indeed, he succeeded in convincing Mulroney that the Constitution Act, 1982, with its Canadian Charter of Rights and Freedoms, was a catastrophic and humiliating imposition on the Quebecois people. It needed to be revamped if the Quebecois political, intellectual, and economic classes were going to be reconciled to Canada. Choosing his words carefully, Mulroney began to make statements to the effect that a Conservative government, given the appropriate political climate and the strong likelihood of a positive outcome, would reopen constitutional negotiations with Quebec. He proposed to redress what the Quebec elite considered the unacceptable outcome of Trudeau's constitution and charter, especially the loss of Quebec's "traditional" constitutional veto.[14]

Clearly, Mulroney believed that the political risks of altering his constitutional position could be managed. His confidence was based on the fact that, as prime minister, he would be negotiating not with a separatist PQ government but with a Liberal government headed by his old friend Robert Bourassa, who he was certain would be eminently reasonable in his constitutional demands. . . .[15] A Mulroney-Bourassa alliance was being forged in the political trenches of Quebec, an unusual alliance that would have an incalculable and far-reaching impact on Quebec and Canadian politics. The alliance would play a central role in Mulroney's quest for a comprehensive and enduring political realignment at the national level, one that had eluded every Conservative prime minister since Robert Borden.

Urged to be more explicit by his Quebec team, Mulroney opted to make a major policy announcement on the Constitution—based on a revised text prepared by Bouchard—during his nomination meeting in Sept-Îles in northern Quebec on 6 August 1984.[16] In a forceful and passionate speech full of codes easily understood by all Quebecois nationalists and secessionists, Mulroney promised to do whatever he had to in order to "convince the National Assembly of Quebec to give its consent to the new constitution with honour and dignity."[17] Mulroney's forthright appeal to Quebecois nationalists proved highly effective. Many Quebecois nationalists, including a large number of PQ, Liberal, and former Union nationale supporters, threw their support behind, and eventually voted for, relatively unknown Conservative candidates. They had come to perceive that Mulroney and not Turner was the appropriate successor to former prime minister Trudeau. Like Trudeau, Mulroney came across as one of their own, a sympathetic and reliable defender of the francophone cause in the Canadian federal system.[18]

The Conservatives were rewarded beyond their wildest dreams. In Quebec, Mulroney successfully convinced a majority of Quebecois that it was essential for them to be part of what was going to be a majority Conservative government. In the election of 4 September 1984, the Progressive Conservative Party defeated the Liberal government of John Turner in a landslide victory, one that surpassed even that of Diefenbaker in 1958. With 50 per cent of the vote, the Tories garnered 211 of 282 seats. . . . The most dramatic and crucial breakthrough came in Quebec. Mulroney and his Quebec campaign team . . . delivered a stunning blow to the Quebec wing of the national Liberal Party by winning 58 of the province's 75 ridings. . . .[19]

Forging the Mulroney-Bourassa Alliance

The Mulroney government's accession to power in Ottawa accelerated the political transition in Quebec. Prime Minister Mulroney's challenge was how best to forge an alliance with the soon-to-be Liberal premier of his home province. . . .

Bourassa's easy victory in a 1985 by-election in the Montreal riding of Bertrand reaffirmed and widened the divisions in Lévesque's demoralized Parti Québécois. Hoping to outmanoeuvre Bourassa on the constitutional question, Levesque welcomed Mulroney's 1984 election promise to undertake constitutional negotiations with the Quebec government. He announced his government's intention to seek a constitutional accord with Ottawa if and when Mulroney became prime minister. Initially agreeing with the militants that the PQ should remain committed to independence, Lévesque then questioned the tactic of turning the next provincial election into a vote on sovereignty-association. At the PQ's convention, backed by a three-to-two margin among the delegates, Lévesque declared that the party would not fight the next election on sovereignty. This decision accelerated the internecine warfare . . . within the party.

In May 1985 Lévesque released a *Draft Agreement on the Constitution: Proposals by the Government of Quebec*. The document set out a comprehensive list of constitutional demands: the recognition of Quebec as a distinct society; the primacy of the Quebec Charter over the Canadian Charter of Rights and Freedoms; Quebec's exclusive jurisdiction over language matters; full financial compensation for opting out of any amendment; the return of Quebec's traditional veto over all constitutional changes; a severe curtailment of federal spending powers; the elimination of Ottawa's powers of reservation of disallowance; and full control over immigration, communications, economic, and manpower policy, and marriage and divorce laws.

In return, the National Assembly would ratify the Constitution Act, 1982. Lévesque's constitutional bottom line read like a vast shopping list of Quebecois nationalists' ever-expanding demands. For a leader running out of time, Lévesque had little option but to hold his fractured party together. . . .

In the interim, Bourassa's Liberal Party made public its own five constitutional conditions for signing the Constitution Act, 1982. Hammered out by Gil Rémillard, a law professor, the five conditions were somewhat less radical but no less far-reaching than those of the PQ. The two crucial demands were constitutional recognition of Quebec as a distinct society in a preamble applying to the entire Constitution and the restoration of Quebec's *de facto* veto over amendments to federal institutions or the creation of new provinces. The three other conditions were the limitation of the federal spending power, Quebec's participation in the appointment of judges to the Supreme Court of Canada, and increased powers for Quebec over immigration.[20] There was nothing in the Liberal package that Mulroney publicly disagreed with, a sure sign that he had been allowed to vet the proposals. The emerging Mulroney-Bourassa alliance would not have to wait in the wings much longer. Surprising everyone, including members of his entourage, Cabinet, and caucus, Lévesque submitted his resignation on 20 June. . . . Undoubtedly facing almost certain defeat in the upcoming election, Lévesque preferred to leave on his own terms rather than face a much-rumoured putsch. . . .

As most political analysts and pundits had predicted, Lévesque's and successor Pierre-Marc Johnson's decision to abandon the PQ commitment to sovereignty-association destroyed the party's raison d'être. Despite Johnson's perceived competence and popularity among the voters, the PQ's chances of re-election were marginal. The political door was opened wide for Robert Bourassa to reassume the office of premier after an absence of nearly a decade. He and his new team of younger, nationalistic Liberals ran a highly effective campaign promoting economic renewal based on Quebec's immense

water and hydroelectric resources, social peace on the language issue, and a promise to regain Quebec's constitutional veto along with special status within the federation. On 2 December 1985 the Parti Québécois was routed. With 56 per cent of the vote, Bourassa's Liberal Party won 99 seats. . . .[21]

The Alliance Pays Off: The Meech Lake Accord

The Mulroney-Bourassa alliance, forged during their respective leadership and election campaigns, produced one of the most unusual constitutional deals in Canadian history. Following a late January 1986 meeting, Mulroney and Bourassa stated publicly that fulfilling the constitutional aspirations of Quebec was the top priority of both governments. They set up teams of trusted advisers, ministers, and senior mandarins.[22] By March 1986, Quebec's intergovernmental affairs minister, Gil Rémillard, announced that the Canadian Charter of Rights would be given precedence over the Quebec Charter. The National Assembly would no longer invoke the "notwithstanding clause" to override sections 2 and 7–15 of the charter. At a conference at Mont-Gabriel, Quebec, on 9 May 1986 . . . Gil Rémillard reiterated Quebec's five conditions for signing the 1982 Constitution. There was one crucial alteration to the initial conditions laid out in the Liberal Party's platform *Maîtriser l'avenir*. Symbolic recognition of Quebec as a distinct society in the preamble to the Constitution no longer sufficed. Recognition had to be explicit and legally meaningful.[23] How this was to be done was eventually spelt out in the Meech Lake Constitutional Accord. The "distinct society" clause, to achieve Quebec's long-term constitutional and political objectives, would function as a powerful interpretive clause applying to the entire Canadian Constitution. In other words, Quebec could use the Supreme Court to reshape the federation in its interests. Rémillard concluded his remarks by warning Canadians that "Quebec nationalism is not dead, far from it. It is thriving more than ever but in a different form. It is no longer synonymous with isolationism or xenophobia but rather with excellence."[24]

The drive for a constitutional accord with Quebec was on in earnest. Mulroney and Bourassa, eager to dispose of the constitutional question in a pragmatic and rapid manner, met on 4 June 1986 to discuss Quebec's five demands. Mulroney, without formally endorsing the five demands, indicated that he was receptive to Bourassa's constitutional initiative. He encouraged Bourassa to convince the premiers, before their annual meeting in Edmonton in mid-August 1986, to give Quebec's constitutional demands serious consideration. Rémillard was dispatched to all the provincial capitals to convince his counterparts to accept Quebec's constitutional agenda. Quebec would not proceed until it had the assurance of provincial support, since some aspects of its package required the application of the unanimity amending formula. Bourassa was well aware that failure would rekindle the fires of Quebecois nationalism and secessionism.

Mulroney wrote the nine premiers before their August meeting urging them to look favourably upon Quebec's demands. His and Bourassa's efforts were partially successful. At the conclusion of their August 1986 meeting, the premiers issued the vaguely worded "Edmonton Declaration" in which they agreed to hold constitutional discussions based on Quebec's demands in order to facilitate "Quebec's full and active participation in the Canadian federation." Nonetheless, most of the premiers remained reluctant to become involved in another round of mega-constitutional politics so soon after their bruising experiences of 1980–1. Their constituents were far more interested in economic development, trade, jobs, and taxation matters than in the Constitution. If they were going to reopen constitutional negotiations, many of the premiers and their constituents had priorities of their own, including Senate reform and the entrenchment of property rights. Brian Peckford insisted on greater control over the Grand Banks fisheries.[25]

Following up on Senator Lowell Murray's advance work, Mulroney launched an intense lobbying blitzkrieg that culminated in the Meech Lake Accord. Already in considerable political difficulty in Quebec, Mulroney had urgently required the political credit that would accompany the constitutional reconciliation of the province. But how was he able to forge the deal, one he was not convinced was possible? The agreement emerged as a result of the negotiating strategy proposed by Senator Murray and his deputy, Norman Spector, and adopted by Mulroney. The prime minister, rather than putting a single constitutional demand for the Canadian government on the table, played the role of broker between his ally, Premier Bourassa, and nine reluctant premiers. On 30 April, Mulroney convened an informal first ministers' meeting at Willson House, located on Meech Lake in Gatineau Park. With no officials in the room and facing the unrelenting pressure tactics of Mulroney, the nine premiers, one at a time, eventually agreed to Bourassa's five demands on condition that four of Bourassa's provisions—the distinct society interpretive clause was reserved for Quebec—be available to them. As one perceptive journalist demonstrates in his account,[26] the premiers hijacked the Quebec round at Meech Lake and transformed both the process and the final accord into a provincial round. The ambiguous accord married asymmetrical federalism for Quebec in the distinct society clause with the nine other premiers' determination to obtain recognition of the equality of the provinces in the clauses pertaining to the limitation of Ottawa's spending power, an amending formula giving provinces a veto over national institutions and the creation of new provinces, bilateral immigration agreements, appointments to the Supreme Court and the Senate, and annual first ministers' conferences. Much to Mulroney's and Bourassa's surprise and ultimate dismay, the premiers' hijacking of the deal set in motion an uncontrollable political chain reaction that contributed to the eventual demise of the Meech Lake Accord three years later.

Throughout the trials and tribulations of the accord, the Mulroney-Bourassa alliance held firm. Mulroney had come to embrace Bourassa's vision of a distinct constitutional role for Quebec in an increasingly decentralized, asymmetrical, bi-national federation called Quebec-Canada. The traditional pan-Canadian dualism of French Canada and British Canada was dead. It had to be transformed constitutionally into a bi-national federation comprising two territorially defined national states: a francophone national state represented primarily by an officially unilingual state of Quebec and an officially bilingual and multicultural national state represented by Canada, the provinces, and territories. . . .

The Bourassa government ratified the Meech Lake Accord on 24 June 1987, despite strong denunciations by the leader and members of the PQ and the Quebecois "chattering classes." In doing so, the premier kickstarted the three-year ratification process. Convinced that the accord offered francophone Quebecers far too little too late, [Jacques] Parizeau declared that a PQ government led by him would use the accord's distinct society clause to advance the cause of independence.[27] Outside Quebec, there was initially little indication that the accord would encounter widespread opposition, since all political leaders appeared to be onside. Polls indicated that the general public was in favour of the deal, while groups committed to the defence of the Charter of Rights remained dormant or disorganized. The leader of the official opposition, John Turner, . . . immediately committed himself and his caucus to the accord despite the fact that the concept of Quebec as a distinct society had been rejected at the November 1986 policy convention. Turner was convinced that supporting the accord was essential to reverse the political realignment underway in Quebec.[28]

Little did Turner realize that his impromptu decision momentarily accelerated the realignment and eventually contributed to his early political demise. Indeed, he foolishly refused to heed a major warning sign. On 27 May 1987, in the *Toronto Star* and *La Presse*, Pierre Elliott Trudeau declared that the accord, if ratified, would render the Canadian state so impotent that it was destined, "given the dynamics of power, to be governed eventually by eunuchs."[29]

A great many prominent Liberals, including Donald Johnson, Jean Chrétien, Marc Lalonde, and Michael Kirby, realized that the future of their party and their vision of Canada were under siege. They waged a relentless and ultimately successful campaign against the accord and the Mulroney-Bourassa alliance.[30]

Aiding and abetting the emerging opposition to the accord was a fundamental disagreement between Mulroney and Bourassa over how to interpret and then sell the distinct society clause to Canadians in general and more specifically to francophone Quebecers. Outside Quebec, Mulroney, his closest advisers, and his government proclaimed immediately and repeatedly that the recognition of Quebec as a distinct society was purely symbolic and did not grant Quebec any additional powers. In contrast, Bourassa, feeling triumphant, argued that the distinct society clause confirmed Quebec's exclusive control over all language matters, including those pertaining to education. "We must acknowledge," he declared in the National Assembly, "that in the distinct society clause we are getting a major gain that is not limited to the purely symbolic, since the country's entire Constitution . . . including the Charter of Rights, will be interpreted and applied in the light of the article on the distinct society. This directly involves the exercise of legislative power, and will allow us to consolidate our gains and make even greater advances."[31] In 1982 Bourassa had made the questionable claim that, under the unacceptable Constitution Act, 1982, the federal government was henceforth "constitutionally required to use all means necessary to enforce respect of [Canada's] territorial integrity."[32] Bourassa then was quick to boast that the Meech Lake Accord's distinct society clause recaptured Quebec's right to national self-determination, a right that it had lost with the Constitution Act, 1982.[33] In time, Bourassa's highly exaggerated interpretation of the distinct society clause lost him credibility among nationalist academics and journalists in Quebec while setting off a political firestorm throughout Canada, one that sealed the fate of his cherished accord.

With all three national parties formally adopting the Meech Lake Accord for a second time in June 1988, the issue was effectively eliminated from the national political agenda during the heated "free-trade election" of that fall. . . . In early May 1989 John Turner instructed the Liberal Party to organize a leadership convention to choose his successor. His erratic political career was over.[34] The barely concealed rift among the rank and file of the party erupted into the open as Jean Chrétien and Paul Martin, to name only two, launched their respective leadership campaigns by taking opposite stances on the Meech Lake Accord.

The crisis in the national Liberal caucus and party emboldened an increasing majority of Canadians to question both the process and the substance of the Meech Lake Accord. It also prompted several political commentators to argue that the process of political realignment . . . was all but irreversible. The national Liberal Party, encouraged by provincial leaders opposed to the Meech Lake Accord—Sharon Carstairs in Manitoba and premiers Frank McKenna of New Brunswick and Clyde Wells of Newfoundland—and its rank and file from coast to coast, appeared to be turning its back on the increasingly nationalistic francophone Quebec electorate and concentrating on rebuilding its political fortunes in Ontario. This analysis was confirmed, in part, by the inordinately influential role exercised by Quebec's sixty-two Tories in the Mulroney caucus and cabinet following the election. In the minds of francophone Quebecers, Mulroney's Conservative Party had replaced the Liberal Party as their preferred political vehicle for defending and promoting their national interests within Confederation. This was a remarkable development. . . .[35]

The Unravelling of the Meech Lake Accord, 1988–1990

The Quebec political realignment precipitated by the Mulroney-Bourassa alliance on the Constitution and the Free Trade Agreement invariably fostered political reaction and political realignment in the rest of the country. Given the fundamental disagreement over the substance of the Meech Lake Accord—reflected in Mulroney's and Bourassa's divergent political strategies to sell it—the three-year ratification period gave its opponents plenty of time to organize at the provincial level. Encouraged by Trudeau's blunt criticism of the accord in September 1987 and the retirement or defeat of premiers in New Brunswick, Manitoba, and Newfoundland, a wide range of "charter groups," Aboriginal organizations, and Preston Manning's fledgling right-wing populist Reform Party in western Canada went to political war against the accord. What ensued was one of the most tumultuous and divisive periods in the history of Canada's political and constitutional development.

The first serious political setback for the Meech Lake Accord occurred in New Brunswick. It was fuelled, in part, by a rapidly growing and increasingly powerful Acadian community and its nationalistic leaders, who felt betrayed by Prime Minister Mulroney's and Premier Bourassa's determination to entrench a territorial conception of dualism, Quebec-Canada, in the Constitution. While favourable to the distinct society clause, Acadian leaders insisted on two amendments. It was essential to include in the accord a constitutional obligation for Ottawa to defend and promote the francophone minority communities as well as the entrenchment of New Brunswick's Bill 88, *An Act Recognizing the Equality of the Two Official Linguistic Communities in New Brunswick*.[36] Conversely, the accord was denounced by right-wing Conservatives—those opposed to any and all forms of official bilingualism or the recognition of Quebec as a distinct society—as a sell-out to Quebecois nationalists and separatists. The young, brash, and relatively inexperienced leader of the New Brunswick Liberal Party, Frank McKenna, used the outcries against the accord to launch his political career. Before a special parliamentary joint committee in late August 1987, McKenna declared that substantive amendments—pertaining to the Charter, linguistic minorities, spending powers, Senate reform, the Supreme Court, and fisheries—would have to be made to the accord before he would ask the New Brunswick Legislative Assembly to proceed with ratification.[37] The strategy paid off. McKenna's Liberals soundly defeated the 17-year administration of Premier Richard Hatfield on 13 October 1987, winning all 58 seats.

For nearly two years, McKenna used grass-roots opposition to the Meech Lake Accord to ward off the incessant campaign by the Mulroney government—led by Senator Lowell Murray—and Premier Bourassa to have his government ratify an unamended accord. McKenna, guarding his leverage, established a committee of the legislature to hear testimony on the accord and to submit a report in the fall of 1989. As expected, the vast majority of those intervening before this committee criticized various aspects of the accord and demanded that it be substantially amended or rejected. Yet many New Brunswickers feared that their premier would cave in to the immense pressure to ratify. McKenna was called upon repeatedly to deny stories of either a provincial cabal against Ottawa or a sweetheart deal with Quebec.[38] Buoyed by the emergence of two other anti-accord premiers—Gary Filmon of Manitoba and Clyde Wells of Newfoundland—McKenna momentarily strengthen his resolve in 1989.[39]

Hard-core political opposition to the accord surfaced among all three parties in Manitoba. The New Democratic Party (NDP) government, led by premier Howard Pawley, a reluctant supporter of the accord, procrastinated. On 8 March 1988 Pawley's shaky government was brought down by vote of non-confidence triggered by an angry backbencher. The defeat of the New Democratic Party in a surprise election on 26 April 1988 produced a minority Progressive Conservative government, with 25 of 57 seats, led by Premier Gary Filmon. The Manitoba Liberal Party, led by the feisty and inveterate pro-Trudeau "anti-Meecher" Sharon Carstairs, emerged from obscurity to form the official opposition in the legislature. She predicted the imminent death of the Meech Lake Accord. Meanwhile, Premier Filmon, still loyal to Mulroney, promised in the Throne Speech to ratify the accord at the first opportune moment.[40]

Considering that over half the Tory caucus was opposed to the accord, particularly the distinct society clause, Filmon's challenge would prove far more difficult than he and Mulroney ever imagined. Sensing the need to recuperate ground lost to the Liberal Party, Gary Doer, Manitoba's new NDP leader, announced within days of the federal election of 21 November 1988 that his party was committed to killing the accord. The combination of free trade and the Meech Lake Accord, he argued, would destroy the political and constitutional integrity of the country.[41]

On 16 December 1988, pressured by Mulroney and Bourassa, Filmon introduced the accord into the Manitoba legislature and spoke passionately in its favour as a powerful embodiment of a renewed phase of cooperative federalism.[42] And yet a delighted Mulroney had no time to rejoice. His alliance with Bourassa was challenged by a Supreme Court ruling on 15 December 1988 striking down the commercial-signage provisions of Quebec's Bill 101 (the provisions mandated the use of the French language exclusively). The decision called for the restoration of bilingual commercial signage with prominence given to French throughout Quebec.[43] On 18 December, Premier Bourassa, pressured by ardent nationalists in his government—Claude Ryan threatened to resign—and vociferous public demonstrations in support of Bill 101, introduced Bill 178. This controversial bill, which clearly violated the letter and spirit of the Supreme Court's ruling, authorized a bizarre and discriminatory outside-inside approach to commercial signage. All outdoor commercial signs had to be exclusively French, while indoor signage could be bilingual as long as French was given priority and predominance. The government invoked the Charter's "notwithstanding clause" to prevent any legal challenges to Bill 178. Bourassa foolishly maintained that if the Meech Lake Accord had been ratified, he would not have had to take this step. Mulroney, pleading privately with Bourassa to refrain from using the "notwithstanding clause," understood immediately that the Meech Lake Accord was on life support. But, fearing that his alliance with the premier was in jeopardy, he kept his public criticism to a bare minimum, thereby fuelling fears that he was a weak defender of the Charter of Rights. Bourassa had opted to preserve the stability of his government and the unity of his party even if his actions meant endangering his cherished accord. Most emphatically, Quebec's interests, not Ottawa's, came first. Facing Jacques Parizeau, a hard-line secessionist at the head of the Parti Québécois, and an angry English-speaking community, Bourassa's government was re-elected on 9 August 1989 with 50 per cent of the vote and 92 of 125 seats. Bourassa had a renewed mandate to push for the ratification of an unaltered accord because, in the words of Lowell Murray, it was a seamless web.[44]

On 19 December, Filmon shocked Mulroney, Bourassa, and the entire nation by withdrawing the accord from the Manitoba legislature. He justified his action by stating that Bourassa's Bill 178 was a "national tragedy" and a harbinger of worse things to come, since the Quebec government might use the Meech Lake Accord to achieve constitutional special status. Early in 1989, Premier Filmon urged Mulroney to refer the distinct society clause to the Supreme Court for a ruling, but the prime minister, fearful of the reaction in Quebec, demurred.[45] Hearings held by the Manitoba legislature's task force on Meech Lake that spring demonstrated the depth and breadth of public resentment over what termed the Mulroney-Bourassa deal.[46] The task force's report, published in October 1989 and endorsed by all three party leaders, called for dramatic amendments to the accord. The Charter of Rights was deemed paramount. A "Canada clause," recognizing the distinct nature of Canada by virtue of its Aboriginal and ethno-cultural communities, encapsulated and constrained the Quebec distinct society clause. The spending power provision and the extension of a veto to all provinces over national institutions and the creation of new provinces were dropped. Premier Filmon had lost all manoeuvring room.[47]

The Mulroney-Bourassa alliance also faced a major political setback in Atlantic Canada. . . . Promising to rescind the accord, Clyde Wells

and the Liberal Party were swept into office in Newfoundland on 20 April 1989 on anti-Meech ticket.[48] Premier Wells, the brilliant, articulate, and determined constitutional lawyer and Trudeauite, preached the gospel of the equality of the provinces and the need for an elected Senate. He criticized the interpretive nature of the distinct society clause because it granted the government and legislature of Quebec "special powers to protect and promote that status." Like Trudeau, Wells contended that this would enable Quebec to achieve constitutional special status, thereby endangering the federation.[49]

Determined, Wells encouraged the Newfoundland House of Assembly to pass a private member's bill condemning the accord on 23 November 1989 and then had the assembly rescind its ratification of the accord on 6 April 1990. . . .

Mulroney, Bourassa, and their advisers were frustrated and shaken. They were convinced they had set the stage for the ratification of an unamended accord. The internal and external pressure on McKenna began to pay dividends. The report of the New Brunswick Select Committee on the Meech Lake Constitutional Accord, released in October 1989, recommended a few substantial amendments but left the accord formally untouched. It embraced both the distinct society clause and the expansion of the veto and recommended the entrenchment of the Charter of Rights as a fundamental characteristic of Canada as well as an obligation by the federal government to preserve and *promote* both official languages. The amendments, set out in a "parallel accord," would be ratified at the same time as the Meech Lake Accord.[50] . . . McKenna was ripe for the picking. Following extensive negotiations with Mulroney's constitutional advisers, the premier dropped the report's demand for a "parallel accord." On 20 March 1990 he introduced resolutions into the assembly calling for the ratification of an unamended Meech Lake Accord followed by the negotiation and ratification of a separate "companion accord" comprising a watered-down version of the select committee report's additional constitutional proposals.[51]

. . . Desperate to legitimize the widely condemned and despised elitist Meech Lake Accord process and consume all the remaining time available to those seeking amendments, Mulroney created a special House of Commons committee to study McKenna's companion resolution. He named an unknown Quebec MP, Jean Charest, as its chairperson and requested a report by 18 May. Ten days later, Bourassa's government supported a Parti Québécois motion stating that Quebec reject all constitutional proposals, including those of New Brunswick, "which would constitute an amendment or modification susceptible to changing the content and the scope of the Meech Lake Accord."[52] . . . The Charest report, submitted to the House on 17 May 1990, called for the ratification of an unaltered Meech Lake Accord by 23 June and recommended a list of 23 additional constitutional amendments—providing, among other things, for recognition of Aboriginal peoples and Canada's multicultural heritage and setting the stage for Senate reform—that the first ministers might include in a "Companion Accord" to be negotiated and ratified at a later stage.[53]

This controversial, tactical report, even before its release, ignited a political firestorm in Quebec City and Ottawa, one that was intended to, but did not, derail the Mulroney-Bourassa alliance. Bourassa and Rémillard, pondering the probability of either the amendment of Meech or its demise, proffered dark warnings that the nation of Quebec would seek a fundamental restructuring of Quebec's association with the "rest of Canada," one that respected its long history as a distinct society. Both reiterated that they would not accept a single amendment to the accord. . . .[54]

Three days later, in the wake of his deliberately provocative telegram to the Parti Québécois—referring to the Quebec people's right to self-determination—sent on the tenth anniversary of the 1980 referendum, an ambitious Lucien Bouchard resigned from cabinet and the Conservative Party. . . .

Mulroney and Bourassa decided that they had no option but to forge ahead—"roll all the dice," as the prime minister later boasted. On 3 June 1990, a Sunday, Mulroney gathered the premiers for a dinner at the Museum of Civilization to prime them for negotiations on the basis of a Charest report embellished by other premiers' demands. Using the threat of another referendum on separatism and sensing that they could logroll the recalcitrant Filmon and Wells, Bourassa and Mulroney convinced the premiers to reconvene the next day for a make-it-or-break-it constitutional conference in the National Conference Centre, Ottawa's old train station.[55] . . . It took the premiers four days to agree to ratify an unamended Meech. . . .

. . . They then reconvened to tackle the even more daunting task of determining the nature and scope of significant amendments destined for a separate constitutional package to be ratified after the Meech Lake Accord came into effect. By late Saturday evening, 9 June, a complicated and ambiguous agreement of sorts was reached. Its main elements were as follows: the three holdout provinces would do everything in their power to ratify Meech before the 23 June deadline; the federal and provincial governments would have three years to achieve an elected, more "equitable," and more effective Senate, failing which there would be automatic changes to seat distribution; a special House of Commons committee would be formed to fashion a "Canada clause" by September 1990; a non-binding legal opinion would be obtained from six constitutional experts clarifying the impact of the interpretive distinct society clause on the Charter of Rights; a series of constitutional conferences with Aboriginal organizations would be held; gender equality and official-language minority rights in the Charter would be strengthened; and a review of the amending procedures would be undertaken. Totally exhausted, Mulroney and the premiers signed a highly questionable "Constitutional Agreement," one that had little chance of surviving the harsh scrutiny of the media and the accord's growing legions of determined critics. Indeed, Premier Wells's signature was conditional. Frustrated and distraught, yet determined not to betray his principles or his supporters, Wells agreed only to put the Meech Lake Accord to referendum or to submit it to the House of Assembly for a vote.[56]

Bourassa, well aware that Quebecois nationalists and secessionists were displeased with the scope of the companion agreement, kept a low profile. McKenna proceeded as promised and the New Brunswick legislature unanimously ratified the accord on 15 June. Meanwhile, Mulroney, Murray, and Norman Spector worked overtime to keep up the full-court press on Filmon and Wells to ratify the accord. In addition, conscious of strong opposition from Ovide Mercredi's Assembly of First Nations (AFN), Mulroney dispatched a federal delegation to make Manitoba's Aboriginal leaders a six-point offer, which was, however, refused. Elijah Harper, an NDP Cree MLA, was instructed by Manitoba chiefs and AFN leaders to deny the Manitoba legislature the necessary unanimous consent to allow the procedural motions required to consider the Meech Lake Accord. Meanwhile, McKenna, Ontario premier David Peterson, and Mulroney appeared before the members of the Newfoundland House of Assembly, urging them to prevent a second Quebec referendum on secession by ratifying the accord. Elijah Harper informed Wells at noon, central time, on 22 June that debate in the Manitoba legislature on the accord would be adjourned at 12:30 without a vote. Wells, outraged at Mulroney's and Murray's ongoing attempts to manipulate the process despite their ignominious defeat in Manitoba, promptly moved to adjourn the Newfoundland legislature without a vote. Following three long years of acrimonious threats and counter-threats, the ill-fated Meech Lake Accord was finally put to rest.[57] . . .

The Canada Round: The Marriage of Convenience Implodes, 1990–1992

The death of the Meech Lake Accord did not terminate mega-constitutional wrangling. Mulroney and Bourassa, surfing the rising tide of Quebecois nationalism and secessionism, forged ahead with a more destabilizing series of constitutional negotiations that produced a highly controversial, comprehensive, yet incomplete constitutional agreement that was rejected by Canadians in a referendum held on 26 October 1992. The unsuccessful "Canada Round," as it was dubbed, severely challenged and then virtually demolished the Mulroney-Bourassa alliance, producing a remarkable but unintended national political realignment, one that altered inextricably the course of Canadian politics. This happened for two reasons: first, because Mulroney and Bourassa were determined to achieve their respective political agendas at almost any price; and second, because Quebecois nationalist and secessionist critics of the accord proved to be far more skilful in "spinning" Meech's demise to their advantage. The accord—like the Conquest of 1759, the Rebellions of 1837–8, the 1980 referendum, and the Constitution Act, 1982—was another humiliating defeat to be used effectively to advance the struggle for an independent Quebec. Quebec *nationalistes* blamed the accord's defeat on the Trudeau-inspired Canadian nationalists who rejected the Quebecois conception of territorial duality, Quebec-Canada, in favour of their own unrealistic conception of pan-Canadian linguistic duality and cultural pluralism.[58]

Quebecois nationalists' claims of victimization were never challenged by Canada's political leaders. On the contrary, their highly questionable interpretation of events was legitimized by some leading anti-Trudeau Canadian nationalists[59] and, more important, by the Mulroney-Bourassa alliance. Acutely conscious that the demise of Meech had fuelled the growing rift in the Quebec Liberal Party and caucus, a development that could lead to the Liberal government's defeat at the hands of Jacques Parizeau's hard-line Parti Québécois, Bourassa embraced a Quebecois neo-nationalism based on a European Union style of sovereignty-association. In an emotionally charged speech in the National Assembly on 22 June, Bourassa offered a prophetic but ominous warning: "English Canada must understand that no matter what anyone says or does, Quebec is today and forever a distinct society, free and able to undertake its own destiny and development."[60] Quebec would achieve distinct society status de facto if not de jure. . . . Bourassa informed Canadians on 23 June that he would not return to the constitutional bargaining table. If the Canadian government came forward with acceptable constitutional proposals, however, Bourassa just might agree to bilateral discussions on a new status for Quebec in the federation, one that reflected the Canada-Quebec territorial duality at the heart of the Meech Lake Accord.

. . . Determined to control and manipulate his caucus and party militants—a neo-liberal, extreme nationalist minority represented by Jean Allaire and Mario Dumont was threatening to bolt—Bourassa urged the constitutional committee of the Quebec Liberal Party, chaired by Allaire, to proceed with its mandate of analyzing Quebec's constitutional options. On 4 September 1990, intent upon harnessing the rising tide of separatist sentiment to his and Mulroney's constitutional agenda, Bourassa had the National Assembly establish a commission to "examine and analyze the political and constitutional status of Quebec."[61] With representatives from provincial and federal parties, nationalist organizations, labour centrals, and business groups, the commission was granted a mandate to consult widely and make recommendations on the full range of constitutional options available to his government, including, if necessary, independence.[62]

The commission, dubbed Bélanger-Campeau after its co-chairs, Michel Bélanger, federalist president of the Quebec-based Banque Nationale, and Jean Campeau, secessionist chairperson of the Caisse de Dépôt et Placement du Québec, was designed to create a sacred union, that is, to rally both Quebec parties and their supporters behind Bourassa's second attempt to obtain the substance of the Meech Lake Accord. Determined to outflank Parizeau and to increase Quebec's *rapport de force* with the rest of Canada, Bourassa appointed the highly popular Lucien Bouchard—recently crowned leader of the Bloc québécois, the new separatist party at the federal level that Bourassa fully endorsed—as

one of the most prominent members of the commission. Determined to achieve his goal at virtually any price, Bourassa pursued a hard-line strategy of putting "a knife to the throat" of Canada.[63] Yet, given the deteriorating state of his health owing to skin cancer, Bourassa quickly lost control of the commission to the extreme nationalists and secessionists, who considered Bouchard their rightful leader. Quebecois politicians, academics, journalists, and a wide range of organizations and citizens' groups—many of whom submitted briefs and/or gave testimony to the Bélanger-Campeau Commission—stoked the fires of secessionism by reinforcing over and over the potentially destructive myth that English Canada was to blame for the defeat of the accord and that francophone Quebecers had no choice but to opt for secession.[64] As was the intention, the commission's hearings legitimized the claim that Quebecois were the victims of Confederation, thereby helping drive support for secession among francophone Quebecers to an all-time high of 64 per cent by November 1990.[65]

At the end of January 1991, the constitutional committee of the Quebec Liberal Party released its report, *A Quebec Free to Choose*. Intended to shock the rest of Canada and undercut the PQ, the Allaire report, as it was known, called for a comprehensive political disengagement of Quebec from Canada while retaining important economic ties: that is, sovereignty-association, a concept heretofore the primary goal of the Parti Québécois. Once the rest of Canada agreed with the report's recommendation for a transfer of powers to Quebec in 22 areas—a highly dubious assumption—a referendum would be held in the fall of 1992 to ratify the new arrangement. If the rest of Canada refused to negotiate, the Allaire report endorsed the holding of a referendum on Quebec's secession from the federation. The Quebec Liberal Party, during its convention on 8–10 March 1991, endorsed the radical Allaire report. Bourassa, deploying his iron-fist-in-a-velvet-glove approach, reminded Canadians that if the federation was not reformed to suit Quebec, he would have no option but to follow his party's constitutional policy. He did open the door to possible negotiations with the premiers if and when an acceptable offer was made to Quebec.[66]

The Bélanger-Campeau report . . . was submitted to the National Assembly on 28 March 1991. It proclaimed that "Quebecers are aware that they form a distinct national collectivity: the language of the majority of Quebecers and their culture, which are in a minority situation in Canada, are unique across the continent." Since Quebecers "have always expressed the need to be masters of their own destiny," it was imperative that they choose their constitutional future with "serenity."[67] The divided commissioners—unable to develop a consensus on either Bourassa's European Union style of a highly decentralized, bi-national, Canada-Quebec federation or Parizeau's call for outright secession with possible future ties with the rest of Canada—recommended that the National Assembly adopt a two-track approach whereby all Quebecers would determine their political and constitutional future. Track one entailed passing a law authorizing a referendum on secession no later than 26 October 1992. Track two called for the creation, by legislation, of two special parliamentary commissions: one would "assess any offer of a new partnership of constitutional nature made by the Government of Canada," and possibly hold a referendum if the offer was deemed acceptable; the other, dear to Parizeau's heart, would evaluate the political complications and economic costs of secession.[68] . . . Putting into action his knife-to-the-throat strategy, Bourassa authorized Bélanger-Campeau's two-track approach in his government's Referendum Bill 150, enacted by Quebec's National Assembly on 20 June 1991.[69] The highly contentious and ambiguously worded law—based on the disputed premise that, under international law, Quebec had the right to secede unilaterally from Canada within a year of a majority vote in a referendum *proposing* sovereignty—was criticized by Prime Minister Mulroney but never legally challenged.

Mulroney's . . . challenge was to set the parameters for the constitutional offer that needed be made to Quebec if a second referendum on secession was to be avoided. To oversee the sensitive process, on 21 April 1991 the prime minister appointed Joe Clark as minister for constitutional affairs and chair of the Cabinet Committee on Canadian Unity and Constitutional Negotiations. On 24 September 1991 the Mulroney government released a document, *Shaping Canada's Future Together*, comprising a pastiche of constitutional reforms drawn from the defunct Meech Lake Accord and the Companion Agreement. . . .[70]

The Mulroney-Clark proposals were put into the hands of a special joint committee on a "Renewed Canada" chaired by the Manitoba Conservative MP Dorothy Dobbie and Senator Gérald Beaudoin, the latter conscripted to rescue the committee from criticism and ridicule (a development that prompted Quebec senator Claude Castonquay to resign in disgust).[71] . . .

The Beaudoin-Dobbie committee's report, released on 1 March 1992, set out Ottawa's radical vision for reshaping Canada's constitutional structure. It encompassed modified elements of the Meech Lake Accord: a circumscribed distinct society clause within an omnibus "Canada clause"; a veto limited to cultural and linguistic legislation and an entrenched Supreme Court with three justices from Quebec; and concurrent federal-provincial powers covering a range of jurisdictions. In addition, the report recommended the strengthening of the economic union, an elected and effective Senate based on four regions (not provincial equality), and the recognition of the Aboriginal peoples' inherent right of self-government with a veto over constitutional changes affecting them, as well as the inclusion of a limited number of social and economic rights in the Charter.[72]

As expected, the report was denounced vehemently by Parizeau and Bouchard. Bourassa characterized the Beaudoin-Dobbie report's conception of federalism as "domineering" and centralist rather that "flexible" and decentralist. Clearly, it did not satisfy his criteria for an acceptable constitutional offer.[73] . . . Yet it was Ontario premier Bob Rae, backed by fellow NDP premiers in British Columbia and Saskatchewan, who altered the course of events. His steadfast refusal, made clear throughout his testimony to the joint committee, to let Ottawa alone determine the constitutional offer to Quebec compelled Mulroney to authorize Joe Clark to chair a series of multilateral meetings of the provincial and territorial ministers responsible for constitutional matters. On 12 March the Continuing Committee of Ministers on the Constitution (CCMC), again at the insistence of Rae, invited representatives of the four national Native organizations, except for the Native Women's Association of Canada, to join the negotiations. During an interview with the CBC's *The Journal*, Bourassa was visibly shocked and dismayed when he learned of the addition of Aboriginal representatives at the negotiating table. He agreed only to send observers, a decision he would later regret because he lost a great opportunity to influence directly the shape of the constitutional offer to Quebec.[74]. . .

Ministers and Aboriginal representatives involved in the closed-door multilateral ministerial conferences, travelling back and forth across Canada, laboured in vain throughout April, May, and June to reach a consensus on both the substance and the scope of a comprehensive constitutional package, one that had to satisfy provincial and territorial leaders, Aboriginal representatives, and Premier Bourassa. They agreed on all five elements of the Meech Lake Accord, a revised omnibus "Canada clause," and the constitutional recognition of the Aboriginal peoples' right to self-government, leading to a "third order" of government. But there was one major condition. In exchange for granting Quebec a veto over the reform of national institutions, Alberta premier Don Getty, with the backing of other premiers, demanded a Triple-E Senate. As with the Meech and Companion Resolution process, Senate reform emerged as an intractable deal breaker. Mulroney convened the premiers on 29 June for lunch at 24 Sussex and warned them to settle their differences on Senate reform or his government, upon his return from a G-7 summit in Munich, Germany, would recall Parliament on 15 July to discuss his government's unilateral set of constitutional proposals for Quebec. Working

under extreme duress, the nine premiers came to an agreement once Ontario's NDP Premier Bob Rae accepted a watered-down version of the Triple-E Senate—elected, equal, but not very effective. Despite conflicting messages, they were given repeated assurances that Bourassa would go along with the complex deal on Senate reform if he got a veto for Quebec.[75]

Clark reconvened the multilateral ministerial conference in Ottawa on 6–7 July at the Lester B. Pearson Building to hammer out the details of its *Final Status Report*, which was to include all the items mentioned above plus an astonishingly radical restructuring of the Senate and its role in the federation. The new Senate would be composed of eight senators from each province and one from each territory. Senators could veto tax and natural resources legislation with a simple majority, while it would take a 70 per cent vote to veto ordinary legislation. Legislation dealing with French language and culture required approval of a majority of the senators and a majority of the francophone senators.[76]

Somewhat shocked that Clark had accomplished the improbable, Mulroney and Bourassa were reluctant to endorse the *Final Status Report*. Mulroney knew that his government's future, his political future, and his legacy were all on the line. Both awaited the reaction in francophone Quebec—which was immediate and negative, especially on the Senate proposals.[77] Responding to the proposals on 9 July 1992, a cautious and conciliatory Bourassa indicated that he and his colleagues would study the report carefully before deciding what amendments might make its recommendations acceptable to Quebec. He warned that the distinct society clause needed to be strengthened by the recognition of Quebec as a sovereign nation and that Quebecers would have to be convinced of the benefits of the Triple-E Senate because under it the province would lose considerable power. Bourassa's ambivalence reflected that of francophone Quebecers.[78] A June CROP poll revealed that a majority remained attached to Canada and over 70 per cent supported the Charter of Rights.

On the other hand, the Quebecois "chattering classes" unanimously rejected the report's proposals as a dramatic watering down of Meech, especially concerning the distinct society clause. For them, Quebec did not get enough new powers to justify accepting the Triple-E Senate and Aboriginal self-government. Their outcry had its effect. Polls soon revealed that nearly 44 per cent rejected the package and 55.5 per cent of francophones supported a second referendum on sovereignty-association.[79] The Canadian and Aboriginal nationalisms expressed in the report had fuelled a counter-reaction from Quebecois nationalists and secessionists.

Nonetheless, encouraged by Bourassa's conciliatory demeanour, eager to avoid a referendum on secession, and fearing that unilateral action would backfire, Mulroney invited him to meet informally with the premiers on 4 August at Harrington Lake. . . . Bourassa consented to participate in a full-scale, closed-door constitutional conference, including territorial leaders and Aboriginal representatives, in Ottawa on 18 August 1992.[80]

Throughout five tense days of negotiations centred on the Canada and distinct society clauses, the Senate, Aboriginal self-government, and the division of powers, the participants agreed on a complex, wide-ranging, ambiguous, and incomplete—25 political accords remained to be negotiated—Charlottetown Consensus Report, named after Charlottetown, Prince Edward Island, where it would be formally signed on 28 August. The vast majority of the document's 60 clauses resembled those of the *Final Status Report* of 7 July except for those amendments required to get Bourassa on board. Bourassa won a partial victory on the interpretative omnibus "Canada clause" 2, which incorporated a distinct society clause 2(1) (c) as well as another clause (2[2]) authorizing the "legislature and Government of Quebec to preserve and promote the distinct society of Quebec." Bowing in part to pressure from francophone and Acadian community leaders, Bourassa agreed to a clause 2(1) (d), which stated that "Canadians and their government were committed to the vitality

and development of official language minority communities." In return for accepting a drastic reduction of the number of Quebec senators from 24 to 6, Bourassa obtained the right for Quebec to appoint its senators, 18 additional seats in the House of Commons, and a guarantee in perpetuity that Quebec would have "no fewer than twenty-five percent of the members in the House of Commons."[81] Bourassa was unable to obtain any limitations on Aboriginal peoples' inherent right to self-government that would lead, in due course, to a "third order" of government in the federation, one that was not subject to the Canadian Charter of Rights and Freedoms. On the division of powers, Bourassa obtained a degree of decentralization but not the radical restructuring of the federation called for in the Allaire report or in his musings about a Canada-Quebec union modelled on the European Union.

The Charlottetown Consensus Report was submitted to Canadian voters for their approval or rejection in a nationwide referendum set for 26 October 1992. . . . In an emotional but rather defensive speech, Bourassa presented his case in favour of the accord in the National Assembly on 9 September. Portraying the accord as fulfilling only the minimum of Quebec's constitutional objectives, he focused on the gains: full control over the integration of immigrants; increased cultural and linguistic security via the distinct society clause working in tandem with section 1, the "reasonable limits" clause, and section 33, the "notwithstanding clause," of the Charter of Rights; appointment of Quebec's senators by the National Assembly; and the strengthening of the Canadian common market, which would enhance Quebec's ability to play a greater role on the international stage.[82]

The reaction of francophone Quebecers to the Charlottetown deal was not what Mulroney or Bourassa expected or needed if they were to win the high-stakes, winner-takes-all referendum. Following the Quebec Liberal Party's ratification of the accord on 29 August, members of the youth wing and Jean Allaire left the party, setting the stage for the emergence of Mario Dumont's Action Démocratique du Québec.

Bourassa and his YES campaign committee were put on the defensive when a late-August private cell-phone conversation between his leading constitutional advisers, Wilhelmy and Tremblay, was taped, transcribed, and then broadcast throughout Quebec on 16 September. During their candid chat, they concurred that Bourassa had caved in completely during the negotiations. Other briefing notes published in *L'Actualité* just before the vote inflicted more damage on the beleaguered YES campaign. These revelations confirmed what Parizeau and Bouchard repeatedly claimed during their increasingly successful NO campaign.[83]

Bourassa and Mulroney responded in two ways. First, they sowed fear by claiming that a YES vote was a vote for Canadian unity while a NO vote would bring about the secession of Quebec. In English-speaking Canada, Mulroney, as he had done in the Meech Lake debate, claimed that a rejection of the Charlottetown deal would be interpreted by francophone Quebecers as a rejection of Quebec. Meanwhile, in Quebec, appealing to *nationalistes*, Mulroney warned that a rejection of the distinct society clause would reduce Quebecois to the sorry state of Louisiana's assimilated Acadians—Cajuns. Both Mulroney and Bourassa also boasted that, with the Charlottetown Accord, Quebec had made the most significant constitutional gains since Confederation. To emphasize this rather questionable assertion, Mulroney ripped up a copy of the Charlottetown deal in front of the cameras, commenting that all Quebec's gains would be lost if the deal were rejected. He was widely ridiculed in the media for this tactic.[84]

Early September polls revealed the YES side leading in Quebec by 10 percentage points, 49 to 38. But, by 2 October, the NO side had reversed the tide and was leading by 14 points. There were two main reasons for this dramatic shift. No doubt, Bourassa's and Mulroney's failure to convince Quebecois nationalist federalists that Charlottetown represented a "Meech Plus" instead of a "Meech Minus" package prompted many of them to reconsider their support. In addition, Trudeau's two well-timed

and highly effective interventions for the NO side accelerated the growing opposition to the deal. In an article published in *Maclean's* and *L'actualité* in September, entitled "Quebec's Blackmail," Trudeau castigated Quebec's corrupt "blackmailing" political culture and fingered Premier Bourassa as the master blackmailer for his dangerous use of the threat of secession to obtain more powers for the province. Then, during his 1 October *Cité libre* dinner speech at the Maison Egg Roll Chinese restaurant in Montreal, Trudeau dissected the Charlottetown deal's contradictions, myths, and questionable principles, all of which, he said, threatened democracy, the Charter of Rights, and national unity by constructing an explosive hierarchy of conflicting collective and individual rights. He then pronounced the deal "a mess that deserves a big No."[85] Once again the sly fox had emerged from his lair to slay the beast of Quebecois nationalism. In doing so, he helped defeat the Mulroney-Bourassa alliance's attempt to establish a decentralized, bi-national confederation, Quebec-Canada, via radical amendments to the Constitution Act, 1982 and the Charter.

When the campaign concluded and the ballots were counted, the pollsters were proven correct. The complex and ambiguous Charlottetown deal, comprising an explosive cocktail of conflicting Canadian, Quebecois, and Aboriginal nationalist dreams, was rejected by a respectable margin of nearly 10 percentage points, 54.4 to 44.6. The Quebec results, 55.4 to 42.4, mirrored the national outcome.[86] . . .

Torpedoed by Quebecois Nationalism: An Unintended Political Realignment

The Mulroney-Bourassa alliance paid the ultimate political price for opening, not once but twice, the constitutional Pandora's box. Their failed attempts at mega-constitutional politics, using Quebecois nationalism and secessionism to entice the rest of Canada onside, brought to a brutal end their respective quests for political realignment. Bourassa failed in his effort to redefine Canada's cultural and linguistic duality into a territorial, state-based duality of Quebec-Canada. Rather than applauding him for his valiant efforts, Quebecois nationalists abandoned his Liberal Party and turned to the secessionist parties, Jacques Parizeau's Parti Québécois and Lucien Bouchard's Bloc québécois, to achieve their dream of independence. Mulroney's dangerous dalliance with Quebecois nationalism and secessionism cost him his jobs as prime minister and leader of the Conservative Party. More important, it ushered in a dramatic but unintended political realignment. His failure to entrench a special constitutional status for Quebec precipitated the wholesale destruction of the Progressive Conservative Party of Canada. Three sectional parties emerged from the political crash, one in western Canada, the second in Quebec, and a third comprising the remnants of the Red Tory wing of the party dispersed through Atlantic Canada and Ontario.

Bouchard, advised by Jean-François Lisée, was cagey enough to leave Bourassa enough room to make one last attempt to obtain the essentials of Meech from the "Rest of Canada." If Bourassa failed a second time, then Bouchard could lead a coalition of nationalist and secessionist forces into a second referendum.[87] During the Bloc's founding convention in June 1991 in Sorel-Tracy, Bouchard set as its goal the winning of more seats than either the Conservatives or the Liberals. When Bourassa agreed to a referendum on the Charlottetown deal, Bouchard quickly denounced the accord as a sell-out by his ally Bourassa and campaigned energetically, and successfully, for its defeat. Bouchard plunged into the 1993 federal election campaign at the head of a Bloc committed to sovereignty-association, with the organizational support and financial backing Parizeau's Parti Québécois. A titanic struggle was under way over which of the two would control the Quebecois secessionist movement in the 1990s.[88]

An exhausted, dejected, and humiliated Mulroney, forced to acknowledge . . . damaging polls, decided to step down as party leader in February 1993. . . . The fortunes of Kim Campbell (the new Conservative leader) and her party plummeted dramatically as Lucien Bouchard and Preston Manning hammered the Conservatives in Quebec and the West, while, coming up the middle, Jean Chrétien—promising to refrain from constitutional negotiations and to rectify the problems of the deficit and the debt—picked up disillusioned Red Tories in Atlantic Canada, Ontario, and British Columbia.[89]

The election of 25 October 1993 was a political watershed. Chrétien's Liberal Party, with 41 per cent of the votes, took 177 seats, enough for a comfortable majority government. The Liberals won every seat in Ontario except one, turning the once mainly Conservative province into the new political bastion of the national Liberal Party. In Quebec, Chrétien's disorganized, old-fashioned party was limited to 19 seats, better than expected but a sign of future troubles to come. The Liberals also garnered every seat except one in Atlantic Canada. Campbell's hapless Progressive Conservative Party, garnering a mere 16 per cent of the votes, was reduced to a humiliating two seats. It was the beginning of a difficult and protracted period that eventually led to the party's demise. Lucien Bouchard's Bloc québécois, with 48 per cent of Quebec votes, won 54 seats, enough to take on the role of official opposition in the House of Commons. Preston Manning's fledgling Reform Party, with 18 per cent of the national vote, 26 per cent outside Quebec, sent 52 MPs to Ottawa, all but one from western Canada.[90] Canada had been carved up into three political fiefdoms, Quebec, Atlantic Canada–Ontario, and the "New West."

Mulroney's dream of political realignment was displaced by other attempts at political restructuring as Manning's populist Reformers and Bouchard's Bloc québécois continued to rearrange the Canadian political landscape over the next decade. That process had been set in motion by Mulroney's and Bourassa's unbridled determination to redraw the political map of Quebec and Canada, each using Quebecois nationalism to that end. Their decision to pursue fundamental alterations to the Constitution Act, 1982 and the Charter of Rights and Freedoms destabilized Canadian politics, a dynamic that was accentuated by the struggle over, and eventual ratification of, the Trade Agreement. The resulting conflict between federal and provincial political elites, dependent upon traditional political cultures of deference, and a wide range of groups and a majority of citizens, all inspired by a democratic approach to constitutional renewal, culminated in the defeat of two

mega-constitutional deals. More important, these dramatic failures had a profound, and perhaps even permanent, impact on Canadian politics and the federation. They generated an unforeseen and unintended political realignment that has thrown national politics into turmoil and weakened Ottawa while giving the Quebecois secessionist movement a second opportunity to achieve its dream of a radical constitutional realignment through the creation of an independent Quebec state with an economic association with what remains of Canada.

Notes

1   John Sawatsky, *Mulroney: The Politics of Ambition* (Toronto: Macfarlane Walter and Ross 1991), 129–56.
2   Ibid., 289–314. Paradoxically, Diefenbaker turned against Mulroney during the leadership race. No doubt he misunderstood and distrusted the bilingual Mulroney's Irish, French-Canadian, and Catholic background and his success as a businessman.
3   Michael D. Behiels, *Prelude to Quebec's Quiet Revolution: Liberalism versus Neo-nationalism 1945–1960* (Montreal and Kingston: McGill-Queen's University Press, 1985); Ramsay Cook, *Canada, Québec and the Uses of Nationalism*, 2nd edn (Toronto: McClelland & Stewart, 1995).
4   Michael D. Behiels, *Canada's Francophone Minority Communities: Constitutional Renewal and the Winning of School Governance* (Montreal and Kingston: McGill-Queen's University Press, 2004).
5   Claude Morin, *Lendemains piégés: De la referendum au nuit de longs couteaux* (Montreal: Boréal, 1988).
6   David V.J. Bell and Donald C. Wallace, "Parliament and Politics," in *The Canadian Annual Review 1980* (Toronto: University of Toronto Press, 1982), 48–58.
7   Michael D. Behiels, "Pierre Elliott Trudeau's Legacy: The Canadian Charter of Rights and Freedoms," in Joseph Magnet *et al.*, eds, *The Canadian Charter of Rights and Freedoms* (Toronto: Butterworths, 2003), 154–8.
8   Lawrence Martin, *The Antagonist: Lucien Bouchard and the Politics of Delusion* (Toronto: Penguin Books, 1998), 84–97.
9   Ibid., 164–75, 214–26.
10   Ibid., 7–21.
11   Robert J. Drummond, "Parliament and Politics," in *Canadian Annual Review 1984* (Toronto: University of Toronto Press, 1987), 10–19.
12   L. Ian MacDonald, *Mulroney: The Making of the Prime Minister* (Toronto: McClelland and Stewart, 1985), 259–67, 272–4, 300–1.

13   Ibid., 288–90.
14   Morin, *Lendemains piégés*, 305–14.
15   MacDonald, *Mulroney*, 299–300.
16   Lucien Bouchard, *À visage découvert* (Montreal: Boréal, 1992), 143.
17   Morin, *Lendemains piégés*, 327, author's translation. See also MacDonald, *Mulroney*, 289. This remarkable statement was repeated during the French-language TV debate, which Mulroney won hands down. His performance had a profound impact throughout francophone Quebec.
18   Lawrence Martin, *The Antagonist*, 98–105.
19   J.L. Findlay and D.N. Sprague, *The Structure of Canadian History*, 3rd edn (Toronto: Prentice Hall, 1989), 504, Table 14; Carol Goar, "The Conservatives' Mandate for Change," *Maclean's*, 17 September 1984, 12–20.
20   Gil Rémillard, "Under What Conditions Could Quebec Sign the Constitution Act of 1982?," in Michael D. Behiels, ed., *Quebec since 1945: Selected Readings* (Toronto: Copp Clark Pitman, 1987), 209–20.
21   L. Ian MacDonald, *From Bourassa to Bourassa: Wilderness to Restoration* (Montreal and Kingston: McGill-Queen's University Press, 2002, 242–3); René Durocher, "Quebec," *Canadian Annual Review 1985* (Toronto: University of Toronto Press 1988), 310–16.
22   Bourassa's team comprised Minister Gil Rémillard and his deputy minister, Diane Wilhelmy; André Tremblay, a constitutional specialist; Roch Bolduc, head of the Quebec civil service; and Jean-Claude Rivest, his alter ego. Mulroney's team was led by Senator Lowell Murray and his deputy minister, Norman Spector.
23   Gil Rémillard, "Unofficial English Language Text of the Speech to the 5 May, 1986 Mont-Gabriel Conference, 'Rebuilding the Relationship; Quebec and Its Confederation Partners,'" in Peter M. Leslie, ed., *Canada: The State of the Federation 1986*

(Kingston, ON: Institute of Intergovernmental Relations, Queen's University, 1986), 97–104.

24 Ibid., 105.

25 Peter Leslie, "Rethinking Basic Relationships," in Leslie, ed., *Canada: The State of the Federation 1986*, 5–6.

26 Andrew Cohen, *A Deal Undone: The Making and Breaking of the Meech Lake Accord* (Vancouver/Toronto: Douglas & McIntyre, 1990).

27 Consult *Le Québec et le Lac Meech: Un Dossier du Devoir* (Montreal: Guérin Littérature, 1987).

28 Donald C. Wallace, "Ottawa and the Provinces," *Canadian Annual Review 1986* (Toronto: University of Toronto Press, 1990), 76–7.

29 Pierre Elliott Trudeau, "Say Goodbye to the Dream of One Canada," *Toronto Star*, 27 May 1987, repr. in Donald Johnston, ed., *With a Bang, Not a Whimper: Pierre Trudeau Speaks Out* (Toronto: Stoddart, 1988), 8–22.

30 Donald Johnston, "A Dismembered Confederation of Fiefdoms?," *Ottawa Citizen*, 16 May 1987; his extensive brief to and testimony before the Senate committee of the whole on the Meech Lake Constitutional Accord, Canada, Parliament, *Debates of the Senate*, 23 March 1988, 2912–21; his testimony to the Legislative Assembly of Ontario, Select Committee on Constitutional Reform, 1987, Constitutional Accord, *Hansard Official Report of Debates*, 7 March 1988.

31 Quebec, *Journal des Débats*, 18 June 1987, 8708.

32 Cited in Vastel, *Bourassa*, 114–15.

33 Quebec, *Journal des Débats*, 18 June 1987, 8709.

34 Greg Weston, "Turner Attacks Bourassa for Quebec Language Policy," *Ottawa Citizen*, 6 April 1989; Susan Delacourt, "Grits Bare Souls on Meech Lake," *Globe and Mail*, 17 April 1989, and "Race Is On as Turner Bows Out," *Globe and Mail*, 4 May 1989; Paul-André Comeau, *Le Devoir*, 4 May 1989.

35 Gretta Chambers, "Federal Liberals Turn Backs on Quebec," *Gazette* (Montreal), 18 May 1989; Michel Vastel, "Le leadership liberal se prepare sur le dos du Québec," *Le Devoir*, 19 June 1989; Richard Cleroux, "Quebec MPs Emerge as Surprise Powerhouse," *Globe and Mail*, 24 May 1989.

36 Behiels, *Canada's Francophone Minority Communities*, 260–2.

37 Frank McKenna, testimony before the Special Joint Committee of the Senate and the House of Commons on the 1987 Constitutional Accord, *Minutes of Proceedings and Evidence*, no. 12, 25 August 1987, 5–19.

38 Michel Vastel, "McKenna veut son petit lac Meech," *Le Devoir*, 27 November 1987; Don Richardson, "Delaying Ratification of Meech Lake," Fredericton *Telegraph Journal*, 17 February 1988; "Murray Confident NB. Will Eventually Throw Its Support to Meech Lake Deal," Fredericton *Telegraph Journal*, 27 April 1988; Bernard Descoteau, "Lac Meech: McKenna envoie paître Bourassa," *Le Devoir*, 18 March 1988; "Le Quebec et le Nouveau Brunswick on fait la paix," *Le Devoir*, 23 August 1988.

39 "McKenna Steadfast on Meech Lake," *Ottawa Citizen*, 13 January 1989; Susan Delacourt, "McKenna Questions Meech Lake Deadline," *Globe and Mail*, 13 January 1989; Roy MacGregor, "McKenna Wants Answers from Mulroney, Bourassa," *Ottawa Citizen*, 24 May 1989.

40 Don McGillivray, "Manitoba Catches Nation by Surprise," *Ottawa Citizen*, 25 April 1989; William Johnson, "Liberal Votes in Manitoba Kill Meech Deal," *Gazette* (Montreal), 27 April 1989; "Filmon Gov't Makes Meech a Priority, Report Says," *Ottawa Citizen*, 21 July 1989.

41 Geoffrey York, "Will Kill Meech Lake, Manitoba NDP Warns," *Globe and Mail*, 23 November 1989; Michel Vastel, "Bourassa paiera cher son appui à Mulroney," *Le Devoir*, 18 December 1989.

42 Cohen, *A Deal Undone*, 194–5.

43 *Quebec v. Ford et al.* [1988] 2 S.C.R. 712.

44 MacDonald, *From Bourassa to Bourassa*, 294–9.

45 Geoffrey York and Benoît Aubin, "Manitoba Premier Ends Meech Debate," *Globe and Mail*, 20 December 1989; "Half Man. PCS Oppose Accord," *Ottawa Citizen*, 21 December 1989; Geoffrey York, "Filmon Urges Judicial Clarification of Accord's Distinct Society Clause," *Globe and Mail*, 12 January 1989.

46 Geoffrey York, "Meech Lake Accord Comes under Attack at Manitoba Hearing," *Globe and Mail*, 7 April 1989; "Opposition to Meech Dominates Hearing," *Globe and Mail*, 12 April 1989.

47 *Report of the Manitoba Task Force Report on Meech Lake*, Summary of Recommendations (Manitoba Legislative Assembly, 21 October 1989), 72–9.

48 Kevin Cox, "Newfoundland Liberals Win Majority," *Globe and Mail*, 21 April 1989; Hugh Winsor, "Newfoundland Liberals' Win Raises Alarms in Ottawa," *Globe and Mail*, 22 May 1989; Don McGillivray, "Federal Tories Blew Nfld. Election," *Ottawa Citizen*, 21 April 1989.

49 Michael Valpy, "Wells a New Star on Political Stage," *Globe and Mail*, 22 May 1989; Hugh Winsor and Kevin Cox, "Wells Pledges to Oppose Meech Lake Agreement," *Globe and Mail*, 22 May 1989.

50 New Brunswick, Select Committee on the 1987 Constitutional Accord, *Final Report on the Constitution Amendment 1987* (Fredericton, October 1989).

51 New Brunswick, *A Guide to New Brunswick's Companion Resolution to the 1987 Constitutional Accord* (Fredericton, March 1990).

52 Darrel R. Reid, "Chronology of Events, 1989–90," in Ronald L. Watts and Douglas M. Brown, eds,

Canada: The State of the Federation 1990 (Kingston, ON: Institute of Intergovernmental Relations, Queen's University, 1990), 253.

53   Canada, Special Committee to Study the Proposed Companion Resolution to the Meech Lake Accord, *Report* (Ottawa, May 1990).

54   Martin, *The Antagonist*, 198–9.

55   MacDonald, *From Bourassa to Bourassa*, 306–7.

56   Patrick J. Monahan, *Meech Lake: The Inside Story* (Toronto: University of Toronto Press 1991), 210–37; Cohen, *A Deal Undone*, 233–56.

57   Cohen, *A Deal Undone*, 258–67.

58   Guy Laforest, *Trudeau et la fin d'un rêve canadien* (Montreal: Septentrion, 1992), 149–71; Pierre Fournier, *A Meech Lake Post-Mortem: Is Quebec Sovereignty Inevitable?* (Montreal and Kingston: McGill-Queen's University Press, 1991), 68–83.

59   Philip Resnick, *Toward a Canada Quebec Union* (Montreal and Kingston: McGill-Queen's University Press, 1991); Kenneth McRoberts, *Misconceiving Canada: The Struggle for National Unity* (Toronto: Oxford University Press, 1997).

60   Cited in William Johnson, *A Canadian Myth: Quebec between Canada and Utopia* (Montreal: Robert Davies Publishing, 1994), 249.

61   *An Act to Establish the Commission on the Political and Constitutional Future of Quebec* (Bill 90), s. 2.

62   Johnson, *A Canadian Myth*, 260–1.

63   MacDonald, *From Bourassa to Bourassa*, 322–3. The expression "a knife to the throat" was first used by a renowned Laval University political scientist, Léon Dion, during his testimony before the Bélanger-Campeau Commission.

64   Max Nemni, "Canada in Crisis and the Destructive Power of Myth," *Queen's Quarterly* 99(1), (1992), 222–39.

65   Kenneth McRoberts, *Quebec: Social Change and Political Crisis*, 3rd edn (Toronto: Oxford University Press, 1993), 449.

66   *A Quebec Free to Choose: Report of the Constitutional Committee of the Quebec Liberal Party for Submission to the 25th Convention* (Quebec Liberal Party, 28 January 1991). This document was called the "Allaire report." Robert Bourassa, interview on the Allaire report, *La Presse*, 2 February 1991.

67   Quebec, *Report of the Commission on the Political and Constitutional Future of Quebec*, 15. This commission was known as the Bélanger-Campeau Commission.

68   Ibid., 79–82.

69   *An Act respecting the Process for Determining the Political and Constitutional Future of Quebec*, s. 1.

70   Canada, *Shaping Canada's Future Together: Proposals* (Ottawa: Minister of Supply and Services 1991).

71   Robert Everett, "Parliament and Politics," in David Leyton-Brown, ed., *Canadian Annual Review of Politics and Public Affairs 1991* (Toronto: University of Toronto Press, 1998), 26–9.

72   Canada, Special Joint Committee of the Senate and of the House of Commons on a Renewed Canada, *A Renewed Canada, in Minutes of Proceedings and Evidence*, 66 (28 February 1992).

73   Robert Bourassa, "Conference de presse," *Le Devoir*, 4 March 1992; *Globe and Mail*, 4 March 1992.

74   Susan Delacourt, *United We Fall: The Crisis of Legitimacy in Canada* (Toronto: Viking, 1993), 138–41.

75   Ibid., 141–66; Johnson, *A Canadian Myth*, 318–20.

76   Canada, Continuing Committee of Ministers on the Constitution, *Final Status Report of the Multilateral Meetings on the Constitution, July 16, 1992* (Ottawa: Government of Canada 1992).

77   Johnson, *A Canadian Myth*, 321–2.

78   Delacourt, *United We Fall*, 166–70.

79   CROP Poll, *L'Actualité*, June 1992, Léger et Léger poll, *Le Journal de Montréal*, July 1992.

80   Delecourt, *United We Fall*, 171–2.

81   *Consensus Report on the Constitution, Charlottetown, August 28, 1992, Final Text*. See also *Draft Legal Text, October 9, 1992*.

82   Quebec National Assembly, *Journal des Débats*, 9 September 1992.

83   Johnson, *A Canadian Myth*, 338–9.

84   Delacourt, *United We Fall*, 176–81.

85   Michael D. Behiels, "Who Speaks for Canada? Trudeau and the Constitutional Crisis," in Andrew Cohen and J.L. Granatstein, eds, *Trudeau's Shadow: The Life and Legacy of Pierre Elliott Trudeau* (Toronto: Random House Canada 1998), 343–8.

86   Robert Everett, "Parliament and Politics," in David Leyton-Brown, ed., *Canadian Annual Review of Politics and Public Affairs 1992* (Toronto: University of Toronto Press 1998), 26–7.

87   Martin, *The Antagonist*, 228-40. Consult Lisée, *The Trickster: Robert Bourassa and the Quebecers, 1990–1992* (Toronto: James Lorimer, 1994).

88   Manon Cornellier, *The Bloc* (Toronto: James Lorimer 1995), 28–31.

89   Trevor Harrison, *Of Passionate Intensity: Right-Wing Populism and the Reform Party of Canada* (Toronto: University of Toronto Press 1995), 239.

90   Ibid., 240–5; Cornellier, *The Bloc*, 84.

⊚ 3.2: Aboriginal Identities and the New Indian Problem

David Newhouse

As an Aboriginal person, I believe that one of the most difficult issues Canada faces today is how to accommodate the continuing presence of Aboriginal peoples who express a strong desire to maintain a distinct identity within the country. This desire and its political expression in the idea of Aboriginal self-government challenge the idea that Confederation is complete. Until Aboriginal peoples are brought into Confederation in ways meaningful and satisfactory to us, Canada will always have what has come to be called an "Indian problem." This is not a new problem.

Since the arrival of Europeans and the establishment of governments in Canada after 1763, government officials have been trying to decide what to do with the Indians; each administration over the years has had a particular view of the Indian problem. At various times, the problem was whether we were human and had souls, how to make us into good Christians, how to live next to us, how to get us to enter into military alliances, how to civilize us, how to assimilate us, or how to get us to become an ethnic group within the multicultural environment of Canada. Each of these views of the Indian problem has led to a particular policy solution and to a set of actions by government officials.

I spoke to staff of the Ontario Native Affairs Secretariat in Toronto as part of their ongoing series of talks from community members. The overall purpose of the talks was to help policy-makers and advisers gain a more complex understanding of the issues and problems facing Aboriginal peoples and the potential solutions. At the time, my fourth-year Native Studies honours students and I were discussing the federal government's White Paper on Indian policy, now commonly known as the "White Paper of 1969"—an ironic name because what it largely proposed was that Indians should become, for all intents and purposes, white. At the start of the discussion, I asked the students: What is the Indian problem that the White Paper was intended to address? How did the framers of the policy see Indian peoples?

The Indian problem is still with us today. However, is it now a problem of new Indians or a new problem with Indians? To answer these questions, I will discuss two things: first, some history to give a sense of the incredible change that has occurred over the past three decades; and second, what I call "modern Aboriginal society"—that is, what appears to be emerging—and the new Indian problem that recent developments constitute.

As I was preparing to talk to the Ontario public servants, I watched an incredible spectacle on the Cable Public Affairs Channel (CPAC): the House of Commons sat for more than 26 hours to deal with the Nisga'a Treaty. Whatever one thinks of the treaty and its implications, one must be struck by the enormous significance of the work and by the marshalling of resources that was necessary to get it approved given the opposition that it had received in many quarters. That a government would use its political energy and goodwill to push through a bill concerning Aboriginal peoples speaks to the changes that have occurred over the past three decades. I am not convinced that 30 years ago such an event could have occurred. How did we get to this place?

A few years ago, there was a similar televised event. On 7 January 1998, the minister of Indian affairs and northern development, Jane Stewart, stood up in a room in the House of Commons and read a statement of reconciliation. We can discuss whether it was an apology and what the words meant. We can also debate whether she should have made it, whether it was sincere, whether it went far enough, and what its effect, if any, has been and will be. However, if we step back and look at the statement in another light, we can see it as the first statement by a government of the "New World" to acknowledge that it had been wrong in its treatment of the people it encountered: "The Government of Canada today formally expresses to all Aboriginal people in Canada our profound regret for past actions of the federal government which have contributed to these difficult pages in the history of our relationship together."[1] Such a declaration has not been made in the United States of America, Mexico, Brazil, Argentina, or Peru. Nor have England, Spain, France, or Portugal made any official statement that comes close to the sentiments expressed here.

Also important is the view of history that Stewart's statement contains. It says explicitly that Aboriginal peoples have lived here for thousands of years, have had their own forms of government, have been organized into nations with distinct national cultures, and have made contributions to the development of Canada. It also says that there has been a deliberate attempt, based on attitudes of racial and cultural superiority, to suppress Aboriginal cultures and values and to dispossess Aboriginal peoples of their lands and territories. And it says that this was wrong. It vows to make amends. It also paints a picture of Aboriginal peoples as having remarkable strength and endurance. We can be cynical about the statement, but we should know that at least in its ideas it conforms to the position held by many Aboriginal peoples. We should also know that it was prepared mostly by Aboriginal peoples working within one of the major Aboriginal political organizations.

What has happened over the past 30 years to allow for these two events?

I divide modern Aboriginal history into before and after the White Paper of 1969. The post-1969 period was a critical and profound time in Aboriginal history, during which we can begin to see the marshalling of Aboriginal political energy into a strong force for change and the glimmerings of unease among Canadian makers of public policy with the status quo, an unease accompanied by a desire to try to do something to solve the Indian problem. Previously, Indians were primarily seen as poor people existing on the margins of Canadian society who needed to be brought into the mainstream of the economy and into full citizenship participation. The period 1969–72 defines what I call the start of modern Aboriginal society.

On 25 June 1969, the government of Canada introduced, for public discussion, "A Statement of Indian Policy." As noted above, it is now commonly referred to as the "White Paper," an ironic name because what it largely proposed was that Indians should become, for all intents and purposes, white. The paper proposed repealing the Indian Act, dismantling Indian reserves, and turning over responsibilities for Indian affairs to provinces, among other things. The introduction of the White Paper—and the subsequent Indian and white responses, which led to its withdrawal—was to have profound effects on Aboriginal peoples' thinking about governments and about themselves. It also led to three decades of political activism and change as well as to a climate of distrust and paranoia about governments and their actions. Over the next three decades, the White Paper, which remains present in many Indian people's consciousness, would become the de facto standard against which all government policies were measured.

It is hard to imagine what the world of 1969 was like. The National Indian Brotherhood, now the Assembly of First Nations, was just starting. The word "Aboriginal" wasn't used to describe the original inhabitants of what is now Canada. The term "First Nations" did not exist. We talked of Indians and Eskimos and Métis and non-status Indians. Aboriginal rights were not part of the popular vocabulary, nor was there any talk of self-government. The government's proposals were met with fear; they didn't seem to mark the start of a thousand years of peace between whites and Indians marked by love for Indian peoples.

In 1970, the Indians, with the support of mainstream activists, started to talk back. The Indian Chiefs of Alberta issued their response, *Citizens Plus*, now called the Red Paper, which said:

> To us who are Treaty Indians there is nothing more important than our Treaties, our lands and the well being of our future generations. We have studied carefully the contents of the Government White Paper on Indians and we have concluded that it offers despair instead of hope. . . .

Indian Lands must continue to be regarded in a different matter than other lands in Canada. It must be held forever in trust of the Crown because, as we say, the true owners of the land are not yet born.[2]

The Union of British Columbia Indian Chiefs issued its Declaration of Indian Rights in the same year. In 1971, the Association of Iroquois and Allied Indians presented their position paper. They rejected all that had been proposed and, more important, set out their own vision of their place in Canadian society and the steps that needed to be taken to move forward.

That new vision is captured best by the response in 1971 of the Manitoba Indian Brotherhood (MIB), titled "Whabung: Our Tomorrows." The Manitoba chiefs said:

Harold Cardinal (standing), leader of the Indian Association of Alberta, which issued *Citizens Plus*, addressing Prime Minister Trudeau (left, with back to camera) and other cabinet members at an Ottawa meeting on 4 June 1970.

The Indian Tribes of Manitoba are committed to the belief that our rights, both aboriginal and treaty, emanate from our sovereignty as a nation of people. Our relationships with the state have their roots in negotiation between two sovereign peoples. . . . The Indian people enjoy special status conferred by recognition of our historic title that cannot be impaired, altered or compromised by federal-provincial collusion or consent.[3]

"Whabung" also called for a comprehensive approach to the development of Indian communities, both as economies and as entities central to Indian life. It called for development to proceed, not in bits and pieces, but according to a comprehensive plan on several fronts. There were three elements to this strategy: (1) a plan to help individuals and communities recover from the pathological consequences of poverty and powerlessness, meaning a focus on individual and community health and healing as well as on adequate health services and community infrastructures; (2) a program for Indian peoples to protect their interests in lands and resources; and (3) a concerted effort at human-resource and cultural development. The MIB plan had at its heart the idea that if change were to lead to increased self-sufficiency, it ought to be directed by Indian peoples themselves so that Indians could consider both individual and communal interests.

The White Paper was formally withdrawn in 1971. It remains to this day a potent political symbol within Aboriginal politics. The Indian reaction to the White Paper was informed by ideas expressed in the 1968 consultations about revisions to the Indian Act. While there was no consensus about changes, there was agreement among Indians about the way forward, particularly the need (1) to recognize the special rights of Indians and the historical grievances over lands and treaties and to deal with them in an equitable manner; (2) to ensure Indians' direct and meaningful participation in making policies that affect their futures; and (3), most important, to maintain and enhance the distinctiveness of Indians.

Indian reaction to the White Paper and its subsequent withdrawal led to profound changes in thinking and in Indians' conceptions of ourselves. We do have some rights. We can mobilize ourselves (and others) to influence government policy. We can be successful in creating change. We now think differently about ourselves than we did in 1969, when self-government was not part of the language of Indian peoples. It is now part of the language of the country. The White Paper galvanized the Indian community in a way that no other event has, with the exception of the Oka Crisis in 1991. The White Paper marshalled the efforts of many non-Aboriginal voices in support of Aboriginal peoples' desire to remain culturally distinct and to be supported in this desire. The Indian-Eskimo Association of Canada, later the Canadian Alliance in Solidarity with the Native Peoples (CASNP), emerged as the main leader of these forces, joined in time by a new and different ally, the judicial system, primarily the Supreme Court of Canada. The White Paper created strong and loud Aboriginal voices that insisted on speaking and being heard. The response also gave voice to our own aspirations and created the political organization necessary to advance them in a more collective and powerful manner.

In the 1970s, the advances piled up. In 1973, the Supreme Court of Canada ruling in the Calder claim, while rejecting the Nisga'a claim on a technicality, upheld the principle of Aboriginal title to land. This case set in motion a whole series of actions by politicians and gave fuel to further court cases and more favourable rulings over the next two decades—to Sparrow, Delgamuukw, and Marshall, among others. In 1975, the Dene Nation of the Northwest Territories made its declaration of nationhood. In 1976, the government of Canada signed

the first modern-day treaty with the Crees of Quebec. This agreement created a form of self-government, giving the Crees varying degrees of control over resources. In 1979, Jack Beaver released his report on economic development, *To Have What Is One's Own*. He argued for a policy of self-direction as the fundamental basis for the economic development of Indian communities and stipulated that the development of Indian communities should be under the guidance of Indian peoples. His report set the blueprint for the future economic development policy of the federal government.[4]

In the early 1980s, progress continued. The Constitution of Canada was patriated from Britain and was rewritten to recognize Aboriginal peoples as including Indian, Inuit (formerly Eskimo), and Métis. The Constitution also affirmed existing Aboriginal rights and called for a series of constitutional conferences between Canada, the provinces, and Aboriginal peoples to determine what these rights were and what self-government meant. In 1983, the House of Commons Special Committee on Indian Self-Government issued its report, which stated that Indian peoples were nations before the arrival of Europeans and had a tradition of government that had been removed. Known as the "Penner Report" after the committee's chair, the document recommended the establishment of a new relationship with Indian peoples, a key element of which would be the recognition of Indian self-government. The report was adopted by the House of Commons in a show of all-party support in November 1985. This appears to be the first official recognition of the idea that Aboriginal peoples had a right to govern themselves. The Penner Report recommended that Indian self-government within the Canadian federation be supported, and the government of Canada agreed.[5]

Two rounds of constitutional discussions, Meech Lake and Charlottetown, then tackled the questions surrounding Aboriginal self-government. There were endless discussions of what it meant, how it should be recognized, how it should be implemented, what powers Aboriginal peoples should have, and so on. The discussion outlined in broad detail the Aboriginal desire and argument for self-government.

The land claims process also occurred during this period. While it got off to a slow and tentative start and lumbered along to much criticism and suspicion, it was at the very least some evidence of talk and of a reluctant willingness to consider the idea of sharing. No one said that it was going to be easy. In February 1997, *Time* magazine said that the process was one of the boldest experiments in social justice in Canada's history.[6] And so we moved from James Bay to Nisga'a in the space of 20 years, with 80 self-government negotiations ongoing and hundreds of small specific claims being discussed. The land claims process—based on the principle of negotiated settlements—brought Aboriginal peoples and governments together in a protracted set of conversations that seems destined to last forever.

The government of Canada agreed in 1993 to divide the Northwest Territories into two: the west, the new Northwest Territories; and the east, to be known as Nunavut, where the majority of residents were Inuk. The latter was viewed as an Aboriginal territory with an Aboriginal government, a public government comprised of both Inuit and northerners. This was done against the background of hundreds of reports from the 1960s to the 1990s containing thousands of recommendations on how to improve the condition of Aboriginal peoples in Canada. Aboriginal issues were on the agenda of virtually every government agency. An extraordinary level of bureaucratic attention was being paid to Aboriginal issues.

In 1995, the government of Canada announced that it would support the policy of the inherent right to self-government for Aboriginal peoples of this country. The Royal Commission on Aboriginal Peoples (RCAP) underlined the importance of this policy and recommended the reconstitution of Aboriginal nations and their governments and the creation of a new relationship between Aboriginal peoples and Canada. In the series of consultations on Indian policy from 1966 to 1968, Indian peoples had not been involved except as informants for the federal committee. The membership of the RCAP, however, consisted of an equal number of Aboriginal commissioners and non-Aboriginal commissioners. We would do a disservice to the historical record if we did not also give credit to two other factors: the courts played an enormously liberating role; and public support was crucial, although it has waxed and waned.

These are remarkable achievements in such a short period of time. We often forget what we have achieved and how we have achieved it. Progress has been made by Aboriginal peoples speaking out, organizing, and pushing hard for their own ideas. Victories have been won in the public debates of courts, legislatures, and policymakers through the creative involvement of political allies, Aboriginal support groups, churches, academics, writers, and activists. From the White Paper in 1969 to the royal commission in 1996, we have moved from an official government policy of termination and assimilation to a reluctant acceptance of the inherent right of Aboriginals to self-government. This evolution shows the great determination, endurance, sacrifice, capacity for hard work, and integrity of Canada's Aboriginal peoples. Yet these political achievements remain masked by poverty and its effects, which are evident in many of our communities.

Political developments have been paralleled in other areas. In the arts, we have seen the development of the Woodland School, based on the work and techniques of Norval Morriseau, and the emergence of new forms of carving, painting, and pottery. There is now a recognized genre of art known as Aboriginal, which includes a wide variety of expression: Inuit stone carving, Iroquois soapstone, Haida masks, Mi'kmaq baskets, Ojibway quill work, and postmodern Aboriginal expressionism (as in the work, for example, of Carl Beam and Joanne Poitras). There is music that goes beyond that of Winston Wuttanee and Buffy Sainte-Marie: we have Kahstin, Red Power, 7th Fire, Robbie Robertson, and Shania Twain; and *Aboriginal Voices Magazine* now lists the top 10 albums in Indian country. There are writers galore: Thomson Highway, Jeannette Armstrong,

Scott Momaday, Sherman Alexi, Drew Hayden Taylor, and Thomas King. In September 1999, the Aboriginal Peoples Television Network was launched. The National Native Achievement Foundation, formerly the Canadian Native Arts Foundation, gives out awards each year to recognize outstanding accomplishments by Aboriginal peoples.

In the area of health and healing, we have seen the emergence of a widespread healing movement that affects almost every Aboriginal person in Canada, as well as the establishment of Aboriginal health centres in many locations across the country. In education, one Aboriginal university and 17 Aboriginally controlled postsecondary institutes are now in place. The last federally run Indian residential school was closed in 1985. All public schools on Indian reserves are now under Indian control. In urban centres, there are Aboriginal survival schools. An increasing number of Aboriginal people are choosing academic careers, working as professors and teachers in the secondary and postsecondary sectors. More than 30,000 Aboriginal students are enrolled in postsecondary institutions, up from 160 when I started my studies in 1972. In large urban centres, an extraordinary array of service and cultural organizations cater to large urban Aboriginal populations. There are almost 130 Aboriginal friendship centres located throughout the country. More than half of the Aboriginal population and about 40 per cent of status Indians live in urban centres.

We have come a long way in three decades. There is now a solid foundation of hard-won legal rights, locally controlled institutions, pride, and a renewed sense of capacity and responsibility. One can begin to see how some of these changes have affected the writing of Aboriginal history. Until recently, we were portrayed in the historical literature as having an almost complete lack of human agency. Rarely were we depicted as human beings attempting to build our communities or shown to act independently in pursuit of our own interests. Rather, it was suggested that we acted mostly in defence or in reaction to the actions of others. Even in the history of the past

25 years, we have been written out of the central part of the play.

Yet this is not the way it was. Over and over again, Aboriginal peoples set out their views in a positive and forceful manner, fully cognizant of what was happening to them. "Whabung," while it may have been a reaction against government policy, was also a positive statement of principles and values by Aboriginal leaders. It outlined a vision of how they wanted the future to unfold. It was an act of human agency. This act has begun to have enormous effect. A burgeoning literature on this new Indian history now makes an effort to show Indians as moral agents who acted on their own ideas and beliefs.

In the area of economic development, we are now starting to think about something that we call an "Aboriginal economy" or "Aboriginal economies." We are now considering the nature and functioning of this economy and the appropriate microeconomic policies needed to develop it. However, we do not yet know much about these economies. According to an Aboriginal Business Canada report, it is impossible to state the size of the Aboriginal economy or to define the relative size of entrepreneurial business in comparison to community-based or on-reserve business. Although we do not have this information, it is significant that the questions are starting to be asked.

We are also moving away from the old idea that business, trade, profit, and hard work were not part of our past. We have seen excellent work by Frank Tough of the University of Saskatchewan, who has written an economic history of Native people in northern Manitoba; by Rolf Knight of the University of British Columbia, with his history of British Columbia Indians in the labour force around the turn of the twentieth century; by Sarah Carter, who has documented the trials and tribulations of prairie Indian farmers in the nineteenth century; by Fred Wien of Dalhousie University, with his economic history of the Mi'kmaq in Nova Scotia; by Douglas Elias, an expert on Aboriginal economic development; by Wanda Wuttunee of the University of Manitoba, who has written on Aboriginal entrepreneurs in the North; by Pamela Sloan and Roger Hill, who have examined how present-day corporations conduct their relationships with Aboriginal peoples; and by Stephen Cornell and Joe Kalt of the Harvard Project on American Indian Economies, who have co-authored a seminal work on Native American economies. These authors' works all have as their premise the fact of an Aboriginal economic history and economic life. Whereas Indian economic history had been relegated to discussions of the fur trade, these recent texts are a start in our journey towards understanding this other part of Aboriginal history. We have also begun to understand that the enormous effort of developing Aboriginal economies is not just the responsibility of economists and businesses, but also involves Aboriginal participation in higher levels of education and improved health, housing, and government, among other things, to which must be added a sense of agency, a sense that we can influence the present and the future because our ideas count.

We are also starting to explore in great detail "Aboriginal government" and the much broader concept of "Aboriginal governance." Governing units on Indian reserves are beginning to be seen as governments. We talk of First Nations instead of Indian bands. A study I have completed with the Union of Ontario Indians-Anishinabek about governance asks questions about their view of good governance.[7] When I look across the country, I see a great number of Aboriginal governments in action, all evolving, all governing, and all trying hard in some way to find a blend of historical-traditional and contemporary governance practices and philosophies. The debate has shifted from its first narrow focus on self-government rights to issues of how to govern. In my view, the philosophical debate about the right to self-government was over with the adoption of the Penner Report. After that time, it was not a question of whether Aboriginal peoples had a right to govern themselves but a question of the form that this self-government should take. We are now debating details, a process that is likely to last forever if experience in other jurisdictions is any indication. Over the past three decades, we

have seen a slow, steady, and laborious debate about powers and jurisdictions and about lands and resources. For the most part, Aboriginal peoples have been winning the debate for greater control over their lives.

This victory has been the legacy of the past three decades. We have begun to have confidence in ourselves, and again we have begun to believe that we can do things for ourselves and that we can affect our futures. We convinced the government of Canada that our approach is the right one for us. We convinced the Royal Commission on Aboriginal Peoples that a comprehensive approach is fundamentally right. We argued for self-determination. We argued for Aboriginal capital corporations, increased loan funds, and equity contributions. Our voices were heard, and in part the government listened and began to respond.

This is the context and foundation of modern Aboriginal societies, which today are confident, aggressive, assertive, insistent, desirous of creating a new world out of Aboriginal and Western ideas, and self-consciously and deliberately acting out of Aboriginal thought. The desire for a new order and the actions of the past three decades have shaped modern Aboriginal society. Urban Aboriginal communities, having reached a critical size, can now grow without additional migration from rural reserve-based communities. Traditional world views, values, and customs are becoming the central informing aspect of Aboriginal life for many individuals. New social, economic, and political institutions are appearing at a rapid rate, supplementing or replacing traditional kinship systems (primarily clans) within Aboriginal society. As individuals, communities, and governments attempt to solve the problems facing them, increasingly specialized organizations are being established. Deliberate and internally defined individual and collective identities are being reinforced, rooted in traditional cultural groups. A textual mode of cultural transmission is beginning to supersede ancient oral transmission, and English is emerging as the lingua franca among Aboriginal peoples. Individuals and groups are now asserting control over the structures and processes of everyday Aboriginal life.

The next 20 years will be a critical time for Aboriginal individuals and communities. During this period, the basic structures and processes of Aboriginal life will be modified and placed under Aboriginal stewardship. Aboriginal governance will become a social and political reality. Much as in the mainstream, modern Aboriginal society will be a society of organizations. These institutions (political, education, cultural, spiritual) will then work to improve the quality of Aboriginal lives. The creative and contemporary interpretation of Aboriginal culture is at the heart of the modernization process. Aboriginal peoples will interpret their cultures (and their cultural institutions) in ways that best fit their everyday lives. We must recognize that Aboriginal cultures are not static; they do not exist under glass but are ever changing in response to influences from within and without. As Aboriginal societies blend their traditions with Western, European ways, the processes and institutions that arise will be varied. No single model will occur or prevail. It is futile and misguided to think that this will happen. The development of modern societies in the world has not resulted anywhere in a uniform set of institutions or structures for everyday life. We can expect nothing different within Aboriginal societies in Canada.

Postcolonial consciousness will be the fundamental condition of modern Aboriginal societies, which have been colonized in many ways and are aware of the implications of this colonization. Aboriginal societies are choosing deliberately, consciously, and systematically to deal with this fact of their shared past. Our societies are coming to terms with what has happened to them and are determined to overcome their colonial legacy.

Many postcolonial Aboriginals are angry and want to dismantle the master's house, or at least to renovate it so that it more readily suits their desires. Postcolonial consciousness exists within a paradox: it wants to go back and start over again, yet it knows that this is impossible for a colonized people. It can never recover the

world that was lost as a result of colonization. It can only go forward. Postcolonial consciousness careens between optimism and pessimism.

How are we to deal with the new Aboriginals, those who are acting through their postcolonial consciousness and whose expectations revolve around self-government and material life? And how are we to deal with the old Aboriginal problem of poverty? Can we address the problem of Aboriginal poverty through self-government? A confident, aggressive, savvy, educated, and experienced leadership has recently emerged that knows how to push hard and how to get what it wants. Behind it are thousands of Aboriginal students in postsecondary education institutions across the country who will move into positions of leadership in many communities over the next decade. These people are determined, well educated, and courageous, and they want the world to be different for them and their children. These groups see Aboriginal self-government within their grasp. They have experienced aspects of it in language training and education, in health care, in economic development, in social work, in housing, and in cultural programs.

The new "Indian problem" for Canadians is about how to accommodate Aboriginal self-government within the governing structure of Canada so that Aboriginal governments can govern effectively. The challenge is made more complex by the wide geographic distribution of the Aboriginal population and its growing concentration in urban centres.

One of the most difficult challenges will be to foster the development of positive public attitudes towards Aboriginal peoples and their governments. The Royal Commission on Aboriginal Peoples recommended a major public education effort aimed at helping Canadian citizens to understand Aboriginal aspirations, cultures, communities, and ways of living. We forget that Aboriginal peoples and Aboriginal governance exist within a Canadian context that has had a hard time coming to terms with a continued Aboriginal presence, let alone a modern, educated Aboriginal population that will challenge the Canadian status quo and assert itself, insisting upon its own place and possessing the legal clout to achieve its aims.

The 1996 *Report of the Royal Commission on Aboriginal Peoples* presented a vision for the incorporation of Aboriginal peoples into the Canadian federation. We used to say, when presented with proposals from governments, "Is this just the White Paper in disguise?" In 1996, the standard became the *Report of the Royal Commission on Aboriginal Peoples*. Now we will say: "How does this accord with the *RCAP*?"

Endnotes

1   Aboriginal Affairs and Northern Development Canada, Notes for an Address by the Honourable Jane Stewart, 7 January 1998. Web: www.aadnc-aandc .gc.ca/eng/1100100157251/1100100015726.

2   Indian Chiefs of Alberta, *Citizens Plus: A Presentation by the Indian Chiefs of Alberta to Right Honourable P.E. Trudeau, June 1970* (Edmonton: Indian Association of Alberta, 1970), 1, 10.

3   Manitoba Indian Brotherhood, "Whabung: Our Tomorrows" (Winnipeg: MIB, 1971), xvi–xvii.

4   Jack W. Beaver, *To Have What Is One's Own* (Ottawa: National Indian Socio-Economic Development Committee, 1979).

5   Canada, "Indian Self-Government in Canada," *Minutes and Proceedings of the Special Committee on Indian Self-Government*, no. 40, 12, and 20 October 1983 (known as the Penner Report).

6   Andrew Purvis, "Whose Home and Native Land?," *Time*, Canadian edn, 15 February 1997, 18.

7   David Newhouse and Kevin Fitzmaurice, *Governing in a Good Way: Report of the Community Consultations on Governance* (Toronto: Union of Ontario Indians, 1999).

PART I

Suggested Readings

Day, Richard J.F. *Multiculturalism and the History of Canadian Diversity*. Toronto: University of Toronto Press, 2000.

Igartua, José Eduardo. *The Other Quiet Revolution: National Identities in English Canada, 1945–71*. Vancouver: UBC Press, 2006.

Kelley, Ninette, and M. Trebilock. *Making of the Mosaic: A History of Canadian Immigration Policy*. Toronto: University of Toronto Press, 1998.

Miller, J.R. *Skyscrapers Hide the Heavens: A History of Indian-White Relationships in Canada*, 3rd edn. Toronto: University of Toronto Press, 2000.

Russell, Peter H. *Constitutional Odyssey: Can Canadians Become a Sovereign People?* 3rd edn. Toronto: University of Toronto Press, 2004.

Vance, Jonathan. *A History of Canadian Culture*. Toronto: Oxford University Press, 2011.

Key Terms

Bill of Rights 1960
governance
"imagined community"
multiversality
October Crisis

"opt-out"
social security
transnational
universality

Questions for Consideration

1. What were the reasons for implementing multiculturalism in 1971?
2. What is meant by "multiversality" and how does it present challenges to the concept and policy approach of multiculturalism?
3. What are the main principles and objectives of Canada's multiculturalism policy?
4. Why was the reception of the Hungarian refugees so much more "successful" than that of the later Chilean refugees?
5. How has the concern for national unity shaped the nature of federal government July 1st celebrations?
6. In what ways have the themes, content, and symbols of July 1st celebrations changed and/or remained the same?
7. Edwardson notes that opposition to government intervention in culture is due to the belief that "art can only flourish in an open atmosphere free from national considerations." Do you agree and why or why not?
8. In what ways are the objectives of government cultural policy similar and/or different from those behind government support for July 1st commemoration?
9. What are the goals of Quebec nationalism and why do Quebeckers believe it is necessary to have an equal partnership between the Quebec government and the federal/other provincial governments?
10. What is the "Indian problem"? How and why has this concept changed since 1968?
11. How have Aboriginal peoples' concepts of themselves and their political goals changed?

Relevant Websites

Canada Council for the Arts—Cultural Policy
www.canadacouncil.ca/aboutus/links/
ew127229064355625000.htm

Canadian Council for Refugees—A Hundred Years of Immigration to Canada 1900–1999
http://ccrweb.ca/en/
hundred-years-immigration-canada-1900-1999

Canadian Museum of Civilization—Four "Constants" in Canadian Cultural Policy
www.civilization.ca/research-and-collections/
research/resources-for-scholars/essays-1/

CBC Digital Archives—A Celebration of Aboriginal Heritage
http://archives.cbc.ca/society/native_issues/
topics/3531

Government of Canada—Forging Our Legacy: Canadian Citizenship and Immigration 1900–1977
www.cic.gc.ca/english/resources/publications/
legacy/

Government of Manitoba—Report of the Aboriginal Justice Inquiry of Manitoba
www.ajic.mb.ca/volume.html

Library and Archives Canada—Royal Commission on National Development in the Arts, Letters, and Sciences 1949–51
www.collectionscanada.gc.ca/2/5/

Maple Leaf Web—Immigration Policy in Canada: History, Administration and Debates
www.mapleleafweb.com/features/immigration-
policy-canada-history-administration-and-
debates

Maple Leaf Web—Official Bilingualism in Canada: History and Debates
www.mapleleafweb.com/features/
official-bilingualism-canada-history-and-debates

Marianopolis College—Quebec History
http://faculty.marianopolis.edu/c.belanger/
quebechistory/

Parliament of Canada—Canadian Multiculturalism
www.parl.gc.ca/Content/LOP/
ResearchPublications/2009-20-e.htm

PART II

Federalism, Liberalism, and Regionalism

TIMELINE

1943–68 Ernest Manning and the Social Credit Party form the government of Alberta

1945 Family allowance program created

1945–6 Dominion-Provincial Conference on Green Book Proposals

1948 Louis St Laurent succeeds Mackenzie King as leader of Liberal Party

1948–57 St Laurent and the Liberals form the government

1949 Newfoundland joins Confederation

1950 Construction of Trans-Canada Highway begins (completed 1970)

1951 Universal Old Age Security introduced

1955 Creation of Atlantic Provinces Economic Council

1955 Creation of Royal Commission on Canada's Economic Prospects

1956 Unemployment Insurance extended to fishery workers

1957 System of equalization grants to the provinces begins

1957 John Diefenbaker and Conservative Party win federal election, defeating Liberals

1957 Hospital Insurance introduced as shared-cost program

1958 Diefenbaker and Conservatives win largest majority since Confederation

1961 New Democratic Party formed from the previous Co-operative Commonwealth Federation

1962 Saskatchewan government of Tommy Douglas introduces medical insurance

1963–8 Lester Pearson and the Liberals form the government in Ottawa

1966 Canada Pension Plan (and QPP in Quebec) established

1966 Canada Assistance Plan established to provide federal-provincial cooperation in social programs

1968 Medicare established as a shared federal/provincial program

1968–79 Pierre E. Trudeau and the Liberals form government in Ottawa

1971 Victoria Constitutional Conference

1971 Expansion of Unemployment Insurance to cover seasonal workers and maternity leave

1972 Increases to Old Age Security pensions and to the Guaranteed Income Supplement

1973 Reform of Family Allowance Act increases the payments but makes them taxable

continued

1979–80	Joe Clark and Conservatives form the government in Ottawa	**1993**	Kim Campbell (Conservative) is first woman prime minister for about four months
1980–4	Pierre E. Trudeau and Liberals form the government in Ottawa	**1993**	Jean Chrétien and Liberals form government in Ottawa (the Bloc is second, with Reform holding third place in the House of Commons)
1980	National Energy Program introduced		
1981	Agreement reached between federal and provincial governments (except Quebec) to patriate the Constitution		
1982	Constitution Act, including Charter of Rights and Freedoms, proclaimed	**1995–2002**	Mike Harris and Conservatives form the government in Ontario and introduce their "common sense" revolution
1984	Liberal John Turner is prime minister for four months	**1995–8**	Ontario Days of Action protest movement
1984–93	Brian Mulroney and the Conservatives form the government in Ottawa	**1996**	Canada Health and Social Transfer replaces Canada Assistance Plan
1986	Cancellation of the National Energy Program	**2000**	Reform Party is renamed the Canadian Alliance
1987	Reform Party is created with Preston Manning as leader	**2003**	Canadian Alliance and Conservative parties merge into a new Conservative Party
1988	Canada–US Free Trade agreement is passed (in effect in 1989)		
1990	Bloc Québécois is formed	**2003–6**	Paul Martin becomes Liberal leader and forms the government
1991	Goods and Services Tax introduced	**2004**	Federal 10-year commitment to increased funding for health care
1992	North American Free Trade Agreement is reached		
1992	Moratorium imposed on cod fishing on east coast	**2006–11**	Stephen Harper and Conservatives form a minority government
1992	Family allowance replaced with a new Child Tax Benefit based on income	**2011**	Stephen Harper and Conservatives win a majority government

Introduction

The post-1945 period undoubtedly saw significant challenges and, thus, both change and continuity in the nature of federal-provincial relations, in the level of government intervention in the economy and in society, and in the realization of the postwar goal of improving the position and well-being of Canadians. These trends led to periods of federal-provincial cooperation in achieving common goals, such as the development of the welfare state, but also facilitated significant regional and provincial dissatisfaction with the union as well as challenges to federal power and the unity of the nation.

The issue of federalism, liberalism, and regionalism in the postwar years divides into two relatively distinct time periods, the first period spanning from 1945 to approximately

1970. Federal-provincial relations—in particular, questions surrounding the jurisdiction and powers of the two levels of government—had been a source of political debate and conflict since the union was formed in 1867. In fact, a series of court challenges in the decades following Confederation made it clear that the constitutional division of powers (enumerated in the British North America Act, 1867) and the relative autonomy of the two levels of government respective of one another were unclear and overlapping in some areas. Thus, while debate about the nature of Canadian federalism was not new to the postwar years, the marked centralization of power in the federal government, concomitant with an increase in government intervention in both the economy and social matters, was a definitive change in the three decades following 1945.

Both centralization and cooperation arose in part from what scholars have generally referred to as the "postwar liberal consensus" or commitment to Keynesian theory and the goals of achieving full employment and economic security for all citizens through government expenditure and policy. Federal government power and intervention in the economy had already increased dramatically during the war years owing to the invocation of the War Measures Act and a general consensus that significant government management and control of production, resources, and labour were necessary to execute a total war effort. With war's end, politicians, policy advisers, and average Canadians pointed to the obvious success of government management in achieving impressive wartime production goals and high employment at good wages while also avoiding problems such as inflation. This evidence of the potential of Keynesian theory, combined with memories of the suffering and devastation of the Great Depression, led to the "postwar liberal consensus." Politicians (regardless of party affiliation) and citizens alike turned to government spending and policy design to stimulate demand and high employment while providing social assistance programs and other social services to guard against economic want and ensure equality of opportunity. Most of the cornerstone programs of Canada's welfare state had developed by the end of the 1960s, many (such as Medicare) through federal-provincial cooperation in design, administration, and funding. While health and welfare lay within provincial jurisdiction, a centralization of federal government power resulted in part from the development of these programs. Recognition of the need for federal funding to achieve these expensive programs and a desire to ensure uniformity across the country led to tax rental agreements and to transfer payments through which the federal government exercised jurisdiction in policy design and regulation. For many politicians, such as Pierre Trudeau, a strong federal government was necessary not only to ensure uniformity but also to pursue equality and the maintenance of national unity.

By the 1960s, however, provincial governments and political parties began to challenge this centralization of power and the concept of federalism underlying it. Rising regionalism, voiced most strongly in Quebec (as discussed in Part I) had emerged from the Quiet Revolution with a distinct and potentially separatist nationalism and led the provinces to reassert their right to exercise power within their own jurisdiction. In the 1960s and early 1970s, a primary site of conflict was Ottawa's involvement in social programs, both shared programs and those specifically under federal control, such as family allowances, the subject of Raymond Blake's article. While Trudeau believed in the necessity of a strong federal government (including in the realm of social programs) to maintain national unity, Blake argues that reforms to the family allowance program in the 1970s resulted from concessions to Quebec nationalism rather than from the initial social policy goal of alleviating the poverty of many families. In a revealing examination of the relationship between social policy and federalism, Blake outlines how family allowance reforms, which gave the provinces greater control over the allocation of the money for the program, stemmed from Ottawa's desire to concede, in part, to Quebec's demand for greater autonomy in social spending in the hope of encouraging Quebec's participation in constitutional reform.

The fact that some Canadians were still plagued by the poverty and economic insecurity that had initiated the debate on family allowance reform in the late 1960s reveals some of the shortfalls of postwar liberalism and the goal of creating a more "just society" for all Canadians. While the postwar years, in general, did witness an overall increase in the economic security and standard of living of the average Canadian, Sean Purdy's article on the difficulties Canadians faced in securing adequate and affordable housing in postwar Toronto "complicates" the picture often portrayed of the effects of postwar prosperity combined with the emerging welfare state. While the factors that created housing problems for some families varied over the course of the time period and certainly increased with the decline of postwar prosperity after 1975, the availability of public housing consistently failed to meet the needs of many families, thus contributing to their poverty, insecurity, and distress.

Certainly the period after 1970 witnessed an increased challenge to these trends of federal centralization and postwar liberalism, particularly in Quebec and western Canada, where opposition to the growing power of the federal government seriously challenged the unity of the nation and any consensus of a commonality of national goals and identity. While Quebec's opposition resulted largely from its desire to protect its distinct culture and identity (a topic covered in the Part I), western regionalism arose in part due to the belief that federal government "national" policies addressed only the needs and demands of central Canada (Ontario and Quebec), neglecting and often harming "peripheral" regions. Yet, western regionalism was not a new phenomenon in postwar Canada, and as Alvin Finkel notes, Alberta under its Social Credit government was "largely hostile" to federal government social and economic intervention even in the 1950s and 1960s, when Manitoba and Saskatchewan embraced the assistance that Ottawa could offer in social policy development. Finkel finds that Alberta's hostility reflected two trends more notable in western regionalism after the 1970s: (1) a social conservatism that challenged the Keynesian faith in government intervention through social spending to promote economic well-being; and (2) Alberta's transition to a "have" province through wealth from oil and gas, which allowed it the means to finance its own policy objectives. Corey Slumkoski, in contrast, questions why Maritime and Atlantic Canada failed to achieve regional unity (and identity) and in that way address the economic and political "marginalization" that characterized the region even before 1970. Focusing on the period from 1945 to 1970, Slumkoski reveals that despite the entrance of Newfoundland into Confederation in 1949, which had the potential to strengthen the political influence of eastern Canada, the region failed to maintain the unity necessary to force the federal government to address economic disparity.

As the country entered the second period of federal-provincial relations, from 1970 to present, the process of decentralization would continue as consecutive governments embraced a neo-liberal agenda and retreated from postwar liberalism. Neo-liberalism, a response to the economic stagnation and problems that plagued many western countries after 1973, dictated a reduction in government intervention in the economy as well as in government spending and debt. Consecutive federal governments after 1980 attempted to reduce spending, including those that gradually began to reduce their commitments to funding social programs. Reduced federal funding contributed to rising regional discontent and assertions of provincial autonomy and power, a trend that has led to a change in federal-provincial relations. The implications of both neo-liberalism and "open federalism" are explored by Brooke Jeffrey in relation to the present government of Stephen Harper. While a significant withdrawal from social policy was expected, Jeffrey finds that political "pragmatism" has led the Harper government to a more moderate approach to social policy, in part a result of the government's minority status, at least until the 2011 election. Neo-liberalism combined with free trade and globalization has similarly weakened the Canadian labour movement in terms of membership and ability to resist the significant economic concessions demanded by both the private and public sectors. As Michael Goldfield and Bryan Palmer reveal, the greater economic security and well-being of average Canadians after 1945 were the result not just of the welfare state but also of the workplace gains achieved by Canadian labour from the 1960s to the early 1970s. Since the mid-1970s, however, the strength of labour and the well-being of workers have declined, in part due to the disproportionate burden of cost-cutting placed on Canadian workers.

CHAPTER **4**

Regional Politics and Identity

◎ **4.1: ALBERTA SOCIAL CREDIT AND THE SECOND NATIONAL POLICY**
Alvin Finkel

Alberta stands out from the other two Prairie provinces in its attitude in the 1950s and 1960s to the social and economic interventions of the federal government that scholars now refer to as the "Second National Policy."[1] The long-running Social Credit government (1935–71), led for most of the postwar years by Ernest Manning (1944–68), was largely hostile to federal programs throughout this period. This article explores the attitude of Manning and his associates to federal policies from 1945 to 1971, when the Social Credit dynasty gave way to a Conservative dynasty. A key concern here is the extent to which Social Credit resistance to the federal agenda was ideological or was simply the reaction of a newly wealthy province to programs that would redistribute wealth from richer to poorer provinces. In terms of ideology, an important consideration is the degree to which Socred attitudes were motivated by social conservatism.

Another explanation could lie in "western alienation." Certainly, the western provinces had historical complaints about the tenor of the original national policies of John A. Macdonald. But Social Credit was not consciously a party of western protest, even though it is possible to explain some of its appeal in Alberta with reference to a general dislike of federal parties whose

power base was in central Canada. As this essay suggests, Alberta did not present its complaints in the pre-1970 period in the discourse of "Prairie complaints" or "western alienation." It could hardly do so, since most of its positions were not shared by the other two Prairie provinces.

Both Saskatchewan and Manitoba largely welcomed the programs that were introduced in the two and a half decades that followed World War II.[2] In Saskatchewan, federal spending was welcomed as a relief to the provincial treasury of a province that pursued an activist social agenda under its Co-operative Commonwealth Federation (CCF) government from 1944 to 1964, an agenda that Ross Thatcher's Liberals only partially undermined from 1964 to 1971. In Manitoba, federal spending was largely seen as an alternative to provincial spending in the days of the penny-pinching Liberal-Progressive administration that ended in 1958, and as a helpful add-on in the more activist years of Duff Roblin's Conservatives. Roblin sided with the private insurance industry against proponents of a national medicare scheme,[3] but he rarely appeared to be a defender of provincial rights per se or an ideological opponent of government involvement in the economy, at least if it was limited to social services and to aid to the private sector.

By contrast, the positions taken by the Alberta government in the area of federal-provincial relations were generally hostile. It has been argued that the bad blood between Ottawa and Edmonton owed its beginnings to the federal government's disallowance of Social Credit's efforts in the 1930s to introduce social credit in the province. The province's efforts to control banks and currency clearly violated federal jurisdictions under the British North America Act, but that had not stopped William Aberhart from running his 1935 electoral campaign on a promise to introduce social credit provincially. Nor did it stop the Aberhart Social Credit government from excoriating the federal government when it asserted its authority in the area of finance and received the total support of the courts. . . .

In 1940, when the federal government proposed a national unemployment insurance program, both the Alberta government and the Social Credit members in Ottawa were early opponents of the legislation. The federal program involved contributions from individuals and from employers as well as a small contribution from the federal government. Social Credit argued that such a program subtracted from, rather than added to, national income. They supported a non-contributory program. So had the communists and the CCF in the 1930s. But while these parties believed that wealthier Canadians should be taxed to provide the funds necessary to sponsor unemployment insurance from general government revenues, Social Credit called for the government simply to print the money necessary to fund the program. This would allow the unemployed to have spending money without taking it from anyone else. The Alberta government, however, wanted to cooperate with Ottawa during wartime and faced pressures from labour groups who were anxious to have unemployment insurance in any form. So in the end the Aberhart government decided to go along with the other eight Canadian provinces and give the federal government the all-province support required to pass a constitutional amendment allowing the federal government to introduce unemployment insurance.[4]

The circumstances of Aberhart's granting of consent to national unemployment insurance suggest that Alberta Social Credit was far from being reconciled to the notion that Ottawa should play a larger role in social programs in Canada. The hostilities that had arisen by the mid-1950s in Edmonton-Ottawa relations may seem simply a continuation of the battles of the 1930s. But any argument that suggests a straight line in Alberta Social Credit relations with the federal government from the 1930s onwards is misleading. In fact, in the early postwar period, before it became clear that Alberta was not destined to remain another Prairie have-not province, overly dependent on the precarious markets for farm products, Alberta cultivated good relations with the federal government. Its attitudes bore some similarities to the other two Prairie provinces on the subjects of social welfare and the relative responsibilities of the two senior levels of government. There were, however, differences that resulted from Social Credit philosophy.

Ernest Manning's willingness in 1945 and 1946 to embrace, even if half-heartedly, Ottawa's blueprint for a welfare state was evident in the round of federal-provincial meetings that stretched from August 1945 to May 1946. The federal government presented in book form an elaborate set of proposals that would have established an advanced welfare state for Canada in one fell swoop. *Proposals of the Government of Canada*, usually referred to as the "Green Book," was imbued with a centralizing philosophy. The federal government would take the primary responsibility for funding a national program of pensions for everyone over age 65 and a national health insurance program to cover all aspects of health care. It would run the former program and set the standards for the latter, which would be provincially administered. The federal government would also extend its role in caring for unemployed Canadians by assuming sole responsibility for the social welfare of unemployed employables who were not eligible to receive unemployment insurance. Finally, it would also provide the lion's share of funds for provincial public works programs to be timed with declines in the business cycle and, in turn, would have to approve the programs to be carried out. So great an assumption of federal powers would not come without a price tag for the provinces. They were expected to agree to let the federal government remain, as it had been in wartime, the sole recipient of personal and business income taxes, as well as estate taxes. While the provinces would receive a small percentage of what the federal government raised, as a grant based on provincial population, their ability to raise taxes on their own would be limited to indirect taxes.[5]

None of the provinces particularly liked the tax arrangements that Ottawa proposed as the price of the 1945 version of the Second National Policy. Privately, Prime Minister Mackenzie King recognized that his government was, in fact, offering the provinces too little independence and too little money if they were to carry out their functions. Eventually, he decided that the programs he was promising to fund would be too costly for the federal treasury. It was best that agreement not be reached with the provinces, provided that the provinces rather than the federal government appeared as the villains.[6] The literature on the Green Book debate sometimes lays the blame for the failure of federal-provincial discussions on certain provinces and sometimes on Ottawa. Those who blame the provinces focus on Ontario and Quebec, but if they wanted to cast the net more widely to blame all the provinces that pushed Ontario's and Quebec's concerns at the conference, they might also blame Nova Scotia, British Columbia, and even Prince Edward Island.[7] Alberta, by contrast, sided with Saskatchewan, Manitoba, and New Brunswick in accepting the tax arrangements as an unpleasant, but acceptable, price to pay to get the programs that the Green Book promised, even though Manning had reservations about financing and control of some programs. . . .

Manning's support, whatever King thought, was lukewarm at best. At the opening of the Dominion-Provincial Conference on 6 August 1945, Manning's preliminary speech was a primer on Social Credit economic and political theory.

Social Credit theory was opposed to centralization and maintained that each level of government could carry out its functions only if it had sufficient control over revenues. Manning complained to the conference that exclusive federal control over banking and currency left the provinces in a poor position to fulfil their duties to provide for the welfare of citizens. "It is plainly the responsibility of the Dominion Government to ensure that Provincial revenues are adequate to enable the Provinces to discharge fully their constitutional responsibilities," argued Manning. This was a position in keeping with the concept of a Second National Policy based on federal underwriting of a substantial proportion of social program costs. But Manning, the Social Crediter, believed Ottawa should acquire the revenues required by both federal and provincial governments to run social programs from monetization of the nation's wealth.[8] Although he was insistent that each level of government should carry out the functions it was assigned, Manning indicated in his preliminary address, as he did several times throughout the conference sessions, his government's willingness to entertain constitutional changes. While he was vague about what responsibilities might be reassigned, subsequent statements by Manning and other ministers indicated they believed that old-age pensions, care of unemployed employables, and housing should be solely federal responsibilities.

Communications between the Alberta government and the federal government regarding Green Book proposals were friendly. W.W. Cross, Alberta's long-time minister of health, made plain that his government wanted a national scheme of old-age pensions to be available at age 65, free of a means test, with "the entire cost provided for out of the consolidated revenue of the Dominion."[9] Provincial Secretary A.J. Hooke, an ardent Social Credit ideologue, received a favourable response when he asked the federal minister of health and welfare whether the proposed national medicare scheme would allow a province to charge a small deterrent fee for hospital stays and medical visits.[10]

Yet Manning, as a Social Crediter, could hardly be happy with Ottawa's approach to the financing of social programs. When the Green Book was tabled at the conference, Manning's first response was that there was too much emphasis on "redistributing purchasing power" as opposed to creating new purchasing power through monetary means. He chided the government for its emphasis on full employment, suggesting that in a mechanized age of mass production, the concept of full employment "is as antiquated as an old maid's dream and as improbable of realization."[11] No doubt, such pessimism on the employment issue encouraged the province's decision to let the federal government take full responsibility for the unemployed. It also encouraged Social Credit to continue its traditional support of non-contributory social insurance programs, financed through monetary expansion, as a key to maintaining consumer purchasing power.

Manning summed up his scepticism regarding the Green Book approach to social programs in an address to the Saskatoon Canadian Club in August 1946:

> Let us not delude ourselves into thinking that the mere redistribution of the national income increases the aggregate by one five cents piece. That, I submit, is the great weakness and inadequacy of the multiplicity of post-war social security insurance schemes and proposals being propagated today. The majority of them are based on the false premise that post-war economic security can be assured by a simple process of redistributing an inadequate over-all consumer income.[12] . . .

Such views on Manning's part, however, raise the question of why he would support the Green Book proposals, federal programs that were to be financed through taxation rather than expansion of the money supply. The answer seems to be simply that Manning was a pragmatic politician. His principal political opponents in the 1944 provincial election had been the socialist CCF, who claimed that the state profits from nationalized industries would provide much of the funding required to operate social programs. Manning

had argued that socialism would mean a state dictatorship over people's lives and that squeezing the monies required for social programs out of productive enterprises was counterproductive. He espoused Social Credit's idea of getting the monies needed for social insurance from monetary inflation. But, of course, as the evidence of the 1930s made clear, a province could play no role in setting monetary policy. The Green Book would let the premier of a poorer province off the hook to some degree. The federal government, whose resources were greater than those available to the Alberta government, would provide the social programs most Albertans appeared to want. This would reduce the CCF's chances of ever ousting Social Credit from power.

As the premiers and the federal cabinet met, Manning was also faced with a concerted campaign by the municipalities in his province to have the province assume the bulk of the costs involved in relief of the unemployed. In 1940, the Aberhart government had taken advantage of the relatively low unemployment rate during the war to pull out of its shared-cost program for unemployed employables ineligible for unemployment insurance. When the war was over and job seekers once again exceeded jobs, the municipalities began to chafe at the provincial government for leaving them holding the bag. British Columbia was reimbursing municipalities for 80 per cent of the costs of relief as well as 50 per cent of the cost of medical services to recipients of old-age pensions, mothers' allowances, and relief allowances.[13] Alberta municipalities, large and small, pressured the province to follow suit. Calgary led the fray in early January 1946 with a resolution calling on the provincial government to follow the British Columbia example. For a month, Manning received a flurry of resolutions from municipalities endorsing Calgary's position.[14]

Still, at the last session of the Dominion-Provincial Conference, Manning's explanation of why Alberta was willing to be one of only four provinces prepared to accept the tax arrangements demanded by the federal government largely ignored the Green Book proposals. Premier T.C. Douglas of Saskatchewan stressed his hesitation in supporting a set of tax arrangements that left unclear where the provinces would find sufficient revenues to carry out their obligations. His adherence to the federal proposals was largely predicated on his government's desire to have Ottawa establish—or help provinces establish—the social programs itemized in the Green Book.[15] By contrast, Premier Stuart Garson of Manitoba simply emphasized that a poor province could raise little revenue on its own from personal, corporate, and succession taxes, and that Manitoba was happier to have the federal government collect these taxes and give the provinces a per capita share.[16]

Manning's reasoning was similar to Garson's, though he was careful not to appear to be grovelling in the manner of the Manitoba premier. He indicated that prospects for Canada's economic growth would be hampered by bickering among governments, since this would create uncertainty among investors. But "the most important reason" for concluding an interim taxation agreement along the lines suggested by Mackenzie King was that the alternative for some provinces was "complete bankruptcy." Provinces "would be faced with the responsibility of collecting, by means of dual taxation, sufficient revenues to maintain their present public services, to say nothing about providing for post-war development." In poorer provinces, it would mean "they would shortly be forced into the position of beggars at the door of the dominion treasury."[17]

Manning's support of the federal government package was by no means unconditional. While his government had publicly supported federal old-age pensions and federal authority in the area of housing, he was adamant that in the areas that remained under provincial responsibility, the federal government should provide "unconditional supplementary grants for social services" rather than directing the provinces as to how they should spend the money. This demand, which reflected Social Credit's concern about centralization, separated Manning from both Douglas and Garson, who were too anxious to get federal funds for social programs to worry about federal efforts to control how these funds were spent.[18] On the whole, though, the positions taken by the government of Alberta on federal-provincial relations in 1945–6 seemed to reflect a realistic assessment that a poor province needed Ottawa's help if it was to establish a level of social programming acceptable to its citizens . . . .

On the whole, then, in early 1948 the Alberta Social Credit government . . . was a supporter of the Second National Policy. It proposed a Social Credit version of the policy, of course, but in general, it was after federal money to help a poorer province fulfil its social responsibilities as well as pursue economic growth through the building of transportation infrastructure.

Indeed, it seemed to take several years after the discovery of the Leduc oilfield before the Social Credit government developed the notion that Alberta was a rich province that could, in fact, look after the social welfare of its citizens without federal help and indeed without control over monetary policy. After the federal government withdrew the Green Book proposals in June 1946, claiming that Ontario's and Quebec's recalcitrance made it impossible to find agreement on the issues raised by the federal proposals, the Alberta government remained open to federal initiatives for some time to come. There was no opposition from Alberta to the federal proposals for a national universal pension scheme in 1951, for example. But by the mid-1950s, there had been a change in the Alberta attitude that seemed to coincide with the change in Alberta's economic fortunes. The attitude shift was manifest in the positions the province took at dominion-provincial conferences and in public statements regarding the allocation of taxing and spending powers between the provinces and the federal government. It was also manifest in a more conservative position on the question of social welfare. In fairness, however, there was continuity in the Alberta government's positions to the extent that, even in 1945–6, it had demanded that there be a strict separation of powers between Ottawa and the provinces and no conditions on monies given by Ottawa to the provinces.

CP PHOTO

Premier Ernest Manning of Alberta, 1950.

At the 1955 federal-provincial conference, Premier Manning protested that federal taxation practices left the provincial government too little money to carry out its responsibilities. Federal revenue collections from the province were 252 per cent higher in 1955 than they were in 1948. But the province had received only a marginal increase in funds from the "tax rental" agreements that the provinces continued to sign with Ottawa, despite the breakdown of the Green Book negotiations. Manning was concerned because in 1954 the debt-averse provincial government had to take $13 million from accumulated surpluses to fund its expenditures, despite a healthy increase in provincial oil royalties.

Manning's proposed solution, which eventually was put into practice, was for each province to set a tax rate as a proportion of the federal tax. Both sets of taxes could be collected by the federal government, which would then send the province its share. Obviously, this method

favoured wealthier provinces over poorer ones. Before Ottawa had acceded to such a demand, it adopted a proposal favoured by Quebec and the Atlantic provinces, along with Manitoba and Saskatchewan: equalization grants. These were meant to be a redistribution of taxes collected from wealthy provinces in favour of the poorer provinces. While they were relatively small and meant mainly to allow the disadvantaged provinces to provide education and social services to their citizens that paralleled those available in wealthy provinces, Alberta begrudged these grants, claiming, as noted below, that it should share in any grants given to the provinces.

From the Social Credit point of view, of course, programs that simply redistributed existing wealth added nothing to the overall economy and gave power to state bureaucrats, if not to the "money conspiracy" itself. But the government, and with it the Social Credit party, was moving away from the idea of large-scale social spending programs, whether financed by redistributing wealth or by printing new money. A committee convened by the Department of Public Welfare in 1956 to review welfare legislation and policy assumed, in its recommendations, that public policy should favour means-tested programs over universal social programs. The committee complained that the federal government had "seen fit to issue assistance to those not necessarily in need, by way of old age security and family allowances." So it wanted the Alberta government to approach Ottawa to "relinquish their present supervisory authority in connection with old age assistance, blindness allowances, disabled persons' allowances." The committee proposed that Ottawa simply give the provinces a grant to help them discharge their responsibilities in these areas.[19]

In an article in December 1956, in the Social Credit League's house organ, *The Busy Bee*, Ernest Manning outlined the government's position on both the purpose of social welfare programs and the desirable relative involvement of the federal and provincial governments in their elaboration and delivery. Manning emphasized that social welfare programs should be residual rather than universal:

> A major objective of organized society should be to assist each citizen to attain through his own enterprise sufficient financial resources to enable him to obtain for himself and his dependents an acceptable standard of social welfare without dependence on state welfare services. To the extent that this is impossible, society collectively must assume the cost of an acceptable standard of social services to bring such services within the financial reach of each individual citizen.[20]

Such a shift from Social Credit's one-time emphasis on handing money to all consumers regardless of their need made sense to many Albertans in the midst of an oil boom. In the 1930s, it would have been dismissed as high Toryism in a province where the Tories would await the 1970s to form a government. Indeed, it reflected a right-wing philosophy rather than the Social Credit philosophy with its blend of right-wing and left-wing ideas, held together uneasily by a focus on the monetary panacea.

Manning's new views on federal-provincial relations still reflected in part the views he had expressed at the time of the discussions on the Green Book. He opposed all conditional grant programs "with the exception of limited national equalization grants," from which Alberta should not be excluded.[21] There should be a clear definition of the responsibilities of all three levels of government and clear sources of revenue for each. There should be no meddling by one level of government in the activities of another. But there was no longer a notion that the goal of full employment was an illusion, nor the view that the province of Alberta needed federal grants to avoid bankruptcy. Alberta's wealth had caused the Social Credit government to put some teeth into its doctrine of opposing centralization. It had less need of the federal government's money and its citizens had, at least from the provincial government's point of view, less need for any government's money. Why, then, should their money and the money that the Alberta government might require as taxation be diverted to Ottawa and, via Ottawa, to other provinces?

This philosophy of minimalist government and opposition to centralization governed most dealings between the Alberta government and the federal government after 1956. Alberta's opposition to a national medicare program, to regional development programs, and to grant-in-aid programs has been documented elsewhere.[22] But to what extent was this opposition based on Social Credit philosophy and to what extent was it based on the social conservative philosophy that was implicit in the Manning government's management of public affairs from the 1940s and explicit after 1963?

Throughout the 1950s, Manning continued to advocate expansion of the money supply to boost consumer purchasing power as an alternative to a tax-and-spend approach to dealing with problems of the business cycle and of poverty. But, as noted above, he also increasingly emphasized that respect for the individual's right to choose, always a key consideration in Social Credit philosophy, was incompatible with universal social programs. His speeches defending private enterprise demonstrated a conversion to the view that the marketplace, rather than government intervention, was the key to economic growth and greater wealth for individuals. Just as Depression-era socialism was watered down in the prosperous 1950s, Depression-era Social Credit lost its messianic fervour. While the conviction remained that reform of the monetary system was the key to forever solving the problems inherent in the business cycle, competing currents in the movement about how the government should ensure that each individual shared some of the benefits of prosperity had been resolved in favour of the right wing of the movement.

Manning let the penny drop in an interview with Southam reporter Charles Lynch in 1963. He argued that Canada was facing a "transition period," a period of political realignment. "Out of this a two-party system will emerge," he said. On the one side would be a party that supported the existing "monetary policies" that were turning Canada into a socialist country that favoured high taxation and increased public debt. On the other side would be a party of "social conservatism" that supported individualism and resisted spending programs that required increased taxation. What would happen to the Social Credit party and its philosophy when this new party was formed? "I do not see this new party of free enterprise as being primarily a Social Credit party. Social Credit is a philosophy first and a party second—it started as an educational approach and there is nothing in the monetary policies or philosophy of Social Credit that ties it to an individual party."[23]

The following year, the provincial Social Credit convention in Red Deer followed their leader's call to take the party into oblivion by agreeing to instruct both the provincial and federal Social Credit organizations "to encourage the realignment of all those who believe in the Free Enterprise Way of Life to band together in a program with as many points on which there can be general agreement."[24] In part, Manning's implicit rejection of the national Social Credit party was simply a recognition of the party's inability to sink roots outside the West. The breakthrough in Quebec in the federal elections of 1962 had simply caused fissures between the western and Quebec wings of the party, with many of the Quebec MPs leaving to form their own party, the Créditistes, under the leadership of Réal Caouette. But the party's failure to win support in most regions was only half the story. Manning's focus on higher taxes and increased debts, as the "monetary policies" he opposed, demonstrated the extent to which he was refashioning Social Credit ideas to make them indistinguishable from the ideas supported by chambers of commerce and conservative ideologues. The Social Credit Party, while being his power base, was worth sacrificing if that could help to fashion a genuine, national conservative party with a chance to form a federal government.

In the interim, however, the national Social Credit party might be a useful forum in which to express the provincial government's criticisms of federal policy towards the province. Manning campaigned for the federal Social Credit party

during the 1965 federal election, in which his young son, Preston, was one of the Socred candidates in Edmonton. The premier's criticism of the federal Tories, and particularly the Tory members from Alberta, was not founded on Social Credit ideology. It seemed to be based in equal parts on social conservatism and on the complaints of a rich province. With regard to the former, Manning criticized the Tories for opposing his government's "co-insurance payments" for hospital patients (a daily fee for staying in the hospital) while allowing other provinces to levy premiums on their citizens for hospital insurance. That Alberta's system meant a tax on the sick while the premium system meant simply an insurance payment was of little concern to Manning, since, from his social conservative point of view, a daily hospital fee was a deterrent to abuse of the system.[25]

The complaints of a rich province were evident in Manning's lashing out at both Tories and Liberals for having "penalized" Alberta in the awarding of equalization grants. The grants were determined by comparing the taxes that provinces were able to collect to the taxes collected by the richest two provinces, Ontario and British Columbia. A formula then determined a grant that provinces with lesser incomes than those of the "big two" would receive. Alberta was the only province to receive nothing because of, as Manning put it, "Ottawa's insistence that revenue from our natural resources be treated the same as revenue from taxes."[26] The Alberta premier complained that the Conservative members from Alberta, who had held the overwhelming majority of the province's federal seats since 1957, had refused to support his call for Ottawa to exclude petroleum royalties from the federal government's calculations of Alberta's provincial revenues.

Both social conservatism and rich-province thinking informed Manning's reaction to the designated-area concept that the Tories had developed under Diefenbaker to help Atlantic Canada diversify its economy, and that the Liberals had extended to all areas of the country marked by poverty and lack of industry. While Manitoba and Saskatchewan welcomed a program that promised subsidies to most areas of their respective provinces, Alberta, which had far fewer designated areas proportionate to its population, was actively opposed to the concept of designated areas and particularly to the idea of encouraging firms to establish themselves in these areas by giving them start-up subsidies as a reward. "This is not in keeping with the free enterprise concept and could well be in direct conflict with economic feasibility so important if Canada is to develop a solid competitive position in world export markets," Manning wrote Lester Pearson.[27]

While Manning's words to Pearson simply suggested social conservatism, his province's efforts to promote industrial development suggest that he saw no violation of free-enterprise principles when a wealthy province built infrastructure with its own monies, which a poor province could not hope to duplicate without federal help. In northern Alberta, as he told the legislature in February 1965, the province planned to provide the capital to the Canadian National Railway to build rail lines to connect undeveloped mineral resource areas in the western portion of the province north of the CN main line, with CN outlets to the ocean. Manning saw subsidization of this sort as simply creating a better climate for investment, and he expressed concerns about the policies of other provinces as well as of the federal government that involved "giving special concessions to a certain industry to locate in a particular area."[28] But Manning had once followed similar policies. In the 1950s, his government had used the Alberta Treasury Branches (ATB) to make interest-free loans to entrepreneurs with plans to diversify the provincial economy. ATB only abandoned this practice after some of these loans were not repaid and the government faced the main scandal of its years in office over the issue of political interference with ATB.[29]

Manning and his ministers felt somewhat alone among the provinces in what they regarded as their principled opposition to federal intrusion in areas of provincial jurisdiction, an intrusion that is key to the concept of a Second National Policy. So, for example, when Alberta health

minister Dr J. Donovan Ross blasted federal minister of health and welfare Judy LaMarsh for recommending a federal-provincial conference on mental retardation, he could not resist taking a swipe at other provincial governments. After affirming that the federal government had no business at all in getting involved in the area of caring for individuals with disabilities, Ross lamented, "No doubt my sentiments may not be shared by other provinces, who too often are concerned with the possibilities of getting additional financial assistance from the federal treasury, rather than following out the principles contained in our major Dominion statute."[30] This was a rather self-righteous observation coming from a Social Credit minister, considering that less than two decades earlier his government had been happy to have the federal government take complete control over provision for the unemployed, the aged, and the inadequately housed. But the sweet smell of gasoline money over those two decades had allowed Alberta to become much tougher in its stance in favour of provincial control over jurisdictions that the British North America Act explicitly or implicitly gave to the provinces.

Manning was so convinced that the other premiers mainly wanted to suck Ottawa dry, forcing the federal government to collect more taxes in Alberta, that he refused to consider working closely with the other provinces in the area of economic development strategy. At the third provincial premiers' conference, held in 1962 in Victoria, Premier Roblin suggested the creation of a body to study the provinces' difficulties in the areas of economic growth and to advise them on the best directions to take to improve economic performance. While most of the premiers liked the idea, Manning poured cold water on it. There was too great an ideological divergence among Canada's provincial governments for this to work, he argued. While some supported belt-tightening, others favoured "pump-priming the economy," usually with the federal government's help. He saw no point in trying to find advisers who could speak at once to the ideologically diverse provincial governments of Canada.[31]

Certainly Ernest Manning was, at times, given reason to believe that he alone among the provincial premiers defended both private enterprise and a clear division of federal and provincial responsibilities. While Manning was hardly alone among the premiers in opposing a national medicare scheme at the federal-provincial conference of 1965, he was completely alone in his opposition to designated-area programs.[32] His long-term efforts to have the federal government rebate federal tax collected from investor-owned firms generating electricity were rebuffed by Finance Minister Walter Gordon, with no argument from the other provinces, if only because Alberta was, at the time, the only province where private companies generated most of the electricity.[33]

Manning phrased his opposition to the tenor of federal policies and the policies of most of the other provincial governments, not in the language of Social Credit, but in the language of social conservatism. The discriminatory treatment of private electrical utilities, he argued, encouraged provinces to nationalize these firms, which was not "in the interests of our national economy or the preservation of our free enterprise form of society."[34]

As for the designated-areas programs, Manning's point of view coincided with the views of Alberta's major magnates. W.O. Twaits, president of Imperial Oil, wrote to Manning in September 1968, sending him a copy of a letter he had sent to the federal minister of mines, energy, and resources in which he had protested federal financial aid to a refinery planned for Come-by-Chance, Newfoundland. Manning responded by indicating his agreement with Twaits, claiming that it was "a glaring example of the inequities that stem from various forms of government subsidies to induce industries to locate in specific locations."

> As you know we have always opposed this policy on the part of the Federal and various Provincial governments, and, frankly, we are much concerned that it is becoming such a widespread practice throughout the country. In addition to being inequitable to Canadian taxpayers, it is grossly unfair to require legitimate private industry to compete in the marketplace with plants which are exempt from carrying a fair and equitable share of the tax load and, in addition in many cases, are receiving substantial bonuses by way of capital funds from the federal treasury.[35]

By the 1960s, then—indeed, by the mid-1950s—the Social Credit government of Alberta can be seen to have become an opponent of the so-called Second National Policy. It did not accept the view that the federal government had an obligation either to raise the living standards of individuals regardless of the province in which they lived or to attempt to favour disadvantaged areas in its efforts to achieve economic development. Rather, the federal government and the provinces should each stick to their own constitutional obligations and should have their own separate funds for their separate programs. . . .

There were, as we have seen, continuities and discontinuities in the Alberta government's attitude to federal proposals for intervention in areas of provincial jurisdiction in the quarter century after World War II. Throughout this period, Ernest Manning argued that a clear division of responsibilities and revenues between the federal and provincial governments was required. But, in the early years after the war, when Alberta could not go it alone, he foresaw a fairly large scope for the federal government, including full responsibility for care of the unemployed and full responsibility for housing. If only because the province was not to be allowed to have any control over currency, he also accepted the idea that the federal government would collect the lion's share of taxes and then distribute a portion of them to provinces on a per capita basis. This would ensure that the poorer provinces received more revenue than if they attempted to collect income and succession taxes on their own. Social Credit thinking argued for a clear division of powers; poor-province thinking argued for compromise with the federal government and for support, however grudging, for the Second National Policy. If the province could not have social credit, it could, at least, have federal funds.

By the mid-1950s, however, the Social Credit government recognized that it did not need federal funds. It soon realized that it also did not need social credit. It had oil—who could ask for anything more? Its earlier convictions—that the new age of technology guaranteed that not everyone could be employed and that therefore employment income could not generate sufficient purchasing power to keep the economy booming—disappeared. In their place came the "social conservative" philosophy that the unimpeded marketplace was indeed generally the guarantor of prosperity for the many. While the social conservative philosophy bore some resemblance to the old Social Credit philosophy—in its emphasis, for example, on devolution of power and in its opposition to socialism—it was marked more by big-business economic liberalism than the by the anti-big-business populism that had inspired the early social credit movement in Alberta. If the Alberta Social Credit government in the 1960s sounded less like its counterpart in the 1940s and more like George Drew's Ontario Conservatives, both in terms of its attitude to the role of the state and its hostility to federal plans in the areas of social insurance and economic growth, it is because Alberta had changed. It had become rich and could not accept that a portion of its new oil revenues was being redistributed to help provinces that remained poor. While a degree of the social credit rhetoric of the early days still popped up from time to time from within the Social Credit governments after 1955, and certainly within the party, it bore no relationship to the reality of the Social Credit administration's goals. The Manning government in the 1960s felt quite alone, among provinces generally as well as among western provinces, in its opposition to the welfare state consensus of tile postwar era, a consensus that, in the pre-petroleum period of its life, Social Credit seemed to welcome. This government, I would argue, is best understood not as a government motivated by social credit ideology or western alienation, but as a government motivated by social conservative and rich-province thinking.

Endnotes

1   The notion that the postwar federal government interventions meant to address the economic problems of disadvantaged provinces constituted a second or new national policy was first discussed in Vernon C. Fowke, "The National Policy—Old and New," *Canadian Journal of Economics and Political Science* 18, no. 3 (August 1952): 271–86.

2   Their welcome of the programs can be judged by the position these provinces took at federal-provincial conferences throughout the period. Saskatchewan's presentations to the Royal Commission on Health Services also emphasized the importance of federal funding and standards for provincial medical insurance programs. Library and Archives Canada (hereafter LAC), RG 33, series 78, Hearings of the Royal Commission on Health Services, vol. 9, file 78, "Submission of the Government of the Province of Saskatchewan," January 1962.

3   Roblin called on the federal government to make per capita grants to the provinces for citizens enrolled voluntarily in comprehensive prepaid medical insurance schemes, privately or publicly operated. LAC, RG 33, series 78, Hearings of the Royal Commission on Health Services, vol. 8, file 48, Honourable Duff Roblin, Premier, Manitoba, January 1962.

4   Alvin Finkel, *The Social Credit Phenomenon in Alberta* (Toronto: University of Toronto Press, 1989), 78. On the attitude of the Aberhart government more generally to the war effort, see William R. Young, "'A Highly Intelligent and Unselfish Approach': Public Information and the Canadian West, 1939–45," *Canadian Historical Review* 62, no. 4 (December 1981): 502.

5   R.M. Burns, *The Acceptable Mean: The Tax Rental Agreements, 1941–1962* (Toronto: Canadian Tax Foundation, 1980), chap. 2.

6   See Alvin Finkel, "Paradise Postponed: A Re-examination of the Green Book Proposals of 1945," *Journal of the Canadian Historical Association*, new series 4 (1993): 120–42.

7   See the addresses given by the various provinces in *Dominion-Provincial Conference (1945): Dominion and Provincial Submissions and Plenary Conference Discussions*, 29 and 30 April 1946 (Ottawa: King's Printer, 1946).

8   *Dominion-Provincial Conference (1945)*, 43–5.

9   LAC, Department of National Health and Welfare papers, RG 29, vol. 23, file 21-2-1, W.W. Cross, Minister of Health, Alberta, to Alex Skelton, Secretary, Cabinet Committee on Dominion-Provincial Relations, 12 October 1945.

10   LAC, RG 29, vol. 23, file 21-2-2, "Memorandum of Correspondence Re Dominion-Provincial Conference on Reconstruction, Proposals of the Government of Canada on National Health Program," G.B. Chisholm, M.D., Deputy Minister of Health, to A.J. Hooke, 29 December 1945.

11   *Dominion-Provincial Conference*, 7 August 1945, 188.

12   Provincial Archives of Alberta (PAA), Premiers' (Manning) Papers, file 2161, "Address to Saskatoon Canadian Club," 14 August 1946.

13   PAA, Premiers' Papers, file 1450, C.W. Lundy, Director of Welfare, Department of Provincial Secretary, Social Assistance Branch, Victoria, to George Thompson, Superintendent, Civic Relief Department, Calgary, 2 February 1946.

14   PAA, Premiers' Papers, file 1450 and 1811, contain letters from 18 municipalities sent between 14 January 1946 and 19 February 1946, endorsing the Calgary position. Beginning with Calgary itself, the municipalities calling on the province to act were Edmonton, Lethbridge, Edson, Cardston, Macleod, Blairmore, Grande Prairie, Leduc, Vegreville, Fort Saskatchewan, Raymond, Wainwright, Coleman, Stony Plain, Magrath, Drumheller, Macleod, and Strathmore.

15   *Dominion-Provincial Conference*, 30 April 1946, 479.

16   Ibid., 444.

17   Ibid., 30 April 1948, 491. Manning's position reflected the general support of Prairie Canadians for the Rowell-Sirois Report recommendation that the federal government distribute tax monies in a way that guaranteed residents of poorer provinces similar social services to those available to residents of wealthier provinces. As Gerald Friesen comments, "This was an important forward step, in the view of Prairie Canadians, because they were henceforth to be protected as much as possible from a disaster like that of the 1930s." Gerald Friesen, *The Canadian Prairies: A History* (Toronto: University of Toronto Press, 1987), 448.

18   *Dominion-Provincial Conference*, 30 April 1948, 495.

19   PAA, Premiers' Papers, file 2141A, Department of Public Welfare, "Report and Recommendations of the Departmental Committee Convened for a Review of Welfare Legislation and Policy."

20   *Busy Bee* 1, no. 7 (December 1956): 3.

21   Ibid.

22   Finkel, *The Social Credit Phenomenon in Alberta*, 148–52.

23   *Busy Bee*, March-April, 1963, 3.

24   Alberta Social Credit Papers, box 2, "Report of Resolutions, Alberta Social Credit League Convention, 25 November 1964."

25   PAA, Manning Papers, box 41, file 418, Ernest Manning to Lester Pearson, 31 December 1963.

26   Ibid., box 10, file 126, "Tele-Facts," 2 November 1965.

27   Ibid., box 41, file 421C, Manning to Pearson, 10 June 1965.

28   Ibid., box 37, file 371c., "Premiers' Address in legislature," 23 February 1965.

29   Revelations about the Alberta Treasury Branch scandal are found in Bob Hesketh, "The Company A, Company B Charges: The Manning Government, the Treasury Branches and Highways Contracts," MA thesis, University of Alberta, 1989. Hesketh largely demolishes the claim that Manning's cabinet provided honest and efficient governance for the province.

30   PAA, Manning Papers, box 41, file 418, Dr J. Donovan Ross to Judy LaMarsh, 20 December 1963.

31   *Proceedings of Third Provincial Premiers' Conference*, Victoria, 6 August 1962 (Ottawa: Queen's Printer, 1962).

32   *Federal-Provincial Conference of the Prime Minister and Premiers*, 19–22 July 1965, 1:25.

33   PAA, Manning Papers, box 41, file 418, Ernest Manning to Lester Pearson, 31 December 1963: *Federal-Provincial Conference*, 19–22 July 1965, 1:45–7.

34   Ibid., box 41, file 418, Manning to Pearson, 31 December 1963.

35   Ibid., box 56, file 607(a), W.O. Twaits to Manning, 12 September 1968; Manning to W.O. Twaits, 12 September 1968.

◎ 4.2: "A Narrow Provincialism": Regionalism in Atlantic Canada, 1945–1970

Corey Slumkoski

Introduction

In a 1948 letter to noted journalist and poet Andrew Merkel, Nova Scotia premier Angus L. Macdonald revived a question periodically raised in the Maritimes—that is, whether regional action could improve the Maritime provinces' depressed position within the Canadian federation. "Would we speak with one voice," he pondered, "and, if so, would the voice be in the proper pitch?" As the premier informed Merkel, "There have been instances not so very long ago where I had hoped that Nova Scotian members, and perhaps members from the other two Maritime Provinces, might have taken a stand, but they did not."[1] Merkel's reply admonished Macdonald for his limited perspective on regional unity, accusing him of "a narrow provincialism of which no doubt we are all guilty."[2] This exchange between Macdonald and Merkel encapsulates the difficulties faced by the Maritime/Atlantic provinces—Nova Scotia, New Brunswick, Prince Edward Island, and, after 1949, Newfoundland—in acting together to remedy their region's economic and political marginalization; rarely did the provinces speak with "one voice."[3]

This paper surveys Atlantic Canadian regionalism following the Second World War. It argues that both the emergence and the decline of Atlantic regionalism between 1945 and 1970 can be linked to Newfoundland's 1949 entry into Confederation. The prospect of a new Atlantic province initially strengthened the regional lobby and lent weight to calls to remedy the region's depressed position in the Canadian federation. While the regional movement began with talk of political union in the late-1940s, it came to focus on a more limited form of regional collaboration in the next decade. In a somewhat ironic twist, however, the very terms by which Newfoundland merged with Canada—and particularly Term 29—served to fracture the regional movement before it was firmly rooted. In this manner, postwar regionalism followed a pattern that can be observed in earlier and later Maritime/Atlantic regional movements, whereby meaningful cooperation was derailed by entrenched provincialism.

This lack of cooperation stemmed largely from the structure of Canadian federalism, which with its focus on provinces, not regions, has tended to impede regional initiatives. Atlantic Canadian regionalism thus reveals itself most clearly when provincial interests converge, for the provinces have been reluctant to support regional initiatives when they bring no promise of corollary provincial benefit. In other words, regionalism is not an altruistic force; it is rooted in the best interests of the individual provinces that compose the region. As a result, regionalism as a "'political stance' . . . [that] can be summoned up when other structures—familial, communal, provincial, national, global—fail" ebbs and flows in relation to perceived benefit.[4] Following the limited successes of the broadly based regional Maritime Rights Movement of the 1920s, collective action lay dormant throughout the 1930s and early 1940s, as the three Maritime provinces jockeyed first for scant federal assistance during the bleak years of the Great Depression and then for elusive wartime contracts.[5] Maritime politicians—conditioned by years of acting in isolation in their efforts to secure federal support—tended to look out for their own interests by acting provincially, not regionally, when it came to courting development programs and determining public policy. By the end of the Second World War, Maritime regionalism was thus at a low point; although the Maritime provinces (and Newfoundland) shared some common experiences—such as underdevelopment, staples-based economies, and a commitment to ocean-going trade—their populations did not (and still do not) conceive of a common identity or imagine themselves as partners in a broader region.

Yet from this postwar nadir there emerged a renaissance in Maritime regionalism, an upswing encouraged in part by actions in the federal sphere. Ottawa's policy increasingly treated the three Maritime provinces as a distinct region. As early as 1946, for example, a series of stamps celebrating the Canadian provinces included just one for the Maritimes—a picture of the newly launched Prince Edward Island ferry.[6] When Newfoundland entered Confederation on 1949, Ottawa's mandarins readily incorporated the new province into the regional framework. Not only did Term 29 of Newfoundland's terms of union specifically tie the new province's standard of economic and social development to "that obtaining generally in the region comprising the Maritime Provinces of Nova Scotia, New Brunswick, and Prince Edward Island,"[7] but during the negotiations preceding the merger, it was specified that "the Island of Newfoundland will be considered as within the Maritime Region for the purposes of the Maritime Freight Rates Act,"[8] while the Newfoundland Railway would "be deemed an extension of the Canadian National Railways service in and through the Maritime Provinces for the purposes of determining freight, passenger and express rates."[9] Since Ottawa increasingly grouped the four Atlantic provinces together as an economically distressed region, it made sense for the provinces to use the same regional framework and to collaborate on issues of common concern. Perhaps by acting together they could improve the region's weak political status, strengthen its underdeveloped economic position, and counter detrimental federal policies. Unfortunately, this strategy met with limited success. As this examination reveals, between 1945 and 1970, upswings in Maritime/Atlantic regionalism consistently disintegrated amid concerns that the provinces could accomplish more independently than they could together; although regional action increased during the postwar era, a narrow provincialism continued to hold sway in Atlantic Canada.

The Context of Postwar Regionalism

Regionalism has been a long-standing feature of Maritime and, after Newfoundland's 1949 entry into Confederation, Atlantic Canadian political discourse. The 1864 Charlottetown Conference was originally intended as a forum for the discussion of Maritime union before the broader platform of a British North American union took centre stage. With Canadian Confederation in 1867, the push for Maritime union fell by the wayside, though regionalism continued to rear its head intermittently. Maritime unity of purpose came to the forefront both with the movement to repeal Confederation in the 1880s and again with the Maritime Rights movement of the 1920s.

With the demise of the Maritime Rights movement in the late 1920s, Maritime regionalism subsided. This process was accelerated by the Great Depression and the Second World War,

which encouraged the Maritime provinces to deal with Ottawa on an individual basis. The onset of the Depression in the 1930s presented the already weak Maritime provinces and municipalities with responsibilities for relief that they could no longer afford. Maritime per capita income was well below the national average; so, too, were the region's relief payments, while unemployment rates were higher. As a result, the impact of the Great Depression was as severe in the Maritimes as it was on the drought-ravished Prairies. So dire was the situation across Canada that the federal government was compelled to take action. Unfortunately for the Maritimes, Ottawa's solution was a series of one-third matching grants, whereby the federal, provincial, and municipal governments would each bear one-third of the cost of administering relief. This system was only as strong as its weakest link, and thus the more affluent municipalities in central Canada could better participate than could the cash-strapped Maritimes. This meant that those areas most immune to the Depression could receive the most relief from it, while areas in greater need were entitled to lower payments. Moreover, since the system was geared towards the provinces, not the regions, it helped to consolidate and entrench provincial cleavages, as each province lobbied individually for its share of relief allocations.

Circumstances improved little with the outbreak of the Second World War. Ottawa's wartime policies, far from alleviating regional inequities, helped to consolidate them. During the war, powerful Minister of Munitions and Supply C.D. Howe, whose task it was to distribute wartime contracts, used the lack of Maritime infrastructure—roads and hydroelectrical facilities—and the region's proximity to the Atlantic seaboard, and therefore to German attack, to justify policies that centralized Canadian industry. Although Maritime provincial governments benefited to some extent from the war—the conflict relieved them of much of their social spending and provided full employment—Ottawa's unwillingness to grant contracts to the Maritimes and the internecine competition among the Maritime provinces for limited funds meant that the region emerged from the conflict fragmented and in an even weaker position relative to the rest of Canada than it had been in during the Depression. As E.R. Forbes has argued, "the region which received the least wartime investment . . . would have the greatest difficulty adjusting to a peacetime economy."[10]

The tendency of the Maritime provinces to act independently of one another continued after war's end. Emblematic of this provincialism were the provincial industrial development programs proposed following the war: Prince Edward Island focused its efforts on securing federal subsidization for the expansion of trade with the potential new province of Newfoundland; New Brunswick lobbied for a canal across the Isthmus of Chignecto to connect the Northumberland Strait with the Bay of Fundy; and Nova Scotia argued for the construction of a fixed link across

FEDERALISM

Federalism refers to a political union, such as Canada, in which formally independent parts (colonies and territories) have been brought together in a nation, with the constituent parts maintaining their individual governments yet also creating a national government. Thus, federalism entails the distribution of powers between the constituent units of a federal union. In the case of Canada, federalism entails the distribution of power to the provincial governments and the national government, first laid out at the time of Confederation in the Constitution (British North America [BNA] Act) and then revised over the years through constitutional amendments.

In a nation like Canada, federalism and the relations surrounding it directly influence the degree to which there is cooperation or conflict between the provincial/territorial and federal governments and thus the extent to which the nation experiences polarizing regionalism or national unity. This results from the fact that Canada is a highly decentralized federal union with important areas of governmental jurisdiction under provincial control, thereby potentially creating strong and independent provincial governments equal to the national government, though separate in their responsibilities. However, Canadian federalism has never been characterized by a strict and distinct separation of provincial powers from federal jurisdictions. Some degree of federal-provincial interdependence has always existed because of shared areas of jurisdiction (such as immigration), both because new areas of policy arise that were not included in the Constitution and jurisdictional responsibility is unclear and because seemingly separate areas of jurisdiction often require both federal and provincial involvement to fulfil policy goals. This last point is particularly pertinent for the post-1945 period owing to the development of the welfare state. With the primary policy areas of health, education, and welfare under provincial jurisdiction, federal involvement was still imperative because of the greater power of the federal government to raise revenues. This led to cooperation between both levels of government to ensure the development of these programs on a nationwide level and the provision of adequate funding to pay for what are undeniably expensive policies. Medicare, the pinnacle of the welfare state, is often used as a primary example of cooperative federalism and equitable relations; it was Saskatchewan that provided the model for the later, national program. Yet disputes over jurisdiction and the demand for autonomy/independence in areas of provincial jurisdiction have led to (and continue to lead to) destabilizing conflict, such as the demand for "special status" for Quebec and the growing question of how to accommodate the "national" demands of the First Nations within Canadian federalism.

For further discussion, see Herman Bakvis, Gerald Baier, and Douglas Brown, *Contested Federalism. Certainty and Ambiguity in the Canadian Federation* (Don Mills, ON: Oxford University Press 2009).

the Strait of Canso to connect Cape Breton Island to the mainland.[11] Created largely in isolation and geared primarily towards provincial—not regional—rehabilitation, these programs undermined the formation of a regional front and weakened the Maritime lobby. Despite this, the federal government continued to treat the three provinces collectively, and as a result, only in Nova Scotia did Ottawa assist with a province's development strategy, by contributing to the construction of the Canso Causeway. By the end of the war, the almost two decades that each Maritime province had spent courting the federal government for support had led to the fragmentation of Maritime regionalism. Yet from this fractured group of provinces a stronger sense of regionalism would soon emerge, prompted in part by the prospect of Newfoundland's entry into Confederation.

The Push for Maritime/Atlantic Union

One of the earliest postwar manifestations of Maritime/Atlantic regionalism can be seen in the push for a formal regional union that emerged in the late-1940s. This union drive was directly related to the declining position of the Maritimes in the Canadian federation. In particular, many Maritimers were concerned about the diminished voice they had in Ottawa. In the years following Confederation, Ottawa had concentrated on settling the west, with the result that newly arrived settlers bypassed the Maritimes. As immigrants moved westward, the Maritimes' relative population fell, and the region's representation in the House of Commons dropped from 43 to 26 seats between 1874 and 1945, while the number of seats in the House increased from 206 to 245 over the same period of time. The drop in the Maritime component of the House of Commons—from 21 per cent to 11 per cent in approximately 70 years—meant that the region's political clout was substantially reduced and regional politicians found it increasingly difficult to protect the interests of their constituents. By the postwar era, many Maritime politicians and private citizens were concerned with their diminished

stature within the federation, and some began to promote regional action and unity of purpose as a means of strengthening the region's position in Ottawa. The prospect of Newfoundland's entry into Confederation was warmly received by these regionalists, for they believed that the added political representation of the new province would strengthen their cause.

Postwar rumblings for union were first heard on 5 June 1946, when an editorial in the *Fundy Fisherman*, published in Black's Harbour, New Brunswick, promoted regional amalgamation as a means of enticing Newfoundland to enter Confederation: "[I]f the Maritime provinces were to join up with Newfoundland in forming one large Maritime Province of the Dominion we are inclined to think the people of Newfoundland would be interested." The union of the Maritimes and Newfoundland made sense, the editor claimed, because "the interests of these territories are almost identical." Moreover, such a union would then be the third-largest province in Confederation, trailing only Ontario and Quebec. As the editor argued, this "combined group would have such a large representation in the federal House of Commons and Senate, they would be able to hold their own very well with the rest of Canada."[12]

The idea of Atlantic union transitioned from editorial fodder to political football on 7 April 1947, when the *Charlottetown Guardian* reported that a Canadian parliamentarian "in close touch with affairs of Newfoundland" had suggested that Newfoundland join with the Maritimes to form one large province.[13] This proposal prompted responses from the Maritime premiers. New Brunswick's John McNair and Prince Edward Island's Walter Jones readily offered their opinions of the proposed merger. "Maritime Union has been suggested at various times," said McNair, who did not "think there is any marked degree of opinion in this province on it." Jones agreed with McNair and pointed out that the idea had been around since the 1864 Charlottetown Conference, but he doubted that the subject would "become a live issue."[14] Although he made no comment at the time, Nova Scotia premier Macdonald's view of regional union is revealed in a 1948 letter to Andrew Merkel, in which he doubted "very much whether any great gain would be effected by Maritime Union."[15]

Although the Maritime premiers were reluctant to endorse the idea of union, New Brunswick Progressive Conservative opposition leader Hugh John Flemming displayed no such reservations. Put off by the lack of regional cooperation that he saw in the ongoing tax-rental negotiations, during which New Brunswick quickly entered an agreement with Ottawa only to find out that those provinces that delayed signing a deal— such as Nova Scotia—brokered more lucrative arrangements, Flemming used his response to the 1947 New Brunswick Speech from the Throne to endorse regional union, stating, "Personally, I am in favour of Maritime union if it could be arranged."[16] Flemming believed that had New Brunswick and Nova Scotia presented a united front on the issue, they would have effected a more generous tax-rental agreement from Ottawa. This did not happen, which underscored for Flemming the importance of regional integration. As Flemming explained, "Down here in the Maritimes we speak with three divided voices. New Brunswick tells its story, Nova Scotia presents its case and Prince Edward Island does likewise." And this allowed the federal government to play one province off against another. This regional division prompted the opposition leader to ask, "When will we realize that we can build up a larger unit by simply working together, cease being divided against ourselves, but speak as one?"[17]

Flemming believed that union would benefit the Maritime provinces. It would allow the region to speak more effectively in federal-provincial negotiations, while trimming expenditures by eliminating the duplication of services. As the New Brunswick opposition leader suggested enthusiastically, "What an advantage it would be to work with Prince Edward Island on potatoes, with Nova Scotia on many things. The ramifications of working together are almost endless."[18] However, Flemming overlooked the political backlash that his call to erode provincial

boundaries would create, and within a month's time he was backpedalling on the issue.

The day following Flemming's remarks in the New Brunswick Legislature, the *Sydney Post-Record* came out strongly against any form of regional amalgamation. In editor H.P. Duchemin's mind, talk of union displayed a basic misunderstanding of the purpose of Confederation itself. According to Duchemin, the British North America Act made provision for a strong central government to deal with international affairs, national defence, and other matters that required a dominion-wide response. The provinces were meant to deal with the administration of local affairs in a "[l]egislative jurisdiction small enough to insure close contacts between the people's elected representatives and their constituents." The three Maritime provinces, claimed Duchemin, all had very different economies and ways of life, and therefore each needed their independent legislatures to serve their widely divergent constituents. As he saw it, "For these unanswerable reasons . . . the bundling of the Maritimes and Newfoundland together under a single 'local government' is miles outside the range of practical politics."[19]

Perhaps owing to this unfavourable media coverage, Flemming began to qualify his endorsement of regional union by publicly suggesting that "[t]he disadvantages of a legislative union, at the present time, would be far greater than the possible advantages."[20] This did not mean, however, that he rejected the idea of Maritime cooperation. In his view, if Prince Edward Island, Nova Scotia, and New Brunswick were to cooperate on matters of common concern, they could "improve their national position and directly attack the grave problems of their economic life."[21] Maritime cooperation, Flemming contended, was a worthwhile goal that had "infinite possibilities." Already the three provinces cooperated in a number of ways, with the Maritime Lumber Bureau and the Maritime Board of Trade being Flemming's foremost examples. What is more, in the years following the war, the time was ripe for regional solidarity. All three Maritime provinces had recently concluded reports on postwar reconstruction that could be used to pinpoint shared areas of need to be jointly developed. At the same time, the differing experiences of New Brunswick and Nova Scotia in their negotiation of tax-rental agreements with Ottawa illustrated for Flemming the pitfalls of not acting in concert and reinforced his belief that the Maritime provinces should cooperate on matters of regional concern.

From Regional Union to Regional Solidarity

Flemming's qualification of his statements regarding regional union serves as a useful demarcation point between the desire among some Maritimers for Atlantic union and the less ambitious goal of developing some form of regional cooperation. It also seems likely that the clamour for formal Maritime political amalgamation began to subside in part because the entry of Newfoundland into Confederation had become a political certainty and the impracticality of merging the Atlantic region into one political body became more readily apparent. This was compounded by the fact that advocates of union were unable to offer any real benefits of such a merger, for they could provide no guarantee that the concerns of each of the Atlantic provinces would be adequately heard once they were part of a larger political entity. After all, would one voice in seven really be any stronger than four voices in ten? With no real assurance that a union scheme would actually strengthen the region's political position or improve its economic prospects, Maritime politicians were highly reluctant to upset the political apple cart for a program that would undoubtedly be a tough sell to their constituents. As a result, they decided that their best chance for economic and political improvement lay in the maintenance of the provincial status quo. Nevertheless, talk of Newfoundland's entry inspired the hope that, even in the absence of formalized political union, the region's elected officials would act together to benefit the Maritimes. As the editor of the *Fundy Fisherman* observed while assessing Newfoundland's impact on the existing political relations between the Maritime provinces, "Few families grow up with the children consistently

harmonious . . . [but perhaps] Newfoundland will be the catalyst that will finally resolve us into some united mass."[22]

Perhaps the most enthusiastic advocate of Maritime regional cooperation during the late-1940s and 1950s was New Brunswick newspaperman C.C. Avard, publisher of both the *Sackville Tribune-Post* and the *Maritime Advocate and Busy East*. Disheartened by what he saw as the increasing marginalization of the Maritimes under Prime Minister William Lyon Mackenzie King, Avard observed as early as 1944: "We are victims of conditions over which we seemingly have little control, but one thing is sure and that is that we can't have a united Canada if some sections are weak and ailing, while other sections are strong and vigorous."[23] By 1947, Avard was suggesting that Confederation had failed the Maritimes, since the trend towards centralization ensured that "the smaller provinces have not always received fair treatment," and he laid the blame for regional problems squarely on the shoulders of the region's long line of Liberal members of Parliament (MPs). As Avard saw it, the Maritime's Progressive Conservative MPs had become the champions of regional causes, while Liberal representatives were constantly hamstrung by party loyalty.[24]

This philosophy was further articulated in a January 1949 article written by an anonymous author using the pseudonym Grant Evans, which argued that years of centralist federal policies had hindered Maritime economic development. But rather than lay all the blame at Ottawa's feet, Evans, like Avard, admonished Maritime federal representatives for not adequately protecting the region's interests. The key to solving the problem of regional representation, according to Evans, was the formation of a *de facto* regional bloc among the Maritime members in the House of Commons. This would not require any large-scale integration of the provincial governments, nor would it even necessitate discussions between Fredericton, Charlottetown, and Halifax regarding how to cooperate on matters of common concern. All that was required was a desire among the region's federal representatives to think regionally and not along party or provincial lines. Since Maritimers would "[p]ledge all candidates of all parties in advance to vote against the party where necessary on each and every Maritime measure that arises from time to time," this Maritime bloc would not be shackled by the customary bonds of party loyalty and could vote against the party line on matters of regional importance.[25]

Just a few months later, Avard used Newfoundland's recently concluded entry into Confederation to promote regional solidarity. In a June 1949 editorial, he trumpeted the cause of regional cohesion and cooperation, and Newfoundland was his catalyst. "Now that Newfoundland has become Canada's tenth province," Avard argued, "the Maritimes comprise four provinces instead of three. This has possibilities for solidarity, for unanimity of action, for a united Atlantic front. If all the representatives from this section of Canada would stand firmly together there would be formed a solid block that could demand Maritime rights from Ottawa instead of being men with their hats in their hands seeking favors from the bigwigs, who for a brief time occupy the seats of the mighty."[26] These sentiments concerning the positive impact of Newfoundland's entry were oft stated across the region. The *Charlottetown Patriot*, for example, had suggested as early as August 1948 that Newfoundland's entry into Confederation would make the Maritime voice in Ottawa better heard, as the new province would add seven members to the House of Commons, creating a "bloc of 33 votes" and adding six new senators. As D'Arcy O'Donnell argued in the *Patriot*, "Once the Newfoundland representatives are elected to the Commons and appointed for life to the Senate, the demands of the Atlantic provinces will carry more weight."[27]

A similar take on Newfoundland's importance to Maritime solidarity had been offered in the 2 November 1948 issue of the *Fundy Fisherman*. In the eyes of the paper's editor, the coming years should see the Maritimes wielding greater say in federal affairs and Ottawa showing increased willingness to assist Canada's eastern provinces. As the editor stated, "The Maritime

Provinces are now the stronghold of Liberalism in Canada. There are only three Liberal Provincial Governments and all three are located in the Maritimes. This places our Atlantic Provinces in a favourable position politically and the Federal Liberal Candidates should not be slow to call the attention of the present Federal government to the political loyalty of the Maritimes and ask for greater consideration of Maritime needs."[28] The editor went on to recognize that, within a year's time, there would likely be a fourth Liberal government in Newfoundland, giving the region even greater say with the federal government. Even H.P. Duchemin, editor of the anti-union *Sydney Post-Record*, endorsed the idea of regional cooperation, as such a tack had in the past born "fruitful results."[29]

The regional solidarity espoused by Maritime papers was almost realized at the Liberal Party's national convention in 1948. At the convention, plans were made for New Brunswick premier McNair to nominate Nova Scotia premier Angus L. Macdonald for the Liberal leadership, ensuring Macdonald a chance to speak to the assembled delegates. In his speech, Macdonald would be able to articulate Maritime grievances and concerns, and in so doing, he would spearhead a united Maritime front that would capture the attention of the convention, the press, and the public at large. After his address, Macdonald would withdraw his name from candidacy.[30] Journalist and political operative Dalton Camp later described the plan as "an entirely plausible, effective, and even dramatic way to make our views known and to demonstrate the unity and strength in which they were held."[31] What is more, Newfoundland's pending entry added to the impact the Maritime politicians could have. As the *Charlottetown Patriot* trumpeted in its coverage of the convention, "Our three Maritime premiers are making them sit up at Ottawa and we also will have the Newfoundland premier with us—that's the idea!"[32] Despite the PEI paper's enthusiasm, Maritime unity failed to appear at the convention. Nova Scotia MP Robert Winters, who was destined for a cabinet position under Louis St Laurent, caught wind of the scheme and dissuaded Macdonald from participating in it. With the

Maritime threat extinguished, Louis St Laurent easily won the leadership on the first ballot.

While regional unity fell prey to party politics at the 1948 Liberal convention, the region's political leaders did band together that same year to oppose an increase in railway freight rates. Early in 1948, after more than a year of contemplation, the Board of Transport Commissioners approved a 21 per cent horizontal increase in rates. This effectively removed the regional subsidies granted under the Maritime Freight Rates Act (MFRA), which since 1927 had helped offset the geographical disadvantages faced by shippers from the region by granting them a 20 per cent reduction in railway freight rates. The rate hike prompted a regional response from the Maritimes: the Transportation Commission of the Maritime Provinces Board of Trade helped coordinate the Atlantic effort to halt the rate increases—an effort that Newfoundland supported even though "the transportation concerns of Canada's newest province differed substantially from those of the Maritime provinces."[33] Likewise, the three Maritime premiers came together, along with their four western counterparts, to protest what was seen as an unfair and unreasonable hike by lobbying Ottawa to appoint a royal commission to investigate the problem of freight rates to the outlying provinces. Such concerted action would ultimately lead to the appointment of the 1951 Royal Commission on Transportation, or the Turgeon Commission. Although the Turgeon Commission would later uphold the rate increase, the Maritime premiers were able to get the 20 per cent subvention granted by the MFRA entrenched in a 1951 Railway Act amendment. Such successes—getting a formal examination of the rate hike and receiving a continuation of the MFRA subsidy—hinted at the merits of united action and helped give rise to the Atlantic Revolution later that decade (see below).

The Atlantic Revolution

The ongoing inability of the region's federal representatives to act as a regional bloc, combined with the apparent success of the Atlantic

and western premiers in securing the desired Turgeon Commission, contributed to the transfer of the locus for regional action from the federal to the provincial sphere. During the 1950s, Maritimers increasingly called for a formal Atlantic lobby to enable the four Atlantic provinces to work together on areas of overlapping interest. Foreshadowing this shift was a proposal by Liberal MLA (member of the Legislative Assembly) Martin Kaufman in the 1949 Nova Scotia Throne Speech debate for the formation of a Maritime-Newfoundland Council. Such an organization would bring together the region's business and government leaders to present a united front to the federal government on matters of common concern.[34] Although nothing came of Kaufman's proposed council, the idea of the region's provincial leaders acting together to protect the region's interest soon manifested itself in what historian W. Stewart MacNutt called the "Atlantic Revolution" of the 1950s.[35]

The Atlantic Revolution was a period when Atlantic business and political elites came together in the hope that state planning and financial support might ameliorate the region's "have-not" status in Confederation. It was rooted in the continuing economic problems faced by the region during the postwar era. By war's end, per capita income in the Maritimes stood at 24 per cent below the Canadian average. Things did not improve in the 1950s. By 1955, per capita income in the Maritimes had dropped to 33 per cent below the Canadian average; factoring Newfoundland— where per capita income was 55 per cent below the national average—into the equation further lowered the region's per capita income to 37 per cent below the Canadian average. Moreover, the net value of secondary manufacturing in the Atlantic provinces was only $94 per person, far below the national average of $405.[36] Declining incomes relative to the Canadian standard prompted more and more Maritimers to leave their farms and fishing villages in search of better work opportunities in the region's urban centres, such as in the expanding fields of construction, banking, and, particularly, government, resulting in an increasingly urban Maritime population.[37]

The Atlantic Revolution was also influenced by a fundamental reconceptualization of the state that occurred during the postwar years. This was the era of Keynesian economics, when government elites called for such things as counter-cyclical financing and a greater state role in the economy. Following the war, governments across Canada turned their attention to massive reconstruction efforts that required of them a far more interventionist role, and the Maritimes proved no exception. New Brunswick built roads, Prince Edward Island expanded its agricultural export trade, and Nova Scotia modernized its fishery, all of which placed additional pressure on provincial treasuries and led Atlantic Canadians to expect more of the state in what it could do to remedy underdevelopment. The federal government had, after all, overseen the centralization of industry in Ontario and Quebec during the war, while the postwar period saw the expenditures of huge sums of money on massive development projects of importance to the central provinces, such as the St Lawrence Seaway. Perhaps concerted action by the Maritime governments could counter this centralizing trend.

A change in political will and leadership also contributed to the Atlantic Revolution. Conservative Hugh John Flemming's defeat of John McNair's Liberals in New Brunswick's 1952 election brought to the premier's office a leader more committed to regional action than his predecessor. Equally important was the ascension of Henry Hicks as premier of Nova Scotia following the 1954 death of Angus L. Macdonald. Macdonald had been a champion of provincial rights during the 1940s, and his steely commitment to that crusade made him ill-suited to the regionalist cause. Hicks, on the other hand, quickly embraced the potential of regional action. Within two weeks of becoming Nova Scotia's premier in 1955, Hicks oversaw the creation of the Atlantic Provinces Economic Council (APEC), a region-wide organization tasked with surveying, studying, stimulating, and coordinating activities relating to the economic well-being of the Atlantic provinces.[38] Not to be outdone, that same year Flemming inaugurated

a series of Atlantic Premiers Conferences (APCs) designed to allow the four Atlantic premiers to discuss matters of common concern. Through initiatives such as APEC and the APC, the cooperative movement of the 1950s enabled the premiers of the four Atlantic provinces to meet on matters of common interest without being compelled to commit themselves to any plan that might prove harmful to their own provinces.[39] These 1950s regional initiatives allowed the Maritime provinces to act in concert in lobbying the 1955 Royal Commission on Canada's Economic Prospects and in making the regional case at the 1955 Federal-Provincial Conference. And such regionally minded actions appeared to have met with success. Not only did the 1956 federal budget include plans for a more equitable equalization formula based on the average income of the two wealthiest provinces, but that same year Unemployment Insurance (UI) benefits were extended to workers engaged in the seasonal fishery, an industry of great importance to Atlantic Canada.

Yet an oft overlooked catalyst of the Atlantic Revolution was Newfoundland's entry into Confederation. Not only did the entrance of Newfoundland quadruple the geographic area of the region, but many Maritimers hoped the new province's additional seats in the House of Commons and Senate would allow the entire region to more forcefully make its case for federal assistance. As a result, Newfoundland became a welcome and integral part of the Atlantic Revolution's cooperative push. Soon after entering Confederation, for example, Newfoundland was warmly welcomed into the Maritime Provinces Board of Trade, whose Transportation Commission coordinated the Atlantic effort to halt increases in freight rates to the region. Moreover, Newfoundland premier J.R. Smallwood was a spirited advocate of Newfoundland and Maritime development. He was quick to criticize the federal government for the centralist policies that had strengthened Ontario and Quebec seemingly at the expense of Atlantic Canada, and pledged that "every bit of [Newfoundland's] strength and energy as a government will be used in this great work of development."[40] As the fiery Newfoundland premier told a 1955 meeting of the Atlantic Association of Broadcasters, "Before we become second-class citizens of Canada we will show the other Maritime provinces how to get out of Confederation."[41]

The concerted efforts of the Atlantic premiers appear to have had some effect on the federal sphere. For example, during the 1957 federal election, in an effort to increase the Progressive Conservative vote in Atlantic Canada, PC leader John Diefenbaker readily adopted the Atlantic Manifesto. This program for regional economic development, created by the five Maritime Progressive Conservative MPs, called for such things as the decentralization of industry, adjustment grants to assist the poorer provinces, and reductions in freight rates.[42] The manifesto did what it was designed to do, and Diefenbaker won a slim seven-seat majority in the 1957 campaign, largely on the support of Atlantic Canadian voters. Although the Liberals tried to jump on the regional development bandwagon during the 1958 election, Atlantic Canadians again voted for Diefenbaker.[43] Yet while Diefenbaker appeared committed to regional development (prior to the 1958 election he did, after all, loan $29.5 million to New Brunswick for the Beechwood power plant and provide over $25 million in Atlantic Adjustment Grants to the four Atlantic provinces), he contributed to the demise of 1950s regionalism when he proved reluctant to entertain Smallwood's claims to special status for Newfoundland under Term 29 of the new province's terms of union.

In 1949, Newfoundland was much more impoverished than its provincial cousins. With Confederation, the Newfoundland government would have to impose new taxes, such as a general sales tax, and increase existing taxes, such as gasoline levies, in order to remain financially viable. As the extent to which the new province's citizenry could afford these taxes was unknown, Term 29 mandated a transitional grant for eight years to assist the provincial government during the early years of its integration into Canada.

Furthermore, it specified that within eight years of Newfoundland's joining Confederation a royal commission be called to determine "the form and scale of additional financial assistance, if any, that may be required"[44] to ensure that Newfoundland's standard of services was equal to that prevailing in the Maritimes after its transitional grant expired. In the fall of 1957, the Royal Commission on Newfoundland Finances began its investigation of Term 29. Headed by former New Brunswick premier John McNair and featuring Queen's University economist John Deutsch and Newfoundland chief justice Albert Walsh, the commission reported remarkably quickly on the status of Newfoundland's finances, tabling its report on 25 July 1958 and recommending the transitional grant paid to Newfoundland be raised to $8 million annually. This was particularly galling to Smallwood, who viewed $15 million as a more appropriate sum.

Smallwood, never one to hold his tongue when he felt he had been wronged, freely aired his discontent with the commission's recommendations. This tactic greatly annoyed Diefenbaker, who already looked unfavourably on Newfoundland for having elected only one Progressive Conservative MP in the recently concluded election, and may have backfired when the prime minister rose in the House of Commons to declare that the $8-million grant recommended by the McNair Commission was the "final and irrevocable" settlement of Newfoundland's terms of union and would only be paid until 1962. Diefenbaker's hard-line stance incensed Smallwood, and the Newfoundland premier began to disassociate himself from his Atlantic counterparts and from the politics of regionalism. At the 1959 Atlantic Premiers Conference, Smallwood publicly stated that he would not ask the other premiers to take an official stance on Term 29 out of fear that their position might be at odds with his and lead to frosty relations in the region. The Newfoundland premier told his counterparts, "It would be a pity if the Atlantic front were broken."[45] Yet, for all intents and purposes, the front had already begun to splinter. Following the Term 29 verdict, Smallwood increasingly backed away

University of Saskatchewan, University Archives & Special Collections, Diefenbaker Archival Collections, JGD 4752

John Diefenbaker (right) and Joey Smallwood (left) in Newfoundland during the 1958 election.

from the politics of regionalism, believing instead that Newfoundland's unique status as Canada's newest and poorest province would prove more persuasive in soliciting federal largesse. In a somewhat ironic turn of events, Newfoundland's entry into Confederation contributed to the emergence of Atlantic regionalism during the 1950s, while the actual terms by which the new province joined the federation—in particular Term 29—helped fracture the regional movement before it could meaningfully alter the region's depressed position within the federation.

Although the Atlantic Revolution would persist into the 1960s, by the end of that decade, Atlantic Canadian regionalism was once again on the wane. The defeat of New Brunswick's Flemming—the *de facto* leader of the Atlantic Revolution—in the 1960 New Brunswick election led to the ascension of Louis J. Robichaud,

who as premier would go so far as to advocate in 1964 for the union of the Atlantic provinces.[46] While Newfoundland premier Smallwood and Nova Scotia PC premier Robert Stanfield, who had replaced Hicks, promised to "study" the idea, PEI premier Walter Shaw refused to commit his province to the idea.[47] Despite the subsequent Deutsch Commission's 1970 endorsement of Maritime union, the only tangible result of the 1960s union movement was the 1971 formation of the Council of Maritime Premiers, which simply formalized the status quo by providing a forum for Nova Scotia, New Brunswick, and Prince Edward Island to discuss issues of common concern. What is more, neither the Deutsch Commission nor the Council of Maritime Premiers incorporated Newfoundland. Newfoundland was now distancing itself from its Maritime cousins, and as a result, the broad cooperative spirit of the Atlantic Revolution was fading, a victim both of a lack of public involvement—women, labour, and rural voters in particular had little say in or understanding of the movement's principles—and the opposition of other provinces.[48] By the early 1970s, concerted Atlantic regionalism as a political strategy was again on the wane.

Conclusion

Historian Christopher Harvie has compared the growth of European regionalism to "a badly organized dinner party" at which the guests "somehow contrive to speak not to but alongside one another."[49] The same could be said about Maritime/Atlantic regionalism itself during the postwar era. The experiences of depression and war had conditioned the Maritime provinces to act independently in lobbying the federal government for assistance. As a result, the early postwar era was characterized by a lack of regional cooperation in the Maritimes, with each province believing it could secure greater federal assistance by going it alone than by tying its fortunes to the regional whole. Yet the 1949 entry of Newfoundland into

Confederation and the federal government's tendency to treat the four Atlantic provinces regionally gradually prompted the re-emergence of regional cooperation in the hope that collective action could improve the region's position in Confederation. An abortive push for regional union developed during the late 1940s, to be replaced by a more limited spirit of cooperation that would blossom into the Atlantic Revolution. However, the gains of such regional initiatives were limited; a lasting sense of regionalism and solidarity did not take root among the four Atlantic provinces between 1945 and 1970, and the region's economic position remained well below the Canadian average. Unfortunately, the seeds of division sown during depression and war remained strongly rooted, and a narrow provincialism continued to trump regional concerns even during the heady days of the Atlantic Revolution.

Author's Note: Portions of this text appeared in Corey Slumkoski, *Inventing Atlantic Canada: Regionalism and the Maritime Reaction to Newfoundland's Entry into Canadian Confederation* (Toronto: University of Toronto Press, 2011). Reprinted with permission of the publisher.

Endnotes

1   Letter from Angus L. Macdonald to Andrew Merkel, 2 September 1948, MG2/934 F31-1/451, Angus L. Macdonald Papers, Nova Scotia Archives and Records Management (hereafter NSARM), Halifax, Nova Scotia.

2   Letter from Andrew Merkel to Angus L. Macdonald, 5 September 1948, MG 2/934 F31-1/449, Angus L. Macdonald Papers, NSARM.

3   The term "Maritime provinces" refers to Nova Scotia, New Brunswick, and Prince Edward Island. The term "Atlantic Canada" arose after 1949 to describe the Maritimes and Newfoundland. In this paper, I have used "Newfoundland" rather than the current political designation of "Newfoundland and Labrador," since "Labrador was treated as a subordinate dependency of Newfoundland" until the late 1960s. See James Hiller, "Robert Bond and the Pink, White, and Green: Newfoundland Nationalism in Perspective," *Acadiensis* 36, no. 2 (Spring 2007): 113.

4   Margaret Conrad and James Hiller, *Atlantic Canada: A Region in the Making* (Don Mills, ON: Oxford University Press, 2001), 6. The formation of regionalism has received considerable scholarly attention. Janine Brody illustrates how Canada's federal policies organized the nation's political economy along a metropole-hinterland spectrum, with wealth increasingly concentrated in the central provinces. This can foster regional identity, and as geographer Randy William Widdis suggests, a region can be "predicated on the idea that geographical borders, by symbolically differentiating 'here' from 'there,' delineate belonging." While historian Colin Howell has cautioned against using this underdevelopment paradigm as the sole one to account for regional identity, it is clear that detrimental federal policies contributed to the rise of regional movements such as the 1920s Maritime Rights crusade and the postwar regionalism analyzed in this study. See Janine Brody, *The Political Economy of Canadian Regionalism* (Toronto: Harcourt

Brace Jovanovich, 1990); Randy William Widdis, "Globalization, Glocalization, and the Canadian West as a Region," *Acadiensis* 35, no. 2 (Spring 2006): 129; Colin Howell, "Economism, Ideology, and the Teaching of Maritime History," in *Teaching Maritime Studies*, ed. Phil Buckner (Fredericton: Acadiensis Press, 1986), 19.

5   See E.R. Forbes, *The Maritime Rights Movement, 1919–1927: A Study in Canadian Regionalism* (Montreal and Kingston: McGill-Queen's University Press, 1979); E.R. Forbes, "Cutting the Pie into Smaller Pieces: Matching Grants and Relief in the Maritime Provinces in the 1930s," *Acadiensis* 26, no. 1 (Autumn 1987): 34–55; and E.R. Forbes, "Consolidating Disparity: The Maritimes and the Industrialization of Canada during the Second World War," *Acadiensis* 15, no. 2 (Spring 1986): 3–27.

6   "Claim PEI on New Stamp but Nova Scotia Omitted," *Summerside Journal*, 5 August 1946, 1.

7   Canada, "Term 29," *An Act to confirm and give effect to Terms of Union agreed between Canada and Newfoundland*, assented to 23 March 1949.

8   "Memorandum by Department of Transport," 8 November 1948, in Paul Bridle, ed., *Documents on Relations between Canada and Newfoundland*, vol. 2: *1940–1949, Confederation, Part I* (Ottawa: Minister of Supply and Services Canada, 1984), 1211.

9   Letter from J.G. Channing to Cabinet Committee on Newfoundland, 23 November 1948, in ibid., 1215.

10   Forbes, "Consolidating Disparity," 4.

11   See Slumkoski, *Inventing Atlantic Canada*, chaps 2–4.

12   "Newfoundland," *Fundy Fisherman*, 5 June 1946, 4.

13   "Maritime-Newfoundland Proposal Stirs Little Interest in Maritimes," *Charlottetown Guardian*, 7 April 1947, 1. The parliamentarian in question was likely A. Neil McLean, a New Brunswick senator, staunch advocate for Newfoundland's entry into Confederation, and owner of the *Fundy Fisherman*.

14   "Newfoundland and Canada," *Sydney Post-Record*, 7 April 1947, 4.

15   Letter from Angus L. Macdonald to Andrew Merkel, 2 September 1948, MS, MG 2/934 F31-1/451, Angus L. Macdonald Papers, NSARM.

16   *Synoptic Report of the Proceedings of the Legislative Assembly of the Province of New Brunswick* (Fredericton: King's Printer, 1947), 96.

17   Ibid.

18   Ibid.

19   "Newfoundland and Canada," *Sydney Post-Record*, 7 April 1947, 4.

20   *Synoptic Report*, 269.

21   Ibid.

22   "Newfoundland," *Fundy Fisherman*, 15 December 1948, 4.

23   C.C. Avard, "Editorial," *Maritime Advocate and Busy East* 34, no. 10 (May 1944): 29–30.

24   C.C. Avard, "Editorial," *Maritime Advocate and Busy East* 37, no. 11 (June 1947): 3.

25   Grant Evans, "What's the Matter with the Maritimes?," *Maritime Advocate and Busy East* 39, no. 6 (January 1949): 8.

26   C.C. Avard, "Editorial," *Maritime Advocate and Busy East* 39, no. 11 (June 1949): 3.

27   D'Arcy O'Donnell, "Maritime Voice to Be Strengthened by Nfl'd Union," *Charlottetown Patriot*, 1 August 1948, 1.

28   "Federal Politics," *Fundy Fisherman*, 3 November 1948, 4.

29   "'Maritime Union' Again Lifts Its Hoary Head," *Sydney Post-Record*, 12 January 1949, 4.

30   For a discussion of Macdonald and the 1948 Liberal leadership convention, see T. Stephen Henderson, *Angus L. Macdonald: A Provincial Liberal* (Toronto: University of Toronto Press), 176–9.

31   Dalton Camp, *Gentlemen, Players & Politicians* (Toronto: McClelland & Stewart, 1970), 5.

32   "Current Comments," *Charlottetown Patriot*, 7 August 1948, 4.

33   T. Stephen Henderson, "A Defensive Alliance: The Maritime Provinces and the Turgeon Commission on Transportation, 1948–1951," *Acadiensis* 35, no. 2 (2006): 47n3.

34   "Council for Newfoundland and Maritimes Suggested," *Halifax Chronicle-Herald*, 18 March 1949, 1.

35   W.S. MacNutt, "The Atlantic Revolution," *Atlantic Advocate* 47, no. 11 (June 1957): 11–13.

36   Margaret Conrad, "The 1950s: The Decade of Development," in *The Atlantic Provinces in Confederation*, ed. E.R. Forbes and D.A. Muise (Toronto: University of Toronto Press, 1994), 401.

37   Margaret Conrad, "The Atlantic Revolution of the 1950s," in *Beyond Anger and Longing: Community and Development in Atlantic Canada*, ed. Berkeley Fleming (Fredericton: Acadiensis, 1988), 60.

38   Ibid., 70.

39   Conrad, "The 1950s," 414.

40   Joey Smallwood, *I Chose Canada: The Memoirs of the Honourable Joseph R. "Joey" Smallwood*, vol. 2 (Scarborough, ON: Signet, 1973), 26.

41   "Newfoundland May Quit Canada Premier's Threat," *Ottawa Journal*, 21 June 1955, 1.

42   Conrad, "The Atlantic Revolution of the 1950s," 82.

43   In the 1957 election, the Progressive Conservatives won 21 seats in Atlantic Canada, which was 16 more than they tallied in 1953. In the 1958 election, the number of Atlantic Canada PC seats increased to 25.

44   Canada, "Term 29."

45   "The Atlantic Conference and the Opening of the Beaverbrook Art Gallery," *Atlantic Advocate* 50, no. 2 (October 1959): 28.

46 Della Stanley, *Louis Robichaud: A Decade of Power* (Halifax: Nimbus, 1984), 116–17.

47 "Untitled," *Atlantic Advocate* 55, no. 3 (November 1964), 14–15.

48 It would not be until 27 October 1999 that Newfoundland and Labrador would be invited to join the Council of Maritime Premiers. Donald Savoie, *Visiting Grandchildren: Economic Development in the Maritimes* (Toronto: University of Toronto Press, 2006), 207.

49 Christopher Harvie, *The Rise of Regional Europe* (New York: Routledge, 1994), x.

CHAPTER 5

The Welfare State

◎ 5.1: "IT WAS TOUGH ON EVERYBODY": LOW-INCOME FAMILIES AND HOUSING HARDSHIP IN POST–WORLD WAR II TORONTO

Sean Purdy

[H]e had his first heart attack in December 21, 1947. In between a couple of times, he brought up blood from the mouth and in March 49, I think it was March the 10, 1949 he came home from work and he had bled the whole day at work. . . . And it was a very, very difficult case and from 1956, he was out of work, on and off, from 1954. And from April 56, he never worked again until the day he died July 21, 1958. . . . I couldn't find a place to live with two children and him . . . in the meantime, we heard about this Regent Park [public housing project], gonna build a new place. It was in the papers and that and he thought we should go down. . . . Well, by the time we got the letter we were accepted, it was about three days before he died.[1]

Such was Thelma Pilkey's painful recollection of her husband's illness and her family's housing hardship in 1950s Toronto. She had always worked, but with two children, her husband's irregular employment, and arduous medical bills, it was difficult to make ends meet. Finding a decent, affordable place to live was particularly hard: vacancy rates in Toronto were persistently low, landlords frequently shunned families with children, and rents were often excessive for low-income earners. Medical problems aggravated the difficulties. Thelma did not want to move the family into public housing, but given the precarious circumstances, she felt there were few options.

The Pilkeys' distressing struggles did not reflect the typical experience of working families in Canada. From the 1940s to the 1990s, Canada became one of the most socially and economically developed societies, with, arguably, the highest overall living standards in the world.[2] Generally, the majority of Canadian workers were able to achieve adequate housing without overwhelming difficulty in the postwar period.[3] However, this fulsome portrait presents an overly generalized view of the concrete situations of many working families. In turbulent economic times such as recessions, depressions, and wars, even employed workers with moderate incomes were disadvantaged and confronted severe shortages of reasonable dwelling spaces.[4] Moreover, the last 25 years have witnessed a marked decline in the social and economic well-being of the Canadian working class that has affected chiefly the housing opportunities of women, single parents, the working poor, and some recent immigrants.[5] In fact, there has always been a sizeable minority of low-income families who have historically experienced a permanent crisis of affordable, quality dwelling spaces.

This article explores the question of housing need in postwar Toronto by looking at the diverse reasons why families applied to the few public housing projects that were constructed after the war. It identifies a number of often-overlapping causes for the housing dilemmas of low-income families, including outright inability to pay, landlord intransigence towards families with children, evictions, illness, overcrowding, deprived housing conditions, racism, and social factors within the family. It aims to make a contribution to a growing body of work that complicates accepted notions of postwar prosperity and the benefits of the welfare state for low-income earners in advanced capitalist countries.[6]

The first section is based on adaptations of various statistical indicators of housing hardship generated by researchers for Toronto's public housing administration as well as analyses by social agencies, contemporary observers, and recent scholarly research. It briefly looks at pre–World War II developments and then chronicles housing need from the 1940s to the 1990s. Various methods and databases were used in these studies, and rarely did they originally attempt to chart processes over time. Nevertheless, we can make a reasonable assumption that this information offers us sound indications, if not exact measures, of the housing difficulties faced by low-income families. . . .

The second section of the article elucidates the informative if partial statistical record of housing need by considering various qualitative sources such as oral testimony, tenant correspondence, and other documentary voices of low-income families.[7] My interests in exploring this subject emanated from a larger study of Regent Park (RP) in Toronto, Canada's first and largest rent-geared-to-income housing project.[8] The archival records, which contain numerous letters from prospective tenants and rare resident case files, and the interviews I conducted with former

tenants of RP, speak directly to the question of housing need. I use the evidence both of families that secured places in RP as well as of prospective tenants who expressed a need for state assistance. By no means does this exhaust the low-income housing experience in Toronto, but it provides readily accessible qualitative evidence to help in the exploration of the question of housing hardship in the postwar era. The article thus highlights individual accounts of housing hardship, allowing us to put a much-needed human face on those left out of the much-vaunted postwar "age of prosperity."

The Low-Income Housing Crisis by Numbers, 1945–2000

. . . World War II ended unemployment, but it exacerbated the housing crisis. Toronto's location as a centre of war industry aggravated the grave shelter situation for many workers. First, the rapid increase in population was not matched on the supply side by dwelling construction; the building industry suffered from a lack of raw materials, and the priorities of industry and government were focused on war production. As a result of family formation, migration, and immigration, the population of the City of Toronto and surrounding municipalities increased by almost 190,000 people from 1931 to 1947, while less than 44,000 new dwelling units were built.[9] Only 2,245 of these units were built as emergency housing by the City of Toronto with assistance from the federal government.[10] The plunge in rental housing construction was particularly acute. Rental controls temporarily eased the crisis but did not address the shortage.[11] The extent of the crisis can be measured by the severity of the emergency measures undertaken to house people during and immediately after the war: families in acute need were placed in community centres, fire stations, police halls, army barracks, and hastily built emergency houses.[12]

Most importantly, there was a glaring lack of suitable apartments and houses that workers could afford. By 1944, prices of individual homes in major urban centres exceeded those at the peak of the 1929 boom.[13] A 1943 study by economist

O.J. Firestone of the housing difficulties of the lowest two-thirds by income among renters in Toronto showed that only 6.4 per cent were paying less than 20 per cent of their annual income in rent.[14] In 1947, housing researcher Humphrey Carver found that the 12 per cent of low-income households that made less than $1,000 a year were paying more than 40 per cent of their income in rent.[15] At least 10,000 families lived in overcrowded conditions of more than one person per room or in dilapidated dwellings. By war's end, 30,000 families in the city were "doubling up," with two or more families sharing a dwelling intended for one family.[16] The *Toronto Star* noted in 1943 that finding a place to live was a "nerve-wracking, heart breaking, time and money consuming experience" for low-income Torontonians.[17]

Unscrupulous landlords made matters worse. In a tight housing market, they had the leverage to demand high rents. Sometimes, they deliberately kept houses vacant in order to make speculative gains in the market. More often, they served notices to vacate and eviction orders for tenants who had difficulties paying the rent in order to secure more "reliable" tenancies such as families without children. By July 1945, 8,391 eviction notices were filed in the twelve largest cities in Canada while smaller communities looked at 15,000 to 20,000 eviction notices. Eric Gold, emergency shelter coordinator for the federal government, reported that landlords in Toronto were "descending during the night and physically forcing the tenants out."[18] Only with the development of a concerted working-class and war veteran protest movement around housing issues in Canada's major cities—often involving mass picket lines around houses to prevent repossession and eviction and angry demonstrations—did the government enact an eviction freeze.[19]

Problems with landlords continued during the late 1940s after the federal government loosened its rent control regulations, relaxing controls for new rental vacancies, which prompted landlords to evict existing occupants in order to hike their rents for new tenants. The Wartime Prices and Trade Board estimated that in Toronto "uncontrolled rents exceed the old rentals by about 100 per cent."[20] The Community Planning Association of Canada noted that over 1,000 families faced eviction in Toronto in January alone and that the numbers could reach 5,000 in the following months.[21] . . .

The housing situation improved somewhat as the chaotic effects of postwar reconstruction finally subsided. A significant number of new dwellings were built in response to critical demand, and there seems to have been general improvements in housing quality.[22] In cities across Canada, home ownership became an option for families with modest incomes who could rely on government home ownership incentive programs or employ extraordinary economic strategies such as having both parents work, taking in boarders, and working extra jobs.[23] However, the grave problem of affordable housing did not disappear in the 1950s and 1960s for those whose incomes were very low. In 1958, the Department of Public Welfare (DPW) in Toronto commented that it was receiving frequent calls from the public about public housing spaces. Numerous enquiries were fielded from British immigrants "amazed" at the lack of "council houses" in Toronto and despairing families from outside the city or those recently arrived who were ineligible for public housing. Department officials lamented that even though many of the requests came from families in houses "unfit for human habitation," they could do little but make futile referrals to the filled-to-capacity Regent Park.[24] The 1961 census reported that 12 per cent of dwellings in Toronto were still overcrowded and over 10,000 houses were in "need of major repair."[25] A 1966 DPW analysis of 2,783 families on welfare who changed addresses also found high rents, overcrowding, eviction or notice to vacate, and landlord dislike of children as key causes of housing hardship.[26] It was in this context that families applied to live in public housing projects.

Public housing initiatives such as Regent Park North (RPN) and Regent Park South (RPS), which totalled 2,139 units, and the few other developments built in the Toronto area in the

City of Toronto Archives, Fonds 2028, Item 132.

First tenants of brick row houses in Regent Park North, April 1949.

1940s–60s, fell far short of the ongoing demand for affordable housing. The 1959 Interim Housing Committee report of the Metropolitan Toronto Housing Authority (MTHA) estimated that there was a need for 10,000 to 15,000 more subsidized units in the region.[27] In all of Metro Toronto, there were only 4,489 such spaces.[28]

Low-income residents in the neighbourhoods cleared for rebuilding had first priority in public housing. Other tenant selection guidelines centred on income, existing housing quality, and veteran status. . . . Even for families clearly eligible and accepted in principle for public housing, an often-interminable wait followed. In a sample of 59 RPN tenant case files, families had waited from one month to five years for a place in the project, with a mean average of two years. By the time a unit became available, many applicants had already moved several times; many had

probably just given up hope for a publicly assisted place.[29] Some complained: "Just a few lines to find out if you could please help me. I have not phoned too often cause I thought you were too busy with other people. I have had my application in since 1962 [three years] but I have not heard nothing [*sic*] from you people. What is the matter, I do not no [*sic*] . . . I just have to get out of here for my kid's sake."[30]

In the 1960s, more and more applications for public housing appear to have been motivated by women's desire to escape from abusive men. Robert Bradley, RPN manager, claimed that applications from "broken families," 98 per cent of them women and the majority fleeing abuse, increased over 100 per cent in 1965.[31] It was for women in situations like this that in 1967 the MTHA established an emergency hostel for women and children who were being evicted or were fleeing abuse. In addition to providing some security for families for a short period (average stay was 13 days), the hostel helped them find spots in both the private rental market and public housing. In its first year, it assisted over 400 women and 1,300 children. Approximately 30 per cent were housed for "domestic problems."[32]

The strategies employed by low-income families to achieve what Robert Murdie and Carlos Teixeira term a "comfortable neighbourhood and appropriate housing"[33] varied considerably among ethnic groups in postwar Toronto. Toronto was the single largest destination of immigrants to Canada in the post-1945 period; yet until the 1970s, the vast majority of public housing applicants and residents in English Canada were of Anglo-Canadian origin.[34] Only in the 1970s and 1980s did larger numbers of Caribbean and Asian families opt for state-assisted housing in Toronto.[35] The single largest immigrant populations to Toronto before the 1970s, the Italians and Portuguese, adopted a very different approach to securing housing. Investing substantial cultural and economic importance in home ownership and close-knit, ethnic neighbourhoods, first in the area due west of the city centre and later in several distinct ethnic suburban enclaves, Italian and Portuguese families relied on extensive community and family ties as well as considerable economic sacrifice to become homeowners. More often than not, this meant relying on private community sources of finance, renting out a part of the owned house to pay the mortgage, living in boarding houses in the first years after arriving in the city, purposely doubling or tripling up with other families to save money, and devoting a disproportionate amount of income to home purchases.[36] . . .

Nevertheless, by the mid-1960s, as Kevin Brushett has thoroughly documented, the housing crisis had come "full circle"[37] for many underprivileged families. Shortages for low-income Torontonians were once again rampant, rents were spiralling, and evictions were increasing. City officials warned migrants, especially the growing numbers of families from the Maritime provinces seeking work in industrial Toronto,

to stay home.[38] Excepting southern European immigrants, the dream of home ownership increasingly became just that for many. Homeowners in Toronto decreased from 71 per cent of occupied dwellings in 1951 to 56 per cent in 1981.[39] Shelter costs also became increasingly burdensome for poor families. In 1962, the *Toronto Star* noted that there were still "Thousands Caught in High-Rent Trap."[40] In 1965, a City of Toronto housing policy committee report argued that fully 20 per cent of the city's families "were unable with their own resources, to provide decent, safe and sanitary housing."[41] A 1966 study of 411 applications to RPN found 62 per cent paying more than 30 per cent of their income towards rent.[42]

Housing affordability problems for those on the bottom rung of the socio-economic ladder persisted into the 1970s. In 1972, 36.9 per cent of Family Benefits (welfare) recipients were paying above 30 per cent of their incomes in rent, while 55.6 per cent were paying more for shelter costs than the shelter allowances granted as part of welfare benefits.[43] *The Rent Race*, a 1974 study by the Social Planning Council of Metropolitan Toronto, verified that social assistance recipients were particularly hard hit by the housing crunch: 30 per cent of those that rented paid more than half their income in rent; 50 per cent lived in substandard housing; 70 per cent paid more in rent than the shelter allowance granted by welfare payments.[44] A study by the same organization in 1981 confirmed that increased housing costs coupled with the inadequacy of shelter allowances for welfare recipients had made living standards considerably worse.[45]

It comes as little surprise then that more and more families on social assistance were applying for public housing, as Figure 5.1 demonstrates. By the 1980s, various measures of housing need confirmed that housing affordability problems worsened for the most disadvantaged. Vacancy rates in Toronto during the 1980s averaged 1 per cent—far below the 3 per cent standard considered to be reasonably advantageous for tenants.[46] In Canada as a whole, the percentage of renters paying more than 30 per cent of their income in rent rose from 23 per cent in 1976 to 27 per cent

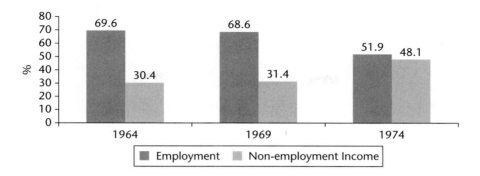

FIGURE 5.1 | Family Housing Applications—MTHA—According to Family Income Source, 1964

Source: Chart adapted from figures in CTA, HAT, RG 28, series B, box 27, file: Housing Registry of Metropolitan Toronto, 1967–8, Quarterly Report of Family Housing Applications, 31 December 1964; CTA, HAT, RG 28, series B, box 27, file: Housing Registry of Metropolitan Toronto 1969, Report of a Survey of Family Housing Applications on File with the Housing Registry of Metropolitan Toronto and Ontario Housing Corporation, 1 May 1969; MTA, MTHA, box 6, file 2.02, Ontario Housing Corporation Housing Registry, "Second Quarter 1974, Applications by Income Source," Table III. Non-employment income includes the following forms of state assistance: welfare, mother's allowance, Department of Veteran's Affairs Pension, Workmen's Compensation, retirement pension, and Old Age Security.

in 1986.[47] In Ontario, renters in core need—those paying more than 30 per cent of their income for shelter—increased by 44 per cent between 1988 and 1991.[48] The Ontario government's Social Assistance Review Committee found that, in Toronto, Ottawa, Hamilton, and Waterloo, more than 70 per cent of social assistance recipients directed more than 40 per cent of their incomes towards rental payments in 1986.[49] As Pierre Filion and Trudi Bunting note, renters, particularly single women with children, were hardest hit by the affordability crunch in the 1980s.[50] It was obscenely incongruous that at the same time as the United Nations declared 1987 International Year for the Homeless, homelessness in Toronto reached frightening levels.[51]

By the 1990s, vacancy rates of less than 1 per cent, high house prices, rental increases twice the rate of inflation, an almost complete lack of rental unit construction, unemployment, government cuts to income distribution programs, and the relaxation of rental controls were intensifying the crisis. This affected all low-income families, including particular recent immigrant groups and refugees who generally had larger families and lower incomes and who coped with racial discrimination in labour and housing markets.[52] Afro-Caribbean immigrants, for example, with a larger proportion of single woman–headed families suffered a double burden in the housing market: they were subject to the oppressive racial and gendered positions of landlords (public and private) as well as the "constrained choice" in housing opportunity owing to their low incomes.[53] By the closing years of the 1990s, record numbers of families, including escalating numbers of single parents, welfare recipients, and poor, visible-minority immigrants, were applying for public housing.

That there was a social necessity for affordable housing in Toronto was evident in the sheer numbers of people who sought assisted housing, an imprecise but useful indicator of housing need. Given the stigma attached to public housing as a "last resort," especially since the 1960s, these numbers show the extent of the problem for those most in need. We can assume that the figures somewhat underestimate the actual number of families in need, since they do not include those people who were either unaware of the state-assisted housing option or believed that it was not possible to obtain a space. As Figure 5.2 illustrates, the 1950s and 1960s saw mounting numbers of households seeking government assistance. Even before RPN had been

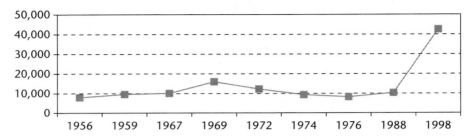

FIGURE 5.2 | Public Housing Waiting Lists—Metropolitan Toronto/Toronto, No. of Families

Source: Chart adapted from the following figures: 1956, RG 28, HAT, series B, box 1, file: A, B 1948–1959, Frank Dearlove to Gordon Ames, 10 February 1956; 1959: MTHA, Regent Park South Annual Report (Toronto, 1960), n.p.; 1967 and 1969: MTHA, "Report on Survey of Family Housing Applications on File" (Toronto, June 1969), 1; 1972 and 1974: MTA, MTHA, RG 5.1, box 6, file 2.02, vol. 9, Summary of Family Applications December 1972–June 1974; 1976: MTA, MTHA, RG 5.1, vol. 16, box 4, file 2, Establishing a Central Registry for MTO, 1976; 1988: John Sewell, "Trapped by Inaction," *Now Magazine*, no. 299 (29 September–5 October 1988): 11; Housing Connections Central Registry Report cited in Jack Lakey, "22-Year Wait for Some Low-Cost Housing," *Toronto Star*, 13 July 1998, B5.

completed in 1957, there were 7,000 applications on file for the project. From the inception of the waiting list for RPS in 1957 to the end of 1959, the MTHA received 13,527 inquiries.[54] By 1959, the waiting list for these units was almost 10,000 names long. By 1970, 38 employees of the Metro Toronto housing registry office were receiving 10,000 calls a month and 2,000 new applications a month. Applications on file reached 16,000 in 1969.[55]

The figures declined somewhat in the 1970s and then shot up dramatically again in the late 1980s and 1990s. Explanations for the decline in the 1970s and early 1980s are only suggestive: there was an expanding availability of state-assisted options from the mid-1970s to mid-1980s,[56] and vacancy rates in the rental market were consistently above the 3 per cent level.[57] In September 1988, 10,400 families, comprising 38,000 people, were waiting for the eight units that opened each day. The situation was so critical at this point that the 1940s predicament of doubling-up resurfaced within public housing itself even though MTHA guidelines strictly prohibited the practice. John Sewell estimates that,

in 1988, 25,000 people were living "unofficially" in public housing in Toronto in addition to the official resident numbers of 100,000.[58]

By 1991, there were 33,000 rent-geared-to-income units in Metro Toronto's public housing system. However, demand for assisted housing always outstripped the limited supply. In 1998, assuming they started at the bottom of the list, families requiring a four-bedroom apartment in MTHA would have to wait an average of 21.8 years for a spot, while the wait for a two-bedroom apartment was 12.9 years.[59] The shelter crisis in Canada's largest city once again resembled the critical war years, except this time the economy was in recession, living standards were deteriorating, and governments at all levels were not expanding, but rather retracting their commitments to assist families in need.

Stories of Housing Need

We know that Toronto experienced a crisis of low-income housing availability and affordability in the postwar period, but we know little of the individual stories and experiences of the actual families who lived through this bleak time. Fortunately, the archival repositories contain numerous case files for public housing residents, letters by prospective tenants, and written comments on both these groups by housing authority officials. Along with oral testimony, these valuable sources allow us to recover some aspects of the lives of the hitherto marginalized low-income families who searched for decent dwelling spaces.[60] This approach promises, as Cynthia Comacchio puts it, to "corroborate historic trends, placing real human beings and real lives into the statisticians' reports."[61]

Despite a general boom in the economy with little unemployment until the 1970s, there was still a considerable proportion of the working population that searched in vain for affordable dwelling opportunities in the postwar period. Housing need would intensify during the extended economic crisis that Canada and other advanced economies would undergo from the 1970s onwards. Various barriers to economic and social mobility obtained: a marked shift from stable, unionized and well-paid employment to increasingly low-wage, casual jobs, inadequate welfare rates, relatively high rents, lack of childcare, and residential discrimination.[62] The simple lack of affordable living space was the primary factor in housing hardship, but this was often complicated by secondary factors such as poor housing environments, overcrowding, and landlord conduct. In fact, usually tenants coped with a number of overlapping difficulties.

Take Ernest Lambert, a returned soldier who worked as a salesman at Eaton's department store for $63 a week, a relatively good salary in the 1950s. With two young daughters, he and his wife were living in a two-room apartment with no bathroom and a shared kitchen when they received a notice to vacate from the landlord in 1953.[63] In 1952, Zachary Thompson, a clerk with the City of Toronto, was served with a notice to vacate his two-room apartment, with shared kitchen and bathroom, along with his wife and four children.[64] Simon Petersen, a laid-off letter carrier, was on unemployment insurance, living with his wife and daughter in a one-room flat

with no kitchen and a shared bath, when they filled out the application for RP; they were paying over 40 per cent of their income in rent.[65] One single working mother with three children wrote RPN officials in 1968 saying the rising cost of living and rents in particular (she paid just under 50 per cent of her income in rent) were forcing her on to welfare since her single salary just could not pay the rent as well as clothes and dental bills for her children: "Am willing to work. I certainly do not drink my money, but the situation is getting worse."[66] Taida Hambleton, her sister, and her parents arrived from war-torn Europe in 1950. They applied to RP because "it was the only independent and separate apartment [where] my parents found. . . . they could afford the rent."[67] Larry Quinto's parents and his two sisters also found public housing a viable option. Larry's father was a lineman at the huge Massey Ferguson plant, and his mother worked as a cook in a local diner. He recalls, "We moved because of the affordable housing, and the project was new, and close to schools."[68]

It was not unknown for people to apply for public housing after losing their houses or businesses to the finance companies. This happened to Ralph Porter, an unemployed 56-year-old father of two. Unable to make his mortgage payments, he applied to and was accepted by RPN.[69] Some families came to RPN unable to pay debts incurred for furniture and cars purchased during better economic times.[70] Dave Norris, his wife, and his four kids had a similar experience. His cleaning business in Toronto went bankrupt, leaving the family in desperate straits. In 1964, they lucked out and received a spot in RP with little wait. He remembered, "I don't really think that we had to but my wife insisted. She said we couldn't afford to live anywhere else."[71]

Families frequently complained that landlords disliked families with children and refused to rent dwellings to them.[72] One early RPN tenant recalled landlords in the 1940s and 1950s saying, ". . . we can't take you," when prospective tenants told them they had children.[73] Larry Furlan, a self-employed bailiff with three kids, was sharing a four-room duplex with another family when the landlord asked him to leave because "children not wanted."[74] Steve Rohan, a shipper and receiver, applied to RP because his wife was pregnant with their third child; they feared that no landlord would rent to them. Nancy Boudreau, a 21-year-old mother of two whose husband worked as a clerk, stated in her 1961 application to RP that the reason she was applying was that "landlords will not take children."[75] One family, citing landlord obstinacy with children, wrote the mayor for help, signing their letter, "We remain a despaired Family of Seven."[76] In 1965, Marian Hartley, a single mother with six children, wrote a heartfelt letter to RPN manager Robert Bradley, affirming, "I have been looking for a place but it is so hard with 6 children, soon as you tell anybody you have 6 children you might as well stay on the sidewalk than to go ask for a place."[77]

Unsanitary, rundown living quarters were also a widespread concern. Theresa and Richard Lampston wrote the Housing Authority of Toronto (HAT), pleading with them to provide healthy accommodations for their two children. The inspection report in their apartment noted an open sewer trap on the kitchen floor, few windows, and an unfavourable location next to a boiler room.[78] Marie Corbeil, who lived with her husband and four children in a badly maintained east Toronto house, articulately described in a letter to housing authorities her family's gloomy housing state:

> The house is very hard to heat and we are cold all the time. There are no heat vents in either kitchen and we have both to turn on gas stoves to heat the kitchen making both our heat (which is at 80–85 degrees all the time) and our gas bill too high and then we are still not warm. The children have running noses since we moved in and my 3-month old girl caught a bad cough and kept bringing up her milk. The bills are piling up and we are having a hard time to keep up. . . . We have been looking for another place but no one is interested in our four children.[79]

. . . Families in the very worst shelter situations risked losing their children to the Children's Aid Society (CAS), the state agency responsible for "neglected" children. One woman beseeched the Toronto Housing Authority (THA) for a vacancy, citing a CAS threat to take her children into care unless she provided a letter stating she had a place in public housing.[80] Certain families willingly gave up their children to foster parents while they sorted out decent accommodation. This extreme predicament is described in the following exchange between an agency official and the father of the family:

> When your children were put into the foster home, was it you who arranged it?
>
> Oh yes, I had to arrange it myself . . .
>
> Why did your children have to leave your place?
>
> Well, we didn't have the housing accommodation at the time, to get someone to come in and look after them at home. The only solution at the time was to have them placed in foster homes—until such time as we could take care of them ourselves.
>
> The place where you were living in at that time wasn't equipped to deal with this kind of problem?
>
> Well, the place we were living in at the time wasn't equipped for anything. Definitely we couldn't get anyone to come in and help out. . . . It was what you might call a lean-to—in fact it has been described as a garage. It consisted of one room roughly 20 feet long by 10 feet wide, and that's about all except there was a small water closet in an additional lean-to.[81]

In the years before state-provided health insurance, medical problems could severely compound general housing difficulties. Walter Davies worked for 25 years in the British coalmines. He took sick after he immigrated to Toronto and was forced to rely on $21 a week from Unemployment Insurance: "[I] never knew a day's sickness till this last two years. . . . I'd like to say that honestly, two years I had lots of trouble, lots of sickness, my expenses have been very heavy and my banking account happens to be nil." As the hospital bills and living expenses mounted, the family began a desperate search for accommodation.[82] David Blackmore's family migrated from the East Coast province of Newfoundland with similar impediments to decent shelter. With five children and a father suffering from persistent medical problems, he moved to Toronto in search of "greater economic opportunities" in the late 1950s. After a lengthy period on the waiting list, they eventually landed a unit at RP.[83] The family of Al Ford, a maintenance worker, lived in a five-room house on the outskirts of RP when the landlord gave them a notice to vacate. His wife and their four-year-old daughter suffered from medical conditions. Their daughter had chronic tonsillitis and Osgood Shlatter's disease, prompting their doctor to write a letter recommending them for admission to RP.[84] Hazel Meere, one of the first residents to move into RP, described for *Maclean's* magazine how housing conditions could be worsened by illness. During the 1930s, her family had relied on relief for long stretches and in a period of 22 years had moved eight separate times. When her husband, Albert, contracted tuberculosis in the late 1940s, the family of eight struggled in vain for three years to find a healthy dwelling before they found a place in RP.[85]

If public housing were a viable choice for the working poor needing housing, it would also be a central option for those living on the minimal incomes of social assistance payments. Scrambling to find stable housing can be a singularly disconcerting experience for people on social assistance payments, principally for single-parent families. As Margaret Little aptly puts it, "[w]ithout stable housing, your life is thrown into constant upheaval, and life is reduced to a desperate scramble to find shelter: temporary, permanent, good or bad. Health suffers and damages your ability to make any long-term plans."[86] Josephine Thomas, a widow with one son and one daughter, had to pester the THA every month, asking for a spot in RP. She described the overcrowded and unsanitary conditions of the large house her family was occupying along with 17 other people and articulated the desperate plight of many families on welfare: "I need a place for my kids. . . . I sincerely hope you will do something for me as I am alone with no relatives anywhere to help me. I have to depend on welfare now as my husband left no insurances of

any kind at all. . . . I hope you will help me in the near future."[87] When Sandy Elster and her husband separated, her husband refused to provide support. She and her four children, surviving on welfare and Mother's Allowance, had few choices but to apply for public housing.[88] When she wrote the authorities requesting a public housing unit, Janice Bukowski, an abandoned spouse with five children, was living in an unwinterized cottage.[89] Neil Ruttle's family found themselves in a similarly thorny situation. With five brothers and two sisters, he remembers the chaotic situation of his father's employment and, after his parents' separation and their move into RP, the difficulties of making do on the limited resources of welfare.[90]

Wife abuse also forced families of women and children to apply for public housing. Cathy Lismer wrote Robert Bradley, RPN manager, in 1966 declaring that she had no choice but to apply for an apartment in RP for herself and her two children: "I will have to separate from my husband because of his physical cruelty and mental cruelty, which is praying [*sic*] on my health. . . . I do not want this for a long period but for a year or two as I am desperate in order to keep working and be of less or no bother to Welfare. All I wish is to stand on my own feet."[91] A growing awareness of violence against women and an expansion of support services, including special housing units, in the 1970s to 1990s nonetheless left much to be desired in terms of availability and accessibility to housing units. Joyce and her four kids, living in a tiny, cockroach-infested flat in the late 1990s, dreamed of a subsidized unit, especially since it was one means of fleeing her abusive partner. The situation was so critical that Joyce said, "I would be willing to go back with him for a few months and get beat up a few times if it meant I would qualify for the special needs list [to facilitate a public housing spot]. If I could keep the abuse to my bedroom, so my kids couldn't see it, I'd do it."[92]

In the 1960s and 1970s, the shift in the profile of Toronto's immigrants from largely white Europeans to visible-minority populations from Asia, Africa, and the Caribbean would also create demand for low-income housing.[93] . . .

John Kumar's family—two parents and three children—immigrated from Tanzania and were forced to tackle two overlapping problems: in addition to having their life savings stolen when they arrived in the country, they had to "build their life over again . . . in a totally hostile environment."[94]

Racial discrimination would become a key factor in housing need in the 1980s and 1990s, but it existed before this period and often intersected with gender oppression. George Fallis and Alex Murray argue convincingly that in a low-vacancy market, landlords can discriminate against those considered to be unreliable tenants: "families with children, especially single-parent families, those with psychological disabilities, or those without long job histories. . . . Landlords can more readily exercise their racial, religious, or other prejudices."[95] During the slum clearance and relocation plans for RPS in the mid-1950s, one family of "New Canadians" told interviewers that discrimination in the housing market influenced their choice of a place to live.[96] John Talbot wrote the HAT in 1966 detailing the racial discrimination his family faced in the housing market. He would frequently answer advertisements for rental vacancies, but no landlord would offer his family a spot. He concluded it was because of "their colour."[97] As Sylvia Novac and Frances Henry have documented, both "overt" and "mediated" cases of outright racial discrimination directed towards immigrant women and men in Toronto continued through the 1990s.[98]

Discriminatory professional practices also shaped some immigrants' housing choices. V.G. Pande arrived in Canada with a PhD and experience as a teacher, guidance counsellor, and administrator. He was eventually able to redevelop his professional career, but the lack of job opportunities on his first arrival to Canada in the early 1970s rendered public housing a practical option.[99] Dr Thompson T. Egbo-Egbo had trained as a physician in Nigeria. After immigrating, his housing options were circumscribed by the near impossibility of ever practising medicine again. He wrote more generally of this common immigrant experience: "Many residents [of RP] are immigrants who bring considerable skills with them. In their country, they were tradespeople and professionals such as teachers, lawyers or physicians. It can be very difficult to re-enter one's field here. Due to 'no Canadian experience,' many immigrants are faced with going back to school and taking expensive exams."[100]

Conclusions

Housing hardship among working families in postwar Toronto was shaped by a variety of broad social and economic developments, such as changes in employment structure, the development of the welfare state, single-parent family formation, and immigration, as well as more specific factors on the demand and supply sides of housing. From the 1940s to 1990s, the single most important feature on the demand side was low financial resources among the working poor and social assistance recipients. Low incomes were complicated by secondary factors such as family size, household size, the particular requirements of immigrants, medical problems, and social dilemmas within the family. On the supply side, the 1940s and early 1950s witnessed absolute dwelling shortages, high rents, low vacancies for rental units, poor-quality dwellings, oppressive landlord practices, and a disruptive slum clearance and rebuilding program. Physical housing quality issues and absolute shelter scarcity became less important by the late 1950s, although the late 1990s saw almost zero growth in rental unit construction. By the last years of the century, high house prices and rents, low vacancy rates, and a dwindling public sector had hastened the latest emergency situation.

Although the specific national and local social formations,[101] especially the differing interventionist strategies of the state, the respective strength of the organized workers' movement, and the vagaries of specific economies, have determined differences in the extent and timing of the housing crisis and, more generally, social marginalization among low-income families, developments in Toronto mirrored those in many other Canadian and American cities in the

1945–90 period. In Canada and the United States in the two decades after the war, sustained economic growth, government incentives, and a desire to be an owner-occupier allowed many working families to purchase or build their own homes, although there was always a sizable minority of poor families who struggled to find affordable accommodation in urban areas.[102] From the 1970s to the 1990s, housing affordability problems in urban areas in both countries worsened considerably among low-income families, especially those led by single women and some new immigrants.[103] . . .

The stories of families interested in public housing reveal a rich array of people and situations relating to housing hardship. In the early period, the vast majority of these families were fully employed workers, confronting serious housing availability and affordability issues. Yet, even in the later decades, families with employment found public housing a suitable shelter alternative, especially if they also endured other social and economic hurdles, such as health problems and racial discrimination. Those families relying on the state for their incomes, of course, faced more urgent housing need since state benefits were always nominal. More than anything, the stories of housing need demonstrate that in the midst of plenty, it was always a struggle for low-income families to find a decent place to live. As Thelma Pilkey earnestly recalled, ". . . it was tough on everybody."[104]

Endnotes

1   Thelma Pilkey, interview by author, Lakefield, ON, tape-recorded, 21 March 1996.

2   While Canada consistently placed first on the United Nations (UN) Human Development index in the late 1990s, it failed to place in the top 10 countries on the UN human poverty index. Andrew Jackson and David Robinson with Bob Baldwin and Cindy Wiggins, *Falling Behind: The State of Working Canada, 2000* (Ottawa, 2000), chap. 1. Moreover, the ratio of social spending to overall government spending has fallen significantly in recent decades. Willem Adema, "Net Social Expenditure," 2nd edn, Labour Market and Social Policy—Occasional Papers No. 52, Paris: OECD, 2001, Tables 7 and A2.1.

3   According to Tom Carter, 63 per cent of households in Canada were owner occupied by 1993, paying on average only 9.5 per cent of their income for shelter. Renters were less well off, but 35 per cent could still afford the mortgage payments on an average two to three bedroom home. Nevertheless, at least 12 per cent or more than 1 million households were living in housing considered officially "unacceptable." Tom Carter, "Current Practices for Procuring Affordable Housing: The Canadian Context," *Housing Policy Debate* 8 (1997): 593. An illuminating discussion of the importance of house and home can be found in Richard Harris, "Housing," in Trudi Bunting and Pierre Filion, eds, *Canadian Cities in Transition: The Twenty-first Century*, 2nd edn (Toronto, 2000), 380–403.

4   Richard Harris, "More American Than the United States: Housing in Urban Canada in the Twentieth Century," *Journal of Urban History* 26 (2001): 470–1.

In other national contexts, consult Gwendolyn Wright, *Building the Dream: A Social History of Housing* (New York, 1981); Seán Damer, *From Moorepark to 'Wine Alley': The Rise and Fall of a Glasgow Housing Scheme* (Edinburgh, 1989), chap. 3; David Widgery, *Some Lives! A GP's East End* (London, 1991).

5   There is abundant evidence that a growing gap existed between the "haves" and "have nots" between the 1970s and 1990s. See Trudi Bunting, "Social Differentiation in Canadian Cities," in Trudi Bunting and Pierre Filion, eds, *Canadian Cities in Transition*, 1st edn (Toronto, 1991), 286–312; Monica Townson, *A Report Card on Women and Poverty* (Ottawa, 2000). The loss of stable, well-paid manufacturing jobs and their replacement by various forms of casual and part-time work are discussed in Henry Veltmeyer and James Sacouman, "The Political Economy of Part-Time Work," *Studies in Political Economy* 56 (Summer 1998): 115–44. For the long-term decline in Canadian capitalism, see Murray E.G. Smith and K.W. Taylor, "Profitability Crisis and the Erosion of Popular Prosperity: The Canadian Economy, 1947–91," *Studies in Political Economy* 49 (Spring 1996): 101–30. On social polarization *within* public housing, note Robert Murdie, "Social Polarization and Public Housing in Canada: A Case Study of the Metropolitan Toronto Housing Authority," in Frances Frisken, ed., *The Changing Canadian Metropolis: A Public Policy Perspective*, vol. 1 (Berkeley, CA, and Toronto, 1994), 303–33.

6   For a summary of these works, see Alan Sears, "The 'Lean' State and Capitalist Restructuring: Towards a

Theoretical Account," *Studies in Political Economy* 60 (Summer 1999): 94–7.

7   It is not my intention to revisit the lively and important methodological debates that swirled in the 1980s between advocates of oral and social science history. Suffice it to say that recently there has been an acceptance of a multiplicity of approaches as well an increasing specialization of oral and social science history into their own discrete realms of historical practice. See Louise Tilly, "People's History and Social Science History," *Social Science History* 7 (Fall 1983): 457–74, reprinted in *International Journal of Oral History* 6 (February 1985): 5–17; see the same issue of the journal for responses by Paul Thompson, Luisa Paserini, Isabelle Bertaux-Wiame, and Alessandro Portelli (19–39), the counter-response of Louis Tilly (40–2), and concluding comments by Ronald Grele (42–6). A recent oral history of laid-off workers in Pennsylvania's Anthracite region by Thomas Dublin and Walter Licht vividly shows how oral history can illuminate the more personal aspects of economic misery: "Gender and Economic Decline: The Pennsylvania Anthracite Region, 1920–1970," *Oral History Review* 27 (Winter/Spring 2000): 81–98.

8   Sean Purdy, "From Place of Hope to Outcast Space: Territorial Regulation and Tenant Resistance in Regent Park Housing Project, 1949–2001" (PhD diss., Queen's University, 2003).

9   City of Toronto Archives (CTA), Toronto Reconstruction Council/Civic Advisory Commission (TRC), RG 249, box 4, file 7, Civic Advisory Council, City of Toronto, Metropolitan Problems Committee, Tables 1–2: Population Growth and Housing Provision for Suburban Municipalities in the Toronto Area, by Years, 1931–1947; and Population Growth and Housing Provision for the City of Toronto, by Years, 1931–1947.

10   CTA, RG 28, Housing Authority of Toronto (HAT), series B, box 25, file: RP North 1947–66 General, Emergency Housing: Projects Undertaken or Financially Assisted by City of Toronto, 1947.

11   John Bacher, *Keeping to the Marketplace: The Evolution of Canadian Housing Policy* (Montreal and Kingston, 1993), 163.

12   Bacher, *Keeping to the Marketplace*, 178. As Bacher details, these emergency housing units would last until the 1960s, housing what were deemed "problem" families. In addition to being substandard, they were managed like private rental housing, effectively making the City of Toronto a "slum" landlord itself (187–8).

13   Bacher, *Keeping to the Marketplace*, 126.

14   Cited in ibid., 169.

15   Humphrey Carver, *Houses for Canadians: A Study of Housing Problems in the Toronto Area* (Toronto, 1948), 75.

16   Kevin Brushett, "Blots on the Face of the City: The Politics of Slum Housing and Urban Renewal in Toronto, 1940–1970" (PhD diss., Queen's University, 2001), 51; and Humphrey Carver, "Toronto in the Housing Crisis," *Planning Action*, October 1947, 246.

17   "Voice of the People, House Hunting," *Toronto Star*, 20 August 1943, 6; also quoted in Brushett, "Blots on the Face of the City," 51.

18   Bacher, *Keeping to the Marketplace*, 174. For a full discussion of wartime shortages, see Brushett, "Blots on the Face of the City," 49–59.

19   Bacher, *Keeping to the Marketplace*, 174–5. On housing protest movements, see Purdy, "Building Homes, Building Citizens," 499–504; Wade, *Houses for All*, chaps 3–4; and Marc Choko, *Crises du logement à Montréal* (Montreal, 1980). For a broad survey of housing struggles in the United States, see Peter Marcuse, "Housing Movements in the United States," *Housing, Theory and Society* 6 (1999): 67–86. For a ground-breaking study of the persistent struggles of public housing tenants, especially black women in Baltimore, consult Rhonda Y. Williams, "Living Just Enough in the City: Change and Activism in Baltimore's Public Housing, 1940–1980" (PhD diss., University of Pennsylvania, 1998).

20   Bacher, *Keeping to the Marketplace*, 197, 193.

21   Community Planning Association of Canada, *Bulletin*, 1 March 1949, 1.

22   On improvements in housing quality, see John Sewell, *Houses and Homes: Housing for Canadians* (Toronto, 1994), 39.

23   Alvin Finkel, *Our Lives: Canada after 1945* (Toronto, 1997), 45.

24   Metropolitan Toronto Archives (MTA), Department of Public Welfare (DPW), RG 5.1, box 2, file 2, vol. 4, Metropolitan Toronto, Department of Public Welfare, Comparative Monthly Operational and Statistical Report, May 1958, 1.

25   Average calculated by author. Dominion Bureau of Statistics, "Census Metropolitan Area of Toronto," *Census of Canada 1961* (Ottawa, 1961).

26   MTA, DPW, RG 5.1, box 8, file 2.09, vol. 2, Department of Public Welfare, Analysis of Questionnaires re: Leaving Accommodation as reported by Recipients of Welfare Assistance, 1965. A 1969 study of applications for public housing revealed the same reasons for housing need: 36.6 per cent found the rent too high; 40.2 per cent lived in overcrowded or substandard dwellings; 10 per cent moved because their house was being sold or re-rented; and just over 5 per cent suffered health problems. Metropolitan Toronto Housing Authority (MTHA), *Report on Survey of Family Housing Applications on File* (Toronto, June 1969), Table 4.

27   MTHA, *Annual Report 1959* (Toronto, 1959), n.p.

28   MTHA, *Metropolitan Toronto Interim Housing Committee Report* (Toronto, 1959), n.p.; and "End the

Buck Passing on Housing," *Toronto Star*, 3 December 1959, 4.

29 CTA, HAT, RG 28, series B, box 29, file no. 2, boxes 29–30. This figure was based on 59 tenant case files where evidence existed of waiting time. Calculations by the author. Albert Rose claimed in 1969 that the wait for a vacancy in Ontario public housing was from six months to two years. See "Brave New Worlds," in Michael Wheeler, *Housing Crisis and Public Policy*, Special Project on Social Aspects of Low-Income Housing, Conference of Mayors and Municipalities, 1967 (Canadian Welfare Council, 1967), 132.

30 CTA, HAT, RG 28, series B, box 9, file: 1965–1968 H, M.H. to Robert Bradley, 9 August 1965.

31 CTA, HAT, RG 28, series B, box 8, file: 1965–1968 C, Robert Bradley to Alfred De Manche, Editor, *Canadian Register*, 25 August 1965.

32 CTA, HAT, RG 28, series B, box 9, files "Hostel Reports 1966–1967," Manager to Robert Bradley, 30 November 1967, and "1968 Hostel Self-Improvement Course," Robert Bradley to RF, 1 March 1968.

33 Robert A. Murdie and Carlos Teixeira, "Towards a Comfortable Neighbourhood and Appropriate Housing: Immigrant Experiences in Toronto," Centre for Excellence in Research on Immigration and Settlement, Working Paper No. 10, 1999.

34 Sewell, *Houses and Homes*, chap. 8.

35 Sean Purdy, "'Ripped Off' by the System: Housing Policy, Poverty and Territorial Stigmatization in Regent Park Housing Project, 1951–1991," *Labour/ Le Travail*, no. 52 (Fall 2003), 45–108, contains a detailed statistical analysis of various socio-economic indicators, including ethnic origin.

36 A thorough synthesis of the literature on immigrant families and home ownership in Toronto during the 1950s and 1960s can be found in Murdie and Teixeira, "Towards a Comfortable Neighbourhood," 20–5. See also Franca Iacovetta, *Such Hardworking People: Italian Immigrants in Postwar Toronto* (Toronto, 1993), ix, chap. 6.

37 Brushett, "Blots on the Face of the City," 353.

38 Ibid.

39 Dominion Bureau of Statistics, "Metropolitan Toronto Region," *Census of Canada*, 1951–1981 (Ottawa, 1951–81). On home affordability in Ontario, see George Fallis, *Housing Programs and Income Distribution in Ontario* (Toronto, 1980), 36. On immigrants and home ownership, see E. Moore and B. Ray, "Access to Homeownership among Immigrant Groups in Canada," *Canadian Review of Sociology and Anthropology* 28 (1991): 1–27; and Harris, "Housing," 390.

40 Robert Cochrane, "Thousands Caught in High Rent Trap," *Toronto Star*, 17 March 1962, 17.

41 Cited in James Lemon, *Toronto Since 1918: An Illustrated History* (Toronto, 1985), 126. Note also

Desmond Morton and Leon Kumove, *Housing: The Predictable Crisis* (Toronto, 1967), 2.

42 CTA, HAT, RG 28, series B, box 32, file: Housing Authority Statistics, 1965–1968, HAT, Analysis of Investigated Applications—Ratio of Rent Paid to Income.

43 Ministry of Community and Social Services, "Housing and Social Policy," brief prepared for the Ontario Advisory Task Force on Housing Policy, 1973, Tables 12 and 13. James Struthers has thoroughly shown that welfare benefits were always less than adequate in Toronto even in the 1960s and 1970s during the federal government's US-inspired "War on Poverty": *The Limits of Affluence: Welfare in Ontario, 1920–1970* (Toronto, 1994), chaps 7–8.

44 MTA, Social Planning Council of Metropolitan Toronto (SPCMT), RG 5.1, file 2.02, box 6, vol. 9, "Summary of the Rent Race," 1–2. For more data on the worsening situation of the very poor, note Jeffrey Patterson and Patricia Streich, *A Review of Canadian Social Housing Policy* (Toronto, 1977). For the affordability problems of renters in Canada as a whole, see Sewell, *Houses and Homes*, chap. 2.

45 MTA, SPCMT, RG 5.1, file 49, box 121, ". . . And the Poor Get Poorer: A Study of Social Welfare Programs in Ontario," 19 May 1981, 2–4.

46 Sewell, *Houses and Homes*, 34.

47 David Hulchanski, *Canada's Housing and Housing Policy: An Introduction* (Vancouver, 1988), 9.

48 J.D. Hulchanski, "The Use of Housing Expenditure-to-Income Ratios: Origins, Evolution and Implications," Ontario Human Rights Commission, Background Paper No. 2, 1994, 21.

49 Social Assistance Review Committee, *Transitions: Executive Summary* (Toronto, 1988).

50 Pierre Filion and Trudi Bunting, *Affordability of Housing*, Focus on Canada series (Ottawa, 1989).

51 Sewell, *Houses and Homes*, chap. 11; and Bacher, *Keeping to the Marketplace*, 259–63.

52 Murdie and Teixeira, "Towards a Comfortable Neighbourhood"; Eric Fong and Kumiko Shibuya, "The Spatial Separation of the Poor in Canadian Cities," *Demography* 37 (November 2000), Table 1; and Mark Edward Pfeifer, "Community, Adaptation and the Vietnamese in Toronto" (PhD diss., University of Toronto, 1999).

53 Robert Murdie, "'Blacks in Near-Ghettos?' Black Visible Minority Population in Metropolitan Toronto Housing Authority Public Housing Units," *Housing Studies* 9 (1994): 435–57. Racist practices by the Ontario Housing Corporation (OHC), responsible for overseeing public housing in the province, also contributed to housing hardship. It was usual for some Afro-Caribbean single mothers to immigrate to Toronto in search of work and then send for their children when the time was appropriate. However, those

desiring to do this who already lived in OHC projects were evicted and put on the bottom of the waiting list when they informed the authorities that their children were coming to Canada. It then became standard practice at OHC to ask applicants if they had children living elsewhere; if they said yes, they would be denied public housing and would have to wait to reapply when the children arrived. See Dorothy Quann, *Racial Discrimination in Housing* (Ottawa, 1979), 33–4.

54   MTHA, *Annual Report 1959*, n.p.

55   "Betty Meredith Really Cares for the People Who Need an OHC Home," *Ontario Housing* 15 (June 1970): 9.

56   Carter, "Current Practices," 601.

57   Sewell, *Houses and Homes*, 32–3.

58   Ibid., 144.

59   Housing Connections Central Registry Report, cited in Jack Lakey, "22-Year Wait for Some Low-Cost Housing," *Toronto Star*, 13 July 1998, B5.

60   I have consciously chosen to mine the files for information that sheds light on the larger question of housing need. For a valuable discussion of how case files can also be fruitfully analyzed as forms of narration and self-representation, see Franca Iacovetta and Wendy Mitchinson, "Introduction: Social History and Case Files Research," in Iacovetta and Mitchinson, eds, *On the Case: Explorations in Social History* (Toronto, 1998), 11–13. The Housing Authority of Toronto papers at the City of Toronto Archives are rich in case files and other documents that permit researchers to probe the lives of low-income families. CTA, HAT, RG 28, series B, boxes 29–30, for example, contain 118 detailed, if inconsistent, case histories of tenants who left RPN in 1962. They include rental histories, incomes, occupation and family composition information, original applications to RP, including inspection reports of their previous housing, reasons for applying to public housing and reasons for acceptance, and miscellaneous information regarding their tenancy in RP. In compliance with Access to Information Guidelines, the files, labelled by names in the archival boxes, were coded by numbers according to their order in the boxes. The names were not recorded. Thus, file no. 1 is the first file and so on. The people referred to in these files have been given pseudonyms. These files will be subsequently cited as "Tenant Case File" with the number of their placement in the archival boxes. Numerous letters from prospective tenants and comments by housing officials on the situations of low-income families can be found throughout the HAT records. Items of correspondence or other documents from all archival collections that may identify non-public persons have been given abbreviations. If the correspondence is directly quoted, pseudonyms have been used. I have used the real names of the interviewees unless they specifically

requested to have pseudonyms. In the latter case, abbreviations have been used in the citations.

61   Cynthia Comacchio, "'The History of Us': Social Science, History, and the Relations of Family in Canada," *Labour/Le Travail* 46 (Fall 2000): 189.

62   See Murdie, "Social Polarization and Public Housing," 295; and Sacouman and Veltmeyer, "The Political Economy of Part-Time Work," 115–17.

63   Tenant Case File 2.

64   Tenant Case File 13. For other families who were asked or ordered to leave by landlords, see files 4, 12, 17, 22–3, 36, 46, 48–9, 57, 59–61, 68, 75, 77, 80, 82, 87, 89, 91, and 99. For the interesting case of a rich woman who pled for public housing for her servant who had been evicted, see CTA, HAT, RG 28, series B, box 36, file: City of Toronto Mayor's Office, 1950–1957, Mrs C to the Mayor, 25 June 1956.

65   Tenant Case File 24. For other families who were paying more than 30 per cent of their income in rent, see files 6, 7, 20, 36, 37, 52, 64, and 116. For overcrowding, see files 3, 17, 33, 56, 58, 71, 79–81, 83, 85–6, 88, 93, 101, 104, 115.

66   CTA, HAT, RG 28, series B, box 8, file: 1965–68 F, HF to Robert Bradley, 20 March 1968.

67   Taida Hambleton to author, 15 January 1996.

68   Larry Quinto to author, 2 January 2002.

69   Tenant Case File 8. For other cases of applicants who had lost their houses, see files 87 and 112.

70   Tenant Case Files 34 and 40.

71   Dave Norris, interview by author, tape-recorded, Cambridge, ON, 7 May 1996.

72   This was a long-standing practice of landlords reaching back to the nineteenth century. See "Evidence of Arthur Short," in Greg Kealey, ed., *Canada Investigates Industrialism: The Royal Commission on the Relations of Labour and Capital, 1889* (Toronto, 1973), 254.

73   Interview, anonymous, *c.* 1956, cited in Albert Rose, *Regent Park: A Study in Slum Clearance* (Toronto, 1958), 109.

74   Tenant Case File 61.

75   Tenant Case File 110. For other residents who explicitly moved into RP because of landlord dislike of children, see files 14, 19, 44, 84, 94, 99, 103, and 110.

76   CTA, HAT, RG 28, series B, box 36, file: City of Toronto Mayor's Office, 1950–7, Tenants to Mayor Lamport, 11 February 1952. See in the same file, Mr and Mrs GC to Mayor Lamport, 11 February 1952.

77   CTA, HAT, RG 28, B, box 9, file "1965–68 H," MH to Robert Bradley, 9 August 1965.

78   Tenant Case File 35.

79   Tenant Case File 19. For other cases of dilapidated housing, see files 6, 8, 24, 27, 37, 39, 40, 51, 56, 58–9, 60–4, 66, 69, 70, 72–6, 78, 97, 100, 103, 105, 108, and 115. See as well evidence from a 1954 report from a doctor describing housing conditions "hardly fit to

house animals," in CTA, HAT, RG 28, series B, box 36, file "City of Toronto, Department of Buildings, 1953–55," Frank Dearlove to Commissioner of Buildings, 31 December 1954.

80 CTA, RG 28, series B, box 8, file: 1965–68 B, Robert Bradley to Mr Borins, Counsel to the Judicial Inquiry on Housing, 15 September 1965.

81 Interview, anonymous, *c.* 1956, cited in full in Rose, *Regent Park*, 110–11.

82 Interview, anonymous, *c.* 1956, cited in full in Rose, *Regent Park*, 109. For more families with medical problems, see files 26, 44, 52–3, 62, and 99.

83 David Blackmore, interview by author, tape-recorded, Toronto, 6 May 1996.

84 Tenant Case File 15.

85 Hal Tennant, "Our Second Chance at Public Housing," *Maclean's*, 20 March 1965, 20.

86 "A Litmus Test for Democracy: The Impact of Ontario Welfare Changes on Single Mothers," *Studies in Political Economy* 66 (August 2001): 18.

87 Tenant Case File 37.

88 Tenant Case File 80.

89 CTA, HAT, RG 28, series B, box 11, file: 1965–1968, MP to Robert Bradley, 7 October 1965.

90 Neil Ruttle, interview by author, tape-recorded, Toronto, 15 May 1995.

91 CTA, HAT, RG 28, series B, box 9, file: 1964–1968 G, CH to Robert Bradley, 15 February 1966.

92 Jack Lakey, "Housing Wait Now 12–22 Years," *Toronto Star*, 17 July 1998, B3.

93 Harold Troper, "History of Immigration to Toronto Since the Second World War: From Toronto 'the Good' to Toronto 'the World in a City,'" Centre for Excellence in Research on Immigration and Settlement, Working Paper No. 12, March 2000.

94 AG, interview by author, tape-recorded, Toronto, 18 May 1995.

95 George Fallis and Alex Murray eds, *Housing the Homeless and Poor* (Toronto, 1990), 54–5, cited in Sewell, *Houses and Homes*, 33.

96 MTHA, *Regent Park South Relocation Study: Interim Report* (Toronto, 1958), 40.

97 CTA, HAT, RG 28, series B, box 8, file: 1965–1968 D, VD to Robert Bradley, 2 March 1966.

98 Sylvia Novac, *A Place to Call One's Own; New Voices of Dislocation and Dispossession* (Ottawa, 1996); and Frances Henry, *The Caribbean Diaspora in Toronto: Learning to Live with Racism* (Toronto, 1994), 230.

99 See the profile in "Candidates for RPCIA Executive," *Regent Park Community News* 1 (March 1973): 3.

100 "Foreword," in David Zapparoli, *Regent Park: The Public Experiment in Housing: A Photographic Exhibit at The Market Gallery*, 13 March–11 July 1999 (Toronto, 1999).

101 Hilary Silver cautions that despite global economic trends, national politics still play a central role in shaping inequality. "National Conceptions of the New Urban Poverty: Social Structural Change in Britain, France and the United States," *International Journal of Urban and Regional Research* 17 (September 1993): 336–54.

102 On the US case, see Peter Marcuse, "Interpreting 'Public Housing' History," *Journal of Architectural and Planning Research* 12 (1995): 240–58. David Ley charts the development of "inner-city populations" in various Canadian cities that faced housing problems. See "The Inner City," in Bunting and Filion, eds, *Canadian Cities in Transition*, 2nd edn, 284–5. On the owner-building option, see Richard Harris, "Owner-Building," in W. van Vliet, ed., *Encyclopedia of Housing* (Beverly Hills, 1998).

103 Harris, "Housing," 398. On housing affordability in the United States, consult Joan H. Rollins, Renee N. Saris, and Ingrid Johnston-Robledo, "Low-Income Women Speak Out about Housing: A High-Stakes Game of Musical Chairs," *Journal of Social Issues* 57 (2001): 277–98; and Janet L. Smith, "Cleaning Up Public Housing by Sweeping Out the Poor," *Habitat International* 23 (1999): 53.

104 Thelma Pilkey, interview by author.

◉ 5.2: INTERGOVERNMENTAL RELATIONS TRUMPS SOCIAL POLICY CHANGE: TRUDEAU, CONSTITUTIONALISM, AND FAMILY ALLOWANCES

Raymond Blake

Introduction

The constitutional and jurisdictional question has been an important part of the debate about family allowances in Canada since the idea of paying families an allowance to support the raising of children was first raised. In 1929, when the Select Standing Committee on Industrial and International Relations of the House of Commons studied family allowances, it paid particular attention to the issue of jurisdiction: were family allowances a federal or a provincial matter? Although the committee was not prepared to recommend family allowances at that time, it advised that the government consider the whole jurisdictional question, which proved to be a perpetual challenge to social policy development in Canada.

Ernest Lapointe, the minister of justice, subsequently asked his deputy, W. Stuart Edwards, for a legal opinion on the matter, and Edwards concluded that family allowances were within Ottawa's jurisdiction because the federal government could raise money and spend it as it wished. However, Prime Minister Mackenzie King was not yet committed to a program of social security for Canada that included family allowances.[1] That commitment would come near the end of World War II. At that time, both Quebec and Ontario argued that Ottawa had exceeded its constitutional reach with the program; King disagreed, using Edwards's decision as support for his position. Moreover, with a strong central government clearly in the ascendancy, King dismissed those who challenged Ottawa's constitutional right to make payments to individual Canadians. The Exchequer Court later confirmed Ottawa's jurisdiction when it ruled in *Anger vs the Minister of National Revenue* in 1957 that the 1945 Family Allowances Act was within Parliament's purview to legislate for the peace, order, and good government of Canada. That ruling did not settle the matter for long.[2]

By the 1960s, support for the centralizing tendencies of the immediate postwar period had waned as a new province-building era began.[3] Quebec led the charge for major changes in the operation of the federation, as it challenged Ottawa's right—as well as its effectiveness—in the delivery of many federal programs, particularly those in the area of social policy. When Canada established its contributory pension plan in 1966, for instance, Quebec opted for its own plan, and not surprisingly, some of the more well-established social programs, notably family allowances, came to play an important role in the Canadian minefield of federal-provincial relations throughout this period. When that happened,

the issue of jurisdiction—that is, which level of government should control the family allowance program—became more important than the social policy embedded in the program.

In the months leading to the Victoria Constitutional Conference in 1971, Quebec demanded a constitutional amendment that would have effectively transferred to the provinces both control over family allowances and the funds that Ottawa expended on the programs.[4] While Quebec often spoke of the need for an integrated approach to social policy that would rationalize and streamline all social policy spending within the province, what it really wanted was to extend to family allowances and other exclusive federal social programs the principle of shared jurisdiction with the proviso that the provinces would prevail in any instance where there was a conflict between the two levels of government.

Constitutional scholars have long been aware of the key role that social policy played in Quebec's ultimate rejection of the Victoria Charter, but they have ignored how federal negotiators attempted to use social policy to achieve their constitutional goals. Peter Russell, Kenneth McRoberts, and others have argued that Quebec's social policy proposals did not fit with Prime Minister Pierre Trudeau's view of Canada, as his government insisted on the importance of national programs.[5] What this analysis ignores is that the Trudeau government used social policy—as had the Bourassa government—as a key strategy in the constitutional negotiations of the early 1970s. Clearly, social policies in Canada have lives long after they are implemented.

This paper considers the impact of intergovernmental conflict on the development of family allowances in Canada. Scholars have previously recognized the role of the state itself in the creation of social welfare policy,[6] and in a diverse and increasingly multinational state such as Canada, where the lines of regional and ethnic cleavage have been particularly strong, some scholars have argued that the social security system has been one way of maintaining national unity.[7] . . . This paper suggests that the conflict between the federal government in Ottawa and the provincial government in Quebec in the late 1960s and early 1970s was a primary force leading to major reforms to the family allowance program in 1973. A few scholars have considered the role federalism plays in the origins and development of social programs in Canada, but they have largely ignored the impact of specific federal-provincial conflict on policy outcomes in specific program areas.[8] Canadian scholars are divided on the impact of the federal system on social policy. Some have suggested that federalism has had a negative impact on the development of the welfare state, as it represents a form of institutional fragmentation;[9] others have argued that federalism actually encourages the growth of the welfare state, as innovative policies adopted in one jurisdiction are copied by others within the federation.[10] In the case of family allowances in the early 1970s, Ottawa attempted a series of reforms to the program to satisfy Quebec's demands for greater autonomy within the Canadian federation during a period of intense constitutional negotiations. These reforms came at a time when Canada and many of the other liberal welfare states, including the United States and the United Kingdom, rediscovered poverty in their midst and realized that reforms were necessary to existing social programs such as family allowances. The reforms to family allowances that were first contemplated by the Trudeau government after 1968 to address poverty in Canada changed radically in the heated constitutional debates of 1971. These reforms, which were implemented in the early 1970s, had more to do with accommodating Quebec than with helping families living in poverty, which had been the primary imperative in reforming family allowances when the issue first arose in the late 1960s.[11]

Jurisdiction and Family Allowances

Despite the heavy expenditure on social security after the end of World War II, it was clear by the 1960s that Canada's social security system had not delivered its intended results. A series of investigations undertaken by governmental and non-governmental agencies reported that poverty continued to be a serious problem. In fact,

there was a new-found consciousness of poverty throughout North America. Not unexpectedly, questions were raised about the efficacy of government expenditure on social security, especially among those in the policy branch of the Department of National Health and Welfare.

Quebec's Family and Social Welfare Minister René Lévesque—who, in 1961, had led the province's nationalization of the hydroelectric power companies—announced in November 1965 that he wanted control of all federal social security programs in his province; in addition, he wanted to limit federal involvement to the funding of the programs.[12] He maintained that Quebec City knew better than Ottawa the particular needs of his province, a claim initially made in the 1963 *Rapport du comité d'étude sur l'assistance publique*, which had recommended that the federal government withdraw from a variety of joint programs and simply provide the province with the financial resources it expended on these programs.[13] Quebec believed that only through an integrated social security program could it deal effectively with poverty and that that could not happen if Ottawa continued to control programs such as family allowances. Lévesque's own plan for social security reform depended, in large measure, on his getting his hands on the $180 million that the family allowance program paid to families in Quebec.

At a federal-provincial meeting of welfare ministers on 7–8 January 1966, Lévesque demanded that Ottawa either radically reform the family allowance program to meet the priorities of Quebec or, barring that, transfer funds for the program to the provinces. He insisted on using "repatriation" to describe the transfer, suggesting that the transfer could be justified on constitutional grounds.[14] Of course, the reforms that Lévesque enunciated followed closely the masters-in-our-own-house rhetoric of a more autonomous Quebec. While the province had opted out of several federal-provincial programs during the 1960s, most notably the Canadian Pension Plan and youth allowances,[15] the withdrawal from family allowances would mark the first separation of Quebec from the trio of long-standing national programs—old age pensions and unemployment insurance, in addition to family allowances—that Ottawa had established as purely federal initiatives to create a national social security program during and immediately following World War II. If Quebec opted out of family allowances—a program seen, in part, by federal political leaders as an important aspect of Canadian citizenship—it would represent the strengthening of provincialism, particularly in Quebec, and an erosion of the strong central government that had emerged in postwar Canada.

Lévesque's request surprised Ottawa, though Judy LaMarsh, the minister of national health and welfare, and some of her colleagues in Lester B. Pearson's minority government, had already become concerned over Quebec's propensity to opt out of national initiatives and demand cash transfers to establish its own parallel programs. In her view, Lévesque was becoming more and more anti-Ottawa, and she contended that the government had decided that it would take a firm position with Lévesque on family allowances.[16] . . . Although officials in the Department of National Health and Welfare, the department responsible for the administration of family allowances, had been concerned for some time that the universal family allowance program was not able to provide the level of assistance low-income families required, Quebec's demands for control of the program accelerated the reform impetus that was slowly taking root in Ottawa. Several provincial governments, notably Quebec, were already showing some interest in making social programs selective rather than universal.[17] The election of Pierre Trudeau as Liberal leader and prime minister in 1968 gave additional impetus to those in National Health and Welfare who had already decided that the universality of the family allowance program limited its effectiveness as an anti-poverty measure. Trudeau told the leadership convention, "In the field of social welfare programs it is my belief that we have enough of this free stuff. . . . We have to put a damper on this revolution of rising expectations. . . . We must not be afraid of this bogeyman, the means test. We must be more selective, to help those who

live on uneconomic land or in city slums."[18] John Munro, Trudeau's minister of national health and welfare, shared his leader's sentiments.[19]

Social Security Reform and the Constitutional Agenda

Trudeau's government also committed itself to constitutional reform in 1968. It launched a series of constitutional conferences with the provinces that culminated in the Victoria Conference in June 1971. At one of the constitutional meetings in December 1969, Ottawa attempted to bring some clarity to the question of jurisdiction in matters such as income security and social policy. Earlier attempts by Ottawa to introduce old age pensions and unemployment insurance had proven difficult because of the constitutional uncertainties surrounding jurisdiction. Greater clarity in the social policy field could be established if the Constitution was reformed. Most of the provinces accepted the principle that both the federal parliament and the provincial legislatures had, and should continue to have, powers to make income support payments to individuals. Others agreed that it might be best if the federal government alone controlled basic income support and income security programs. Quebec stood alone, however, in insisting that the provinces should have exclusive jurisdiction in these fields.[20] Constitutional reform and social policy reform subsequently became fused.

Ottawa began work on a White Paper on social security to assess each of its programs, consider the constitutional implications of each, and propose a series of initiatives and reforms that might lead to a more effective social security system. Family allowances became part of this wider reconsideration of social policy, and when Munro tabled the *White Paper on Income Security for Canadians* in Parliament on 30 November 1970, it proposed to restructure the existing family allowances in favour of a Family Income Security Plan (FISP) to deal particularly with low income families. It set out a preferred course of action that embodied four steps: first, retain income tax exemptions for dependent children; second, terminate family allowances for families with incomes exceeding $10,000; third, tax family allowances and include them in the income of the parent who claimed the exemption for any dependent children; and fourth, significantly increase the benefits for children in families with up to $4,500 of family income by using the amounts recovered from taxing family allowances and withholding payments to higher income families, and provide graduated benefits to families with incomes between $4,500 and $10,000. The new program would provide a monthly benefit of $16 for each child under 16 in families with incomes up to $4,500. For families with incomes between $4,500 and $10,000, monthly benefits would be reduced by $1 for each $500 of income above $4,500, and benefits would cease once incomes reached $10,000.[21] The Family Income Security Program would have more than doubled the amount paid to families living below the poverty line, but would have eliminated benefits for 1.2 million or 39 per cent of Canadian families.[22] . . .

Ottawa announced its plans for social security just weeks before Quebec released its study of social welfare, the *Report of the Commission of Inquiry on Health and Social Welfare* (the Castonguay-Nepveu Commission). The report made four points: first, it accused the federal government of fragmenting social and income security policies; second, it insisted that a policy approach geared to providing a guaranteed income commensurate with essential needs was the only means of alleviating the consequences of poverty; third, it claimed that such a policy required a complete harmonization and coordination of federal and provincial programs in the field of social policy; and fourth, it maintained that an integrated approach was possible only if the provinces were given overriding responsibility for the social policy framework and objectives.[23] Castonguay described FISP as "piecemeal" and insisted, Munro told his colleagues, that Quebec have primary responsibility in social policy. Only then could Quebec implement an effective social security system to help its citizens, particularly

the working poor. Castonguay told the Federal-Provincial Conference in January 1971 that Quebec required "primary responsibility in the conception of social policy, the primacy of the power to legislate, [and] even in certain cases, the exclusivity of such power," but Ottawa would have to finance and even administrate the various legislative measures.[24]

Quebec dismissed the proposals contained in the White Paper. So, too, did many in the middle class who would have seen their benefits eliminated.[25] Even though Munro and his department realized quickly that there were serious problems with the reforms they had proposed in the White Paper, they would not have the opportunity to respond to those criticisms, as family allowance reform became inextricably linked to constitutional change. When that happened, Munro saw his authority on the subject disappear as responsibility for reforming the family allowance program moved to the prime minister's office.[26]

Although Trudeau had high hopes for constitutional reform, he failed to appreciate that there were fundamental differences between Ottawa and the English-speaking provinces on the one hand, and Quebec on the other. While Trudeau and the English-speaking premiers sought fairly modest changes to protect linguistic and cultural rights and entrench a modest charter of human rights, they did not envision any fundamental change to the relationship between the two levels of governments. They wanted to modernize the British North America Act by removing certain articles that had fallen into disuse and to patriate the Constitution with a new amending formula. Quebec had much more aggressive constitutional aspirations. It wanted to clarify and enlarge the legislative and fiscal autonomy of the provinces with the goal of creating a national government in Quebec City. This aim was no more evident than in the area of social policy as outlined in the Castonguay-Nepveu Report. It recommended a new and radical approach to social policy, and it provided Quebec with further ammunition to insist that provincial legislative primacy in the area of income security had to be enshrined in the Constitution.[27]

Quebec wanted the best of both worlds when it came to income security. It insisted that provincial legislatures had paramountcy (or primary constitutional authority) to legislate in the field of social policy and income security, but that both levels of government shared the responsibility and the power to finance and operate programs within the policy objectives and priorities established by the provinces. The federal government was uncomfortable with such an approach, but it realized, too, that any confrontation with Quebec over the control of social policy would prevent it from patriating and amending the British North America Act—a policy objective of considerable urgency for Trudeau. Moreover, any confrontation with Quebec would have serious implications for Canadian unity. Such were the concerns over Quebec's stand on social policy that Mitchell Sharp, the secretary of state for external affairs, recommended to the cabinet that the federal delegation avoid the subject of social policy in the Constitutional Conference scheduled for 8–9 February 1971.[28] Such avoidance was quite unlikely, however, given that Bourassa had made social security reform one of his major priorities. . . .

This position became abundantly clear at a February 1971 federal-provincial constitutional meeting. R. Gordon Robertson, the clerk of the Privy Council and cabinet secretary, communicated regularly by telephone with his counterpart in Quebec City, Julien Chouinard, and four days before the conference, Robertson briefed Prime Minister Trudeau. He told the prime minister that if Ottawa was willing to give Quebec what it thought it needed to meet objectives as laid out in the Castonguay-Nepveu Report, then social policy might be kept separate from the constitutional file.[29] Such a concession was unlikely given the position of many of the senior officials in the government. Robertson had R.B. Bryce, his predecessor, convene a meeting of the government's senior officials. . . . They recommended, too, that the prime minister reassure Bourassa that the federal government would endeavour to formulate and operate its social policies in a manner that would contribute to provincial social objectives while permitting each province the maximum flexibility in developing its own social policies.

Bryce advised Trudeau that he should be clear in private with Bourassa that Ottawa had no intention of surrendering its right to provide family allowances in Quebec, nor should Bourassa expect a guaranteed income, as it would necessitate an unacceptable increase in the level of taxation. As Bryce wrote in his memorandum to the prime minister, "[t]hey [Bourassa and Castonguay] should not expect us to tax other provinces . . . in order to provide them with the funds necessary to finance a more advanced social program than we are able and prepared to finance in other provinces."[30]

As the federal government anticipated, Bourassa made it clear at the Third Working Session of the Constitutional Conference, on 8–9 February 1971, that social policy was a major issue for Quebec; it had to be included on the agenda for the conference scheduled for Victoria in June 1971.[31] The communiqué from the meeting acknowledged the impasse between the federal and provincial governments: social policy was fundamental to any constitutional change for Quebec, yet Ottawa offered only a coordinated approach that might lead to greater cooperation between the federal and provincial governments and even allow the provinces to achieve their social policy priorities; but Ottawa would not transfer the sums it expended on social policy to the provinces.[32] New Brunswick premier Richard Hatfield insisted that it was crucial that Ottawa maintain its spending power in social policy to protect the national interest, and Saskatchewan premier Ross Thatcher stated that if Quebec secured greater powers, it would mean the end of Ottawa's authority to deal with national problems. Thatcher was blunt in his assessment, noting, "If Quebec persists with the demands she [sic] is making today, perhaps she [sic] should become a separate nation."[33] Despite the gulf between Quebec and the other governments, social policy was put on the agenda for the Victoria conference.

For the Trudeau cabinet, then, the question became one of working out a mutually acceptable approach with Quebec as it kept in mind the interests of the other provinces.[34] The cabinet had decided some time earlier that it would continue to make direct payments to individuals. Yet Quebec had proposed an income security system that would see the existing programs—federal as well as provincial—folded into a unified structure, and it insisted that the provinces had priority in the conception of income security policy, if not primacy in matters of determining benefits and administration. In others words, if the province decided to move into an area where the federal government operated, Ottawa would simply withdraw and turn over to the province the fiscal equivalent of all monies spent in that particular province.

An overwhelming concern for Trudeau became the need to satisfy the interests of Quebec.[35] The Cabinet Committee on Federal-Provincial Relations took control of the file in early 1971 as the discussions on social policy accelerated and broadened. Bryce, by this time the economic adviser to the prime minister on the Constitution and chair of the Interdepartmental Committee on Federal-Provincial Social Policy Issues, played the leading role. He realized that the success achieved in the discussions on social policy would have an important bearing on Quebec's willingness to approve the proposals for constitutional revision that Ottawa was preparing for the First Ministers' Constitutional Conference scheduled for June. . . .

Victoria Conference

When he opened the Constitutional Conference in Victoria on 14 June, Trudeau said that repatriation and an amending formula had been the main objective of the conference, but social policy had emerged as a major issue. He acknowledged that Quebec had proposed that the provincial legislatures be given the authority to limit the power of the federal Parliament to make income security payments, such as family allowances, in the provinces. If the federal government acceded to the demands of Quebec to divert federal spending for social policy to the provincial treasuries and allow each province to determine how to spend the funds, it would not only lead to the erosion of the federal presence in such areas, but also might undermine Ottawa's ability to collect taxes in affluent provinces to support provincial programs in have-not provinces.[36] The federal government was faced with a dilemma. On the one hand, it had decided that it would not consider any constitutional change that emasculated federal spending power and ability to redistribute monies in relation to individuals; but it still wanted to provide "the necessary minimum to Mr. Bourassa" that would allow him to win support for the constitutional package in the National Assembly of Quebec.[37]

After three days of debating various constitutional proposals, the conference concluded at midnight on 16 June with a new Canadian Constitutional Charter. The Victoria Charter addressed a variety of issues, including political and language rights, the appointment of Supreme Court judges, and an amending formula; but the major issue at the conference came down to the issue of jurisdiction over social policy, which, as one commentator noted, was a microcosm of the larger issue of the division of legislative and taxing powers.[38] As mentioned above, the federal government was willing to go only part way to meet Quebec's demands for legislative primacy in social policy. Trudeau insisted that Ottawa would not surrender its power to make direct payment to individuals, but he agreed that federal legislation in social areas could "dovetail with their [Quebec] legislation in social areas and if there is a conflict, ours [federal legislation] will have to adjust to theirs."[39] The federal government agreed to amend section 94, but the proposed amendment did not satisfy Quebec. While the amendments recognized provincial paramountcy in the fields of family allowance and other income security measures, it did not prohibit Ottawa from participating in income support programs, nor did it offer to provide financial compensation to the provinces if they chose not to participate in a new federal initiative.[40] The final communiqué from the conference, which promised that the premiers would meet shortly to discuss all aspects of the federal-provincial fiscal arrangements, did not give Quebec the decentralized federalism it sought. . . .

Even as Bourassa considered the Victoria Charter with his cabinet, Ottawa continued to search for ways to solve the impasse over social policy with Quebec. It was R.B. Bryce again who suggested a way forward. He recommended a solution that would "assist" Quebec without additional cost to the federal treasury, without loss of ultimate control of future federal programs, and without creating the impression that Trudeau was doing anything special for Quebec. He proposed that Ottawa allow all provinces—not just Quebec—the option of determining how the federal benefit for each recipient would be made within their province. This proposal was in keeping with the cabinet's insistence that "in developing the federal position on the substance of social policy it [was] important to bear in mind the need to avoid giving the appearance of a substantive concession to Quebec alone."[41] The federal government would continue to administer the program and send cheques directly to parents. Bryce's plan would allow Quebec, for example, to determine how its envelope of funds were distributed in that province; it could decide the amount of the benefit paid to each child, and it could, for instance, increase benefits for the fourth child and subsequent children in a family at the cost of some reduction in the scale of payments for other children. The added incentive for Ottawa, Byrce suggested, was that only Quebec was likely to be interested in such an option.[42] Bryce's plan conformed to Trudeau's vision of federalism, which was determined to reverse the trend towards special status for Quebec by allowing all provinces to make special arrangements with Ottawa in the delivery of social programs.[43]

Bryce said that the proposals should be put to Premier Bourassa on 23 June "if it appears that such action is needed and has a good chance of success in gaining Quebec's approval to the Charter." Bryce added that there seemed to be a "reasonable chance of reaching a conclusion on this proposal by Monday, June 28, the deadline for governments to approve the Charter." The cabinet liked the proposal but made it clear that Ottawa's intention should be kept secret from Quebec until after the Quebec cabinet had met on the evening of 21 June. The cabinet did not think that Bourassa would make a decision on Victoria at that meeting, and it wanted to be prepared with additional incentives if the Quebec cabinet wavered on the constitutional proposal. Trudeau's cabinet was clear in its objectives, as the Record of Cabinet Decisions shows: concessions on family allowances could be an important bargaining chip with Quebec ministers.[44] A few days later, on 22 June, the federal cabinet agreed that "if the action was needed and had a good chance of making possible Quebec's acceptance of the Canadian Constitutional Charter 1971," then the prime minister should inform Premier Bourassa of Ottawa's willingness to change the Family Income Security Plan to accord broadly with changes proposed by Quebec and enrich the plan by the allocation of an additional $150 million. . . .

The next day, 23 June 1971, Bourassa formally rejected the Victoria Charter. Ottawa had counted on Bourassa waiting until the 28 June deadline before he rendered a final decision; his announcement caught Ottawa by surprise and pre-empted Ottawa's strategy. Trudeau's proposed amendment to the British North America Act, "to guarantee prior consultation of the provinces before changing federal income security measures and to protect provincial social allowance plans from interference by parallel federal programs," was too little to satisfy Quebec.[45] A statement issued by Bourassa's office gave a measure of hope to Ottawa; it was enough to ensure that family allowances would remain at the top of the federal-provincial agenda. Bourassa insisted, "Federalism constitutes for Quebecers the best way of attaining their economic, social and cultural objectives" and noted the failure of the constitutional reforms to deal adequately with social policy. "The texts dealing with income security," the statement noted, "leave an uncertainty that meshes badly with the objectives inherent in any idea of constitutional revision. If this uncertainty were eliminated, our conclusions could be different." He and Trudeau decided to meet in a week or so, but Bourassa had made it clear to the prime minister that success was contingent on new powers for Quebec in the social security field. Trudeau also told the House of Commons on 25 June that further negotiations with Quebec were likely, pointing out that Bourassa had said that "ambiguities" in language were the source of difficulty with the Victoria Charter.[46]

While Bourassa may have been misleading the Liberal government in Ottawa and English Canadians generally over what was necessary for Quebec to agree to constitutional reform, Ottawa believed that an agreement could be reached with Quebec. Bourassa's insistence on social policy reform continued to have a major impact on policy-making in Ottawa. The cabinet decided on 25 June to push ahead with the proposals for the Family Income Security Plan that it had previously approved. Ottawa could not withdraw the $150 million it had committed to lure Quebec into signing the Victoria Charter; to do so would have caused a split in the cabinet and, above all, shown how the Trudeau government had attempted to use social policy to manipulate the constitutional agenda. However, the federal government dropped its proposal to allow provinces to play a greater role in family allowances; it alone would determine the structure of the benefits, perhaps in retaliation for Quebec's rejection of the Victoria Charter. . . .

On 2 September 1971, [Premier Bourassa] wrote Trudeau that he hoped to find a way of "averting conflict" in the area of family allowances. Bourassa continued to insist that the province required supremacy in the design of social security programs to meet its own social policy priorities. He wanted the proposed federal legislation to reform family allowances to conform to any existing terms, conditions, and regulations of the family allowance legislation in Quebec. He also wanted the province to have control over designating the recipients, the nature and the amount of the allowances, the scale of benefits, and the total amount payable to the citizens in that province. Trudeau was optimistic because Bourassa had intimated that it was possible to find a legislative solution to the social policy

question rather than a constitutional one, which had derailed the Victoria Conference earlier that summer.[47] . . .

There was no legislative action taken on the new Family Income Security Plan (Bill C-264) tabled on 13 September 1971 after it received first reading, as Ottawa struggled to meet Quebec's demands. The federal government had good reason to be patient because Bourassa had told *Le Devoir* in late September that after Quebec had found a workable solution with Ottawa on family allowances, it would begin new constitutional discussions: "Mais . . . je ne veux pas m'engager, et je l'ai dit clairement au premier ministre du Canada que je ne veux du Québec qui déterminera le moment opportun de reprendre le débat constitutionnel." Quebec's ultimate goal was to obtain sole jurisdiction over all social policy, or legislative primacy, although it appeared at times to be willing to contemplate something less. Quebec's preferred approach was to have a provincially designed basic plan for children under 18, with a supplement for larger families included in a single plan. While it was agreeable to having the federal government issue the cheques, it wanted the province to play an important role in the following: having income statements verified by the province; identifying the province on the application forms, on all literature relating to the program, and, most importantly, on the cheques issued to parents; and having the province determine final benefit amounts using the provincial definition of income.[48] . . .

Family Allowance Reforms

On 9 March 1972, in response to Quebec's demands for a redesigned, more flexible Family Income Security Plan, which would allow them to meet their own provincial social policy objectives, Prime Minister Trudeau offered each province the right to redesign FISP for operation within the province, subject to certain minimum federal standards. This had been proposed in the period leading to the Victoria constitutional conference. In a letter to Premier Bourassa, Trudeau wrote, "Acceptance of a plan along these lines would represent, as you will appreciate, a very important change so far as the federal government is concerned." For the first time, a federally financed and administered program, legislated by Parliament, would be subject to modification by the provinces even though the amount of financial participation by the provinces would be small in comparison with that of the federal government. Provinces with family allowance programs, providing a supplement amounting to at least 15 per cent (not 20 per cent as the federal interdepartmental committee had recommended) of the total spent on family allowances in that province, would be given the right to alter the monthly benefit rate, the reduction rate, and the income threshold for FISP, provided that total federal spending on FISP did not exceed the amount that would have been spent had this right not been exercised. The benefits per child could not be set below 80 per cent of the national benefit rate, the threshold could not be set below the income tax exemption level, and provincial definitions of residence could not be more restrictive than the federal definition. Trudeau insisted that the federal definition of income would have to be used for the purpose of federal payments. He also said that the literature describing the program would indicate clearly that the plan in each province had been designed in accordance with provincial legislation, and there would be recognition of provincial financial participation.[49]

Trudeau also told Bourassa and the other premiers that the federal government would proceed with the Family Income Support Plan legislation in the current session, but the bill that would be presented to Parliament would not include the provision for the kind of flexibility he now suggested. He reassured Bourassa, however, that Ottawa would amend the bill to do so as soon as the provinces agreed to his proposal. What must have been encouraging, particularly for Bourassa, was Trudeau's suggestion that "the principles involved [with FISP] are clearly capable of extension to other income support programs" and might pave the way for constitutional change in matters relating to social security: "While the difficulties are considerable, the federal government would be prepared to consider this kind of extension of the principles I am proposing if a satisfactory constitutional basis can be found and if it solved the problem of social security which remained to be cleared up to permit further progress in the process of constitutional review."[50] Bourassa telexed the prime minister on 17 March expressing his satisfaction with the proposal and telling Trudeau, "I have a conviction that we shall soon arrive at developing a successful formula for family allowances."[51] Constitutional reform was clearly on Trudeau's mind. In fact, when Trudeau met with Bourassa earlier in February, the prime minister had insisted that "[l]es allocation familiales et la question constitutionnelle" be the first item on the agenda for the meeting.[52]

In Trudeau's view, he had conceded little to Quebec. The federal government claimed that it did not recognize in the changes to FISP any provincial supremacy in this particular social program, as it retained the undiluted right to make direct payments to individuals anywhere in Canada. Trudeau and his advisers had realized much earlier that there was considerable division within the Quebec cabinet over social security policy. Trudeau knew, however, that Bourassa was his best chance for finding a solution within the current framework of Confederation. Trudeau's offer, in his view, had simply allowed Bourassa to claim victory. The premier had described it as a "great step forward." As Trudeau said in an interview with TVA television news, there were many people in Quebec who did not want to see any agreements between the federal and provincial governments. Trudeau realized that the agreement on family allowances showed that Confederation continued to work, and he expected a more cooperative attitude from Premier Bourassa in the future on other important national issues.[53] . . .

Bill C-170 died on 7 July 1972, the last day of the session, when it failed by one vote to receive the unanimous consent that was necessary for Third Reading before Parliament was adjourned. Parliament did not meet again before the federal election on 30 October 1972.

In that election, Canadians sent Prime Minister Trudeau and the Liberals a strong message that they were not impressed with their handling of affairs, returning them to a minority government. In the unsettled period following the election, Trudeau reorganized his priorities to win support from the New Democratic Party (NDP) by promising action on social policy and a program to increase the presence of the state in the national economy. These changes kept the Liberal government in office until 8 May 1974, but the compromise with the NDP effectively stymied any fundamental change to the family allowance program that targeted low-income families through selective measures contained in the FISP. Trudeau must have been appalled that his important constitutional plans had foundered on something as unimportant (to him) as social policy, and he handed the National Health and Welfare portfolio to Marc Lalonde, his former private secretary and constitutional adviser, to fix the social policy problem with Quebec. Trudeau had made it clear to Lalonde that he wanted a major review of Canada's social security system to integrate federal and provincial social security policies and reform the various programs based on a number of specific principles around which a national consensus of opinion might be formulated. This approach was designed to avoid the constitutional impasse that had derailed the earlier constitutional agreement in 1971.[54] In the January 1973 Throne Speech, the federal government promised "that Canada's total social security system—including both federal and provincial elements—must be reconsidered and reorganized, and made more sensitive to the needs of people in different parts of the country."[55] Castonguay could have written the words himself, and it showed that Canada had entered a new period of harmonic federalism on social policy, at least.

The review of Canada's social security system began when Lalonde tabled the *Working Paper on Social Security* (the Orange Paper) in the House of Commons on 18 April 1973. The *Working Paper* was the federal government's contribution towards a joint federal-provincial review of Canada's social security system, and the provinces all agreed to participate in the exercise.[56] The cabinet wanted to avoid putting a series of proposals on the table that would clash with the objectives of the provincial governments, particularly those of Quebec; but the cabinet wanted a concrete family allowance proposal put before the provinces at the April meeting of welfare ministers.[57] This effort would reassure Canadians that the Liberal government was committed to substantial and immediate benefits through universal family allowances, as well as provide tangible evidence that the government was serious about meaningful social reform. It was also clear that the principle of universality in social programs would not be threatened as long as the Liberals remained in a minority position in Parliament.[58]

The *Working Paper* proposed that family allowances be increased from an average of $7.21 per child per month to an average of $20 per child, and be made taxable. The 1970 White Paper recommendation to eliminate the universality of family allowances had fallen victim to the political pressures of keeping the minority government in office and the need for provincial approval. Further evidence of the political practicalities was Lalonde's proposal that the level of benefit be reviewed periodically in relation to changes in the Consumer Price Index (as Old Age Security had been several months earlier). Lalonde suggested that, subject to a national minimum and assuming the development of a consensus regarding provincial flexibility and national norms, the precise amount paid for each child would be left to the provinces, as with the proposed FISP. Provinces could choose to vary the amount paid either by the age of the child or the size of the family. With an obvious reference to Quebec, Lalonde noted that it was a major constitutional innovation to permit the provinces to determine the benefits paid to individual Canadians by the Government of Canada, within the limits set by Parliament.[59] This flexibility allowed provinces to design their own income support and supplementation programs for families and would mark the introduction of a new—yet much discussed and anticipated—approach to federal-provincial relations in the social security field.[60] . . .

On 16 July 1973, Marc Lalonde introduced in Parliament the new reforms to the family allowance program, claiming they represented a new formula for federal-provincial cooperation in the area of social security.[61] Only three provinces took advantage of the federal offer that provinces be allowed to determine benefits. Not surprisingly, Quebec was one; Alberta and Prince Edward Island were the others. The increase now gave Quebec control of $8 of federal payment when it had only asked for control of $7.21—the average monthly federal expenditure per child on family allowance when Quebec asked Ottawa to transfer control of the program to Quebec City. Even though Ottawa had insisted there was no additional money, with the reforms the family allowance program cost nearly $1 billion.[62] When Premier Bourassa announced Quebec's plan on 19 September 1973—just days before the provincial election—he said that it "constituted an admirable example of a type of federalism which is both flexible and beneficial for Quebec." It was Social Welfare Minister Claude Castonguay who championed the new Quebec family allowance program that would cover all children up to the age of 17, thus eliminating Quebec's schooling allowances that had been created when the province opted out of the federal youth allowance program. The province set the benefits according to the number and age of the children, as provided under the provisions of the bill before Parliament. Federal monthly allowances were pegged at $12 for the first child, $18 for the second, $28 for the third, and $31 for the fourth and each additional child in the family. Additionally, the basic allowance was supplemented by an age premium of $5, paid for children between the ages of 12 and 17 years. The Quebec government administered and financed a separate Quebec scheme that provided additional monthly allowances of $3 for the first child, $4 for the second, $5 for the third, and $6 for each additional child. The Quebec benefits were administered through the Quebec Pension Board, which was already in charge of family and school allowances. . . .

Conclusions

The example of the family allowance program suggests that Canada's federal system had an important impact on the development of family allowances, especially as the two levels of government attempted to resolve outstanding constitutional issues. When a nationalist Quebec government demanded that Ottawa withdraw from the social policy field and transfer monies expended on such programs to the provinces, family allowances became intricately involved in the minefield of Canadian intergovernmental relations. Because family allowances were one of the few programs shared by all Canadian families and one of the means of building social cohesion across the country, the federal government initially refused to allow any provincial involvement in the program. By the early 1970s, however, family allowances were elevated from sectoral or "low politics" to the realm of "high politics."

Family allowances had rarely been the concern of the prime minister except when the program was introduced in 1945, but during the constitutional negotiations in 1970 and 1971 this issue moved to the centre of Canadian politics. Prime Minister Pierre Trudeau proved willing to make changes to the family allowance program as a means of enticing Quebec premier Robert Bourassa to amend the British North America Act. In those intergovernmental negotiations to patriate the Constitution, family allowances played an instrumental role. Ottawa promised certain reforms to the program to satisfy some of Quebec's social and constitutional objectives and its demands for greater autonomy within the Canadian federation as a way to move the constitutional file to a conclusion. The changes made to family allowances, to allow the provinces to determine how the benefits were allocated to parents, came as a result of the political manoeuvring with Quebec. Even so, Trudeau realized—as Mackenzie King had much earlier—that family allowances served as a link between the federal government and individual Canadian citizens in various regions and especially in Quebec. Even as the program was being reformed, the federal government made certain that family allowances remained a nation-building tool to help foster a pan-Canadian citizenship and attachment to the Government of Canada. The federal government, it might be concluded, designed some of its family allowance reforms to counter the province-building project in which the Quebec provincial government was so heavily involved. . . .

Note: A version of this paper appeared in the Saskatchewan Institute of Public Policy's Public Policy Paper Series in December 2007. The author wishes to acknowledge the generous financial assistance of the Social Science and Humanities Research Council of Canada that made the research for this paper possible.

Endnotes

1   Library and Archives Canada (hereafter LAC), Department of National Health and Welfare (hereafter DNHW), accession 85-86/343, box 12, file 3201-3-3, pt 3, "Family Allowances—Jurisdiction of the Parliament of Canada," 24 December 1979.

2   *Canada Law Reports*, Exchequer Court of Canada, 1957 (Ottawa: Queen's Printer for Canada, 1958), 83–7. When his claim for the $300 exemption for his children was denied by the Income Tax Board, François-Albert Anger, a Quebec taxpayer, took the matter to court, claiming that the board's decision constituted "an attack upon the legislative attributes of the Province in the matter of civil rights and family authority." The court ruled that the Act was within the legislative competence of the Parliament of Canada: it was "a national benevolent measure assimilated in the good government of Canada clause."

3   See R.A. Young, Philippe Faucher, and André Blais, "The Concept of Province-Building: A Critique," *Canadian Journal of Political Science/Revue canadienne de science politique* 17, no. 4 (December 1984): 783–818.

4   See Keith Banting, *The Welfare State and Canadian Federalism*, 2nd ed. (Montreal and Kingston: McGill-Queen's University Press, 1987), 120–1.

5   Peter H. Russell, *Constitutional Odyssey*, 3rd ed. (Toronto: University of Toronto Press, 2004), 85–91; and Kenneth McRoberts, *Misconceiving Canada: The Struggle for National Unity* (Toronto: Oxford University Press, 1997), 146.

6   Theda Skocpol, *Protecting Soldiers and Mothers: The Political Origins of Social Policy in the United States* (Cambridge, UK: Cambridge University Press, 1992); Richard Splane, "Social Policy–Making in the Government of Canada," in *Canadian Social Policy*, ed. Shanker A. Yelaja, rev. ed. (Waterloo, ON: Wilfrid Laurier University Press, 1987), 224–44; and Daniel Patrick Moynihan, "The Professionalization of Reform," *Public Interest* 1 (Fall 1965): 9.

7   T.H. Marshall, *Citizenship and Social Class and Other Essays* (Cambridge, UK: Cambridge University Press,

1950); Keith Banting, "Social Citizenship and the Multicultural State," in *Citizenship, Diversity, and Pluralism*, ed. Alan C. Cairns *et al.* (Montreal and Kingston: McGill-Queen's University Press, 1999); and Janine Brodie, "Citizenship and Solidarity: Reflections on the Canadian Way," *Citizenship Studies* 6, no. 4 (December 2002): 377–94.

8   Keith Banting, "Institutional Conservatism: Federalism and Pension Reform," in *Canadian Social Welfare Policy: Federal and Provincial Dimensions*, ed. Jacqueline S. Ismael (Montreal and Kingston: McGill-Queen's University Press, 1985), 48–74.

9   Harold Laski, "The Obsolescence of Federalism," in *The People, Politics and the Politician*, ed. A.N. Christensen and E.M. Kirkpatrick (New York: Henry Holt and Company, 1941), 111–17; Banting, *The Welfare State and Canadian Federalism*; and Banting, "Institutional Conservatism," 48–74.

10 Pierre Elliott Trudeau, "The Practice and Theory of Federalism," in *Social Purpose for Canada*, ed. M. Oliver (Toronto: University of Toronto Press, 1967), 371–93.

11 Rick Van Loon, "Reforming Welfare in Canada," *Public Policy* 27, no. 4 (Fall 1987): 470–505.

12 *Le Devoir*, 20 November 1965.

13 Government of Quebec, *Report of the Study Committee on Public Assistance* (Quebec City, 1963), commonly referred to as the Boucher Report.

14 LAC, DNHW, vol. 2361, file 264-1-8, "Brief of the Province of Quebec for the Federal-Provincial Conference on the Canada Assistance Plan," Ottawa, 7–8 January 1966, and "A note of Quebec's Proposal to Revise the Family and Youth Allowances Programs," prepared by Research and Statistics Division, 10 January 1966.

15 Quebec had pioneered the idea of youth allowances in 1961, a program that Canada adopted for the whole country in 1964.

16 See Judy LaMarsh, *Memoirs of a Bird in a Gilded Cage* (Toronto: McClelland & Stewart, 1969), 123–4; and *Ottawa Evening Citizen*, 25 November 1965.

17 In Canada, many commentators and academics have associated "selectivity" with cutbacks in social spending and an attempt to dismantle the welfare state. For example, see Allan Moscovitch, "The Welfare State Since 1975," *Journal of Canadian Studies* 21, no. 2 (Summer 1986): 83, where he writes, "One means of eroding social welfare has been through the use of more selectivity, or means testing benefits."

18 LAC, Grace MacInnis Papers, vol. 12, file Social Security 1966–74, "A Social Policy for Canada." The memo attributes the quote from Trudeau to the Canadian Manufacturing Association publication *Industry* (May 1968). In January 1969, the principle of selectivity was introduced into the family allowance program in the United Kingdom. See J.I. Clark, "Recent Trends and Developments in Guaranteed Income," paper prepared for Nuffield Canadian Seminar on Guaranteed Annual Incomes: An Integrated Approach, Canadian Council on Social Development, April 1972.

19 Quoted in Rodney S. Haddow, *Poverty Reform in Canada, 1958–1978: State and Class Influences on Policy Making* (Montreal and Kingston: McGill-Queen's University Press, 1993), 92. Munro told the *Globe and Mail* in May 1969 that, personally, he had considerable doubt about paying family allowance benefits to high-income families, but, he hastily added, the government had not yet considered the issue.

20 Provincial Archives of New Brunswick (hereafter PANB), Records of the Department of Finance (hereafter RDF), file 01-01-00, Ottawa—Conférence constitutionelle 1969, Summary of Proceedings.

21 LAC, DNHW, acc. 85-86/343, box 28, file 3301-3-C14, Privy Council Office, Record of Cabinet Decision, 19 November 1970.

22 LAC, DNHW, acc. 85-86/343, box 28, file 3301-3-C14, Memorandum to Cabinet, 29 July 1970, and Memorandum to Cabinet, 1 September 1970.

23 LAC, DNHW, acc. 85-86/343, box 28, file 3301-3-C8, pt 1, Memorandum to Cabinet from Mitchell Sharp, 1 February 1971.

24 LAC, DNHW, acc. 85-86/343, vol. 1937, file R234/100, "Summary of the Steps that have been taken to Accommodate Quebec's Point of View," 15 June 1972.

25 Munro later disbanded a secretariat he had created in the department to answer questions about the plan because of the lack of queries it had received. *Winnipeg Free Press*, 20 September 1972.

26 LAC, Pierre Elliott Trudeau fonds (hereafter Trudeau fonds), MG 26 O7, vol. 117, file Memorandum to the Prime Minister, Meeting of Cabinet Committees on Federal-Provincial Relations, prepared by E. Gallant, 2 February 1971. In the memorandum, Gallant noted that there was "a certain amount of annoyance shown that Mr. Munro has come forward with major [social policy] proposals at the last minute. Mr. Munro's only active support came from Mr. Andras."

27 LAC, DNHW, vol. 1605, file 6, Constitutional Conference, 3rd Working Session, 8–9 February 1971, "Statement of Conclusions," 8–9.

28 LAC, DNHW, vol. 1605, file 6, Memorandum to Cabinet from Mitchell Sharp, 1 February 1971. Sharp said in the cabinet on 7 May 1970, in a discussion on the Quebec situation and national unity, "[T]he government had to do everything possible to assist the new Premier of Quebec [Robert Bourassa] because it might well be the last chance to solve the problems in Quebec." LAC, Privy Council Office, vol. 6359, Cabinet Conclusions, 7 May 1970.

29 LAC, DNHW, acc. 85–86/343, box 28, file 3301-3-C8, Memorandum for the Prime Minister, prepared by Gordon Robertson, 4 February 1971. The memorandum was based on Robertson's telephone conversation with Chouinard.

30 LAC, DNHW, acc. 85-86/343, box 29, file 3301-3-C6, Memorandum for the Prime Minister, Re: Quebec's Proposals in Social Policy, prepared by R.B. Bryce, 5 February 1971. Bryce also reminded the prime minister that if an arrangement on social policy were worked out with Quebec and then announced to the other provinces without any prior notice, it would cause trouble in getting them to agree on a package to patriate the Constitution, "which most of them believe they are doing in order to help Mr. Bourassa."

31 LAC, DNHW, vol. 1937, file R234/100, Summary of the Steps That Have Been Taken to Accommodate Quebec's Point of View, 15 June 1972.

32 PANB, RDF, file 01-03-00, Ottawa—Conference—Constitutional, 1971, Statement of Conclusions.

33 John Saywell, ed., *Canadian Annual Review of Politics and Public Affairs 1971* (Toronto: University of Toronto Press, 1972), 44.

34 See Trudeau fonds, MG 26 O7, vol. 117, Memorandum to the Prime Minister, Meeting of Cabinet Committees on Federal-Provincial Relations, prepared by E. Gallant, 16 February 1971.

35 Privy Council Office, Cabinet Minutes, 25 February 1971; and Trudeau fonds, MG 26 O7, vol. 117, Memorandum to the Prime Minister, Meeting of Cabinet Committees on Federal-Provincial Relations and Social Policy, prepared by R.B. Bryce, 1 March 1971.

36 John Saywell and Paul Stevens, "Parliament and Politics," in *Canadian Annual Review of Politics and Public Affairs 1971*; and Saywell, *Canadian Annual Review*, 51–2.

37 Trudeau fonds, MG 26 O7, vol. 103, file 306.21—June 1971, Memorandum for the Prime Minister, Strategy at Victoria, 7 June 1971. The memorandum is marked "Confidential" and signed by R. Gordon Robertson.

38 Saywell and Stevens, "Parliament and Politics," 56.

39 Quoted in ibid., 58–79.

40 Ibid., 48–9, 63. The Victoria Charter can be found at www.solon.org/Constitutions/Canada/English/Proposals/Victoria_Charter.html.

41 Trudeau fonds, MG 26 O7, vol. 117, Memorandum to the Prime Minister . . . E. Gallant, 16 February 1971.

42 LAC, DNHW, acc. 85–86/343, box 28, file 3301-3-C8, pt 2, Memorandum, Re: Provincial Options to Modify Federal Family Income Security Plan, 20 June 1971, prepared by Bryce. Bryce noted in his memorandum that the proposals should be put to Premier Bourassa on 23 June.

43 See Richard Simeon, *Federal-Provincial Diplomacy* (Toronto: University of Toronto Press, 1972), 66–8.

44 LAC, DNHW, vol. 1629, file 1, Record of Cabinet Decision, 18 June 1971.

45 Saywell and Stevens, "Parliament and Politics," 48–9, 63. See also Jeremy Webber, *Reimagining Canada: Language, Culture, Community, and the Canadian Constitution* (Montreal and Kingston: McGill-Queen's University Press, 1994), 97–9; and Haddow, *Poverty in Canada*, 94–6.

46 Saywell and Stevens, "Parliament and Politics," 63–4, 68.

47 LAC, DNHW, acc. 85–86/343, box 37, file 3303-3-A16, Bourassa to Trudeau, 2 September 1971, and Trudeau to Bourassa, 17 September 1971 (unofficial translation of both letters); and ibid., vol. 1929, file 1, Memorandum to Cabinet 14 October 1971. Prime Minister Trudeau tabled the letter from Premier Bourassa in the House of Commons on 15 September 1971.

48 Trudeau fonds, MG 26 07, vol. 332, file 363.44, Lalonde to Trudeau, "Conversation téléphonique avec l'honorable Bourassa," 6 December 1971; and LAC, DNHW, acc. 85–86/343, box 28, file 3301-3-C1, Memorandum to Cabinet, 10 December 1971.

49 Trudeau fonds, MG 26 07, vol. 332, file 363.44, Lalonde to Trudeau, "Rencontre avec l'honorable Bourassa," 17 January 1972.

50 Trudeau fonds, MG 26 07, vol. 105, file 306.4, Trudeau to Bourassa, 9 March 1972; LAC, DNHW, vol. 1610, file 6, Trudeau to Bourassa, 9 March 1972; and Department of National Health and Welfare, acc. 85-86/343, box 84, file 3201-3-3, pt 3, Memorandum on Policy Consideration Underlying the Design and Development of the Family Income Security Plan, 4 January 1980. Trudeau tabled the letter in the House a few days later. On the issue of the federal definition of income, Claude Castonguay had stated emphatically in September 1971 that Quebec required that determination of income reside with its Department of Revenue. This issue was important because income levels determined the level of allowance. See *Montreal Gazette*, 16 March 1972.

51 Trudeau fonds, MG 26 07, vol. 105, file 306.4, Bourassa to Trudeau, 17 March 1072; LAC, DNHW, acc. 85-86/343, box 27, file 3301-3-A16, Telex to

the Prime Minister from Robert Bourassa, 17 March 1972. Bourassa wrote in the telex, "I think that the proposals in your letter are in keeping with the talks we have been having on this matter for some months and that they make an appropriate framework within which we shall be able to draw up the specific terms and conditions for an agreement at further meetings" (translation in Trudeau fonds). See also *Journal de Montréal*, 14 March 1972.

52 Trudeau fonds, MG 26 07, vol. 332, file 363.44, Lalonde to Trudeau, "Rencontre avec l'honorable Bourassa," 17 January 1972.

53 See LAC, DNHW, acc. 85-86/343, box 27, file 3301-3-P15, "Basis of Federal Approach, March 1972"; *Montreal Gazette*, 14 March 1972; and *Le Devoir*, 14 and 15 March 1972, for instance.

54 On this point, see Splane, "Social Policy–Making in the Government of Canada," 237.

55 Stevens and Saywell, "Parliament and Politics," 105.

56 The Joint Review of Canada's Social Security System turned out to be a long and complicated process, and its final outcome is beyond the scope of this paper. The reform of family and youth allowances and the decision to integrate the federal family allowance program with the provincial schemes were a part of the review, but family allowance reforms were completed by the end of 1973. Family allowances did not figure prominently in the review after that date.

57 LAC, DNHW, acc. 85-86/343, box 26, file 3301-3-A3, pt 2, A.W. Johnson to Lalonde, 26 March 1973. John Turner wrote to Marc Lalonde on 23 March 1973, suggesting that a family allowance proposal be put to the provinces in April.

58 MacInnis Papers, vol. 15, file: Social Security, 1966–1974, "Speech Delivered by the Honourable Marc Lalonde to the Montreal Chamber of Commerce on Canada's Social Security Policy," 5 February 1973.

59 LAC, DNHW, acc. 85-86/343, vol. 31, file 3301-3-C47, News Release, Health and Welfare Canada, 18 April 1973.

60 As P.E. Bryden has argued for the Quebec and Canada Pension plans, this shared approach to the administration of family allowances also represented a new method of negotiating with the provinces that served to enhance the role of the federal government while, at the same time, strengthening national unity. See P.E. Bryden, *Planners and Politicians: Liberal Politics and Social Policy* (Montreal and Kingston: McGill-Queen's University Press, 1997).

61 Ottawa had also bowed to the pressure to maintain the universality feature of family allowances and permitted every Canadian family the privilege of receiving a monthly cheque, although it introduced a measure of income redistribution through the tax system. In a period of rising living costs, the Liberal government could boast that with its new social security legislation,

it added $840 million to the incomes of mainly low- and middle-income families. The total cost for family allowances was then $1.83 billion annually. See LAC, DNHW, vol. 2081, file 20-2-2, pt 3, News Release, Minister Introduces New Family Allowance Legislation, July 1973. It was estimated that the tax recovery for the Federal Treasury would be $350 million and for the provincial treasuries a further $115 million.

62   Leonard Shifrin, "Income Security: The Rise and Fall of the Federal Role," in *Canadian Social Welfare Policy: Federal and Provincial Dimensions*, ed. Jacqueline Ismael, 24–5.

CHAPTER **6**

From Postwar Liberalism to Neo-liberalism

◎ 6.1: CANADA'S WORKERS MOVEMENT: UNEVEN DEVELOPMENTS

Michael Goldfield and Bryan D. Palmer

Within the context of North America, Canada's economy, politics, and labour movement, as well as the country's diverse cultures, have a dual, almost divided, character. On the one hand, they exhibit highly independent and distinctive features; on the other, they are deeply entwined with—indeed operating in the shadow of and influenced greatly by—the imperialist colossus to the south. An advanced capitalist nation in its own right, and one with an imperialist arm reaching into the Caribbean and elsewhere, Canada nevertheless remains very much within an "American" sphere of influence.[1]

Historicizing National Difference

. . . Over the course of the twentieth century, Canada-US relations solidified as more and more of Canadian economic and cultural life came to be dominated by the dynamic expansion of United States capitalism, which, on a world scale, was unprecedented, especially in the post–World War II years.[2] Today the Canadian and US economies, and the politico-cultural trajectories that arise out of them, are integrated to the point that it is difficult to discern where they are differentiated, where one stops and another begins.[3]

That said, the Canadian bourgeoisie has generally been an independent wing of world capitalism, in contrast to its Mexican counterparts, who have usually functioned as US subsidiaries.[4] The protection of Canadian home industries was often compromised in the face of US capital's capacity to extend its influence. Yet, the Canadian state produced extensive networks of tariffs and other trade restrictions that, up until the 1980s, at least, allowed Canada's ruling class to preserve significant levels of autonomy.[5]

With the development of so-called free-trade agreements with the United States and Mexico (the Free Trade Agreement, or FTA, in 1989, and the North American Free Trade Agreement, or NAFTA, in 1994), the Canadian bourgeoisie has succumbed more to the economic dominance of US capital. Bourgeois independence has subsequently suffered a series of blows, some of which are material, others ideological. The picture is complicated by the unevenness of the developments, but on balance it can be said that the neo-liberal restructuring of the free-trade era has not in fact strengthened Canadian capital in relation to its US counterparts. Foreign ownership rose marginally in the period 1988–96, increasing from 27 percent to

31.5 percent, but more surprisingly the much-predicted expansion of the manufacturing sector did not materialize, and Canadian dependency on staples exports has remained a key feature of economic life. This is due in part to low levels of productivity in particular sectors, specific lags in technological development, and, perhaps critically, the bellicose nature of the Bush administration, which is more willing than any previous US governing political elite to simply insist that its arbitrary economic provisions be adhered to, however much they fly in the face of established trade agreements (softwood lumber, etc.).[6]

. . . [T]here remains much that is similar in the Canadian and US economies. Both, for instance, gained immensely from the post-1945 prosperity, being among the few developed Western economies in the Northern Hemisphere that survived World War II with their productive capacities intact. The occupational and industrial structures of both Canada and the United States have experienced similar changes in the last half-century, with strong expansion of the service sector and the resulting explosion of white- and pink-collar jobs. Postwar immigration has played a critical role in sustaining labour market growth. Institutions of social provisioning—hospitals, clinics, universities, research complexes, media of all sorts—are important components of a recognizable "North American" way of life in which the consumption side of a Fordist regime of accumulation seemingly predominates.[7]

The Labour Regime and National Welfare: Standards, Entitlements, and Race

Yet for all of the similarities, Canada and the United States are also quite different, especially in terms of the "climate" of expectation and entitlement as it is lived out in the broad population and articulated within the workers movement. The labour relations environment has, since the consolidation of a modern post–World War II system of industrial pluralism, been different in Canada than in the United States.[8] Far more social democratic than their US counterparts,

Canadians, with a somewhat lower standard of living (which has experienced a long, slow slide since the end of World War II, one accelerating markedly in the 1990s),[9] nonetheless have deeply ingrained appreciations of programs of social universality. Especially evident in terms of health care, this Canada-US difference also appears in education and inner-city infrastructure. Canadians experience, moreover, nowhere near the level of contact with debilitating poverty that characterizes the contemporary United States. The racialization of this destitution, while evident, is simply not comparable in the two countries. Canadian cities tend to be cleaner, safer, and less desperate places than those in the United States, recognized by Americans as well as Canadians as more liveable.

Evidence suggests that this difference is indeed fading, and if the free-trade era has produced change in Canada, it is in the structural narrowing of specific historical gaps between the Canadian and US ways of grappling with economic inequality. The share of Canadian government expenditure in the gross domestic product, for instance, has fallen considerably between 1992 and 2001, bringing Canadian experience more in line with that of the United States.[10] The historic association of Canadian identity with universality and a relatively strong welfare state nonetheless remains an important component of contemporary political culture. And this is buttressed, in terms of comparison with the United States, by the significantly different levels at which racialization of poverty, welfare, and labour market segmentation have operated in the two countries.[11] . . .

The history of racial oppression in the United States, compared to that of Canada, is also inseparable from key political-economic differences. Canada has a much smaller low-wage manufacturing sector, where workers are permanently trapped in poverty. There is, of course, an obvious Canadian gap between rich and poor, but not the ostentatious street visibility of this separation, evident in acute form in the United States. Canada's social safety net, however ragged in its capability of catching the most egregious instances of individuals falling from economic grace, is, while under attack and constantly threatened by growing state cutbacks and erosions, far more generous in its provisioning than what has historically existed in the United States. Health care, unemployment insurance, housing provisions, and welfare entitlements remain, whatever their precariousness, better in Canada than in its neighbour to the south. And public discussion of this, even in an age of market-driven priorities, reflects recognition that this matters to Canadians. . . .

Public Sector Workers and the Social Wage

Not surprisingly, and . . . undoubtedly related to the preservation of minimal levels of institutionalized, state-orchestrated welfare, Canada's public sector is proportionately far larger than that of the United States, employing roughly one-third of the labour force, approximately 72 percent of which is unionized. Yet it needs to be recognized that these organized public-sector workers occupy rungs on a welfare state economic ladder that are being chopped at viciously by state policies of retrenchment and outright attack, many of them ideologically fuelled by the political culture of the United States and the worldwide dominance of the neo-liberal agenda. Even if unionized, such workers routinely toil at tasks that are ill paid, poorly regarded, and without status; they are more likely to be women, persons of colour, or recently arrived immigrants and, as a result, are often marginalized and undermined. A Calgary wildcat strike of laundry workers in 1995, illegal nurses' walkouts in Quebec and Saskatchewan in 1999, and British Columbia's hospital employees' struggles over the period 2002–4, which came close to precipitating a province-wide general strike, all indicate that such public-sector workers, for all of their strength, are currently under considerable pressures. They often face demoralizing defeats that are a consequence of recalcitrant state forces and union officialdoms less than resolute in commitment to safeguard the material well-being of their memberships.[12]

Roughly one in three Canadian workers nevertheless belongs to a union, and this figure is understandably compared favourably to the dramatic decline in union density in the United States.[13] (Historically, it is worth noting that this is almost exactly the same level of union organization as existed in Canada in 1948, after the postwar surge of industrial unionism and a wave of mass strikes in important sectors of the economy.) Moreover, precisely because unionism's relative well-being in Canada has been in part premised on a climate of moderate social democratic sensibility and sustained somewhat by the presence of a public sector in which women workers figure centrally, the Canadian labour movement's modern addressing of gender issues has historically been more direct and forceful than what has unfolded in the United States. This is of course again no cause for self-congratulation given what remains to be confronted and changed and the uneven development of feminist consciousness and practice across different unions and regions in both Canada and the United States.[14]

The Canada-US comparison, then, raises warnings as well as highlighting clear differences. Union density in the United States reached levels of over 35 percent in 1945 and 1953, at that time higher than such figures in Canada. Since this historical peak, the steady, continuous erosion of the percentage of the workforce organized in the United States has dipped to the point where, in 2005, less than 12 percent of the non-agricultural workforce carried a union card. The picture of union membership in Canada is, to be sure, not pretty, there being an ongoing decline in the percentage of the workforce organized from the mid-1990s to the present, dropping from 36 percent in 1994 to 30 percent in 2005. . . . Even if such figures compare well with those of the United States, giving credence to the existence of differentiated "labour regimes," there is no denying that unions in Canada are on the defensive and whatever modest gains they register annually are coming nowhere near keeping pace with the growth in the workforce.[15] . . .

The 1960s: A Watershed Decade

The main divergence between Canada's and the United States' labour movements undoubtedly began during the late 1940s, with the more thorough purge of communists and other leftists and militants in the United States. But this separation took on added salience during the 1960s and 1970s, a product of three different developments. First, highly militant public-sector unions emerged in Canada—a trend that was paralleled in both the United States and Mexico—that had no ostensible ties, through common employers or organizations, to unions in the United States. These unions coloured the climate of class struggle in Canada, their attention inevitably directed at provincial and federal state policies, thereby providing a national focus to workers' demands rather than limiting demands to a narrow and less political set of contractual negotiations with the common multinational corporations faced by the private-sector unions. Moreover, such public-sector battles tended to be able to extract more from the Canadian state of the 1960s. The liberal hegemony of the Trudeau era, something of a last gasp of postwar affluence, was more able to bankroll worker-demanded reform and related social justice, anti-poverty, and welfare initiatives than was possible in the Vietnam War–entangled United States.[16]

Second, the flowering of Quebec nationalism and the development of a far more radical labour movement in a province seething with discontent created a broad workers movement with a distinct culture and identity, one that often veered in the direction of a revolutionary program. The October Crisis of 1970, in which the Front de Libération du Québec signed its own death warrant with the kidnapping of James Cross and Pierre Laporte and the execution of the latter, actually gave way to an October 1971 "Blue Collar" Crisis. Striking workers at *La Presse* mobilized thousands and clashed with police, leaving one young supporter dead. By March-April-May of 1972, 210,000 public-sector workers had walked off their jobs; a "Common Front" brought together the historically divided Quebecois working class; strikes and protests took on an insurgent quality as worksites were occupied, radio stations seized, and union leaders jailed.

"Not since the days of the Industrial Workers of the World . . . has a North American union movement been so dedicated to the tradition of revolutionary syndicalism," proclaimed Marcel Pepin of the Confederation of National Trade Unions (CNTU).[17]

Third, one wing of the generalized North American youth radicalization of the 1960s opted in Canada for an increasingly left-inflected nationalism. This dissident contingent intersected with elements of organized labour that were then chafing under the bureaucratic yoke of a US-dominated "international" unionism that was strongly economistic in its day-to-day dealings with employers and conventionally conservative in its relations with the political culture of the time. The result was a small, but growing, contingent of left-nationalist trade union forces that precipitated a politically influential breakaway movement of unions that separated themselves out from the US-headquartered AFL-CIO [American Federation of Labor–Congress of Industrial Organizations] unions. Often this coming together of radical youth and independence-minded trade unionists broke through barriers of complacency to try to organize the unorganized or bring union protections to the most vulnerable, immigrant workers.[18] Over the course of the 1960s and early 1970s, this fusion of youth radicalism and labour nationalism exercised a considerable impact among West Coast smelter and metal-working tradesmen, pulp and paper workers, energy and chemical labour, retail clerks, and building tradesmen, and within the Ontario and Quebec garment trades, where Kent Rowley and Madeleine Parent were standard-bearers of an alternative unionism.[19] This contrasted sharply with the US experience. There, an entrenched anti-communist but often reform-sympathetic labour leadership had countenanced a tenuous alliance with the elements of a revived early 1960s left. But as the mid-1960s saw growing militancy around opposition to the war in Vietnam, a shift from civil rights activism to black power, and the countercultural challenges of youthful rebellion, US trade union leaders moved decisively to marginalize student rebels and radical African-American activists.

New Leftists and organizations like the League of Revolutionary Black Workers found themselves excluded from any possible positions of common work or influence in the trade union movement.[20] . . .

Significant gains were thus registered by trade unions in Canada over the course of the 1960s, 1970s, and into the 1980s. . . .

These class struggles at the point of production paved the way for social democratic success in the political arena as the New Democrats [NDP] were elected to govern provincially, first in Manitoba, and then later in Saskatchewan and British Columbia in 1971–2. On the federal stage, David Lewis and the NDP, campaigning against the "corporate welfare bums" in 1972, rode the trough of Trudeau's faltering Liberals, managing to win enough seats to give them the balance of power over the deadlocked Liberals and Conservatives, who found themselves separated in the final House of Commons tally by a mere two seats. In this context, workers benefited from legislation that raised minimum wages, protected jobs, and restructured labour-capital relations. Plant shutdowns and strikebreaking were subjected to labour movement–orchestrated research reports and studies, pressuring provincial governments to draft acts and policies in line with workers' interests. The numbers of workers organized almost doubled between 1960 and 1975, rising from just under 1.5 million to roughly 2.9 million, with the percentage of the non-agricultural workforce unionized fluctuating from a low of 29.4 percent in 1964 to a high of 36.8 percent in 1975. This rising union density would peak in the mid-1980s, with 40 percent of Canadian workers organized in trade unions.[21]

The 1970s: Class Struggle and the Beginnings of the Downturn

This high-water mark of seeming union strength was, however, about to recede. The relations of class forces turned against the Canadian working class as the global crisis of capital accelerated with the recession of the 1970s. The oil crisis of 1973, the end of the international gold standard, the collapse of the ideological edifice of Keynesianism, along with a decade or more of economic stagnation, persistent unemployment, and seemingly unstoppable inflation, were all signals, rather than causes, of a crisis of Western capitalism. Overproduction and a generalized falling rate of profit were taking place in the historically unprecedented context of a post–World War II Fordist compromise, in which high wages and union organization in the pivotal economic sectors and welfare state provisioning to sustain more marginal milieus were traded for the stability of peaceful class co-existence. Given Canada's dependency on international trade and exports, the global slump precipitated in the 1973–5 years quickly translated into a fiscal crisis of the state.[22] With Canada's capacity to compete in the manufacturing sector slipping as the national measure of a unit cost of labour rose, peaking in 1976, and international demand for Canadian natural resources spiralling downward, a 1970 Canadian trade balance surplus of $3 billion turned into a $450-million deficit five years later. Coincident with the rise of the New Right in the United States and the United Kingdom, Canada's largely liberal and social democratic federal and provincial states followed suit, waging war on the working class, especially targeting government employees in the public sector.[23]

As Leo Panitch and Donald Swartz have demonstrated convincingly, the 1975–84 years saw an unprecedented wave of state assault on trade union freedoms, commencing with anti-inflation measures that, for all the rhetoric of curbing wages *and* prices, placed meaningful restriction only on the former. Canadian labour fought back, threatening general strikes and mounting political protests; intense years of class struggle such as 1972, 1974, and 1976 saw anywhere from 20 to 50 percent of all organized workers involved in strike action. But this militancy was not without its counter-reaction. Labour found itself on the receiving end of state discipline. Back-to-work legislation in the public sector proliferated, with the rising record of coercion unmistakable: between 1950 and

1970, Canadian federal and provincial governments legislated striking workers back to their jobs only 16 times; in the 1970–84 years, this figure soared to 63. With the federal election of Brian Mulroney and the Conservative Party to power in 1984, the trend continued. Complaints of violations of trade union rights by Canadian labour bodies to the United Nations–affiliated International Labour Organization climbed from 3 in the entire 1950–73 years to 27 in the 1973–91 period; four provinces were censured by the ILO for their clampdowns on government clerks in 1985–6 alone.[24]

This repressive message was read loudly and clearly, including in the private sector. The number of strikes waged over the period 1982–5 declined precipitously and was, on annual average, down more than 30 percent from comparable figures for the 1970s. More and more class battles were initiated by employers, who often opted to lock their workers out. By the late 1980s, wage settlements below the rate of inflation had climbed to 87 percent, up almost 40 percent from the first half of the decade, and whole sectors of the economy, including the building trades of the prairie West, had been reduced from strongholds of unionism to open shop enclaves. As early as 1984 almost 300,000 Canadian workers were bound by 136 collective agreements that called for either a wage freeze or a pay cut; salary hikes for corporate executives, in contrast, were poised to climb 22.5 percent.[25] Strikers as a percentage of the workforce organized, whose numbers had rarely dipped below 10 percent over the course of the entire 1970s, tapered to a paltry 4.4 percent in 1985. Not since the early 1960s had the number of days lost to class conflict been so low. In 1990, time lost to strikes dropped by 66 percent in one short year.[26] . . .

Compromising Class Struggle: The Fruit—Bitter and Sweet—of Unevenness in the 1980s

In broad outline, for both Canadian and US workers the periods of militancy (1960s and 1970s) as well as the years of relative quiescence (1980s and 1990s) have closely paralleled one another.

Yet Canadian workers have engaged in a number of impressive displays of solidarity and struggle in the 1980s and 1990s that are often presented as the envy of US leftists and labour militants. If these battles do indeed need to be recognized, they must also be seen for what they were: defeats that led to demoralization, undermined by union leaders who failed, almost to a person, to mount anything approximating an adequate opposition to the concerted intransigence of employers and the state. The unending record of missed opportunities, in which rank-and-file commitment to class struggle was squandered by a layer of trade union officialdom that persistently snatched defeat from the jaws of potential victory, reaches from the debacle of British Columbia's Solidarity movement of 1983 into the steady erosion of Quebec's painfully constructed Common Front union solidarities of the 1970s and early 1980s. By 1987, the much-heralded proletarian Quebecois militancy that was, in 1972, widely regarded as a potentially revolutionary cutting edge of North American syndicalism was but a pale reflection of its former self.[27] . . .

Days of Action/A Decade of Defeat

This art of trade union leaders stroking labour's foes rather than struggling resolutely against them was perhaps nowhere more evident than in Ontario's Days of Action campaign against the Mike Harris Tory "Common Sense Revolution" of the mid-to-late 1990s. Background to this momentous uprising was the sorry social democratic capitulation of the Bob Rae–led New Democratic Party. It swept to a surprising Ontario electoral victory in 1990 only to abandon much of its campaign promise of reform, retreating in the face of a fiscal crisis passed on to it by the predecessor Liberal government. Attacks on the unions followed, gutting collective bargaining in the public sector, leaving trade unions prey to the successor ideologues of reaction in the far-right Conservative Party, once Rae and the NDP went down to inevitable defeat.[28] As Harris unloaded on the working class, changing the voluntary Rae Days (government-enforced non-paid "holidays") into pink slips, promising cutbacks to the public sector that would have eliminated tens of thousands of jobs, closed hospitals, dismantled the welfare state, eliminated important trade union rights, and targeted much-maligned teachers' unions, the labour bureaucracy was forced by a rank-and-file mood of revolt to rise to the threatening occasion.

The Ontario Days of Action were initiated by a Canadian Auto Workers/public-sector unions/social movements coalition, which prodded the Ontario Federation of Labour [OFL] to act. Workers and a broad array of groups representing women, welfare recipients, anti-poverty activists, minorities, students, and environmentalists were brought together. The goal was to protest the policies of the Harris government by holding one-day general strikes in conjunction with another day of mass political protests and demonstrations. Focusing on one city at a time, the ostensible purpose came to be to build towards a province-wide general strike. Beginning in London, Ontario, in December 1995, and spreading to 10 other cities, including Hamilton, St Catharines, North Bay, Peterborough, Toronto, and Kingston, the Days of Action eventually encompassed hundreds of thousands of people. Unfolding over two and a half years, the last strike-protest gathering was organized in June 1998. The mobilization grew more and more spirited, sustaining radical critiques of the provincial government, creating an increasingly rebellious atmosphere. Toronto's massive work stoppage and anti-Harris demos saw the city's inner core of government-related institutions and businesses brought to a standstill on a Friday. A day later, as many as 250,000 protesters were in the streets. This much-publicized success was followed by an unprecedented education strike at the end of October 1997. The province-wide teacher walkout, involving 125,000 members of five separate unions/federations, closed elementary and secondary schools, forcing the state to petition the courts unsuccessfully for an injunction to end the conflict.[29]

The teacher job action, rare in its coordinated bringing together of historically divided federations of classroom educators organized by gender, religion, and level of schooling, was widely perceived as an illegal work stoppage. For a week it had the province open-mouthed in awe. Yet it signalled the beginning of the end. The embattled teachers went down to defeat, not because the rank-and-file strikers, the students, or even parents and their associations and local boards of education faltered in the face of the Harris government attacks, but rather because three of the teacher federation leaders capitulated and broke the strike, declaring the struggle over without so much as meeting with their striking memberships and explaining what had been gained and what could be lost. It was a demoralizing denouement to an exhilarating battle.[30]

As went the teachers, so went the province's workers as a whole. The impressive accomplishment of trade unionists and their allies challenging the state by the hundreds of thousands, rallying to the standard of protest, defying laws in the insistence that their economic power be used to create and maintain a better society was, in the final instance, undermined by labour's leaders. . . . While they undoubtedly pursued a path determined to develop initial impressive protest showings, they also eventually abdicated and at a critical juncture downloaded all responsibility for the ultimate organization of a general strike onto the somewhat wobbly table of OFL officialdom. There it soon dispersed into inaction and worse. Amidst the militancy and success of the October 1997 Toronto strike-protest, OFL President Gord Wilson grew astonishingly mild mannered, going so far as to sound apologetic about the "disruptions" of job actions. Smaller and more isolated cities were targeted, in the hope that the mobilization would fizzle. When the possible election of an NDP candidate in a Windsor by-election seemed to caution against rocking the autoworking centre with widespread plant shutdowns and mass protest, the plug was quietly pulled on the scheduled walkouts and demonstrations. After the Kingston Day of Action was a resounding success, drawing not only a huge local contingent, but militants from across the province and, indeed from the United States and Quebec, newly elected OFL head Wayne Samuelson scotched the notion that a general strike was in the offing. What had gone up with a bang, came down, ultimately, with a whimper. The Days of Action were unobtrusively terminated. . . .

Lean Production and the Politics of Accommodation: The Case of the CAW

Ontario's Days of Action were followed by the Canadian labour bureaucracy's abstentionist distancing of the trade union movement from the activities of radical youth–led protest that challenged the Free Trade Area of the Americas Summit, held in Quebec City in late April 2001. As perhaps 100,000 demonstrators converged on Quebec City, the protest quietly bifurcated as tens of thousands of militants battled police and assailed the symbolic fence that separated and "protected" bourgeois power from its radical opponents. In contrast to the spirited anti-capitalist challenge mounted by the left, labour's leadership did its best to channel union forces away from the main battle, marching their ranks to an empty parking lot on the outskirts of a city where the agitational fires of resistance burned in the streets and tear gas wafted over thoroughfares and alleyways congested with the antagonism of the rowdy ranks of potential revolt. There organized workers largely sat out the fight. Many, of course, had followed the non-labour protesters into battle, but others no doubt wondered why they had bothered to make the trek to Quebec City.[31]

Five months later the events of 9/11 drove many in the labour bureaucracy into postures even more cautious and conservative. Among those whose anti-terrorist rhetoric revved higher as 2001 closed was Buzz Hargrove, widely recognized as the most "radical" of Canada's labour bosses, a "social" unionist of progressive views and the leader of the most powerful private sector union in the country. As such, Hargrove garners significant media attention and has privileged access to television and newspaper outlets to promote not only the cause of the working class,

but broader social agendas of reform, justice, and fairness as well. If there is a union and a working-class leader who might be expected to be in the forefront of the struggle for social change in Canada, the Canadian Auto Workers [CAW] and Hargrove would be on everyone's list.

Yet in the last decade, in spite of rhetorical militancy, Hargrove has come to be seen as highly mercurial, incapable of sustaining a radical orientation towards class struggle. He demonstrates, precisely because of his seeming progressive, social unionist stance, the extent to which labour officialdom, *as a whole*, is incapable of developing and sustaining an unwavering opposition to capital and the state. Moreover, because the CAW occupies a unique and pivotal place in Canada's industrial heartland, the autoworkers having a historic and ongoing centrality to class struggle in the most powerful province in the dominion, Hargrove's stance is especially noteworthy. The CAW leadership under Hargrove also illuminates how the restructuring of capitalist workplaces with the pressures of free-trade globalization has inevitable and debilitating consequences on the politics of the labour bureaucracy. In the end, however "social" the union pronouncements of certain trade union tops, they retreat into the "business" unionism of their class politics. For without a program of socialist class struggle, union leaders invariably compromise and capitulate in the ongoing struggle that pits capital and labour against one another.

Autoworker unionism in Canada has, in the last 40 years, been buffered somewhat by the 1960s-developed protectionist legislation of the Canada–United States Auto Pact, which insured certain levels of production and state support to this critical economic sector. Between 1965 and 2002, Canada's automotive-producing sector employment soared from 75,000 to almost 500,000, while the vehicles that came off the Canadian assembly lines climbed from 846,000 to 2.6 million. In 2002, the auto industry accounted for 12 percent of Canadian GDP. The Auto Pact, however, was abolished as a consequence of World Trade Organization discussions over the course of 1999–2001, arguably one of the most important consequences of neo-liberal globalization to hit central Canadian workers. With the massive restructuring of the North American automobile industry over the course of recent decades, its Canadian component has been in an irreversible slide.[32]

During the period of the Auto Pact's existence, Hargrove, who followed on the leadership heels of Dennis McDermott and Bob White, and was schooled in their classroom of labour officialdom, could mouth the rhetoric of class struggle without paying its full price. He knew full well that, unlike his US counterparts in Detroit's UAW [United Auto Workers] Solidarity House, he could rely on a measure of Canadian state support for the country's protected auto plants. As militancy flared in the 1980s and 1990s, with the CAW one of the seemingly few bright spots on the horizon of union resistance, Hargrove utilized the muscle of organized labour's ranks to sustain plant occupations and flying squadrons of picket and protest-supporting autoworkers.[33] He also lent material aid to radical movements such as the Ontario Coalition Against Poverty [OCAP], which was among the most forceful anti-capitalist agitators in Ontario's ongoing and escalating war against economic retrenchment. But as OCAP found itself locked into a no-holds-barred battle with Mike Harris, presenting almost the only fighting front against the mean-spirited Tories in the aftermath of the Days of Action debacle, Hargrove, embarrassed by the refusal of the anti-poverty movement to play with the stacked deck of legalism and opposed to its raucous office occupations of Conservative cabinet ministers and resulting charges of criminal trespass, pulled the plug on CAW donations to OCAP coffers.[34] It was a direct attempt to silence and starve into submission a critical voice on the margins of the labour movement.

The flying squadrons were also subdued. Once given something of a free rein, they had come to be recognized throughout labour and left circles as a corps of working-class self-activity. They are now nothing of the sort, reduced to a merely military arm of the CAW hierarchy, kept on a very tight leash by Hargrove and his immediate circle in the union's National Office.

Dissidents in the CAW, who in earlier years of Hargrove's reign had been given something of a hearing, have increasingly found themselves more and more muzzled and marginalized. When a Hargrove opponent, Willie Lambert, had the temerity to challenge the CAW head for the presidency in 2006, running on a platform opposing concessionary bargaining, the auto-worker bureaucracy came down quite heavily on the upstart leadership bid. It did not so much want to defeat Lambert as crush him, providing a strong message to Hargrove rivals that they would be in for some very tough sledding if they dared to strike out against the entrenched CAW leadership. A union bureaucracy that routinely extolled the virtues of democracy in its public pronouncements barely countenanced it in its private practices of governance.[35]

Lambert's campaign highlighted a growing concern among many in the UAW ranks. The last years have seen the Canadian Auto Workers' historic refusal to engage in concessionary bargaining, always promoted by both Hargrove and his predecessor Bob White as *the* key and strategic line of demarcation separating them (and, indeed, the Canadian union) from the officials of the UAW, compromised and, ultimately, jettisoned. Hargrove has exerted pressure on locals to abandon past collective bargaining gains, arguing that such give-backs are necessary if Canada's auto industry is to survive in the difficult and growingly competitive era of globalization. . . .

What explains this on-again, off-again labour bureaucratic politics? As Bruce Allen, a left dissident within the CAW and vice-president of Local 199 in St Catharines, Ontario, has suggested, the complex trajectory of autoworker politics is not unrelated to the material context of the last 15 years, in which the lean production methods of the "Toyota Way" have aligned with the globalizing thrust of free-trade agreements to produce a continuous downsizing of central Canada's critically important the auto workforce. One measure of declining union density in Canada is of course the extent to which this quintessentially Fordist workforce has been whittled down, figuring forcefully in the falling

rate of unionization among private-sector workers. The pivotal CAW GM [General Motors] Local
222 in Oshawa lost approximately 4,000 members in the 1996–2001 years, and a further round
of job cuts was announced in 2006. In February
2007, the Chrysler Group stated that it planned
to eliminate 2,000 jobs, or 20 percent of its
entire Canadian workforce, in the working-class
strongholds of Windsor and Brampton. Plant clo-
sures and massive layoffs have thus been particularly acute in the automobile industry–sensitive
manufacturing of Ontario and Quebec, rivalling
in their impact a previous set of consequences
of the economic downturn of the late 1980s
and early 1990s. The devastation runs, ripple-
effect like, through smaller factories in the auto-
supplying economy and extends into clothing
and textile manufacturers and a pulp and paper
sector crippled by the negative effects of a high
Canadian dollar. Over the course of the last half-
decade, from 2001 to 2006, 200,000 Canadian
manufacturing jobs, or just under 10 percent of
the country's total, have succumbed to economic
restructuring, almost half of this staggering loss
occurring in 2005 alone. The state-subsidized
expansion of non-union auto-manufacturing
operations by Toyota and Honda in central
Canada complicates the current scene even further, leading to an intensification of competition
in the auto industry and an ongoing weakening of
industrial-unionist struggles that puts a leash on
the entire labour movement.

At the bargaining table this has resulted in
the "Big Three" automakers demanding concessions from the CAW and handouts from the
Canadian state as the price for doing business.
The neo-liberal, free-trade setting is one where
the now dismantled Auto Pact no longer guarantees specific levels of production. Desperate
to stop the bleeding away of jobs and dues,
Hargrove and the CAW officialdom have done
their part by conceding to the demands of the
auto corporations for "flexible" contracts. This
has been especially evident in the case of recent
Oshawa negotiations, where a concessionary
"shelf agreement" opened up the contract and
bargained away important workplace rights long

protected by collective agreements. Ratified
in early March 2006, the CAW-GM agreement,
which the union officialdom pushed on its ranks
with all the "hard sell" techniques at its disposal,
spelled a decisive end to claims that the Canadian
autoworkers are resisting concessions. The union
agreed to work cooperatively with the company
in "restructuring" endeavours. It allowed out-
sourcing of janitorial work throughout the life
of the agreement. Significant ground was given
on issues related to early retirement. The daily
relief time allowed shift workers was decreased,
thereby exacerbating the problems associated
with ongoing speed-up of production and all
of the attendant stresses and complications that
undermine the health and occupational safety
of line workers. Finally, the CAW caved in to
management's insistence that it be allowed to
use temporary workforces in "product launch
situations." Ten short years ago these give-backs
would certainly have precipitated strike action,
mobilization of flying pickets, even, possibly,
plant occupations and sit-down work stoppages.
But now they are lauded by the CAW as grounds
on which concessions must be made, opening
up collective agreement language to employer
demand and the voracious pressure of ever leaner
production methods.

Such Hargrove-endorsed concessions are the
union *quid pro quo* for state handouts to the companies. As was obvious in the recent 2006 Ontario
government Oshawa General Motors bailout, the
automakers are pressing harder and harder for
dual concessions, in which unions *and* the state
cough up enough to sweeten the likelihood of the
assembly lines remaining operational. . . .

Left on the sidelines, however, is the Ontario
working class, which faces an ongoing restructuring of work environments that results in intensification of the labour process, concentration of
workplace power in the hands of an aggressively
demanding, union-hating managerial element,
and reductions in the cost of production that are
invariably extracted from the hide of the working class. With this happening to arguably the
most powerful and militant union in Canada, led
by the seemingly most progressive trade union

leadership in the country, the writing on the wall of class struggle is telling an increasingly depressing tale. Its storyline, evident since the late 1980s, was presented starkly in the 1990s and has been ongoing ever since.[36] . . .

Note: This essay is part of a larger project, tentatively entitled *Entwined Fates: The North American Working Classes*, the co-authors of which are Dan La Botz, Michael Goldfield, and Bryan D. Palmer.

Endnotes

1   For relevant discussions of this Canadian political economy, in which debate still dominates as to whether dependency or the capitalist logic of accumulation and the terms of class struggle best defines the nature of a political program of resistance, see, among many useful studies, Kari Levitt, *Silent Surrender: The Multinational Corporation in Canada* (Toronto, 1970); Steve Moore and Debi Wells, *Imperialism and the National Question in Canada* (Toronto, 1975); Wallace Clement, *Continental Corporate Power: Economic Linkages between Canada and the United States* (Toronto, 1977); Glen Williams, *Not for Export: Toward a Political Economy of Canada's Arrested Industrialization* (Toronto, 1983); Murray E.G. Smith, "Political Economy and the Canadian Working Class: Marxism or National Reformism?," *Labour/Le Travail* 46 (Fall 2000): 343–68; and Paul Kellogg, "Kari Levitt and the Long Detour of Canadian Political Economy," *Studies in Political Economy* 76 (Autumn 2005): 31–60.

2   For a brief summary of US world economic dominance after World War II, see Michael Goldfield, *The Color of Politics: Race and the Mainsprings of US Politics* (New York, 1997). Note as well the discussions in Philip Armstrong and Andrew Glyn, *Capitalism since 1945* (Oxford, 1991); and Robert Brenner, *The Economics of Global Turbulence: The Advanced Capitalist Economies from Long Boom to Long Downturn, 1945–2005* (London, 2006), 43–51.

3   This deep continentalist integration is a feature of much of the literature addressing free-trade agreements and Canada in the age of globalization. See, for instance, Christina Gabriel and Laura Macdonald, "'Of Borders and Business': Canadian Corporate Proposals for 'Deep Integration,'" *Studies in Political Economy* 74 (Autumn 2004): 79–100. See, also, of course, an older work: Clement, *Continental Corporate Power*.

4   See, for instance, James D. Cockcroft, *Mexico's Hope: An Encounter with Politics And History* (New York, 1998).

5   For a raucously extreme statement that questions the independence of the Canadian ruling class, see R.T. Naylor, "The Rise and Fall of the Third Commercial Empire of the St. Lawrence," in Gary Teeple, ed., *Capitalism and the National Question in Canada*

(Toronto, 1972), 1–42. More judicious is the argument and theoretical elaboration in Leo Panitch, "The Role and Nature of the Canadian State," in Panitch, ed., *The Canadian State: Political Economy and Political Power* (Toronto 1977), 3–27.

6   Andrew Jackson, "The Free Trade Agreement—A Decade Later," *Studies in Political Economy* 57 (Spring 1999): 141–60; Jackson, "A Tale of Two Economies," *Canadian Dimension* 40 (May-June 2006): 33–6; Jeffrey Ayres, "Power Relations under NAFTA: Reassessing the Efficacy of Contentious Transnationalism," *Studies in Political Economy* 74 (Autumn 2004): 101–23; William K. Carroll and William Little, "Neoliberal Transformation and Antiglobalization Politics in Canada: Transition, Consolidation, and Resistance," *International Journal of Political Economy* 31 (Fall 2001): 42; Jim Stanford, "Economic Models and Economic Reality: Free Trade and Predictions," *International Journal of Political Economy* 33 (Fall 2003): 28–49; Stanford, "Back to the Hinterland," www.caw.ca/ (17 December 2003); Stanford, "The Northern Tiger's a Kitten—But Do Voters Care?," *Globe and Mail*, 10 May 2003; and Mel Watkins, "The Clash of Ideas: Neoclassical Trade Theory versus Canadian Political Economy," *International Journal of Political Economy* 33 (Fall 2003): 90–101.

7   For a still useful discussion of Fordism, see David Harvey, *The Condition of Postmodernity: An Enquiry into the Origins of Cultural Change* (Oxford, 1989).

8   For an overview accenting this "labour regime" difference, see David Kettler, James Struthers, and Christopher Huxley, "Unionization and Labour Regimes in Canada and the United States: Considerations for Comparative Research," *Labour/Le Travail* 25 (Spring 1990): 161–88. Note as well Peter McInnis, *Harnessing Labour Confrontation: Shaping the Postwar Settlement in Canada, 1943–1950* (Toronto, 2002). On union culture in modern Canada, see D'Arcy Martin, *Thinking Union: Activism and Education in Canada's Labour Movement* (Toronto, 1995).

9   On Canada's slipping standard of living, see Daniel Shaw, "Canada's Productivity and Standard of Living: Past, Present, and Future," Government of Canada, Depository Services Program, dsp-psd.pwgsc.gc.ca/.

Heather Schofield, "Equality Myth Seen Holding Canada Back," *Globe and Mail*, 18 January 2007, notes that a Conference Board of Canada report points out that Canada's standard of living, as measured by per capita income, has slipped from ranking fifth among the developed countries of the world in 1990 to tenth place in the same rankings in 2005.

10   Robert Johnson and Rianne Mahon, "NAFTA, the Redesign and Rescaling of Canada's Welfare State," *Studies in Political Economy* 76 (Autumn 2005): 7–30; and David A. Green and Jonathan R. Kesselman, eds, *Dimensions of Inequality in Canada* (Vancouver, 2006).

11   For evidence that the political culture of Canada remains different than that of the United States and has not been vanquished and "Americanized" from above by neo-liberal restructuring, see Watkins, "The Clash of Ideas," and Sam Gindin, "Beyond NAFTA," *Canadian Dimension* 38 (March-April 2004): 29–31.

12   See David Camfield, "Neoliberalism and Working-Class Resistance in British Columbia: The Hospital Employees' Union Struggle, 2002–2004," *Labour/Le Travail* 57 (Spring 2006): 9–42.

13   On this demise, see Michael Goldfield, *The Decline of Organized Labor in the United States* (Chicago, 1987); and Goldfield, "The Impact of Globalization and Neo-liberalism on the Decline of US Unions," in Debdas Banerjee and Michael Goldfield, eds, *Labour, Globalization, and the State* (London 2008).

14   See, for instance, the accounts in Julie White, *Sisters and Solidarity: Women and Unions in Canada* (Toronto, 1993); Linda Briskin and Patricia McDermott, eds, *Women Challenging Unions: Feminism, Democracy and Militancy* (Toronto, 1993); Meg Luxton, "Feminism as a Class Act: Working-Class Feminism and the Women's Movement in Canada," *Labour/Le Travail* 48 (Fall 2001): 63–88. For the US, see Dorothy Sue Cobble, *The Other Women's Movement: Workplace Justice and Social Rights in Modern America* (Princeton, 2005).

15   For discussions of Canadian union density, see Barry Brennan, "Canadian Labor Today: Partial Successes, Real Challenges," *Monthly Review* 57 (June 2005): 46–61; and Andrew Jackson, "Solidarity Forever? Trends in Canadian Union Density," *Studies in Political Economy* 74 (Autumn 2004): 125–46.

16   There were, of course, limits to this era of free collective bargaining, but compared to the post-1970 climate of repression, it offered cautious and conservative union leaderships some room for manoeuvre. See Leo Panitch and Donald Swartz, *The Assault on Trade Union Freedoms: From Wage Controls to the Social Contract* (Toronto, 1993), 7–20. For a discussion of state initiatives and popular mobilizations surrounding the period's "War on Poverty," see James Struthers, *The Limits of Affluence: Welfare in Ontario, 1920–1970* (Toronto, 1994), 211–30; Honourable David A. Croll, Chairman, *Poverty in Canada: A Report of the Special Senate Committee on Poverty* (Ottawa, 1971); and Ian Adams *et al.*, *The Real Poverty Report* (Edmonton, 1971).

17   The writing on Quebec unions and radicalization in this period is extensive. See, as an introduction only, Daniel Drache, ed., *Quebec—Only the Beginning: The Manifestoes of the Common Front* (Toronto, 1972); Black Rose Books Editorial Collective, ed., *Quebec Labour: The Confederation of National Trade Unions Yesterday and Today* (Montreal, 1975); Dimitri Roussopoulos, ed., *Quebec and Radical Social Change* (Montreal, 1974); Louis Fournier, *F.L.Q.: The Anatomy of an Underground Movement* (Toronto, 1984).

18   R.B. Morris, "The Reverter Clause and Break-aways in Canada," and Charles Lipton, "Canadian Unionism," in Teeple, ed., *Capitalism and the National Question in Canada*, 89–119; Philip Resnick, *The Land of Cain: Class and Nationalism in English Canada, 1945–1975* (Vancouver, 1977); Ed Finn, "Prospects for an Autonomous Labour Movement," *Canadian Dimension* 1 (September-October 1968): 4; and Finn, "The Struggle for Canadian Labour Autonomy," *Labour Gazette* 70 (November 1970): 766–74.

19   Rick Salutin, *Kent Rowley: The Organizer—A Canadian Union Life* (Toronto, 1980); Andrée Lévesque, ed., *Madeleine Parent: Activist* (Toronto, 2005); Philip Resnick, "The Breakaway Movement in Trail," and Paul Knox, "Breakaway Unionism in Kitimat," in Paul Knox and Philip Resnick, eds, *Essays in BC Political Economy* (Vancouver, 1974), 42–59; Wayne Roberts, *Cracking the Canadian Formula: The Making of the Energy and Chemical Workers Union* (Toronto, 1990), 149–64; Joan Sangster, "Remembering Texpack: Nationalism, Internationalism, and Militancy in Canadian Unions in the 1970s," *Studies in Political Economy* 78 (Autumn 2006): 41–66.

20   Peter B. Levy, *The New Left and Labor in the 1960s* (Urbana, 1994); Dan Georgakas and Marvin Surkin, *Detroit: I Do Mind Dying* (Boston, 1998); and James A. Geschwender, *Class, Race and Worker Insurgency: The League of Revolutionary Black Workers* (Cambridge, 1977).

21   The above paragraphs draw on Bryan D. Palmer, *Working-Class Experience: Rethinking the History of Canadian Labour, 1800–1991* (Toronto, 1992), 298–339. On other matters raised in this paragraph, see Marc Zwelling, *The Strike Breakers: The Report of the Strikebreaking Committee of the Ontario Federation of Labour and the Labour Council of Metropolitan Toronto* (Toronto, 1972); John W. Eleen and Ashley G. Bernadine, *Shutdown: The Impact of Plant Shutdown, Extensive Employment Terminations*

and *Layoffs on the Workers and the Community* (Toronto, 1971); David Lewis, *Louder Voices: The Corporate Welfare Bums* (Toronto, 1972); and Steven High, *Industrial Sunset: The Making of North America's Rust Belt, 1969–1984* (Toronto, 2003).

22 On the wider, global context, see Brenner, *Economics of Global Turbulence.*

23 For an important contextual and conceptual discussion, see Murray E.G. Smith and K.W. Taylor, "Profitability Crisis and the Erosion of Popular Prosperity: The Canadian Economy, 1947–1991," *Studies in Political Economy* 49 (Spring 1996): 101–30.

24 Ernest Mandel, *The Second Slump: A Marxist Analysis of Recession in the Seventies* (London, 1978); and Panitch and Swartz, *The Assault on Trade Union Freedoms.*

25 CEO salaries and benefits have soared in the recent past and are a measure of the widening gap of inequality that suggests the worsening lot of labour and the poor in our times. The current gap between CEO remuneration and the working-class wage is not as wide in Canada as it is in the United States, but as the *Globe and Mail* noted in an 8 January 2007 editorial, "What's a CEO Worth," "the disparities in Canadian income levels have similarly grown to unhealthy levels." The Canadian Centre for Policy Alternatives noted that in 2005 Canada's top 100 CEOs averaged annual earnings of $9 million. The average earnings of a Canadian worker, by comparison, were $38,000. Thus, even the lowest-paid Canadian CEOs earned in three and a half days what it took most Canadians a year to take home in pay.

26 For a general discussion, see Palmer, *Working-Class Experience*, 340–416.

27 For a thorough critique of the Solidarity experience, see Bryan D. Palmer, *Solidarity: The Rise and Fall of an Opposition In British Columbia* (Vancouver, 1987); and for a comparison of Quebec and British Columbia, see Palmer, *Working-Class Experience*, 361–70. For a particularly irksome reading of the BC Solidarity movement by arguably one of the most antediluvian of trade union leaders, see Jack Munro and Jane O'Hara, *Union Jack: Labour Leader Jack Munro* (Vancouver, 1988), 1–17.

28 For this unfortunate chapter in a generalized contemporary crisis of social democracy, see Stephen McBride, "The Continuing Crisis of Social Democracy: Ontario's Social Contract in Perspective," *Studies in Political Economy* 50 (Summer 1996): 65–94; George Ehring and Wayne Roberts, *Giving Away a Miracle: Lost Dreams, Broken Promises, and the Ontario Ndp* (Oakville, ON, 1993); Thomas Walkom, *Rae Days: The Rise and Fall of the NDP* (Toronto, 1994); and Panitch and Swartz, *Assault on Trade Union Freedoms*, 159–88. For the Harris assault on the public sector, see David Rapaport, *No Justice,*

No Peace: The 1996 Opseu Strike Action against the Harris Government In Ontario (Montreal and Kingston, 1999).

29 For a rather uncritical approach to the Days of Action, see Marcella Munro, "Ontario's 'Days of Action' and Strategic Choices for the Left in Canada," *Studies in Political Economy* 53 (Summer 1997): 125–40. There is also much of relevance, including considerable discussion of context, in Yonatan Reshef and Sandra Rastin, *Unions in the Time of Revolution: Government Restructuring in Alberta and Ontario* (Toronto, 2003). We are obviously more inclined to endorse the views in Bryan D. Palmer, "Slowdown in Ontario: Build the General Strike," *Canadian Dimension* 30 (May-June 1996): 21–6; and Palmer, "Where Ya At, General Strike?!," *Canadian Dimension* 32 (September-October 1998): 20–4.

30 Bryan D. Palmer, "Halloween in Harrisland: Teachers, Bureaucrats, and Betrayal," *Canadian Dimension* 32 (January-February 1998): 29–32.

31 For one account, see Kevin McKay, "Solidarity and Symbolic Protest: Lessons for Labour from the Quebec City Summit of the Americas," *Labour/Le Travail* 50 (Fall 2002): 21–72.

32 For a recent example of the CAW's political nostalgia for the days of the auto pact, see Jim Stanford, "A New Auto Pact, for a New Auto Industry," *Globe and Mail*, 29 January 2007. On the history and importance of the Auto Pact, see Dimitry Anastakis, "Between Nationalism and Continentalism: State Auto Industry Policy and the Canadian UAW, 1960–1970," *Labour/ Le Travail* 53 (Spring 2004): 89–125; Anastakis, "Requiem for a Trade Agreement: The Auto Pact at the WTO, 1999–2000," *Canadian Business Law Journal* 31 (February 2001): 313; and Anastakis, *Auto Pact: Creating a Borderless North American Auto Industry* (Toronto, 2005).

33 On background and development of this history, see Bryan D. Palmer, "'Taking It': Ontario Workers' Struggles," in W.J.C. Cherwinski and Gregory S. Kealey, ed., *Lectures in Canadian Labour and Working-Class History* (St John's, NL, 1985), 183–98; Robert Simms and Joanne Wallador, "Auto Strikers Occupy GM Plant in Ontario," *The Militant*, 28 October 1996; Don Whelman, "No More Mandatory Overtime," leaflet by Local 222 Shop Committee Chairperson on Behalf of the GM Unit Shop Committee, 1996; and D.W. Livingstone and Reuben Roth, "Workplace Communities and Transformative Learning: Oshawa Autoworkers and the CAW," *Convergence* 31 (1998): 12–23.

34 On the Ontario Coalition Against Poverty and Hargrove, see Bryan D. Palmer, "What's Law Got to Do with It? Historical Considerations on Class Struggle, Boundaries of Constraint, and Capitalist Authority," and John Clarke, "Social Resistance

and the Disturbing of the Peace," in *Osgoode Hall Law Journal* 41 (Summer/Fall 2003): 465–504; and Jonathan Greene, "Whatever It Takes: People's Organizing, OCAP, and Social Struggle," *Studies in Political Economy* 75 (Spring 2005): 5–28.

35   Alex Levant, "Reflections on the Canadian Labour Congress Convention," *Autonomy & Solidarity*, http://auto_sol.tao.ca (accessed 7 January 2007).

36   The above paragraphs draw on the important analytic statement in Bruce Allen, "Inside the CAW Jacket," *New Socialist* 57 (July-August 2006): http://newsocialist.org (accessed 7 January 2007); and "Chrysler to Axe 2000 Jobs," *Globe and Mail*, 8 February 2007. See also Sam Gindin, "Concessions in Oshawa: The End of an Era?," *MRZine*, at http://mrzine.monthlyreview.org (accessed 8 January 2007); Gindin, "Auto Concessions: Yesterday's Defeat . . . Tomorrow's Revival?," *Canadian Dimension*, at

http://canadiandimension.com (accessed 8 January 2007), which accents the importance of health care differentials in Canada and the United States as a cause of Big Three demands for concessions in Canada; and Freda Coodin, "The CAW Turn: Bargaining versus Building," *Canadian Dimension* 39 (November–December 2005): 36–8. James Rinehart, Christopher Huxley, and David Robertson, *Just Another Car Factory: Lean Production and its Discontents* (Ithaca, NY, 1997); and Jeffrey Liker, *The Toyota Way: 14 Management Principles from the World's Greatest Manufacturer* (New York, 2003), present insights into lean production, while Alan Sears, *Retooling the Mind Factory: Education in a Lean State* (Peterborough, ON, 2003), indicates that the principles of lean production have permeated many sectors of social/economic life. See, as well, Jackson, "Tale of Two Economies," 34–5.

◎ 6.2: THE HARPER GOVERNMENT AND OPEN FEDERALISM

Brooke Jeffrey

We can create a country built on solid Conservative values . . . a country the Liberals wouldn't even recognize, the kind of country I want to lead.

—*Stephen Harper, 2004*

Long before he became prime minister, Stephen Harper made it clear that he had a much different vision of Canada than his Liberal predecessors, and especially former prime minister Pierre Trudeau. Like other Canadian conservative leaders—including Robert Stanfield, Joe Clark, and Brian Mulroney—Harper also espoused a different approach to federalism, one that typically gave priority to provincial autonomy and interpreted Confederation in terms of the compact theory. As Senator Michael Kirby noted, this decentralist approach was epitomized by the Mulroney government's failed Meech Lake Accord, a constitutional reform package diametrically opposed to the Trudeauvian vision of a strong national government and the supremacy of individual rights.[1]

However, there are several new aspects to Harper's vision of federalism that make it more extreme and inflexible than the traditional

conservative approach. Harper recognized this fact by introducing a new term, "open federalism," to better reflect and distinguish his views from those of traditional Tories. Harper spelled out this vision in statements he made as a Reform member of Parliament (MP), president of the National Citizens' Coalition, and leader of the Alliance Party and the new Conservative Party, all before taking office in 2006.

Since then, Harper has been confronted with several unanticipated policy dilemmas that challenged his vision. On some occasions, his determination to chart his own course has been evident. On others, it appears he has been obliged to temper his views with a pragmatism born of political necessity, a reality reinforced by his government's minority status from 2006 until the May 2011 election.

Nevertheless, a number of developments since 2006 suggest that Harper has not lost sight of his unique federal vision. This article outlines the theoretical basis of open federalism and then examines the Harper government's record with a view to determining whether the operation of Canadian federalism has changed significantly. A concluding section explores the potential impact of any such changes for the welfare state.

Open Federalism in Theory

In 1992, as the party's policy adviser, Stephen Harper was instrumental in convincing Reform leader Preston Manning to oppose the Charlottetown Accord. Harper particularly rejected the special status offered to Quebec in the accord. The subsequent failure of the Charlottetown deal played a major role in bringing down the Progressive Conservative (PC) government of Brian Mulroney and his successor, Kim Campbell, providing an opening for the Reform Party in the 1993 federal election. Although the Chrétien Liberals were returned to power with a majority government, Reform came tantalizingly close to forming the official opposition, falling just two seats short of the Bloc Québécois (BQ).

Harper was among the MPs elected in the 1993 Reform sweep of western Canada. Soon after, he was appointed the party's intergovernmental affairs critic. When the PQ government in Quebec launched the 1995 sovereignty referendum, Harper drafted a comprehensive package of reforms that he argued would strengthen national unity by reducing the role of the federal government. The changes, he said, "will assert the autonomy of the provinces and the power of the people well into the future."[2] When challenged to explain how national unity could be reinforced by such measures—in a federation that was already among the most decentralized in the world—Harper insisted that stronger provinces would create a stronger country. He also denied that this approach was inconsistent with his earlier rejection of special status for Quebec. That province, he said, would only benefit from the decentralization of power, like the other provinces. Mindful of Mulroney's two failed attempts at constitutional reform, Harper

was also quick to point out that he believed his changes could be implemented without recourse to the Constitution, since they were "administrative" in nature and "simply require a federal government that is willing to act."[3]

Until then, Harper's stated views on Canadian federalism had not deviated significantly from traditional Tory positions. His emphasis on provincial rights was perhaps more emphatic, but nothing in his earlier comments foreshadowed the more extreme positions he would now take. Indeed, over the next decade, as his views on the appropriate functioning of the federal system were spelled out in detail, it became clear that Harper's concept of Canadian federalism differed from the traditional conservative approach in several important ways.

To begin with, Harper favoured the total withdrawal of the federal government from areas of provincial or even shared responsibility, rather than a more collaborative approach in which the provinces and the federal government shared equal billing. In his party's 2005 platform, there was a predictable commitment to "the federal principle and the notion of strong provinces within Canada." But this was followed by a pledge to "ensure [that] the use of the federal spending power in areas of provincial jurisdiction is limited" and another to "authorize the provinces to use the opting out formula with full compensation if they want to opt out of any new or modified program" in areas of exclusive provincial or shared jurisdiction. (This approach, it should be noted, is reminiscent of the language found in the ill-fated 1999 Social Union Framework Agreement [SUFA] promoted by Alberta's Ralph Klein and Ontario's Mike Harris, two right-wing premiers who shared Harper's extreme decentralist views and ideology.)

In a speech in Quebec City during the 2006 election campaign, Harper expanded on his platform pledges. He spoke of allowing the provinces *to take the lead* on social policy and the social union, and declared that any government he led would limit the federal role to "complementing and supporting" the activities of the provinces, an unprecedented ceding of federal involvement.[4]

This voluntary retrenchment predictably was criticized by Liberals as an abdication of responsibility and a threat to national unity. More surprising was the criticism coming from Harper's presumptive colleagues. After the "merger" to create the new Conservative Party in 2003, former Progressive Conservative prime minister Joe Clark declared he would vote for the Martin Liberals as the lesser of two evils. "I'm that concerned with the imprint of Stephen Harper," Clark said, "not only what he has stood for in the past . . . but the way he has led this party. This is not my party. This is something entirely new."[5] His views were echoed by his former intergovernmental affairs minister, Senator Lowell Murray, who insisted on retaining his designation as a Progressive Conservative in the Senate along with several colleagues. At the time, Murray declared the new party was "fundamentally different" and "incompatible" with Progressive Conservative values.

Several former Mulroney cabinet ministers also declined to be identified with Harper's new Conservative Party, and one, Sinclair Stevens, aggressively criticized the new party and its leader for their radical views on the federation: "This is the first time in Canadian history that a national political party has embraced a provincial rights agenda."[6]

Nevertheless Harper finally secured a minority victory for his own party in the 2006 election. Shortly after, he declared that he would consider his government a success if it was able to limit federal activities to defence, foreign policy, and the economic union.[7] This led one journalist to describe Harper's approach as more American than Canadian, one that envisaged a mere "night watchman" role for the federal government.[8] This view was confirmed during the next election campaign, in 2008, when Harper made further concessions to the provinces. Rather than simply allowing provinces to opt out of federal programs, Harper now declared that no new programs would be introduced unless the majority of provinces agreed.

Harper justified his determination to see the federal government withdraw from the social union by introducing a second new element in

CP PHOTO/Jeff McIntosh

Conservative leader Stephen Harper speaking after winning the federal election, Monday, 23 January 2006, in Calgary.

his federal vision, namely the need to return to a classic form of federalism. Like other Progressive Conservatives before him, he had long argued that Canadian federalism suffered from a failure to adequately respect the formal allocation of responsibilities between the two levels of government. But Harper went further, famously criticizing Ottawa for "sticking its nose into provincial and local matters" and at the same time for "neglecting what it had to do."[9] In his view, the "watertight compartments" defined by political scientist Kenneth Wheare were an accurate reflection of the Constitution and the intentions of the Fathers of Confederation.[10] During the 2008 election, Harper made this point explicitly, declaring that it was time "to return to the original principles of the constitution."[11]

Harper's insistence on this strict interpretation of the Constitution is all the more surprising because it is technically incorrect, as historian Michael Behiels, among others, has noted.[12]

The British North America Act of 1867 did not meet the "watertight compartment" criteria of Wheare. In fact, it specifically provided for areas of shared jurisdiction, such as agriculture and immigration. In addition, it conferred on the federal government several tools—such as the Peace, Order and Good Government clause (POGG), the federal spending power, the disallowance provision, and the assignment of residual powers—that were specifically designed to ensure the supremacy of the federal government. Harper himself recognized the importance of these provisions and the intent of the drafters. He repeatedly criticized "this outrageous spending power," which he saw as "giving rise to a domineering and paternalistic federalism," despite the fact that this power is not only constitutional but deliberately unrestrained.[13]

Equally important, Harper's proposed "return to classic federalism" ignores much of the history of Canadian intergovernmental relations. Since the 1930s, the evolution of Canadian federalism has involved a considerable degree of federal-provincial cooperation. Indeed, the notion of watertight compartments, while never accurate, could only have been possible in the early years of Confederation, when no government was expected to do much more than provide the basics of defence, currency, transportation, and a postal service. With the advent of two world wars and a global depression, governments everywhere began to take on more responsibilities and, notably, to implement the programs that collectively came to be known as the welfare state.

For Canada, creating the welfare state proved a constitutional conundrum. On the one hand, the provinces had jurisdictional responsibility for most of the policy areas involved. On the other hand, they were unable to fund such programs because of their limited capacity to raise revenues. Lacking an amending formula, the federal government and the provinces turned to administrative solutions. The federal government agreed to use its spending power to share the cost of such programs in exchange for provincial agreement that these programs would meet minimum national standards.

Many scholars have described these developments as a sort of golden age of Canadian federalism. For Harper, however, the era of "cooperative federalism" represents the unwarranted and aggressive intrusion of the federal government into areas of exclusive provincial jurisdiction. Here, too, the historical reality he paints is problematic As one senior official involved in the early negotiations pointed out, "it is difficult to believe that . . . Stephen Harper is a true believer in such a myth-based misreading of federal-provincial bargaining. . . . Ottawa did not barge in. Initially it was dragged in."[14] Indeed, the adoption of the Quebec model for the Canada Pension Plan, and of Saskatchewan's medicare plan to form the basis of the Canada Health Act, underlines the importance of provincial governments in serving as incubators for national policies, a point emphasized by American president Bill Clinton in a speech at the first Forum of the Federations conference at Mont Tremblant in 1999.

Progressive Conservative politicians of the day were supportive of the welfare state and the intergovernmental process by which it was achieved. Their differences with the Liberals were primarily over details of funding and implementation. Over time, the range and scope of such federal-provincial cost-sharing arrangements greatly expanded under Liberal and Tory governments. In many cases, they were not only a practical solution to the jurisdictional impasse, but a logical response to the increasingly horizontal nature of many policy areas. As a result, any serious attempt to rein in the federal spending power and "return to classic federalism"—as proposed by Harper—would represent a major break with his PC predecessors and inevitably have significant implications for the welfare state.

At the same time, it is important to note that Stephen Harper's federal vision is not exclusively decentralist. Again, unlike his Progressive Conservative predecessors, he has consistently emphasized his determination to maintain and even expand the role of the federal government in areas of exclusive jurisdiction. In an article entitled "My Plan for Open Federalism," he stressed "the need to re-establish a strong central government that focuses on genuine national priorities like defence and the economic union."[15] He also made it clear that he saw little or no need for federal-provincial dialogue and hardly any role for the provinces in the economic union.

This emphasis on a strong central government initially appears to contradict the decentralist thrust of much of Harper's federalist discourse. However, this apparent contradiction can be resolved by recognizing the importance of neo-conservative ideology in the formulation of his federal vision.

Ideology and Open Federalism

Unlike Progressive Conservative prime ministers before him, Stephen Harper's origins lie in the defunct Reform and Canadian Alliance parties. When those parties merged with the remaining fragments of the decimated Progressive Conservative party, he became the first leader of the new Conservative Party and ultimately that party's first prime minister. This unusual path to power is significant for a number of reasons, but most importantly for the unprecedented philosophical perspective Harper brought to national politics. In many respects, his views placed him outside the traditional parameters of political debate. He recognized this fact partly by tempering those views with pragmatism when he believed it was necessary for political gain, but also by asserting that one of his overarching objectives was to alter the political culture and "create a country based on solid conservative values."[16]

Not surprisingly, some of Harper's most revealing comments were made when he was not in power. Having resigned as a Reform MP in 1997 after taking issue with party leader Preston Manning, Harper was appointed vice president of the National Citizens Coalition (NCC), a right-wing advocacy group whose motto is "more freedom through less government." Shortly after, he delivered a speech to the Council for National Policy, a right-wing American think tank. Harper referred to Canada disparagingly as "a Northern European welfare state in the worst sense of the term, and very proud of it." He urged his audience not to "feel bad" about Canada's unemployed, because

"they don't feel bad about it themselves, as long as they're receiving generous social assistance and unemployment insurance." And he criticized the Progressive Conservative party, whose membership he described in unflattering tones as "officially in favour of the entrenchment of our universal, collectivized health care system and multicultural policies in the constitution of this country."[17]

Some four years later, Harper was one of six signatories to an open letter to Alberta premier Ralph Klein. Published following the 2000 federal election, in which Klein's health care policies had been criticized by the federal Liberals, the letter defended Klein's controversial creation of "truth squads" to promote the benefits of privatization and his repeated demands that no conditions be attached to federal funding for health care. The "Firewall Letter" took the defence of provincial rights into uncharted waters, urging Klein to adopt an Alberta agenda that would isolate the province from the federal government as much as possible. Recommendations included withdrawing from the Canada Pension Plan and "resuming provincial responsibility for health-care policy." The authors argued that "each province should raise its own revenue for health care," dismissing the problems of poorer provinces relying on equalization. Finally, they urged the premier to fight any federal attempt to challenge the legality of these moves, especially concerning the Canada Health Act. "If we lose, we can afford the financial penalties that Ottawa may try to impose," they wrote.[18]

Harper also dismissed as "not only useless but dangerous" the efforts of the newly created Romanow Commission on Health Care appointed by Prime Minister Chrétien. His position, summarized by the *Globe and Mail*, was that "a fully socialized system is incapable of generating or efficiently allocating the funds to meet growing health-care demands." The solution was "provincial experimentation with market reforms and private delivery options."[19]

As the above quotes suggest, Harper's main focus at the time was the economy. Promoting a classic neo-liberal agenda, his speeches generally called for lower taxes, smaller government, and less state intervention in the economy, while praising the benefits of an unfettered market economy. Meanwhile he continued to eschew the social conservatism of Preston Manning, Stockwell Day, and many of the Reform/Alliance MPs, assuming any mention of the so-called theo-con issues would be politically fatal.

But his party's failure to make sufficient electoral headway by using the strategic approach of targeting alienated westerners, Red Tories, and Quebec nationalists—as revealed later by senior policy adviser Tom Flanagan[20]—eventually prompted him to stress rather than downplay the social conservative side of his thinking. A crucial component of a conservative victory,

GLOBALIZATION AND NEO-LIBERALISM

In its most common usage, the term "globalization" is applied to economies. In this sense, it refers to the increasing integration and interaction of national economies to others, thereby creating a world, or global, economy. Globalization has been characterized by an increase in free trade and the free flow of capital, technologies, and production.

The term "globalization" is fairly recent, probably appearing for the first time in the 1960s. However, the process has existed for a long time, with periods of increased integration and inter-connection of national economies followed by periods of retreat and trade restriction. Globalization is one outcome of the vast improvements to transportation and communication that have occurred since the sixteenth century, which have allowed for the movement of people, products, ideas, and technologies and for business to operate over long distances. The pace of technological change since the Second World War, particularly in communications with the advent of the Internet, has dramatically increased the pace of globalization. As a term denoting this change, "globalization" has been used extensively since the 1990s.

The pace of globalization in Canada has also accelerated greatly since the 1980s, with the rise of neo-liberalism as the country's dominant political ideology. As an economic theory, neo-liberalism calls for a reduction in government intervention in the economy, reduced government spending on social programs, and greater reliance on the private sector to facilitate economic activity and growth. Thus, neo-liberal proponents also support free trade and the move towards a "global" economy because they believe that a relatively free, competitive marketplace that is on a global scale and unfettered by government trade and economic restrictions is the best means for nations to achieve economic well-being. These ideas led to the 1988 free-trade agreement between Canada and the United States, which was subsequently expanded to include Mexico and named the North American Free Trade Agreement (NAFTA) in 1994.

Critics of globalization and neo-liberalism, in Canada and elsewhere, argue that these trends pose a threat to social programs (including medicare) and to labour standards, wages, and benefits (as well as other standards such as environmental regulations). They argue that the terms of international agreements such as NAFTA have the potential to restrict the government from implementing policies to protect the well-being of their citizens. Furthermore, governments may be forced to lower labour and other regulations as well as employer contributions to pension or health programs in order to attract foreign companies or to allow Canadian companies to be competitive. Thus, the combined impact of globalization with neo-liberal ideology is viewed as providing further justification for governments to reduce spending on costly social programs, such as welfare, health, and education.

he now believed, was to follow the lead of New Right Republicans in the United States and form a coalition of right-wing interest groups. In his seminal June 2003 speech to the Civitas Society, a secretive group of conservative and libertarian thinkers, Harper spoke directly to this point. Polishing his neo-con credentials, he argued for a greater emphasis on the social conservative side of the equation because "serious conservative parties simply cannot shy away from values questions." This, he said, was because "on a wide range of public policy questions, including foreign affairs, defence, criminal justice and corrections, family and child care . . . social values are increasingly the really big issues." Harper argued that the party needed to emphasize the social conservative aspect, since "a growing body of evidence points to the damage the welfare state is having on our most important institutions, particularly the family." Even such disparate areas as defence and foreign affairs were affected, he stressed, stating that "emerging debates on foreign affairs should be fought on moral grounds" as well.

Another important element of the speech was Harper's vehement rejection of liberalism. He saw the "real challenge" posed by liberal cultures and governments to be their social, not their economic, agendas, and went on to decry the "social relativism, moral neutrality and moral equivalency" of a liberal culture in which secularism, pluralism, and social justice are highly valued. He equated modern liberal philosophy with something "darker" than relativism. "It has become a moral nihilism" he argued. His ultimate objective after forming a government, therefore, was to alter the political culture to one in which conservative values predominate and the welfare state is greatly reduced.

The speech was also informative about Harper's views on the role of government institutions. Underpinning his world view is a Hobbesian approach to government and the role of the state. Simply put, he sees such institutions as obstacles for conservatives precisely because they were created by liberals and therefore inevitably promote liberal ideology. Similarly, he views many bureaucratic practices and

parliamentary traditions with scepticism because they allow for organized dissent, a concept at odds with the conservatives' view that they are right and those who oppose them are not simply in disagreement but wrong.[21]

Harper admitted that this new value-driven neo-conservative policy agenda might cause the party to lose some voters, such as red Tories and members of the business community. However, he emphasized that "this is not all bad . . . a new approach can draw in new people. Many traditional Liberal voters, especially from key ethnic and immigrant communities, will be attracted to a party with strong traditional views of values and family. This is similar to the phenomenon of the Reagan Democrats in the United States, who were so important in the development of the conservative coalition there." At the same time Harper agreed wholeheartedly with Tom Flanagan's cautionary approach to implementing the conservative agenda. "The explicitly moral orientation of social conservatives," Harper declared, "makes it difficult to accept . . . the incremental approach. Yet, in democratic politics, any other approach will certainly fail."[22] As would soon become evident, he had embraced Flanagan's call for pragmatism as an essential technique for acquiring and maintaining power. For guidance in how to achieve this, he turned to the successful model of the New Right in the United States.

The Influence of the American New Right on Open Federalism

Harper's reference to the Reagan Democrats in his Civitas speech was no accident. His familiarity with, and approval of, the New Right's strategy of co-opting special interest groups and southern Democrats to forge a new coalition has been well documented.[23] It resulted in the adoption of many of the same strategies by his new Conservative Party. More importantly, the Republicans' use of federalism for conservative ends was clearly influential in shaping Harper's concept of open federalism.

For decades, two overarching themes of American neo-conservatives have been states' rights and small government. Both have implications for the functioning of a federal system. In the first instance, the term "states' rights" has served as a code for the dismantling of liberal policies and programs introduced by the federal government. In the early years, these included desegregation and the right to an abortion. More recent targets include affirmative action and environmental protection programs. The primary argument of states' rights activists has been framed as a legal/constitutional one, namely, that the federal government has encroached on state jurisdiction and there must be a return to a strict or "originalist" interpretation of the Constitution that would see the federal government's powers reduced. The underlying purpose of this approach is to allow right-wing legislators at the state level to effectively dismantle the offending liberal programs.[24]

The Federalist Society, an organization of well-known conservative lawyers and judges who support the originalist interpretation of the Constitution, has proven quite successful in promoting this cause through a combination of court challenges and presidential appointments to the Supreme Court. President Reagan alone appointed several prominent Federalists, including Antonin Scala, Sandra Day O'Connor, and Samuel Alito, while another nominee, Robert Bork, was only unsuccessful due to fierce resistance in Congress. Over the course of the Reagan, Bush, and Bush Jr administrations, the Federalists also succeeded in placing their members in key positions ranging from attorney-general and five assistant attorneys-general to senior White House counsel and counsel to the Senate Judiciary Committee. Some critics have argued that the ultimate expression of their influence came with the Supreme Court decision to reject Democratic presidential candidate Al Gore's appeal and install George W. Bush in the White House.

Meanwhile cases such as the 1999 *American Trucking v. EPA* decision, which saw federal environmental protection standards declared *ultra vires*, and the 1996 decision to allow California's anti-affirmative action Proposition 209 to stand, have been widely cited as classic examples of the success of the Federalist states' rights approach through court challenges.

As we have already seen, Stephen Harper's insistence on the watertight compartments interpretation of the Canadian Constitution and the withdrawal of the federal government from areas of provincial jurisdiction lies at the heart of his concept of open federalism. Similarly, he and other members of his government, including his justice and public safety ministers, have repeatedly demonstrated their distrust of the Supreme Court and vowed to alter the appointments process.[25] The importance that Harper attributes to the Court was evident in his 2008 election claim that voters could safely entrust his party with a majority because the public service and the courts were filled with Liberal appointees who could not be replaced for some time.

The second, equally important theme of the American New Right—the need to reduce "big government"—is also one in which federalism has an important role to play. Liberal initiatives can be minimized or eliminated by reducing the size of the federal government as well as by diffusing its power.

As economist Grover Norquist, a favourite of Ronald Reagan, famously declared, the simplest way to reduce the size of government is to "starve the beast." In practical terms, this means cutting taxes as well as programs and spending, thereby reducing the revenue available to the federal government to pursue any liberal initiatives. At the same time, the removal of federal regulations and standards will allow the development of "market-preserving federalism," in which unfettered competition among the subnational units will force a race to the bottom.[26]

It is this economic aspect of the New Right's federal vision that explains Harper's determination to further centralize some powers at the federal level in order to pursue his neo-liberal economic agenda. As Canadian economist Adam Harmes has demonstrated, there are many tools available to the federal government to implement that agenda nationwide if it chooses.[27] And there is considerable evidence that Harper is well aware of this economic theme. In a speech to the Montreal Board of Trade in 2006, shortly after winning the federal election, the new prime minister declared that tax reduction is "the ultimate decentralization," promising significant tax cuts and offering tax room rather than any increase in transfer payments to the provinces. Columnist John Ibbitson described this commitment as "Mr. Harper's most important liberal initiative."[28]

Meanwhile political scientist Peter Leslie has described Harper's stated objectives of "developing" the social and economic unions in opposing federalist directions as entirely consistent with a world view of the role of the state that is both minimalist and assertive. Such objectives, Leslie argued, "not only call for a review of the conduct of intergovernmental relations, but open up questions of broad scale political design. . . . At stake is the kind of country that Canada is and should become."[29]

This leads logically to the question of whether Harper, as the first prime minister to espouse such extreme views, has been able to alter the operation of the federation through the exercise of political will.

Open Federalism in Practice: The Social Union and the Welfare State

Stephen Harper had barely been elected when he acted on his commitment to withdraw the federal government from areas of provincial jurisdiction. For the most part this retrenching involved the social union. It also produced important changes to intergovernmental relations. For example, Harper immediately killed the national child care strategy established by the Chrétien and Martin governments. This strategy was part of the National Children's Agenda developed over a decade of negotiations with the provinces. Interestingly, that agenda had been praised by the premiers for the flexibility and discretion it accorded to the provinces. This was particularly true of two components of the agenda, the National Child Benefit and the Early Childhood Development Initiative, both of which actually were criticized by the National Council of

Welfare because low-income families across the country received very uneven benefits as a result of this provincial discretion.

However, the most ambitious element of the agenda was the Multilateral Framework Agreement on Early Learning and Child Care program, whose primary objective was to increase the total number of child care spaces. The program was agreed to in late 2003 by all first ministers except Quebec's, since that province had already instituted a major child care program and would receive funding automatically. The 2005 federal budget committed $5 billion over five years to the program and identified four principles that the provinces were to follow in implementing the plan—namely, quality, universality, accessibility, and development. In addition, the funding could only be spent on non-profit child care. Between April and November 2005, the federal government signed bilateral agreements in principle with nine provinces. Three of them—Manitoba and Ontario, as well as Quebec—had also released detailed action plans and signed final funding agreements with the federal government.

On taking office in January 2006, the Harper government almost immediately gave notice that it was unilaterally invoking the one-year termination clause found in the umbrella Social Union Framework Agreement. Subsequently, the 2006 Speech from the Throne provided several indications that this decision to cancel the child care deal was driven by ideology as much as by a concern for constitutionally watertight compartments. First, the government established the new Choice in Child Care Allowance ($1,200 per year), which went directly to families for each child under the age of six. Basically a non-targeted credit, it was seen as a counterproductive measure that did nothing to encourage the use of quality child care or increase the number of spaces. Moreover, when the government finally did respond to growing pressure concerning its inaction on child care spaces, its solution was to announce a 25 percent tax credit for businesses that created child care spaces in the workplace, and an allocation of some $250 million to provide incentives for businesses to do so.

WELFARE STATE

The welfare state refers to a political system in which the government and therefore society as a whole is responsible for the economic and social well-being of citizens. This objective is accomplished primarily through programs to provide social/economic assistance when needed and through universal, state-funded health care and education.

The welfare state in Canada, as in most Western, capitalist countries, began to develop in the early twentieth century, but the most important aspects of the welfare state were finalized and implemented during the post-1945 period. This was a result of the fact that the concept of the welfare state intersected with the ideology of postwar liberalism and Keynesian economics, which became dominant in the postwar years. The principle underlying the welfare state is the belief in the need for the state (society) to offset the social and economic inequality that naturally results from a capitalist economy. While Keynesian economics dictated that governments could stabilize the natural trend of capitalist economies to experience periods of acute boom and bust through control of monetary policy, the welfare state was to complement these initiatives by addressing the inequality of opportunity and economic position similarly intrinsic to capitalism. Thus, the welfare state in Canada encompasses two components. Social assistance programs exist to provide income support to those facing temporary distress—for example, due to unemployment—and to those unable to support themselves owing to such factors as disability. The second components of Canada's welfare state are social services, primarily medicare and education up to the level of high school. These important social services are universal and state-supported, reflecting the belief that equality of access improves opportunity for all Canadians.

Canada's welfare state developed in a piecemeal, somewhat haphazard fashion, with its most important parts introduced in the 1960s. The main components of Canada's welfare state include Old Age Security (1952), the Canada Pension Plan, and universal medicare (the latter two introduced in 1966), but there is also a range of social assistance measures operated and funded by all three levels of government. The piecemeal nature of Canada's welfare state is particularly notable in these social assistance programs. While the concept of universality for pensions and medicare has long been considered a right of citizenship, the idea of providing economic security through a single program by which no citizen would fall below a basic minimum income needed to ensure their "welfare" has been far more controversial. It has been debated in government and social-planning circles over time, but to date this idea of a "guaranteed annual income" program has been rejected, in part because of traditional liberal values that hold the individual and the family responsible for their own well-being. As a result, most social assistance measures in Canada are directed towards providing temporary relief or assisting those citizens deemed worthy of state support due to circumstances, such as unemployment or disability, that prevent them from caring for themselves. This factor has led to the large number and variability of programs as well as of methods of administration.

Nevertheless, most of the funding that had been set aside by the Martin government for its child care strategy was returned to general revenue.

An even more dramatic withdrawal of federal activity took place in the area of Aboriginal policy, when the Harper government, shortly after its election in 2006, announced that it would not implement the Kelowna Accord. This refusal to honour the agreement reached in November 2005—after months of negotiation involving federal, provincial, territorial, and Aboriginal leadership—was particularly striking, since the federal government's constitutional responsibility for First Nations peoples under the Indian Act is unquestioned. The accord, however, made a 10-year commitment to improve the situation of *all* Aboriginal Canadians in four key areas: education, housing, health, and a new relationship. It was announced at the conclusion of a two-day meeting of leaders of the federal government, ten provincial governments, three territorial governments, and four national Aboriginal organizations, and followed three earlier sets of meetings in September 2004, May 2005, and November 2005. The accord pledged $5.1 billion over the first five years for the various programs announced in the accord. The appendix contained a detailed set of tables outlining the breakdown of funding, along with specific commitments in all four subject areas. In addition, a tripartite agreement was signed between the federal government, the government of British Columbia, and the Leadership Council of First Nations in British Columbia, detailing how the accord would be implemented in that province.

The Kelowna meeting was called "historic" by many of the participants. Premier Gordon Campbell of British Columbia described the meeting as offering "a seat at the Table of Confederation" for Aboriginal Canadians, and concluded, "We have an obligation to build on the legal framework of our Constitution, to extend the same rights, entitlements and opportunities to aboriginal Canadians, on and off reserve or treaty lands."[30] His views were shared by PEI premier Pat Binns, who declared that the accord "will be the test of our nationhood and its federalist underpinnings."[31] A press release by Phil Fontaine of the Assembly of First Nations (AFN) echoed these sentiments, stating, "We are making history by taking the first steps towards creating a new Canada and a new federation; a federation where first peoples of this land enjoy the same quality of life as other Canadians, and where we control the decisions that affect our lives."

During the 2006 federal election that followed almost immediately, the Martin Liberals highlighted the agreement as one to which they were firmly committed. Meanwhile Conservative candidate Jim Prentice stated that the terms of the Kelowna Accord would be followed if the Conservatives won.[32] Yet with the Conservative victory later that month the Kelowna Accord was shelved.

The government's explanations for its refusal to honour the accord varied. The most frequent objections raised were, first, that the accord had not actually been signed and therefore was not legally binding and, second, that it did not represent a meaningful consensus because Aboriginal leaders from Quebec had not been in attendance. This latter argument, surprisingly, was made by the new minister of Indian affairs and northern development, Jim Prentice.[33] Virtually all the participants disagreed. The degree of detail provided, the financial commitments, the existence of the signed tripartite agreement with British Columbia, and the statements of the various participants at the time were all seen as concrete proof that the deal was considered binding. Inuit Tapirisat leader Mary Simon further noted that "the Kelowna Accord committed to the achievement of targeted outcomes and allowed for a high level of accountability to the public in the measurement of progress towards those outcomes." An irate Premier Jean Charest of Quebec stated that he had specifically addressed the absence of his province's Aboriginal leaders in his opening remarks in Kelowna, stressing that they had already been consulted in detail and, while choosing not to attend for political reasons, were effectively represented.

A number of academic studies subsequently examined the Kelowna Accord to determine its legal and constitutional status. Many concluded that the agreement technically was not legally binding but argued that it should be treated as such. Most also found that the accord should be considered a political convention and that the Harper government's decision to renege on the deal constituted a violation of that convention.[34] Several premiers also noted that if the federal government could renege on the deal with impunity, it would likely feel free to do so on a number of other federal-provincial agreements, something which they clearly wanted to discourage.

Despite these protestations, the government's Throne Speech and subsequent budgets made no mention of the accord. The surprise passage of Paul Martin's private member's bill calling on the federal government to implement the accord and a similar move in the Senate were ignored. Provincial premiers were unanimous in their criticism of Harper's rejection of the deal. Premier Ralph Klein of Alberta chaired a meeting of western premiers in June 2006 that collectively called on the Harper government to fulfil its obligations under the Kelowna Accord. By 2008, provincial anger had only increased. Quebec's Jean Charest, the chair of the annual meeting of the Council of the Federation in July of that year, told reporters, "We are doing everything in our power to offer the federal government an opportunity to sit down with us."[35]

The picture with respect to a third policy area, social housing, is somewhat different and appears to demonstrate Harper's willingness to be pragmatic when necessary to guarantee political success. Initially, Harper had indicated that his government was planning to pull out of the social housing field as well, despite the existence of a number of multi-year federal-provincial agreements. He also mused about the possibility of shutting down the federal government's window on the industry—the Canada Mortgage and Housing Corporation (CMHC)—since it represented an "unacceptable" intrusion into both provincial jurisdiction and the private sector.[36]

However, the advent of a worldwide recession less than a year later forced Harper to adapt. In addition to leaving the social housing agreements in place, he moved to avoid the appearance of a looming housing crisis and the likelihood his minority government would shoulder the responsibility. He directed CMHC to offer more guaranteed mortgages and to do so at 0 percent interest over 40 years. The American subprime disaster of mid-2008 effectively forced Finance Minister Flaherty to order a return to 5 percent interest and a 35-year amortization, but this remained an exceptionally favourable (or risky) situation for Canadian borrowers.

The government also ordered CMHC to approve high-risk borrowers in order to keep credit levels up. According to CMHC records, the approval rate for risky loans rose from 33 percent

in 2007 to 42 percent in 2008 alone, resulting in a 9.3 percent increase in Canadian household debt between June 2008 and June 2009. As economist Murray Dobbin has noted, "Every single U.S. lender specializing in sub-prime has gone bankrupt. The largest sub-prime lender in the world is now the Canadian government."[37]

Unquestionably, the social policy area in which the Harper government has trod most carefully is health care. Fully aware of the difficulties Stockwell Day encountered in that minefield, Stephen Harper stressed from the beginning that his government would respect the primacy of a publicly funded health care system, ignoring his earlier comments when outside of political life. In reality he had little choice, given the Martin government's 2004 negotiation of a 10-year, $41-billion agreement with the provinces to "fix health care for a generation," an agreement that *was* signed and would run until April 2014 under the Canada Health Transfer (CHT).

This reality was doubtless reinforced for Harper by countless public opinion polls showing that health care remains the top priority of Canadians. In the May 2011 election, with the prospect of a majority government on the horizon, Harper repeatedly assured voters (and provincial premiers) that his government would continue the 6 percent annual health transfer payments guaranteed in the 2004 agreement. He also promised that his government would begin negotiations with the provinces for a new health deal "sooner rather than later."[38]

In an interview the day after the election, Harper confirmed the 6 percent commitment, but added, "[W]e do want to sit down as we renegotiate to look at how to ensure better and clearer results," a reference to the fact that many provinces failed to follow through on promises made in the 2004 agreement.[39] The next day, Harper said he was aware that some provinces were experimenting with alternative ways to deliver services and he believed this should be encouraged. He emphasized that he was not contradicting his support for a "universal public health-care insurance system," but also promised that Ottawa would not impose solutions on provinces. "This is a discussion that will be collaborative," he declared.[40] In addition, the prime minister made it clear that no new initiatives, such as a national pharmacare plan or homecare plan, would be on the table, despite widespread consensus among social policy experts that these measures were long overdue and could serve to reduce some elements of health care costing if properly implemented.

Three months later, Ontario premier Dalton McGuinty delivered a speech to the Ottawa Chamber of Commerce arguing that Harper should begin negotiations immediately. By November 2011, with the federal government's fiscal situation deteriorating rapidly in light of the global recession and developments in the European Union, Finance Minister Flaherty's economic update declared the 6 percent annual CHT escalator could not be guaranteed for more than two years after the end of the existing health accord in fiscal year 2013/14.

Meanwhile, various leaked federal documents indicated that the federal government was considering moving to an equal per capita allowance of the CHT in 2014/15, a move that would uniquely benefit the province of Alberta.[41] By early December, a First Ministers Conference on health care issues still had not been scheduled and an exasperated group of premiers announced that they would hold their own special conference on the issue in early January in Victoria.

With most observers concluding that Harper was delaying as long as possible in order to better position his government for the negotiations, many health care experts expressed serious concern that a frank dialogue on the underlying issues affecting public health care delivery might not take place. This concern was heightened when one prominent economist predicted that, if unchecked, health care costs in Ontario would consume nearly 100 percent of that province's budget within 20 years.[42] As a result, and undoubtedly to the satisfaction of the Harper government, the economic viability of a publicly funded health care system—rather than its merits, delivery options, or best practices—was rapidly becoming the primary focus of political debate.

Then, in December, Finance Minister Jim Flaherty appeared briefly at a meeting of provincial health ministers and laid an unprecedented unilateral "take it or leave it" offer on the table. There would be no federal-provincial negotiations of any kind. Instead, Flaherty announced that after 2014 the funding formula for federal transfers would be tied to the rate of economic growth in each province. He also confirmed that there would be no more "strings" attached. Provinces were free to experiment.

Subsequently the premiers met on several occasions to express their shock and outrage at the federal government's high-handed treatment, which they claimed would reduce their funding by $36 billion over 10 years. They also raised concerns over the fate of equalization, whose agreements are also set to expire in 2014. Significantly, they began to plan common approaches to issues such as drug pricing and wait times in the absence of federal direction.

Meanwhile the Harper government's reluctance to participate in shared-cost programs with the provinces has been accompanied by a willingness to act unilaterally to promote an alternative social agenda in areas it considers to be of exclusive federal jurisdiction. It has eliminated long-standing social and environmental programs and regulatory regimes and created new programs to promote family values and the missionary work of fundamentalist religious groups.[43] The federal government's law and order agenda has resulted in escalating provincial costs, while its proposal to permit private ownership of property on reserves has met with fierce resistance from Aboriginal chiefs concerned about the potential for non-Native takeovers, the lack of consultation, and the failure to address more important issues.

Conclusion

Having obtained a majority in the May 2011 election, Harper now finds himself in an unprecedented position of power. The four-year window of opportunity presented by the election results, coupled with a weak parliamentary opposition and a greatly diminished voluntary sector, suggests that any further efforts to reduce the welfare state can only be seriously challenged by provincial premiers, in effect reversing the traditional roles of the federal and provincial governments. Interestingly, there is already some evidence to suggest that this may well be the case. Apart from the collective response of the provinces on health care, there has been vocal and aggressive resistance by the Quebec government to the Harper Conservatives' changes to the Criminal Code with respect to sentencing, parole, and the treatment of young offenders. More recently, Quebec premier Jean Charest has threatened a court challenge to the federal government's plans to destroy records collected under the gun registry. In addition, in the absence of federal action on the environment, the premiers of Ontario and Quebec have launched a comprehensive joint plan of their own. Similarly, many provinces have followed the lead of former BC premier Gordon Campbell in calling on the federal government to initiate negotiations on measures to improve the Canada Pension Plan and the Employment Insurance system, both areas of federal responsibility. Perhaps most significantly, the recent election of Alison Redford (a self-described Red Tory and critic of the Harper government) as premier of Alberta and the likely election of an NDP government in British Columbia, may signal a continuing trend towards the emergence of more liberal regimes in many provinces in response to the more extreme conservative agenda being promoted in Ottawa.

As a result, it may be too soon to predict that the social union will suffer further and even more serious reversals under the Harper government's watch. At the same time, with the Harper government having reduced federal revenues substantially even before the 2008–9 recession by means of tax reductions, its priority of restoring a balanced budget quickly and at all costs may allow the Conservatives to argue that a lack of revenue precludes any increased investment in cost-sharing programs or other initiatives to bolster the welfare state. At a minimum, this will result in a lack of progress that by the next election, in 2015, will represent a lost decade for the development of the Canadian social union.

Endnotes

1   Michael Kirby, "Meech Lake Pact Reflects Traditional Tory Views," *Toronto Star*, 4 June 1988.
2   Sinclair Stevens, "One Canada or Ten?," 2006 (accessed at www.BLOC-HARPER.com).
3   Stephen Harper, "The New Canada Plan" (Ottawa: Reform Party of Canada, 1995).
4   Peter Leslie, "The Two Faces of Open Federalism," in *Open Federalism: Interpretation, Significance* (Kingston: Institute of Intergovernmental Affairs, Queen's University, 2006), 39–66.
5   "Joe Clark Says He'd Choose Martin over Harper," CTV News, 26 April 2004.
6   Stevens, "One Canada or Ten?"
7   L. Ian Macdonald, "A Conversation with the Prime Minister," *Policy Options*, February 2007, 5–11.
8   John Ibbitson, "Judicial Reform: It's the Newest 'Liberal' Initiative," *Globe and Mail*, 21 February 2007, A7.
9   Stephen Harper, "Prime Minister Outlines His Government's Priorities and His Open Federalism Approach," speech delivered to the Montreal Board of Trade, Montreal, 20 April 2006.
10 Kenneth Wheare, *Federal Government*, 5th ed. (Oxford: Oxford University Press, 1967).
11 Canadian Press, 2008.
12 Michael Behiels, "Harper Finds a Use for the Premiers," *Ottawa Citizen*, 17 November 2008, A11.
13 Stephen Harper, "Harper Announces Conservative Platform for Quebec," speech delivered to the Quebec City Chamber of Commerce, 19 December 2005.
14 Tom Kent, "The Harper Peril for Canadian Federalism," *Policy Options*, February 2008, 12–15.
15 Stephen Harper, "My Plan for Open Federalism," *National Post*, 27 October 2004, A19.
16 Ibid.
17 Stephen Harper, speech delivered to the American Council for National Policy, Montreal, 1997.
18 Stephen Harper *et al.*, "An Open Letter to Ralph Klein," *National Post*, 24 January 2001.
19 *Globe and Mail*, 23 March 2002.
20 Tom Flanagan, *Harper's Team* (Montreal and Kingston: McGill-Queen's University Press, 2009), 369.
21 Christian Nadeau, *Rogue in Power* (Toronto: Lorimer, 2010), 157.
22 Originally reproduced in the *Citizens Centre Report* of June 2003 and then posted on the Christian Coalition International website, the speech has been removed and is now unavailable except on the website of Cannabis Culture, at www.cannabisculture.com/v2.
23 Brooke Jeffrey, "Prime Minister Harper's Open Federalism: Promoting a Neoliberal Agenda?," in Gordon DiGiacomo and Maryantoinette Flumian, eds, *The Case for Centralized Federalism* (Ottawa: University of Ottawa Press, 2010), 108–36.

24   Robert Reich, "The Republican Strategy," www
      .robertreich.org.
25   Kirk Makin, "The Coming Conservative Court: Harper
      to Reshape Judiciary," *Globe and Mail*, 13 May
      2011.
26   Barry Weingast, "The Economic Role of Political
      Institutions: Market-Preserving Federalism and
      Economic Development," *Journal of Economics and
      Organization* 11, no. 1 (1995): 1–31.
27   Adam Harmes, "Neoliberalism and Multilevel
      Governance," *Review of International Political
      Economy* 13, no. 5 (December 2006).
28   John Ibbitson, "Judicial Reform: It's the Newest 'Liberal'
      Initiative," *Globe and Mail*, 21 February 2006, A7.
29   Peter Leslie, "The Two Faces of Open Federalism,"
      Open Federalism: Interpretation, Significance
      (Kingston: Institute of Intergovernmental Affairs,
      Queen's University, 2006), 39–66.
30   Carey Hill *et al.*, "Dangling Participants: Is the
      Kelowna Accord Constitutionally Binding as a
      Federal-Provincial Agreement?," paper presented to

the annual meeting of the Canadian Political Science
      Association, Waterloo, ON, 13 May 2011.
31   Canadian Intergovernmental Conference Secretariat,
      Press Release, December 2005.
32   As reported by CBC News, 11 January 2006.
33   House of Commons, *Hansard*, 2 June 2006.
34   Hill *et al.*, "Dangling Participants"; and DiGiacomo and
      Flumian, *The Case for Centralized Federalism*, 287.
35   Sean Gordon, *Toronto Star*, 17 July 2008.
36   Teresa Healy, *The Harper Record* (Ottawa: Canadian
      Centre for Policy Alternatives, 2010), 501.
37   Murray Dobbin, "Why Canada's Housing Bubble
      Will Burst," *The Tyee*, 22 October 2010.
38   Healy, *The Harper Record.*
39   John Ivison, "A Good Night for Harper," *National
      Post*, 3 May 2011.
40   Mark Kennedy, *Ottawa Citizen*, 4 May 2011.
41   Ibid., 10 November 2011.
42   Don Drummond, *Toronto Star*, 10 November 2011.
43   Jonathan Malloy, "Hidden in Plain Sight: The Tory
      Evangelical Factor," *Ottawa Citizen*, 13 April 2011.

PART II

Suggested Readings

Clarkson, Stephen, and Stephan Wood. *A Perilous
Imbalance: The Globalization of Canadian
Law and Governance*. Vancouver: UBC Press,
2010.

Conrad, Margaret, and James Hiller. *Atlantic Canada:
A Region in the Making*. Don Mills, ON: Oxford
University Press, 2001.

Finkel, Alvin. *Social Policy and Practice in Canada:
A History*. Waterloo, ON: Wilfrid Laurier Press,
2006.

Palmer, Brian D., and Joan Sangster, eds. *Labouring
Canada: Class, Gender, and Race in Working-Class*

History. Don Mills, ON: Oxford University Press,
2008.

Rocher, Francois, and Miriam Smith. *New Trends
in Canadian Federalism*. 2nd ed. Toronto:
University of Toronto Press, 2003.

Stevenson, Garth. *Unfulfilled Union: Canadian
Federalism and National Unity*. 5th ed. Montreal
and Kingston: McGill-Queen's University Press,
2009.

Young, Lisa, and Keith Archer, eds. *Regionalism and
Party Politics in Canada*. Don Mills, ON: Oxford
University Press, 2002.

Key Terms

Auto Pact
Fordist
Keynesian economics
neo-liberal
provincialism

social conservatism
social credit theory
social democratic
"western alienation"

Questions for Consideration

1. What were the main concerns/problems that the Atlantic provinces sought to address through regional unity in the years after 1949?
2. How do the concerns of western Canada differ from those of the Maritime/Atlantic provinces?
3. What is "social credit" ideology and how does it differ from social conservatism? How did these two ideologies influence Alberta's opposition to federal involvement in social policy?
4. What are the main reasons why Alberta differed from Saskatchewan and Manitoba in its response to federal government initiatives in the 1950s and 1960s?
5. How does Sean Purdy's article contribute to and "complicate" existing ideas about the impacts of the welfare state for low-income Canadians?
6. What were the primary reasons that led to housing problems and how did these reasons change over the decades of the postwar years?
7. In what ways are the reforms to family allowances in the 1970s a shift away from the principles that shaped the creation of the welfare state? And in what ways are they a deviation in the ideology of Pierre Trudeau?
8. What were the main reasons that led to the growth and strengthening of labour in the postwar years?
9. Goldfield and Palmer argue that the strength of labour has been jeopardized in part due to the "failure" of the labour leadership to mount an effective opposition. To what extend do you agree with this opinion? What additional factors would explain the diminishing strength of labour?
10. What are the implications of "open federalism" for the welfare state?
11. Why have federal governments since 1984 sought to encourage a decentralized federalism and an expansion of provincial autonomy?

Relevant Websites

Canada. A Country by Consent—Newfoundland Joins Confederation
  www.collectionscanada.gc.ca/2/5/
  www.canadahistoryproject.ca/1949/1949-02-nfld-history.html

Canadian Council on Social Development—Links to material on social policy and related topics
  www.ccsd.ca/links.html

Centre for Research on Globalization
  www.globalresearch.ca

The Encyclopedia of Saskatchewan—Western Alienation
  www.esask.uregina.ca/entry/western_alienation.html

Federalism-E—Undergraduate journal about federalism published by Laval and Queen's
  www.queensu.ca/iigr/pub/Ejournals/federalismE.html

Government of Canada, Department of Intergovernmental Affairs
  www.pco-bcp.gc.ca/aia/index.asp?lang=eng&page=federal

Government of Newfoundland, Royal Commission on Renewing and Strengthening Our Place in Canada, Report (on regional development programs)
  www.gov.nl.ca/publicat/royalcomm/research/savoie.pdf

Institute for Research on Public Policy—Publications on Federalism
  http://archive.irpp.org/pubs/index.php

Maple Leaf Web—Federalism in Canada: Basic Framework and Operation
  www.mapleleafweb.com/features/federalism-Canada-basic-framework-and-operation

Newfoundland and Labrador Heritage
  www.heritage.nf.ca/law/win_lose.html

William Aberhart Historical Foundation
  www.aberhartfoundation.ca/Pages/Premier.htm

Canada and the World

TIMELINE

1944	Creation of the International Monetary Fund and the World Bank
1944–6	Founding of the United Nations
1946	Gouzenko Affair reveals Soviet spy ring in Canada
1947	Lester Pearson delivers the Gray Lecture
1947	Canada is a signatory to the General Agreement on Tariffs and Trade (GATT)
1949	North Atlantic Treaty Organization (NATO) created
1948	Inauguration of World Council of Churches
1949	Independence of Indonesia achieved
1949–57	Construction of three radar defence systems, including the DEW Line in the North
1950–3	Korean War; Canada participates in a UN force
1953	Canada establishes diplomatic relations with and assigns aid to Indonesia
1954	Canada joins the International Commission for Supervision and Control in Vietnam (ICSC)
1955	Royal Commission on Canada's Economic Prospects appointed
1956	Canada and US sign the Defence Production Sharing Agreement
1956	Suez Crisis
1957	Lester Pearson wins the Nobel Peace Prize for his role in the Suez Crisis
1958	Canada enters the North American Air Defence Agreement (NORAD) with the US
1959	Diefenbaker government cancels the Avro Arrow project
1961	Canadian University Service Overseas (CUSO) created
1962	Cuban Missile Crisis
1963	Bomarc missile (nuclear weapons) debate diminishes support for Diefenbaker
1963	Canada suspends aid to Indonesia
1965–6	Canada re-establishes trade and aid with Indonesia
1965	Lester Pearson's speech at Temple University calls for cessation of bombing in Vietnam
1965	Merchant-Heeney Report
1968	Trudeau re-commits Canada to a non-nuclear policy and begins to reduce Canada's NATO commitment
1968	Canadian International Development Agency (CIDA) formed

continued

1969	American oil tanker travels through Canadian Arctic without asking permission	**1985**	American *Polar Sea* travels through Northwest passage without asking permission
1972	Trudeau government introduces the "third option"	**1988**	Canada and US sign the Free Trade Agreement
1973	Canada withdraws from the International Commission for Supervision and Control in Vietnam (ICSC)	**1988**	Canada-US Arctic Waters Cooperation Agreement
		1992	North American Free Trade Agreement signed
1973	Foreign Investment Review Agency (FIRA) created by federal government	**1993**	GATT is ended and replaced (in 1995) by the World Trade Organization
1975–99	Canada opposes East Timorese independence from Indonesian control	**1997**	Canada negotiates the ban on anti-personnel landmines
1982	UN Convention of the Law of the Sea enacted; includes the Arctic Waters Pollution Prevention Act	**1998–9**	Canada supports self-determination for East Timor

Introduction

Since 1945, one of the most notable changes for Canada has been the vast increase in its involvement in international affairs and multinational organizations. While the extent of Canadian involvement in foreign affairs, the nature of that involvement, and the objectives underlying it have changed over the postwar years (and been the source of significant debate among scholars), Canada has remained active in the international field.

Canada emerged from the Second World War strengthened, both militarily and in its political voice in Allied decision-making. The Allies, including Canada, had begun planning for the development of intergovernmental agencies to enhance international peace and security and to encourage economic cooperation in the postwar world. These negotiations led to the official creation of the United Nations and the International Monetary Fund in 1945, both of which Canada joined. Yet it was not clear what type of international role Canada would be given or would accept in the postwar world. However, in January, 1947 Secretary of State for External Affairs Louis St Laurent gave his Gray Lecture, in which he asserted the five principles of Canada's foreign policy; his inclusion of Canada's "acceptance of international responsibility" is often cited as the point indicating Canada's commitment to internationalism, its active involvement in international affairs in pursuit of international security and aid for the world's peoples.

Profound changes in the world further influenced the course of Canadian action and explain its move to more active involvement. Canada remained committed to the British Commonwealth of Nations, and many Canadians viewed Britain as Canada's most important ally; yet the reality was that Britain had declined as a world power. In its place, the United States and the Soviet Union had arisen as the world's new "superpowers." This new world order was evident even before the war was over, but the advent of the Cold

War in the immediate postwar years solidified the division of the world into two opposed and antagonistic political and ideological groups. Canadians quickly and resolutely came to believe that the Soviet Union and the countries that allied around it (either by choice or force) constituted a threat to world security and to Western institutions and values. For Canada, the deciding moment is often cited as the Gouzenko Affair in September 1945, when Igor Gouzenko, a clerk at the Soviet embassy, revealed the existence of a Soviet spy network within Canada during the war years. Under these circumstances, Canada firmly allied itself with the Western camp, led by the United States, against communism and the Soviet Union, joining the North Atlantic Treaty Organization (NATO), an alliance of western Europe and North American countries, in 1949. Continental defence issues further strengthened Canada's alliance with and adherence to US leadership, owing to its geographical position between the two contending superpowers. The North American Air Defence Agreement (NORAD) agreement, signed in 1957, committed the United States and Canada to cooperation in continental defence, with the US as the dominant partner.

Postwar events propelled Canada's active participation in world affairs through numerous multinational organizations; yet there remained the question of the nature of Canada's participation. The period from 1947 to 1957 has come to be known as Canada's "golden age" of diplomacy, a time when the nation was influential in world events but also acted according to the principles of internationalism, in particular with respect to its commitment to the peaceful resolution of conflict through collective means and with objectivity. In his paper in chapter 7, Hector Mackenzie examines the origins of this belief—as well as its nature and validity—in the writings of Escott Reid. Like other recent scholars, he suggests that the idea of a golden age is a myth; while Canada did experience a significant change in its international relations and activity in the postwar years, this change was not the result of a change in "will or guidance" (originating from the leadership of Lester Pearson in External Affairs) but a result of the changing dynamics of the international situation. In fact, Canada's actions are better understood as having been influenced by its allies, rather than as having been the consequence of a concerted commitment to internationalism.

The question of Canada's commitment to internationalism versus its foreign policy actions based on alliance politics and/or national self-interest continued into the 1960s, even as Canada's golden age came to an end. Andrew Preston examines this question in relation to Canada's highly controversial diplomatic efforts in the midst of escalating tension between the United States and North Vietnam in the early 1960s. Canada could exercise "quiet diplomacy" through its position on the International Control Commission (established in 1954 to oversee the "peace" between North and South Vietnam) and through its strong relationship with the United States. Yet, as Preston notes, Canada has been accused of "quiet complicity" for acting strictly as an agent of the United States and for reaping economic advantages through selling defence materials to the United States as it began to militarize. However, in a detailed examination of Canada's actions in relation to the United States, Preston concludes that although Canadian diplomats supported the US objective of communist containment in Vietnam, they viewed US actions as reckless and antithetical to a peaceful resolution and thus sought to achieve a difficult position between "loyal ally, international referee, concerned participant and . . . sometime critic of American policy."

The two essays in chapter 8 shift the focus from Canada's role in the Cold War politics of superpowers and alliances towards the role Canada and Canadians can play in the developing world, with its need for development aid. In his article on Canadian-Indonesian relations, Daniel Webster notes that since countries like Indonesia have been peripheral to Canada's primary international concerns, such relations are instructive as to the nature of Canada's internationalism. If Canada as a middle power was driven by the principles of humanitarianism and maintaining peace (through support for the decolonization of countries and social justice for their citizens), these principles would be evident in Canada's actions and sustained involvement in these peripheral regions. Instead, Webster finds that Indonesia was not a priority for Canadian policy-makers; in fact, they ignored human rights abuses and made decisions based primarily on the interests of the Western allies or on Canada's economic national self-interest. Ruth Brouwer's article shifts the focus from governments' to non-governmental organizations' involvement in the developing world. Through a study on changes in the nature of missionary work carried out by the mainstream Christian churches through the 1960s, Brouwer reveals a transition among church mission societies from a commitment to evangelization to the provision of social and economic development aid, based on the growing recognition and critique of colonialism and racism that characterized social movement politics of the 1960s (see Part IV). Yet, despite these changes, Brouwer argues that young "globally minded" Canadians rejected participation in the church mission societies in favour of joining secular aid organizations, such as Canadian University Service Overseas (CUSO).

Since the end of Second World War, a dominant concern shaping both foreign and national policy and debate within Canada has been Canada's relations with the United States. Shaped by the Cold War alliance politics highlighted in chapter 7, this relationship has also been a product of the growing interdependence and integration of the Canadian and US economies. Economic nationalism, as Stephen Azzi reveals, existed prior to 1945, but in the postwar years, it found expression in concern over American investment in, and thus ownership of, Canadian industry. Azzi describes the changing nature of Canadian concern over US dominance and Canadian "sovereignty" in the postwar years, showing how it has been shaped by several factors and particularly heightened during times of economic prosperity. Robert Huebert examines another long-standing issue of Canadian-American relations, one that has acquired greater primacy in the postwar years: the "protection" of Canadian Arctic sovereignty. Focusing on Canadian efforts to exert control over shipping through the Northwest Passage (two key examples being Canada's response to the challenges issued by two American ships that sailed through the passage without Canada's permission), Huebert identifies several trends in Canadian government efforts to assert its Arctic sovereignty. Both of these studies suggest the ongoing importance of these issues to Canada and Canadians today.

CHAPTER **7**

Finding a "Middle-Power" Ground in the Postwar World

◎ 7.1: THE "REVOLUTION" IN CANADA'S INTERNATIONAL POLICIES
Hector Mackenzie

Analyses of Canada's international policies have characterized the period immediately after the Second World War as a time when Canadian foreign policy underwent a transformation or "revolution" culminating in an enlightened internationalist outlook. This has often been associated with a "golden age of Canadian diplomacy." This article traces the origins and content of this belief to the writings of Escott Reid, assesses its validity, and briefly summarizes how subsequent analysts have employed this belief not only to celebrate past achievements but also to lament later disappointments. Finally, the article considers how this myth has affected recent pronouncements about Canada's international policies.

The Gospel According to Reid

As a commentator on Canadian foreign policy, Escott Reid was highly influential. His sway on interpretations of the history of Canada's international relations, through his memoirs and narratives of events in which he was involved, was greater than his impact on policy-making when he was in the senior ranks of the Department of External Affairs.[1] His depiction of policy-making and policy-makers was persuasive, especially as he reinforced his recollections with scrutiny of departmental files and personal sketches of the participants. His treatment of the negotiation of the North Atlantic Treaty Organization (NATO), *Time of Fear and Hope*, still influences assessments of the negotiators and the outcome.[2]

Reid's analyses have affected evaluations of how Canada's external relations in the war and its aftermath differed from what preceded and what followed. An article about Canadian foreign policy for the *International Journal* first applied the label "golden decade" to the 1940s, which were recalled and celebrated as a period when the Canadian government not only accepted its international responsibilities but increased its overseas obligations and pursued global collaboration.[3]

Often overlooked in assessing these years is another seminal article by Reid. Perhaps the comparative neglect of this earlier essay may be explained by its publication by the Indian Council of World Affairs, whose printed materials were not readily available in Canada. Reid's appraisal of what he dubbed "The Revolution in Canadian

Foreign Policy 1947–1951" merits attention, not only for its argument and evidence but also for its impressions.[4] Reid drew upon this analysis in his later work, and his depiction of this period as one of dramatic change in Canada's attitude and conduct has been echoed by later analysts.

This paper will examine not only that article but also the concept of a "revolution" in Canada's international relations after the war. Reid's text will be evaluated, as well as the context and factors that later authors have cited to elaborate on Reid's initial themes and emphases. For his part, Reid made a vital distinction that others have not—between conduct driven by circumstances and the deliberate revision of policies determined by changes in personnel. The purposes of Canadian foreign policy, he contended, remained unaltered, but "the methods of achieving those broad objectives," including "associations, alliances and armaments," differed substantially. Later commentators described a sea change, but Reid did not suggest a wholly new course. His provocative use of "revolution" undoubtedly compounded subsequent misunderstandings.

For Reid, defence expenditures and military commitments measured a country's engagement in world affairs. In 1947, Canada was "virtually a disarmed nation." From a wartime peak of 800,000, its armed forces had dwindled to only 43,000, with a focus on national defence, narrowly defined. The lesson from 1940 that Canada's "first line of defence" was abroad had apparently been forgotten. Canada's soldiers and airmen, after contributing so much to Germany's defeat, had been withdrawn from Europe and abstained from occupation duties. Canada's navy, fourth largest in the world at war's end, no longer maintained a significant overseas presence. The Canadian government ignored those less fortunate in the world, providing no aid to development. Canada apparently had retreated to the aloof stance of the 1930s, the "low, dishonest decade."[5]

As Reid depicts it, the transformation from 1947 to 1951 was extraordinary, with a sevenfold increase in the defence budget. "Canada, for the first time in its history, became in peacetime a member of a military alliance"—NATO—with forces stationed in Germany. The Canadian

government and people strongly supported international endeavours, including "an army brigade and naval units fighting in Korea under United Nations [UN] Command." As for help for developing nations, "Canada became a member of the Colombo Plan for co-operative economic development in South and South-East Asia." In other words, Canada acted responsibly in world affairs.

According to Reid, this reversal was governed by external events. The communist coup in Czechoslovakia and the invasion of South Korea altered Canadian attitudes and ultimately prompted major shifts in policy. The onset of the Cold War sparked Canada's revolution. In Reid's reckoning, the reaction to these events in Ottawa and across Canada not only explained Canada's response to new international bodies such as the UN, but also redefined its relationship to familiar institutions such as the Commonwealth.

Reid briefly mentioned Canada's attitude to the UN, its more internationally minded economic policies and actions, its closer collaboration with the United States (US) to defend North America, and the implications of Newfoundland's entry into Confederation.[6] In his later work, he paid more attention to the UN: that institution assumed a central place in mythology surrounding Canada's primordial internationalism, but its beginning predated the revolution, so it was downgraded in this analysis. Reid excluded Canada's role in the founding of the UN, an engagement that later commentators, himself included, would extol and exaggerate. A colleague in the Canadian foreign ministry contended that Reid had also undervalued the impact of the American rise to global power.[7] After all, it was war under American leadership on the Korean peninsula, formerly distant from Canada's interests and concerns, that prompted the escalation of defence expenditures.[8] Thereafter, allocations were greatest for NATO and for continental defence—commitments that reflected Canada's traditional partnerships with the US and the United Kingdom (UK), as well as understandable concern about the fate of Europe. The Canadian cabinet ultimately supported the Colombo Plan to bolster a vulnerable region against communism, but only after acrimonious discussions about how much to contribute.[9]

Reid's assessment ignored a factor that contemporary journalists had highlighted and that he and others would later stress: the influence of ministers and officials who differed from their predecessors.[10] The presence or absence of William Lyon Mackenzie King from decision-making was not mentioned, nor was the advent of Louis St Laurent and Lester B. Pearson.[11] Reid did not condemn Canada's past posture and performance, but post-revolutionary Canada was unquestionably more enlightened and responsible. This new era coincided with the peak of Reid's policy-making influence, likely reinforcing his approval.[12]

Questioning Beliefs

Reid twice revised his dates for Canada's zenith in world affairs. Four years afterward, he contended that "the heyday of Canadian foreign policy was from 1943 to 1949," when the agencies and institutions associated with the UN and NATO were developed. Later still, he back-dated the beginning of the "golden decade" to 1941.[13] Reid's preferred periods do not coincide with new leadership. Instead, a prime minister rarely identified with "internationalism" or with fundamental change, King, remained at the helm; moreover, King regarded Canada's postwar position as consistent with past attitudes and policies, not indicative of bold departures.[14] Rather than address these contradictions, most accounts of Canada's international relations after the Second World War relegate or omit King—one author even excludes him when discussing postwar prime ministers.[15] Most assign him a peripheral role in policy-making, viewing him as having been eclipsed by those who purportedly favoured more robust overseas involvements. That interpretation was advanced by King's first posthumous biographer, who interviewed dissatisfied and frustrated subordinates, and the caricature of King as a querulous bystander prevails.[16]

Others, notably Pearson and Canadian diplomats, may have chafed at King's direction of national affairs and Canada's external relations, but his successor, St Laurent, did not hasten the retirement of his predecessor and mentor; nor did he abandon a cautious course that had served the country and governing party so well. Shortly before he became prime minister, St Laurent stressed the hopes for the UN, the threat posed by "totalitarian and imperialistic Communism," and the need for a North Atlantic pact—all themes that King had addressed. St Laurent's metaphor to justify NATO—house insurance against fire—would have appealed to King and most Canadians as prudent and cautious.[17] As careful scrutiny of the decisions of King's last government proves, his influence remained formidable, often conclusive, until he resigned on 15 November 1948.[18] Arguments for a major reorientation that emphasizes the ascendance of new leadership must be qualified.[19]

Still, most analyses focus on the impact of St Laurent and Pearson. The Gray Lecture delivered by St Laurent at the University of Toronto in January 1947 has been treated as heralding a new outlook.[20] Though Reid does not mention it in either article, that address is surely the most frequently cited speech about Canada's international relations. It is invariably depicted by scholars as forward-looking and a break with the past.[21] According to one later pundit, "St Laurent articulated the principles of an activist foreign policy."[22] Pearson claimed that the speech "remained a guide" to him as foreign minister.[23] Yet closer scrutiny of the text demonstrates that the Gray Lecture stressed continuity and consensus, not bold leadership or innovation.[24] However, its contents may help to determine whether or not there was a revolution in Canada's foreign policy after the war.

"A policy of world affairs, to be truly effective," St Laurent observed, "must have its foundations laid upon general principles which have been tested in the life of the nation and which have secured the broad support of large groups of the population." The foreign minister identified five "general principles" that directed Canada's foreign policy: "national unity . . . political liberty . . . the rule of law in national and international affairs . . . the values of Christian civilization . . . [and] the acceptance of international responsibility in keeping with our conception of our role in world affairs."

St Laurent also described the "practical application" of these maxims, again under five headings: the Commonwealth, the United States,

CANADA AND NATO

Canada emerged from the Second World War with both a determination and the potential to be active in global affairs for the first time in its short history. This resulted from its strong economic and military strength and its heightened status among the Allies owing to its significant contribution to the war effort. Canadian politicians and diplomats believed that Canada was in a position to act as a middle power, that it could and should take an active role in facilitating peace and security in the postwar years. The creation of the United Nations (UN), an international organization intended to ensure collective security and deal with other international problems, presented the possibility for Canada to pursue its own national objectives within a forum in which it could exercise a voice.

However, events soon led to concerns about Canada's ability to achieve these goals. By 1947, the expansionist Soviet Union appeared ever more threatening to many Western nations, as it had acquired large parts of eastern Europe and promoted communist insurgency in other parts of the world. The communist coup in Czechoslovakia in 1948 brought the communist threat closer to the Western, "democratic" world. The threat of communist domination coincided with a growing scepticism among Canadians officials within Foreign Affairs (and others in the foreign affairs community in Canada and among its allies) about the ability of the UN to protect the security of its members. With escalating tension and the increased willingness of the Soviet Union to use its veto as a permanent member of the UN Security Council, the UN appeared potentially ineffective. Canadian officials were also concerned that the United States might return to a position of isolationism, leaving the West further weakened.

In response to these concerns, Canadian officials were among the first to suggest the idea of creating a security organization (or alliance) among the Western allies. In separate speeches in 1947, Foreign Affairs official Escott Reid, followed by the minister, Louis St Laurent, advocated a need for such an organization to protect the security of members. The North Atlantic Treaty Organization (NATO), signed in 1949, committed its members to mutual defence in the case of military aggression against any participant by an external force or nation. The initial members included Canada, the United States, Britain, and other countries of western Europe. Through this alliance, the members of NATO sought to protect themselves against potential Soviet aggression, either directly or indirectly. As well, the creation of NATO committed the US firmly to an active role in the leadership of the Western nations.

Canada was also actively involved in the drafting of the treaty for NATO. Article 2 (known as the "Canadian article") in particular was initiated and promoted by Canada despite initial opposition by both the US and Britain. It committed members to economic and social cooperation, as many Canadian officials believed that NATO would better achieve its security goals if its members were interconnected in matters beyond military alliance.

France, "the support of constructive international organization," and the growth of the Canadian foreign service. In each instance, he emphasized how the contemporary situation had developed from Canada's history. Moreover, he highlighted those values and interests that Canada shared with its traditional allies, not its distinctiveness.[25]

His foremost concern, as for predecessors and successors, was Canadian unity. To St Laurent, acting "as a united people" entailed, "through reflection and discussion," arriving "at a common understanding of our interests and our purposes." That consensus was articulated in current policies and firmly rooted in past experience. As Gerry

Riddell, who wrote the speech, observed, the remarks were intended to be "constructive and non-controversial," reflective rather than prescriptive.[26]

The first four principles, neither exceptional nor novel, were interwoven in Canadian statements and speeches in the interwar and wartime years. The fifth principle, St Laurent conceded, had been the slowest to gain popular acceptance in Canada; others since have noted that it was the least likely to appeal to King. However, it was depicted not as a departure but as a product of Canada's wartime experience and postwar circumstances. Curiously, the implications of Canada's extraordinary interest in international commerce were omitted from the inventory. A tendency to stress how St Laurent's acceptance of international responsibility differentiated him from King is misleading when the postwar government is reviewed. The most consequential changes for Canadian foreign policy concern the other side of the ledger—the practical application of the agreed precepts.

For the Canadian government, the British Empire and Commonwealth had long been an exceptional international forum, an informal alliance, and the framework within which Canada gradually developed its autonomy.[27] So close was the relationship with the United Kingdom that Canada's world view tended to be shaped by British perceptions and engagements, even when Canadian policy-makers disagreed with British stances. Consultation within the Commonwealth enabled Canada and other dominions to influence a great power. As the events of 1939 demonstrated, the Anglo-Canadian relationship also had the capacity, unlike any other, to involve Canada in war, without a treaty obligation. That bond also divided Canadians over potential entanglements. The UK mattered to Canada after the war, but its relative decline meant that it was unlikely still to commit Canada overseas. Moreover, a combination of change in the Commonwealth and Cold War alignment rendered collaboration with Britain less controversial in Canada than before.[28]

The continental relationship underwent even greater change as the United States assumed leadership in a divided world. The onset of the Cold War enhanced mutual understanding and partnership in North America and extended that collaboration overseas. As St Laurent stressed, however, the interconnections were myriad and long-standing, with bilateral questions simply resolved according to prevailing common values and interests. The Second World War broadened and deepened economic and military collaboration, characteristically expressed in informal declarations, not treaties.[29] After the war, both countries participated in various multilateral agencies and organizations. Nonetheless, the bilateral relationship was still defined and sustained by a common outlook and the practical demands of sharing a continent.[30] The distinction between national and continental defence, blurred in wartime, was effectively erased as the neighbours collaborated closely to protect their neighbourhood from intruders, with greater attention to circumpolar threats and the North.[31] In Canada, global and continental circumstances boosted popular support for external commitments. An obvious foreign threat overcame differences within Canada over priorities and choices.[32]

St Laurent had highlighted Canada's relations with France to underline the priority he assigned to national unity, not France's importance. As for "support of constructive international organization," St Laurent did not intend that as backing the UN (nor did his audience likely interpret it as such), however much later readers regarded it thus. When he spoke, the UN was unproven and a great power deadlock nullified its authority. Canada's faith in—and reliance on—the UN in the 1940s was neither firm nor unquestioning.[33] St Laurent had to be persuaded that Canada should stand for a term on the UN Security Council (UNSC), because he was initially not convinced of the UN's effectiveness and that Canada's participation would be worthwhile.

Canada's performance on the UNSC indicated that it viewed international events primarily as a Western ally would, not a UN devotee.[34]

Canadian representatives acted responsibly but cautiously. In the Korean War, the government increased its contribution under pressure from the US and from Canadian public opinion, not out of concern for the UN.[35] Canada was rarely out of step with its allies. That caution characterized Canada's approach generally to global issues in the "golden age." St Laurent stressed "the limitations on the influence of any secondary power," not bold leadership, and he did not equate Canadian internationalism with support for the UN.[36]

As for the last item on St Laurent's list, the Department of External Affairs and the Canadian foreign service expanded in the 1940s and 1950s, but that was not exceptional in postwar Canada. Generally, according to St Laurent's criteria, there was no "revolution in Canadian Foreign Policy 1947–1951."

Even so, Canada acted differently in world affairs before and after the war. The Canadian government, in words and deeds, was no longer indifferent to overseas questions. However, "revolution" misrepresented what had happened and why, however much the word pleased Reid's immediate audience and others. The apparent shifts in Canada's foreign policy were adaptations, not departures, cautious not bold.

What changes in circumstances had the greatest impact? The relative decline of the UK and rise of the US were parts of a larger realignment after the war, with Germany and Japan defeated and much of Europe and Asia devastated. The breakdown of the victorious wartime alliance and the reordering of the world had major implications for Canada, as for all nations. The unmentioned opponent in the Gray Lecture—the Soviet Union—assumed a global significance much greater than before.

The Cold War framed Canadian decisions in international affairs. The division of the world into hostile camps, with the US and the USSR as the principal adversaries, made international engagement more likely (and more popular) in Canada, even as it eliminated choices. Canada's alignment was definite, and consequently so were its alliances and commitments. This was no triumph for an abstract concept of "internationalism," but rather recognition of friends and foes in a dangerous situation. Mediation—Canada's supposed vocation as a middle power—was neither welcomed by the rivals nor likely to succeed.[37] Moreover, Canadian public opinion would not then have countenanced that pretension. Canada was located between the two most likely foes in the next world war. Neutrality was unthinkable.[38] His successor was more forthright, but King was equally sure of Canada's appropriate response and the impossibility of simply cheering from the sidelines.

The greatest reversal of past policies, initiated while King was prime minister, was the Canadian government's unprecedented commitment to a military alliance in peacetime, NATO. That pledge reflected a dire threat to Canada and its traditional allies as well as an acute appreciation of western Europe's vulnerability. NATO was conceived as a remedy for the UN's failure to assure collective security. To Canadians, NATO linked Canada more closely to its principal allies, the US and the UK, and to western Europe. Involvement in that alliance kept Canada in familiar and reassuring company.

Perception of a global Soviet threat also prompted Canada's enlightened attitude to redefining Commonwealth membership to accommodate a republican India as a potential bridge to Asia for the West,[39] and that anxiety also extracted more money from Ottawa for the Colombo Plan. However, the King government and its successor both stayed out of a major test of Western resolve, the Berlin Airlift, in spite of pleas from Canada's closest allies and overwhelming support for participation from Canadians. Even in the context of the Cold War, Canada's internationalism clearly had limits.[40]

The proliferation of international organizations from wartime deliberations and declarations generated increased diplomatic activity by all nations. Opportunities for international engagement over global problems multiplied, so that some increase in Canada's participation in world affairs simply reflected enlargement of the international system. Thus, Canada's greater engagement in global economic institutions corresponded with an elaboration of a multilateral framework. Canadian delegates helped design and implement the International Monetary Fund, the International Bank for Reconstruction and Development (or World Bank), and the General Agreement on Tariffs and Trade. Canada contributed to the Marshall Plan as an off-shore supplier of goods for western Europe funded by American dollars. Meanwhile, Canada took advantage of its exceptional position as an international creditor at the end of the war to finance its exports to the UK, western Europe, and elsewhere. Canada identified its prosperity with international commerce, but its multilateral zeal was tempered by self-interest and opportunity.[41]

Another factor was Canada's temporary wartime and postwar power and influence. With so many countries vanquished or devastated, Canada assumed an unprecedented importance. It was consequently more likely to be seen as a valuable ally or as a potential contributor to solutions to the world's problems. Almost by default, not by design, Canadian ministers and officials became more involved in deliberations and assumed greater prominence in conferences and organizations addressing global issues. For Canada, this sway was ephemeral, as others would recover and regain power. However, it did mould Canadian assumptions and expectations.

Former diplomat and policy analyst John Holmes, who scrutinized Canada's contribution to postwar world affairs in his superb two-volume study *The Shaping of Peace*, aptly titled a later book on the subject *No Other Way*.[42] Holmes warned about nostalgia for a "golden age," a "myth" that ignored more complex explanations for Canada's approach to international affairs and for its rise and fall in influence.[43] To Holmes, the causes of Canada's relative decline "were natural and not discreditable."[44] Throughout his work, Holmes stressed how circumstances explained Canada's outlook and actions, as well as its sway.

Differences with past policies were often imperceptible. Justifiably, Denis Stairs has described Canada in these years as "a status quo power of modest capacity."[45] The celebratory

depiction of Canada's international relations in the 1940s and 1950s does not withstand closer scrutiny. The change in Canadian foreign policy in the 1940s was more evolutionary than revolutionary. Canada's conduct was neither so autonomous nor so influential as commonly understood. Its alignment in the early years of the Cold War was predictable, with its policies and actions conceived within the setting of traditional alliances and national interests.[46] The altered course suggested by rhetoric and actions after the war was less bold and distinctive than most accounts contend. In this reckoning, global context explains much more than does Canadian leadership. However, that reappraisal, which has been scorned by at least one true believer, has not yet overturned the orthodox view of Canada's past and its appropriate role in the world.[47]

Articles of Faith

Since Reid first advanced the notions of a "revolution" and a "golden decade," there has been a profound consensus that Canada's external relations changed fundamentally. More attention has been paid to explaining that shift than to testing its validity. Memoir writers and pundits have burnished the lustrous image. Some have enlarged the momentous decade to a golden age, and many have shifted the focus forward, particularly to the halcyon days from 1948 to 1957, when St Laurent was prime minister and Pearson was secretary of state for external affairs.[48] Other than one early sceptic,[49] most Canadian commentators echoed Reid's assertion of a break with the past. However, his emphasis on circumstances as determinants of what happened in Canadian international policies was forgotten, ignored, or downplayed in later evaluations. Consequently, an image of robust internationalism, often personified as "Pearsonian," has become identified with revolutionary change and venerated as an essential myth about Canada's role in the world.[50]

Pearson stands rather awkwardly on the pedestal erected for him by admirers. Those who worship him as an icon for internationalism have parsed his speeches to confirm his faith and ignored contradictions, whether in words or deeds. However, a careful reading of what Pearson said when he was foreign minister demonstrates that his most vivid rhetoric was that of a convinced cold warrior, not an idealist striving to save the world. His biographer has depicted someone who was cautious and pragmatic.[51] To Geoffrey Pearson, his father's perspective and conduct simply expressed "practical idealism."[52]

Nonetheless, Pearsonian internationalism has been venerated. Survey texts have invariably depicted a postwar transformation in attitudes and actions, including a "revolution in Canadian diplomacy," that has been traced to the arrival of St Laurent and Pearson and to the departure of King.[53] In most accounts, Pearsonian internationalism was best expressed at the UN, one scholar describing it as the "cornerstone of Canada's post-war multilateralist foreign policy." As a middle power, Canada has been enlightened and relatively disinterested, with a predilection and talent for mediation and a willing acceptance of international responsibility.[54] To some, this expressed Canada's mission or purpose.[55] Later foreign ministers, diplomats, scholars, and editorialists have summoned Pearson to justify or to criticize choices in Canadian foreign policy, as when one journalist moaned, "Where are you, Mike Pearson, now that we need you?"[56] Of his successors, his most devoted admirer was Lloyd Axworthy, who often invoked Pearson in support of his own initiatives. To one observer, Axworthy aimed to make "Pearsonianism Permanent."[57] His most recent popular biographer has revived the idealistic portrait of Pearson and again employed that reputation to lament the failings of successors.[58]

Internationalism has been treated as being distinctly Canadian, differentiating Canada from other nations, especially its powerful neighbour. The determination to better the world makes Canada different.[59] Internationalism has been installed as a national faith. Peacekeeping, in which Canada had initially participated to help its allies, was exalted as a Canadian invention as well as its appropriate task—so much so that when a Canadian government broke a string

of consecutive involvements in such ventures, that decision was deemed newsworthy and controversial.[60] That reaction reflected a long-standing tendency to exaggerate the importance of the UN to Canada's international policies and to downplay the importance of Canada's alignment in the Cold War to its overseas commitments. Most regard NATO as less significant. In the overall reckoning, engagement in the UN has usually been the litmus test for Canada's internationalism.

After the Revolution

When later governments made less of a difference or seemed less internationalist, these shortcomings were disparaged as unworthy and un-Canadian. The "revolution," the triumphs of the "golden age," and Pearson's legacy were frequently cited by critics in their lamentations over what happened since. Former diplomat Arthur Andrew blended memoir and history to chronicle *The Rise and Fall of a Middle Power*, whose demise was associated with the cumulative impact of John Diefenbaker, Pierre Trudeau, and Brian Mulroney, all of whom strayed from the true path.[61] The most persistent and prolific mythologist has been Andrew Cohen, whose veneration of Pearson culminated in a recent hagiography.[62] Holmes once mocked those who employed the remembrance of a better past to lament the later fall from grace as "melancholics who enjoy our tragic situation as a lost cause."[63] Even so, when prime ministers and foreign ministers assign priority to Canada's national interest, this is seen as heresy.[64] Most commentators deny that Canada's internationalism "was based on a very hard-boiled calculation of the Canadian national interest rather than on woolly-minded idealism."[65]

As prime ministers, neither Diefenbaker nor Pearson could match past glories.[66] The Trudeau government's review, *Foreign Policy for Canadians*, was pilloried as parochial and narrowly self-interested.[67] Pearson scrawled disparaging remarks on his copy.[68] Mulroney was rebuked for overzealousness over improving relations with the US and over the importance of international trade to Canada's prosperity, though some stances of his government, notably on apartheid in South Africa, were consistent with "Pearsonian internationalism."[69] Cohen scolded the government of Jean Chrétien for cleaving to "the national interest" in its foreign policy review, *Canada and the World*.[70] That government's subsequent emphasis on domestic issues such as national unity and fiscal prudence earned it further rebukes. The most common standard for judging Canada's international policies has been an abridged and idealized interpretation of the postwar "revolution" in Canadian foreign policy.

Not surprisingly, academics have tread more warily in this interpretative minefield than ex-diplomats, politicians, and journalists. However, most still perceive an internationalist mission after the war and regret subsequent performance as less impressive or worthy.[71] The editors of *Canada among Nations* have contributed to the malaise with volumes entitled *A Big League Player?*, *A Fading Power*, and *Split Images*.[72] The most prominent recent plaints about Canada's alleged fall from grace, *While Canada Slept* by Andrew Cohen and *At Home in the World* by Jennifer Welsh, both endorse the myth of the golden age.[73] Advocates and critics alike believe that Canadians, supposedly primordial internationalists, expect their governments to take stands on global issues and to help others. This belief skews the debate over Canada's international policies and actions.[74]

Revolution Renewed

In distinct ways and with different emphases, Canada's most recent prime ministers have pledged to restore Canadian prominence in world affairs. In his government's international policy statement, Paul Martin vowed to define and uphold *A Role of Power and Influence in the World*. After a prolonged preoccupation with the federal government's deficit and the understandable priority to security at home and abroad, Martin pledged to "make a difference" with a steadfast commitment to what he called "the new multilateralism." Five major themes (and corresponding responsibilities) were enumerated that would guide Canada's

international policies in diplomacy, defence, development, and commerce.[75] The political reception was predictably partisan, indirectly meeting the government's desire to differentiate itself from its opponents as well as from its predecessor.[76] Throughout, the statement recalled past glories and asserted a unique Canadian contribution. Pearson was invoked on the second page of the booklet on *Diplomacy*, and there was a detailed inventory of proposals that were clearly regarded as consistent with his legacy.[77] The resolve of the Martin government was never tested, as it was defeated in the next general election.

The Conservative government led by Stephen Harper was certainly keen to chart a different course. The prime minister rejected another foreign policy review, though the government's pronouncements and speeches by the prime minister and his foreign ministers conveyed firm convictions. The new government's approach was described as "certainly more muscular, with an emphasis on alignment with the US and a strengthened military."[78] When he governed for more than four years with a minority of seats in the House of Commons but even more so after his party won a majority, Harper articulated an international vision that upheld Canada's "values and interests." As foreign minister John Baird declared, the Conservatives had developed and implemented a "principled foreign policy" and consequently refocused on Canada's partnerships and alliances. The government undertook to promote "freedom, democracy, the rule of law and human rights around the world," to help others in need and to safeguard the security and prosperity of Canadians through collaboration with "our friends and allies."[79] Before and especially after Canada lost its bid for a seat on the UN Security Council, the UN ceased to dominate Canadian engagement in the world. When the UN was mentioned in ministerial speeches, it was as likely to be cited for failures or limitations as for achievements.[80]

That did not mean that the Harper government looked inward. On the contrary, the prime minister stressed the impact of global developments on Canada and Canadians. The summits of the G8 in Muskoka, Ontario, and the G20 in Toronto provided platforms for the prime minister as host, which he used effectively to define an agenda and a role.[81] Moreover, his speeches asserted that the world could learn from Canada's experience, in financial policy and governance. The specific themes—such as "enlightened sovereignty" and the affirmation that "Canada does not 'go along' in order to 'get along'"—differed from earlier ones, and the lessons for others were not those associated with Pearsonian internationalism.[82] Pearson vanished from statements and speeches, which cited instead his partisan adversary, Diefenbaker.[83] Nonetheless, the principles articulated as the bases of Canadian policy now are reminiscent of those promulgated by St Laurent in January 1947. The major differences—an emphasis on the global economy and on safeguarding Canada's prosperity—were identified earlier as omissions from the Gray Lecture. Perhaps the consistency in the preoccupations of Canadian governments in dealing with world affairs simply confirms the long-standing consensus in Canada surrounding the key precepts as well as the validity of St Laurent's original stress on continuity.

Canada's international policies have always been more conservative than most analyses and Canadian political rhetoric have suggested.[84] There may or may not be a revolution in Canada's international policies currently underway, but if so, it is deliberately cast as consistent with what matters most to Canadians, as defined and tested over the years. As one commentator has observed, Harper's foreign policy "leans without ambiguity to our traditional values and long-standing allies, beginning with the United States."[85] That prudence and pragmatism may not shelter Harper from critics who prefer the approach associated with the interpretations advanced by Reid and his followers, but they do remind us that circumstances still frame how Canada's values and interests are applied to the conduct of international relations.

Author's Note: The views in this paper are those of the author, not the Department of Foreign Affairs and International Trade. The author would like to thank Professor Norman Hillmer of Carleton University for invaluable comments and suggestions in the drafting and redrafting of this article.

Endnotes

1   Greg Donaghy and Stéphane Roussel, eds, *Escott Reid, Diplomat and Scholar* (Montreal and Kingston: McGill-Queen's University Press, 2004).

2   Escott Reid, *Time of Fear and Hope: The Making of the North Atlantic Treaty, 1947–1949* (Toronto: McClelland and Stewart, 1977).

3   Escott Reid, "Canadian Foreign Policy, 1967–1977: A Second Golden Decade?," *International Journal* 22, no. 2 (Spring 1967): 171–81.

4   There is a copy in Library and Archives Canada (hereafter LAC), Escott Reid Papers, MG 31 E46, vol. 3. See also Kim Richard Nossal, *The Politics of Canadian Foreign Policy*, 3rd ed. (Scarborough, ON: Prentice-Hall Canada, 1997), 154–9.

5   James Eayrs, "'A Low Dishonest Decade': Aspects of Canadian External Policy, 1931– 1939," in Hugh L. Keenleyside *et al.*, *The Growth of Canadian Policies in External Affairs* (Durham, NC: Duke University Press, 1960), 59–80.

6   Reid, "The Revolution in Canadian Foreign Policy, 1947–1951."

7   MacKay to Reid, 10 May 1957, MG 31 E46, vol. 34, file "MacKay," LAC.

8   Robert Bothwell, "The Cold War and the Curate's Egg: When Did Canada's Cold War Really Begin? Later Than You Might Think [1945–1950]," *International Journal* 53, no. 3 (Summer 1998): 407–18.

9   Douglas LePan, *Bright Glass of Memory, Memoirs by Douglas LePan* (Toronto: McGraw-Hill Ryerson, 1979), 145–226; and David R. Morrison, *Aid and Ebb Tide: A History of CIDA and Canadian Development Assistance* (Waterloo, ON: Wilfrid Laurier University, 1998), 29–30.

10   Bruce Hutchison, *The Incredible Canadian: A Candid Portrait of Mackenzie King: His Works, His Times, and His Nation* (Toronto: Longmans Green, 1952), chaps 42–5.

11   St Laurent became secretary of state for external affairs in September 1946, with Pearson as his undersecretary. In September 1948, Pearson succeeded St Laurent as minister, shortly before St Laurent succeeded King as prime minister (in mid-November 1948). They remained in tandem as prime minister and foreign minister until the Liberals were defeated in June 1957.

12   Escott Reid, *Radical Mandarin: The Memoirs of Escott Reid* (Toronto: University of Toronto Press, 1989), 241.

13 Hector Mackenzie, "Golden Decade(s)? Reappraising Canada's International Relations in the 1940s and 1950s," *British Journal of Canadian Studies* 23, no. 2 (2010): 199–206.

14 Hector Mackenzie, "King's Exit: The Prime Minister and Canada's International Relations, 1945–1948," *London Journal of Canadian Studies* 24 (2008/09), 106–31.

15 John Kirton, *Canadian Foreign Policy in a Changing World* (Toronto: Thomson Nelson, 2007), 111.

16 Hutchison, *Incredible Canadian*; and Mackenzie, "King's Exit."

17 Louis St Laurent, "Canada and World Affairs," 11 November 1948 (Department of External Affairs, *Statements and Speeches*, no. 48/59).

18 Mackenzie, "King's Exit."

19 Norman Hillmer, "The Foreign Policy That Never Was, 1900–1950," in Serge Bernier and John MacFarlane, eds, *Canada, 1900–1950: Un pays prend sa place/A Country Comes of Age* (Ottawa: Organization for the History of Canada, 2003), 141–53.

20 Louis St Laurent, *The Foundations of Canadian Policy in World Affairs: Duncan and John Gray Memorial Lecture* (Toronto: University of Toronto Press, 1947).

21 Nossal, *Politics of Canadian Foreign Policy*, 54–5; David B. Dewitt and John J. Kirton, *Canada as a Principal Power: A Study in Foreign Policy and International Relations* (Toronto: John Wiley & Sons, 1983), 48; and Andrew Cohen, *Lester B. Pearson* (Toronto: Penguin Canada, 2008), 127.

22 Andrew Cohen, *While Canada Slept: How We Lost Our Place in the World* (Toronto: McClelland & Stewart, 2003), 127.

23 John A. Munro and Alex I. Inglis, eds, *Mike: The Memoirs of the Right Honourable Lester B. Pearson*, vol. 2: *1948–1957* (Toronto: University of Toronto Press, 1973), 26. Pearson then quotes extensively from the text of the lecture (26–8).

24 Hector Mackenzie, "Shades of Gray? 'The Foundations of Canadian Policy in World Affairs' in Context," *American Review of Canadian Studies* 37, no. 4 (Winter 2007): 459–73; and Hector Mackenzie, "Gerry Riddell: A Golden Age Idealist?," in Greg Donaghy and Kim Richard Nossal, eds, *Architects and Innovators: Building the Department of Foreign Affairs and International Trade, 1909–2009/ Architectes et innovateurs: Le développement du ministère des Affaires étrangères et du Commerce international, de 1909 à 2009* (Montreal and Kingston: McGill-Queen's University Press, 2009), 169–87.

25 St Laurent, *Foundations*.

26 Mackenzie, "Shades of Gray?," 461; and Mackenzie, "Golden Age Idealist?," 175.

27 Norman Hillmer, "Defence and Ideology: The Anglo-Canadian Military 'Alliance' in the Nineteen

Thirties," *International Journal* 33, no. 3 (Summer 1978): 588–612.

28 Robert A. Spencer, *Canada in World Affairs: From UN to NATO 1946–1949* (Toronto: Oxford University Press, 1959), 365–8, 379–83.

29 C.P. Stacey, *Canada and the Age of Conflict*, vol. 2: *1921–1948, The Mackenzie King Era* (Toronto: University of Toronto Press, 1981), 307–17.

30 Robert Bothwell, *Alliance and Illusion: Canada and the World, 1945–1984* (Vancouver: UBC Press, 2007), 41–72; and James Eayrs, *In Defence of Canada: Peacemaking and Deterrence* (Toronto: University of Toronto Press, 1972).

31 Joseph T. Jockel, *No Boundaries Upstairs: Canada, the United States and the Origins of North American Air Defence, 1945–1958* (Vancouver: UBC Press, 1987); and Shelagh Grant, *Sovereignty or Security? Government Policy in the Canadian North, 1936–1950* (Vancouver: UBC, 1988).

32 Hector Mackenzie, "Canada's International Relations in the Early Cold War: The Impact and Implications of the Gouzenko Affair," in J.L. Black and Martin Rudner, eds, *The Gouzenko Affair: Canada and the Beginnings of Cold War Counter-Espionage* (Manotick, ON: Penumbra Press, 2006), 15–37.

33 John English, "'A Fine Romance': Canada and the United Nations, 1943–1957," in Greg Donaghy, ed., *Canada and the Early Cold War 1943–1957* (Ottawa: Department of Foreign Affairs and International Trade, 1999), 73–89.

34 Hector Mackenzie, "Knight Errant, Cold Warrior or Cautious Ally? Canada on the United Nations Security Council, 1948–49," *Journal of Transatlantic Studies* 7, no. 4 (December 2009), 453–75.

35 Denis Stairs, *The Diplomacy of Constraint: Canada, the Korean War and the United States* (Toronto: University of Toronto Press, 1974); and Steven Hugh Lee, *Outposts of Empire: Korea, Vietnam and the Origins of the Cold War in Asia, 1949–1954* (Montreal and Kingston: McGill-Queen's University Press, 1995).

36 Munro and Inglis, *Mike*, 2, 25.

37 John Holmes, *Canada: A Middle-Aged Power* (Toronto: McClelland & Stewart, 1976), v–vii; J. King Gordon, ed., *Canada's Role as a Middle Power* (Toronto: Canadian Institute of International Affairs, 1966); and Kim Richard Nossal, Stéphane Roussel, and Stéphane Paquin, *International Policy and Politics in Canada* (Toronto: Pearson Canada, 2011), 55.

38 King Diary: 9 July 1946.

39 Hector Mackenzie, "An Old Dominion and the New Commonwealth: Canada and Republican India, 1947–49," *Journal of Imperial and Commonwealth History* 27, no. 3 (September 1999): 82–112.

40 Leigh E. Sarty, "The Limits of Internationalism: Canada and the Soviet Blockade of Berlin, 1948–1949," in J.L. Black and Norman Hillmer, eds, *Nearly Neighbours, Canada and the Soviet Union: From Cold War to Détente and Beyond* (Kingston: Ronald P. Frye & Company, 1989), 56–74; Mackenzie, "Cold War and Limits"; and John C. Milloy, *The North Atlantic Treaty Organization, 1948–1957: Community or Alliance?* (Montreal and Kingston: McGill-Queen's University Press, 2006).

41 Hector Mackenzie, "The White Paper on Reconstruction and Canada's Post-war Trade Policy," in Greg Donaghy, ed., *Uncertain Horizons: Canadians and Their World in 1945* (Ottawa: Canadian Committee for the History of the Second World War, 1997), 167–88.

42 John W. Holmes, *The Shaping of Peace: Canada and the Search for World Order, 1943–1957*, 2 vols. (Toronto: University of Toronto Press, 1979 and 1982); and John W. Holmes, with Ian Smart *et al.*, *No Other Way: Canada and International Security Institutions* (Toronto: Centre for International Studies, University of Toronto, 1987).

43 John W. Holmes, "Merchant-Heeney Revisited: A Sentimental View," in Lauren McKinsey and Kim Richard Nossal, eds, *America's Alliances and Canadian-American Relations* (Toronto: Summerhill Press, 1988), 180–99.

44 John W. Holmes, "Canadian External Policies Since 1945," *International Journal* 18, no. 2 (Spring 1963): 137–47 (quotation, 146).

45 Denis Stairs, "Realists at Work: Canadian Policy Makers and the Politics of Transition from Hot War to Cold War," in Donaghy, *Canada and the Early Cold War*, 91–116 (quotation 92).

46 Mackenzie, "Cold War and Limits"; Greg Donaghy, "Coming off the Gold Standard: Re-assessing the 'Golden Age' of Canadian Diplomacy" (Saskatchewan Institute of Public Policy, 2005— www.suezcrisis.ca/pdfs/Coming%20off%20the%20Gold%20Standard.pdf); and Adam Chapnick, "The Golden Age, a Canadian Foreign Policy Paradox," *International Journal* 64, no. 1 (Winter 2008–9): 205–21.

47 Cohen, *Pearson*, 128–9.

48 Mackenzie, "Golden Decade(s)?"; Donaghy, "Coming off the Gold Standard"; and Chapnick, "The Golden Age."

49 Trevor Lloyd, *Canada in World Affairs, 1957–1959* (Toronto: Oxford University Press, 1968), 1–10, 245–7.

50 Hector Mackenzie, "Canada's Nationalist Internationalism: From the League of Nations to the United Nations," in Norman Hillmer and Adam Chapnick, eds, *Canadas of the Mind: The Making and Unmaking of Canadian Nationalisms in the Twentieth Century* (Montreal and Kingston: McGill-Queen's University Press, 2007), 89–109.

51 English, "Fine Romance."

52 Pearson, *Seize the Day*, 7.

53 Nossal, *Politics of Canadian Foreign Policy*, 58; Andrew F. Cooper, *Canadian Foreign Policy: Old Habits and New Directions* (Scarborough, ON: Prentice Hall Allyn and Bacon Canada, 1997), 40; Kirton, *Canadian Foreign Policy*, 109; and Nossal *et al.*, *International Policy*, 135–40.

54 Adam Chapnick, "The Canadian Middle Power Myth," *International Journal* 55, no. 2 (Spring 2000): 188–206; and Paul Gecelovsky, "Constructing a Middle Power: Ideas and Canadian Foreign Policy," *Canadian Foreign Policy* 15, no. 1 (Spring 2009): 77–93.

55 Richard Gwyn, "We Are a Missionary Society," *Hill Times*, 13 May 2002; and Michael Valpy, "The Foreign Policy Myth, Our image of Canada as a Positive Force for Good Dies Hard," *Globe and Mail*, 30 June 2008.

56 Sandra Gwyn, "Where are you, Mike Pearson, now that we need you? Decline and Fall of Canada's Foreign Policy," *Saturday Night* 93, no. 3 (April 1978): 27–35.

57 Richard Gwyn, "Lloyd Axworthy Makes Pearsonianism Permanent," *Policy Options*, December 1999, 13–16.

58 Cohen, *Pearson*, 186–7.

59 According to a Canadian bookseller, Indigo Books and Music, "the world needs more Canada."

60 Joseph Jockel, *Canada and International Peacekeeping* (Toronto: Canadian Institute of Strategic Studies, 1994); Norman Hillmer, "Peacekeeping: Canadian Invention, Canadian Myth," in Sune Akerman and J.L. Granatstein, eds, *Welfare States in Trouble* (Uppsala, Sweden: Swedish Science Press, 1995); and Sean Maloney, *Canada and Peacekeeping: Cold War by Other Means* (Toronto: Vanwell, 2002).

61 Arthur Andrew, *The Rise and Fall of a Middle Power: Canadian Diplomacy from King to Mulroney* (Toronto: James Lorimer, 1993).

62 Cohen, *Pearson*.

63 Holmes, *Middle-Aged Power*, vii.

64 Gwyn, "We Are a Missionary Society."

65 John W. Holmes, "The Role of Usurper," in Holmes, *Middle-Aged Power*, 6.

66 H. Basil Robinson, *Diefenbaker's World: A Populist in Foreign Affairs* (Toronto: University of Toronto Press, 1989); and Denis Smith, *Rogue Tory: The Life and Legend of John Diefenbaker* (Toronto: Macfarlane, Walter & Ross, 1995). The most recent biography of Pearson prolongs the golden age to include developments when he was prime minister. Cohen, *Pearson*, 70, 78.

67 See the contributions to a special issue in Winter 1970–1 (vol. 26, no. 1) of the *International Journal*.

68 John English, *The Worldly Years: The Life of Lester Pearson, 1949–1972* (Toronto: Alfred A. Knopf Canada, 1992), 385.

69   Nelson Michaud and Kim Richard Nossal, eds, *Diplomatic Departures: The Conservative Era in Canadian Foreign Policy, 1984–93* (Vancouver: UBC Press, 2001).

70   Andrew Cohen, "Canada in the World: The Return of the National Interest," *Behind the Headlines* 52, no.4 (Summer 1995).

71   Cohen, *Pearson*, 126–31; and Mike Trickey, "Canada's Fall from Grace on World Scene," *Ottawa Citizen*, 8 July 1998. Some academics cite the myth of the golden age without necessarily endorsing it. Bothwell, *Alliance and Illusion*, 391–2; Norman Hillmer and J.L. Granatstein, *Empire to Umpire: Canada and the World into the 21st Century* (Toronto: Thomson Nelson, 2008), chap. 7; and Kirton, *Canadian Foreign Policy*, 39, 110.

72   Fen Osler Hampson, Michael Hart, and Martin Rudner, eds, *Canada among Nations 1999: A Big League Player?* (Don Mills, ON: Oxford University Press, 1999); Norman Hillmer and Maureen Appel Molot, eds, *Canada among Nations 2002: A Fading Power* (Don Mills, ON: Oxford University Press, 2002); and Andrew F. Cooper and Dane Rowlands, eds, *Canada among Nations 2005: Split Images* (Montreal and Kingston: McGill-Queen's University Press, 2005).

73   Cohen, *While Canada Slept*; Jennifer Welsh, *At Home in the World: Canada's Global Vision for the 21st Century* (Toronto: HarperCollins, 2004).

74   Mackenzie, "Canada's Nationalist Internationalism." John Holmes described internationalism in Canadian policy-making circles as "almost a religion after the Second World War." Holmes, *Shaping of Peace*, 2, 119.

75   Government of Canada, *Canada's International Policy Statement: A Role of Pride and Influence in the World: Overview; Diplomacy; Defence; Development; Commerce* (Ottawa: Government of Canada, 2005); and Brian W. Tomlin, Norman Hillmer, and Fen Osler Hampson, *Canada's International Policies: Agendas, Alternatives, and Politics* (Don Mills, ON: Oxford University Press, 2008), 198–9. For scholarly reaction to the international policy statement, see especially the contributions to Cooper and Rowlands, *Split Images*.

76   Andrew F. Cooper and Dane Rowlands, eds, *Canada among Nations 2006: Minorities and Priorities* (Montreal and Kingston: McGill-Queen's University Press, 2006), notably articles by Hugh Segal, John Kirton, and Adam Chapnick.

77   Government of Canada, *Canada's International Policy Statement: Diplomacy*, 2.

78   Tomlin *et al.*, *Canada's International Policies*, 199.

79   Baird's remark about a "principled foreign policy" was widely reported in the Canadian press on 19 May 2011, including the *Ottawa Citizen*.

80   Speech 2011/30, "Address by the Honourable John Baird, Minister of Foreign Affairs, to the United Nations General Assembly," 26 September 2011, posted by Foreign Affairs and International Trade Canada on its website (www.international.gc.ca). For a critique, see Kim Richard Nossal, "Baird Mixes Up His 'P' Words at the UN," *Embassy*, 5 October 2011.

81   Keith H. Christie, "Setting a New High-Water Mark for Canadian Multilateralism: Canada's 2010 G8 and G20 Summits," *Canadian Foreign Policy* 16, no. 2 (2010): 143–8.

82   Harper first employed the phrase "enlightened sovereignty" in an address to the World Economic Forum in Davos, Switzerland, on 28 January 2010. It also featured in remarks by Baird to UNGA on 26 September 2011, as did the reworking of the admonition to "go along to get along."

83   Baird referred to Diefenbaker and quoted him in his speech to UNGA on 26 September 2011. On 19 September 2011, the former city hall of Ottawa, now a federal government office building whose tenants include parts of the Department of Foreign Affairs and International Trade, was named for Diefenbaker. Government of Canada, *News Release*, 19 September 2011.

84   Adam Chapnick, "Peace, Order, and Good Government: The "Conservative" Tradition in Canadian Foreign Policy," *International Journal* 60, no. 3 (Summer 2005): 635–50.

85   Colin Robertson, "Harper Charts a Course for Canada," *Ottawa Citizen*, 17 October 2011.

◎ 7.2: BALANCING WAR AND PEACE: CANADIAN FOREIGN POLICY AND THE VIETNAM WAR, 1961–1965

Andrew Preston

"A settlement is hard to envisage in the heat of battle," Canadian prime minister Lester B. Pearson declared on 2 April 1965, "but it is now imperative to seek one."[1] With these words, the leader of America's closest ally publicly expressed growing frustration with, and opposition to, American military intervention in Vietnam. In a speech at Temple University in Philadelphia, Pearson called on the administration of President Lyndon B. Johnson to halt unilaterally the bombing and seek a negotiated settlement with the Democratic Republic of Vietnam (DRV). The private, growing rift between Canadian and American foreign policy toward Vietnam was now very open and very wide. Incensed over the timing and location of the speech as much as its content, LBJ immediately summoned Pearson to Camp David; unsurprisingly, the Temple speech was the main issue that Johnson wanted to discuss. The resultant scene, during which LBJ berated Pearson for over an hour and eventually grabbed the prime minister by the lapels of his coat, is a familiar one.[2] It is also instructive: regarding Southeast Asia, the differences between the American and Canadian perspectives had, by mid-1965, widened so much as to be irreconcilable. Canada and the United States disagreed fundamentally over the strategic importance of Vietnam, and over America's ability to achieve its goals in Southeast Asia.

The Temple–Camp David episode is thus emblematic of these differences, and of the frustrations borne of the divergence in foreign policy outlook between the two intimate allies. On one hand, Canada indeed supported America's policy of sponsoring and maintaining a non-communist South Vietnam, condemned the communist North Vietnamese for instigating and perpetuating an aggressive war, and feared the effects of falling dominoes, at least those of a psychological nature. On the other hand, the Canadians, through their experience on the International Control Commission for Vietnam (ICC), believed not only that American military escalation was a threat to world peace, but also that it was futile. The conclusion was that negotiating, not fighting, would best achieve American aims while simultaneously avoiding the spread of a wider war. . . .

Canadian diplomacy during the Vietnam War has been the subject of a very small, but hotly contested, historiographical debate. The dominant interpretation has argued that Canadian politicians and diplomats in the early to mid-1960s helped facilitate US policy and were thus partners to an American crime. Known primarily as the "complicity thesis," this school of

thought was first postulated by Charles Taylor's *Snow Job* and James Eayrs's *Indochina: Roots of Complicity*.[3] Instead of limiting a rapacious American foreign policy, Canada eased its path and betrayed its obligations to both the ICC and the Vietnamese people. . . .

Ramesh Thakur's *Peacekeeping in Vietnam*, a comparative study of national foreign policies within the ICC (India and Poland were the other commission members and subjects of the book), posited that Canadian "leaders either viewed the conflict entirely in American categories or subordinated their perceptions to dictates of prudence in Canada–United States relations." Thakur's thesis did not castigate Canadian foreign policy for deliberate complicity; rather, it centred on the subordinate—and unavoidable—role played by Canada in its relations with the United States. His findings derived from a presumption that Ottawa would do just about all it could to avoid ruffling the eagle feathers of its giant neighbour to the south.[4] . . .

The other major work that developed the complicity thesis was the aptly titled *Quiet Complicity* by Victor Levant. . . . Levant argued that Canadians profited economically from the Vietnam War, that Canada had a vital trade relationship with East and Southeast Asia to protect, and that the Canadian government, whether Liberal or Conservative, shared an identical geopolitical view of the world with Washington. The record of Canadian participation on the ICC, then, "was characterized by partisan voting, willful distortion of fact, and complicity in U.S. violations of both the [1954] Geneva and [1973] Paris agreements." Like Thakur, Levant believed the heavy imbalance intrinsic to the Canadian-American relationship to be at the root of Canadian actions.[5] . . .

Coincidentally, a rival interpretation emerged simultaneously to counter the complicity thesis. In *Vietnam: The Ten Thousand Day War*, journalist Michael Maclear defended Canadian diplomacy as an effective means of diverting American decision-making away from the deployment of tactical nuclear weapons.[6] But it was the book *In the Interests of Peace*, by political scientist Douglas

A. Ross, that most forcefully challenged the view that Canada had aided and abetted America in Vietnam. Instead, Ross argued, Canadian officials "aimed prudentially at conciliation of critical disputes" between the warring parties. Ottawa made "every reasonable effort to facilitate serious negotiations between Hanoi and Washington," due mainly, Ross believed, to an overwhelming fear among Canadian officials that the Vietnam War would spark a general nuclear war. Ross also directly addressed the chief tenet of the complicity thesis. "Reduced to its essentials," he exhorted, "the record of Canadian policy-making and diplomacy is not cause for shame. Successive Canadian governments accommodated the policy imperatives of various American administrations not because they believed in the wisdom or practicality of intervention but because they hoped to constrain the play of policy in Washington."[7] . . .

. . . Canadian diplomacy intended to prevent the United States from becoming mired in the Vietnamese quagmire. . . . [F]rom 1961 to 1965, the Kennedy and Johnson administrations confronted a rapidly deteriorating position in South Vietnam and made difficult choices in committing America to war. This was also a crucial time for Canada, as the conflict between its alliance duties to the United States and its peacekeeping duties to the ICC sharpened to the extent that it debilitated Canadian policy. Since it had reluctantly agreed to monitor the illusory peace in Indochina by joining the ICC in 1954,[8] Canada had become convinced of the culpability of the communists—the National Liberation Front (NLF) in South Vietnam and, especially, the DRV in the North—for the instability and chaotic conditions in Vietnam. To most Canadian officials it was, put simply, a case of foreign aggression, a slow invasion of the South by the North. This conviction only hardened over time, so that by the early 1960s it had become a truism in Ottawa. While serving on the ICC, however, Canadian officials also had a unique perspective of South Vietnamese politics and society—namely, the incompetence, authoritarianism, and inherent unsteadiness of the government of President Ngo Dinh Diem in

Saigon. After November 1963, Diem's carnival of successors made their predecessor seem like a model of stability. And with direct experience in the Korean War not long behind them, the Canadians feared that in its bid to prevent the collapse of South Vietnam, the United States would again provoke Chinese intervention and thus instigate the next world war.[9] Canadian officials thought the American anti-communist cause in Indochina laudable—perhaps even noble—but not worth a war. In other words, while the Canadians maintained broad agreement with American aims—the preservation of a non-communist South Vietnam—they came to disagree sharply with the methods used: military intervention, escalation, and eventually war. Moreover, after mid-1964, not only did Ottawa disagree with Washington's means, but it also believed that the end was no longer attainable, at least at any acceptable cost.

The challenge for the Canadian government, then, was to effect a change in American policy, but without causing a significant and perhaps irrevocable breach between Ottawa and Washington, which would obviously be much more catastrophic for the former than for the latter.[10] Affecting US behavior would not be a simple task, as even the most sympathetic American officials saw Canadian concerns and opinions as, at best, peripheral. . . .

Because of its place in the hierarchy of international relations, the framework within which Ottawa devised foreign policy was self-consciously called "middle-power" diplomacy. The task of a middle power was to attain successfully its own goals within the constraints delineated by both the international system and the great powers. Although Canada in the 1960s lacked the stature, might, and authority of a great power, it nonetheless had its own interests to pursue and possessed its own vision of how the international system ought to work (multilateral institutions and United Nations conflict resolution and peacekeeping being those with the highest priority). In order to bring their influence to bear on the course of international relations, Canadian policymakers could use only the limited, invariably diplomatic tools that a middle power had at its disposal.[11] . . .

A corollary to middle-power diplomacy—one that was not conceived with Indochina in mind but was nonetheless perfectly suited for it—was "quiet diplomacy," which was used specifically to remove Canada from the horns of its America-Vietnam dilemma. Differences in outlook and policy were best settled, it was believed, privately and quietly between the Canadian and American governments. In theory, quiet diplomacy, as expressed in the bilateral 1964 report "Principles for Partnership," was intended to serve as the mutually beneficial foundation for Canadian-American relations: "In the abiding interests of both countries . . . divergent views between [the] two governments should be expressed and if possible resolved in private, through diplomatic channels."[12] In practice, it offered the Canadian government one of its only means to influence the direction of American policy. Open dissent by Ottawa would not only fall on deaf ears in Washington; it would also ruin the Canadians' credibility with the Americans. As Pearson reflected in his memoirs: "Canada has its own role to play in the world. . . . We have our own values to develop and to offer, our own identity to realize as something worth preserving. These things can be done, but not by mirrors or miracles, or by considering our relations with the United States as a matter for rhetoric rather than realism."[13] This realism would face an enormous challenge in Vietnam, where Canada had to act simultaneously as loyal ally, international referee, concerned participant, and, most inauspiciously, sometime critic of American policy.

The first real challenge came in May 1961, when Kennedy sent Johnson, who was then vice-president, on a tour of South and Southeast Asian capitals. Johnson's most important stop was in Saigon, where he pledged to South Vietnamese president Ngo Dinh Diem further American economic and military assistance. Charles J. Woodsworth, the Canadian commissioner to the ICC, believed that the augmentation of the US Military Assistance Advisory Group (MAAG), which was one of the measures proposed by Johnson, would openly violate the limits imposed by the Geneva Accords on foreign military participation. As recently as January 1961, the Canadian delegation had been willing and able to argue successfully to the ICC that the reasons for the introduction of US military helicopters were justifiable,[14] but by the spring such allowances had been nullified by the increasing size and scope of the American military buildup. Canada, as both a member of the ICC and a close ally of the United States, was now faced with a difficult choice: ignore the American buildup and discredit the ICC, or cite the MAAG increase as a violation and risk incurring the wrath of Washington. Woodsworth believed that the United States must postpone the buildup, and he informed Ottawa that the Canadian delegation "took [the] stand [that] we could not support any further MAAG increase. . . . We suggested that [the] USA explore every possible avenue of accomplishing [its] objective without increasing MAAG[']s military strength beyond its present ceiling."[15] Woodsworth also passed this suggestion on to the American ambassador in Saigon, Frederick Nolting.[16] An open breach of the Geneva limits by the United States would not only discredit the ICC; it would also signal its demise and possibly clear the path for an enlarged conflict. "If the ICC were forced to leave," Woodsworth wrote, "the greatest danger would be [the] vacuum created. . . . Undoubtedly both sides would wish to fill in, possibly sparking a conflagration."[17]

The Department of External Affairs (DEA) in Ottawa agreed with Woodsworth's analysis but not his recommendation.[18] Both scenarios—openly siding against the American position or acquiescing in deepening military intervention—would ruin the ICC and thus be disastrous for Canada's Indochina policy. The solution, a typically Canadian compromise, was to agree with the Americans but press them to make all changes and increases as quietly and inconspicuously as possible. Norman A. Robertson, the undersecretary of state for external affairs, outlined the tactic to the minister, Howard Green. "It is apparent that the Americans and the South Vietnamese are determined to go ahead with their intention to increase strength of . . . [MAAG] in Vietnam," Robertson explained to the minister. "We entirely agree as to the seriousness of the situation in South Vietnam which has led them to this decision." If Washington simply went ahead with a public increase, Robertson feared, the ICC would inevitably be compelled to rule against the United States and South Vietnam for violating the limits on foreign military personnel mandated by the Geneva Accords. But a quieter, more subtle, and less noticeable increase could be handled much more easily:

> In this difficult situation, it might be useful to the Americans if we were to have an informal discussion with them to outline what we anticipate. . . . (a) Regardless of what the South Vietnamese and U.S.A. authorities intend to do in practice, it would be unwise for the South Vietnamese Government formally to notify the Commission of its intentions; (b) It would be better for the South Vietnamese to continue operating (for the time being at least) under the terms of the Commission's letter which made no reference to an authorized ceiling.[19]

What Robertson was suggesting, and what the minister approved, was tacit acceptance of a slight American increase in its military presence in South Vietnam. . . .

In October, Kennedy responded to the continuing crisis by sending two of his closest advisers, military aide General Maxwell D. Taylor and Deputy National Security Adviser Walt W. Rostow, to South Vietnam for an assessment. . . . The Canadians were kept informed. On 17 November, Assistant Secretary of State Walter P. McConaughy told Arnold Heeney, the Canadian ambassador to Washington, "As [a] result [of the] Taylor mission . . . we believe it [is] now necessary [to] take offensive action against [the] Viet Cong." Although American combat troops would not be sent, McConaughy warned that "nothing currently envisaged rules this out should it become necessary."[20] Rostow sought to allay Ottawa's fears of a wider war. Somewhat

disingenuously, he told Heeney that ground troops had not been sent because Kennedy was hoping that the ICC would broaden its investigations and strengthen its authority to enforce communist compliance with the Geneva Accords. But Rostow also refused to "preclude the possibility of further and more drastic measures being taken by [the] USA."[21] Following Rostow's suggestion, Ambassador-at-Large W. Averell Harriman, one of Kennedy's top lieutenants on Southeast Asia, told Heeney of the administration's "desire that [Canada] press in the Commission" for citations against the DRV. Harriman also conveyed the "request that [Canada] do everything possible to have [the] Commission accede to [American and South Vietnamese] requests . . . for increased patrolling of important areas."[22] More cynically, Harriman revealed to the British ambassador to Washington, David Ormsby Gore, that the Americans believed the ICC to be of great political value as a "shield against demands for other forms of international action."[23] Harriman also told Heeney that, for the time being, negotiations over the fate of Vietnam were unfeasible.[24]

Aside from their tough rhetoric, Rostow and Harriman told the Canadians exactly what they wanted to hear. The ICC was, to unending Canadian dismay, a convoluted body in which squabbling and tension were endemic. It is not surprising that West-oriented Canada and communist Poland did not cooperate very well: aside from representing opposing ideologies and strategic interests, each was also committed to a powerful ally that had vital interests of its own in Southeast Asia. . . . By forestalling the "drastic measures" hinted at by Rostow, Ottawa hoped to counterbalance Polish obstinacy and maintain solidarity with India. The ICC also had no means to enforce its decisions, which was a crippling deficiency. Ottawa's perennial goal was a stronger, more emboldened ICC that would be able to enforce the Geneva Accords strictly. The biggest hurdle over which the Canadians had to jump was American, and hence South Vietnamese, cooperation; now that this seemed to be forthcoming, the Canadian delegation acted. Frank Hooton, who had replaced Woodsworth in October as commissioner, told

Nolting of Ottawa's desire to "push for [the] immediate creation of [a] mobile team to undertake investigation at once."[25]

A mobile, empowered team of ICC investigators was anathema to the DRV leadership, however, and it was clear that they would refuse to allow such an intrusion into their half of Vietnam. Working in tandem with Hanoi, the Polish delegation to the ICC killed the initiative by initially agreeing to its desirability and subsequently drowning it in the committee stage with technical concerns.[26] . . . Unfortunately, the situation continued to deteriorate. Hooton reported to the DEA in early February 1962 that the situation in South Vietnam "has worsened and that it may continue to deteriorate for some months before it improves." The commissioner felt that if the insurgency were not quelled at some point in the near future, the United States would feel "obliged to reassess [the] situation and take what action seemed necessary to avoid South Vietnam coming under Communist control."[27] The rapidly declining state of South Vietnamese political stability and military security and the concomitant deepening of American involvement—and the possible introduction of ground troops, which continually cast a pall over Canadian policy—would once again sharpen the conflict between Canada's role on the ICC and its status as an intimate American ally. Preventing an Americanized war was Canada's goal, but in its pursuit Ottawa would run the risk of antagonizing Washington.

The Americans did their Canadian counterparts no favours by introducing to South Vietnam—in a "rather ostentatious way," as State Department official Benjamin C. Wood confessed to a British diplomat—military helicopters launched from an aircraft carrier.[28] The arrival of the military hardware at the beginning of 1962 not only represented the most flagrant US violation of the Geneva Accords to date; it also destroyed Robertson's carefully quiet strategy of tacitly accepting the growing American presence in South Vietnam. From London, R.L. Seconde of the British Foreign Office sympathized with the Canadians. In a letter to the embassy in Washington, he wondered why the Americans insisted on "making life difficult for their friends on the International Control Commission." While Seconde praised the Canadians' "splendidly robust" attitude, he feared that it, along with the ICC itself, would suffer irreparable damage from the American reinforcements.[29] The British High Commission in Ottawa relayed to London the DEA's concern that it would now be much more difficult to persuade the Indians that the United States was merely responding to prior aggression. Canadian diplomats felt strongly that the American military buildup "can only be unhelpful so far as the Commission is concerned."[30] . . .

While neither Ottawa nor the Canadian delegation was "prepared [to] adopt [the] position that [a] breach by one party justifies [a] breach by the other," they were intent on more assertively pressing the South Vietnamese and American complaints to the ICC and doing "what they can [to] avoid or minimize possible citations against" Saigon and the United States.[31] In discussing the issue with the American embassy, the DEA expressed its agreement with the US position on subversion, but warned "they do not feel they can support it in [the] ICC or that they would get anywhere if they tried. However," the Canadians continued, "they doubt if it [is] necessary [to] approach [the] problem in precisely this manner."[32] A DEA aide-memoire, passed to the State Department with "an attitude of sympathy for USA objectives in Vietnam,"[33] presented the dilemma and a solution. Not only had the balance of the 1954 ceasefire "been upset by the increase in the strength of the North Vietnamese military forces; the North Vietnamese authorities have also unquestionably been responsible in very large part for the incitement and direction of subversive and terroristic activities in [South Vietnam]." It followed, then, that Ottawa agreed with Washington's position that "the question of Northern subversion and American assistance are directly and intimately linked." As a member of an international commission, however, Canada could not be expected to endorse American violations of the Geneva Accords simply because North Vietnam had already done so. Instead, the paper concluded that the Canadian delegation would work for a report condemning communist violations, which would place South Vietnam and the United States on the moral and legal high ground and make the terms of Geneva more enforceable.[34] The conflict in the South could then de-escalate, stability would return to Saigon, and—it was hoped—American escalation would be avoided. Until the Canadians could convince the Indian ICC delegation to join in a majority report against communist subversion, Ottawa asked the Kennedy administration not to react to provocations.[35]

The Canadian delegation pressed its case, particularly to the Indian delegation, throughout the first half of 1962. As early as January, for example, Heeney confided to Wood that "the Canadians were trying to be as helpful as possible and in talking to the Indians they always stressed that increased American military aid should be viewed in the light of the long-standing and large-scale interference by North Vietnam in the internal affairs of the South."[36] The Kennedy administration was certainly expectant of a legal and political victory on the ICC,[37] and the Canadians did not disappoint. The ICC's special report of 2 June 1962 reflected the Canadian opinion that the DRV was to blame for the war in the South, although there were also lesser charges cited against the South and the United States for the continuing introduction of American military personnel. Overall, the report was more favourable to the United States.[38] . . . The verdict of the special report, it was hoped, would have enough political and legal authority to force a change in the communists' tactics, thereby avoiding a crisis that would eventually draw American troops to Vietnam. Less enthusiastically, the State Department agreed with this rationale. "We believe the ICC," stated a policy paper, "does still perform a useful function by somewhat restraining the overtness of Communist aggression."[39] The Canadian strategy was a very legalistic—and highly improbable—remedy to a problem that had long crossed such reasonable limits.

The release of the special report did not have the mitigating effect for which the Canadians hoped. The North Vietnamese denunciations were expected, but they nonetheless made for increasingly difficult relations on the ICC between Canada and Poland. The Indians—always the swing vote on the ICC—also began to stiffen their stance into one less amenable to American and South Vietnamese considerations. The Indian commissioner revealed his second thoughts about the special report to Hooton, stating that despite mounting evidence of Northern infiltration, the American military presence in South Vietnam could not be "justified."[40] . . .

Thus, it was with great alarm that the Canadian ICC representative in Hanoi reported extensive talks in late 1962 between leaders of the DRV and the NLF, with the former promising to support the latter's struggle "more actively" and "more wholeheartedly."[41] If Diem was finding it difficult to suppress the insurgency in 1962, an intensified communist campaign would almost certainly topple his government—unless, that is, the United States could offset the North Vietnamese effort with an increased role of its own. Gordon Cox, who arrived in Saigon at the end of 1962 as Hooton's replacement, was immediately aware of this discouraging trend. Judging from the ineptitude of Diem and his government, it was one that could only end in an Americanized war. "The very great extent to which the Americans here are involved in actual military operations," Cox wrote upon arrival in South Vietnam, "must be very worrying."[42] . . . But while the Kennedy administration relied on the overly optimistic claims of progress and improvement emanating from both American and Vietnamese sources in South Vietnam, Canadian officials were not so sanguine. . . .[43]

The Buddhist crisis, which began on 8 May and lasted throughout the summer and fall of 1963, decimated the sense of progress and proved the pessimists in the DEA to be correct. A dispute between the Catholic Diem regime and the Buddhist population over the right to fly religious flags in the city of Hue exploded into a national clash between the government and the people it purported to serve, crippling both parties in the process. The government's violent but ineffectual tactics in responding to the crisis made it appear as incompetent as it was authoritarian. Not only did the Buddhist crisis hamstring the government's effort against the NLF; it also robbed it of crucial American support. As the DEA wrote to Cox, the "apparent continuing failure of [Diem] to come to terms with an issue involving 90 percent of [the] population is bound to give rise to widespread lack of confidence in [Diem's] handling of [the] situation."[44] The Kennedy administration, through internal byzantine intrigues of its own, withdrew its support for Diem and quietly sponsored a coup that finally ousted him from power. Three weeks later, the assassination of Kennedy brought about a change in American leadership.

A change in leadership in Saigon and Washington did not necessarily mean a change in policy, at least as far as Ottawa was concerned. Cox informed General Duong Van "Big" Minh, the putative head of the new government in Saigon, that Canada remained in "full agreement" with Saigon's view that the conflict was solely the work of North Vietnam.[45] There was a new government in Ottawa as well, after Pearson and the Liberals formed a minority government in the election of April 1963. Robertson and the new minister for external affairs, Paul Martin, agreed with each other and with Cox that the war in Vietnam was "characterized essentially by the carrying out of a subversive war directed by North Vietnam against the authorities of [South] Vietnam."[46] Moreover, for both the Pearson and Johnson governments, Vietnam remained a crisis-in-waiting, an insoluble problem with which neither wanted to deal. At their first meetings, in January 1964, the two leaders touched upon Vietnam briefly, and only as it related to the equally sticky issue of recognizing the PRC [People's Republic of China].[47]

The situation in South Vietnam continued to deteriorate rapidly. After Diem's ouster, the reports of military, social, and political progress were exposed as fraudulent. The junta led by Big Minh was itself overthrown by General Nguyen Khanh at the end of January. Most ominously, the pace of the insurgency quickened. In the early spring of 1964, Johnson administration officials began planning for the drastic measures about

which Rostow had fatefully warned in 1961. But although LBJ was willing to expand the war to include operations against the North in order to prevent a collapse of the South, he was not especially eager to do so, particularly during a presidential election year. While planning for war proceeded in Washington, Johnson also sought to render any such preparations irrelevant. Since 1954, the United States and North Vietnam had had virtually no direct communication; they had neither official diplomatic relations nor the sort of informal contacts that can sometimes lead to fruitful discussions. American officials needed a reliable interlocutor to approach the DRV leadership and warn it of the adverse repercussions of defying American resolve. Accompanying the stick was the proverbial carrot, a promise of American financial assistance for North Vietnamese development after the cessation of fighting.

After determining that an approach to Hanoi should be made, the Americans next had to choose the third party. . . .

Canada was not an odd choice. As a member of the ICC, Canada had a permanent representative in Hanoi, and the Canadian high commissioner frequently travelled from Saigon to Hanoi to meet with DRV officials. Hooton and Cox had done so several times; Cox was even known to DRV prime minister Pham Van Dong as "mon cher ami."[48] Indeed, Cox had once emphasized the likelihood of deepening American involvement should the conflict in the South continue to escalate, while Pham Van Dong had stressed that "the real difficulty was that [the North] had no means of communication with the USA and that they would welcome any expression of [American] views, interests, and intentions."[49] And Canadian ICC officials, who held no sympathy for either the NLF or the DRV or their cause, could be relied upon to deliver faithfully an American message. . . .

With this in mind, Rusk flew to Ottawa to meet with Pearson and Martin on 30 April. By this time it was clear that J. Blair Seaborn, an expert on communism whom Martin later praised as "one of our ablest diplomats,"[50] would head to Saigon as Cox's replacement. Lodge did not have a very high regard for Cox and was happy to deal instead with Seaborn.[51] Rusk found Pearson and Martin to be "in close concert" with American thinking and "willing to cooperate with us." The secretary of state formally requested that Seaborn be employed as an interlocutor, and he touched upon four main points that should comprise the message to Hanoi. First, Seaborn should determine "what is on Ho Chi Minh's mind," whether he was confident or anxious. Second, "Seaborn should get across to Ho and his colleagues the full measure of US determination." This was the heart of the matter for Rusk, the stick that he and Lodge believed would convince North Vietnam to halt its infiltration and destabilization of the South. Third, "Seaborn should spread the word that he is puzzled by Hanoi's intentions. . . . If Hanoi would leave its neighbors alone, the US presence in the area would diminish sharply." And finally, Seaborn should present the carrot, although it was not a very substantial or convincing one: the Americans, Seaborn should say, "recognize North Viet Nam's need for trade, and especially food, and consider that such needs could be fulfilled if peaceful conditions were to prevail." Almost as an afterthought, Rusk also mentioned briefly that Seaborn should carefully observe Polish behavior on the ICC.[52] A few days later, Lodge toughened the rhetoric to be conveyed by Seaborn—"We intend to stay. We intend to win," he wrote—but the focus and purpose of the message did not change.[53] Thus, as historian Fredrik Logevall has pointed out, Rusk, Lodge, and the Johnson administration did not aim merely to convince the North Vietnamese; they sought to compel. The message carried by Seaborn was, in Lodge's words, "more nearly an ultimatum."[54]

For their part, Pearson and Martin were concerned about a wider, Americanized war, and they welcomed the opportunity for Canada to serve as an intermediary between the belligerents. They also thought that the American ploy could work. Martin had shared his "doubts about the direction of United States policy on South Vietnam" with Richard Austen Butler, the British foreign secretary, who had visited Ottawa in February. But additionally, Martin had been intrigued by rumours that "the State Department had been contemplating the issue of an ultimatum to Hanoi." While this might provoke Chinese intervention, bringing "another Korean-type war on our hands," Martin also believed that "a strong line of this kind might prove effective."[55] There were other incentives for Ottawa's participation. A virulent new strain of pessimism had arisen among Canadian officials about the future of the ICC, which continued humiliatingly to be rendered ineffectual and moribund by both the lack of an enforcement mechanism and the internal disputes among its members.[56] A new, independent role as an honest broker would thus continue Canada's efforts to prevent a major war in Indochina; as Seaborn recalled, Pearson and Martin envisioned that the secret channel to Hanoi would eventually lead to broad talks.[57] Just as importantly, it would continue to ensure Ottawa a primary role in Vietnam. . . . For the Americans, the ultimatum—plus any observations by Seaborn—constituted the primary component of the mission. For the Canadians, however, the potential opening of a dialogue between the United States and the DRV was the most important element.

The details were arranged at the end of May. Pearson went to New York on 28 May to meet with Johnson and National Security Adviser McGeorge Bundy. Pearson expressed a desire to cooperate but "indicated some concern about the nature of the 'sticks.'" The president responded that the United States had no intention of expanding the war—Bundy put it as "a less than 50% chance"[58]—and needed Seaborn's services simply "to carry the message of US attitudes to Hanoi."[59] To be sure, American resolve was the main component of the intended message, but Johnson made it clear to the prime minister that the United States had no current intentions of expanding the war. Pearson seems to have been won over by LBJ: after stating unequivocally that Canada could not abide the use of nuclear weapons, he agreed that limited retaliatory strikes against North Vietnam could be warranted in certain situations. . . .[60]

After establishing his credentials in Saigon as the new Canadian commissioner, Seaborn travelled to Hanoi to meet with the North Vietnamese leadership and relay the American message. Granted an interview with Prime Minister Pham Van Dong, Seaborn iterated that while "President Johnson was [a] man of peace . . . he was determined that [South Vietnam] would not fall under communist control as a result of subversion and guerilla warfare." Pham understood the importance of the message and said that he appreciated Canada's efforts as an intermediary. He responded that the United States would first have to withdraw militarily from Vietnam before a settlement—one based on the neutralization of South Vietnam—could be reached.[61] Seaborn also recorded his observations of life in Hanoi and the temper of its people: he detected an abundance of stoicism, no signs of war-weariness, and no factionalism within political circles.[62] From an American perspective it was a gloomy assessment, predictably so. Pham did not seem to be at all concerned about the possibility of war with the United States, and the general mood in Hanoi seemed to support the prime minister's confidence. Marcel Cadieux, who had recently replaced Robertson as under-secretary, wrote to Martin with this in mind: "Mr. Seaborn's first and very tentative conclusion is that there may be fewer pressures on the North Vietnamese to reach an accommodation with the United States than the Americans may themselves believe."[63]

As Seaborn's and Cadieux's initial thoughts made clear, the conclusion that Canadian officials were drawing was that North Vietnam was ready and willing to go to war with the United States and that any opening for a negotiated solution—such as Pham Van Dong's hint about neutralization of the South—should be explored. American officials, on the other hand, gleaned a much different lesson. Sullivan agreed that Seaborn's report "provided a sobering picture," but this only "illustrated the size of the job there was to do for [South Vietnam] and [the] USA."[64] Whereas Seaborn and the DEA thought that Pham's clear reference to neutralization was a hopeful development, the State Department disagreed, dismissing it as mere propaganda.[65] And

while Seaborn was eager to return quickly to Hanoi to continue the dialogue and capitalize on potential breakthroughs, the Americans thought it best to move slowly. "In our view," the new ambassador to Saigon, Maxwell Taylor, wrote to Rusk, "[the] ball [is] now in Hanoi's court and their views should be volunteered rather than solicited."[66] Of course, the chief American intent for the Seaborn mission—the delivery of a warning, if not an ultimatum—had been fulfilled. The opening of a productive, continuing dialogue with the North would certainly be a bonus, but it was not the main purpose.

In August, the Johnson administration made good on its ultimatum. On 2 August, North Vietnamese gunboats attacked a US destroyer in the Tonkin Gulf; two days later, another attack was reported to have occurred. LBJ responded with air strikes against targets inside the DRV and secured from Congress a joint resolution guaranteeing the president whatever support he needed to prosecute the war. There was a sense of bewilderment among most observers, and the crisis appeared to be more unstable than at any other previous time. Why would the North be so flagrantly provocative, especially when it did not necessarily seem to serve its interests? An aggressive naval exchange in the gulf initiated by the North "defies rational explanation," the Canadian representative in Hanoi wrote to Seaborn.[67] The attacks defied rational explanation for two reasons, neither of which was available to most people at the time. First, the North Vietnamese were reacting to raids by the South Vietnamese and Americans under the now-infamous OPLAN-34A. Second, the attack of 4 August is now considered not to have even occurred.[68] The Canadians were generally pleased—and relieved—at the scope of the American reprisal, which was seen as limited in relation to what had been anticipated. "I am quite sure that the United States government would limit . . . their action," Pearson told the House of Commons, "to the requirements of the situation and to meeting an attack on their forces, in this case by a Communist dictatorship in North Viet Nam."[69] . . . In July, Seaborn had arranged to meet with DRV officials during a routine ICC visit to Hanoi in August. The incidents in the Tonkin Gulf now complicated matters for Seaborn tremendously, but the American position remained unaffected. The message—a profession of peace, a delivery of an ultimatum—would not change, although the absence of carrots in Seaborn's diplomatic bag was now conspicuous. In Washington, Assistant Secretary of State William P. Bundy told Ambassador Ritchie what type of statements Seaborn should present to Pham Van Dong: "What do you think you are doing? Do not say that you did not attack us because we know you did. We also do not intend to escalate. Our basic position remains unchanged from the time of Seaborn[']s last visit."[70] The official instructions, which conveyed the same basic meaning, followed shortly: American air strikes were retaliatory and limited, not aggressive; the United States was "at a loss to understand [the] DRV motive"; and, in a reiteration of the original warning, Seaborn was to say that the United States would escalate its attacks on North Vietnam in the event of further provocation.[71]

Seaborn met again with Pham Van Dong on 13 August in an atmosphere that was much less cordial than it had been in June. The DRV prime minister reacted angrily to the messages that Seaborn carried, saying that the United States was responsible for an "act of aggression." North Vietnam was interested in peace but it would fight a "defensive and patriotic war" alongside its fraternal allies, the USSR and the PRC. He added a note of defiance to the determination: "[The] more [the] USA spreads war [the] greater will be its ultimate defeat." He concluded the monologue on a hopeful note by asking Canada to prod the ICC into a more active and assertive role "to stabilize the situation and to seek a solution."[72]

Once again, Canadians and Americans reacted differently to the fruits of Seaborn's labour. It was clear that compellance would not work and that the North Vietnamese were becoming, if anything, even more inflexible. But there were remaining openings, particularly in the oblique reference to the ICC. Seaborn himself thought that behind Pham's tough, discouraging words there lay a potential opening. . . .[73]

The American response was not so ambivalent; nor was it enthusiastic. Michael V. Forrestal of the State Department reported, with listless fatalism, that nothing more could be done.[74] Both the North Vietnamese and the Americans seemed content to rely upon their respective strategies—as opposed to a negotiated settlement facilitated by outsiders—to achieve their very different goals for Vietnam.

The two Seaborn missions marked a watershed. To the Americans, the missions served their purpose: the DRV had been fairly warned, and Seaborn had provided insight into their leaders' mindset. To the Canadians, the missions were only the beginning of a search for a negotiated settlement; their efforts to this end would now be doubled. After the presidential election in November, in which Johnson scored a landslide victory, the United States moved more firmly toward finding a military solution. The Vietnam Working Group, an inter-agency task force under the direction of William Bundy, began preparing a strategy for an expanded, but not open-ended, American war effort that included air strikes against North Vietnam. Canada moved in the opposite direction, beginning a frantic and often disjointed search for a diplomatic solution.

Profound doubt and a gnawing sense of futility also infused the Canadians' thinking on their role in Vietnam and on the ICC. Seaborn not only doubted his capacity as a messenger; he also doubted that Canada could play a useful part on the ICC while remaining a close ally of the United States. . . .[75]

Rather than abandon the ICC and Indochina altogether, Pearson and Martin decided to pursue more actively a diplomatic denouement to the conflict. Events, however, soon quickly outpaced the Canadians. In early February, Johnson sent McGeorge Bundy to South Vietnam for an emergency appraisal of the situation. While he was there, the NLF staged their largest attack on Americans to date with a raid on the American base at Pleiku. Johnson responded immediately with retaliatory bombings on targets in the North. On 2 March, a sustained bombing campaign, appropriately codenamed ROLLING THUNDER, began pounding North Vietnam. The war had taken a decisive turn. . . .

Undeterred, Canada set out to reverse the irreversible trend. On 10 February, three days after the raid on Pleiku and the day after another attack, this time against the American base at Qui Nhon, Pearson made a speech that called for a halt to the fighting, endorsed a recent Indian proposal to convene a new international conference on a settlement for Vietnam, and asked for patience and tolerance for his government's method of quiet diplomacy.[76] Responding to a question, Pearson told the House of Commons "that a conference of some sort may well prove necessary and desirable to work out a more durable settlement for Viet Nam."[77] Martin and Cadieux supported the idea of an international conference as well, albeit with a few caveats, such as a guarantee that all communist military activity and preparations would be stopped.[78] Martin also sent word to the Soviets requesting that they restrain their North Vietnamese ally.[79] . . .

These efforts were doomed to fail, however, as neither North Vietnam nor the United States was willing to compromise their positions enough to consent to negotiations. Nor was either side willing to submit to a political process that could force them to abandon their interests. India, moreover, could not reconcile itself to Canada's sympathy for American objectives and increasingly began to side with Poland on ICC decisions. Canadian diplomacy seemed to have run out of options.

The onset of a larger war did not augur well for Canadian policy. In Saigon, Seaborn was told by Deputy Ambassador U. Alexis Johnson that he would not be needed to pass an American message and that if one were needed in the future, Moscow, not Ottawa, would be contacted.[80] Pearson's logical precondition for India's plan for an international conference— "a conference [is] hardly possible while serious fighting [is] taking place"[81]—was to be perpetually unfulfilled with the launch of ROLLING THUNDER. Pearson had not decided that negotiations were undesirable because of continuing

fighting; rather, he had determined that under such conditions an international conference simply would not work. . . .

Canadian diplomacy now became much less quiet. The sustained bombing of the North greatly troubled Pearson, and under pressure from a number of close friends and advisers, he decided to take advantage of a speaking engagement at Temple University in Philadelphia and call publicly for a bombing pause. . . . Although Pearson slightly tempered some of the more caustic language, on 2 April he delivered a relatively stinging rebuke of US policy in Vietnam. American "motives were honourable" and "neither mean nor imperialistic," Pearson declared. But because "continued and stepped-up intensification of hostilities in Vietnam could lead to uncontrollable escalation," the only practicable solution was a negotiated settlement. "What are the conditions for such a settlement?" Pearson asked, and then answered his own question: "First, a ceasefire." It was one thing to call for a ceasefire, but Pearson's next remarks crossed the threshold of what LBJ would tolerate, as the prime minister would soon find out. "[T]here does appear to be at least a possibility that a suspension of such air strikes against North Vietnam, at the right time," the prime minister continued, "might provide the Hanoi authorities with an opportunity, if they wish to take it, to inject some flexibility into their policy without appearing to do so as the direct result of military pressure."[82]

Despite the qualifying and cautious language, Pearson clearly called for a unilateral, unconditional American pause to the hostilities. The speech would probably have been considered imprudent even had it been given in Canada, but to criticize American policy on American soil was just too much for LBJ. At the sudden invitation of the president, the next day Pearson and Ritchie went to Camp David ostensibly to confer with Johnson and some of his advisers.

What actually occurred was the unseemly and altogether unlikely scene of one national leader berating another to the extent that Pearson was literally grabbed by his coat lapel while Johnson continued to yell. The fact that

The Associated Press/CP

Prime Minister Lester B. Pearson (left) and President Lyndon B. Johnson talk with the media at Camp David on 3 April 1965, one day after Pearson delivered a speech at Temple University in which he called on the US to halt bombing in Vietnam.

Pearson, a Nobel laureate for his efforts to defuse the 1956 Suez crisis, was at Temple to receive a World Peace Award did not help matters; nor did the fact that in four days Johnson was to give a peace and redevelopment speech of his own, at Johns Hopkins University, and the prime minister had just stolen his thunder. LBJ's 7 April speech was extremely well received, but to the president's doubtless fury Pearson was given credit for moving Johnson in the right direction. The *New York Times*, for example, intoned in its lead editorial that LBJ "has given wings to long-pending, imaginative proposals by men such as . . . Canada's Prime Minister Lester Pearson."[83]

Although it marked a moral victory of sorts for Pearson, the Temple speech neither changed the course of the war nor changed the minds of those in the Johnson administration. Instead, it had the opposite effect. Despite its merits—indeed, probably because of its merits—it served to stiffen Johnson's Vietnam policy, lest the president of the United States, particularly one as intensely insecure as LBJ, seem to be dictated to by a foreign leader. Pearson tried to make

amends with an apologetic and clarifying letter, but the damage had been done.[84] . . .

Perhaps more than during any other major twentieth-century war, the belligerents in the Vietnam War were targeted by third parties wishing to mediate the conflict. No nation, including the United States and North Vietnam, wanted a prolonged war to engulf Southeast Asia. Communist, anti-communist, and non-aligned states alike indefatigably sought to broker a way out of the conflict. The ICC can thus be seen as a microcosm of the international diplomacy that surrounded the war but was, ultimately, peripheral to it. Without a proper means to enforce its decisions, and without a bureaucratic method through which to secure a consensus, the ICC could neither maintain a state of peace nor impose a new one when serious fighting broke out in the early 1960s. . . . The anti-communist lenses through which policy-makers in Ottawa and Washington viewed the conflict in Vietnam were very similar, and with the notable exception of Pearson's speech at Temple University, Canadians in Ottawa and Saigon offered consistent public support for the American objective. This was not Canadian "complicity" in America's war, as some critics have suggested; rather, it was an attempt by the smaller member of an intimate alliance to alter what it perceived to be the potentially dangerous behaviour of the dominant—and often domineering—partner. That such a close ally as Canada could not alter American policy is evidence of Washington's blinkered anti-communist approach toward Southeast Asia. Canada's goal was, to some extent, unattainable; the commitment to South Vietnam was too firmly embedded within the general framework of US foreign policy. America was simply more committed and beholden to a policy of global anti-Communism than were allies like Canada.

Moreover, Canadian diplomats and politicians never provided their American counterparts with a feasible plan to disengage from South Vietnam without triggering a quick collapse of non-communist rule. This, too, undermined the credibility and force of Canada's dissent over

Vietnam. Like Undersecretary of State George Ball, the most prominent and prescient dove in the Johnson administration, Canada could repeatedly warn of the perils of intervention, but it could not provide a viable alternative. Without a solution, complete withdrawal, even under the cover of a diplomatic settlement or the political neutralization of Southeast Asia, remained anathema to Washington.[85] Perhaps this is why LBJ tolerated Canadian objections on Vietnam (with the exception, of course, of the Temple–Camp David episode), as he did Ball's dissent, without really paying them much attention. In Johnson's eyes, Ball was the in-house devil's advocate; Canada was simply the international version.[86]

Canada's ulterior motive, the strategy behind its middle-power tactics, was to constrain American policy and prod it toward a negotiated settlement. Obviously, Canadian policy failed: a major war came, and went badly for the United States; South Vietnam was not "saved" from communist domination; and, in the process, a breach between the Johnson administration and the Pearson government opened, and then widened, as the war intensified and U.S. military intervention escalated. It seems, then, that Canadian foreign policy toward the American war in Vietnam was destined to be frustrated under either quiet diplomacy or open protestation; that, in its middling position, Canada was ill-equipped to alter the course of a committed ally fighting an intractable war.

Author's Note: The author is grateful to Robert Bothwell, Kurk Dorsey, Ann Foster, John Lewis Gaddis, James G. Hershberg, Mark Atwood Lawrence, Fredrik Logevall, Hang Nguyen, John A. Thompson, and the three anonymous reviewers for their encouragement and constructive criticism on various drafts of the essay. Earlier versions of this paper were presented at: the American Historical Association annual meeting, Boston, 7 January 2001; the Centre of International Studies, Cambridge University; the Cold War History Group, University of California-Santa Barbara; and the Society for Historians of American Foreign Relations annual meeting, Toronto, 23 June 2000.

Endnotes

1   Bruce MacDonald, "Pearson Urges U.S. Curb North Vietnam Strikes," *Globe and Mail* (Toronto), 3 April 1965.

2   The episode is recounted by its participant and a witness in, respectively, Lester B. Pearson, *Mike: The Memoirs of the Right Honourable Lester B. Pearson*, vol. 3, *1957–1968* (Toronto, 1975), 138–41; and Charles Ritchie, *Storm Signals: More Undiplomatic Diaries, 1962–1971* (Toronto, 1983), 80–3. Pearson's biographer provides the best secondary account of the speech and its aftermath. See John English, *The Worldly Years: The Life of Lester Pearson*, vol. 2, *1949–1972* (Toronto, 1992), 362–9.

3   Charles Taylor, *Snow Job: Canada, the United States, and Vietnam, 1954–1973* (Toronto, 1974); and James Eayrs, *In Defence of Canada*, vol. 5, *Indochina: Roots of Complicity* (Toronto, 1983).

4   Ramesh Thakur, *Peacekeeping in Vietnam: Canada, India, Poland, and the International Commission* (Edmonton, AB, 1984), 4, 15. See also Ramesh Thakur, "Peacekeeping and Foreign Policy: Canada, India and the International Commission in Vietnam,

1954–1965," *British Journal of International Studies* 6 (July 1980): 142, 146–7, which is considerably more lenient toward Canadian policy in Vietnam.

5   Victor Levant, *Quiet Complicity: Canadian Involvement in the Vietnam War* (Toronto, 1986), 2, 3, 5.

6   Michael Maclear, *Vietnam: The Ten Thousand Day War* (Toronto, 1981), 95–9, 118–20, 124–5.

7   Douglas A. Ross, *In the Interests of Peace: Canada and Vietnam, 1954–1973* (Toronto, 1984), 7, 8. Ross delighted in attacking proponents of the complicity thesis. Eayrs, for example, was prominently exposed in the pages of *In the Interests of Peace* for fervently supporting an anti-communist foreign policy for Canada in the 1950s, long before he changed tack and criticized Canadian diplomacy on those very grounds. See ibid., 70n. For Ross's thesis, see also Douglas A. Ross, "Middlepowers as Extra-Regional Balancer Powers: Canada, India, and Indochina, 1954–62," *Pacific Affairs* 55 (Summer 1982): 185–209.

8   Canada neither sought nor desired a place on the ICC. See Robert Bothwell, "Eyes West: Canada and the Cold War in Asia," in *Canada and the Early Cold War, 1943–1957*, ed. Greg Donaghy (Ottawa, 1998), 59–70, 68.

9   On the Canadian role in the Korean War and the important issue of restraining American diplomatic and military exuberance, see Denis Stairs, *The Diplomacy of Constraint: Canada, the Korean War, and the United States* (Toronto, 1974).

10   The literature on Canadian-American relations is vast, but for useful introductions, see especially Seymour Martin Lipset, *Continental Divide: The Values and Institutions of the United States and Canada* (New York, 1990); J.L. Granatstein and Norman Hillmer, *For Better or for Worse: Canada and the United States to the 1990s* (Toronto, 1991); Robert Bothwell, *Canada and the United States: The Politics of Partnership* (Toronto, 1992); and John Herd Thompson and Stephen J. Randall, *Canada and the United States: Ambivalent Allies*, 2nd ed. (Athens, GA, 1997).

11   On middle powers, see Carsten Holbraad, *Middle Powers in International Politics* (London, 1984). Much has been written on Canada as a middle power, but see especially J. King Gordon, ed., *Canada's Role as a Middle Power* (Toronto, 1966); John W. Holmes, *Canada: A Middle-Aged Power* (Toronto, 1976); Tom Keating, *Canada and World Order: The Multilateralist Tradition in Canadian Foreign Policy* (Toronto, 1993), especially 16–20; Arthur Andrew, *The Rise and Fall of a Middle Power: Canadian Diplomacy from King to Mulroney* (Toronto, 1993); and Norman Hillmer and J.L. Granatstein, *Empire to Umpire: Canada and the World to the 1990s* (Toronto, 1994), 181–284 *passim*. Australia, India, Indonesia, the Netherlands, Sweden, and Yugoslavia have also, at one time or another, been identified as middle powers. For a particularly trenchant critique of Canada's status as a middle power, see Adam Chapnick, "The Canadian Middle Power Myth," *International Journal* 55 (Spring 2000): 188–206.

12   Quoted in Hillmer and Granatstein, *Empire to Umpire*, 275–6. The "Principles for Partnership" report was co-authored by Canadian Arnold Heeney and American Livingston Merchant, who had each recently served as ambassador to the other's country.

13   Pearson, *Mike*, 3:116–17. The notion expressed by Pearson is what one scholar has called "pragmatic idealism." See Costas Melakopides, *Pragmatic Idealism: Canadian Foreign Policy, 1945–1995* (Montreal and Kingston, 1998).

14   Telegram 16, Charles J. Woodsworth (Saigon) to DEA, 18 January 1961, Record Group 25 (hereafter RG), Vol. 8187, File 7266–P–1–40, Pt 1.2, NAC.

15   Telegram 120, Woodsworth to DEA, 20 May 1961, RG 25, Vol. 4668, File 50052–A–13–40, Pt 2, NAC.

16   Telegram 1752, Frederick Nolting (Saigon) to Dean Rusk (secretary of state), 16 May 1961, NSF/CF, Vietnam (hereafter NSF/CF/VN), Box 193, JFKL.

17   Telegram 150, Woodsworth to DEA, 22 June 1961, RG 25, Vol. 4668, File 50052–A–13–40, Pt 2, NAC.

18   Telegram Y–305, P.A. McDougall (DEA) to Woodsworth, 26 May 1961, RG 25, Vol. 4668, File 50052–A–13–40, Pt 2, NAC.

19   Memo, Norman A. Robertson (undersecretary of state for external affairs) to Green, "South Vietnam–U.S.A. Proposal to Increase Strength of Military Assistance Advisory Group (MAAG)," 31 May 1961, RG 25, Vol. 4668, File 50052–A–13–40, Pt 2, NAC. The letter to which Robertson referred was from 1960, mandating that Saigon inform the ICC of the introduction of foreign troops or any increases in its own armed forces.

20   Telegram, Circular 966, 18 November 1961, NSF/CF/VN, Box 195, JFKL.

21   Telegram, Arnold Heeney (Washington, DC) to DEA, 20 November 1961, RG 25, Vol. 4668, File 50052–A–13–40, Pt 2, NAC.

22   Telegram 3790, Heeney to DEA, 15 December 1961, RG 25, Vol. 5240, File 7266–P–1–40, NAC. Harriman repeated this advice to Kennedy. See George McT. Kahin, *Intervention: How America Became Involved in Vietnam* (New York, 1986), 136.

23   David Ormsby Gore (Washington, DC) to Alec Douglas-Home (foreign secretary), 17 April 1962, Foreign Office File 371/166722, Public Record Office, Kew (hereafter FO, PRO).

24   Telegram 3804, Heeney to DEA, 16 December 1961, RG 25, Vol. 5240, File 7266–P–1–40, NAC.

25   Telegram 685, Nolting to Rusk, 21 November 1961, NSF/CF/VN, Box 195, JFKL. In May, Rostow had impressed upon Kennedy the desirability of a strengthened ICC. Memo, Rostow to John F. Kennedy, "One Approach to a Dialogue with the Chairman," 11 May 1961, NSF, Regional Security Series, Southeast Asia (General), Box 231, JFKL.

26   Mieczyslaw Maneli, *War of the Vanquished* (New York, 1971), 55–7. See also William P. Bundy, "Vietnam Memoir," unpublished manuscript, chaps 8–10, William P. Bundy Papers, Manuscripts and Archives, Sterling Memorial Library, Yale University, New Haven, Connecticut (hereafter W. Bundy, "Vietnam Memoir," SML).

27   Telegram 19, Frank G. Hooton (Saigon) to DEA, 2 February 1962, RG 25, Vol. 4643, File 50052–A–6–40, Pt 2, NAC.

28   J.B. Denson (Washington, DC) to R.L. Seconde (Foreign Office), 25 January 1962, FO 371/166717, PRO.

29   Seconde to Denson, 19 January 1962, FO 371/166717, PRO.

30   D.J. McCarthy (Ottawa) to J.I. McGhie (Foreign Office), 4 January 1962, FO 371/166717, PRO.

31   Telegram 780, Livingston Merchant (Ottawa) to Rusk, 16 February 1962, NSF/CF/Canada, Box 18, JFKL. See also telegram 974, Rusk to Saigon

embassy, 9 February 1962, *Foreign Relations of the United States, 1961–1963* (Washington, DC, 1988), 1:117–19 (hereafter *frus*, followed by appropriate year). Not only did Canadian officials disagree, on both political and legal grounds, with the Americans' argument that a breach by one party nullified the terms of the accords, but they also felt constrained by the Indian delegation, which strenuously objected to the American interpretation. In other words, even had the Canadians agreed with the American argument, they would not have been able to act upon it for fear of alienating the Indians on the ICC. Memo, Robertson to Green, "Vietnam Commission," 14 May 1962, RG 25, Vol. 4646, File 50052–A–10–40, Pt 4, NAC.

32 Telegram 906, Ottawa to Rusk, 17 March 1962, NSF/CF/VN, Box 196, JFKL.

33 Telegram 817, Heeney to DEA, 15 March 1962, RG 25, Vol. 4643, File 50052–A–6– 40, Pt 2, NAC.

34 Aide-memoire, unsigned, 5 March 1962, RG 25, Vol. 4639, File 50052–A–1–40, Pt 2, NAC. The document was passed by the Canadian embassy to the State Department's Bureau of Far Eastern Affairs on 12 March. Telegram 817, Heeney to DEA, 15 March 1962, RG 25, Vol. 4643, File 50052–A–6–40, Pt 2, NAC. For other expressions of this Canadian strategy, see McCarthy to A.S. Fair (Commonwealth Relations Office), 16 February 1962, FO 371/166719, PRO; and Denson to Seconde, 23 February 1962, FO 371/166720, PRO.

35 Telegram 1119, George Ball (undersecretary of state) to Saigon, 20 March 1962, NSF/CF/VN, Box 196, JFKL.

36 Denson to Seconde, 25 January 1962, FO 371/166717, PRO. Wood reported the substance of his conversation with Heeney to John Denson, of the British embassy in Washington; Denson then relayed the information to the Foreign Office in London.

37 Telegram, Circular 1947, 15 May 1962, NSF/CF/VN, Box 196, JFKL; and telegram, 1539, Nolting to Rusk, 31 May 1962, NSF/CF/VN, Box 196, JFKL. See also memo of conversation, Kennedy and Harriman, drafted by Michael V. Forrestal (NSC Staff), 6 April 1962, *frus, 1961–1963* (Washington, DC, 1990), 2:309.

38 Relevant portions of the special report are published in *American Foreign Policy: Current Documents, 1962* (Washington, DC, 1966), 1103–6. In its entirety, with attached dissents and appendices, the special report is in RG 25, Vol. 9522, Folder 7, NAC, and, under a cover memo, William H. Brubeck (State Department) to Bromley K. Smith (National Security Council Staff), 23 June 1962, NSF/CF/VN, Box 196, JFKL. See also W. Bundy, "Vietnam Memoir," 5:13–14, SML, and Ross, *In the Interests of Peace*, 212.

39 Paper drafted by Benjamin C. Wood, "What Can the ICC or the UN Do in Viet-Nam," 8 November 1961, NSF/CF/VN, Box 194A, JFKL.

40 Hooton to DEA, "Aftermath of Special Report," 7 August 1962, RG 25, Vol. 4646, File 50052–A–10–40, Pt 5, NAC.

41 Memo, L.J. Wilder (Hanoi) to Peck (Saigon), "The Visit to North Vietnam by a Delegation of the South Vietnam Liberation National Front," 5 November 1962, RG 25, Vol. 4639, File 50052–A–1–40, Pt 3, NAC.

42 Gordon E. Cox (Saigon) to DEA, "Notes on Arrival—Part II," 5 December 1962, RG 25, Vol. 4639, File 50052–A–1–40, Pt 3, NAC.

43 Telegram, Cox to DEA, 22 February 1962, RG 25, Vol. 4646, File 50052–A–10–40, Pt 5, NAC.

44 Telegram, DEA to Cox, 22 August 1963, RG 25, Vol. 4639, File 50052–A–1–40, Pt 4, NAC.

45 Telegram 228, Cox to DEA, 30 November 1963, RG 25, Vol. 10122, File 21–13–VIET–ICSC, Pt 1.2, NAC.

46 Memo, Robertson to Martin, "Draft Reply to a Possible Question on the Vietnam Commission," 20 December 1963, RG 25, Vol. 10122, File 21–13–VIET–ICSC, Pt 1.2, NAC.

47 State Department memo of conversation, part 4 of 14, "Far East and Southeast Asia," 22 January 1964, NSF/CF/Canada, Box 167, Lyndon B. Johnson Library, Austin, Texas (hereafter LBJL). On the issue of the recognition of China—which successive Canadian governments had aimed to do, including Pearson's, and Washington had always strenuously forbade—see Stephen Beecroft, "Canadian Policy towards China, 1949–1957: The Recognition Problem," in *Reluctant Adversaries: Canada and the People's Republic of China, 1949–1970*, ed. Paul M. Evans and B. Michael Frolic (Toronto, 1991), 43–72; and Don Page, "The Representation of China in the United Nations: Canadian Perspectives and Initiatives, 1949–1971," in ibid., 73–105. Canada recognized the People's Republic in 1970.

48 Telegram, Cox to DEA, 4 December 1962, RG 25, Vol. 4639, File 50052–A–1–40, Pt 3, NAC.

49 Telegram, Cox to DEA, 10 June 1963, RG 25, Vol. 4644, File 50052–A–8–40, Pt 1, NAC.

50 Paul Martin, *A Very Public Life*, vol. 2, *So Many Worlds* (Toronto, 1985), 424n4.

51 Lodge insisted that Cox, who was "simply not discreet and occasionally anti-American," be kept uninformed of the existence of the Seaborn mission. Telegram 2357, Lodge to McGeorge Bundy (special assistant for national security affairs), 31 May 1964, NSF/CF/VN, Vol. X, Box 5, LBJL.

52 Telegram 1821, Rusk to Lodge, 1 May 1964, *frus, 1964–1968* (Washington, DC, 1992), 1:281–2.

53 Telegram 1621, Lodge to Rusk, 4 May 1964, NSF/CF/VN, Vol. VIII, Box 4, LBJL.

54   Fredrik Logevall, *Choosing War: The Lost Chance for Peace and the Escalation of War in Vietnam* (Berkeley, 1999), 156. The Lodge quote is from ibid., 155.

55   Record of meeting between Richard Austen Butler (foreign secretary) and Martin, 11 February 1964, Prime Minister's Office, File 11/4794, PRO. Another record of this meeting can be found in telegram 242, Patrick Dean (New York) to Foreign Office, 12 February 1964, FO 371/175493, PRO.

56   For example, during this time, Cox sent to Ottawa an uncommonly lengthy, bleakly written cable on the ICC's future. Telegram 183, Cox to DEA, 4 May 1964, RG 25, Vol. 10122, File 21–13–VIET–ICSC, Pt 1.2, NAC.

57   J. Blair Seaborn, interview with author, 5 January 2000, Ottawa. See also Martin, *So Many Worlds*, 424–5; and Martin's comments in Peter Stursberg, *Lester Pearson and the American Dilemma* (Toronto, 1980), 257. State Department official William H. Sullivan and Chester L. Cooper of the CIA were charged with coordinating the mission from Washington, and neither of them thought that Seaborn's main purpose was as blunt as Lodge and Rusk did. Sullivan recalled that by using Seaborn, the United States was trying "to get the North Vietnamese to the negotiating table." William H. Sullivan interview, 21 July 1971, 14, Oral History, LBJL (hereafter OH/LBJL). Cooper simply felt that "the Seaborn thing was really an attempt to find out what the hell was on Hanoi's mind." Chester L. Cooper, interview 1, 9 July 1969, 23, OH/LBJL. George Ball, the Johnson administration's in-house sceptic on Vietnam, thought that the Seaborn initiative was a "genuine effort to get discussions going." George Ball interview, 8 July 1971, 39, OH/LBJL. See also Chester L. Cooper, *The Lost Crusade: America in Vietnam* (New York, 1970), 326.

58   Memo for the record, Robinson, 29 May 1964, RG 25, Vol. 3092, File 29–39–1–2–A, NAC.

59   Telegram 2133, Ball to Lodge, 30 May 1964, NSF/CF/VN, Vol. X, Box 5, LBJL.

60   Memo for the record, McGeorge Bundy, 30 May 1964, NSF/CF/Canada, Box 165, LBJL.

61   Telegram 273, Seaborn (Saigon) to Arnold Smith (DEA), 20 June 1964, RG 25, Vol. 10113, File 20–22–VIET.S–2–1, NAC.

62   Telegram 282, Seaborn to Smith, 22 June 1964, RG 25, Vol. 10113, File 20–22–VIET.S–2–1, NAC.

63   Memo, Marcel Cadieux (undersecretary of state for external affairs) to Martin, "Mr. Seaborn's Mission to North Vietnam," 24 June 1964, RG 25, Vol. 10113, File 20–22–VIET.S–2–1, NAC.

64   Telegram 2278, Washington, DC, embassy to Smith, 24 June 1964, RG 25, Vol. 10113, File 20–22–VIET.S–2–1, NAC.

65   Telegram 69, Ball to Saigon embassy, 8 July 1964, *frus, 1964–1968*, 1:543.

66   Telegram 314, Seaborn to Smith, 5 July 1964, RG 25, Vol. 10113, File 20–22–VIET.S– 2–1, NAC; and telegram 74, Maxwell D. Taylor (Saigon) to Rusk, 11 July 1964, NSF/CF/VN, Vol. XIII, Box 6, LBJL.

67   Memo, R.D. Jackson (Hanoi) to Seaborn, "USA–DRVN Naval Engagements," 6 August 1964, RG 25, Vol. 9510, File 100–7–2, Pt 1, NAC.

68   See Edwin E. Moise, *Tonkin Gulf and the Escalation of the Vietnam War* (Chapel Hill, NC, 1996), 106–207; and David Kaiser, *American Tragedy: Kennedy, Johnson, and the Origins of the Vietnam War* (Cambridge, MA, 2000), 331–6.

69   Canada, House of Commons, *Debates*, 5 August 1964, Vol. 6 (1964), 6418.

70   Telegram 2848, Charles Ritchie (Washington, DC) to Smith, 7 August 1964, RG 25, Vol. 10113, File 20–22–VIET.S–2–1, NAC.

71   Telegram 169, Rusk to Ottawa embassy, 8 August 1964, NSF/CF/VN, Vol. XV, Box 7, LBJL; and telegram 2872, Washington, DC, embassy to Smith, 8 August 1964, RG 25, Vol. 10113, File 20–22–VIET.S–2–1, NAC.

72   Telegram 419, Seaborn to Smith, 15 August 1964, RG 25, Vol. 10113, File 20–22–VIET.S–2–1, NAC; record of conversation, "Conversation with Prime Minister Pham Van Dong–Hanoi, August 13, 1964," 17 August 1964, RG 25, Vol. 10113, File 20–22–VIET.S–2–1, NAC; letter 312, Seaborn to Cadieux, "DRVN: Conversation with Prime Minister Pham Van Dong," 18 August 1964, RG 25, Vol. 10113, File 20–22–VIET.S–2–1, NAC.

73   Telegram 426, Seaborn to Smith, 17 August 1964, RG 25, Vol. 10113, File 20–22–VIET.S–2–1, NAC. With his own degree of scepticism, Taylor reported to Rusk on the hopes Seaborn placed in further communication with Pham Van Dong. Telegram 467, Taylor to Rusk, 18 August 1964, NSF/CF/VN, Vol. XVI, Box 7, LBJL.

74   Telegram 2974, Ritchie to Smith, 17 August 1964, RG 25, Vol. 10113, File 20–22–VIET.S–2–1, NAC. See also Logevall, *Choosing War*, 208–10.

75   Letter, Seaborn to Rogers, 31 August 1964, RG 25, Vol. 10113, File 20–22–VIET.S–2– 1, NAC.

76   Telegram Y–74, DEA to Washington, DC, embassy, 10 February 1965, RG 25, Vol. 10122, File 21–13–VIET–ICSC, Pt 1, NAC; and English, *The Worldly Years*, 361.

77   Canada, House of Commons, *Debates*, 16 February 1965, Vol. 11 (1964–5), 11372.

78   Memo, Cadieux to Martin, "Vietnam: Statement by U Thant," 13 February 1965, RG 25, Vol. 10122, File 21–13–VIET–ICSC, Pt 1.1, NAC.

79   Telegram Y–82, Martin to Moscow embassy, 12 February 1965, RG 25, Vol. 10122, File 21–13–VIET–ICSC, Pt 1, NAC. The Soviets could do nothing of the kind to the independently minded leaders in Hanoi. But the USSR was, at the same time, putting

out its own feelers to the United States on the prevention of a war that might eventually drag in the USSR. Ilya Gaiduk, *The Soviet Union and the Vietnam War* (Chicago, 1996), 30–1; see also Ilya Gaiduk, "Containing the Warriors: Soviet Policy toward the Indochina Conflict, 1960–1965," in Lloyd C. Gardner and Ted Gittinger, eds, *International Perspectives on Vietnam* (College Station, TX, 2000), 58–76. It is extremely doubtful that Martin's ploy had any effect on Soviet policy.

80 Telegram 177, Seaborn to DEA, 27 February 1965, RG 25, Vol. 3092, File 29–39–1– 2–A, NAC.

81 Telegram Y–128, Delworth to New Delhi, 18 February 1965, RG 25, Vol. 10122, File 21–13–VIET–ICSC, Pt 1.1, NAC.

82 Quoted in Pearson, *Mike*, 3:138.

83 "The President Opens the Door," *New York Times*, 8 April 1965. The same happened in the Canadian press, although it likely escaped Johnson's notice. See Bruce MacDonald, "Johnson Offers Peace Talks, $1 Billion Aid Plan for Asia," *Globe and Mail*, 8 April 1965; and Blair Fraser, "Backstage at Camp David," *Maclean's*, 1 May 1965.

84 The text of the letter is in Pearson, *Mike*, 3:142–3.

85 On this point, see Logevall, *Choosing War*, xxiii–xxiv, 402–3.

86 For Ball and Vietnam, see David DiLeo, *George Ball, Vietnam, and the Rethinking of Containment* (Chapel Hill, NC, 1991); David M. Barrett, *Uncertain Warriors: Lyndon Johnson and His Vietnam Advisers* (Lawrence, KS, 1993), 27–34, 52–4; and James A. Bill, *George Ball: Behind the Scenes in U.S. Foreign Policy* (New Haven, CT, 1997). The differences between Canada and the United States over Vietnam did not seem to affect other policy priorities. In January 1965, LBJ and Pearson signed the Autopact, a trade deal on automotive parts that greatly benefited the Canadian economy. At LBJ's behest, the US Senate ratified the Autopact in the summer of 1965, after Pearson's Temple speech. See Robert Bothwell, "Canada's Moment: Lester Pearson, Canada, and the World," 28; and Greg Donaghy, "Minding the Minister: Pearson, Martin and American Policy in Asia, 1963–1967," 137–8; both in *Pearson: The Unlikely Gladiator*, ed. Norman Hillmer (Montreal and Kingston, 1999).

CHAPTER **8**

Canadians in the Developing World

⊚ 8.1: EYEING THE INDIES: CANADIAN RELATIONS WITH INDONESIA, 1945–1999

David Webster

When Theodore Newton, in 1958, became Canada's second ambassador to Indonesia, his reaction summed up his new station's peripheral place in Canada's foreign relations:

> Indonesia? The other side of the world! Visions of watery islands, brown hordes struggling to assert themselves, equatorial jungles, smoking volcanoes, gorillas and other bizarre forms of life flashed through my mind. . . . The die was cast, but my ignorance of my future parish was colossal and what little knowledge I possessed of it was bookish and remote.[1]

Indonesia mattered: it was the fifth most populous country in the world, the largest Muslim-majority country, and a trailblazer of non-alignment. Yet as Newton noted, even the capital city of Jakarta was a "confusing South Seas metropolis," pioneer territory for Canadian diplomats.[2]

Canadian involvement with Indonesia began when Canada's Security Council delegation played a significant role in the United Nations–brokered peace settlement that saw the Netherlands accept the independence of its Indonesian colonies in 1949. The two countries exchanged embassies in 1953, and Canadian development aid commenced

in the 1950s. Cordial if low-key relations continued until 1963, when the remaining British colonies in the region joined the Federation of Malaya to form a new independent Malaysia. This angered President Sukarno, who embarked on a "confrontation" with the new Commonwealth member state.[3] The Canadian government lent strong support, even including some military aid, to Malaysia, and suspended aid to Indonesia. It welcomed the military coup that toppled Sukarno in 1965–6 and began to seek closer trade and aid ties with the authoritarian "New Order" regime headed by General Suharto. Ottawa made Indonesia a "country of concentration" for development aid in 1970, and Indonesia rose as high as second among bilateral-aid recipients in the years that followed. While Canadian governments cultivated closer economic relations with Indonesia, human rights were not a major factor. Only after the fall of Suharto in 1998 did any Canadian government press very hard on rights issues, giving support to the 1999 decolonization of Timor-Leste (East Timor). Human rights were again subordinated to economic interests in Canadian policy towards the democratizing governments of Indonesia in the first decade of the twenty-first century.[4]

For most of this period, Indonesia was important globally but peripheral to Canadian policy-makers' perceptions of the national interest. Their mental maps, their ways of picturing the world, placed the North Atlantic at the centre of the zone of "civilization," as Prime Minister Louis St Laurent called it, with most of the world as periphery.[5] This was the natural result of their upbringing in a Canada that was very much part of the British Empire. Lester Pearson considered that Canada could be most effective as an "honest broker" in areas on the periphery of Cold War clashes.[6] Examining a relationship peripheral to the imagined interests of Canadian governments permits a clearer look at the themes of Canadian foreign policy. The idea that Canada played the role of an idealistic "middle power" has been debunked thoroughly by historians who have identified the importance of alliance politics.[7] If there was indeed a strain of idealistic mediation running through Canadian foreign policy, it might be expected to be more visible in areas at the edge of the Cold War, as Pearson suggested. In Indonesia—a land almost impossibly distant to many in Ottawa—it was not. Part of the reason was that Asia and the rest of the less-developed world were seen as peripheral. Racialized perceptions underpinned and reinforced mental maps.

Many Canadians have spelled out their own diplomatic self-image of Canada as benevolent peacemaker and humanitarian internationalist power with respect to relations with the global South. In a 1960 Dominion Day speech delivered on Radio Indonesia, Newton offered as clear a statement of the Canadian sense of mission as any: "We aim to be considered honest brokers in world affairs. We wish to help the less developed and the less fortunate nations of the world toward a fuller life."[8] A case study of Canadian policy towards Indonesia, however, shows that policy-makers made decisions about Indonesia in ways that would serve the interests of Canada's alliances and multilateral associations—the Commonwealth and the North Atlantic Treaty Organization (NATO) above all. Over time, it increasingly meant serving the

interests of Canadian capital by promoting trade and investment.[9]

Canada and Asia: The Bases of Trans-Pacific Relations

Canadian interactions with Asia are long-standing, but Asia began to appear on the horizons of Canadian policy-makers only gradually. Pearson argued that Canada, in approaching Asia after the Second World War, had "not so much been opening a new chapter as opening a whole new volume; for, until recently, Asia to most Canadians was a closed book."[10] There had in fact been connections, including an embassy in Tokyo opened in the 1920s, but Canadian public and private interest in Asia was mostly concerned with Christian evangelization, commerce, and immigration. In 1950, 46 per cent of Canada's diplomatic corps was stationed in Europe, with just 12 per cent in Asia.[11] The image of Asia was still filtered through Orientalist preconceptions. Cabinet minister Paul Martin Sr, for instance, could speak of Asia as having for many years "fallen into lethargy. Their civilizations have been like sleeping giants, lying in caves, surrounded by the treasures which are the memorials of their past greatness." But, he added, "[t]hese nations are now stirring from their long sleep."[12] Canada's postwar engagement with Asia should be seen in the context of shifting styles of Orientalism. Canadians saw Asia as teeming millions who sprawled from the "martial races" of Afghanistan to the "stone age cannibals" of New Guinea—peoples more primitive than themselves. For some, that meant Asia was benighted; for others, that Canada might have a mission to help Asians develop and perhaps even a model to offer.

The study of Canada-Asia interactions permits a broader understanding of the scope of Canadian foreign relations. It is useful to draw on Steven Hugh Lee's typology, which considers Canada-Asia relations in four realms: diplomacy and foreign relations; trade and investment; migration; and missionary work.[13] As Ruth Compton Brouwer points out, the space once occupied by missionaries increasingly passed to development workers (even while those workers denied direct connections).[14] Like many missionaries, development workers preached a gospel of modernity and sought to transform Asian societies, making them more like Canada. An exclusive focus on "high politics" can miss important non-state aspects of foreign relations. As one Indonesian diplomat noted, a "Canada-Indonesia community" of businessmen, non-governmental organizations (NGOs), exchange students, and others became "the real driving force in the relations between our two countries."[15] Nor is this non-state community new. In 1958, for instance, 65 of the 146 Canadians in Indonesia were working for American oil companies; another 67 were missionaries, teachers, or development workers; and just 14 worked in other jobs, including at Canada's embassy.[16] This article therefore explores non-state relations alongside state-to-state relations, using Indonesia as a Canada-Asia case study in the four realms of diplomacy, trade, migration, and missions/development.

Diplomacy and Foreign Relations

Canadian involvement with Indonesia began with that country's revolution to secure independence from Dutch rule. Canadian attitudes towards decolonization were entangled with Cold War concerns and mediated through the prism of relations with the Netherlands. Canada hosted a large Dutch-Canadian community; its government saw the Netherlands as a like-minded "middle power" and North Atlantic partner; and Canadian troops forged new, stronger ties in 1944–5 as they liberated the Netherlands from German control. When Ottawa sent postwar reconstruction aid to Europe, the East Indies were the only colonial territory to receive a loan, extended since they were considered vital to the recovery of the Dutch metropolitan economy.

Canadian policy-makers used their own country's past as a model, preferring orderly evolution towards independence to revolutionary breaks. Commonwealth-style empire was

no negative in Canada, where empire's image was burnished by the tales of Rudyard Kipling and Somerset Maugham, by cartoons featuring the adventures of heroic colonialists in tropical jungles, and so on. Ottawa thus had considerable sympathy with the Dutch proposal that Indonesia be "linked to the Home Country as in our own Commonwealth by the Crown."[17] They had less for Indonesian nationalists who declared an independent republic with Sukarno as president in 1945. Canada's entry onto the UN Security Council in 1948 forced Ottawa to take an interest in the situation, guided by a perceived need to restore the Indies' economic production for use in world trade.

Indonesia's revolution was soon embroiled in Cold War politics. After Sukarno crushed a communist uprising in 1948, his government's image was burnished in the United States, which joined India and Australia at the Security Council in criticizing Dutch intransigence. When the Dutch spat back stiff-necked defiance, Canadian diplomats stepped in with a compromise formula that led to the creation of a federal United States of Indonesia, locked into a Commonwealth-style Netherlands-Indonesian Union. Although later writers hailed this as an early example of Canadian mediation, a close reading of the archival record reveals that Canadian actions aimed at preventing a breach between the UN and the Netherlands, especially between Dutch and American governments during the years when NATO was being negotiated. Canadian mediation was not between Dutch and Indonesian positions, but rather between Canadian allies, in ways designed to ensure the survival of alliances important to Canada.

Jakarta was the first Southeast Asian city to host a Canadian embassy. It opened with staff housed in cramped offices borrowed from a Dutch bank, with additional work done on the verandah of the Hôtel des Indes, and with office stationery shelved in Ambassador George Heasman's hotel room.[18] "Because this is such a populous, strategically located and potentially wealthy new state," the undersecretary of state for external affairs wrote, "there is a political interest in seeing that it maintains its contacts with the western world and does not fall under the Communist influence, whether Russian or Chinese."[19]

Hopes for post-independence Dutch-Indonesian friendship were doomed by another decolonization dispute, over West New Guinea (now known as West Papua or, sometimes, simply Papua). This territory had been part of the Indies, but the Dutch held on to it when they accepted Indonesia's independence, arguing that the dark-skinned, curly-haired Papuans were ethnically distinct from Indonesians. The struggle to "regain" this territory became the central Indonesian nationalist struggle. When diplomatic efforts failed, Sukarno in 1957 expelled all Dutch citizens and nationalized the Dutch-owned businesses that dominated Indonesia's economy. Three years later, responding to plans for Papuan independence, he broke relations and embarked on a military buildup fuelled by Soviet bloc aid and arms. The West Papua conflict threatened to drive Indonesia into the camp of communism; decolonization once again intertwined with the Cold War.

Indonesian diplomats turned to the Canadian government in search of mediation. But for all the efforts of Ambassador L.N. Palar, Indonesia's image in Canada had plummeted. "The West cannot afford to lose the democratic leaders of Asia, because if you lose them, you are lost too," Palar told audiences on a 1958 tour of Canada. The West had to "let us finish our fight against the old colonialism and you will see how we treat this new [communist] danger."[20] His efforts had little impact, and the Diefenbaker government rebuffed mediation requests. That job went instead to US president John F. Kennedy, who forced the Dutch to accept Indonesian rule starting in 1963, with a few forms of window dressing to preserve the forms of self-determination. Papuans remain independence-minded today.[21]

The settlement offered hope that Indonesia would return to a pro-Western path, but the rapprochement careened off track later that year when Malaysia was formed. Sukarno and others saw the new country as a front for a continued British informal empire. Indonesia was back on a path of opposition to a Western power—except now it was Britain rather than the Netherlands, and there was little chance of American intervention. Both the US government (under Lyndon Johnson) and the Canadian government (under Lester Pearson) distanced themselves from Sukarno but resisted breaking all links. Canadian Conservatives joined American Republicans in demanding the termination of all aid. Conservative external affairs critic Wallace Nesbitt denounced Pearson for "a two-faced, fence-sitting, wishy-washy foreign policy in southeast Asia" and compared Sukarno to Hitler. Why, an internal Conservative memorandum asked, was Canada "giving free flour to [Indonesia] . . . while she is waging war on one of our youngest and most vulnerable Commonwealth brothers"?[22] Only after Indonesia left the United Nations and tried to form a rival UN called the Conference of the New Emerging Forces did Pearson's government suspend aid to Indonesia and start giving military training and supplies to Malaysia. This earned Canada a place on Sukarno's list of "imperialists with white skins" and an invitation from one Indonesian newspaper to "go to hell," marking a low point in bilateral relations.[23]

In 1965, a group of plotters assassinated some of Indonesia's top generals. Suharto, the highest-ranking general not targeted for assassination, blamed the Indonesian Communist Party. Encouraged by American diplomats, the army launched a campaign of violence in which hundreds of thousands—some estimates say a million or more—were killed and many others imprisoned.[24] Canadian policy-makers showed few signs of being disturbed by the mass violence. Canada's ambassador praised Suharto, who moved to replace Sukarno as president, as "a moderate, sensible and pragmatic leader."[25] So he remained, in diplomatic reports, for more than three decades. Indonesian and Canadian diplomats collaborated effectively on the 1970s Indochina truce commission. Ottawa welcomed Suharto's low-key pro-Western policies, although each country remained largely peripheral to the other in the diplomatic realm.

© epa/Corbis

Indonesian President Suharto waves in Jakarta, Indonesia, 23 December 1991.

A decolonization issue once again came to the fore when Portuguese Timor (now Timor-Leste, or East Timor) declared independence in 1975. Indonesian policy-makers told Western counterparts that they feared "a second major danger" alongside communist Vietnam, "another Cuba" in their backyard.[26] Most Western governments, including Canada's, offered broad sympathy, easing Suharto's decision to invade. From 1975 to 1999, East Timor was under Indonesian military control. No accurate death count is possible, but estimates range from somewhat over 100,000 to 250,000, in a country with a population of fewer than one million people.[27] Canadian governments occasionally mentioned the Indonesian army's human rights violations in private but steadfastly opposed Timorese independence until the late 1990s.

By the 1990s, Indonesia no longer seemed peripheral to Canada. It was "un partenaire de plus en plus important en Asie," the Department of Foreign Affairs briefed Jean Chrétien's first foreign minister.[28] Although the record shows some concern over human rights violations in East Timor, it does not show that human rights were allowed to interfere much with good relations. It was only in 1996, as East Timor became a more troublesome aspect of Indonesia's overall foreign relations, that Foreign Minister Lloyd Axworthy offered to mediate. Indonesia said no: its foreign minister believed that "Canadian NGOs are the most ferociously anti-Indonesian in the world and he is sceptical, therefore, of the Canadian government's ability to resist domestic political pressure and maintain its neutrality."[29] Canada instead opened a "bilateral human rights dialogue" with Indonesia in 1997, which aimed to defuse domestic criticism by creating a closed-door forum for exchange of views. Axworthy was even willing to apologize to Suharto for the protests mounted by Canadians against Suharto's human rights record.[30]

Axworthy and his department, however, did act effectively to support Timorese self-determination after the fall of Suharto in 1998. Ottawa backed a UN-sponsored referendum and pressed (unsuccessfully) for an international peacekeeping presence. The lack of such a presence allowed Indonesian generals to spur violence after 78.5 per cent of voters opted for independence in the 1999 referendum.[31] UN and other multilateral pressure, with useful Canadian involvement, forced the Indonesian government to accept Timorese independence. After this brief window of advocacy, however, Canadian support for human rights again faded. It is in non-diplomatic realms that the relationship continues to develop.

Trade and Investment

The Sukarno years spelled disappointment for Canadian hopes that Indonesia would be a valuable market and trade partner. In the Suharto years, those hopes were realized, and the drive to promote Canadian trade and investments in Indonesia came to dominate the relationship.

In Canada as elsewhere, there are long-standing images of the "oriental riches" and vast potential markets of Asia. The revolutionary Indonesian Republic played to trade hopes, pledging to welcome investment and even claiming a "right to export" Indonesian raw materials to fuel the world economy.[32]

Ottawa's chief Asia specialist, Arthur Menzies, was far from alone in his hopes for "the development of considerable trade between Canada and Indonesia."[33] The post of Canada's first ambassador fell to George Heasman, head of the Trade Commissioner Service, who had been assistant trade commissioner to the East Indies in the 1920s. Officials hoped that high wheat sales (by 1953 in excess of $6 million, 27 per cent of total Canadian exports to Indonesia) could lead an expansion of trade.[34] Disappointment soon set in. Trade reached $1 million each way in the mid-1950s, but this was well behind the prewar levels (in 1941, Canadian exports to the East Indies exceeded $3.6 million and imports were almost $4.6 million).[35] By the end of the decade, prospects seemed so poor that the position of Jakarta trade commissioner was abolished. Even the wheat market was lost to Australian competition. Canadian wheat exports to Indonesia continued, but Ottawa paid for them under the "food aid" label. Faltering trade hopes contributed to a downgrading of bilateral relations. "In the realm of economics," one Canadian ambassador sniffed, "many Indonesians still live in a socialistic dream world of their own creation."[36]

Although trade would increase, it is in foreign direct investment that the Canadian presence in Indonesia became most significant. Investment ties were long-standing: for instance, Bata Shoes has operated continuously in Indonesia since the 1950s. By 1999, a total of 46 Canadian companies had Indonesian offices, operating in financial services, fast food, engineering, consultancy, transport, communications, and electronics.[37] Canada loomed especially large in the mining and oil and gas sectors. The forerunner to Royal Dutch/Shell was formed to funnel Indonesian oil to European markets. Indonesia doubled its oil production in the 1950s, pushing it to just shy of a third of total exports, and ranked as the world's twelfth-largest producer.[38] Production was in the hands of three big oil companies, Shell plus two American conglomerates. To counter this dominance, Jakarta opened the doors to smaller oil independents, including several based in Canada. For instance, Refinery Associates of Canada, a subsidiary of a California company based in Toronto for tax purposes, entered Indonesia in 1957 in partnership with the Indonesian army.

Another key independent was Calgary-based Asamera Oil, formed in 1957. The company insisted it was a Canadian enterprise, but the Department of Trade and Commerce disagreed, arguing that just 7 per cent of stock was Canadian owned. Its owners, the embassy in Jakarta reported, were "a very mixed bag indeed and certainly not noticeably Canadian." They included a shady majority stockholder who was "some sort of Greek-Swiss combination," an American retired general, and "a British naturalized White Russian."[39] Denied embassy support, the company bribed its way to a contract and found its own army patrons.[40] Asamera then won a contract to explore for oil in the northern half of the island of Sumatra. It found natural gas in the rebellious Aceh province in 1962 and parlayed this into corporate respectability. In the process, it fuelled tensions in Aceh by creating a wealthy enclave economy that delivered little profit to local people. Conflict over resources combined with conflict over politics and religion to create a regional rebellion that raged from the 1970s to 2005.[41] Once Asamera struck oil, Canadian embassy staff embraced the company as a true national standard-bearer. "I was most favourably impressed with this Canadian company's operations in Indonesia," one ambassador enthused in 1969.[42] Asamera was eventually absorbed into Gulf Canada, then into the ConocoPhilipps empire, but many other Canadian oil companies remained present.

Mining was also important. Canadian investors expressed interest in nickel deposits on the Indonesian island of Sulawesi in the 1950s, but their "bustling Bay Street approach" won few friends and they opted for other opportunities.[43]

In 1968, Toronto-based Inco won a contract from the Suharto government to any minerals found in a vast area covering an entire province and parts of two others on Sulawesi. When the company found nickel, it was able to open Indonesia's second-largest mine and vault Canada to the number-four spot among Indonesia's foreign investors. It was assisted with a $57-million credit from the Canadian government, even while trimming staff at its mine in Sudbury, Ontario. "Our only trouble here is that there is just too damned much nickel lying around," one Inco official said.[44]

Canada today is one of the superpowers of global mining, home to over three-quarters of the mining and exploration companies on the planet.[45] Indonesia is no exception. In the last days of the Suharto era, Canadian companies continued to explore and seek the close ties with the regime necessary to do business in Indonesia. One firm, Bre-X, made headlines when it claimed to have struck gold in Borneo. Those present in 2010 were led by controversial Barrick Gold. Canadian mining companies, supported by Prime Minister Stephen Harper's government, successfully resisted a move that year to legislate their human rights and environmental conduct overseas and deny them the sort of government financing that helped Inco become a mining giant in Indonesia.

The precedence of business over human rights advocacy is a trend that goes back to the Trudeau government's "third option," a move to diversify trade away from dependence on the United States. The third option concentrated on Europe and Japan, but also included cultivation of the countries of the global South, including Indonesia. This accelerated in the Chrétien years, with "Team Canada" trade missions as the tool of choice. The trade drive performed ritual contract-signing ceremonies and tried to link Canada with Asian "miracle" economies. By 1994, Canadian investment in Indonesia stood at $3 billion, with Canadian exports above $50 million. "Indonesia offers the best fit for Canadian economic interests I have seen," one Canadian ambassador declared.[46] In 1996, Team Canada broke all previous records to become the largest trade

delegation ever to visit Indonesia. Investment soon doubled again, to $6 billion. Canada also scrambled to sell wheat, regaining the number-two spot among Indonesian suppliers. The frenzy slowed only when financial crisis swept through Asia in 1998. Nevertheless, trade and investment remain central to bilateral relations.

Missions and Development

Canadians first approached Asia as merchants and missionaries—groups who wished to change Asian societies. Many diplomats were "mishkids," the children of missionaries. Missionary reports and visits home shaped Canadian images of Asia. Missionaries suffered the loss of the China mission field in the 1950s as the People's Republic cast off Western influences. But the missionary stress on schools, hospitals, and literacy could easily spill into a new mission: to "lift up" less-developed societies through a renewed gospel of progress. It makes sense, then, to consider development as the postwar inheritor of the missionary strand in Canada-Asia interactions.

Indonesia had not been a significant mission field for Canadians, although a few evangelists were part of American-run missions to Muslim-majority Indonesia. Canadian development work in Indonesia also began slowly, as part of the Colombo Plan for economic development in South and Southeast Asia. This plan was conceived at a 1950 Commonwealth meeting as a means to channel Western funds into India and other former British colonies in Asia in ways that would reduce the temptations of communism and keep them integrated into the Western-dominated global economy.[47] Canadian diplomats did not, contrary to some accounts, play a prominent role in launching the plan, but they increasingly embraced it as public support grew. Canadian participation was informed by Canada's own recent experience in economic development, which Ottawa perceived as relying not on aid, but on foreign investment and Canadian ingenuity. Canadians did not go forth to proclaim the virtues of their country as a model for others to follow, but the pattern of the Canadian past and Canadian development experiences nevertheless influenced policy-makers.

In Colombo, Canadian diplomats began a habit of approaching South and Southeast Asia through the prism of India, its leading Commonwealth member. Indonesia appeared as a smaller and more exotic version of India and accordingly received smaller and slower aid. Canada began with technical assistance, sending advisers with specialized skills and providing fellowships for Indonesians to study in Canada. Capital aid began later in the 1950s, in the form of aircraft and (as commercial prospects dwindled) wheat flour. But total Canadian aid to Indonesia from 1950 to the fall of Sukarno in 1965 was little more than $5 million, less than 1 per cent of total Canadian bilateral aid for Asia, and came overwhelmingly in the form of wheat and technical training.[48]

Yet there was much more to development work in Indonesia than bilateral aid. As with the missionaries, Canada's engagement with Indonesia came primarily in the non-state realm. Two projects began in the 1950s and grew strong during the Suharto regime: one in development planning and one in Islamic education.

McGill University economist Benjamin Higgins became the first key figure in Indonesia's State Planning Bureau, a joint project between the Indonesian government and the United Nations Technical Assistance Administration (TAA). Other Canadians also influenced the bureau. TAA operations chief George Cadbury, for instance, brought the model of social-democratic development from his previous post as top economic adviser to the Co-operative Commonwealth Federation government of Saskatchewan. The bureau mapped out a path towards a developmentalist state seeking foreign direct investment. Although not adopted in the Sukarno years, this precisely anticipated the direction of the Suharto regime's National Development Planning Agency (Bappenas). So did many of the personnel. Bappenas chief Widjojo Nitisastro, for instance, started his career as an assistant to another Canadian posted to the Planning Bureau, statistician Nathan Keyfitz.

The technocratic project begun in the Planning Bureau became one key prop to Suharto's military government, as economists lacking public support teamed up with generals who had the ability to enforce their will. After the army crushed the Indonesian Communist Party, the sole remaining threat to its rule appeared to lie in political Islam. A second major prop, therefore, came from religious scholars who worked to depoliticize Islam. This support, too, was rooted in Canadian assistance going back to the 1950s. McGill University opened an Institute of Islamic Studies in 1951, directed by Wilfred Cantwell Smith, a former Presbyterian missionary in what is now Pakistan. The institute aimed to modernize Middle Eastern understandings of Islam, but turned out to be most influential in Indonesia. Islam, Smith was convinced, "is living through in our day a transformation comparable in scope and profundity, though not in form, to the Protestant Reformation in the history of Christianity." He hoped to see his institute "make a notable contribution to that Islamic renascence and reformation" and even "conceivably [act] as a kind of midwife for the Islamic Reformation which is struggling to be born."[49] It proclaimed itself to be a modern, rational alternative to traditional centres of religious learning in the Middle East. McGill graduate Abdul Mukti Ali became Suharto's most influential minister of religion; fellow alumnus Harun Nasution redesigned Indonesia's Islamic universities system according to the model of McGill's religion curriculum; and other members of the "McGill mafia" also worked to redirect Indonesian Islam into "modern" channels that fit the Suharto regime's emphasis on "apolitical" economic development.

Pioneered without government funds, the Canadian International Development Agency would pick up the McGill connection for subsequent major funding. Western development aid was crucial in bolstering the Suharto regime in its early days, both through the funds provided and the symbolism of international support for Suharto. CIDA picked Indonesia as the first "country of concentration" for Canadian aid outside the Commonwealth and *la francophonie*. Owing

Foreign Aid and Non-governmental Organizations

Foreign aid, in the form of financial and/or technical assistance to help developing or impoverished countries or their citizens, has increased significantly since 1945, both as an instrument of foreign policy used by governments and through the efforts of private organizations driven by humanitarian motives.

As an instrument of foreign policy, foreign aid has been used by countries such as Canada to promote international security and build alliances or positive relations with receiving countries by stabilizing them or encouraging greater economic and social interactions. Canada's foreign aid has increased due to its participation in multilateral organizations such as the United Nations and the World Bank, which has encouraged a greater sense of obligation to aid the impoverished and dispossessed throughout the world. Development aid has also increased owing to the growth of non-governmental organizations (NGOs), non-profit volunteer organizations dedicated to a range of concerns, including the provision of assistance to the impoverished in many areas of the world or to emergency relief in times of humanitarian crisis—such as displacement or famine.

Government foreign aid is distributed either directly to the receiving country or through funding to multilateral organizations, such as the UN High Commission for Refugees. In 1968, the federal government created the Canadian International Development Agency (CIDA) to coordinate its foreign aid policy. Prior to its demise in 2013, CIDA often turned to—and funded—NGOs, both Canadian and in the receiving country, which have provided the service and personnel to fulfil Canada's aid goals.

NGOs proliferated in Canada in the postwar years as a part of the general growth of social movement politics, of groups or organizations dedicated to addressing social and economic problems and to encouraging greater equity and opportunity in Canada and throughout the world. NGOs dedicated to development aid in impoverished countries were often motivated by a determination to provide both aid to their fellow human beings and by a desire to redress the poverty and oppression often viewed as a product of colonialism and imperialism, in both the past and the present. A significant component of the work of NGOs has been in the form of emergency relief during humanitarian crises. Longer-term aid work involves the provision of personnel and goods in such areas as education and medical or health services/programs, as well as assistance in developing infrastructure for purposes such as improved water quality or economic development.

to Indonesia's clear need for assistance, its ability to absorb aid (albeit with much siphoned off by corruption), and the government's reliability in Western eyes, Canadian aid soared. By the end of the Trudeau years, Indonesia ranked second only to Bangladesh among bilateral Canadian aid recipients. It remained a top recipient in the Mulroney and Chrétien years. This was not altruistic. Canadian aid, rather, was designed to "facilitate Indonesia's transformation from aid recipient to trading partner."[50]

At only one point did Canadian willingness to send substantial aid to Indonesia falter, and then only in part. At the Cold War's end, the Mulroney government promised to link aid with human rights. The first test case came in East Timor, where, weeks after Mulroney's declaration, Indonesian troops opened fire on pro-independence protesters, killing 263 people. There had been many previous massacres, but none in the presence of Western journalists. As the killings grabbed world headlines, Ottawa froze future aid for Indonesia while leaving existing projects untouched. The effort to use aid suspensions to leverage human rights improvements did not go far—perhaps because it was never permitted to cross into the trade realm. On taking office in 1993, Jean Chrétien's Liberal government approved new aid. Canadian support for the Suharto regime's developmentalist project would not waver again. Even as CIDA moved to focus Canadian aid on fewer countries, Indonesia remained on the list of priority aid recipients, while poorer Timor-Leste was dropped.

An unintended consequence of Canadian aid to Indonesia brings the story back to the non-state side. Canadian aid has involved a focus on boosting civil society, which includes sectors that lie outside government and the marketplace. While the largest aid projects continued to be institutional partnerships with Indonesian state agencies, a significant chunk went to support Indonesian NGOs. The Suharto regime aimed to transform the highly mobilized civil society of the Sukarno years into a passive "floating mass" of people concentrated on developing the country.[51] Suharto, dubbed the "Father of Development," hoped to become a hero to his people for delivering economic progress. He certainly became a hero to Western donors, who proved willing to make Indonesia the largest single aid recipient in the world.[52] Canadian aid to Indonesian civil society supported new action on issues ranging from environmental law to the treatment of political prisoners. Suharto's fall in 1998 came partly amidst financial crisis, but it was also spurred by pro-democracy protests. Indonesian civil society organizations were vital in these protests. Although CIDA priorities shifted, the legacies are there to be seen in organizations that survive without ongoing CIDA support.[53]

Migration

The Indonesian-Canadian community is much smaller and more recent than the large and long-present communities of Chinese, Japanese, Filipino, and South Asian descent. Indonesian migrants are therefore less of a factor in Canadian foreign relations. Nevertheless, the fourth realm of Canada-Asia interactions—migration—has influenced relations.

The factor of race has not received much attention in Canadian foreign relations history.[54] However, it has done much to shape Canadian perceptions of Asia and thus Canadian relations with Asia. Racist politics at home led to severe restrictions and, for many years, outright bans on immigration from China and India, as well as to a "gentleman's agreement" to restrict immigration from Japan. Anti-Asian laws culminated in the forcible relocation of Canadians of Japanese descent during the Second World War. Important work by recent historians elaborates on the centrality of racialized perceptions and policy-making in Canadian foreign relations as well as in immigration policy, suggesting that foreign relations and immigration cannot be rigidly separated.

The documentary record contains repeated references to Indonesians' alleged excitability, indolence, and lack of maturity. On the other hand, Canadian mental maps have given privileged space to the Netherlands, a country whose positive image was renewed each year as the tulips bloomed in Ottawa. A typical External Affairs memorandum pointed out: "Often Canada and the Netherlands have had very much the same point of view on NATO matters, and to a lesser extent on United Nations matters and their delegates, consequently, have kept in close touch."[55] From 1946 to 1955, 114,777 Dutch nationals moved to Canada.[56] Many of these migrants came directly from the Netherlands, especially as many Dutch women married Canadian soldiers, but others were Dutch citizens leaving Indonesia. When Sukarno expelled 47,000 Dutch residents in 1957, potential Dutch migration to Canada became an issue and an opportunity. The people in question were not the European colonial administrators of the previous wave of Dutch migration out of Indonesia; many were "Indos," the mixed-race descendants of Dutch fathers and Indonesian mothers. They often held elite positions in the East Indies, but they also included many lower-income people.

The chance to attract skilled Dutch citizens appealed to officials in the Ontario town of Newmarket. Robert Bullock, Newmarket's industrial commissioner, suggested that "another opportunity is presenting itself to the Canadian Government to achieve a trade success" by scooping up "the entire managerial force of a country." Offering this group a haven, Bullock argued, would boost Newmarket's development and promote trade with Indonesia "under the Canadian flag . . . before Red China can draw Indonesia into its orbit."[57] There was some sympathy in External Affairs and cabinet for the notion, but the Department of Immigration blocked it. In the end, the vast majority of the Dutch in Indonesia went to the Netherlands.

Canada did admit some Indonesians of ethnic Chinese descent after waves of anti-Chinese violence in 1965–6 and 1998. In the 1950s and early 1960s, Chinese-Indonesian political parties and associations thrived. Sukarno welcomed this and cultivated close relations with the People's Republic of China. In 1965–6, the situation reversed itself, with the army blaming China for supporting the Indonesian Communist Party. The Suharto regime brought in a series of measures restricting expressions of Chinese culture and identity. More mobile than other Indonesians and tending more towards Christianity than Islam, ethnic Chinese were better able to migrate, and some landed in Canada. Thanks to this group, Indonesian became one the languages of Catholic masses in Toronto and Vancouver.

The 1998 protests that toppled Suharto also included a welling-up of anti-Chinese violence. This inspired investigations and advocacy by Indonesian human rights groups, as well as the mobilization of the Chinese-Indonesian community in several cities in Canada. Toronto community members formed a group called "Canadians Concerned about Ethnic Violence in Indonesia" (CCEVI), then broadened their critique beyond the treatment of Chinese-Indonesians to include all aspects of ethnic discrimination and human rights. CCEVI was able to influence immigration decisions and make human rights more of a concern.

Timorese migration to Canada was miniscule—just three students accepted as refugees in the 1990s—but still had an impact. The Portuguese-Canadian community included a handful of Portuguese who had served in colonial government or military capacity in East Timor. A community with a growing presence and a stable of Portuguese-language newspapers filled the role of a diaspora concerned with policy towards East Timor, even while there were few Timorese in Canada. Meanwhile, the three Timorese refugees became representatives of East Timor's independence movement, creating links to the worldwide Timorese diaspora and adding strong, "authentic" voices to the East Timor lobby in Canada. One of them, Bella Galhos, made national headlines and was able to best the Indonesian ambassador in a press battle after he tried to silence her by pressuring her family at home. Galhos and her supporters managed to get the story into Canadian newspapers, and Foreign Minister Axworthy called the ambassador in for a severe scolding.[58] The episode showed that even a tiny Timorese presence in Canada could affect policy. Migration, no matter how small, affected bilateral relations.

Conclusion

Canadian policy towards Indonesia was grounded in what the government saw as Canadian national interests, dominated by Cold War allegiances and trade imperatives. This would be a bland and unsurprising conclusion if not for the common belief that Canadian foreign policy has been driven by idealism, peacemaking, and rights promotion. This belief in a benevolent Canada is central to Canadians' diplomatic self-image, yet it has rarely been an actual factor in government policy.

Diplomatic relations between Canada and Indonesia do not reveal the Canada of fond imagination, a helpful and friendly mediator and friend to the global South. Instead, Canada was a loyal (if independent-minded) member of the Western alliance system. It promoted decolonization, but in ways that mirrored Canada's own evolutionary path to independence, with ties to the former colonial power and to global trading networks. Canada also offered itself as a model for economic development, its doors open to foreign investment and full integration into the global capitalist economy. Development work drew on a missionary legacy that aimed to make other countries more like Canada. It also aimed, as did diplomacy during the Suharto years, to promote trade and investment. The Canadian government worked in the interests of Canadian business. A backlash from Canadian civil society demanded that human rights be added to the agenda. The influence of migration from Indonesia and East Timor, albeit small in numbers, added to this pressure and to the emergence of a counter-policy that insisted that human rights stand at the centre of the relationship.

An examination of policy in the four realms of diplomacy, development, trade, and migration makes non-state factors more visible. Development groups, migrants, and corporations have all exerted important influences. Each of these sectors must be considered for one to gain a full picture of the Canada-Indonesia relationship. The same is likely to be true in other cases of Canadian foreign relations: the complete story has both state and non-state aspects.

It is important, too, to see the role of images, of racialized perceptions, and of the mental maps that underpin policy decisions. No minister or diplomat made foreign policy decisions based solely on an image of Indonesians as lazy and excitable, or of Afghans as warlike, or of Chinese as wily and inscrutable. Yet this sort of perception formed the background to policy debates. Understanding the role of images and perceptions is important if we are to understand policy. The images have shifted from Theodore Newton's sketches of a watery parish of volcanoes and gorillas to images of a distant land of terrorism and mining opportunities. But those earlier images are still there, informing policy and reinforcing themselves.

Author's Note: I am grateful to Steven Hugh Lee and Robert Bothwell for comments.

Endnotes

1   Theodore Newton, "South Seas Envoy: Memoirs of a Canadian Ambassador" (unpublished manuscript, Library and Archives Canada (henceforth LAC), Newton Papers, MG 31 E74, vol. 3, file 8), 1.

2   Newton to High Commissioner in Pakistan, 22 October 1958, LAC, MG 31 E74/3/1.

3   Like many Indonesians, Sukarno has only one name; frequent references to his name being Ahmed are incorrect.

4   David Webster, *Fire and the Full Moon: Canada and Indonesia in a Decolonizing World* (Vancouver: UBC Press, 2009).

5   Louis St Laurent, "The Preservation of Civilization," 27 October 1950, External Affairs, *Statements & Speeches* 50/43.

6   John Hilliker and Donald Barry, *Canada's Department of External Affairs*, vol. 2: *Coming of Age, 1946–1968* (Montreal and Kingston: McGill-Queen's University Press, 1995), 30.

7   Greg Donaghy, "Coming Off the Gold Standard: Reassessing the 'Golden Age' of Canadian Diplomacy" (paper presented at the University of Saskatchewan, 28 September 2009); and Robert Bothwell, *Alliance and Illusion: Canada and the World, 1945–1984* (Vancouver: UBC Press, 2007).

8   Newton radio speech, 1 July 1960, LAC, MG 31 E74/3/5.

9   Todd Gordon, *Imperialist Canada* (Winnipeg: Arbeiter Ring, 2010); and Cranford Pratt, "Dominant Class Theory and Canadian Foreign Policy: The Case of the Counter-consensus," *International Journal* 39, no. 1 (1983): 99–135.

10 Lester B. Pearson, "The Development of Canadian Foreign Policy," *Foreign Affairs* 30, no. 1 (1951): 17–30.

11 Mel Himes, *Canadian Foreign Policy Handbook* (Montreal: Jewel Publications, 1996), 37; and John Meehan, *The Dominion and the Rising Sun: Canada Encounters Japan, 1929–41* (Vancouver: UBC Press, 2004).

12 Paul Martin speech to Kiwanis Club in Westboro, ON, 22 August 1950, cited in "Canadian Policy in the Far East," *External Affairs* 2, no. 9 (September 1950): 326.

13 Steven Hugh Lee, "The Canadian-Asian Experience: An Introductory Synthesis," *Journal of American-East Asian Relations* 4, no. 3 (1995): 193–222.

14 Ruth Compton Brouwer, "When Missions Became Development: Ironies of 'NGOization' in Mainstream Canadian Churches in the 1960s," *Canadian Historical Review* 91, no. 4 (2010): 661–93.

15   Quoted in Elizabeth McIninch, ed., *Friendship beyond Borders: Celebrating Fifty Years of Indonesian-Canadian Bilateral Ties* (Ottawa: Indonesian Embassy, 2003), 13.

16   Memorandum to the minister, 23 July 1958, LAC, RG 25/6148/50409-40 [3.1].

17   David England, "Indonesians to Make a New United States," *Saturday Night*, 11 January 1947, 9.

18   "Annual Report of the Work of the Jakarta Office for 1953," LAC, RG 25/6464/5495-G-40 [2.1].

19   Arnold Heeney to deputy minister of trade and commerce, 31 December 1949, LAC, RG 25/6218/5495-G-40 [1.1]; and Secretary of State for External Affairs to Jakarta, 19 August 1953, LAC, RG 25/6613/11129-40 [3.1].

20   "Democracy and Rebellion," notes for speeches by L.N. Palar, McGill University Archives (henceforth MUA), RG 84/72/866; Palar address to Lake Couchiching conference, 11 August 1959, in "Recent Developments in Indonesia," *External Affairs* 11, no. 9 (September 1959), 283–7; Harold Greene, "Spirit of Democracy Lives Despite Failures in Asia: Ambassador," *Globe and Mail*, 12 August 1959; and "Indonesian Explains Asian View of Soviet," *Globe and Mail*, 13 August 1959.

21   John Saltford, *The United Nations and the Indonesian Takeover of West Papua, 1962–1969: The Anatomy of Betrayal* (London: RoutledgeCurzon, 2002); and Eben Kirksey, *Freedom in Entangled Worlds* (Durham, NC: Duke University Press, 2012).

22   Wallace Nesbitt statement in Parliament, 6 August 1964, *Canada House of Commons Debates* (henceforth *CHCD*) 1964, 6:6479–81; Nesbitt statement, 22 May 1964, *CHCD* 1964, 4:3496-7; "The Commonwealth," unattributed note, LAC, Wallace Nesbitt Papers, MG 32 C56/6/External Affairs Committee 1963–1964.

23   Canadian Embassy Jakarta to External Affairs, 16 March 1965, LAC, RG 25/8917/20-INDON-1-3-MLSIA [8]; "'Go to Hell,' Canada, Says Indonesian Paper," *Vancouver Sun*, undated clipping [August 1964], LAC, MG 32 C56/6/External Affairs Committee 1963–1964.

24   John Roosa, *Pretext for Mass Murder: The September 30 Movement and Suharto's Coup d'Etat in Indonesia* (Madison: University of Wisconsin Press, 2006); Bradley R. Simpson, *Economists with Guns: Authoritarian Development and US-Indonesian Relations, 1960–1968* (Stanford, CA: Stanford University Press, 2008).

25   Canadian Embassy Jakarta to External Affairs, 3 March 1967, LAC, RG 25/10283/27-1-2-INDON.

26   Canadian Embassy Jakarta to External Affairs, 11 January 1978, LAC, RG 25/10861/20-INDON-2-2.

27   *Chega! The Report of the Commission for Reception, Truth and Reconciliation in Timor-Leste* (Dili, 2006), Web, 20 May 2011, www.cavr-timorleste.org/en/

chegaReport.htm; and John Roosa, "How Does a Truth Commission Find Out What the Truth Is? The Case of East Timor's CAVR," *Pacific Affairs* 80, no. 4 (2007–8): 569–80.

28   Information Memorandum for the Minister, 15 July 1994, Foreign Affairs file 20-TIMOR.

29   Action Memorandum for the Minister, 25 October 1996; Canadian Embassy Jakarta email, 3 November 1998, 20-TIMOR.

30   Memorandum on Axworthy meeting with Indonesian Foreign Minister, 30 July 1997, University of British Columbia Archives, BC Civil Liberties Association (BCCLA) Papers, APEC Inquiry exhibits, box 1.

31   Geoffrey Robinson, *"If You Leave Us Here, We Will Die": How Genocide Was Stopped in East Timor* (Princeton, NJ: Princeton University Press, 2009).

32   A.K. Gani, "The Indonesian Republic Has a Right to Export," *Fakta dan Dokumen2* [Facts and Documents] (n.p., n.d.) 3:2, 88.

33   Menzies to USSEA, 31 December 1949, LAC, RG 25/6218/5495-G-40 [1.1].

34   Department of Trade and Commerce memorandum, "Canadian-Indonesian Trade Relations," [1956], LAC, RG 25/6465/5495-G-40 [2.2].

35   "Canadian-Indonesian Trade Relations," Department of External Affairs briefing paper, n.d.; Netherlands East Indies trade summary, 14 November 1949, LAC, RG 25/2850/1529-40 [1].

36   Jakarta letter 522, 23 November 1962, LAC, RG 25, vol. 6789, file 1529-40 [2.2].

37   List of Canadian companies in Indonesia, 1999, ETAN Papers.

38   Economic Commission for Asia and the Far East, "Mining Developments in Asia and the Far East 1960," United Nations document E/CN.11/956, pp. 6–7; Alex Hunter, "The Indonesian Oil Industry," in Bruce Glassburner, ed., *The Economy of Indonesia* (Ithaca: Cornell University Press, 1971), 266; and *Petroleum Press Service* (*PPS*) 30 (January 1963): 4.

39   External Affairs memorandum, 18 July 1958; and J.R. McKinney to Far Eastern division, 9 September 1958, both at LAC, RG 25/6985/5495-G-1-40.

40   Canadian Embassy Jakarta to External Affairs, 5 and 8 September 1958, LAC, RG 25/6985/5495-G-1-40; and US Embassy Jakarta to State Department, 25 August 1960, United States National Archives, RG 59, 898.2553.

41   Tim Kell, *The Roots of Acehnese Rebellion, 1989–1992* (Singapore: Equinox, 2010); and Jacques Bertrand, *Nationalism and Ethnic Conflict in Indonesia* (Cambridge: Cambridge University Press, 2004).

42   Canadian Embassy Jakarta to External Affairs, 9 December 1969, LAC, RG 25/10861/20-INDON-2-2.

43   Canadian Embassy Jakarta to External Affairs, 14 November 1957, and J.E. Lancaster, commercial

secretary Jakarta, to Trade & Commerce, 11 November 1957, LAC, RG 25/2850/1529-40 [1].

44 Canadian Embassy memorandum on Inco operations, 22 June 1971, LAC, RG 25/10861/20-INDON-2-2.

45 Foreign Affairs and International Trade Canada, "Building the Canadian Advantage: A Corporate Social Responsibility (CSR) Strategy for the Canadian International Extractive Sector." Web, 20 May 2011, www.international.gc.ca/trade-agreements-accords-commerciaux/ds/csr-strategy-rse-stategie.aspx; and Liisa North, Tim Clark, and Viviana Patroni, eds, *Community Rights and Corporate Responsibility: Canadian Mining and Oil Companies in Latin America* (Toronto: Between the Lines, 2006).

46 *Indonesia: A Guide for Canadian Business, 1995–96* (Ottawa: Queen's Printer, 1995).

47 Ademola Adeleke, "Ties Without Strings? The Colombo Plan and the Geopolitics of International Aid" (PhD diss., University of Toronto, 1996).

48 Figures calculated from *A Report on Canada's External Aid Programs 1965–66* (Ottawa: External Aid Office, 1966).

49 Wilfred Cantwell Smith, "Interim Note on Scope and Objective," and Smith's proposal to James, 7 May 1951, both at MUA, RG 2/208/5586.

50 Quoted in Sharon Scharfe, *Complicity: Human Rights and Canadian Foreign Policy—the Case of East Timor* (Montreal: Black Rose Books, 1996), 131.

51 Benedict Anderson, "Old State, New Society: Indonesia's New Order in Comparative Historical Perspective," *Journal of Asian Studies* 42, no. 3 (1983): 477–96; and Ali Murtopo, *The Acceleration and Modernization of 25 Years' Development* (Jakarta: Yayasan Proklomasi, 1973).

52 Howard Dick, Vincent J.H. Houben, J. Thomas Lindblad, and Thee Kian Wee, *The Emergence of a National Economy: An Economic History of Indonesia, 1800–2000* (Sydney, Australia: Allen & Unwin, 2002), 206.

53 Edward Aspinall, *Opposing Suharto: Compromise, Resistance and Regime Change in Indonesia* (Stanford: Stanford University Press, 2005); and Edward Alden, "The Poor Are Finally Fighting Back in Indonesia," *Vancouver Sun*, 28 May 1997.

54 John Price, *Orienting Canada: Race, Empire and the Transpacific* (Vancouver: UBC Press, 2011).

55 European Division memorandum, December 1957, LAC, RG 25/6148/50409-40 [2.2].

56 Memorandum to the Minister, 27 August 1957, LAC, RG 25/6148/50409-40 [1.1].

57 Bullock to Secretary of State for External Affairs, 14 January 1958, LAC, RG 25/6985/5495-G-40 [3.1].

58 Indonesian Embassy to Department of Foreign Affairs, 30 January 1996, and Canadian Embassy Jakarta emails, 31 January 1996 and 8 February 1996, both at DFAIT file 20-TIMOR.

◎ 8.2: WHEN MISSIONS BECAME DEVELOPMENT: IRONIES OF "NGOIZATION" IN MAINSTREAM CANADIAN CHURCHES IN THE 1960S

Ruth Compton Brouwer

. . . In the small high school that I attended in Atlantic Canada, my friendly competitor for good grades was a girl very different from my self-absorbed teenage self, someone whose all-round seriousness and involvement with church work led some of us to understand that, like her Uncle Roy, she would become a United Church of Canada missionary. Instead, in 1966, after graduating from Mount Allison University with arts and education degrees and teaching for a year in Labrador, my friend joined CUSO. Originally called Canadian University Service Overseas, CUSO was established in 1961, the same year as the Peace Corps. The first distinctively Canadian non-governmental organization (NGO) to undertake development

work from a secular stance and in post-colonial and decolonizing contexts, CUSO sent volunteers to some 40 countries during its first decade.[1] In my friend's case, the destination was Kenya.

Had she joined CUSO out of frustration with a church hidebound by missionary traditionalism and out of touch with the mood of the times? Almost certainly not.[2] During the 1960s, the United Nations (UN) Development Decade,[3] Canada's mainstream churches made a significant break with their missionary past, espousing numerous causes that fit comfortably under the rubric of development. The shift was most pronounced in the United Church of Canada, the largest and most liberal of Canada's Protestant denominations, founded in 1925.[4] This article highlights changes in organization, discourse, and practice that characterized the missions-to-development trajectory in the United Church during the 1960s and some of the ironies that arose from those changes. Despite the church's decidedly non-evangelistic approach to missions in this decade, globally minded young Canadians were not won over: they overwhelmingly chose to express their interest in development work through secular organizations like CUSO, even when, like my friend, they had had a traditional church upbringing and sometimes youthful dreams of a missionary career. Yet, even if it had won their loyalty, the United Church could not have accommodated them, given a decline in the funds available to sponsor mission personnel and the church's new policy of sending its workers to overseas placements only when and where they had been invited. Indeed, when circumstances brought development-minded volunteers their way as would-be missionaries, the church's missions officials frequently referred them to organizations like CUSO, viewing such organizations as acceptable alternatives for expressing a Christian compassion in the developing world. This perspective was not reciprocated. CUSO's organizers were prepared to accept practical, start-up help from the missions community, but like the majority of their volunteers they were anxious to avoid the taint of the *M* word and the distasteful associations with proselytization and colonialism that it evoked.

Conversely, many conservative Canadian churchgoers in the 1960s favoured a more traditional approach to mission, and to Christianity generally, than that promoted by the leadership of the United Church and other mainline churches. In the course of the decade, such people increasingly gravitated to more evangelically inclined faith groups. While the overseas outreach of the United Church and of other like-minded mainline Canadian churches survived these and other challenges in the tumultuous 1960s, it was in a greatly changed and attenuated form. In the new world of international development, they had become faith-based NGOs.[5] Though they spoke and acted from a distinctive ethos and a much longer history, in

practice their everyday concerns in the developing world often had little to distinguish them from the concerns of their young, secular counterparts. . . .

Revisioning and Rebranding Mission in the 1960s

The most striking irony of "NGOization" in the mainline churches was the timing: CUSO was founded just as they were beginning to make a dramatic break with historic patterns of mission. The change was just one element in a much larger pattern of social upheaval affecting the churches in 1960s Canada. The eclipse of the "Liberal Protestant Establishment" on university campuses was a particularly significant transformation.[6] But across the country analogous changes were taking place as "what had been a creeping process of secularization became an avalanche."[7] Reflecting this new climate within Canada and responding to needs, attitudes, and aspirations in recently decolonized countries and in those still struggling to throw off colonial rule, the United Church's missions establishment orchestrated sweeping changes in its understanding and practice of mission.

From its antecedent denominations, Methodists, Presbyterians, and Congregationalists, the church had inherited mission work in India, China, Japan, Korea, the Caribbean, and Angola.[8] The 1960s changes in the church's approach to work in—and beyond—these inherited "fields" were so far-reaching that one is tempted to speak of a paradigm shift.[9] Such a characterization runs the risk of minimizing the degree to which, between the two world wars, much of the United Church's overseas activity already resembled development work and was non-proselytizing, despite accounts for home-base consumption that often suggested otherwise.[10] Nevertheless, from the perspective of liberal missionaries and former missionaries at mid-century who favoured more in the way of service-oriented mission work or who looked back with regret on the colonialist context of missions and the emphasis on evangelization, the churches still had a long way to go. The liberal perspective was increasingly characteristic of the World Council of Churches (WCC), inaugurated in 1948,[11] and in the United Church, a founding WCC member, it appeared strongest among missionaries who had served in China and whose careers there had ended with the triumph of communism.

One such missionary was Donald K. Faris, who would later play a crucial if indirect role in the founding of CUSO. Faris served with the church in China from 1925 to 1942. Early in his missionary career he shifted his focus from evangelism to rural development. After the Second World War Faris worked on UN relief and rehabilitation projects in China, and in the 1950s and 1960s he administered UN-sponsored development projects in Korea, Thailand, and India. But in the 1950s he still wanted to do development work as a United Church missionary. With the door to that possibility closed in China, he sought similar work in India. His vision of grassroots agricultural initiatives linked to national goals and undertaken in a consultative but unconfining relationship with the United Church's India mission was not supported. Facing this reality, Faris concluded that the kind of work he wanted to do and for which his experience had prepared him was "something that the church has no machinery or thinking prepared to use. It forces me to a conclusion that . . . my best contribution to the world now, perhaps is outside the church organization. . . . The exodus from China and growing sentiment in all countries of the world . . . make the older concept of mission a complete impossibility." In a similar vein, a year later another former United Church China missionary, Katharine Hockin, also reflected on the future—and the past—of her church's mission work. "Where do we go from here . . .? Does it not mean the whole missionary venture needs re-vamping and a consecrated self-examination?"[12]

The kind of revamping that Hockin perhaps had in mind in 1951 and in which she would play a significant role did not begin for another decade, but when it did, the changes were far-reaching. They began with the restructuring of the United Church's missions bureaucracy and with

new terminology. In 1962, the Board of Overseas Missions became the Board of World Mission (BWM). The new adjective and the dropping of the *s*, a change already made by the WCC,[13] signified that the board's sense of responsibility now went beyond its historic mission fields. . . . Meanwhile, in the same year that the new BWM came into existence, the church's Twelfth General Council commissioned "an independent and fundamental study of how The United Church of Canada can best share in the World Mission of the Church." By the time that the resulting *Report of the Commission on World Mission* was issued in November 1966, many of its recommendations were already being adopted or put into practice by the BWM.[14] These included a call for a broader, more flexible, more ecumenical approach to the church's "task in mission": "technical assistance," for instance, and refugee and emergency aid; repentance for "all arrogance, whether racial, cultural or ecclesiastical" in past mission practice; and "dialogue with people of other faiths." As well as partnerships with autonomous Third World churches, there was to be cooperation with governments and international aid organizations in a mission field now understood to be of global dimensions.[15] Overall, as A.C. Forrest, the editor of the church's official periodical, the *United Church Observer*, pointed out, the recommendations signalled a "serious and radical departure from what many people still consider 'missions.'"[16]

With the publication of the commission's *Report*, and then, in 1972, with another bureaucratic change, the folding of the Board of World Mission into the new Division of World Outreach (DWO), the United Church of Canada signalled the nature of the changes that were already taking place in the philosophy and practice of its overseas work and its future directions. Not only was the very word *mission* absent from the new organization's name; under the heading "Responsibilities," the DWO constitution contained nothing that could be construed as evangelizing.[17] . . .

New Partnerships and Post-Colonial Soul-Searching

Whether undertaken overseas or within Canada, many of the specific changes sought during this decade by the United Church's core group of mission reformers were interrelated. They were also fraught with challenges and internal contradictions. The church's struggle to work out a new relationship with the Christian community in the Malwa region of Madhya Pradesh, India, provides a vivid example of the challenges. Malwa's Christian community dated from the 1870s, when Canadian Presbyterians had begun work in the city of Indore.[18] In the decade following India's independence, the United Church had increasingly devolved responsibility for Christian work in the region to the Malwa Presbytery (later Council), beginning with evangelistic work. But it could not so easily devolve financial responsibility to that tiny and impoverished Christian community. India remained by a wide margin the single largest recipient country for BWM dollars in the mid-1960s. While some of this money went to institutional activities in other parts of India, the work in Malwa was the single biggest cost.[19] In addition to evangelism, the financial burdens included extensive educational and medical undertakings dating back to the nineteenth century as well as some more recent forms of community development.

By the mid-1960s, the BWM had largely disengaged from direct evangelism in Malwa. Ordained Canadian missionaries and lay workers who still functioned in some sense under the rubric of "evangelistic" workers did so on request in seminaries or colleges or within select indigenous Christian communities. Even in educational work, the BWM seemed eager to reduce its direct ties and obligations to the Malwa Church Council in order to free up funds for work not under the council's control.[20] In 1956 the BWM's predecessor had set a timeline for reducing its then-current levels of funding to the council: five years for evangelistic work and 10 years for educational and medical work. In practice, the legacy of almost a century of

dependence on Western funding proved difficult to escape, with administrators in the council continuing to press for rescue from financial dilemmas over which the BWM had no control and over which it felt intense frustration.[21]

The issue was not simply that of a Western church seeking to cut its ties and obligations now that it was no longer in charge. Nor were the Malwa Council's dilemmas simply those resulting from local poverty and the small size of the Christian community. They were also the product of the mission's history and the kind of Christian community it had brought into existence. Many of the early converts had been among the most vulnerable and marginal members of society. Over the years, many of their descendants had come to look upon the local church and its institutions as a kind of employment or welfare agency on which they and their families had particular claims. . . . The Malwa Christian community was by no means the only Christian community in India struggling during these years with the challenges of poverty and marginalization and with the legacy, and spoils, of mission colonialism.[22] But Malwa was, perhaps, a particularly egregious example. Thus, for the United Church's BWM, "partnership" with this particular indigenous Christian community was proving to be, in every sense, a problematic concept.

In these circumstances, the board thought it prudent to facilitate closer relationships with the ecumenical United Church of Northern India, of which the Malwa Church Council was a part. It also sought to channel more of its resources into the Malwa Economic Development Society (MEDS, 1963) and Action for Food Production (AFPRO, 1966), agencies that, while still having links to the Malwa Council, were at one remove. Though neither would prove to be an entirely satisfactory vehicle for delivering aid efficiently, each seemed to represent a step forward. AFPRO arose as an ecumenical response to a local famine, and because of its cooperative approach and its outreach "without regard for race, class, community or creed," it won support from local secular agencies and from the government of India.[23] Meanwhile, in 1968, Canada's federal government began using the United Church and MEDS as non-government conduits for directing funds into development work in India, the single largest recipient country at this time of Canadian government-to-government aid.[24] A MEDS project for manufacturing water-drilling rigs was chosen to receive a total of $100,000 from the Canadian government via the United Church, with the church itself providing a technician to operate one such rig.[25]

In 1968 the federal government formalized and expanded its use of voluntary agencies, including faith groups, to facilitate its development work in India and elsewhere. Canada's External Aid Office was reborn as the Canadian International Development Agency (CIDA). Maurice Strong, CIDA's first president, believed in providing robust support to NGOs and to that end established a special NGO division within CIDA.[26] Cooperation between the federal government and the United Church on international relief and development work had certainly taken place prior to this CIDA initiative but seemingly just on an ad hoc basis.[27] From 1968 onward, there would be more funding and increasing areas of development work in which the church and the federal government would have overlapping interests and cooperative relationships. These relationships, as well as less congenial church-state relations, will be considered below.

Meanwhile, for the United Church, ecumenism was another expression of partnership, and as noted, it received strong emphasis in the *Report of the Commission on World Mission*. The ecumenical concept in mission was certainly not, in itself, a new phenomenon.[28] What was distinctive in the 1960s was the geographic and denominational reach of the new ecumenism and the kinds of tasks that it undertook. Now, too, a good deal of ecumenical work involving mainstream Protestant denominations was being initiated or orchestrated through the Geneva-based WCC. The United Church was a committed and enthusiastic partner. In 1961 it endorsed the WCC's call in New Delhi for "Joint Action for Mission." Following a 1963 WCC gathering in Mexico City, the BWM publicized and supported its recommendation that member

churches and their missionary societies should become increasingly "international, inter-racial and interdenominational." Reflecting this spirit, former BWM secretary Floyd Honey was relocated to New York in 1965 to join the WCC as its secretary for mission and service. In Toronto, Katherine Hockin became dean of studies of the Ecumenical Institute of Canada, formerly the Canadian School of Missions.[29] . . .

The BWM's increasing involvement in projects such as drilling for water, agricultural training, and family planning and its cooperation in secular and ecumenical aid and development work was accompanied by a range of critiques of colonialism. An early and frequent target was the Portuguese colony of Angola, where the United Church at the time of union had inherited Canadian Congregationalists' mission work, dating back to the 1880s. The BWM was at first only mildly critical of the Portuguese government for its handling of recent uprisings and politely urged it to move towards granting the colony self-government. Despite its initially moderate tone, several of its missionaries were denied visas to return to Angola after furloughs or subjected to delays as a result of their comments about the Portuguese regime. In 1963 BWM associate secretary Roy Webster met with Canada's external affairs minister to exchange information and discuss "our mutual concern regarding the situation in Angola."[30]

By the late 1960s the BWM and some of its most prominent Angola missionaries had become far more critical of Portuguese policy in the colony and had come to believe that by continuing to work there they appeared to condone the colonial regime and its brutal treatment of freedom fighters or, if they were known for their criticisms of the regime, to put African associates at risk. The most vocal critic was veteran medical missionary Sidney Gilchrist, who opted to relocate to a base in the Congo where he could be part of "a team to train front-line fighters for a healthier Africa."[31] Back in Canada in 1970, a woman missionary who had served in Angola from 1941 reflected that she had perhaps made the wrong decision by opting to stay silent in order to remain working in the colony: was she any different, she asked herself, from Christians who had stayed silent in Hitler's Germany?[32]

As a non-British colony and one in which Canada had few if any economic or strategic interests, Angola was a region on which the church and the government generally could confer with little likelihood of conflicting agendas.[33] Increasingly, however, in the late 1960s and early 1970s the federal government became the target of board criticism and advice on matters related to several other regions struggling against direct or indirect forms of colonialism and racism. These regions included Rhodesia (Zimbabwe), South Africa, Vietnam, and Brazil, though it was only in the last country that the United Church had its own mission personnel. A telegram signed by board secretaries Roy Webster and Garth Legge at the time of the board's 1968 general meeting was typical of the tone generally adopted. The telegram urged the government to make further efforts through the Commonwealth to end the Smith regime in Rhodesia. The situation there, they wrote, should be recognized as "fundamentally part of the wider issue constituted by a ring of white minority–dominated states around the southern end of the African continent."[34] A year later the BWM was more specific, but still polite, in its recommendation: if all else failed to end the Smith regime in Rhodesia, "Canada should support the use of necessary police action under the United Nations." . . .

But what about the impact of such verbal position-taking within Canada? In his conclusion to a collection of essays on Canadian churches and foreign policy published in 1990, political scientist Robert Matthews observed that while the churches' tactics had become "increasingly sophisticated" over the years, their actual influence on government policy remained "marginal." His colleague Cranford Pratt, who was dealing more broadly with "humane internationalism," concurred.[35] So far as the United Church was concerned, clearly, some of its recommendations to the federal government in the 1960s, such as one from the BWM in 1969 urging it to double its aid and development budget,[36] stood no chance of being implemented. Nonetheless, as the largest and most mainstream Protestant denomination in Canada, one whose

official periodical had an estimated readership of close to one million people and was widely cited in other media,[37] the United Church certainly had the potential to raise Canadians' consciousness on development issues and through that means to put pressure on government, especially when it lobbied in concert with other organizations.[38] . . .

Mission concerns about colonialism's misdeeds were not new. From the late nineteenth century onward such concerns had periodically been expressed by individual missionaries and even by mission board secretaries. But usually their unease had been conveyed privately or unofficially.[39] Now the concerns were routinely a part of official board statements, an aspect of its new understanding of mission. Political stances were also expressed in financial aid to like-minded organizations, as with a small donation in 1969 to the Canadian Committee for Zimbabwe. More controversially, in 1971 the board decided to fund a WCC initiative that channelled aid to anti-racist groups in southern Africa, notwithstanding the acknowledged reality that some of the aid might wind up supporting guerrilla organizations.[40] The new approach to critiquing colonialism extended to more generalized criticisms of the West's ongoing negative impact in the developing world, through industrial pollution, for instance, and exploitation of its resources. Newly elected moderator A.B.B. Moore referred to both issues in a 1970 address in the context of calling for a new sense of what mission and evangelism should mean in the new era.[41] . . .

Recruiting—and Redirecting— Would-Be Missionaries

Not surprisingly, recruiting and appointing missionaries in this tumultuous decade was in every sense a problematic endeavour, commencing with the very word *missionary*.[42] How was the United Church to reach out to idealistic young people who were interested in the developing world but disengaged from traditional church language? Norman MacKenzie, who had become BWM secretary for personnel recruitment after missionary service in China and India, raised this question at the board's 1968 general meeting in the context of reporting on changes in the format for World Mission Night, the annual service at which the church introduced its new missionaries. There were still many church youth, he believed, wanting to "give their lives in dedicated Christian service," but unable to "describe their inner convictions in words . . . traditionally accepted by the Church." The board followed up on MacKenzie's question in two ways. Missionary applicants, it declared, need not use the traditional language of the Handbook, but they must have "a Christian faith that is real and a relationship with Christ that is alive." This appeared to mean that while their motivation was to come from personal faith, they were under no obligation to present Christianity as inherently superior to other faith traditions. The distinction, however, was not made perfectly clear. The board also decided to appoint a study committee on recruitment and to ask the General Council for advice.[43]

The resulting document, "Some Reflections on Recruiting Personnel for the Board of World Mission," made pertinent observations about dilemmas facing the board and raised questions about future directions. It was agreed that the policy of recruiting "only in response to requests from overseas organizations" had to be maintained. And yet how was the board to deal with such challenges as the fact that while increased food production was clearly an essential need in the developing world, not a single agriculturalist had been requested during the preceding year? And how should the board respond to ongoing requests for teachers of academic subjects when it knew that in India and some other countries there were numerous unemployed young people with arts or other degrees? Given frequent requests from volunteers for short-term appointments, often three to five years, *and* the board's increasing inability to offer longer-term appointments, was there even a future for career missionaries? Moreover, weren't there now plenty of other opportunities for Canadian Christians to serve in the developing world? This question seemed so pertinent that it was formulated in several different ways: "Has the time come when we should encourage the young to join CUSO, the middle-aged to join External Aid, and the older to join Canadian Executive Service Overseas? . . . Should the Board of World Mission be finding more outlets for its staff in service with secular agencies such as local national governments? . . . With the increasing number of government and private agencies becoming involved in development programs overseas, does the Board of World Mission have a distinct role to play or should it encourage Christians to become involved in these secular organizations?"[44]

To the extent that the board answered its own questions, it continued both to send out its own short-term missionaries on request and to encourage and support women and men with an interest in serving overseas under secular agencies such as CUSO. As an *Observer* editorial put it, "The idea is you don't have to wear a church label, let alone a denominational label, to witness effectively to your faith in the neediest parts of the world."[45] . . .

A lack of volunteers was not the foremost recruitment and appointment challenge facing the church in the mid- to late 1960s. Indeed, the idealism of the time and the new global consciousness made opportunities for travel and service in the developing world enormously appealing to young Westerners. Within the church, Norman MacKenzie attracted a record number of young people to overseas service, effectively reversing the recruitment "crisis" of the early sixties.[46] The church, however, did not have the funds to appoint all qualified applicants, even supposing there had been requests for all of them from indigenous churches. And there were some countries, such as Angola and India, where, though indigenous church partners might still want Canadian personnel, increasing national restrictions were being put in place.[47] . . .

These were particular dilemmas, overseas, confronting a liberal mission board. Meanwhile, on the home front, there was a larger, more general, dilemma. Throughout the 1960s, the BWM had struggled to tutor its Canadian constituency into a new understanding of mission. Yet as it entered the new decade, board spokesmen experienced a sense of frustration that their message was not being heard. As board chairman in

1971, C.W.M. Service, a practising surgeon in Lindsay, Ontario, and a former China medical missionary, gave an address on "The Changing Face of Mission." In it he declared that the "man in the pew" was "still generally living with a Nineteenth Century concept of Mission." Even the clergy seemed unaware of "what this Board is doing and what it stands for in the 70's. The Communication Gap is *colossal*." To illustrate his message, Service presented a "Then" and "Now" list—a list of the ways that missionaries, and understandings of mission, had changed in the course of a century.[48]

Service's exasperation was palpable: despite a decade of effort, it appeared that neither the United Church's "man in the pew" nor many of its clergy were attuned to "the changing face of mission." It should thus come as no surprise that neither those organizing CUSO in 1961 nor many of the young adults who became its volunteers were able to see beyond outdated stereotypes. CUSO was determined to create something fresh and new, an organization for overseas service free of mission associations and the odious taint of colonialism. That, at least, was the goal. In reality, there would be significant links as well as tensions between this new secular NGO and the mainline Protestant and Catholic churches.

CUSO: A Secular Alternative and Sometime Partner in Development

By the time CUSO was officially established in the June 1961 meeting of the National Conference of Canadian Universities and Colleges, there were already nascent student-initiated development organizations at three Canadian universities. The first and most solid of these groups, Canadian Overseas Volunteers (COV), was based at the University of Toronto.[49] Before merging with CUSO at the end of 1962, COV sent two cohorts of volunteers to Asia. COV's founder, Keith Spicer, a doctoral student researching Canada's role in the Colombo Plan, had been motivated by reading Donald Faris's 1958 study, *To Plow with Hope*.[50] Inspired by a brief passage in which Faris had

called on educated young Westerners to get involved in development, Spicer and a handful of supporters approached service clubs, businesses, and churches for funding. They also turned to the churches for help with such matters as orientation for would-be volunteers.

Unlike Spicer and COV, CUSO's organizers initially wanted to keep the churches and the missions establishment entirely out of their plans. No representatives of missionary societies were invited either to CUSO's June founding meeting or to an earlier consultative meeting in March. However, the mission groups did have a pipeline to the March consultation in the person of Donald Wilson, attending as a representative of the national SCM (Student Christian Movement). Wilson also represented the SCM in the missionary department of the Canadian Council of Churches (CCC), an ecumenical organization of mainly liberal Protestant denominations. Following the March meeting, he reported back to the CCC that there had been "a general air of not wishing to accept anything from the churches, apart from money, and the rather obvious feeling on the part of some members present that the whole movement must be kept clear of any religious implications."[51] Several months later, following a recruitment tour of western Canadian universities for CUSO, on whose first executive he served, Wilson reported a climate of distaste for anything associated with the churches' missionary work. University students, he wrote, would consider it to be "a compromise of their integrity" to "go overseas under church auspices." Though most volunteers going out under CUSO had come from Christian homes, many of them were "deliberately choosing a secular channel rather than the church." Nor was the negative attitude to missions confined to students. "By and large," Wilson reported, "the university community has a complete emotional and intellectual bloc to the word 'missionary' as they understand it."[52]

The antipathy, then, was both clear and widespread. Yet within Canada at this period it was *only* the churches' missions establishments that had extensive direct knowledge and long-term experience of life in the developing world. Given this reality, CUSO soon found itself turning to those very churches for early guidance as well as financial assistance. In the autumn of 1962, CUSO's first full-time executive director, formerly with COV, asked the CCC's Department of Overseas Missions for assistance with such matters as orientation for newly selected volunteers.[53] During the next few years, Protestant and Catholic church personnel were also involved with CUSO's recruitment and selection activities and overseas placements. A young Presbyterian missionary, for instance, coordinated CUSO's first years of work in Nigeria, while a Roman Catholic priest with decades of experience as a missionary educator in southern Africa remained a leading figure in CUSO's recruitment, selection, and orientation programs well into the 1970s.[54] In Asia, Africa, and Latin America, there would be numerous placements for volunteers in educational and medical institutions founded by missionaries from all parts of the Western world. . . .

Furthermore, other links with the mainline churches emerged by the late 1960s—links based not on dependency but rather on strategic considerations and a desire to influence government policy and public opinion. As the United Church and CUSO itself became more politicized, they increasingly interpreted the problems of the developing world as outcomes of colonialism, neo-colonialism, and racism rather than as temporary difficulties that could be resolved with large doses of Western-style modernization. Thus, as well as turning their critical gaze on themselves for their own past failures or naïveté, they joined in criticizing shortcomings in the Canadian government's development and foreign policies. "The Black Paper: An Alternative Policy for Canada towards Southern Africa," published in 1970, was a striking example. BWM secretary Garth Legge and University of Toronto political science professor Cranford Pratt were the lead authors of this pamphlet, but two CUSO returned volunteers (RVs) were contributors. All four had experience working in eastern or southern Africa. "The Black Paper" provided a critical analysis of the Trudeau government's proposed policies on

southern Africa as set out in its recently released White Paper on foreign policy before making proposals for alternative policies. Canada, it urged, should take a more critical, activist, clearly anti-racist approach to the region, including non-military aid to liberation movements (aid such as Sweden and some NGOs were already said to be providing), and it should cease trading with South Africa.[55]

In the 1970s more such ad hoc coalitions would follow, involving other secular NGOs and other Protestant and Catholic church groups. Some of their initiatives, such as support for projects to aid refugees who had fled from Rhodesia (Zimbabwe) to Zambia, would engender sharp criticism. Critics in the media and elsewhere suggested that, even if only indirectly, such projects made use of Canadian government funds to assist terrorist- or communist-front groups.[56] Such disapproval notwithstanding, activities of this kind demonstrated just how much understandings of mission, and even development itself, had changed in Canada in the course of the 1960s.

Faith in Development and Faith-Based Rifts

. . . To speak of a missions-to-development trajectory and a process of "NGOization" in the churches is by no means to suggest that for those orchestrating the changes their Christian faith had become irrelevant. Sources as different as the files of the CCC's Department of Overseas Missions and late-twentieth-century essay collections on the church coalitions written by scholars and practitioners[57] testify to the concern of the men and women involved to witness to their Christian faith in a relevant way in a rapidly changing world. . . .

Nonetheless, a common theme stands out in trends across the mainline Canadian churches by the end of the 1960s: the churches' social activism had become "unhitched" from its original mandate to further the evangelizing of the wayward at home and to win overseas souls for Christ.[58] The downplaying of evangelism had been a slow and uneven process until the 1960s, even in the ultra-liberal United Church, but by the end of that decade, as one senior churchman observed, evangelism had become a word likely to "turn people off"; he "felt he almost had to apologize for bringing it up at all."[59] Significantly, for the first time in its history, in 1968 the United Church chose a layman, Bob McClure, as its moderator. McClure's exuberant showmanship on behalf of the church's development work following a high-profile career in China and India made him excellent copy in mainstream media as well as the church press. Two years earlier, when the CBC was preparing for its first colour telecast, it sent a documentary crew to India to profile McClure's "war on leprosy, polio, TB, and the population explosion." Following his term as moderator, the now-retired McClure undertook a survey of family-planning needs in Southeast Asia for Oxfam, at the same time looking for a hospital where he could do further volunteer work. Like Legge . . . , McClure had a personal faith life that was important to him, but it was his quotable challenges to traditional Christian theology and his medical activism in the developing world ("he would rather preach family planning than salvation," wrote his biographer) that made him such an appropriate ambassador for the new face of mission.[60] . . .

By the beginning of the 1970s, then, Canada's mainline Protestant churches could frequently make common cause in their overseas work with the federal government and secular NGOs as well as with like-minded Catholic groups. Meanwhile, however, the mainline denominations' new approach to their role in the developing world had been evoking a negative reaction among conservative Christians. The response of conservatives to the waning of the evangelical character of missions was part of a larger response to what was perceived as excessive liberalization on a broad range of social and moral issues in contemporary Canada. One outcome was the formation in 1966 within the Anglican and United churches of conservative subgroups: the Anglican Evangelical Fellowship and the United Church Renewal Fellowship. Members of the Renewal Fellowship were, among other things, "zealous supporters of foreign missions," and for them, the church's

emphasis on social issues was "a diversion from its main business of converting individuals."[61] Many like-minded Christians defected altogether from the United Church and from other mainline denominations. Conservative Christian groups never became as numerous, as politically influential, or as single-mindedly opposed to liberal ideologies and practices within Canada as they became in the United States in the late twentieth century.[62] Nevertheless, by the early 1960s Canadian Protestants who took a strong interest in overseas missions were already showing their preference for an approach that continued to give primacy to evangelization. A 1962 survey conducted by the CCC revealed that by far the largest number of Canadian Protestant missionaries was serving with conservative Canadian mission boards (i.e., boards not affiliated with either the CCC or the WCC) or with congenial US mission boards.[63] *Observer* articles at the beginning of the 1970s confirmed the trend and acknowledged that the gulf "between the liberal social action churches and the conservative evangelicals" was growing all across North America.[64]

Conclusion

The NGOization of the mainline Protestant churches in the 1960s resulted in a progressive bleeding of support to evangelically oriented missionary organizations while failing to capture the imagination and hold the allegiance of young, development-minded, church-raised Christians like my high-school friend. . . . [A]s interviews with some 50 RVs from this era have revealed, by the time they attended university and became CUSO volunteers, many of them were opting out of the religious observances and moral codes of their parents' generation and drawn to the new zeitgeist. The very notion of mission, even in NGOized form, simply did not capture their enthusiasm or speak to their idealism in the way that the new organization did. Thus, while CUSO entered the 1970s with more than 1,300 volunteers serving in more than 40 countries, the United Church, the largest of the mainline Protestant mission-sending agencies, had just 232 personnel, including wives, serving in 24 countries.[65]

Given the defections from the mainline Canadian churches in the 1960s to secular NGOs like CUSO, on the one hand, and to conservative mission organizations, on the other, it might appear that insofar as those mainline churches were concerned a more apt title for this article might have been "When Missions Became Irrelevant." Yet churches like the United Church of Canada did not simply give up on the idea of mission in the tumultuous 1960s. Rather, they sought to reshape it as a mission of service to the developing world in partnership with indigenous churches and in collaboration with inter-church coalitions, secular NGOs, and government agencies like CIDA. Inevitably, there were challenges and ironies aplenty as they sought to escape the legacies of missionary colonialism. To the men and women on the receiving end of interventions by Canadian NGOs, it was perhaps neither important nor easy to determine whether assistance was coming from a secular or a faith-based organization. But within Canada the shift that occurred in the 1960s in the country's historic engagement with non-Western societies was unquestionably significant: the mainline churches that for close to a century had offered humanitarian aid as part of an evangelistic package had reinvented themselves as faith-based NGOs and given way in numbers and importance to secular development agencies like CUSO. It was a particularly telling example of the extent to which, during this transformative decade, the dual forces of secularization and a new global consciousness reshaped Canadian society.

Author's Note: I presented earlier versions of this article at conferences in Vancouver and Bergen in 2008 and at a stimulating research seminar at King's University College in 2009. Richard Allen, Ramsay Cook, Bruce Douville, Karen Dubinsky, and Marguerite Van Die commented insightfully on a later version, as did the editors of this journal and their anonymous reviewers. I thank all of these people for helping to improve this article while taking full responsibility for remaining errors and omissions.

Endnotes

1. Bill McWhinney and Dave Godfrey, eds, *Man Deserves Man: CUSO in Developing Countries* (Toronto: Ryerson Press, 1968); and Ian Smillie, *The Land of Lost Content: A History of CUSO* (Toronto: Deneau, 1985), are valuable insider accounts.

2. My friend died before I began the research on CUSO that led to this article. Her family provided generous access to her letters and diaries.

3. Gilbert Rist, *The History of Development: From Western Origins to Global Faith*, 3rd ed. (London: Zed Books, 2008), 90.

4. General histories of the Canadian churches include John Webster Grant, *The Church in the Canadian Era* (Burlington, ON: Welch Publishing, 1988); and Terence Murphy and Roberto Perin, *A Concise History of Christianity in Canada* (Toronto: Oxford University Press, 1996). David M. Thompson and John Webster Grant have emphasized the uniqueness of the United Church union: Thompson, "Ecumenism," in *Cambridge History of Christianity*, vol. 9, *World Christianities, c. 1914–2000*, ed. Hugh McLeod (Cambridge: Cambridge University Press, 2006), 63; and Grant, "What's Past Is Prologue," in *Voices and Visions: 65 Years of the United Church of Canada*, ed. Grant (Toronto: United Church Publishing House, 1990), 125. Two recent studies of mainline Protestantism dealing with changes analogous to the shift examined in this article are Catherine Gidney, *A Long Eclipse: The Liberal Protestant Establishment and the Canadian University, 1920–1970* (Montreal and Kingston: McGill-Queen's University Press, 2004); and Gary Miedema, *For Canada's Sake: Public Religion, Centennial Celebrations, and the Re-making of Canada in the 1960s* (Montreal and Kingston: McGill-Queen's University Press, 2005).

5. Tim Brodhead and Brent Herbert-Copley, with Anne-Marie Lambert, *Bridges of Hope? Canadian Voluntary Agencies and the Third World* (Ottawa: North-South Institute, 1988). These authors identify faith-based NGOs as having a religious or denominational basis or origin but as doing little in the way of pastoral work or proselytizing. Compare Brian K. Murphy, "Canadian NGOs and the Politics of Participation," in *Conflicts of Interest: Canada and the Third World*, ed. Jamie Swift and Brian Tomlinson (Toronto: Between the Lines, 1991), 165, 171, 186–7.

6   Gidney, *Long Eclipse.*

7   Don Schweitzer, "The Changing Social Imaginary of the United Church of Canada," 8. Schweitzer kindly shared this and several other draft chapters for a forthcoming history of the United Church of Canada under his editorship. The meaning and timing of secularization in the West is, of course, much contested. Nonetheless, recent influential works as different as Callum G. Brown, *The Death of Christian Britain: Understanding Secularization, 1800–2000* (London: Routledge, 2001); Hugh McLeod, *The Religious Crisis of the 1960s* (Oxford: Oxford University Press, 2007); and Charles Taylor, *A Secular Age* (Cambridge: Harvard University Press, 2007), concur that the 1960s marked a fundamental shift in the role of religion as lived experience. For relevant Canadian statistical data, see Stuart Macdonald, "Death of Christian Canada? Do Canadian Church Statistics Support Callum Brown's Theory of Church Decline?" in *Historical Papers 2006/Canadian Society of Church History*, ed. Brian Gobbett, Bruce L. Guenther, and Robynne Rogers Healey, 135–56.

8   Jesse H. Arnup, *A New Church Faces a New World* (Toronto: United Church of Canada, 1937).

9   David J. Bosch, *Transforming Mission: Paradigm Shifts in Theology of Mission* (New York: Orbis Books, 1991).

10   Ruth Compton Brouwer, *Modern Women Modernizing Men: The Changing Missions of Three Professional Women in Asia and Africa, 1902–69* (Vancouver: UBC Press, 2002); and Compton Brouwer, "Canadian Protestant Overseas Missions to the Mid-Twentieth Century: American Influences, Interwar Changes, Long-Term Legacies," in *Empires of Religion*, ed. Hilary Carey (Basingstoke: Palgrave Macmillan, 2008), 288–310; also Robert Wright, *A World Mission: Canadian Protestantism and the Quest for a New International Order, 1918–1939* (Montreal and Kingston: McGill-Queen's University Press, 1991). William R. Hutchison and Jeffrey Cox have explored this "re-thinking missions" process in the United States and Britain. See Hutchison, *Errand to the World: American Protestant Thought and Foreign Missions* (Chicago: University of Chicago Press, 1987), esp. chaps 5 and 6; and Cox, *The British Missionary Enterprise since 1700* (New York: Routledge, 2008), esp. chaps 10 and 11.

11   Marlin VanElderen, *Introducing the World Council of Churches* (Geneva: WCC Publications, 1990). Critiques of the liberalizing WCC include Harvey T. Hoekstra, *The World Council of Churches and the Demise of Evangelism* (Wheaton, IL: Tyndale House, 1979); and Ernest W. Lefever, *Amsterdam to Nairobi: The World Council of Churches and the Third World* (Washington: Ethics and Public Policy Center, 1979).

12   Faris to son Ken, 5 February 1951, from Hong Kong, in Donald K. Faris Family Papers, privately held. Hockin's remarks are in Donna Sinclair, *Crossing Worlds: The Story of the Woman's Missionary Society of the United Church of Canada* (Toronto: United Church Publishing House, 1992), 91.

13   Hoekstra, *World Council of Churches*, 27. Hoekstra sees the change as a regrettable outcome of the integration of the International Missionary Council into the WCC at its historic assembly at New Delhi in 1961: "So strong were . . . [the winds of change] that the 's' was blown right off the word 'missions.'. . . Only later would many realize that much more than a change in spelling was involved."

14   *World Mission: Report of the Commission on World Mission* ([Toronto]: General Council, United Church of Canada, 1966), 3. For the organizational changes described in this paragraph, see 68.

15   Ibid., "Recommendations," 135–9.

16   A.C. Forrest, "Radical Change in Mission," *United Church Observer*, October 1966, 10 (hereafter *Observer*).

17   Roy E. Webster to "Dear Friends," 20 June 1972, writing for BWM, with attached DWO constitution, in file 11, Agenda, BWM, 1972, box 3, BWM, United Church of Canada (UCC), United Church of Canada Archives (hereafter UCA). As well as the former BWM, the DWO included the Committee on Overseas Relief and Inter-Church Aid and the Committee on World Development and Relief.

18   Ruth Compton Brouwer, *New Women for God: Canadian Presbyterian Women and India Missions, 1876–1914* (Toronto: University of Toronto Press, 1990), chap. 4.

19   *World Mission*, 62, 78–85. For 1966, the BWM's total financial commitment for programs in 14 areas of the world was just under $3 million, of which $794,341 was earmarked for India (85). The Malwa Council was part of the United Church of Northern India (UCNI), and while mission boards in various parts of the world supported the UCNI, the BWM was evidently the only external agency supporting the work in Malwa.

20   Executive Committee Minutes, 9 June 1967, 299–300, file 2, box 2, Minutes of Annual General Meeting (AGM) and Executive Committee meetings, BWM, UCC, UCA.

21   See Introduction, "Records of the Area Secretary Relating to India," Division of World Outreach, United Church of Canada, series 8, Finding Aid 321, UCA, for an overview of the changes under consideration and the proposed timeline. BWM executive members Floyd Honey and Wilna Thomas provided lengthy reports on visits to India. File 21, box 5 and file 15, box 7, BWM-Records Relating to the India Mission Work, UCC, UCA. Thomas regarded the ecumenical UCNI as a more reliable partner than the Malwa Council itself.

22 The problems created for Christian medical work in India by corrupt or self-serving Christian leaders was a recurring theme during these years in the *Journal of the Christian Medical Association of India* (hereafter *CMAI Journal*). See, for example, "Secretarial Notes," January 1966, 41–5; and J.C. David, "The Challenge," October 1967, 491–2.

23 "Food for India," *Observer*, 1 September 1966, 10; "Preventive Medical Secretary's Notes," *CMAI Journal*, March 1969, 155 (for quotation).

24 David R. Morrison, *Aid and Ebb Tide: A History of CIDA and Canadian Development Assistance* (Waterloo, ON: Waterloo University Press, in collaboration with the North-South Institute, 1998), app. C, provides statistics on government-to-government aid.

25 Joint meeting of Executive Committee and Policy and Strategy Committee, 21 June 1968,115, and of Interim Executive Committee, 20 September 1968, 145, file 3, box 2, Executive Committee and AGM Minutes, 1968, BWM, UCC, UCA. The AGM minutes, p. 72, in ibid., refer to an enquiry from Ottawa to the Canadian Council of Churches "regarding possible participation in new external aid projects by mission boards" and commend the federal government for its increased support for international development. See also "Well-digger to India," *Observer*, 15 February 1966, 35; and "More Water for India," *Observer*, 1 July 1967, 21.

26 Morrison, *Aid and Ebb Tide*, 21, 68–70.

27 See, for example, "The Norman MacKenzie War on Poverty," *Observer*, 1 February 1968, 12–15, 40; minutes of Interim Executive Committee, 18 January 1962, 27, and 14 December 1962, 200, in file 1, box 1, Minutes, BWM, UCC, UCA. MacKenzie, on furlough from his missionary work in India, had been funded by the External Aid office in 1961 as an agricultural adviser in Nigeria. In 1962 Ottawa and the church also cooperated to get powdered milk into targeted areas of Africa.

28 Brouwer, "Canadian Protestant Overseas Missions."

29 Minutes of BWM, AGM, 13 April 1964, 58–9, file 4, box 1, Minutes, 1964, BWM, UCC, UCA, for quotation, and, regarding Honey, minutes of AGM beginning 22 March 1965, 296, in ibid., file 6. Katherine Hockin, "My Pilgrimage in Mission," *International Bulletin of Missionary Research* 12, no. 1 (January 1988): 23–30.

30 Minutes of Executive Committee meeting, 8 June 1962, including "Draft Statement on Angola," 145–6, file 1, box 1, and, regarding Webster's meeting with Paul Martin Sr, minutes of Executive Committee meeting, 7 November 1963, 422, file 2, BWM, UCC, UCA.

31 Walter Strangway, "Terror in Angola," *Observer*, 1 February 1968, 3; Sidney Gilchrist, "My Africa," *Observer*, 15 April 1968, 11 (for quotation); and Patricia Clarke, "Hanging on in Angola: Is the Price Too High?," 15 November 1968, 6.

32 Frances Walbridge, "I Must Speak Out about Murder," *Observer*, September 1970, 18–20.

33 Still, in one of his many statements on Angola in 1968, Dr Gilchrist was sharply critical of the Canadian government for abstaining from voting at the UN, even when "votes of censure against Portugal for its colonial policy are passed by tremendous majorities." "The Truth about Angola," *Observer*, 15 February 1968, 3–4. Canadian policy is discussed in Robin O. Matthews, "Canada and Anglophone Africa," in *Canada and the Third World*, ed. Peyton V. Lyon and Tareq Y. Ismael (Toronto: Macmillan, 1976), 67–71.

34 At the same meeting the board asked the church's General Council to press the federal government on the subject of Vietnam and urge it to call on the US government to halt its bombing campaign. Minutes of General Meeting beginning 18 March 1968, 37–9, 45–6, file 3, box 2, Executive Committee Minutes, BWM, UCC, UCA.

35 Robert Matthews, Conclusion, in *Canadian Churches and Foreign Policy*, ed. Bonnie Greene (Toronto: James Lorimer, 1990), 161; Cranford Pratt, *Canadian International Development Assistance Policies: An Appraisal*, ed. Cranford Pratt (Montreal and Kingston: McGill-Queen's University Press, 1994), chaps 4 and 13. "Most scholarly commentators," Pratt writes, "have concluded that humanitarian considerations have played little role within government in the shaping of . . . [aid] policies" (334). There appear, however, to be few close-grained analyses of specific efforts to influence such policies. An exception from this period involving both the churches and CUSO is Donald Barry's "Interest Groups and the Foreign Policy Process: The Case of Biafra," in *Pressure Group Behaviour in Canadian Politics*, ed. A. Paul Pross (Toronto: McGraw-Hill Ryerson, 1975), 117–47.

36 "Seek More Aid," *Observer*, 15 June 1969, 31.

37 *Observer*, July 1970, back cover, citing information from Magazine Advertising Bureau of Canada, and page 5, for the current circulation figure of 302,396.

38 Canada's tendency to take a moralizing tone in foreign policy pronouncements even if it did not follow through with corresponding actions perhaps owed something to the church's position-taking. See Norman Hillmer and J.L. Granatstein, *Empire to Umpire: Canada and the World into the Twenty-First Century* (Toronto: Nelson Thomson, 2008), 347, for the tart observation cited there that Canada "all too often sounded like the United Church at the United Nations."

39 Brouwer, *New Women*, 180–1; A. Hamish Ion, *The Cross and the Rising Sun: The Canadian Protestant Missionary Movement in the Japanese Empire, 1872–1931* (Waterloo, ON: Wilfrid Laurier University Press, 1990), 188–9.

40   Interim Executive Committee Minutes, 16, file 4, box 2, BWM, UCC, UCA; "Should Christians Support Guerrillas?," *Observer*, November 1970, 11; and "Board Supports Grants for African Liberation," *Observer*, January 1971, 46–7.

41   Addresses on "Mission in the 70s" in minutes of annual meeting beginning 23 November 1970, file 5, box 2, Minutes, BWM, UCC, UCA.

42   *World Mission*, 99.

43   Minutes of AGM beginning 18 March 1968, 21–2, file 3, box 2, BWM, UCC, UCA. The personal and professional qualifications required of missionaries in the Handbook were reprinted in *World Mission*, 95–6. The first two personal qualifications *did* seem to require some form of evangelistic outreach, hence the board's readiness in 1968 to distance itself from the language of the Handbook.

44   Minutes of Interim Executive Committee, 21 February 1969, app. C, "Reflections," 22–3, file 4, box 2, BWM, UCC, UCA.

45   Editorial, *Observer*, 1 May 1968, 10. References to CUSO as an alternative way to serve one's "fellow men in developing countries" became something of a refrain in the mid- to late 1960s; for example, "Quotes from Our Missionaries," *Observer*, 15 October 1966, 24.

46   "Missionaries and Mission," *Observer*, 1 June 1969, 10; and "The Crisis in the United Church," *Observer*, 1 March 1960, 7.

47   "Only the Skilled Wanted," and Editorial, *Observer*, 1 May 1968, 5, 10.

48   "Board of World Mission/Chairman's Report/ November 1971," with agenda for AGM beginning 1 November 1971, file 10, box 3, BWM, UCC, UCA.

49   McWhinney, Introduction, in *Man Deserves Man*; and Smillie, *Land of Lost Content*, chap. 2. The major repository for CUSO records to the early 1980s, including those of COV, is Canadian University Service Overseas, I 323, MG 28, Library and Archives Canada.

50   Keith Spicer, *Life Sentences: Memoirs of an Incorrigible Canadian* (Toronto: McClelland and Stewart, 2004), chap. 5; and Donald K. Faris, *To Plow with Hope* (New York: Harper & Brothers, 1958).

51   Donald Wilson to John Conway, 22 March 1961, containing copy of Wilson's confidential memo "To members of the D.O.M. [Department of Overseas Missions], Sub-Committee on 'Volunteer Service,'" in file 1, box 22, Canadian University Service Overseas, John S. Conway fonds, University of British Columbia Archives.

52   Donald Wilson, "Volunteers for Overseas Service," presented as part of CCC's Department of Overseas Missions Report of Annual Meeting, 21–2 February 1962, file 6, box 4, BWM, subseries 1, Canadian Council of Churches, Department of Overseas Missions (hereafter CCC/DOM), BWM, UCC, UCA.

53   The CUSO request is discussed in R.M. Bennett to Dear Friends, 19 October 1962, in ibid., file 4, box 4, Correspondence. Bennett, a veteran Baptist missionary, had initially been wary of COV/CUSO.

54   Smillie, *Lost Content*, chap. 5; and "Father G. [Guilbeault] Honored in Lesotho," *Forum* 6, no. 3 (1978): 23–4.

55   *The Black Paper*, first published in the September 1970 issue of *Behind the Headlines*, was later made available as a pamphlet by the Canadian Institute of International Affairs. As John S. Saul notes, *The Black Paper* became a benchmark document in articulating anti-apartheid sentiment; see Saul, "Liberation Support and Anti-Apartheid Work as Seeds of Global Consciousness," in *New World Coming: The Sixties and the Shaping of Global Consciousness*, ed. Karen Dubinsky *et al.* (Toronto: Between the Lines, 2009), 135–6.

56   The most extreme criticism would be made in Branka Lapajne's *CUSO and Radicalism* (Toronto: Citizens for Foreign Aid Reform, 1983). While specifically targeting CUSO, this work depicted various Protestant and Roman Catholic groups as fellow travellers in a "terrorist-support network" (Introduction).

57   Christopher Lind and Joe Mihevic, eds, *Coalitions for Justice: The Story of Canada's Interchurch Coalitions* (Ottawa: Novalis, 1994); and Cranford Pratt and Roger Hutchison, eds, *Christian Faith and Economic Justice: Towards a Canadian Perspective* (Burlington, ON: Trinity, 1988).

58   Grant, *Modern Era*, 242.

59   "Why Don't People Listen to the Church?," *Observer*, April 1971, 6; also David Plaxton, "'We Will Evangelize with a Whole Gospel or None': Evangelicalism and the United Church of Canada," in *Aspects of the Canadian Evangelical Experience*, ed. George Rawlyk (Montreal and Kingston: McGill-Queen's University Press, 1997), 106–22.

60   "The New Moderator/Dr Bob McClure," *Observer*, 1 October 1968, 10–12, 26; "McClure Off and Running," *Observer*, June 1971, 47; and "Incredible Dr McClure," *Star Weekly*, 3 September 1966 (for first quotation and reference to CBC documentary). Munroe Scott's two-volume biography of McClure portrays him as an iconoclastic and larger-than-life figure: *McClure: The China Years of Dr Bob McClure* (Toronto: Canec, 1977); and *McClure: Years of Challenge* (Toronto: Canec, 1985), also issued as a Penguin paperback. The quotation is from the 1985 Penguin edition, 111.

61   Miedema, *For Canada's Sake*, 60. Quoted statements about the Renewal Fellowship are from Grant's "What's Past Is Prologue," in *Voices and Visions*, 141.

62   John G. Stackhouse, Jr, "Bearing Witness: Christian Groups Engage Canadian Politics since the 1960s"; and Sam Reimer, "A Generic Evangelicalism? Comparing Evangelical Subcultures in Canada and the United States," in *Rethinking Church, State and*

Modernity: Canada between Europe and the USA, ed. David Lyon and Marguerite Van Die (Toronto: University of Toronto Press, 2000), chaps 6 and 12.

63   Minutes, including "Report of Survey on the Canadian Missionary Overseas," 19 November 1962, file 6, box 4, BWM, subseries 1, CCC/DOM, UCC, UCA.

64   Leslie K. Tarr, "Let's Look at My Evangelical Friends," *Observer*, April 1971, 16–19; and "New Hope for Evangelism," *Observer*, March 1972, 10 (for quotation). Tarr argued against the tendency to portray evangelicals as lacking in "social consciousness."

65   "CUSO Facts and Figures," leaflet in file 11, box 6, CUSO, Conway fonds, UBC Archives; *United Church of Canada Year Book* [1972], 2:200. In this article

I have done no more than touch on the gendered dimensions of NGOization. Given the fact that the majority of missionaries had traditionally been women and that women were proportionately overrepresented in CUSO, the shift in their loyalties warrants further investigation. It may well reflect an element of what Callum Brown, writing of 1960s Britain, calls "the end of evangelical femininity and piety," for him a crucial factor in the "death" of "Christian Britain" (*Death of Christian Britain*, 196). Certainly, the lure of development work for women came much earlier than Barbara Heron suggests in *Desire for Development: Whiteness, Gender, and the Helping Imperative* (Waterloo, ON: Wilfrid Laurier University Press, 2007), 159n21, and, I suspect, for more complex reasons.

CHAPTER 9

Canada and the United States

◎ 9.1: FOREIGN INVESTMENT AND THE PARADOX OF ECONOMIC NATIONALISM

Stephen Azzi

In postwar Canada, economic nationalism has usually taken the form of opposition to foreign investment. At other times in the country's history, however, economic nationalism meant something quite different. The case of John Charles Rykert demonstrates this point. Rykert, the Conservative member of Parliament for Lincoln, Ontario, from 1878 to 1891, advocated a protective tariff, one high enough to restrict imports and shelter domestic industry. He thus fit into the long line of economic nationalists who believed that protectionism was necessary to preserve Canada's very existence. Yet Rykert's views would have been disconcerting to later nationalists. In 1879 he argued that the tariff would help to provide employment for Canadians by "bringing a large amount of capital into Canada": "The Americans, if debarred from our markets, would start manufacturing establishments here."[1] American investment was not a threat to his concept of nationalism but an integral part of it. Although Rykert's views had no significant impact on the Canadian intellectual tradition, they illustrate the paradox of economic nationalism in Canada. One form of the ideology, protectionism, led to widespread American ownership of Canadian industry, which a later generation of nationalists thought threatened Canada's economic and political life. . . .

For many years John A. Macdonald's National Policy dominated Canada's approach to international economic issues.[2] Implemented in stages beginning in 1879, the policy consisted of a high tariff wall designed to discourage the import of manufactured goods. The tariff, which before the National Policy had been set at 17.5 per cent for most manufactured goods, generally rose to between 20 and 35 per cent. The average duty increased from 21.4 per cent in 1878 to 26.1 per cent in 1880 and to 31.9 per cent in 1888.[3]

American companies increasingly manufactured their products in Canadian branch plants. Many factors explain the establishment of these factories in Canada, including the abundance of natural resources, the stable market, the proximity to the United States, and the common language and similar culture of the United States and English Canada. The main motives, however, were to avoid paying the onerous tariff and to comply with Canada's 1872 patent law, which required firms to establish Canadian manufacturing facilities within two years to maintain their patent rights.

The National Policy did not signal the beginnings of foreign investment in Canada. Outside capital had been entering the country for as long as there had been investment opportunities. In the 1840s and 1850s high levels of British portfolio investment (usually bonds sold to investors) had helped to finance the railway and other Canadian infrastructure. The National Policy did, however, signal a turn from British to American capital and from portfolio to direct investment (the controlling ownership of companies operating in Canada), a shift that largely resulted from the federal government's policy of using the tariff to promote domestic manufacturing. Provinces and municipalities also adopted a policy of encouraging investment, using tax breaks, cash incentives, and free land, water, and electricity to lure investors.[4] Long before the word "globalization" entered the vocabulary, corporations dangled the promise of economic development before competing jurisdictions in an effort to secure financial concessions.

The impact of the National Policy was unmistakable and was no surprise to those interested in public affairs. Throughout the 1880s and 1890s, as historian Michael Bliss has observed, the press reported on the role of the tariff in fostering investment, showing no particular concern about the growth of foreign ownership.[5] During a worldwide depression, which had hit in 1873 and had lingering effects until as late as 1896, no one suggested that Canada should refuse to accept, or even discourage, new investment from the United States. In the laissez-faire world of nineteenth-century economic thinking, the notion of state intervention in global capital flows was alien; at most, the state could bait the hook by providing incentives for foreign investors.

Macdonald's policy endured for more than half a century, in part because he had artfully presented it in a patriotic package. By using the term "National Policy," by emphasizing that protectionism would lead to the development of industry in Canada, and by arguing that it would prevent American annexation, Macdonald turned the tariff into a national symbol. Tariff protection, in the words of historian Craig Brown, had taken on "a much larger meaning than mere tinkering with customs schedules."[6] From a later perspective, however, the policy does not seem nationalist at all. Although it did stimulate industry in Canada, it created a reliance on foreign ownership. Moreover, like other nationalist policies, it dealt less with the concerns of Canada as a whole than with those of certain areas and classes. It helped to build industry in Ontario and Quebec, stimulating employment in both provinces but not in the rest of the country. . . . [7]

The National Policy remained in place long after Macdonald's death. A policy of significant tariff reduction, at least on American products, was for many years political suicide in Canada. Subsequent governments preserved the tariff with only minor adjustments, leaving the National Policy largely intact for almost 60 years. They also continued to court foreign investors. At the turn of the century, for example, the Liberal government of Sir Wilfrid Laurier encouraged Francis H. Clergue, an American promoter, to develop the area around Sault Ste Marie, Ontario, where he created a hydroelectric power development, a pulp mill, a mine, iron smelters, and a railway.[8] Doubts occasionally surfaced about these policies in the early years of the century, but such voices were seldom heard.[9]

In 1911 Laurier's government negotiated a trade agreement with the United States, removing the duties on most natural products and a few other commodities. Fearing that this was the first step toward free trade in manufactured goods, critics attacked the policy, arguing that the presence of foreign direct investment was proof of the effectiveness of the tariff.[10] At a large public meeting shortly after the agreement was announced, Hamilton mayor George Harmon Lees declared that the 33 American factories in his city "were brought to Canada by tariff restrictions. . . . The proposed pact is more than likely to change all this."[11] Voters agreed, particularly in southern Ontario, the area that benefited most from Canada's branch-plant economy.[12] On election day, they rejected Laurier and his trade policy.

Laurier's defeat in 1911 meant that Canada would stay the protectionist path and would thus continue to foster foreign ownership. . . .

The Liberals returned to office in October 1935. Before the year's end Prime Minister Mackenzie King negotiated a trade agreement with the United States, the first since 1854 and one that the two countries extended in 1938 with a more comprehensive deal.[13] Tariffs remained high, but the process of their reduction—that is, the process of dismantling the National Policy—had begun. During the Second World War, King's government agreed to the free movement of defence products across the Canadian-American border, an arrangement recorded in the Hyde Park declaration of 1941. After the war, the pattern of tariff reduction continued. Canada was one of the 23 original signatories of the 1947 General Agreement on Tariffs and Trade (GATT), an agreement that internationalists hailed, believing that the movement of goods and capital across national borders was essential to world peace and economic development. Major tariff reductions negotiated under GATT in 1947 and 1951 further advanced their cause. King even considered free trade with the United States in 1948, although he backed away, fearing that he would be accused, as his mentor Sir Wilfrid Laurier had been in 1911, of taking steps that would lead to the American annexation of Canada.[14] Still, because of gradual, multilateral reductions, Canadian tariffs dropped 25 per cent between 1939 and 1955.[15]

At the same time, the federal government continued to promote foreign investment. Policymakers wanted to ensure the maximum growth of the economy and, with memories of the Great Depression still fresh, did not believe that they should spurn outside capital; rather, they now believed that they had to compete more vigorously for capital. Canada no longer enjoyed its privileged position as a home for American investment, as other countries were becoming increasingly effective at luring capital. Minister of Trade and Commerce C.D. Howe believed that to facilitate development he had to encourage all investment and not discriminate against non-Canadians, a policy that included selling federal Crown corporations to foreign buyers. Howe sold Victory Aircraft to the British-owned A.V. Roe Company, Research Enterprises Limited to Corning Glass of the United States, and Canadair Limited to a group of its executives, who then sold it, with Howe's help, to the American-owned Electric Boat Company (later General Dynamics). Although Howe did not use the tariff as a tool, his goal of attracting foreign funds to develop industry in Canada was essentially the same as the one pursued by Macdonald in the previous century.[16] Howe's program was the National Policy by other means.

Short descriptions of investment levels in Canada are inevitably misleading, with both supporters and opponents of foreign capital using official statistics to bolster their arguments. On the one hand, outside investment in non-financial industries stood at $9.9 billion in 1955, having increased by at least $700 million in each of the four previous years. Most imported capital came as direct investment, bringing with it control of Canadian companies. Furthermore, it was concentrated in certain sectors, with 63 per cent of the petroleum and natural gas industry and 58 per cent of mining and smelting held by foreigners in 1955. On the other hand, foreign investment was not growing significantly faster than the Canadian economy as a whole. Foreign capital stood at 32 per cent of all investment in Canada in 1948 and had increased only to 33 per cent by 1955.[17] As the nationalist economist Cy Gonick pointed out, "Most of the American-owned companies in Canada were already established by the end of 1920."[18]

The statistics are not particularly helpful in explaining why economic nationalism shifted, beginning in the mid-1950s, from trade protectionism to a preoccupation with foreign-owned firms. Perhaps the most common interpretation is the one advanced by economist Peter Karl Kresl: "By 1955 or 1960 . . . the economic dependency of Canada on the United States had developed to such an extent that an increasing number of Canadians were able to recognize that dependency for what it is, and to feel uneasy about it."[19] The available statistics, however, do not bear out this interpretation. Canada's dependence on the

United States, if measured by the proportion of Canadian industry owned by Americans, was not much greater in 1955 or 1960 than it had been in 1930 or 1948.[20] A more satisfying analysis is one that places the rise of concern over investment within the broader contexts both of burgeoning anti-Americanism and of a growing affluence that allowed some Canadians to believe that the country did not need more American capital.

The early postwar years were a period of exceptional growth for Canada. In real terms, the gross national product per capita doubled between 1939 and 1955.[21] This economic expansion was reflected in a noticeable improvement in Canadian living standards. In 1941 almost all homes were heated with coal or wood, 40 per cent lacked piped water, less than half had a bath or shower, barely more than half had flush toilets, and 80 per cent stored food in iceboxes.[22] Over the next 30 years the

situation changed dramatically as most Canadians installed gas or oil furnaces, flush toilets, bathtubs, and refrigerators. Only one in nine Canadians owned an automobile in 1941; by 1971 the figure was one in three.[23] All regions of the country benefited from the postwar boom but some more than others. Most foreign subsidiaries were in Ontario and Quebec, areas that had higher average wages and lower unemployment levels than the rest of the country. . . . In the period before 1939 few Canadians could imagine doing without foreign capital, which had built hundreds of factories and employed thousands of workers. In the context of postwar prosperity, some Canadians, particularly in southern Ontario, began to flirt with the idea that they could be selective about the investment that they would allow into their country.

In 1955, against this backdrop, the federal government appointed Toronto business person

Library and Archives Canada, Mikan No.: 4297995

Members of the Royal Commission on Canada's Economic Prospects, an inquiry established to investigate the long-term prospects of the Canadian economy.

Walter Gordon to chair the Royal Commission on Canada's Economic Prospects, an examination of the long-term outlook of the country's economy. In this position, Gordon played an essential role in redefining Canadian economic nationalism. At the outset of the investigation, Gordon announced that he would be interested in foreign economic influence and encouraged those submitting briefs or testifying before the commission to address the subject. Many witnesses responded to Gordon's prompting. Organized labour was the most vocal critic of foreign ownership, complaining that it meant fewer manufacturing jobs because foreign-owned companies were more likely to export Canadian natural resources to the United States for processing. Supporters of foreign investment, including the government of British Columbia, the Canadian Manufacturers' Association, and a few large corporations, insisted that outside capital was necessary for Canada's development.[24] This clash of ideas sparked the first widespread and critical consideration of foreign investment in Canada's history.[25]

After the hearings, the commission issued two widely circulated reports, a preliminary report in December 1956 and a final report in November 1957. The two documents raised doubts about the value of foreign ownership, suggesting that *perhaps* foreign-owned firms *might* be less likely to employ Canadians and to purchase their supplies and components in Canada. Despite saying that "it would be unfair to overstress these unfavourable operating patterns," the commission proposed measures to encourage the sale of some shares to Canadians, thus ensuring a Canadian point of view in the management of foreign-controlled companies.[26]

The commission also hinted at a link between economic and political dependence: "Many Canadians are worried about such a large degree of economic decision-making being in the hands of non-residents or in the hands of Canadian companies controlled by non-residents" because it "might lead to economic domination by the United States and eventually to the loss of our political independence." The report did not, however, put forward any argumentation to support this concern or even say whether the commissioners thought it justified.[27] Despite the vagueness of the reports, they generated widespread interest in the investment issue, largely because of the media's coverage of the commission's activities.[28] Recognizing that this issue was catching the public's attention, several Conservative politicians began in 1956 to speak out against foreign control.[29] "Canadians should declare their economic independence of the United States," Conservative leader George Drew told a Hamilton audience days after the commission completed its public hearings.[30] These comments foreshadowed the position that the Tories would take during the historic pipeline debate. In May and June 1956 Parliament engaged in a heated battle over a government bill that would allow a largely American-financed company to build a pipeline to transport natural gas from Alberta to Ontario. The opposition denounced the government, both for trying to curtail debate on the bill and for expanding American economic power in Canada.

The pipeline debate signalled the end of a long period of Liberal dominance that had stretched from 1935. In the 1957 general election, a new Conservative leader, John Diefenbaker, exploited the developing scepticism about American economic power to bring his party to power with a minority government. Throughout the campaign he attacked foreign investment and the development of the country's resources by Americans.[31] He continued the assault in the election of 1958, when his party won a sweeping majority of the seats in the Commons. "There is a very definite feel of nationalism in Canada—anti-Americanism if you will," Walter Gordon wrote to Liberal leader Lester Pearson in 1958, "and the Tories capitalized on this."[32]

Yet, once in power, Diefenbaker did little to carry out the promise of his campaign speeches. As prime minister, he frequently peppered his remarks with nationalist rhetoric and may well have considered himself an economic nationalist, but his ability to develop policy was limited, and his cabinet, particularly Finance Minister Donald Fleming, opposed measures that would upset the party's business supporters in Toronto and Montreal. The government did introduce some nationalist measures, such as legislation to restrict foreign control of insurance companies, broadcast outlets, and firms applying for oil and gas leases in the North and offshore. And although the 15 per cent withholding tax on interest and dividend payments was extended to non-residents, this measure was designed less to reduce foreign control than to address unemployment and foreign exchange problems.

These measures did not affect ownership in any but a few narrow areas, and Diefenbaker shunned policies that would have a broader effect. Concerned about Canada's economic dependence on the United States, the prime minister announced in 1957 that he would divert 15 per cent of the country's trade to Britain, but he backed away from the proposal almost immediately. He buried the Gordon report, distrusting the Liberal ties of the commission's chair. When the governor of the Bank of Canada, James Coyne, pursued a tight monetary policy to reduce foreign ownership, the government, concerned about the impact on unemployment, publicly denigrated him and forced him from office. This record is not surprising. An economic downturn began in 1957, a slump that preoccupied the government for the better part of four years and diminished public support for nationalist measures. By the time the Diefenbaker government fell in 1963, it had accomplished little to assert Canada's economic independence from the United States. Indeed, during its six years in office, American capital had increased from 26 to 28 per cent of all investment in Canada.[33]

Gordon became finance minister when the Liberals returned to power in 1963, but he was no more able than Diefenbaker to implement nationalist measures. For Gordon, the problem was not a shortage of ideas. He had spent much of the previous decade developing strategies to limit foreign investment in Canada. His difficulty was that he never convinced the public, the Liberal Party, or even his cabinet colleagues of the value of his plans. In his first budget as finance minister, Gordon introduced both a 30 per cent tax

on foreign takeovers of Canadian firms and tax incentives to encourage foreign companies to sell shares to Canadians. Faced with vehement opposition from the business community and lacking support in cabinet, the finance minister was forced to withdraw the takeover tax. In his remaining two years in the finance portfolio, Gordon accomplished little to reduce the level of foreign investment in Canada. He advised Prime Minister Lester Pearson to call an election in 1965 and resigned when it failed to produce a Liberal majority. Out of cabinet, as a backbench member of Parliament, he tried to have the Liberal Party adopt his ideas at a policy conference in October 1966, but the delegates soundly rejected his proposals.

Gordon returned to the Pearson cabinet in 1967, determined to tackle the problem of foreign ownership. Entrusted with drafting a report on the issue, he recruited eight university economists, including Mel Watkins, Abraham Rotstein, Stephen Hymer, and Ed Safarian. The resulting study, known as the Watkins Report after the task force's chair, was the most reasonable of the era's several government reports on the issue. The economists rejected the idea that the government force "any wholesale substitution of domestic for foreign capital over any short period of time." Canadians had to accept a high level of foreign investment but could work to maximize its benefits and reduce its costs. One of the costs was extraterritoriality, the application of foreign laws to foreign-owned companies in Canada. The United States' Trading with the Enemy Act, for example, banned American-owned companies, including those in Canada, from doing business with countries designated as enemies of the United States. This led to one of the most publicized cases of extraterritoriality: Ford Motors' 1958 decision to prevent its Canadian subsidiary from selling trucks to China. The Watkins Report recommended measures that would stop American law from limiting the operations of companies located in Canada. The task force was also concerned about a lack of competition in the Canadian economy, the result of the dominance of a few large, foreign firms. In response, it urged the government to strengthen anti-combines legislation and to reduce the tariff.[34] This was a view influenced by economist John Kenneth Galbraith, who argued that multinational corporations were powerful enough to shape the larger economic environment and that government had to act as a "countervailing power."[35] These recommendations were far from radical, but the Pearson government refused to endorse the report, and Gordon again resigned from cabinet, having never convinced his colleagues of the need to limit foreign capital.

Gordon's political defeat came at the dawn of a new nationalist era. Opposition to foreign ownership flourished in Canada in the late 1960s and early 1970s. The country was experiencing unprecedented growth in personal income, an economic boom that changed how many viewed American capital. Foreign investment might have been necessary in an earlier age, said Gonick in 1970, but "now our income is among the highest in the world—and we are one of the greatest savers in the world."[36]

A significant demographic shift further bolstered the opposition to foreign control. Canadian politics became radicalized as the first baby boomers came of age and an increasing number of young people became engaged in public debate. The *Toronto Star*, the largest circulation newspaper in the country, reflected the new mood and promoted policies to distance Canada from the United States, printing nearly all of Walter Gordon's pronouncements on the front page. A 1967 poll showed that 60 per cent of Canadians thought that Canada now had "enough U.S. capital," compared with 46 per cent just three years earlier.[37] Gordon himself helped to foster this flourishing movement, providing funding for nationalist organizations and for the publication of books critical of federal economic policies. Although defeated in cabinet, he now found that many Canadians were heeding his call.

Much of Gordon's success in developing a nationalist movement can be attributed to circumstances beyond his control. In the late 1960s and early 1970s an ugly side of the United States emerged with that country's war in Vietnam, the struggle over civil rights, and riots in American cities and on college campuses. The result, in the words of historian Frank Underhill, was that Canadians could not "discuss our relations with the United States in a cool, rational frame of mind."[38] Increasingly, the two countries appeared to have profoundly different values, as Canada's neighbour came to symbolize violence both at home and abroad. American corporations looked no better. Galbraith's influential books *The Affluent Society* and *The New Industrial State* portrayed an unhealthy marketplace controlled not by individuals but by large corporations that moulded consumer behaviour.[39] Although often dismissed by mainstream economists, Galbraith's work was widely read in Canada and throughout the English-speaking world. American lawyer and consumer advocate Ralph Nader also received much attention in Canada after publishing *Unsafe at Any Speed*, a book that exposed the automotive industry's lack of concern for public safety.[40] Ignored originally by the American networks, Nader made his North American television debut in November 1965 on the CBC program *This Hour Has Seven Days*.[41] His book helped to inspire the consumer protection movement in both the United States and Canada, which in turn led to many more disturbing revelations about the activities of large multinational corporations.

The growing suspicion of both the United States and American corporations found its outlet in the New Nationalism, a movement with intellectual roots in the Gordon Commission of the mid-1950s. Concern centred on the impact of branch plants on both the economy and Canadian sovereignty. "The Americanization of Canada is first and foremost a function of the penetration of the Canadian economy by American monopoly capital," wrote political scientist Ian Lumsden in 1970.[42] For the nationalists, everything else—trade, culture, defence, foreign policy—was subordinated to the investment question. . . .

Nationalists had three fundamental concerns about the large American economic presence in Canada, ideas first expressed tentatively in the Gordon Commission reports. First, they charged that foreign ownership had long been increasing at a rapid pace, an argument that implied that it would not be long before Americans owned all Canadian business. Nationalists usually advanced this claim either without evidence or with the support of figures demonstrating a rise in the dollar value of American investments. Ignored were statistics revealing that the percentage of the Canadian economy owned by Americans was increasing only marginally, if at all, and that a surge in domestic investment matched the growth in foreign ownership. Second, nationalists criticized the performance of branch plants, repeating the Gordon Commission's suspicions about the unwillingness of foreign-owned companies to conduct research in Canada or to seek export markets and the preference of these companies for importing parts and for hiring non-Canadian executives and professional firms. Third, nationalists expressed concerns about the impact of foreign investment on Canadian sovereignty. They asserted vaguely and without much explanation that foreign control of Canadian business would eventually lead to the loss of the country's independence. More specifically, and more convincingly, they objected to extraterritoriality, the intrusion of foreign laws into Canada.

Why was anti-American sentiment channelled into a movement to restrict foreign capital rather than into efforts to cut flows of American goods or culture? One reason was that high tariffs were falling from favour. Nationalist intellectuals understood the relationship between the tariff and investment, much as John A. Macdonald had in the previous century. Support for trade protectionism largely disappeared, as many nationalists advocated lowering tariffs to remove a key incentive for companies to create and maintain branch plants.[43] High tariffs also found little public backing, as Canadians were unwilling to forego the American consumer goods that had become such an important part of Canadian life. Many Canadians might have thought that they could turn away future American investment, but they did not want to live without American televisions or stereos.

Canadians had also developed a taste for American music, television, movies, and magazines, so cultural nationalism could never win as much support as opposition to foreign ownership.

The government created Canadian-content regulations for television and radio and amended the tax laws to help Canadian magazines, but these measures had limited appeal for most nationalists. Mel Hurtig, a prominent leader of the movement, dismissed the government's decision to end special tax breaks for *Time* and *Reader's Digest*, saying that this measure was 43rd on a list of 45 nationalist priorities.[44]

Economic nationalism had widespread appeal in the late 1960s and 1970s and, in the words of sociologist Gordon Laxer, "became part of what it meant to be Canadian," at least for a time.[45] Michael Bliss, now a historian largely sympathetic to foreign investment, was full of praise for Walter Gordon in late 1965. He wrote to the former finance minister, saying that Gordon had "done Canada a great service" and that "when the history of these years is finally written your economic policies will shine in comparison to the narrow doctrines of compromise and acquiescence of your opponents."[46] Bliss has since written some of this history himself, but Gordon's policies have not shone, either in his work or in that of others.[47] Paul E. Martin, later a Liberal prime minister, wrote to Gordon in a similar vein in 1970. Although the two differed over policy details, Martin found "that the greater my grasp of Canadian business, the more confirmed an economic nationalist I become."[48] It was a time when everyone seemed to be a nationalist, and those who were not were often labelled "continentalists" or "compradors," words often used as synonyms for "traitors."[49]

The New Nationalism was not a homogeneous movement but consisted of two distinct streams, each preoccupied with a different half of the question of American capital, one opposing American influence and the other, private capital. For the Waffle movement, the radical left wing of the New Democratic Party, the problem was not so much American investment as the entire capitalist system. The group's 1969 "Manifesto for an Independent Socialist Canada" suggested that American and Canadian owners were essentially the same, both primarily motivated by the pursuit of profit. The solution to the problem of American control was to nationalize all industry in Canada, regardless of the owner's citizenship. Other nationalists were troubled not by the capitalist system but by the economic impact of the United States. Partly in response to the Waffle, Walter Gordon and his allies formed the Committee for an Independent Canada in 1970. The organization's vague "Statement of Purpose" called for the government to reduce foreign control through a variety of measures, including the creation of an agency to screen new investment and to oversee the operations of non-Canadian firms. Despite their major ideological differences, both camps preferred an interventionist approach to the economy, one embracing Karl Marx's idea of total control of production by the proletariat, the other adopting the ideas of John Maynard Keynes, who accepted the capitalist system but called for more active government involvement.

Both the anti-American and the anti-corporate sides of the nationalist movement drew support from the same regions. Nationalism was strongest in southern Ontario, precisely the part of Canada that was wealthiest and had the most American-owned industry—in other words, the area that could most afford to be discriminating about future investment. When pollsters asked Canadians in 1973 whether they were prepared to accept a lower standard of living as the cost of reducing or eliminating American ownership, only in Ontario did more residents respond "yes" than "no."[50] The West and the Atlantic provinces, hungry for new industry, were much less enthusiastic. . . . Francophone Quebecers, preoccupied with throwing off the economic domination of English Canada, had little interest in this other struggle.

The New Nationalism had a class dimension. Political scientist Philip Resnick has shown that most of the movement's support came from the new petty bourgeoisie—salaried professionals often in the public sector—who "played *the decisive role* in the eruption of English Canadian nationalism after 1965." They "dominated" both the Committee for an Independent Canada and the Waffle movement.[51] As several Quebec intellectuals, including University of Montreal law professor Pierre Trudeau, argued in a 1964 manifesto, "nationalist policies in Canada or in

Quebec are generally advantageous to the middle class though they run counter to the interests of the majority of the population in general, of the economically weak in particular."[52] Walter Gordon, one of Canada's richest men, declared once that he was "prepared to pay a high price to be a Canadian."[53] Working-class Canadians could not afford quite so high a cost.

Distrustful of economic nationalism, but also concerned about American hegemony, Prime Minister Pierre Trudeau accepted, often half-heartedly, many nationalist proposals.[54] In 1971 his government created the Canada Development Corporation (CDC), which pooled domestic capital to purchase firms that might otherwise fall into non-Canadian hands. Trudeau also appointed cabinet minister Herb Gray to supervise a study of the impact of foreign capital. The resulting document, known as the Gray Report, argued that foreign ownership resulted in the "truncation" of the Canadian economy. Parent companies restricted the scope and activities of branch plants, the result being "potentially less decision-making and activity in Canada—fewer export opportunities, fewer supporting services, less training of local personnel in various skills, less specialized product development aimed at Canadian needs or tastes, and less spillover economic activity."[55] Nationalists scored victories in the mid-1970s both with the government's acceptance of the report's recommendation to establish a permanent agency to screen outside investment, the Foreign Investment Review Agency (FIRA), and with the founding of Petro-Canada, a publicly owned oil company.

The case of FIRA reveals much about the Trudeau government's weak commitment to economic nationalism. Lacking a majority in the Commons from 1972 to 1974 and under pressure from the New Democratic Party, which held the balance of power, the Liberals created the agency in 1973. Under the legislation, foreigners intending to purchase a Canadian company or to establish a new business in Canada had to first submit a formal proposal to FIRA. Concerned only with the larger transactions, the agency assessed the cases individually to decide whether a proposal provided a "significant benefit" for Canada.[56] FIRA had the power to negotiate with potential investors to improve the performance of their Canadian plants. It could work to have firms export more from their Canadian branches, purchase more components on the domestic market, hire more Canadian managers, or appoint more Canadian directors. After reviewing each case, the agency recommended whether the government should accept the investment proposal, accept it with conditions (such as performance requirements), or reject it. This procedure, however, did not satisfy most nationalists, who noted that FIRA approved the vast majority of the applications it received.

In the 1970s there were already indications that the New Nationalism was on the decline. Many of the ingredients that had combined to form the movement in the late 1960s and early 1970s no longer existed a decade later. Frequently radical in their youth, baby boomers, once they held mortgages and had children to support, became much less willing to take economic risks, either with their personal finances or in how they voted. Moreover, the economic climate had changed, with the Canadian economy hitting an unexpected bump in the mid-1970s and struggling to regain its footing for much of the next 20-year period. As in most Western industrialized countries, economic growth in Canada fell sharply after 1973, while inflation and unemployment rose. The interventionist ideas once so widely accepted seemed like folly, as it became increasingly clear that economists' models did not fully correspond to the real world. In the 1970s foreign investment in Canada fell as a percentage of gross national product, largely because of rising labour costs, declining productivity, the continued lowering of tariffs under GATT, and competition for capital from newly industrializing countries such as South Korea, Brazil, and Mexico.[57] "The nationalist movement is in trouble," said Mel Hurtig, president of the Committee for an Independent Canada, after the organization's 1976 annual meeting drew only 68 members.[58]

When the Liberal government regained its majority in the 1974 election, it began to distance itself from FIRA. In 1976 Jean Chrétien became minister of industry, trade, and commerce (the minister responsible for FIRA) and quickly made it clear that Canada welcomed foreign firms. He said that he distrusted nationalists, people who were often "using the flag for their own interests." He knew of "a lot of places in Canada where people don't give a damn who owns what." "They want a job," he said.[59]

Economic nationalists were successful again in the early 1980s when the Trudeau government created the National Energy Program, a policy to increase Canadian ownership of the oil industry and to maintain domestic prices below international levels. As with most nationalist policies, this one divided the country on regional lines. Oil-producing Alberta (and to a lesser extent British Columbia and Saskatchewan) denounced the policy, which primarily benefited Ontario and Quebec, the two largest consumers of energy in Canada.

Yet years of recession had dampened ardour for economic nationalism, even in Ontario. A 1984 poll showed that 67 per cent of Canadians thought that the government should encourage foreign companies to invest in Canada.[60] When Brian Mulroney became prime minister in 1984, he dismantled the Trudeau government's concessions to the nationalists. His Conservative government privatized both the CDC and Petro-Canada, and it replaced FIRA with Investment Canada, an agency dedicated to courting foreign capital. Mulroney cultivated closer relations with the United States and began negotiating a free-trade agreement with Canada's neighbour.

The 1988 election campaign showed that nationalism was still alive but again changing shape. Many nationalists spoke out against Mulroney's free-trade agreement with the United States, arguing that it prevented the federal government from regulating American investment, diminished Canadian sovereignty, and endangered social programs and cultural policies. But they were also concerned that the removal of tariffs would result in the deindustrialization of Canada as multinational companies shifted production to the United States.[61] After the agreement was signed, numerous plants closed and many jobs were lost, but this erosion of Canada's manufacturing base was largely attributable to massive shifts in the structure of global industry. Some nationalists lamented the loss of American investment, further illustrating the paradox of Canadian economic nationalism. As Peter C. Newman wrote in 1989, "It's difficult for those of us who fought so hard against the colonial concept of Canada as a branch-plant economy to look back at those mostly American-owned branch factories with something close to nostalgia. But at least those bastions of foreign capitalism actually manufactured things here, did their own product research and employed many thousands of Canadians."[62] Canada was back to where it had been before. Nationalists were favouring tariffs to keep foreign-owned plants operating in Canada. John Charles Rykert would have grasped only too well the debate of the late 1980s.

In the last decade of the twentieth century, as the Canadian economy began to improve and a new generation (the so-called baby boom echo) came of age, opposition to foreign ownership re-emerged. The debate had much in common with that of 30 years earlier, although the vocabulary had changed. Globalization became the key word, and its opponents, who now shunned the word "nationalism," argued that governments were losing power because of deregulation, privatization, and the growth of the multinational corporation. The phrase "American investment," so common in the 1970s, was seldom used at the century's end, as Nike, Coca-Cola, and Microsoft were seen less as American corporations than as entities that operated without regard to international borders and beyond the reach of governments, even that of the United States.

Canadian opponents of corporate globalization linked with like-minded people from around the world to oppose international trade and investment agreements. A diverse group of churches, anarchists, Marxists, trade unionists, anti-poverty activists, environmentalists, cultural agencies, health care associations, women's groups, farmers' organizations, and human rights advocates found common ground, despite their often unrelated and even contradictory objectives. They were concerned about the effect of globalization on their own countries, but also on developing nations and on the world as a whole. They spoke of the environment, natural resources, labour standards, job creation, human

rights, culture, social programs, education, and democracy. Some wanted to abolish capitalism, or at least they painted "Capitalism sucks!" on public buildings. While the New Nationalism of the 1960s and 1970s often seemed too narrowly focused, the movement of the 1990s appeared at times to have no focus at all. . . .

Canadians also led the opposition to the proposed Multilateral Agreement on Investment (MAI), an international pact to prevent discrimination against foreign capital. The 29 members of the Organization for Economic Cooperation and Development began the MAI negotiations in 1995. Reflecting Canada's long-standing pre-occupation with foreign investment, the issue resonated in Canada more than elsewhere, with the possible exception of France. An international coalition of non-governmental organizations launched a broad campaign against the agreement and succeeded in closing down the talks. Guiding the opposition was Maude Barlow, head of the Council of Canadians, who, according to veteran Canadian trade negotiator Simon Reisman, "almost single-handedly killed" the MAI.[63]

Opposition to the MAI was merely one of the most recent forms of economic nationalism. Over more than 150 years, the ideology has had often contradictory meanings in Canada. On occasion, support for foreign investment was part of a nationalist platform, but at other times nationalists saw outside capital as the main threat to the country's existence. Opposition to foreign ownership generally emerged as a component of the nationalist discourse in periods of peace and economic growth, primarily in affluent areas of the country and among comfortable members of the middle class. Prosperity, from time to time, brought with it the luxury of turning away foreign capital, a policy that served as a safe way for some Canadians to express their disapproval of the United States or the capitalist system.

Author's Note: I am grateful to Norman Hillmer, Duncan McDowall, and Hector Mackenzie, each of whom offered extensive critical advice on this article.

Endnotes

1   Canada, House of Commons, *Debates*, 28 March 1879, 789, 794.

2   Here, I use the term "National Policy," as Macdonald did, in reference to the tariff. Historians later employed the same term, "national policy" (though in lower case), to describe Macdonald's program of railway construction, western settlement, and protectionism.

3   O.D. Skelton, "General Economic History, 1867–1912," in Adam Shortt and Arthur G. Doughty, eds, *Canada and Its Provinces: A History of the Canadian People and Their Institutions*, vol. 9 (Toronto: Edinburgh University Press, 1913), 153; and Canada, *Report of the Department of Trade and Commerce for the Fiscal Year Ended June 30, 1905* (Ottawa: Department of Trade and Commerce, 1906), 15.

4   Michael Bliss, *Northern Enterprise: Five Centuries of Canadian Business* (Toronto: McClelland & Stewart, 1987), 303. On the Ontario government's efforts to create a "manufacturing condition" in that province, see H.V. Nelles, *The Politics of Development: Forests, Mines, and Hydro-Electric Power in Ontario, 1849–1941* (Toronto: Macmillan, 1974), esp. 48–107.

5   Michael Bliss, "Canadianizing American Business: The Roots of the Branch Plant," in Ian Lumsden, ed., *Close the 49th Parallel etc.: The Americanization of Canada* (Toronto: University of Toronto Press, 1970), 31–3.

6   Robert Craig Brown, "The Nationalism of the National Policy," in Peter Russell, ed., *Nationalism in Canada* (Toronto: McGraw-Hill, 1966), 157.

7   Kenneth H. Norrie, "The National Policy and Prairie Economic Discrimination, 1870–1930," in Donald H. Akenson, ed., *Canadian Papers in Rural History* (Gananoque, ON: Langdale Press, 1978), 1:13–32; and T.W. Acheson, "The Maritimes and 'Empire Canada,'" in David Jay Bercuson, ed., *Canada and the Burden of Unity* (Toronto: Macmillan, 1977), 87–114.

8   Duncan McDowall, *Steel at the Sault: Francis H. Clergue, Sir James Dunn, and the Algoma Steel Corporation, 1901–1956* (Toronto: University of Toronto Press, 1984).

9   Gustavus Myers, *A History of Canadian Wealth* (Toronto: James Lorimer, 1972), 1:iii; and Edward Porritt, *Sixty Years of Protection in Canada, 1846–1907: Where Industry Leans on the Politician* (London: Macmillan, 1908).

10   Bliss, "Canadianizing American Business," 29–30.

11   "Monster Meeting Protested against Reciprocity Pact," *Hamilton Spectator*, 22 February 1911, 11.

12   A 1934 examination of 1,030 American-owned industrial plants in Canada showed that 66 per cent were located in Ontario; see Herbert Marshall, Frank A. Southard, Jr, and Kenneth W. Taylor, *Canadian-American Industry: A Study in International Investment* (Toronto: Ryerson, 1936), 222.

13   Ian M. Drummond and Norman Hillmer, *Negotiating Freer Trade: The United Kingdom, the United States, Canada, and the Trade Agreements of 1938* (Waterloo, ON: Wilfrid Laurier University Press, 1989).

14   J.W. Pickersgill and D.F. Forster, eds, *The Mackenzie King Record* (University of Toronto Press, 1970), 4:267, 269.

15   Tom Kent, *Inside the Gordon Report*, Winnipeg Free Press Pamphlet No. 27 (Winnipeg: Winnipeg Free Press, 1958), 14.

16   David A. Wolfe, "Economic Growth and Foreign Investment: A Perspective on Canadian Economic Policy, 1945–1957," *Journal of Canadian Studies* 13, no. 1 (Spring 1978): 18.

17   Canada, *Canada's International Investment Position: Historical Statistics, 1926 to 1992* (Ottawa: Statistics Canada, 1993), 54, 225, 227, 228, 232.

18   C.W. Gonick, "Foreign Ownership and Political Decay," in Lumsden, ed., *Close the 49th Parallel*, 62.

19   Peter Karl Kresl, "Before the Deluge: Canadians on Foreign Ownership, 1920–1955," *American Review of Canadian Studies* 6 (Spring 1976): 119–20.

20   American ownership was 23 per cent in 1930, 23 per cent in 1948, 25 per cent in 1955, and 27 per cent in 1960, a shift insufficient to explain the burst of nationalism in the mid-1950s; see Canada, *Canada's International Investment Position*, 232.

21   The calculation is based on F.H. Leacy, ed., *Historical Statistics of Canada*, 2nd edn (Ottawa: Statistics Canada, 1983), series F13 (gross national product), A1 (population), and K8 (consumer price index).

22   John M. Miron, *Housing in Postwar Canada: Demographic Change, Household Formation, and Housing Demand* (Montreal and Kingston: McGill-Queen's University Press, 1988), 183–8.

23   Leacy, ed., *Historical Statistics*, 2nd edn, series A1 (population) and T148 (registration of passenger automobiles).

24   For the complete submissions to the commission, see Library and Archives Canada (LAC), Records of the Royal Commission on Canada's Economic Prospects, RG 33/35, reels C-1533 to C-1545. Summaries of the briefs, with an emphasis on their statistical content, can be found in *Canada's Economic Future: Digests of One Hundred and Twenty-Five Submissions to the Royal Commission on Canada's Economic Prospects* (Toronto: Cockfield, Brown, 1956).

25   Stephen Azzi, *Walter Gordon and the Rise of Canadian Nationalism* (Montreal and Kingston: McGill-Queen's University Press, 1999), 34–65.

26   *Preliminary Report* (Ottawa: Royal Commission on Canada's Economic Prospects, 1956), 87; and *Final Report* (Ottawa: Royal Commission on Canada's Economic Prospects, 1957), 391–3.

27   *Preliminary Report*, 83; and *Final Report*, 388–90.

28 Newspaper headlines tell much about the tone of the discussion; see "Who Owns Canada?," *Hamilton Spectator*, 13 February 1956; "A Dollar's Nationality Does Matter," *Vancouver Province*, 24 March 1956; "Is the Pace of Expansion Worth the Price We Pay?," *Financial Post*, 7 April 1956; Michael Barkway, "The Great American Flood," *Financial Post*, 14 April 1956; "The Danger is Very, Very Real," *Calgary Herald*, 14 January 1957; and "Foreigners to Control Canada's Destiny?," *Toronto Star*, 26 January 1957.

29 John Diefenbaker charged that Canada was about to "become a virtually forty-ninth economic state in the American union," Léon Balcer talked of an "economic invasion by our neighbours to the south," and E. Davie Fulton warned that "economic domination" would lead "to ultimate political domination as well"; see Peter C. Newman, "Who *Really* Owns Canada?," *Maclean's*, 9 June 1956, 11; Canada, House of Commons, *Debates*, 11 April 1956, 2825–6, and 17 April 1956, 2995.

30 Joseph Barber, *Good Fences Make Good Neighbors: Why the United States Provokes Canadians* (Toronto: McClelland & Stewart, 1958), 119.

31 See, for example, "Diefenbaker Keeps Drawing Big Crowd," *Vancouver Sun*, 23 May 1957, 22; and David Ghent, "'Pipeline Profits to Gov't Puppets,' PC Chief Charges," *Toronto Telegram*, 8 April 1957, 3.

32 LAC, Lester B. Pearson Papers, MG 26 N6, vol. 12, Walter Gordon file, "Notes for Mike," 18 April 1958.

33 Canada, *Canada's International Investment Position*, 232.

34 Task Force on the Structure of Canadian Industry, *Foreign Ownership and the Structure of Canadian Industry* (Ottawa: Privy Council Office, 1968), 91, 401–3, 407–10.

35 Ibid., esp. 345–6. Galbraith outlined his ideas on this issue in *American Capitalism: The Concept of Countervailing Power* (Boston: Houghton Mifflin, 1952). Although he favoured a higher degree of state intervention, Galbraith generally disassociated himself from efforts to regulate the nationality of corporate ownership; see Robert McKeown, "John Kenneth Galbraith Says Yes," *Weekend Magazine*, 25 March 1967, 26, 28–30, 32–3.

36 C.W. Gonick, "Economist: 'Canada Is Financing Its Own Sell-Out,'" *Toronto Daily Star*, 28 November 1970, 22.

37 "U.S. Investment Not Needed," *Ottawa Citizen*, 12 February 1972.

38 Frank Underhill, "Foreword," in Russell, ed., *Nationalism in Canada*, xix.

39 John Kenneth Galbraith, *The Affluent Society* (Boston: Houghton Mifflin, 1958), and *The New Industrial State* (Boston: Houghton Mifflin, 1967).

40 Ralph Nader, *Unsafe at Any Speed: The Designed-In Dangers of the American Automobile* (New York: Grossman, 1965).

41 Ralph Nader, Nadia Milleron, and Duff Conacher, *Canada Firsts* (Toronto: McClelland & Stewart, 1992), xiii.

42 Ian Lumsden, "American Imperialism and Canadian Intellectuals," in Lumsden, ed., *Close the 49th Parallel*, 322.

43 See, for example, Task Force on the Structure of Canadian Industry, *Foreign Ownership*, 402, 406; Kari Levitt, *Silent Surrender: The Multinational Corporation in Canada* (Toronto: Macmillan, 1970), 33; Eric W. Kierans, "Towards a New National Policy," *Canadian Forum*, January-February 1972, 53; and W.H. Pope, *The Elephant and the Mouse: A Handbook on Regaining Control of Canada's Economy* (Toronto: McClelland & Stewart, 1971), 81.

44 LAC, Walter L. Gordon Papers, MG 32 B44, vol. 38, file 7; and Roger Rickwood and Mark Sandilands, "The Fading of the Committee for an Independent Canada: An Examination of Organizational Rise and Decline," paper presented to the Canadian Political Science Association, Halifax, 29 May 1981.

45 Gordon Laxer, "Surviving the Americanizing New Right," *Canadian Review of Sociology and Anthropology* 37, no. 1 (February 2000): 64.

46 LAC, Walter L. Gordon Papers, MG 32 B44, vol. 3, file 8, J.M. Bliss to Gordon, 11 November 1965.

47 In his history of Canadian politics, Bliss portrays Gordon as a man who "bungled budget-making more thoroughly than any finance minister in the country's history" and who "disregarded clear warnings that his schemes were unworkable"; Gordon was a "deeply foolish finance minister" who "crippled the government's" reputation and whose policies fell "into the dustbin of history." See Michael Bliss, *Right Honourable Men: The Descent of Canadian Politics from Macdonald to Mulroney* (Toronto: HarperCollins, 1994), 225, 230.

48 LAC, Walter L. Gordon Papers, MG 32 B44, vol. 28, file 10, Paul E. Martin to Gordon, 11 December 1970.

49 Wallace Clement used the word "comprador" repeatedly in *The Canadian Corporate Elite: An Analysis of Economic Power*, Carleton Library No. 89 (Toronto: McClelland & Stewart, 1975). The Canadian Liberation Movement, an organization dedicated to overthrowing capitalism and American imperialism, printed stickers with the slogan "Continentalism Is Treason"; see William Ready Division of Archives and Research Collections, McMaster University, Canadian Liberation Movement Archives, box 1, file 61, "Continentalism Is Treason" sticker. The phrase also appeared in S.M. Crean, *Who's Afraid of Canadian Culture?* (Don Mills, ON: General Publishing, 1976), 275. In the view

of historian Leo Johnson, Canadian politicians and corporate executives were traitors: "Nowhere is there ever the assertion that Canada is not for sale. The only question is the price. In other places and other times, men who sold out their country were called traitors"; see Leo Johnson, "We Must Not Let Them Give Canada Away," *New Canada*, September 1970, 8.

50 J. Alex Murray, "Independence Oui, Lower Living Standard Non," *Windsor Star*, 24 January 1973.

51 Philip Resnick, *The Land of Cain: Class and Nationalism in English Canada, 1945–1975* (Vancouver: New Star Books, 1977), 167 (italics in the original). Sceptical of Resnick's Marxist approach, I looked for evidence to refute it while conducting my own research for *Walter Gordon and the Rise of Canadian Nationalism*. What I found confirmed Resnick's thesis: the New Nationalism, with few exceptions, was predominantly a middle-class affair.

52 Albert Breton *et al.*, "An Appeal for Realism in Politics," translated by P.M. Pitfield, *Canadian Forum*, May 1964, 32–3. The argument in this piece was more fully outlined in Albert Breton, "The Economics of Nationalism," *Journal of Political Economy* 72, no. 3 (June 1964): 376–86.

53 Walter Gordon, cited in Alan Heisey, *The Great Canadian Stampede: The Rush to Economic Nationalism—Right or Wrong* (Toronto: Griffin House, 1973), 45.

54 Trudeau's views on economic nationalism and American domination are stated succinctly in Ron Graham, ed., *The Essential Trudeau* (Toronto: McClelland & Stewart, 1998), 96–7. A useful

summary of Trudeau's views of the United States can be found in Thomas S. Axworthy, "'To Stand Not So High Perhaps but Always Alone': The Foreign Policy of Pierre Elliott Trudeau," in Thomas S. Axworthy and Pierre Elliott Trudeau, eds, *Towards a Just Society: The Trudeau Years* (Markham, ON: Viking, 1990), 32.

55 *Foreign Direct Investment in Canada* (Ottawa: Government of Canada, 1972), 42–3.

56 Foreign Investment Review Act, 1973–4, c. 46, s. 2 (2).

57 Duncan McDowall, *A Fit Place for Investment? Foreign Investors' Perceptions of Canada in a Changing World* (Ottawa: Conference Board of Canada, 1984), 8.

58 Ian Urquhart, "The Welcome Wagon," *Maclean's*, 1 November 1976, 40x.

59 Ibid., 40n, 40p; and Jean Chrétien, "Foreword," *Foreign Investment Review*, Autumn 1977, 2.

60 "Majority Favors Investment from Abroad: Gallup," *Toronto Star*, 14 June 1984, A3.

61 Mel Watkins, "Ten Good Reasons to Oppose Free Trade," *This Magazine*, April 1986, 14; and Mel Hurtig and Duncan Cameron, "No Longer Will Canada Make Sense," *Globe and Mail*, 14 November 1988, A7.

62 Peter C. Newman, "Opting Out of the 21st Century," *Maclean's*, 23 October 1989, 38. Maude Barlow and Mel Hurtig made similar arguments; see Maude Barlow, *Parcel of Rogues: How Free Trade Is Failing Canada* (Toronto: Key Porter, 1990), 52–81, 205–34; and Mel Hurtig, *The Betrayal of Canada* (Toronto: Stoddart, 1991), 23.

63 Heather Scoffield, "Grassroots Group Takes on Global Goliaths," *Globe and Mail*, 5 June 1999, A6.

9.2: The Transformation of Canadian Arctic Sovereignty and Security: From Myth to Reality?

Rob Huebert

. . .

The true north, strong and free
From far and wide, O Canada
We stand on guard for thee.

—Canadian National Anthem

Introduction

One of the most enduring themes in modern Canadian foreign policy is concern over Canadian Arctic sovereignty.[1] Canadians have long feared that the United States or other outside actors might want to take over part or all of the Canadian north. As a result, there has been a heightened sensitivity to foreign and particularly American actions in the Arctic. Even when the United States had no actual interest in the region, Canada has viewed American action in the North with suspicion.[2] The irony in this is that, for the most part, the United States has shown very little interest in "taking over" any section of the Canadian north and has generally preferred to work cooperatively with Canadians to address what it sees as shared challenges. The purpose of this article is to examine the concerns Canada has had over the protection of its Arctic sovereignty and the efforts that it has taken in this regard. To a very large degree, Canada's protection of its Arctic sovereignty has been more theoretical than actual. Historically its efforts can best be characterized as reactive, piecemeal, and ad hoc. Only in very recent times has there been evidence that Canada is now attempting to develop a more coordinated set of policies.

Canadian concerns about American northern intentions have existed since the US purchase of Alaska in 1867, although the settlement of the Alaska boundary dispute and the end of the Klondike gold rush in the early 1900s mitigated these concerns.[3] However, concern over American intent re-emerged in earnest during the Second World War. Canada was required to work with the United States in its northern region for the common defence against the Japanese and German military threats.[4] But as soon as this conflict ended, Canada again found itself engaged with the Americans in their mutual defence against the threat from the Soviet Union. As part of this effort, vast areas of the Canadian north were developed so that a defensive system could be employed against Soviet bombers and missiles. Prime Minister Mackenzie King and other Canadian leaders became concerned that in allowing the Americans on Canadian soil to build these systems, Canadian Arctic sovereignty could be compromised, but these concerns subsequently turned out to be unfounded.[5]

The Americans did not threaten Canadian Arctic sovereignty, and there were never any indications that their intentions involved anything other than the defence of North America against a common enemy. But a legacy was created that continues to worry Canadian political elites and the general public: just what *might*

the Americans do in Canada's Arctic? The insecurity felt by Canadian decision-makers can be attributed to the challenge of undertaking any project in the Canadian north. Anything that the Canadian government wants to do in the North will be very demanding and very expensive. This is compounded by the political reality that Canadian culture identifies very closely with the North and thus any action (or inaction) is usually closely scrutinized.

Confounding the efforts of Canadian leaders to protect its Arctic sovereignty are the realities of this part of Canada. The location is geographically vast, there is almost no infrastructure, the population is very small, and as a result, it is very difficult and costly to operate in the North. Canadian leaders may want to protect Canadian Arctic sovereignty, but more southern concerns generally overshadow northern needs.

While Canada has wrestled with the issue of Arctic Sovereignty in a general way ever since Great Britain transferred title to Canada in the late 1800s, it has only been with resource and technological developments, combined with climate change, that it became possible for southerners to consider the actual development of the Canadian north. It is critical to recognize that people—the Inuit and other northern indigenous peoples—lived in this region long before the arrival of European and Asian explorers, missionaries, soldiers, and business people. But it is this modern concern over the arrival of non-Canadians to the region that has defined the Canadian understanding of the need to protect Arctic sovereignty. In 1969 the significance of the issue was brought home to the Canadian government by the voyage of the American ice-strengthened oil tanker ss *Manhattan*.[6] It was sent to test the viability of shipping oil from the newly discovered North Slope deposits through the Northwest Passage to American East Coast markets. By failing to ask for Canada's permission, the United States did not acknowledge Canadian sovereignty over the waterway. Nevertheless, Canada assisted in the voyage to ensure that it proceeded in a safe and environmentally responsible fashion. But following the voyage, the Canadian government began to explore ways in which its Arctic sovereignty could be better protected. A similar crisis developed in 1985, when the Americans sent the icebreaker *Polar Sea* through the Northwest Passage, again without asking permission from the Canadian government.[7]

So the question arises: what is the foreign policy problem facing Canada with regard to the protection of its Arctic sovereignty? For that matter, is there really a problem? How have successive Canadian governments responded to this issue? How successful or unsuccessful have these efforts been? Can any commonalities or trends be identified? If so, what does this say about Canada's efforts to secure its Arctic sovereignty?

The History

The first "Canadian" Arctic sovereignty crisis occurred before there was a Canada. It was caused by the European and Asian (i.e., Russians in Alaska) movement into what was to become the Canadian Arctic. The area at that time was inhabited by the Inuit and other indigenous populations.[8] While these peoples did not employ a state system similar to the Europeans', they did occupy the region and had their own system of governance.[9] However, as Europeans and Russians moved into the region, they simply annexed the territory and began to enforce their own sovereignty without regard to the existing peoples. This was, in effect, a sovereignty crisis: Europeans and subsequently Americans and Canadians took over the land as if the Inuit were not there. There is the assumption that this "takeover" was not as violent as what more southerly North American indigenous peoples experienced, but that is not known with any certainty. The bottom line is that the homelands of the Inuit and northern peoples were simply absorbed into the modern Canadian (and American) state. It is difficult not to think of this as the first "Canadian" Arctic sovereignty crisis.

This aspect of Arctic sovereignty—of Arctic history and development—was ignored in the past, but now Inuit leaders such as Mary Simon are pointing out that the Inuit lived and prospered in this region long before the arrival of the

Europeans.[10] This is an area where there is a need for much more thought and research. Canada has utilized the presence of the Inuit to justify its claim of sovereignty. But what does it mean to have the peoples within the region simply ignored as new systems of governance are introduced by a foreign set of nationals? This question needs further and careful consideration, more than can be accomplished within the confines of this article. But the continued existence of the Inuit within these lands remains a critical element of Canada's claim to sovereignty.[11]

The first issue involving Canada as a state and others regarding Arctic sovereignty was initiated with the discovery of gold in the Klondike region in 1897–9. The arrival of a large number of Americans who had made their way to the Yukon looking for gold gave rise to the concern that this influx could lead to a northern version of the American manifest destiny.[12] Furthermore, at the time, the boundary between Alaska and the Yukon remained disputed. While the gold was quickly mined out, the lingering problem of the boundary remained.[13]

The boundary dispute arose when the United Kingdom and Russia signed a treaty in 1825 in an attempt to delimit their territories in the region. This treaty, however, did not adequately delimit the land boundary between the holdings of these two states in the region. Following Russia's sale of Alaska to the United States and the British granting of self-rule to Canada, both in 1867, there was a growing need to determine the actual border. In the early 1900s an international tribunal was established to resolve the boundary dispute. Composed of three representatives selected by the Americans and three selected by the United Kingdom for Canada, the tribunal was mandated to resolve and determine the boundaries of the region. The British selection of two Canadian representatives and one British representative had a major ramification for the resolution of the dispute.

Great Britain was becoming increasingly aware of the military challenge presented by Germany at this time. Consequently, one of its core foreign and defence policies was to develop improved relations with countries such as the

United States. Thus, when the tribunal made its decision regarding the Alaskan boundary, the single British delegate sided with the three American delegates and favoured the US proposed border over the Canadian proposal. The result was that the Alaskan Panhandle was redrawn largely according to the American preference. This led to considerable resentment in Canada against the United Kingdom and contributed to an increasing mood of Canadian nationalism.[14]

It was during the Second World War that the protection of Canadian Arctic sovereignty again became an important issue. When Japanese forces invaded two islands in the Aleutian Islands chain (Kiska and Attu), the United States became concerned over the possibility that the Japanese might invade Alaska and the West Coast.[15] Accordingly, they made the decision to build a highway that would allow them to resupply forces in Alaska if the Japanese used the islands to invade the Alaskan mainland.[16] The Alaska Highway was an engineering feat that was constructed in record time. While there were some concerns in Canada that the large American presence could pose a threat to the long-term control of the region, as soon as the Americans finished its construction of the highway, they left.[17]

But security issues following the end of the Second World War soon reignited these concerns. While the Soviet Union had been an important ally in the defeat of the Germans, its relations with the Western Allies quickly deteriorated to open hostility in the postwar era. With the advancement in weapons technology and specifically the development of nuclear weapons and missiles, the Canadian Arctic became an important theatre of operation.[18] Once again Canada and the United States cooperated in the development of weapons systems to respond to the Soviet threat. In particular, they developed the Distant Early Warning system (DEW Line), first to detect a Soviet bomber attack and then to warn of a ballistic missile attack. As before, the Americans built and paid for the bulk of the system.[19] There were concerns among Canadians that the Americans would not leave once the

system was constructed, but as in the case of the construction of the Alaska Highway, the Americans did in fact leave as soon as the system was operational.

Overall, while Canadian political leaders may have harboured concerns regarding American intentions, at no time did the Americans make any claims that would undermine Canadian sovereignty. While one can speculate that the Americans may not have been so accommodating if Canada had opted to adopt a neutral foreign policy, this was never given serious consideration, as the Soviet threat was seen as real, dangerous, and aimed against the West in general.

In many ways the position of the Canadian government can be viewed as being quite shrewd. Canada was able to ensure that its security against the Soviet threat was protected, but it also was able to ensure that its own sovereignty was not challenged by the United States. Furthermore, once the Americans had built the system and transferred it to Canada, Ottawa had an improved ability to assert control over the region. With the new instruments, it was able to know what was happening in its North and was therefore better prepared to protect Canadian sovereignty. And importantly, it had gotten someone else to foot the bill!

It was not until the end of the 1960s that the first modern US threat to Canadian Arctic sovereignty emerged. This was over the status of the Northwest Passage. The United States has maintained since 1969 that the passage is a strait used for international navigation, while Canada took the position that the passage is internal waters. The main impact of these different approaches revolves around the control of international shipping. If the Americans are right, Canada cannot stop international maritime traffic from transiting the passage as long as international maritime standards are respected. If the Canadians are right, then Canada has the right to grant or deny permission to whomever it wishes. However, despite the limited scope of the issue—it only concerns international shipping—it has achieved emotional status and is known as the "Arctic sovereignty dispute."

DEW LINE AND ARCTIC SOVEREIGNTY

In the 1950s Canada and the United States agreed to joint participation in the construction and manning of radar defence systems on Canadian soil for the purposes of continental defence. These defence systems, particularly the Distant Early Warning system (DEW Line), constructed through the Canadian Arctic, again raised the issue of Canada's sovereignty over its Arctic.

Canada and the United States had already begun to cooperate militarily to ensure defence of the North American continent during the Second World War, through initiatives such as the Permanent Joint Board on Defence created in 1940. By the late 1940s, events necessitated even greater mutual defence projects and cooperation. The Cold War hostility between the United States and the Soviet Union heightened and became more threatening by the early 1950s, when the Soviets developed nuclear weapons and aircraft to carry these missiles. With Canada geographically positioned between the two powers and the likelihood that a Soviet attack would come over Canadian airspace, plus the close proximity of major US population centres to Canadian ones, the need for Canadian involvement with the United States to guard against a Soviet attack was clear. Thus, there was little opposition to the idea of building radar defence systems to detect Soviet bombers and to their placement on Canadian soil. Three radar defence lines were subsequently built through the 1950s, the Pinetree Line (along the 50th parallel, approximately), the Mid-Canada Line (the 55th parallel), and finally the DEW Line, a vast system of 63 radar centres from Alaska through the Canadian Arctic to Greenland.

Given the belief in a real potential threat, plus the commitment to mutual defence, Canadian government officials were in agreement on the need for Canadian participation in the construction and administration of these radar lines and on the need for substantial American involvement. However, the nature of both Canadian and American involvement in the Arctic-based DEW Line quickly raised questions about Canada's sovereignty in the area. The problem was that the project, both its construction and its operation, would mean a large American military presence in the Arctic. This was a result of the extensive cost of both building and manning the DEW Line, a factor that led to the agreement that the Americans would fund and build the DEW Line and the Canadians would take responsibility for the much less costly Mid-Canada Line. However, given the sparse population and lack of government institutions and personnel in the Arctic, a consequence of the DEW Line would be a larger American than Canadian presence in the area, potentially challenging one of the requirements of "sovereignty." As a result of these concerns, the Canadian government did place some Canadian military personnel on the line to man it, even if the American contingent was always much larger. Similarly, Canadian officials emphasized the Canadian role in funding and administering the Mid-Canada Line. Ultimately, the threat to Canada's sovereignty was more imagined than real. Once construction was completed, the majority of Americans left the area and the Canadian military did take over operational control in 1968.

The Arctic sovereignty dispute began in 1969 after the discovery of oil along Alaska's North Slope in the mid-1960s. Once this discovery was found to be substantial, the Americans needed to determine the best means of bringing the oil to market. The two main options considered were to build a pipeline north to south across Alaska or to ship the oil out by tanker in the summer months. To test the feasibility of shipping by tanker, Humble Oil chartered a supertanker—the

Manhattan—which it modified for use in ice-covered waters.[20] The US Coast Guard provided an icebreaker to escort this vessel through the Northwest Passage from the east coast to the Alaska northern coast.

The Canadian response was to grant the United States its "permission" and to send a Canadian icebreaker—the CCGS *John A. Macdonald*—to assist in the voyage. The Americans stated that they had not asked for permission, as they had the right to transit through the passage without Canadian permission. However, they were happy to receive the assistance of the extra icebreaker. The voyage proved to be much more difficult than expected. Without the assistance of the Canadian icebreaker and information on ice conditions provided by the Canadian ice services, there is serious doubt that the Americans would have been successful. The challenges of making the voyage convinced the Americans that

the construction of the pipeline was the preferable means of transporting the Alaskan oil.

However, the American refusal to acknowledge Canadian control of the Northwest Passage had serious ramifications and led to widespread public concern. In the summer of 1969 the voyage became front-page news in Canada. The recently elected Trudeau government decided that it needed to take action. There were those in the cabinet who believed that the best course of action would be to declare complete Canadian sovereign control over the passage. However, this was determined to be too provocative and beyond what international law allowed. Instead, the government opted for a more innovative but less challenging course. They declared that the delicate environmental conditions of the Arctic required special protection. To provide this, the Canadian government enacted the Arctic Waters Pollution Prevention Act (AWPPA), the purpose of

© Bettmann/CORBIS

The SS *Manhattan* (right), attempting the Northwest Passage, follows the Canadian Coast Guard icebreaker *John A. Macdonald* toward the Prince of Wales Strait, 12 September 1969.

which was to give Canada the power to unilaterally require all foreign (and domestic) vessels to follow Canadian marine environmental regulations. It was hoped that this action would be seen as less provocative than if the government had simply announced its right to control all aspects of shipping in its northern waters. Ottawa assumed that, with the focus on the environment, there would be more international support for Canada's actions.[21]

At the same time, the Trudeau government also went on a campaign to seek international support for its position. Canada called for a meeting of Arctic nations, but Soviet suspicions and American coolness prevented such a meeting from occurring. However, the Canadian government was successful in bringing the international need for better northern maritime environmental protection into the Law of the Sea negotiations that were conducted throughout the 1970s. Ultimately, when the negotiations were completed in 1982, Canada's efforts were rewarded with the inclusion of Article 234 in the final draft of the United Nations Convention on the Law of the Sea (UNCLOS). Known either as the "Canadian Article" or the Ice-Covered Water Article," this clause gave states that had maritime regions that were ice-covered for most of the year the right to unilaterally create stronger environmental regulations for activity in such waters. However, any such rules needed to be applied in a non-discriminatory fashion and could not favour domestic shippers.[22]

While Canadian officials hoped that the inclusion of this clause gave them international recognition of their control over the Northwest Passage, they were not completely confident. Therefore, they issued a reservation to the International Court of Justice that Canada would not allow an international challenge on the Act to proceed. Second, while the Act appeared to require all international and domestic vessels to comply with Canadian rules, the reality was quite different. To ensure compliance, the Government of Canada created a reporting system known as the Vessel Traffic Reporting Arctic Canada Traffic Zone (NORDREG). Vessels

entering Canadian Arctic waters were expected to report to a Canadian Coast Guard Marine and Communications Traffic Service centre (MCTS). At this point the ship's captain would provide information to let Canadian officials know whether the ship met the requirements of the AWPPA. If it did, it would be allowed to sail into Canadian Arctic waters. If it did not, it would presumably be denied entry, thus demonstrating Canadian control. The problem was that until very recently, the right of foreign vessels to report remained optional. It was only in 2010 that the Canadian government made the reporting system mandatory for all vessels—domestic and foreign—entering these waters.

In addition, the Canadian government did not develop the actual instruments necessary to provide for the surveillance and enforcement of Canadian laws in this region. Because of the difficulty experienced by the *Manhattan*, there was little actual international shipping in the region. Therefore, having made its point, the Trudeau government did not deem it necessary to spend the money building the surveillance and enforcement systems that would allow Canada to enact control over the region.

The next chapter in this dispute began in the winter of 1984–5. The Americans have required their Coast Guard icebreaking fleet to provide services in both the western and eastern Arctic. In the 1980s the western region was serviced by the *Polar Sea*, which was home-ported in Seattle. Specifically, the *Polar Sea* was required to service various research projects in the waters north of Alaska. The main requirement in the eastern Arctic was to resupply the military base in Thule, Greenland, annually. This was normally done by the *Northwind*, an older vessel, but when it went in for normal servicing in the fall of 1984, significant mechanical problems were found. The decision was made not to spend resources to fix these problems, and the vessel was retired. This left the Americans with the problem of meeting both of their commitments with only one vessel. Canada was approached with a request to provide the resupply to the Thule base. Its Auxiliary Oil Replenishment (AOR) supply vessels had a limited ice-strengthened capability, and one of them could have made the voyage. But all had been committed, and the Canadian government declined the Americans' request.[23]

Senior American Coast Guard officials then met with their Canadian counterparts to see if an alternative arrangement could be made. While there was time for the *Polar Sea* to travel from Seattle through the Panama Canal and then proceed to Thule, there was not enough time for it to return the same way to fulfil it commitments in Alaska. The Americans were aware of the political sensitivities of sailing through the Northwest Passage and asked the Canadians of they could still do this. They offered to issue a statement in which both sides would agree that the voyage was only for operational needs and would in no way prejudice either side's position. An agreement was reached by late winter, and the voyaged seemed set to go. However, when both the Canadian media and senior officials from External Affairs learned of the forthcoming voyage, a political storm erupted. The media presented the voyage as an effort by the Americans to undermine Canadian sovereignty, while External Affairs dissociated itself from the earlier agreement and demanded that the United States ask permission. The Americans did not do this, but Canada still "granted" the Americans permission and once again sent one of its icebreakers to sail with the *Polar Sea*.

Ultimately the voyage went ahead. But it created a large media and public outcry. This in turn led the Mulroney Conservative government to want to "do something." That something was a six-part policy platform announced in September 1985. Of these promises, the government moved quickly to implement three that did not require new resources: (1) declaring straight baselines to enclose the Arctic; (2) passing Canada's Law Offshore Application Act; and (3) removing Canada's reservation to the International Court of Justice on its claim to the Northwest Passage. Each of these was completed quickly. However, of the three actions requiring new resources, only one was actually completed. The promised Polar 8 icebreaker was cancelled within four years of the announcement that it had been built to defend Canadian Arctic sovereignty.

The Mulroney government also stated that it was going to improve the military commitment to air and sea sovereignty patrols. In reality it did almost nothing. There was a marginal increase in over-flights by Aurora long-range patrol aircraft of the Arctic region, but there was no meaningful increase in capability (except for the purchase of three additional stripped-down Aurora-type long-range patrol aircraft called Arcturus). The government considered buying nuclear-powered submarines, but these were deemed too expensive and were also abandoned.[24]

The last of the six promises dealt with efforts to negotiate a deal with the Americans over the use of the Northwest Passage. Considerable political and diplomatic effort went into the negotiations. After two years, direct discussions between Prime Minister Brian Mulroney and President Ronald Reagan led to the Arctic Waters Cooperation Agreement of 1988. The agreement begins with the statement that it does not prejudice the position of either state on the status of the passage. It then states that the United States will ask the consent of Canada when it wants to send its icebreakers through the passage and that Canada in turn is expected to give its consent. It is a limited agreement, but it did ensure that there would be no repetition of the 1985 crisis over the sailing of the small fleet (two vessels at the time).[25]

The issue then receded from public attention until the beginning of the 2000s. It was at this time that there was a growing awareness that climate change was transforming the Arctic. Specifically, as temperatures increased, the ice cover of the Arctic was melting. As the ice melted, the use of the Northwest Passage as a navigable route for surface vessels increasingly came to be seen as a possibility. In the minds of the Canadian public and media, there was a renewed sense of the need to take action.[26]

The Martin Liberal government studied the situation to determine how serious the challenge was. In its foreign and defence policy papers—published in *Canada's International Policy Statement*—there was recognition that Canada faced a future in which there would be increased international use of its Arctic waters.[27]

An examination of Canada's domestic Arctic issues was coming to the same conclusion but was never completed. Under the Martin government, Canadian naval vessels started to visit the North again and northern defence exercises resumed. In addition, it seems that Canada decided that its new replenishment vessels would be given some abilities to operate in limited ice conditions.[28]

In the 2006 federal election campaign, the Conservative Party under Stephen Harper made the protection of Canadian Arctic sovereignty an election issue. Following his party's success, his government began to develop plans to improve Canada's limited ability to enforce its will in the Arctic. These included the building of six to eight Arctic/Offshore Patrol Ships (AOPS), the construction of a large icebreaker, the building of a resupply port in Nanisivik, and an Arctic training base at Resolute Bay. Since becoming prime minister, Harper has also kept protection of Canadian Arctic sovereignty as a priority of his government. He is the only prime minister who has made it a point of policy to visit the Arctic on an official basis every year.[29]

Since 2008, the Harper government has made Canada's response to the international economic crisis one of his government's core priorities. This has created some concern that the promises relating to the enforcement of Canadian Arctic sovereignty may be watered down or abandoned in a manner reminiscent of the Mulroney government's second term. The resupply port in Nanisivik has been scaled back, and in 2012 the actual construction of the AOPS and the new icebreaker had yet to begin. However, officially the government remains committed to all of these plans. What has been noted is that the rhetoric used by the government has been toned down. Harper no longer talks of "using it or losing it" in regard to Arctic sovereignty.

The Problem

Having gone through the history of the Arctic sovereignty issue, we can now answer several of the questions raised in the introduction to this article. One of the greatest challenges in understanding the protection of Canadian Arctic sovereignty as

a foreign policy issue lies in the complexity of the term "Arctic sovereignty." The government, the media, and academics have ascribed multiple meanings to the term (and have often been inconsistent even with the term that they have used). This has made it difficult to determine what was actually being "protected" or even what needed protection. In the minds of many Canadians, the entire Arctic has been at risk. The fear has been that some foreign entity (often the United States) wanted the region for itself and would take either military or political actions to seize part or all of it. A sub-theme of this concern has been that the Arctic has been perceived to be at risk partly because of preceding Canadian governments' failure to "do something" to protect the region.

However, these public (and sometimes political) concerns were largely misplaced. As shown, there is little evidence that there has been some lurking international actor secretly plotting to seize the land territories of the Canadian north. Since the 1930s, any possible interest in Canadian northern land territories has been eliminated with the exception of a very small island, Hans Island. The issues that have lasted into the current era are all associated with Canadian maritime regions in the Arctic. Thus, the protection of Canadian Arctic sovereignty really means the determination of the international legal status of Canadian land (Hans Island) or maritime regions. By protection, Canada means that it wants to retain for itself the right to make the final authoritative decision over the region that is claimed.

Ultimately, the protection of any sovereignty is predicated on an understanding of the term. Originally developed as a core international legal concept that served to shift power from the Church to the ruling monarchy, "sovereignty" is understood to have three core elements.[30] First, sovereignty needs a prescribed geographic boundary. Historically, the focus was only on land territories, but this is now changing and an ever-increasing zone of control over adjacent ocean territory has complicated the existing concepts of sovereignty (this issue will be elaborated upon below). Second, there needs to be a population within the territory. The numbers can be small, as is the case in the Canadian Arctic, but the territory must contain some people. Thus, the Antarctic does not have its own sovereignty, since no people are living in the territory beyond the scientists of various countries. Third, sovereignty requires the existence of a government that has the ability to exercise control over the people within the territory. This control is both absolute and authoritative, which means that there are no other decision-making bodies that are able to make decisions that override the decisions of the state. A fourth element of sovereignty is that it must be recognized by the international community. If a government asserts sovereignty over its territory but no other state recognizes its claims, then it is said not to have sovereignty over the region. Of course, there are situations where a state asserts sovereignty without many other states recognizing its assertion. These contested areas are possible points of tension, and conflict can emerge in such regions.

Complicating the concept of sovereignty in the Canadian Arctic is the evolving nature of maritime sovereignty.[31] When the concept of sovereignty was first developed, it only referred to the land territory of a state. With the exception of a three-nautical-mile strip immediately adjacent to the coastline, the oceans were considered open to all. By the end of the Second World War, this had begun to change. Coastal states began to claim larger areas of water as part of their sovereign territory. Ultimately, a series of international conferences led to the adoption of the United Nations Convention on the Law of the Sea. This international treaty creates a series of coastal zones that provide for sovereign rights over adjacent coastal waters. Without our getting into a detailed discussion about the different zones of control, it is sufficient to say that the further away from the coastline one moves, the more limited the sovereign rights become. The convention also clarifies several key maritime concepts of law, including those relating to international straits. It also grants a state that has ice-covered waters the right to impose strict environmental laws that exceed existing international laws as long as the laws are applied on a non-discriminatory basis. All of these aspects of international law have had a major impact on the actual nature of the sovereignty issue.

The main modern Arctic sovereignty issue is the international legal status of the Northwest Passage. The dispute is between Canada and the United States and is centred on the question of whether the Northwest Passage is a strait used for international navigation or part of the internal waters of Canada. If it is a strait used for international navigation, then it is subject to the rules governing international shipping. These are determined through international agreement, and specifically the International Maritime Organization (IMO), and Canada cannot unilaterally control the international shipping that enters these waterways. On the other hand, if these are internal waters, then Canada has absolute sovereignty over them and can create the rules and regulations governing domestic and foreign shipping through waters. Canada can even deny passage to foreign vessels if it so chooses. The issue is only about the control of international shipping. Canada, under the terms of international law, has complete sovereignty over the resources that are found in the waters.[32]

The challenge, however, lies in the fact that the definition of the issue—the protection of Canadian Arctic sovereignty—has evolved in much broader terms in the Canadian political discourse. The term has been used to also describe other Arctic boundary disputes—for example, the division of the Beaufort Sea, the dispute over Hans Island, and the possible dispute over the division of the extended continental shelf. Technically speaking, these are only boundary disputes, but many Canadians do not make such a distinction and include them as challenges involving Canadian Arctic sovereignty. The Canadian government itself has sometimes included these terms and sometimes not.

Many northern Aboriginal leaders have used the term in connection with the needs of northern indigenous Canadians. Mary Simon, for example, the current leader of the Inuit Circumpolar Council (ICC), has repeatedly made the point that sovereignty must be about the protection of Canadians.[33] She focuses on northern indigenous peoples' need to receive better education, health care, and employment opportunities. As well, the protection of Canadian Arctic sovereignty, in her view, is also principally about the protection of the environment.

For others, the protection of Arctic sovereignty includes the provision of better security of the land masses of the Arctic Archipelago. The Canadian government frequently talks of the use of Ranger patrols (an element of the Canadian forces that includes northern Aboriginal peoples) to protect Arctic sovereignty through expanded patrols of the land. Prime Minister Harper has also talked extensively of the need to "use it or lose it" in regard to the protection of Canadian Arctic sovereignty; he has used this term for both the waterways and the land mass.[34] There is no modern international challenge to Canadian land territory (with the exception of tiny Hans Island) and hence no land sovereignty challenge. Yet the implication of Harper's rhetoric is clear. He is clearly suggesting that action needs to be taken to protect Canada's Arctic waters and lands. This is also an underlying theme in the understanding of most Canadians.

Until very recently, Canada has been fortunate in that few non-Canadian actors have entered the waters and lands of the Canadian north. While the Americans did so in 1969–70 and 1985, they did so very briefly. Hence, as concerned as Canadian leaders and the general public may have been over the possibility of the foreign interests coming to the region, the reality has been that few were interested in—or even capable of—doing so on a long-term basis.

This is now changing. With the acceleration of the impacts of climate change, the improvement of technology, and the promise of resource development in the region, it is becoming apparent that international interest in the region is growing. Thus, there is growing concern that Canadian Arctic sovereignty will face new demands and challenges on a sustained basis. It is not clear, however, who will make these challenges and even what form they will take. Once again, the only challenges to Canadian Arctic sovereignty that could occur will be over the status of the Northwest Passage. While no other country besides the United States has actually challenged the Canadian claim, it is possible that in the future the European Union or an Asian state such as China could publicly and officially support the American position, thereby directly challenging Canadian claims of sovereign control.

A second possible direct challenge to Canada may come when Canada announces the outer limits of its continental shelf. Under the terms of UNCLOS, coastal states have the right to determine whether they have an extended continental shelf that goes beyond the 200-mile exclusive economic zone (EEZ).[35] If they are able to demonstrate through scientific means that they do, they can claim the sovereign right over the soil and subsoil of this region. Canada has been engaged in an extensive multi-year mission to map its seabed. It is expected that by November 2013 it will announce the boundaries of this new zone of control. What is not known is whether the new boundaries will overlap with the Russian and Danish boundaries currently being determined by each of these states. It may be that there will be no overlaps, but it is also possible that there will be. If the latter is the case, then UNCLOS will provide a number of means by which the three states can resolve the issue. While this is clearly a boundary delimitation issue, it is entirely likely that the Canadian public and media will view it as a sovereignty issue.

The real challenges facing Canada, given growing international interest in the Arctic, will come from the need to respond to increased activity beyond Canadian jurisdiction. Such activity will not be an attempt to challenge Canadian sovereign control, but it will occur in and near Canadian Arctic territory. Canada will need to adapt to increased international shipping, including growing international cruise traffic. It is also possible that as the ice continues to melt, there will be increased fishing in waters open to international fishing fleets—which include the waters over the Canadian extended continental shelf, since Canada's international control is restricted to the soil and subsoil and not to the water column. These activities will not challenge Canadian Arctic sovereignty, but they will have a major impact on the Canadian north and will require further Canadian action.

Finally, and perhaps most importantly, the protection of Canadian Arctic sovereignty is really about means and not ends. In other words, the protection of Canadian Arctic sovereignty is really about the start of the story and not the end of it. Even though Canadian leaders and the Canadian public have been fixated on the issue of protecting Canadian Arctic sovereignty, one question has not been asked: "For what purpose?"

If the government is attempting to protect Canadian Arctic sovereignty, it does not do so simply to be able to say it is protecting sovereignty. Instead, it wants to have that sovereignty consolidated so that it would then have the authority to control and regulate activities within Canada's Arctic territories. In other words, the issue is not about having the right to say that the Northwest Passage is Canadian (recognizing that, for some, the nationalistic joy they might receive from such utterances could be a major benefit), but rather about being able to regulate all activity, both foreign and domestic, so as to protect and promote Canadian interests. So the protection of Canadian Arctic sovereignty is merely the first step in protecting Canada's Arctic interests.

This step, however, is often portrayed as the only step. For example, despite all of the attention given to the protection of Canadian Arctic sovereignty relating to the Northwest Passage, no Canadian government has ever addressed the issue of what it wants to use the passage for. Does Canada see the need to limit or even ban international shipping within these waters, or does it wish to encourage shipping? There has never been a policy announcement on this or an examination one way or the other. Instead, the focus of successive Canadian governments has just been on supporting Canada's claim that the passage is Canadian. Why it needs to be Canadian has never been explained.

Thus, as one seeks to understand the problem of Canadian Arctic sovereignty, several themes emerge. The first is that the term "the protection of Canadian Arctic sovereignty" has taken on many meanings. Technically, it expresses the need to ensure that Canada retains the authoritative right to make final decisions within a defined boundary. No outside power has the right to make decisions unless the Government of Canada confers that right. While there have been lingering concerns about the control of Hans Island, the current issues are maritime in nature. They are about the status of the Northwest Passage, the boundary with the

United States in the Beaufort Sea, and possibly disputes with the Russia and Denmark over the seabed relating to any future continental shelf claims.

However, the general Canadian public and many political elites have a broader understanding of what the protection of Canadian Arctic sovereignty entails. In general, they understand the term in a more emotional manner, for they see the threat to the Canadian Arctic in a more general way, one that blurs the difference between the land and waters of the region. The fact that there is a difference between the perception and reality of the problems facing Canadian Arctic sovereignty means that any effort to respond to threats has become problematic. Successive Canadian governments have found it necessary to respond to the technical and legal issues surrounding the specifics of Canadian sovereignty, but at the same time they have found it necessary to take action that responds to the public expectation that they "do something." As a result, the government's plans are often tailored to demonstrate decisive action following a perceived challenge to Canadian Arctic sovereignty. Usually, this has occurred in a crisis. As such, the responses tend to be hurried and reactive. This means that as a crisis fades, the government inevitably retreats on many of the promises it has made to defend Arctic sovereignty—particularly if fulfilling the promises involves large expenditures. In time, Canada has been left with a somewhat hollowed-out set of policies regarding the protection of Canadian Arctic sovereignty. This article will now evaluate how Canada has met the challenges to its Arctic sovereignty.

Conclusion

So what have Canadian governments done to "protect" Canadian Arctic sovereignty? Several trends can be identified. First, much of Canadian policy has developed over the years in the context of responding to a crisis involving a perceived international challenge. This means that when the government does develop a policy response, it does so with the full attention of senior policy-makers. This has resulted in some very powerful policy plans. The problem is that when the crisis subsides and the government's attention goes elsewhere, the policy commitments that have substantial resource implications tend to be scaled back or cancelled.

The second trend is that the policy that is developed is often drawn from policies that really have little to do with the substance of Arctic sovereignty but permits a "repacking" that allows the government of the day to claim that it has a robust set of policy options.

The third trend is that with respect to policy initiatives that are resource neutral, Canadian officials have been both innovative and effective. The passage of the Arctic Waters Pollution Prevention Act, the inclusion of Article 234 (the Ice-Covered Waters Article) in the United Nations Convention on the Law of the Sea, and the negotiations of the 1988 Canada-US Arctic Waters Cooperation Agreement have all been important means of asserting Canadian control in the region. All of

these have succeeded in strengthening Canadian efforts to extend its control in the region. In other words, Canadian policy-makers have good ideas—as long as they do not cost money.

In effect, Canadian policy has a lot of flash, but little substance—except in terms of intellectual power. However, there are indications that recent Canadian governments have recognized the need to alter the way they "protect" Canadian sovereignty. Commencing with the Martin government but continuing with Harper's, there has been a growing desire to make Arctic sovereignty policy a high priority, but in non-crisis environments. There has also been a desire to ensure that the policy initiatives requiring substantial resources that are now being considered are actually developed. As of 2012, it is too soon to determine whether this will happen, but the possibility is good.

Endnotes

1   There is a wide and rich literature on this. For some of the best, see Edgar Dosman, ed., *The Arctic in Question* (Toronto: Oxford University Press, 1976); Nigel Banks, "Forty Years of Canadian Sovereignty Assertion in the Arctic," *Arctic* 40 (1987); Franklyn Griffiths, ed., *Politics of the Northwest Passage* (Kingston and Montreal: McGill-Queen's University Press, 1987); and Ken Coates, Whitney Lackenbauer, William Morrison, and Greg Poelzer, *Arctic Front: Defending Canada's Interests in the Far North* (Toronto: Thomas Allen, 2008).

2   P. Whitney Lackenbauer, "Right and Honourable: Mackenzie King, Canadian-American Bilateral Relations, and Canadian Sovereignty in the Northwest, 1943–1948," in *Mackenzie King: Citizenship and Community*, ed. John English, Kenneth McLaughlin, and P.W. Lackenbauer (Toronto: Robin Brass Studios, 2002), 151–68.

3   David G. Haglund and Tudor Onea, "Victory without Triumph: Theodore Roosevelt, Honour, and the Alaska Panhandle Boundary Dispute," *Diplomacy and Statecraft* 19, no. 1 (2008).

4   Galen Roger Perras, *Stepping Stones to Nowhere: The Aleutian Islands, Alaska, and American Military Strategy, 1867–1945* (Vancouver: UBC Press, 2003); and Shelagh Grant, *Polar Imperative: A History of Arctic Sovereignty in North America* (Vancouver: Douglas & McIntyre, 2010), 31–3.

5   P. Whitney Lackenbauer and Mathew Farish, "The Cold War on Canadian Soil: Militarizing a Northern

Environment," *Environmental History* 12, no. 3 (2007): 920–50.

6   Edgar Dosman, "The Northern Sovereignty Crisis 1968–70," in Edgar Dosman, ed., *The Arctic in Question* (Toronto: Oxford University Press, 1976).

7   Rob Huebert, "Polar Vision or Tunnel Vision: The Making of Canadian Arctic Waters Policy," *Marine Policy* 19, no. 4 (July 1995), 343–63.

8   Andrew Curry, "Ancient Migration: Coming to America," *Nature* 485, no. 7396 (2 May 2012), www.nature.com/news/ancient-migration-coming-to-america-1.10562.

9   Jessica Shadian, "From States to Polities: Reconceptualizing Sovereignty through Inuit Governance," *European Journal of International Relations* 16, no. 3 (September 2010): 485–510.

10 Mary Simon, "Inuit History Is Canadian History," *Hill Times Online*, 24 September 2012, www.hilltimes.com/opinion-piece/2011/10/31/inuit-history-is-canadian-history/28618.

11 Canada, House of Commons, *Debates*, 1st Session, 33rd Parliament, 10 September 1985, 6462–4.

12 William Morrison, *Showing the Flag: The Mounted Police and Canadian Sovereignty in the North: 1894–1925* (Vancouver: UBC Press, 1985).

13 Christopher Sands, "Canada's Cold Front: Lessons of the Alaska Boundary Dispute for Arctic Boundaries Today," *International Journal*, Winter 2009–10, 209–19.

14 William Morrison, "Eagle over the Arctic: Americans in the Canadian North 1867–1985," *Canadian Review of American Studies* 18, no. 1 (1987): 63–76.

15 Galen Roger Perras, *Stepping Stones to Nowhere: The Aleutian Islands, Alaska, and American Military Strategy, 1867–1945* (Vancouver: UBC Press, 2003).

16 K.S. Coates and W.R. Morrison, *The Alaska Highway in World War II: The American Army of Occupation in Canada's Northwest* (Norman: University of Oklahoma Press; Toronto: University of Toronto Press, 1992).

17 Coates *et al.*, *Arctic Front*, 55–63.

18 James Eayrs, *In Defence of Canada: Growing Up Allied* (Toronto: University of Toronto Press, 1980), 278–9.

19 Alexander Herd, "A Practical Project: Canada, the United States, and the Construction of the DEW Line," in *Canadian Arctic Sovereignty and Security: Historical Perspectives, Calgary Papers in Military and Strategic Studies*, Occasional Paper No. 4, ed. Whitney Lackenbauer (Calgary: Centre For Military And Strategic Studies, 2011), 171–200.

20 John Kirton and Don Munton, "Protecting the Canadian Arctic: The Manhattan Voyages, 1969–1970," in *Canadian Foreign Policy: Selected Cases*, ed. Kirton and Munton (Toronto: Prentice-Hall, 1992), 206–21.

21 Jack Granatstein and Robert Bothwell, *Pirouette: Pierre Trudeau and Canadian Foreign Policy* (Toronto: University of Toronto Press, 1990), 76–81.

22 Don McRae and D.J. Goundrey, "Environmental Jurisdiction in Arctic Waters: The Extent of Article 234," *University of British Columbia Law Review* 197 (1982): 197–256.

23 Huebert, "Polar Vision or Tunnel Vision," 343–7.

24 Ibid.

25 Christopher Kirkey, "Smoothing Troubled Waters: The 1988 Canada–United States Arctic Co-operation Agreement," *International Journal* 50 (1995): 401–26.

26 Rob Huebert, "Climate Change and Canadian Sovereignty in the Northwest Passage," *Isuma: Canadian Journal of Policy Research* 2, no. 4 (2001): 86–94.

27 Canada, *Canada's International Policy Statement, A Role of Pride and Influence in the World Overview* (Ottawa, 2005).

28 Rob Huebert, "Renaissance in Canadian Arctic Security?," *Canadian Military Journal* 6, no. 4 (2005–6): 17–29.

29 Whitney Lackenbauer, *From Polar Race to Polar Saga: An Integrated Strategy for Canada and the Circumpolar World*, Foreign Policy for Canada's Tomorrow series, no. 3 (Toronto: Canadian International Council, July 2009).

30 James Allan, *Sovereign Statehood* (London: Allen & Unwin, 1986).

31 R.R. Churchill and A.V. Lowe, *The Law of the Sea*, 3rd edn (Manchester, UK: Manchester University Press, 2002).

32 For the best review of the Canadian legal position, see Donat Pharand, *Canada's Arctic Waters in International Law* (Cambridge: Cambridge University Press, 1988).

33 Mary Simon, "Inuit and the Canadian Arctic: Sovereignty Begins at Home," *Journal of Canadian Studies* 43, no. 2 (Spring 2009): 250–60.

34 Kirstin Bartenstein, "'Use it or lose it': An Appropriate and Wise Slogan?," *Policy Options*, July-August 2010, 68–73.

35 Elizabeth Riddell-Dixon, "Canada and Arctic Politics: The Continental Shelf Extension," *Ocean Development and International Law* 39, no. 4 (2008): 343–59.

PART III

Suggested Readings

Bothwell, Robert. 2007. *Alliance and Illusion: Canada and the World, 1945–1984*. Vancouver: UBC Press.

Bow, Brian J., and Patrick Lennox. 2008. *An Independent Foreign Policy for Canada? Challenges and Choices for the Future*. Toronto: University of Toronto Press.

Coates, Ken, P. Whitney Lackenbauer, Bill Morrison, and Greg Poelzer. 2008. *Arctic Front: Defending Canada in the Far North*. Toronto: Thomas Allen & Son.

Froese, Marc D. 2010. *Canada at the WTO: Trade Litigation and the Future of Public Policy*. Toronto: University of Toronto Press.

Hillmer, Norman, and J.L. Granatstein. 2008. *Empire to Umpire*. 2nd ed. Scarborough, ON: Thomson Nelson.

Key Terms

colonialism
decolonization
ecumenical
evangilization
imperialism

internationalism
multilateral
non-alignment
racialized

Questions for Consideration

1. What is meant by a "revolution" in foreign policy after 1945 and why/how may this be an overstatement?

2. What is "Pearsonian internationalism" and how does it influence post-1970 interpretations of Canada's foreign policy approaches?

3. What world factors shaped Canada's foreign policy in the years from 1947 to 1967 and how did they influence Canadian action?

4. Why was it so difficult for Canada to exercise "quiet diplomacy" and influence US policy during the Vietnam War?

5. Did Canada fail to act according to its reputation as a peacemaker and humanitarian in its involvement in "peripheral" countries/regions during the postwar years?

6. Why did young, service-minded Canadians increasingly reject church missions as the means to pursue development work?

7. In what ways did the United Church practices and ideology towards "missions" change over the course of the 1960s?

8. Why did Canadians become concerned about American foreign investment and ownership in the postwar years? How was this a "nationalist" position?

9. What are the main trends in the Canadian response to concerns about Arctic sovereignty?

10. Compare the nationalist concerns highlighted by both Azzi and Huebert to the cultural nationalism studied in chapter 2.

Relevant Websites

Foreign Affairs, Trade and Development Canada
www.international.gc.ca/arctic-arctique/arctic_policy-canada-politique_arctique.aspx?lang=eng

Canadian Defence and Foreign Affairs Institute
www.cdfai.org

Canadian International Development Agency
www.acdi-cida.gc.ca/acdi-cida/acdi-cida.nsf/eng/home

Canadian Military Journal
www.journal.forces.gc.ca

Canadian War Museum
www.warmuseum.ca

Foreign Affairs, Trade and Development Canada
www.international.gc.ca/department-ministere/index.aspx.

North Atlantic Treaty Organization
www.nato.int/cps/en/natolive/index.htm

United Nations. Oceans and Law of the Sea
www.un.org/Depts/los/convention_agreements/convention_overview_convention.htm

Walter and Duncan Gordon Foundation
www.gordonfoundation.ca

PART IV

The Rights Revolution

TIMELINE

1946	Gouzenko Affair and investigation lead to suspension of civil and legal rights
1946	Viola Desmond begins fight against segregation in Halifax movie theatres
1946	Committee for the Repeal of the Chinese Immigration Act formed
1947	Chinese Immigration Act repealed
1947	First Bill of Rights introduced in Saskatchewan by CCF government of Tommy Douglas
1948	Signing of the UN Universal Declaration of Human Rights
1951	Ontario government passes the first anti-discrimination laws (Fair Employment Practices Act and Fair Accommodation Practices Act, 1954)
1951	Ontario government passes first equal pay for equal work law
1951	Ban on potlatch and sun dance removed
1954	Women's Bureau in Department of Labour formed
1956	Federal government introduces federal equal pay for equal work law
1960	Status Indians receive the franchise
1960	Diefenbaker government enacts the Canadian Bill of Rights
1961	Halifax decides to raze Africville and relocate its citizens
1962	Racial and ethnic discrimination is removed from the Immigration Act
1962	Ontario establishes first Human Rights Code and Human Rights Commission (rest of the country follows suit by 1977)
1962	Creation of the BC Civil Liberties Association
1963	Founding of the Ligue des droits de l'homme in Montreal
1967	Pearson government creates the Royal Commission on the Status of Women
1968	Celebrations held on anniversary of UN Declaration on Human Rights
1968	Black United Front established in Nova Scotia
1969	White Paper on Indian Policy introduced and withdrawn
1969	Official bilingualism and biculturalism introduced by federal government
1970	Report of the Royal Commission on the Status of Women released
1970	October Crisis and implementation of the War Measures Act in Quebec
1971	Multiculturalism is made official government policy

continued

1971	Federal government establishes maternity leave and maternity benefits	**1989**	Montreal Massacre directs attention to issue of violence against women
1972	National Action Committee on the Status of Women created	**1992**	Canadian Army ends discrimination against homosexuals
1974–9	Series of racial attacks occur in Toronto	**1993**	Case of *Rodriquez v. BC* seeks to have assisted suicide legalized under the Charter
1975	Wilson Head releases study on *The Black Presence in the Canadian Mosaic*	**1995**	In Egan decision, Supreme Court extends Charter equality rights protection to sexual orientation
1977	Toronto appoints Task Force on Human Relations to examine racism	**1999**	Supreme Court rules that same-sex relationships must be treated equally under the law (with the same rights as heterosexual common-law relationships)
1977	Quebec first province to add sexual orientation to its human rights code		
1978	Frances Henry report concludes that racism is widespread in Toronto	**2001**	*R. v. Latimer* case seeks to overturn the second-degree murder conviction of a father for taking the life of his daughter
1979	Cardinal Carter examines the treatment of visible minorities		
1981	Bathhouse riots in Toronto	**2001**	Case of religious freedom involving Trinity Western University
1982	Charter of Rights and Freedoms enacted	**2003**	Ontario Court of Appeal rules that preventing same-sex marriages violates the equality provisions of the Charter
1985	Indian Act amended to treat women in the same way as men in the determination of Aboriginal status		
1988	Supreme Court rules that abortion law violates the Charter	**2005**	Federal Civil Marriage Act legalizes same-sex marriage

Introduction

Some of the most definitive changes in Canada since 1945 have resulted from the promotion, protection, and endorsement of civil and human rights and equality of opportunity. From 1945 to the present, the activism of civil and human rights groups, combined with that of organizations of collective minorities, has succeeded in achieving legislative and policy gains that now protect the rights and freedoms of all Canadians and facilitate equality of opportunity.

Civil and human rights groups first appeared in the 1930s, but extensive organization and activism only began in earnest in the immediate postwar years. The devastating poverty experienced by many Canadians and the oppression of political and racial minorities during the Depression years led some intellectuals, socialists, and communists to demand measures that would address economic security and protect civil rights. The end of the war, however, brought with it a greater awareness of racism and discrimination, as well as a determination to protect and ensure the freedoms of all citizens. The reality of systemic and state-sanctioned genocide, the extermination of racial and religious minorities throughout the war, and the decline of British power seriously challenged the sense of racial superiority held by many of British and northern European descent.

This ideological construct existed on a wider international scale, as evidenced by the United Nations Universal Declaration of Human Rights in 1948. As the postwar years continued, several factors further fuelled the growing awareness of and organization around human rights. Economic prosperity and a higher standard of living allowed a growing middle class to examine issues of social justice. With the overall rise in the level of education, many Canadians became aware of and began to critique inequality, discrimination, and rights violations in Canadian society. In the United States, the black civil rights movement became a potent symbol of the violation of individual rights and a model for rights activism, an example further strengthened by the decolonization movements throughout the developing world. By the 1960s, youthful baby boomers added both significant numbers to these groups and a renewed critique of inequality within all areas of Canadian society.

In the immediate postwar years, many human rights groups emerged in the form of civil liberties associations in major Canadian cities. In their campaigns against violations of civil liberties, they were joined by groups representing racial, ethnic, and religious minorities, as well as labour and church organizations. Many of these church and minority groups had existed previously, but in these years they were galvanized around the human rights cause. A notable example was the Jewish Labour Committee, formed in 1936, which joined with the civil liberties organizations, labour groups, and black Canadians in a successful campaign that led to the enactment of the first anti-discrimination laws in Ontario, the Fair Employment Practices Act and the Fair Accommodation Practices Act. Carmela Patrias examines the origins and enactment of the first human rights bill in Canadian history, the 1947 Saskatchewan Bill of Rights. Although the bill has often been seen as originating solely through the efforts of the Co-operative Commonwealth Federation (CCF) government of Tommy Douglas, Patrias reveals the roles played by social democrats, including Jews, labour, and Christians, both within and outside of the CCF, in the development of the bill, as well as how social democratic ideology encompassed the idea of equal rights for all, regardless of race and religion. In these early years, the goal of human rights advocacy was the achievement of laws banning discrimination based on race, ethnicity, national origin, and religion. As Catherine Briggs notes, the human rights discourse of the immediate postwar years did not recognize sex as a potential basis for discrimination. Yet, as she reveals in her study of the Women's Bureau, some women were beginning to acknowledge and argue for state action to address the inequality faced by women, particularly in the labour force. The bureau, in the years preceding the activism of the women's movement, sought to bring attention to the inequities experienced by women, and ultimately it influenced the development of major equality legislation, such as maternity leave and benefits. The passage of the Canadian Bill of Rights in 1960, a federal law enacted by the government of John Diefenbaker, was a significant achievement.

From 1960 to approximately 1980, the human rights movement became a major political force and placed the ideology of human rights into the mainstream consciousness of Canadian society. The overall number of groups grew significantly, and they were joined by new groups representing minorities who argued that they too experienced discrimination based on a collective characteristic beyond race, religion, or ethnicity. Women, gays and lesbians, and First Nations peoples organized, demanding their inclusion in anti-discrimination laws, government action to promote equality of opportunity, and, in the case of the First Nations, recognition of land rights. Such activity expanded not only the concept of rights but also the understanding of systemic and institutional causes of discrimination. In his study of the Ligue des droits de l'homme (Montreal), Dominique Clement examines changes in its membership and organization, as well as the goals of rights movements from the first period (after the Second World War) to the second (starting in the late 1960s). Demographics, in particular the large influx of youth, the increased level of education and wealth of members, and expanding sources of funding all had a significant impact on the nature of these movements, not only expanding the membership of rights movements but also broadening the scope of the grievances they sought to address. By the 1970s, the impact of the rights movements was so profound that many Canadians increasingly identified themselves according to the civic virtues of tolerance and equality, exemplified by the adoption of official multiculturalism in 1971. Consequently, as Malgorzata Kierylo reveals, an upsurge of racial violence in 1970s Toronto significantly challenged this "national narrative" of tolerance, leading to a number of enquiries to determine the reasons. In the end, it came to be recognized that systemic and institutional causes perpetuated racism in Canadian society and that prejudice could not be eradicated strictly through equality laws and awareness at the individual level.

The ultimate achievement of the human rights movements was the enactment of the Charter of Rights and Freedoms in 1982. The Charter provides the constitutional entrenchment of the rights and freedoms of all Canadians and the legal framework for protecting those rights from the actions and policies of government. As such, it is a much more powerful guarantor of rights than had existed earlier; moreover, it has led more individuals and groups to seek equality in Canada, as it has empowered the judiciary to enforce the terms of the Charter and to strike down laws, policies, or regulations in violation of it. The power of the Charter lies also in the fact that it is the result of the wide acceptance and inculcation of the human rights ideology within Canadian society. Miriam Smith explores the impact of the Charter and judicial empowerment on equality-seeking and the expansion of rights since 1982. Using the gay and lesbian rights movement as a case study, Smith shows how the Charter provided gays and lesbians with a new strategy and strengthened their fight for equal treatment. Gay and Lesbian rights advocacy changed after 1982 from lobbying government to using the courts to challenge existing laws that treated gay and lesbian couples and families differently, a successful strategy that ultimately led to the 2005 legalization of gay marriage. Chance Minnett and Matthew Hennigar also examine the issue of the use of judicial power to make political policy. However, they focus on the Evangelical Fellowship of Canada (EFC) to explore whether socially conservative groups have been able to achieve policy goals through the courts to the same extent as equality-seeking groups have. Minnett and Hennigar find that, unlike the latter groups, the EFC was relatively unsuccessful in achieving its goals through the courts, and when it did succeed, the objective was more often to maintain existing policy rather than to reform it or strike it down.

CHAPTER 10

Early Human Rights Movements

◎ 10.1: THE "SOCIAL ANSWER": THE DEVELOPMENT OF MATERNITY AND CHILD CARE PROVISIONS IN THE 1960S

Catherine Briggs

In 1964, Marion Royce, the first director of the federal Women's Bureau, made a speech in which she spoke of the "social answer" to issues surrounding the growing employment of mothers in postwar society, a common theme in her speeches. Royce argued that Canadian society needed first to accept the inevitability of women's employment outside of the home and then to move forward to develop the "supporting services" that would allow women to fulfil their responsibilities as wives, mothers, and workers. Having ambivalence towards or ignoring the reality of mothers' employment was no longer a viable option.[1] The "supporting services" envisioned by Royce included expanded state-supported child care and maternity protection policies (encompassing maternity leave and benefits).

At the time she delivered this speech, Marion Royce and the Women's Bureau were advocating and developing policy to provide for both these services. Created in 1953 and the only federal agency specifically devoted to women's issues, the Women's Bureau, as a division of the Department of Labour, was responsible for studying "the problems peculiar to women

workers."[2] In the years before the surge of women's rights activism after 1970, the bureau, under the leadership of Royce, acted as a strong voice for women's right to work and to do so on the basis of equality with men. The equality and rights discourse of the bureau challenged the social values of the time, when society adhered strongly to traditional gender and family values and the issue of sex discrimination had not yet entered the public discourse. However, the focus on women's workplace problems as issues of inequality had become problematic in the early 1960s as the bureau turned its attention to the problems of working mothers. Maternity protection and child care had entered the policy agenda of the Department of Labour by that time, but the equality discourse competed with ideologies of income support, protection of children, and health and safety to shape the resulting legislation. While the bureau played an important role in the development of legislation providing for maternity leave and benefits and for a limited state-sponsored child care program, these "equality" measures were shaped more by concern for family welfare than for women's labour force equality. Nonetheless, they did constitute the "social response" envisioned by Royce, as they provided some assistance to women trying to balance motherhood with employment.

Women's Bureau in the 1950s: Women Workers and "Inequality"

The Women's Bureau was the first government agency within the Canadian state specifically created to address the problems of women. Yet, its creation at a time before "status of women" issues entered the public agenda raises questions about the government's real intentions for this agency. Undoubtedly, the government hoped to calm the voice of organized women who had actively lobbied since the Second World War on a number of women's issues, such as equal pay for equal work. A women's branch in the Labour Department, equivalent to the one that had existed in the United States since 1920, had been one of those demands.[3] The results of the 1951 census added further fuel to this demand for government action on issues arising from female employment. Despite the glorification of home and family as women's primary place in postwar popular culture, the 1951 census revealed a startling increase in married women's labour force participation, from 10 per cent of all female workers in 1931 to 30 per cent in 1951.[4] Growing public awareness and concern about the social implications for family life and the economy strengthened the voice of the women's organizations in their demand for government action.[5] The potential of the new bureau to effect change, however, was questionable in 1954 owing to a mandate limited to researching the issues facing women workers, a small budget, and staff of only a director, an administrative assistant, and one to two clerks in its first two decades.[6] These conditions led *Chatelaine* editor Doris Anderson to reflect in 1966 that most observers thought the bureau would be nothing more than an "inexpensive and useless cipher."[7]

Clearly, the Women's Bureau might well have become a "useless cipher" and certainly not a voice for women's equality had it not been for the tireless energy and ideological convictions of its first director, Marion Royce. Speaking in her first public appearance as director in 1954, Royce addressed the Canadian public on the CBC (Canadian Broadcasting Corporation) radio program *Canada at Work*. Referring to the "traditional attitudes" that structure society, Royce assured the public that "[w]omen are, and will continue to be, at the centre and heart of family life." Still, she declared, "a woman is a person in her own right, and there is need . . . to explore the causes and extent of occupational inequalities and to work for their removal."[8]

Most striking about Royce's assertion is her use of the concept of human rights and equality to define the problems faced by wage-earning women. The postwar period, as many scholars note, saw growing support for the principle of human rights, characterized by widespread knowledge and abhorrence of prejudice and discrimination and the growth of multiple organizations dedicated to developing measures to define and provide institutional protection of individual rights and to facilitate equality of opportunity. However, as Carmela Patrias and Ruth A. Frager note, the concept of *human* rights did not include *women's* rights; sex was rarely mentioned as one of the grounds on which discrimination could be based. Government legislation concurred; early human rights legislation, such as the Fair Employment Practices Act (FEPA) of 1953, prohibited discrimination but only on the grounds of race, national origin, colour, and religion. Sex discrimination was simply not a concern of the human rights movement during the 1950s and early 1960s because women were not considered equal to men.[9]

Influenced by the ideological construct of the postwar period, Marion Royce assumed the position of director with a strong commitment to the principle of individual rights and freedoms. Unlike her contemporaries in the human rights movement, however, she believed that sex, like race or religion, was a characteristic that had little effect on individual abilities. This is not surprising given her professional and intellectual background. As consultant on social and international questions with the world's YWCA in the 1940s, Royce had participated in the UN Commission on the Status of Women (UNCSW) and monitored the activities of the International Labour Organization (ILO). While human rights organizations in Canada ignored the question of sex discrimination throughout the 1950s, both the UN and the ILO had begun to address the issue with the 1946 establishment of the UNCSW. The 1948 Universal Declaration of Human Rights included sex as one of the forms of discrimination, as did a number of subsequent conventions of the ILO. Thus, Royce was not alone, but she was most certainly in the minority when, in the early 1950s, she began to use the language, concepts, and methods of the human rights discourse to argue against sex discrimination in all facets of life.[10]

Drawing on the equal rights perspective, Royce strove throughout the 1950s to redefine the problems of wage-earning women as issues of equality. In her public speeches, in the bureau's publications, and in policy proposals, Royce steadfastly declared women's *right to work* outside of the home, regardless of marital status and age, and to do so on the basis of equality of opportunity with men. Under Royce, the bureau focused on public education and policy development to address the "occupational inequalities"[11] faced by women, including low wages, job segregation in low-status sectors, inadequate training and education, inaccessibility to promotion, and primary responsibility for care of home and children. This view contradicted the dominant discourse of the postwar period in which the well-being of the family structured most debate on the wage-earning wife and mother, even among supporters.[12] For Royce, however, economic equality, achieved in part through participation in the

Canada Department of Manpower and Immigration/Library and Archives Canada

Under the direction of Marion Royce, the Women's Bureau advocated for Canadian women's right to work on the basis of equality of opportunity with men.

workforce, was fundamental to the advancement of women in Canadian society. "Dignity and worth as persons," she declared, derived from occupational status and wage earning potential. Women in the home, despite their crucial role in society, were "without economic entity."[13] Utilizing this ideological framework, the bureau achieved notable success in publicizing the problems of wage-earning women and promoting possible solutions, despite the very real limitations imposed by its limited mandate and resources. Much like the liberal feminists who would follow her, Royce optimistically believed that the inequality faced by wage-earning women could be removed by state action. It was this work that led Doris Anderson to her 1966 conclusion that the bureau had surmounted its meagre position within government, primarily through the energy, commitment, and insight of Marion Royce.[14]

The 1960s—New Directions: Working Mothers Enter the Public Agenda

By the early 1960s, further changes in the composition of the female labour force came to light, raising renewed concerns about women's role in society and forcing a reorientation in the focus of the work of the Women's Bureau. The "problem" of the wage-earning woman was becoming more complex as the issue of working mothers came to the forefront. Once again, the census (1961) revealed a steady increase in the labour force participation of married women, but those numbers now included married women with children. Although the actual labour force participation rates of women with young children were still relatively low, they provided little assurance to a society that equated *all* motherhood with a full-time commitment to home care and child-raising.[15]

This new evidence led to a renewed concern with the problems of female workers, but with the focus now on *mothers*, the public debate began to examine these questions as they related to postwar concerns with family stability and the idealization of home and family that characterized these years. "Familism," as it has come to be called, "extolled home and family centredness, pronatalism, and heterosexuality" within the "security of traditional gender roles for men and women."[16] Real changes in the nature of postwar society, including in the roles of women, as evidenced by their rising labour force participation, led to anxiety about the stability of the family. This anxiety became conflated with fears of communism; the superiority of the traditional nuclear family was equated with the perceived superiority of Western democracy and capitalism.[17] As the traditional nuclear family unit became the basis of morality and political security, familism was established as a predominant ideological current.

Within this familial discourse, then, it is not surprising that public debate about wage-earning mothers was characterized by "deep concern . . . even hostility."[18] The belief that young children should be cared for only by their mothers (and thus, that women with young children should not work) was "powerfully strengthened in the postwar period by psychoanalytic themes of 'maternal deprivation.'" Most of the opposition to paid employment for mothers centred on the harmful effects it was presumed to have on children. Wage-earning mothers were charged with neglect and selfishness, and working outside the home was presented as a cause of mental health problems, juvenile delinquency, and rising divorce rates.[19] In part because of the popularity of psychology and the social sciences in the postwar period, these ideas found expression in the popular press. These shifts in the familial discourse of postwar society left some space for married women to pursue activities outside the home (whether for personal growth or for economic reasons), but restricted their focus and field of activity exclusively to home and child-raising once they became mothers.

For the Women's Bureau, working mothers, given the societal equating of mothers with family, presented very difficult ideological barriers with the issue of balancing motherhood and employment. The discourse of human rights served well when the bureau's primary focus was on the problems (and hence the rights) of married woman in the labour force. By the late 1950s, the bureau no longer seemed a radical voice in its concern for the rights of wage-earning women. As Joan Sangster notes, throughout the decade, a "grudging acceptance" developed for married women's right to participate in paid employment (although not necessarily on the basis of equality of opportunity). Yet, the anxiety about family stability that permeated postwar society ultimately separated mothers from this growing acceptance of women's right to employment. When the issue of working mothers arose, the arguments used to examine this question centred on the consequences for children, husbands, and family stability, and rarely on women's rights.[20]

By the early 1960s, additional factors were drawing greater attention to women's issues. The "second wave" began to emerge and would, over the course of the 1960s, strengthen the women's movement significantly in numbers but also in the discursive construction of women's issues as questions of equality. New organizations formed, staffed by young baby boomers with higher levels of education; they joined with the existing groups to demand government action to address the barriers to equality faced by women in both employment and the home.[21] By the mid-1960s, the growing size and voice of the women's movement combined with an international climate conducive to assessing women's issues. The international community, in which Canada sought active involvement, provided leadership and an example for action against human rights abuses, including sexism. By 1958, once Canada joined the UN Status of Women Commission, women's organizations began to point to the conventions of both the UN and the ILO, arguing the moral imperative that government should follow the example of the international community and legislate against sex discrimination.[22] Ultimately, the leadership of the international community did provide some impetus for federal action in many areas, including maternity protection and day care. While the government was under no obligation to conform to these standards, many officials

in the Department of Labour argued that Canada should be able to "justify" any decisions to deviate from those standards.[23]

As a result, over the course of the 1960s, working women's issues—including those of working mothers—gradually became more prevalent in the policy debates and initiatives of the Department of Labour. When Royce chose "working women with family responsibilities" as the theme of the 1965 conference, both the deputy minister and the assistant deputy minister spoke approvingly, noting that the theme was "timely" and relevant to departmental considerations regarding future legislation.[24] The 1966 creation of the Royal Commission on the Status of Women (RCSW) definitively placed women's issues onto the government agenda.[25] Initially, the Department of Labour delayed action on women's issues with the pretence of waiting for the commission's report. In general, though, the knowledge that the commission would undoubtedly review, critique, and recommend action on many outstanding women's issues provided an important stimulus to departmental action. In April 1967, the deputy minister wrote to the heads of all branches. Noting the increasing support of maternity leave within the House of Commons and the likelihood that the RCSW would also support the measure, he argued that legislation was inevitable.[26] The bureau would play a definitive role in this policy debate as the sole voice on women's issues within the federal government.

First Actions of the Women's Bureau: Child Care and Maternity Protection

Although the issues of maternity protection and child care emerged around 1960, the "problem" of the working mother had received some tentative exploration in the early research of the bureau. On several occasions in the 1950s, Royce voiced her recognition that women with children and pregnant women might soon form a significant component of the labour force, bringing with them different and potentially more challenging problems. In a speech in 1954, Royce conceded that while the "community rightly assumes that the first duty of the wife and mother is to her family," nonetheless, "it is a matter of vital social concern to discover whether women can carry the double responsibility of a job outside with the adequate care of children especially when they are small."[27] Consequently, the Women's Bureau's first major research project on "married women working for pay in eight Canadian cities" [*MWWP*] expanded its focus beyond the married woman to include examination of the child care provisions and problems experienced by women who were also mothers.[28] In the early 1950s, however, Royce did not have specific ideas about the needs of wage-earning mothers and rarely spoke of government-supported child care or maternity provisions as potential solutions.

This early conceptualization was the bureau's starting point as it began its public advocacy and research on the experiences of wage-earning mothers. Given the assumption that a problem existed, the main issue became the potential inability of women to balance the demands of child and home with paid employment successfully. The difference by 1960 was the bureau's assertion that *society* had a responsibility to help women find a balance between their work and family responsibilities. Thus, the problem and the potential solutions were moved from the private to the public sphere, and policy initiatives, such as state-supported child care, entered the agenda. In her early speeches, Marion Royce acknowledged the societal opposition to and concern about working mothers, but asserted that opposition or "ambivalence" was no longer a viable solution. Society needed to accept the reality that mothers would continue to enter the labour force and would develop viable community responses to the problems that arose.[29] Speaking in 1964, Royce argued: "The social answer must begin from recognition of the fact that women have become an integral part of the labour force and accepting community responsibility for the supporting services that are needed to enable them to fulfil their various responsibilities effectively."[30] Her statements did not challenge the fundamental responsibility of mothers to care for their children and homes. Still, she argued, they could not successfully fulfil these responsibilities along with those of paid employment without the provision of services. The social response Royce envisioned was state-supported, community-based child care services (along with maternity leave and benefits).

As a first step towards developing a child care policy, the bureau argued for further research to supplement the cursory results obtained in *MWWP*. This was an understandable position given a very real lack of information about the issues surrounding wage-earning mothers and child care. As Royce noted in a 1962 speech, "[O]ne of the very real obstacles to tackling the problem" of child care was a lack of information about rudimentary issues like the number of wage-earning mothers and the ages of their children. In particular, Royce believed that a study was needed to assess the availability and form of existing facilities and to determine their adequacy for meeting demand. To achieve this end, she suggested in 1962, family and child welfare agencies could be utilized to conduct the survey or at least be used in a consultative role.[31]

The Women's Bureau succeeded in convincing the government to study child care. In August 1965, the National Employment Committee (NEC) passed a resolution in support of the Canadian Welfare Council (CWC) undertaking a study of the availability and adequacy of child care facilities for wage-earning mothers. Subsequently, the CWC submitted a proposal for the study, which the NEC approved with a recommendation that the Department of Labour fund the survey.[32] Initial support within the department went beyond simple support of the research project. In comments to Royce, the deputy minister suggested that the important questions centred on the adequacy of existing facilities and the potential involvement of government in expanding child care. The CWC survey was divided into two parts: the purpose of the first was to assess existing facilities, while that of the second was to determine the need or adequacy of these facilities to meet demand. Referring to this division, the deputy minister, G.V. Haythorne, argued: "The most important question, I would think, is *how* can we attack the problem of determining outstanding needs and of developing adequate facilities for meeting them. *These* latter questions need attention *now* not in 2 years time [emphasis his]!"[33]

Royce concurred, agreeing there was a need for "immediate action." In previous speeches, it was clear that Royce perceived the survey as a precursor to establishing more facilities through government initiative. "We need careful surveys of the existing need in individual communities," she argued in 1962, "to ensure that adequate facilities be made available."[34] The deputy minister, it appears, also saw potential for government action in creating child care facilities as a result of the initial studies.

In the early 1960s, the bureau devoted most of its early advocacy and policy development efforts towards the issue of child care, although it was equally convinced that a maternity protection policy was needed. The difference in focus between the two issues resulted from the belief that there was not an equivalent need to study maternity protection. A long history of debate on maternity protection had begun with the 1919 convention of the ILO, and precedents already existed as examples for potential legislation, such as the maternity-leave provisions of the federal civil service, established during the war years owing to the hiring of married women.[35] At the provincial level, only British Columbia and Alberta had provisions for maternity leave in their labour legislation, and the provisions in both cases were weak and clearly inadequate. Royce was already aware of this inadequacy and believed that implementation of new regulations by all provinces and by the federal government was necessary. When the bureau commissioned a study of the existing maternity-leave provisions in Canada in 1967, its purpose was to highlight what it had been arguing for years— that the existing provisions were inadequate and inconsistent.[36]

Throughout the early 1960s, the bureau lobbied in support of federal legislation on maternity leave. In 1962, Royce expressed surprise that Canada did not already have government-legislated maternity leave. Noting the lack of federal and provincial legislation (except for weak provisions in British Columbia and Alberta), she asserted that Canada had been "curiously dilatory about the matter of maternity protection."[37] Following this revelation, the bureau began to focus its lobbying efforts on pushing for federal initiatives in the area. Invoking the idea of federal "leadership" in labour matters to the provinces, Royce, in her 1966 recommendations, argued for the need for federal legislative measures for maternity leave, to serve as a model for the provinces and to "ensure a high standard of working conditions within its jurisdiction."[38]

Attention to the question of maternity benefits (to accompany the period of leave) arose at a later date, with the ensuing debate and policy advocacy occurring primarily as a subsidiary or follow-up issue to the maternity-leave question. In the early 1960s, discussion of such benefits was sporadic, although the issue did come up at the bureau's various conferences and in speeches.[39] As support for maternity leave grew within the department, a concern developed that many wage-earning women would refuse to take a leave or would perceive it as a problem because of the lost wages entailed.[40] Thus, in policy debates, Royce gradually began to include the question of benefits as an adjunct to maternity-leave legislation. The objective of a maternity-leave program would be lost if women refused to take time off work because their families could not withstand a reduction in income.

Conceptualizing "Mothers" in Human Rights Discourse

As the Women's Bureau began to lobby in support of child care and maternity protection, it faced an ideological hurdle. The postwar human rights discourse that had informed its previous work was based on the "eighteenth-century liberal conception of the independent and autonomous self"—an ideology focused on the individual rather than on the collective and was premised on a classless, genderless, and colourless individual. This liberal concept of rights provided a clear basis for arguing women's right to equal access to the male-dominated public sphere, but it was problematic when applied to the "differences" between men and women, particularly those occasioned by the physical and familial demands of child-bearing. Ultimately, the postwar concept of equality of opportunity required only that women be treated the same as men; it did not provide for measures based on differences such as maternity leave.[41] This ideological problem could be overcome by enlarging the concept of rights to encompass women's reproductive labour as a factor in their equality in the workplace and thus to demand special provisions for women as a means of surmounting the additional obstacles to equal competition resulting from their primary responsibility for childrearing. In her advocacy of child care and maternity-leave policies in 1965, Royce

argued that they were necessary "to enable the working woman with family responsibilities to work on a basis of equality with those who are less burdened by family cares." Thus, it seems that Royce could expand her concept of rights to allow for "special" rather than "equal" treatment, but such ideas were still not widely embraced before the 1970s.

Another ideological impediment stemmed from the very real—and ongoing—separation of the "public" and the "private." As Annis May Timpson has shown, questions arising from women's unpaid labour in the home and those surrounding employment equity have been continuously "driven apart" throughout the period from 1945 to the present, making it very difficult to link child care policy to women's employment equity.[42] The placement of private

LIBERAL FEMINISM

Liberal feminism evolved from the political theory of liberalism that developed in Western countries during the Renaissance. As a political philosophy, liberalism focuses on the autonomy of the individual and holds to the concept that all citizens have basic civil and political rights/freedoms. The role of government, thus, is to ensure or further these civil and political rights. As an offshoot of liberalism, liberal feminism developed during the nineteenth century and had become the most common form of feminism held by women's rights advocates by the twentieth century.

Liberal feminism extends liberalism to women, arguing that women are equal to men and should have rights and opportunities equal to those of men in all facets of life. Thus, liberal feminism rejects the concept of women and men having different roles and thus opportunities based on their physiological and psychological differences. Women's inequality (historically and in the present) is conceptualized as a result of gender ideology, which is reinforced by laws or other rules and restrictions that have enforced an inequitable position for women, such as laws that disenfranchise women or by the employer practice of paying female employees less than males. While liberal feminists do not necessarily agree on which measures or policy initiatives will best achieve equality, they often turn to the state to implement measures to reduce the legal or institutional obstacles to women's equality or to introduce measures to promote the equality of women with men. Such measures have included "equal pay" laws, employment equity programs to encourage the hiring of women, and anti-discrimination laws that prohibit discrimination based on sex.

While this form of feminism was not new in the 1960s, it became the dominant expression of the women's movement during the "second wave" of activism from the late 1960s to the 1980s. Its prominence stemmed from the growth and ideology of the civil rights (and human rights) movements. Membership in this movement and exposure to its ideology led to a recognition among many women that sex discrimination existed alongside racial and religious discrimination and that such inequality could be addressed by similar methods and measures.

familial matters within the realm of public concern was limited and still tentative by the early 1960s. The expansion of government responsibility into areas of family life stemmed primarily from growing concern about the material welfare and stability of the family unit after the shock of two decades of war, Depression, and social unease, and was manifested in the development of a large number of government-sponsored "welfare" programs.[43] The lore of "mother care" and the familism of postwar society meant that women's issues became matters of public concern primarily in their relation to questions of family stability and welfare. Little space was left for competing discourses that could challenge the naturalness and primacy of women's role in the home and in the lives of children.

To overcome the ideological obstacles to policy development, Marion Royce began to argue that maternity protection and child care legislation was necessary to provide financial and health support to families unable to meet the male breadwinner ideal. These ideas fit comfortably into the bureau's existing arguments regarding both the inevitability of paid employment for many women, including mothers, and the need for services to allow mothers to combine the demands of home and children with paid employment. They were also compatible with the ideas of the social work community, which had already defined child care as an "anti-poverty and/or 'families in need' policy" and had become influential in determining social policy in the postwar period.[44] In the case of maternity protection, this welfare discourse combined with the prewar protective labour laws that had placed special restrictions on women's labour force participation, usually with the justification that these restrictions protected women's health and morality. Premised on the notion that the role of women in society was as a mother and wife, not as a labourer, the laws were intended to ensure women's child-bearing health for the future.[45] For the bureau, the dominance of "welfare" and "protection" in the discursive context of the postwar period provided the definitive construct for

policy relating to wage-earning mothers. The idea that the gendered and hierarchical division of labour in the family was the source of the burden and inequality faced by women had little resonance in postwar society—though it was voiced on occasion by Royce—and thus, it was gradually overpowered by arguments that presented maternity protection and child care—not equality initiatives—as family welfare matters.

Need/"Protection"—The Welfare Discourse

The conception of family welfare as the dominant discourse structuring the child care issue was evident in the bureau's first tentative exploration of the issue in its publication *MWWP*. *MWWP* revealed the importance of women's wages to a family's standard of living and thereby provided the bureau with a defence for mothers' employment that it would utilize throughout the debate. A summary of the study declared that one of its "main findings" was that married women, especially those with children, worked primarily for economic reasons.[46] With respect to married women who worked just for the extra money, the bureau emphasized their right to work on the basis of the importance of employment for women's equality because of the value attributed to wage earning in society.[47] Given the ideology surrounding motherhood, the bureau narrowed its defence of the working mother to a focus on familial economic *need* as it began to lobby in support of child care. This defence invoked the existing and acceptable concept of child care services as "welfare" or anti-poverty measures directed towards the most disadvantaged families. For these families, society had already grudgingly accepted the necessity of paid work for mothers.[48] In research studies and policy statements by the bureau, the concept of "need" became a prominent theme in discussions concerning the employment of mothers. In 1964, Royce argued that women's work outside the home was permanent and inevitable, in part because "their contribution to the maintenance of the family has become a necessity."[49] Having established the inevitability of paid employment for many mothers, the bureau could invoke the argument that society needed to move forward to develop the necessary supporting services.

Related to the welfare discourse, the Women's Bureau also employed the concept of child care as a "protective" measure to guard against the potential social problems often associated with neglect or poor care. Following the publication of *MWWP*, the bureau pointed to the study's results to argue the "growing urgency" to assess child care facilities, because "society" could not afford to have its children neglected.[50] In emphasizing the need to protect children from neglect or poor care, the bureau drew on existing arguments from child care advocates who stressed that many working mothers had to accept poor and inadequate child care arrangements.[51] Like these advocates, Royce criticized the prescription of many commentators that mothers simply should not work by noting the poverty that compelled many of them to enter labour force. Community-sponsored child care, Royce argued, had to be seen as a necessary social response rather than as an inducement to employment for mothers. The issue, she argued in 1964, was not about the employment of mothers but rather about how to "protect the children" and ensure "quality" child care while mothers were at work.[52] Child care advocates also argued for state-funded and -regulated care that would provide not just "spaces" but an environment that facilitated the development of emotionally, psychologically, and intellectually healthy future citizens.[53]

Ultimately, these ideas found legitimacy by invoking a social responsibility to protect children, both directly by saving them from neglect or poverty and indirectly by ensuring their healthy socialization for the future. Protection of children had long been deemed a necessary state intervention. Economic need placed the child care issue within the discourse of the necessity of welfare and social responsibility for a basic minimum standard of living. The bureau did point out the importance of child care for facilitating women's access to employment, but only sporadically. The discourses of

welfare and protection would find the greatest resonance given the preoccupation of society with the centrality of mothers to child welfare. According to Alena Heitlinger, the "ideology of maternal deprivation" meant that "public debates about childcare services focused only on the needs of children; little was heard of the employment needs of the mother."[54] This was an important line of argument because it reoriented the debate from whether or not mothers should work to whether child care was a social responsibility. Still, this meant a shift away from the bureau's primary focus on women's equality as workers to a discourse focused on children, protecting the weak, and family welfare.

The issue of maternity leave went through a similar process of definition over the 1960s, mainly through the competing discourses on women's rights and protection. Conceptually, maternity leave was a much less contentious issue, but it did involve two potentially competing ideas by the early 1960s. First debated and defined in the early twentieth century at the ILO, maternity leave had developed as a protective measure designed to ensure the health of mother and baby around the time of childbirth. Consequently, the 1919 convention stated that a woman "shall *not be permitted* to work during the six weeks following her confinement [emphasis mine]" and called for maternity benefits "for the full and healthy maintenance of herself and her child." By the early 1950s, informed by the growing equal rights movement, maternity leave concepts began to include the idea that women should both be protected from dismissal during the leave and be able to return to their job at the same level of seniority.[55]

These competing discourses of rights and protection found expression in the debate over maternity leave in Canada, presenting ideological difficulties for the bureau. As a protective measure designed to ensure the health of the mother and child, maternity leave held more poignancy within Canada than if defined as an issue of rights, especially given the country's past history of protective laws. For Royce, however, protective laws were an impediment to women's access to and equal participation in the labour force. The solution lay in defining maternity leave as both a health issue and an equality issue, as well as in redefining the purposes of protective laws. While Royce frequently spoke of the need for legislation "to safeguard the health of women workers and their children before and after childbirth,"[56] she drew an important distinction between the demand for these services and the protective labour laws of the prewar period. In a speech outlining the trends in labour laws since the Second World War, Royce noted the shift from the "protection of women as a separate category" to the "promotion of greater equality of opportunity and treatment." However, she argued, women, like all workers, still required protection from dangers and health risks.[57] Consequently, maternity protection was to be understood as a health and safety measure rather than as a means to restrict women's labour force participation in favour of their role as mothers. In speeches on maternity protection, Royce often combined the concepts of women's rights and women's protection to justify the measure. In 1965, she argued, "[P]olicies and services are needed to assist [women] in combining the two roles . . . to ensure their position in employment . . . as well as to safeguard the health and welfare of themselves and their families."[58] While these statements continued to emphasize women's "right to return to employment" following their leave, the notion of maternity leave as a workplace health and safety measure gradually assumed dominance.

Accompanying the maternity-leave question was the issue of whether women should receive benefits, although discussion of benefits within the bureau was sporadic through the early 1960s. Over time, however, discussion of maternity benefits increased, justified within the postwar discourse of welfare as an income support program based on need. Increasing support for maternity leave within the bureau coincided with the recognition that many wage-earning women would reject taking a leave or feel concern about the lost wages that would accompany the leave. According to reports, some wage-earning women had already tried through "subterfuge" to qualify for Unemployment Insurance benefits during periods when they were unable to work after giving birth.[59] Gradually, Royce began to emphasize financial need to justify a maternity benefits program. In 1966, Royce noted that maternity-leave provisions were problematic if not accompanied by some "social provision" for lost wages. Many families simply could not afford to lose the wife's wages, especially during a period of increased costs for health and other needs.[60] Gradually, the idea of maternity benefits was constructed into the discourses of financial need and social security; women's rights as workers and the need to readjust the gendered division of labour in society never entered the discourse of maternity benefits.

Policy Development and Outcome

Despite the Department of Labour's decision to participate in the Canadian Welfare Council survey, commitment to the child care issue within the department gradually diminished. Concern over the high cost of the proposed survey led to the approval of a smaller, more limited study. Funding was granted to the CWC to assess only the existing facilities for child care in Canada; the more important question of the adequacy of these facilities was put aside for a later date because it constituted the more expensive component.[61] Convinced of the urgency and importance of the second question, the Women's Bureau developed a means for assessing, on a much more limited scale, the question of need by having a supplementary questionnaire attached to the monthly Labour Force Survey conducted by the department. The questionnaire examined the child care arrangements made by wage-earning mothers and the problems encountered. Through this period, Royce struggled to reorient the department's focus towards the question of whether more child care facilities were needed, recognizing that government action was contingent on that question.[62] However, these lofty goals for the study were not realized. In the end, it was a minor compilation of statistics.[63] The question of adequacy would not be revisited by the Labour Department, as child care was redefined as an issue within the mandate of Health and Welfare by 1970.

As the question of child care policy was moving off the policy agenda of the Department of Labour, the issue of maternity protection was assuming ascendency. By the late 1960s, the department was moving steadily towards legislation ensuring both leave and benefits for pregnant women. In late 1966, the Women's Bureau prepared for the department's consideration a detailed report outlining the history of maternity-leave provisions within Canada, examining the major issues, and making specific recommendations for federal legislation. The deputy minister forwarded the report with his comments to the assistant deputy ministers; the comments did not question the inevitability of legislation but were concerned with the most expedient legislative means of introducing maternity leave.[64] By April 1967, the deputy minister wrote to the heads of all branches. Noting the increasing pressure within the House of Commons in support of maternity leave and the likelihood that the Royal Commission on the Status of Women would support the measure, he argued that legislation was inevitable.[65] As, unlike child care, this was clearly a labour issue, the department was comfortably moving towards legislation by mid-1967, with only the questions of legislative form and content to determine.

A number of factors combined to limit the government action on (and study of) the child care issue and to move the issue ideologically and institutionally from labour to welfare. One was the conflict of values evident throughout the debate on child care. Demand for expanded and state-supported child care required an acceptance of the permanency of mothers' employment. The majority of Canadians continued to hold the lingering belief that maternal care of children was superior to other forms of care and that child care was a private family issue. This conflict of values led to a social ambivalence that stifled and limited debate on the problems of mothers' employment. As the bureau's 1965 conference concluded, "We shall never get anywhere with this problem of day care until we resolve our conflicting attitudes to the working mother . . . Reluctance to accept the need for day nurseries is the real obstacle to action. We do not accept the fact that substantial numbers of mothers of young children are employed."[66]

Ultimately, this conflict led to an emphasis on economic need to justify state involvement in child care. The problem with an emphasis on economic need, however, is that it undermines the notion of women's right to paid employment if they choose. While arguments stressing economic need have been more successful at placing the issue on the government agenda, they have also indirectly undermined women's claim to equal access to and opportunity in the workforce and implicitly upheld the idea that mothers should not work if they do not have to.[67] Thus, the transition of the child care issue out of the Department of Labour's mandate by the mid-1960s diminished its potential to be conceptualized as a women's rights issue. Finally, the emphasis on need further restricted the available policy options by solidifying the traditional association of child care with charity. Although child care advocates like Royce frequently stressed the benefits to be gained—by children, as well as by society overall—from "quality" child care, these ideas were overshadowed by a definition of child care that saw it as a necessary measure to be available only to disadvantaged families. For the majority of Canadians, government-supported child care remained an acceptable social program only for those unfortunate women who could not afford to stay home.

The association of state-supported child care with charity and poverty was embodied in the Canada Assistance Plan (CAP) of 1966. One of the cornerstones of Canada's welfare state, CAP provided federal support for social assistance and welfare services through a fifty/fifty cost-sharing formula with the provinces; after 1966, it became the primary means of government support for child care facilities. The requirement of means testing to determine eligibility to receive the services covered under CAP institutionalized child care in Canada as a welfare service provided only to those demonstrating socio-economic need.

For the majority of Canadians, including the growing middle class, the provision of child care remained a private matter negotiated on the free market.[68]

Maternity leave, while clearly a labour issue, was further constructed as a health measure designed to protect women and children rather than a women's equality measure during the course of debate about legislative form. Royce's initial legislative proposal was that leave be provided through an amendment to the new federal Labour Standards Code. The provisions recommended included six weeks of prenatal leave followed by eight weeks postnatal leave, with protection from dismissal during this period and a guarantee of reinstatement to a job with equivalent responsibility and seniority. Royce believed these requirements were matters related to working conditions and workers' rights and thus fell appropriately under the concept of "standards."[69] Interestingly, in the departmental debate that ensued, Haythorne questioned whether the standards code was the appropriate means and pointed to the recently passed Canada Labour (Safety) Code, where maternity-leave provisions could easily be slotted into existing regulations, while inclusion in the standards code would require an amendment.[70] While Haythorne's comments emphasized ease of implementation, department correspondence increasingly emphasized the "health and safety aspects of maternity protection" in discussions of legislative form.[71] By slotting maternity leave into the safety code, the construction of this issue as a health matter rather than one of women's rights was reinforced, even if in the end Royce's recommendations would be implemented. Ultimately, as the Canadian Advisory Council on the Status of Women was to note a decade later, "pregnancy is still looked upon as an illness."[72]

In the case of benefits, the spectre of family poverty meant that economic need became the dominant justification for the development of a maternity benefits program. As a result, the proposals suggested that the benefits be separate from the leave provisions and subsumed under the income maintenance system. Royce argued in her 1966 recommendations that "wage-related maternity benefits" would have to be considered "within a total program of income security."[73] The consensus that benefits should be provided through the social welfare system led to a search for a means to implement the program. As in the case of the leave legislation, officials sought to slot the benefits program into existing provisions to avoid the difficulty of creating a new social program (and of spending time doing it). Most commentators recognized that benefits would have to be supplied through the federal government, since neither the provinces nor employers agreed to the economic costs involved.[74] Gradually, the focus turned to the Unemployment Insurance (UI) program. Referring to the upcoming review and revision of the UI Act, Royce raised the possibility of including maternity benefits within that program in January 1967. The bureau's 1967 report on maternity protection also argued for provision through UI because of the assumption that an alternative social insurance program would not be developed. Since the UI system had the administrative apparatus in place for processing claims, it seemed the logical choice. Further, as Royce pointed out, many women were already seeking income replacement through the UI system while on maternity leave.[75] Both arguments became the primary reasons for the eventual decision to implement federal provision of maternity benefits through the UI system.[76] Undoubtedly, she perceived a greater chance of success in realizing the goal of maternity benefits if a means could be found to slot it into an existing program.

Conclusion

Royce retired from the Department of Labour in January 1967 with the knowledge that gains had been made in achieving the twin goals of maternity leave and maternity benefits and that the Women's Bureau had played an important role in shaping the policy outcome. Maternity leave was provided to federal employees by an amendment to the Labour Standards Act in 1971; at the same time, maternity benefits were implemented through the UI system. Certainly, the outcome of the child care debate was more equivocal. A limited provision of state support of child care was included in CAP in 1966. However, the department's interest diminished, as reflected in the lack of support for further research.

Still, it is important not to diminish the work undertaken by the Women's Bureau on these two important equality measures. Marion Royce did advocate for these measures from the perspective of women's right to equality of opportunity in the workforce. Faced with competing and conflicting ideologies, and, in particular, with a societal reluctance to accept child care and familial matters as equality issues, she was ultimately unable to define child care and maternity benefits as labour and equality issues. Maternity leave did encompass the important concept of a woman's right to return to work, in an equivalent position, following the birth of a child, even if it was also defended as a health policy. Still, the bureau played an important part in achieving these two equality measures, even with their limitations. As Canada entered the 1970s and the women's movement surged forward, maternity protection would be considered an equality gain, and expanded state-supported child care would become one of the major goals—a goal that to this day remains elusive as child care and

women's employment continue to be "driven apart." As well, the bureau's argument that society needed to develop programs and services to help wage-earning mothers balance home and work responsibilities was radical for the time. The "ambivalence" of which Royce often spoke revealed that the challenge in these early years was to engage society and government in a debate about the repercussions of mothers' employment. For this reason, the bureau's 1967 study on maternity protection concluded with the following suggestion:

> Perhaps we can think less about "working mothers," with the old connotation of fearful neglect, latch keys and cold suppers. Perhaps we can think more about "employed women with family responsibilities," with the new connotation of a brave effort to combine two jobs in a new way. This latter attitude could be the starting point to further much needed medical research into the problems involved, and for the development of social policies and amenities to the needs of a changed and changing society.[77]

These comments suggest that the Women's Bureau realized that the process of responding to a changing Canadian society was only beginning.

Endnotes

1 Library and Archives Canada (LAC), Marion Royce Papers (MR Papers), MG 30C206, vol. 1, file 5, Speech by Marion Royce to the Soroptimist Club of Peterborough, 25 November 1964, 10.

2 Canada, House of Commons, *Debates*, 14 May 1953, 5420.

3 Important among these groups were the National Council of Women (NCW), the Business and Professional Women's Clubs (BPW), and the Young Women's Christian Association (YWCA). The decision to create the Women's Bureau is examined in more detail in Catherine Briggs, "Fighting for Women's Equality: The Federal Women's Bureau, 1945–1967: An Example of Early 'State Feminism' in Canada" (PhD diss., University of Waterloo, 2001).

4 Married women's participation rates continued to rise, reaching 49.8 per cent in 1961 and 56.9 per cent in 1971. Canada, Department of Labour (Women's Bureau), *Women at Work in Canada* (1957); Canada,

Department of Labour (Women's Bureau), *Women at Work in Canada* (1964); Canada, Labour Canada (Women's Bureau), *Women in the Labour Force, Part I: Participation* (1983).

5 Mona Gleason, *Normalizing the Ideal: Psychology, Schooling, and the Family in Postwar Canada* (Toronto: University of Toronto Press, 1999); Katherine Arnup, *Education for Motherhood: Advice for Mothers in Twentieth-Century Canada* (Toronto: University of Toronto Press, 1994); and articles in Joy Parr, ed., *A Diversity of Women. Ontario, 1945–1980* (Toronto: University of Toronto Press, 1995).

6 The budget remained small throughout the 1950s and 1960s. In 1964, it totalled only $35,000, as compared to its counterpart in the United States, which had a staff of 76 and a budget of over $700,000 in 1964. Mollie Gillen, "Marion Royce: Expert on Canadian Women," *Chatelaine*, September 1964, 89; and Linda Geller-Schwartz, "An Array of Agencies: Feminism

and State Institutions in Canada," in *Comparative State Feminism*, ed. Dorothy McBride Stetson and Amy Mazur (Thousand Oaks, CA: Sage Publications, 1995), 45.

7   Doris Anderson, "Will Twelve Good Years Go Down the Drain," *Chatelaine*, November 1966, 1.

8   LAC, Department of Labour Papers, RG 27, vol. 1903, file 38-2-2 pt. 1, Text of talk given by Marion Royce on CBC radio program *Canada at Work*, 7 November 1954.

9   Carmela Patrias and Ruth A. Frager, "'This Is Our Country, These Are Our Rights': Minorities and the Origins of Ontario's Human Rights Campaigns," *Canadian Historical Review* 82 (March 2001): 2–3.

10   Other active women in Canada similarly applied the concept of human rights to women in the 1950s, most notably those in "feminist" organizations like the BPW. In organizations like the NCW, the discourse on women's issues was mixed, invoking a mixture of equal rights feminism with maternal feminism that extolled women's special nurturing qualities and primary role as mothers. Dorothy McBride Stetson, "The Oldest Women's Policy Agency The Women's Bureau in the United States," in *Comparative State Feminism*, ed. Dorothy McBride Stetson and Amy Mazur (Thousand Oaks, CA: Sage Publications, 1995), 261.

11   LAC, Department of Labour Papers, RG 27, vol. 1903, file 38-2-2 pt 1, Text of talk by Marion Royce on the role of the Women's Bureau on CBC radio program *Canada at Work*, 7 November 1954, 3.

12   Joan Sangster, "Doing Two Jobs: The Wage-Earning Mother, 1945–70," in *A Diversity of Women: Ontario, 1945–1970*, ed. Joy Parr (Toronto: University of Toronto Press, 1995), 106.

13   LAC, Department of Labour Papers, RG 27, vol. 1903, file 38-2-2 pt.1, Talk by Marion Royce on role of the Women's Bureau on CBC radio programme "Canada at Work," 7 November 1954, 4; LAC, MR Papers, MG 30C206, vol. 1, file 5, Talk by Marion Royce to the Soroptimist Club entitled "Changing Expectations," 25 November 1964, 9.

14   Anderson, "Will Twelve Good Years Go Down the Drain," 1. Mollie Gillen, a reporter on staff at *Chatelaine*, also credited the bureau's research with "offering a solid take-off point for arguments against the discrimination deplored by all thinking Canadians," in "The Woman Who Knows about Women," *Chatelaine*, October 1970, 93.

15   The 1961 census showed that among women in the child-bearing years of 25 to 34, 57.4 per cent without children were in the labour force compared to 25 per cent with one child and 12.9 per cent with two or more. These figures come from Canada, Department of Labour, *Women at Work in Canada*, 22.

16   Sangster, "Doing Two Jobs," 102; and Doug Owram, *Born at the Right Time: A History of the Baby Boom Generation* (Toronto: University of Toronto Press, 1996), 3–30.

17   Mariana Valverde, "Building Anti-delinquent Communities: Morality, Gender, and Generation in the City," in *A Diversity of Women: Ontario, 1945–1980*, ed. Joy Parr (Toronto: University of Toronto Press, 1995), 19–20.

18   Joan Sangster, *Earning Respect: The Lives of Working Women in Small-Town Ontario, 1920 to 1960* (Toronto: University of Toronto Press, 1995), 233.

19   Alena Heitlinger, *Women's Equality, Demography and Public Policy: A Comparative Perspective* (London: St Martin's Press, 1993), 222; Mona Gleason, "Growing Up to Be 'Normal': Psychology Constructs Proper Gender Roles in Post–World War II Canada, 1945– 60," in *Family Matters: Papers in Post-Confederation Canadian Family History*, ed. Lori Chambers and Edgar-André Montigny (Toronto: Canadian Scholar's Press, 1998), 40–2; Arnup, 1994, 149–52.

20   Sangster, "Doing Two Jobs," 104.

21   Jill Vickers argues that there was remarkable continuity from 1945 through the second wave, both in a gradual progression of ideas and methods and in the personnel and groups working for women's equality. Jill Vickers, "The Intellectual Origins of the Women's Movements in Canada," in *Challenging Times: The Women's Movement in Canada and the U.S.*, ed. Constance Backhouse and David H. Flaherty (Montreal and Kingston: McGill-Queen's University Press, 1992), 39–40.

22   Catherine Briggs and Sandra Burt, "The Canadian Women's Bureau: Leading the Fight for Justice and Fair Play," in *Canada, Confederation to Present*, ed. Bob Hesketh and Chris Hackett (Edmonton: Chinook Multimedia, 2001), 6–7.

23   LAC, Department of Labour Papers, RG 27, vol. 4159, file 722-4-2, Letter from John Mainwaring to Mr H.J. Waisglas (Director General, Research and Development), 3 February 1969.

24   LAC, Department of Labour Papers, RG 27, vol. 1906, file 38-6-6-6, pt 1, Memo from W.R. Dymond (Assistant Deputy Minister) to Marion Royce, 12 January 1965; Handwritten reply to Marion Royce on original memo sent by Royce to G.V. Haythorne outlining proposal for 1965 conference, 8 January 1965.

25   Annis May Timpson, *Driven Apart: Women's Employment Equality and Child Care in Canadian Public Policy* (Vancouver: UBC Press, 2001), 29.

26   LAC, Department of Labour Papers, RG 27, vol. 1904, file 38-11-6-3, Memo from G.V. Haythorne to Assistant Deputy Ministers, 18 April 1967.

27   LAC, Department of Labour Papers, RG 27, vol. 1903, file 38-2-2, pt 1, Text of broadcast on CBC Radio's *Canada at Work* program on the Women's Bureau, November 1954.

28   Canada, Department of Labour (Women's Bureau), *Married Women Working for Pay in Eight Canadian Cities* (1958). *Married Women Working for Pay* (MWWP) examined why married women worked, the

attitudes of the women to their work, and their plans for the future. As well, it delved into how these women blended waged work with home responsibilities by examining the distribution of housework, the attitudes of husbands, the impact on children, and the provision of care for children. The main questions of the study were how did women balance the dual demands of employment and family and what were the resulting familial problems.

29 LAC, MR Papers, MG 30C206, vol. 2, file 28, Speech by Marion Royce in the Proceedings of the CBC Conference on "The Real World of Women," 6–9 September 1962, 73.

30 LAC, MR Papers, MG 30C206, vol. 1, file 5, Speech by Marion Royce to the Soroptimist Club of Peterborough, 25 November 1964, 10.

31 LAC, MR Papers, MG 30C206, vol. 2, file 28, Proceedings of the CBC Conference on "The Real World of Women," 75.

32 LAC, Department of Labour Papers, RG 27, vol. 1903, file 38-11-6-41, Draft proposal prepared by the Canadian Welfare Council for Department of Labour regarding Studies of Day Care for Children, 1 December 1965.

33 LAC, Department of Labour Papers, RG 27, vol. 1903, file 38-11-6-41, Copy of resolution from National Employment Committee meeting with handwritten comments by G.V. Haythorne to Marion Royce, 25 November 1965; Reply from Marion Royce to G.V. Haythorne, 30 November 1965.

34 LAC, MR Papers, MG 30C206, vol. 2, file 28, Proceedings of the CBC Conference on "The Real World of Women," 75.

35 In 1958, the regulations provided leave without pay for two months before the birth and six months after, a standard that exceeded the ILO's recommendation of 12 weeks (most to be taken after the birth). In 1962, these regulations were further strengthened when maternity leave was made a right for women in the civil service.

36 Canada, Department of Labour (Women's Bureau), *Maternity Protection for Women Workers* (1967).

37 LAC, MR Papers, MG 30C206, vol. 2, file 28, Proceedings of the CBC Conference on "The Real World of Women," 6–9 September 1962, 77.

38 LAC, Department of Labour Papers, RG 27, vol. 1904, file 38-11-6-3, "Notes relating to a project for maternity protection legislation in the Federal Jurisdiction," prepared by the Women's Bureau, November 1966, section VII.

39 LAC, Department of Labour Papers, RG 27, vol. 1905, file 38-6-6-3, Memo from Marion Royce to G.V. Haythorne, "Women's Bureau meeting with trade unionists on Thursday, March 7th," 11 March 1963.

40 LAC, Department of Labour Papers, RG 27, vol. 1908, file 38-9-9, Letter from Marion Royce to Grace McInnis, 2 June 1966; RG 27, vol. 1904, file 38-11-6-3, "Notes Relating to a project for maternity protection legislation in the Federal Jurisdiction," prepared by the Women's Bureau, November 1966.

41 Heitlinger, *Women's Equality*, 27-8.

42 Timpson, *Driven Apart*, 12.

43 Annalee Gölz, "Family Matters: The Canadian Family and the State in the Postwar Period," *Left History* 1, no. 2 (Fall 1993): 11–12.

44 Rianne Mahon, "The Never-Ending Story: The Struggle for Universal Child Care Policy in the 1970s," *Canadian Historical Review* 81 (December 2000): 587, 593.

45 On the subject of "protective" labour laws, see Jane Ursel, *Private Lives, Public Policy: 100 Years of State Intervention in the Family* (Toronto: Women's Press, 1992), 93–4, 136, 234–5.

46 Canada, Department of Labour, *Labour Gazette* (1958), 148.

47 See Briggs, "Fighting for Women's Equality," chap. 2.

48 Alvin Finkel, "Even the Little Children Cooperated: Family Strategies, Childcare Discourse, and Social Welfare Debates 1945–1975," *Labour/Le Travail* 36 (Fall 1995): 98–102, 98.

49 LAC, MR Papers, MG 30C206, vol. 3, file 8, Speech by Marion Royce to the BC Vocational Education Association, 2 December 1964.

50 Canada, Department of Labour, *Married Women Working for Pay*, 58.

51 Finkel, "Even the Little Children Cooperated," 110.

52 LAC, MR Papers, MG 30C206, vol. 3, file 8, Speech given at the Meeting of the BC Vocational Education Association, Vancouver, 2 December 1964, 11.

53 Mahon, "The Never-Ending Story," 593.

54 Heitlinger, *Women's Equality*, 222.

55 International Labour Organization, Maternity Protection Convention 1919, Maternity Protection Convention (Revised) 1952, ILO Website, http://www.ilo.org. The "Maternity Protection Recommendation" of 1952 included additional recommendations for legislation, such as article 4 (3) which stated, "During her legal absence from work before and after confinement, the seniority rights of the woman should be preserved as well as her right to reinstatement in her former work or in equivalent work paid at the same rate."

56 LAC, MR Papers, MG 30C206, vol. 2, file 28, Speech by Marion Royce included in the proceedings of the CBC Conference on "The Real World of Women," 6–9 September 1962, 77.

57 LAC, MR Papers, MG 30C206, vol. 2, file 5, Notes for a speech on "the I.L.O. and women," dated 1961.

58 Canada, Department of Labour (Women's Bureau), *Report of a Consultation on the Employment of Women with Family Responsibilities* (1965), i.

59 LAC, MR Papers, MG 30C206, vol. 3, file 13, Memo from Marion Royce to Mrs J. Findlay, "Legislative Concerns of the Women's Bureau," 19 January 1967.

60   LAC, Department of Labour Papers, RG 27, vol. 1908, file 38-9-9, Letter from Marion Royce to Grace McInnis, 2 June 1966; RG 27, vol. 1904, file 38-11-6-3, "Notes Relating to a project for maternity protection legislation in the Federal Jurisdiction," prepared by the Women's Bureau, November 1966.

61   LAC, Department of Labour Papers, RG 27, vol. 1903, file 38-11-6-41, Minutes of Meeting of Interdepartmental Committee to discuss draft proposal, 9 December 1965.

62   LAC, Department of Labour Papers, RG 27, vol. 1904, file 38-11-6-4-2, Letter from Marion Royce to W.I. Moore (Special Surveys Division, Dominion Bureau of Statistics), 1 December 1966.

63   Canada, Department of Labour (Women's Bureau), *Working Mothers and Their Child-Care Arrangements* (1970).

64   LAC, Department of Labour Papers, RG 27, vol. 1904, file 38-11-6-3, "Notes relating to a project for maternity protection legislation in the Federal Jurisdiction" prepared by the Women's Bureau, November 1966; Memo from G.V. Haythorne to Marion Royce regarding the above "Notes," 3 January 1967.

65   LAC, Department of Labour Papers, RG 27, vol. 1904, file 38-11-6-3, Memo from G.V. Haythorne to Assistant Deputy Ministers, 18 April 1967.

66   Canada, Department of Labour, *Report of a Consultation on the Employment of Women with Family Responsibilities*, 17.

67   Katherine Teghtsoonian, "Work and/or Motherhood: The Ideological Construction of Women's Options in Canadian Child Care Policy Debates," *Canadian Journal of Women and the Law* 8, no. 2 (1995): 429–31.

68   Heitlinger, *Women's Equality*, 225.

69   LAC, Department of Labour Papers, RG 27, vol. 1904, file 38-11-6-3, "Notes relating to a project for maternity protection legislation in the Federal Jurisdiction,"

70   LAC, Department of Labour Papers, RG 27, vol. 1904, file 38-11-6-3, Memo from G.V. Haythorne to Marion Royce, 3 January 1967.

71   LAC, Department of Labour Papers, RG 27, vol. 1904, file 38-11-6-3, Memo from G.V. Haythorne to Assistant Deputy Ministers, 18 April 1967.

72   Canada, Canadian Advisory Council on the Status of Women, *Recommendations of the CACSW by Subject* (1981), 58.

73   LAC, Department of Labour Papers, RG 27, vol. 1904, file 38-11-6-3, "Notes relating to a project for maternity protection legislation in the Federal Jurisdiction," prepared by the Women's Bureau, November 1966, sections VI and VII.

74   The ILO recommended that benefits be provided through a national social insurance fund and not through a charge on employers. Canada, because of its federal system, lacked a *federal* social insurance fund that provided income maintenance to workers who had suffered a loss of wages due to illness, disability, etc. This type of fund was envisioned as the best form for maternity benefits. See LAC, Department of Labour Papers, RG 27, vol. 4159, file 722-4-2, pt 2, Report of the Working Party Committee on Maternity Leave entitled "Legislative Guidelines," December 1968, 8–9.

75   LAC, MR Papers, MG 30C206, vol. 3, file 13, Memo from Marion Royce to Jessica Findlay on "Legislative concerns of the Women's Bureau," 19 January 1967; and Canada, Department of Labour, *Maternity Protection for Women Workers*, 39.

76   Leslie A. Pal, "Maternity Benefits and Unemployment Insurance: A Question of Policy Design," *Canadian Public Policy* 12, no. 3 (September 1985): 553–4.

77   Canada, Department of Labour, *Maternity Protection for Women Workers*, 53.

◎ 10.2: SOCIALISTS, JEWS, AND THE 1947 SASKATCHEWAN BILL OF RIGHTS

Carmela Patrias

"I would suggest, Mr Speaker, that this is perhaps the most important bill that ever came before this house . . . in importance, it will rank with the British North America Act."[1] With these words Attorney General J.W. Corman introduced the Saskatchewan Bill of Rights Act in the provincial legislature in March 1947. The bill, the first of its kind enacted in Canada, was designed to protect a broad range of civil liberties and human rights. It reaffirmed freedom of religion, speech, association, and assembly, freedom from arbitrary arrest and imprisonment, and the right to exercise the franchise in regularly held elections—freedoms its framers believed to be implicitly protected by the principles of British common law. It also affirmed, for the first time, the right of every person in the province, without discrimination on racial and religious grounds, to obtain employment, to engage in any occupation or business or enterprise, to membership in any professional or trade association, to rent or purchase any property, to service in public places such as hotels and restaurants, and to education in schools and universities. The Act also guaranteed freedom from group libel and slander by way of publication or broadcasting of material that tended to restrict the rights of citizens as set out in the Act.[2]

At a time when denial of employment [and] refusal to sell or rent housing and provide service in restaurants and hotel accommodation, on religious or racial grounds, were all legal elsewhere in Canada, the significance of Saskatchewan's enactment of a bill with such a comprehensive list of rights appears undisputable. Only two other provinces, Manitoba and Ontario, had legislated against racial discrimination, and their statutes were much more limited in scope. A 1934 amendment to the Manitoba Libel Act provided for an injunction to prevent "the publication of a libel against a race or creed likely to expose persons belonging to the race or professing the creed to hatred, contempt or ridicule, and tending to raise unrest or disorder among the people." Ontario's 1944 Racial Discrimination Act prohibited the publication or display of signs, symbols, or other representations expressing racial or religious discrimination.[3] Premier Drew's Conservative government rejected all proposals to expand the Act to cover discrimination in employment or the provision of services. At the federal level, a Senate committee pondered the introduction of a Canadian Bill of Rights in the late 1940s, but action was not taken until 1960. . . .

[T]his study attempts to demonstrate that the Saskatchewan Bill of Rights is worthy of historical analysis. As the growing literature on the history of human rights campaigns and legislation makes clear, racist prejudice and discrimination were still widespread in 1940s Canada.[4] Therefore,

carefully organized campaigns by human rights activists were necessary to convince various levels of government in Canada to introduce anti-discrimination legislation. The initiative taken by the Saskatchewan (Co-operative Commonwealth Federation (CCF) played an important role in these campaigns. Indeed, the origins and enactment of its Bill of Rights underscore the central role played by social democrats—and especially by Jews among them—in the development of human rights legislation throughout the country and the concomitant reconsideration of the place of racialized and religious minorities in Canadian society. Even the bill's shortcomings, especially the failure to test its provisions in the courts, are of interest to historians. Not only do they shed light on the trials and errors of the quest by early human rights activists for the most effective ways to legislate against discrimination, they also point to some of the obstacles that they encountered in Canada.

The Saskatchewan Bill of Rights marked the culmination of the CCF's long-time commitment to the defence of civil liberties and human rights. The party's founding program, the 1933 Regina Manifesto, called for "equal treatment before the law of all residents of Canada irrespective of race, nationality or religious or political belief." Implicit in the manifesto's preamble was the view that racist, religious, and political intolerance were the products of competitive capitalism. By contrast, the new co-operative social order envisioned by the CCF would be a tolerant and pluralistic one in which racial and religious minorities would be free to enjoy their cultural rights. The collective organization of economic resources—the socialist foundation on which it would be built—would make possible the building of such a society.[5]

Responding to both Canadian and international developments, CCF members grew increasingly concerned about safeguarding civil liberties and human rights during the later 1930s and the 1940s. Domestically, they were reacting to the intensification of anti-Semitism in the late 1930s, Duplessis's 1937 anti-communist Padlock

Law, the detention of communists and the seizure of Ukrainian Labour and Farmer Temple Federations halls at the outbreak of the Second World War, the expulsion of Japanese Canadians from the West Coast in 1942 and the deportation of many of them to Japan at war's end, and the arrest and detention of suspected communists without trial following Soviet embassy clerk Igor Gouzenko's defection in 1945. Internationally, they were reacting to the rise of fascism and Nazism in Europe and the deliberations of the United Nations on human rights. As they considered the forces that endangered civil liberties and human rights, the centrality of economics to their analysis became more clearly articulated. Delegates at CCF conventions during the Second World War, for example, argued that the treatment of Japanese Canadians was not simply the consequence of wartime tensions, but the product of long-standing racism that had for decades offered economic advantages to capitalists. Since they saw economic insecurity in a competitive society as the main cause of racial antagonism, social democrats believed that such antagonism would disappear with the introduction of full employment and a social security net comprising such measures as insurance for those whose earning capacity was interrupted by illness.[6]

The belief that state-guaranteed social and economic rights provided the basis for protecting human rights distinguished CCF human rights advocacy from the plans of the Conservative and Liberal parties. A key factor behind the Liberal government's failure to endorse a national bill of rights in the late 1940s, for example, was fear that such a bill might imply state responsibility for guaranteeing the right to medical care and employment.[7] Since the CCF advocated such rights in any event, it could promote a Canadian bill of rights without reservations. Indeed, social democratic plans for an interventionist state account for the CCF's unequivocal support for a national bill of rights as a means to ending racism and discrimination in Canada. Yet as left-wing critics have pointed out, the CCF's proposals for such legislation stopped short of including social and economic rights. The omission of such rights at this stage, however, did not signify a retreat from socialist principles. Rather, Canadian social democrats believed that incorporating such rights in a bill of rights would be unenforceable. Separate social security and health insurance legislation would be far more effective in guaranteeing social and economic welfare.[8] ...

Secular humanist ideas, as well as evolving notions of Canadian citizenship, also motivated CCF human rights advocates. British Columbia member of Parliament (MP) Angus McInnis believed that "accepting an individual because he is a human being and has rights and privileges with every other human being, regardless of race," was "of the essence of socialism."[9] Norman Black, president of the Vancouver Consultative Council, an organization aiming to safeguard the rights of citizens in wartime, argued that "distinctions made on the basis of racial stock are contrary to the spirit of Canadian institutions."[10] Speaking out in Parliament against the deportation of Japanese Canadians, Alistair Stewart, CCF MP from Winnipeg, employed the language of rights: "Any citizen of this country, whether he be Jew or Gentile, Catholic or Protestant, black, white or yellow, believer or unbeliever," he argued, "has exactly the same rights as any other citizen."[11]

Eastern-European Jewish immigrants and their children, members of Jewish socialist organizations such as the Labour Zionists and the Workmen's Circle, and labour unions such as the International Ladies' Garment Workers Union and the Amalgamated Clothing Workers played a leading role in shaping the party's human rights policies. Although their number in Canada was not large, they were the most influential non-Anglo-Celtic group within the CCF. For them, the fight against racism and discrimination was far more than a question of principles. When they raised the matter of anti-Semitism at party conventions, they were speaking as the victims of growing racism and discrimination in Canada and Europe.[12] In Canada, they were excluded from various jobs, especially white-collar ones, from "better" neighbourhoods, and from resorts. During the Depression specifically, Jews faced economic boycotts in Quebec. In both Quebec and Ontario, moreover, their properties were on occasion the targets of vandalism and they themselves of violence. Even as Canadian Jews learned with growing alarm about the plight of Jews and socialists in Nazi-occupied Europe, anti-Semitic immigration practices prevented them from rescuing Europeans friends and relatives by offering them refuge in Canada.

Yet their faith in the ability of socialism to eradicate anti-Semitism specifically, and racism more generally, did not flag. We get a glimpse of the great hopes they attached to the power of socialist governments to counteract prejudice and discrimination from a congratulatory letter the American representative of the General Jewish Workers' Union of Poland sent to the CCF government of Saskatchewan following its election in 1944. Although he acknowledged that the CCF victory, signalling a new socialist way of life, could not "return life to the already slaughtered and tortured Jewish victims of Nazism and Fascism," he was confident that socialism would "guarantee for all a lasting peace among people and nations, based on economic stability and equality, real freedom and real democracy." Socialism would create "conditions . . . for the Jewish masses, scattered throughout the world, to live among other people on an equal footing, with equal rights for their future cultural and national advancement, an order where anti-Semitism will be outlawed and definitely erased from the surface of the earth."[13]

Driven by the urgency of their concerns, Jewish social democrats were not content to rest their hopes on future CCF electoral victories. Some of them established a special agency, the Jewish Labour Committee (JLC), to fight against anti-Semitism and to promote human rights in Canada. [The JLC was a branch of the American organization known by the same name, and its] aims at its inception in 1936 were to fight against fascism and Nazism and to save as many European Jews and socialists as possible. Although the organization's primary focus was on Jews and anti-Semitism, its members subscribed to broader socialist goals of improving the lot of all workers, regardless of race and religion. The founders' children, many of them

Canadian-born, increasingly emphasized these universalistic goals over narrower Jewish interests. Maishe Lewis, the JLC's secretary during the Second World War, a Yiddish-speaking socialist garment worker from Russian Poland, typified activists of the older generation. His son David, educated at McGill and Oxford, secretary of the CCF and future leader of the New Democratic Party, represented the younger generation, whose influence grew after the war. He worked tirelessly with his father to publicize the plight of Jews and socialists in Europe, raise money, and in other ways help these refugees to circumvent Canadian regulations against the admission of Jewish refugees from Nazi Europe. But he was also among those responsible for reorienting the JLC work after the war from fighting anti-Semitism to the promotion of human rights in Canada. As he explained in his memoirs, because he was seeking an answer to anti-Semitism in the 1940s, "the struggle against discrimination and for universal human rights remained for me the most important battle and the democratic socialist movement the most important vehicle."[14]

Under the leadership of Kalmen Kaplansky, a Lewis family friend and fellow socialist, the JLC provided the funding and organizational framework for the main labour campaigns against racist discrimination in Canada. Jewish labour activists believed that racism was used by labour's enemies to weaken the labour movement: "Anti-Semitism, anti-Negroism, anti-Catholicism, anti-French, anti-English as the case may be, and union smashing are all parts of a single reactionary crusade of hatred and destruction."[15] These Jewish socialists also saw a close link between the fight against racism and social democracy. Since economic hardship intensified the search for scapegoats, labour's struggle within unions and in the political arena to improve economic conditions and achieve economic security for workers automatically contributed to the elimination of prejudice and discrimination. Thanks to its ties to American organizations, the JLC became the main vehicle for transmitting American anti-racist literature to Canadian social democrats.[16] . . .

The election of a CCF government in Saskatchewan in 1944 provided social democratic advocates of human rights with the opportunity to put their convictions into practice. Given that the province, with its exceptionally high proportion of people of Continental European descent, had witnessed intense anti-foreign movements during the 1920s and again at the outbreak of the Second World War,[17] the Douglas government's actions in this regard were both innovative and courageous. Shortly after the election, the Ministry of Education distributed a pamphlet it had received from the Canadian Jewish Congress (CJC), *The Races of Mankind*, to 5,000 Saskatchewan teachers. Written by Columbia University anthropologists Ruth Benedict and Gene Weltfish, the pamphlet debunked widespread misconceptions about race. During the same year, the CCF overturned Saskatchewan's anti-Chinese traditions by granting Chinese Canadians the right to vote. Despite federal jurisdiction over Indian affairs, the new provincial government, concerned with the plight of Aboriginal nations in Saskatchewan, encouraged the formation of the Union of Saskatchewan Indian Chiefs to speak on their behalf.[18] Even before the end of the war with Japan, moreover, Premier Douglas invited Japanese Canadians to settle in Saskatchewan. The wording of his invitation rankles today, and it evoked criticism from some rank-and-file CCF members in 1944: "We did not think that British Columbia should be saddled with the entire Japanese population of this country," Douglas explained, "but that these people should be allocated to each of the provinces so that all will be accepting their fair share of responsibility, rather than asking British Columbia to assume the entire burden."[19] But at a time when communities throughout Canada attempted to prevent Japanese Canadians from settling in their midst, or admitted them only on condition that they would leave at the end of the war, Douglas's offer was remarkable. His government followed up the invitation by retaining lawyer Andrew Brewin—an active member of the CCF—to fight against Ottawa's attempt to deport Japanese Canadians.[20] . . .

The determination of leading social democrats such as Tommy Douglas and M.J. Coldwell, and of Jewish and other rank-and-file members, to safeguard civil liberties and human rights was essential for steering the course of the party's human rights campaign. They faced opposition from within, as well as from outside, the CCF. Some party supporters, including anti-Catholic Orangemen and people uncomfortable with the entry of Jews into the upper levels of the provincial civil service, still carried the burden of inherited stereotypes and racist views.[21] But the most serious opposition within the party arose in response to the appointment of Japanese Canadians to important positions by the Saskatchewan government. Prominent CCF members in British Columbia believed that such a policy would annihilate the party's electoral prospects.

Their objections centred on the 1946 appointment of Japanese Canadian lawyer George Tamaki as legal adviser to the chairman of the Economic Planning Commission of the Province of Saskatchewan. Tamaki, just one of the Japanese Canadians appointed to important civil service positions by Premier Douglas, was born in New Westminster, BC.[22] He obtained a bachelor of arts with honours in economics and political science from the University of British Columbia in 1938. Leaving the West Coast to escape discrimination against Japanese Canadians, he attended law school at Dalhousie University in Halifax, earning a bachelor of law in 1941. Despite the fact that he was among the top students in the school, the Barristers' Society of Nova Scotia decided that it would be "unwise" to admit him to the Nova Scotia Bar because of the "international situation." Tamaki then tried, unsuccessfully, first to get into the Canadian Army and then to get a civil service job in Ottawa.[23] When the CCF government of Saskatchewan finally offered Tamaki a position in keeping with his talents and education, Harold Winch, leader of the CCF in British Columbia, told Douglas that "the entire CCF caucus in British Columbia were convinced that they might as well shut up shop if word got out about Tamaki's appointment." Douglas replied,

"If the existence of the CCF movement in British Columbia or anywhere else depends upon our bowing to racial intolerance, then in my opinion the sooner it folds up, the better."[24]

Despite the phrasing of his 1944 encouragement of Japanese-Canadian settlement in Saskatchewan, Douglas's vision of Canada was pluralistic. "The time is long past," he wrote a year before the enactment of the Saskatchewan Bill of Rights, "when one racial group in Canada can set itself up as superior to others, or when any one group is singled out for discrimination. Gradually, I think, we are coming to realize that this nation's greatness depends not upon uniformity but upon diversity, and that the mosaic of our national life is composed of the tesserae of every racial and ethnological group."[25] At the Dominion-Provincial Conference of 1945, two years before his own government introduced a bill of rights, Douglas declared his support for the revision of the British North America Act by "placing certain fundamental religious, racial and civil liberties in a Bill of Rights, amendable only by the unanimous consent of the provincial legislatures concurrently with the dominion parliament."[26]

Douglas's commitment to a pluralistic, tolerant Canada was essential in preparing the ground for the Saskatchewan Bill of Rights, but the central figure behind drafting and implementing it was Morris Shumiatcher. Shumiatcher was one of the talented young people drawn to Saskatchewan from across Canada following the election of the CCF by the opportunity to participate in building a more egalitarian society. He was both a Jew and a socialist, but unlike David Lewis or Kalmen Kaplansky, he did not come from a socialist background. Shumiatcher was born in Calgary in 1917 to middle-class Polish Jewish immigrants. His mother had studied at the University of Warsaw, and his father, who had been prevented from obtaining higher education in Poland by poverty and prejudice, earned a law degree after settling in Alberta. In Calgary, members of the Shumiatcher family, including Morris, were active in mainstream Jewish organizations. By his student days at the University of Alberta in Edmonton, however, Morris distanced himself from other Jewish students, whom he saw as "ghetto-ridden," reasoning that any connection with them would impede his progress. "Do you think that if I associated with the Jewish crowd I would be on the Student's Union," he asked in a letter to his parents, "or that my opinion . . . would count for anything at all on the Campus, as I am glad to say it does? Certainly not!"[27] Perhaps an ambitious Shumiatcher was simply making strategic decisions in distancing himself from other Jewish students. Perhaps acknowledging anti-Semitism would have undermined his confidence and hence the momentum of his career. Whatever the reason, in 1939 young Shumiatcher blamed the clannishness of Jewish students themselves rather than anti-Semitism for their marginalization.[28] Not until many years later did he acknowledge the role of racism in his decision to study law, instead of pursuing graduate studies in English literature. Learning of Shumiatcher's plan to teach English literature at university, one of his professors told him that being of Jewish rather than British background, he was unsuited to do postgraduate work in this field.[29]

Whether or not he acknowledged the role of anti-Semitism in his career choice in 1941, Shumiatcher was aware of discrimination and intended to use his legal training to combat it. He obtained a bachelor of law in Edmonton and a master's and doctorate of law at the University of Toronto. While at the University of Toronto, in 1942, he worked with Professor Jacob Finkelman, research chairman of the Joint Public Relations Committee (JPRC) of the Canadian Jewish Congress and B'nai B'rith. Finkelman and the congress were just then engaged in documenting racist employment discrimination in war industries in order to pressure Ottawa to act against it. The two men became close, and as Shumiatcher informed his parents with great excitement, "Fink" offered him a job investigating anti-discrimination legislation throughout America so that the congress could make recommendations to Ottawa about how best to fight employment discrimination.[30] Whether he took the job is unclear, but in 1944 he contemplated running for the CCF in Alberta because it was the only party in which a Jew could rise to the top.[31] Even before he started to work for the CCF in Saskatchewan, Shumiatcher expressed interest in using his legal expertise to combat unjust treatment of First Nations in Canada.[32] Personal ties underscored his concern about the fate of racialized minorities beyond his own group. His interest in Canada's Aboriginal people was first awakened by his high-school teacher John Laurie, secretary of the Indian Association of Alberta.[33] An interest in Japan not only earned Shumiatcher a travelling scholarship to Japan in 1940, but also led him to befriend young Japanese Canadians, including George Tamaki, during a vacation in Vancouver.[34]

Like his socialist contemporaries, Shumiatcher blamed capitalist competitiveness and inequality for racial prejudice and discrimination. Anti-Semitism, he believed, "would disappear when our society is overhauled and the dog-eat-dog principles of capitalism are displaced by the cooperative principles of the CCF." Like David Lewis, Kalmen Kaplansky, and other young Jewish human rights activists, moreover, Shumiatcher clearly envisioned collaboration between Jews and other racialized minorities in the struggle. "Ours is not an isolated problem," he wrote in 1947.

> If we condemn injustices against ourselves, we must condemn injustices against others. Discrimination against the Japanese citizens of Canada is as much our problem as discrimination against Jewish persons; restrictions upon Jehovah's Witnesses should concern us as much as the anti-Semitism emanating from the same quarters; the advocacy of restrictions of the civil liberties of Mennonites in Manitoba and Alberta is as much a matter of concern to us as the program of Adrian Arcand in Quebec. Discrimination against Negroes because of their colour should arouse us as much as discrimination against Jewish persons because of their faith.[35]

On the eve of the Saskatchewan elections of 1944 Shumiatcher expressed his hope that the CCF victory would "lay the foundations for a better society—not only in Saskatchewan, but throughout Canada . . . a system more interested in the welfare of the human beings of the country, than in the ledgers and profits of monopolistic enterprise."[36] Consequently, he was pleased when Premier Douglas and Attorney General J.W. Corman invited him to join the Saskatchewan public service. He had come to their attention because of his work on labour law and on the administration of debt legislation in western Canada.[37] But following his appointment as Premier Douglas's legal adviser, Shumiatcher became the key figure behind the government's human rights policies. The controversial appointment of George Tamaki was instigated by Shumiatcher. He represented the government at the founding of the Union of Saskatchewan Indian Chiefs and wrote the organization's constitution.[38] Shumiatcher not only drafted the Saskatchewan Bill of Rights, but also convinced Attorney General Corman that the bill's enactment prior to the 1948 elections would be politically astute, because it would enhance the CCF's standing in the province.[39]

Shumiatcher's contacts in the Jewish community helped with the drafting of the Bill of Rights. Aware of the activities of the Canadian Jewish Congress in promoting anti-discrimination legislation in Canada, in 1945 Shumiatcher wrote to its president, Samuel Bronfman, and requested copies of the research materials that the organization had collected to this end. The CJC responded not only by sending Shumiatcher materials in their possession, but also by enlisting the help of the Commission on Law and Legislation of the American Jewish Congress. The JLC also showed great interest in Shumiatcher's work. Kalmen Kaplansky asked him to serve on the organization's national executive and supplied him with materials developed by American labour and human rights organizations.[40] . . .

Members of the opposition seized on the bill's introduction in the legislature to denounce the socialist and labour policies of the government. They argued that the CCF was particularly ill-suited to defend civil liberties and human

Bryan Schlosser/Regina Leader-Post. Reprinted by permission.

Morris Shumiatcher, pictured here in 1994, authored the 1947 Saskatchewan Bill of Rights.

rights because it trampled on the freedom of private enterprise through such policies as the nationalization of certain industries, new labour legislation recognizing the right of workers to collective bargaining, compulsory check-off and the prohibition of company unions, and compulsory no-fault automobile insurance.[41] The *Saskatoon Star Phoenix* suggested that the bill would permit the socialist government to interfere with the freedom of contract. Lamenting the refusal of a Regina hotel manager to serve an African American in its dining room, the paper nevertheless declared that the government threat to suspend the hotel's licence was tantamount to tyranny.[42] The Liberal member from Rosthern, P.J. Hooge, equated the bill's enactment to "Satan signing scriptures for his own purposes."[43]

Cold War ideology suffused such criticisms of the "socialist" bill. Opponents alluded

to similarities between the policies of the CCF government and those of communist dictatorships.[44] They argued that under the guise of educational reforms, the provincial government waged a publicly funded propaganda campaign that appealed to class, promoted prejudice, and encouraged envy.[45] Newspapers such as the *Moose Jaw Times-Herald* depicted the bill as a tool for enhancing communist influence in the province. The prohibition against discrimination on the basis of "creed," the paper suggested, would make it impossible to expel communists from any organizations in the province.[46] The Canadian Institute of Public Opinion reported in 1947 that many Canadians saw "left-wing political movements, including communism and socialism" as the "biggest single danger" to their personal liberties.[47]

It was no accident that, amid their anti-socialist harangues, the bill's critics scarcely acknowledged its provisions for racialized and religious minorities. They argued that the bill was meaningless, a matter of window dressing, an act of political opportunism. Some of them maintained that no racial discrimination occurred in Saskatchewan,[48] while others, who, acknowledged that prejudice and discrimination did exist in the province, held either that it was impossible to legislate an end to such attitudes and practices or that legislation already existed to safeguard the rights that the new bill was designed to protect.[49]

Confident in its legislative majority (48 of 55 seats), the government party tackled such objections head on. D.M. Lazorko (CCF member for Redberry), for example, pointed to discrimination against residents of eastern European origin, who comprised a very substantial proportion of the province's population. He noted that he knew young men and women who had graduated from university but were unable to obtain employment because their names ended with "a -chk or a -ski."[50] Attorney-General Corman countered objections to the compulsory features of the legislation in general, and specifically its interference with free enterprise. All legislation, he argued, had compulsory features that served the common good. The Act did not prevent an owner from selling or leasing property to whom he liked, "as long as his decision was not based on religious or racial grounds." Similarly, the landlord could exclude tenants, but not on racist and religious grounds.[51] According to Corman, the bill's most innovative feature was to extend protection to racial and religious minorities. He attributed cries against the denial of "freedom of enterprise" to fears that the bill would deny capitalist employers the right to hire and fire whom they liked.[52] The CCF did not object to legitimate enterprise, Corman maintained, only to the combines, monopolies, and cartels that oppressed the "little man." Powerless to deal with this form of inequality, the provincial government legislated against those who would deny the freedom and security of minorities.[53] Education Minister Woodrow Lloyd argued that "enterprise never has been free and never can be free under monopolistic capitalism."[54] Both he and Corman believed that the farmers of Saskatchewan, having experienced years of depression followed by years of war, did not hold what is called "free enterprise" in as high regard as the opposition, and that, in any event, the Bill of Rights emphasized human rights as opposed to property rights.[55]

Despite the heated, lengthy debate, the Bill of Rights Act was passed unanimously. According to the bill's supporters, no one wanted to be seen to oppose principles that were "so patently acceptable to the large majority of people throughout this country."[56] Since the CCF held the overwhelming majority of seats in the legislature, the bill's passage was guaranteed in any event.

The drafter of the bill, Morris Shumiatcher, intended to test it in provincial courts, thus to build a body of jurisprudence on human rights. Shumiatcher assured those who were inclined to dismiss the bill as merely enunciating pious hopes that it "had teeth." Anyone who contravened the bill, he emphasized, was liable to a fine or an injunction.[57] Over the next decade, however, only three cases were tried under the bill's provisions, and only one of them related to the protection of minority rights, which the

bill's advocates saw as its most innovative feature. . . .

Premier Douglas's and Attorney-General Corman's conviction that the Bill of Rights' chief function would be educational helps to explain the failure to test its provisions more extensively in court. Douglas maintained that "the strength of this act is not in the fact that it will force equality but, rather, that it puts into words the belief of the people of Saskatchewan in the inherent right of all Canadians to equality in education, employment, the right to own and occupy property, the right to access to public places." At the time of the bill's passage, Corman expressed the hope that it would "throw the fear of the Lord into people who break it" and thus prevent further acts of discrimination. Reflecting upon the bill some years later, he recalled that he believed that even if cases of discrimination were reported to his department, prosecution would be unnecessary. An explanation of the bill and a warning would suffice to ensure compliance.[58] Such views help to explain why the Attorney General's Office did not make clear who would initiate prosecution in discrimination cases, nor did it designate specific civil servants to hear complaints or to investigate such cases.

Given Douglas's and Corman's faith in the educational value of the bill, however, it is less clear why the Saskatchewan government did relatively little to publicize the bill or to inform members of racialized minorities of the legal protections that it afforded them. After the heated discussions that accompanied its introduction in the legislature abated, the CCF government's publicity materials and the press said little about the bill. The CCF may have seen as more urgent and hence allocated more resources and attention to such programs as the reorganization of the school system, a universal hospital services plan, compulsory no-fault automobile insurance, and new trade union legislation.[59] Emphasizing such undertakings followed naturally from the social democratic belief that the eradication of economic and social inequality and concomitant competitiveness were prerequisites for the disappearance of discrimination. The inexperience of many of the new CCF cabinet ministers, the absence of a sufficiently developed public service, and the range and scope of the new policies that the social democratic government introduced during its first term also help to explain the limitations of its human rights policy. But, as we shall see, Premier Douglas's response to a number of attempts to lay charges in cases of racist discrimination suggests that anxiety generated by Cold War accusations that the CCF government was repressive and totalitarian also contributed to the reluctance to resort to the courts.

Not surprisingly, in the absence of publicity and administrative preparations, only a few minority group members in Saskatchewan were apparently willing and able to invoke the Bill of Rights when they faced discrimination. . . .

Awareness of the inability or reluctance of the victims of discrimination to institute proceedings under the bill motivated the Joint Public Relations Committee of the western division of the Canadian Jewish Congress not only to investigate cases that came to its attention, but also to monitor any public expressions of discrimination.[60] In the decade and a half following the bill's enactment, the Jewish human rights organization became the Saskatchewan government's main source of information for acts of discrimination. It alerted Morris Shumiatcher (even after he left the provincial government's employ in 1949) or the Attorney General's Office with the intention that, where appropriate, the Attorney General's Office would institute proceedings under the Bill of Rights.

The case of M.E., a Jewish physician who sought the aid of the JPRC in 1951, revealed the inability of the bill to deal with certain types of discrimination. The Canadian-born and -trained M.E. wanted to buy the practice of a deceased doctor in Davidson, Saskatchewan. The response to his telephone inquiries about the practice was positive. But by the time that M.E. met with Mayor J.A. Vopni and Liberal member Herman Danielson, who represented Davidson in the Saskatchewan legislature, the two had learned that he was Jewish. Vopni informed M.E. that Davidson already had a Jewish doctor and a Jewish dentist and that several deputations from

the public had approached Vopni to indicate that "they did not wish another Jewish doctor in the town." Danielson said that he too had been approached by townspeople, and even by the reeves of two neighbouring municipalities, who asked that the new doctor should be a gentile. In case these warnings did not suffice, Vopni added that no one would come to M.E. because the other Jewish doctor was unpopular and the townspeople would think that the two would conspire because Jews, like Catholics, "stick together."

When M.E.'s protests that the decision should be based on his qualifications not on his Jewishness were to no avail, he contacted the JPRC with the intention of fighting this type of anti-Semitism.[61] Upon further reflection, however, he decided to open a practice elsewhere and dropped the matter. Without the doctor's participation, the case could not be prosecuted. But Morris Shumiatcher believed that the involvement of two public officials, the mayor and an MLA, called for some kind of action. The case had special significance for Canadian Jews, who viewed the liberal professions as the route that might permit them to circumvent discrimination barring them from many other white-collar jobs. Although they had to contend with discriminatory policies of medical, dental, and law schools, training hospitals, and leading legal firms in the mid-twentieth century, once they succeeded in obtaining professional degrees, they hoped to become self-employed practitioners. Reactions like those of Davidson's citizens and officials therefore presented a serious obstacle to their plans.[62] In the end, however, Shumiatcher merely mentioned M.E.'s case to CCF politicians. "I have no doubt," he wrote to the JPRC, "that reference will be made from time to time in well placed circles concerning this question." In cases such as this, the Bill of Rights was clearly of no assistance.[63]

Cases of discriminatory advertising seemed simpler to prove and hence to prosecute. Yet human rights activists soon discovered that despite its pioneering role in instituting human rights legislation, the CCF government was disinclined to test it in court.[64] In August 1947, the

Regina Leader Post published an advertisement for the position of cook at the Anderson Café in Weyburn, stating that the restaurant employed "all white help." Shumiatcher suggested to Attorney General Corman that prosecution could be instituted both against the restaurant's owner and against the *Leader Post* for carrying the discriminatory advertisement. Shumiatcher believed that prosecuting such cases was important to demonstrate that the bill was not "mere 'window dressing,'" as some of its opponents alleged. Corman agreed. Premier Douglas, however, believed that prosecution would be ill-advised, since it would "make martyrs of the newspaper which has so consistently been attacking us." This would give the appearance that the CCF government—the target of Cold War accusations of totalitarianism and tyranny—was violating freedom of expression. Douglas advised instead that the paper's editor be warned.[65] . . .

Why was the CCF government so intent on keeping human rights violations out of court and hence the public eye? Why did it prefer to deal with infringements of the Bill of Rights through persuasion, behind the scenes? American experience, followed closely by Canadian human rights activists, suggested that publicizing the punishment of human rights violations operated as a deterrent to discrimination.[66] Although at the time of its enactment the government triumphantly described the bill as an expression of the values of the people of Saskatchewan, a decade later, leading CCF politicians still seemed to believe that their constituents would view the prosecution of human rights violations in the courts as expressions of excessive state power. Despite its repeated re-election in Saskatchewan during the height of the Cold War, the CCF appeared to fear public suspicion of its social democratic orientation. . . .

Because so few cases were tried under the Saskatchewan bill, most human rights activists gradually lost faith in its effectiveness.[67] Some Canadian activists pointed to the contrast between the publicity surrounding American cases and the failure of the Saskatchewan Bill of Rights to attract public attention as evidence of the bill's inadequacy.[68] Drawing on the experience of their American counterparts, these activists came to favour legislation targeting specific areas of discrimination such as in employment or accommodation, with enforcement machinery in the form of commissions to investigate infringements. Not only would commissions be staffed by "experts" in the field, but their responsibility would extend to the development of educational programs to increase public awareness of the existence of prejudice and discrimination and the need and means to overcome them. Moreover, since appeals would be free and far less complicated than prosecution through the courts, commissions could deal efficiently with many more cases. These cases, in turn, would heighten public awareness and act as deterrents.[69]

Frank Scott, one of the CCF's leading legal experts, pointed to another great weakness of the Saskatchewan bill. The failure to test it in the courts meant that the power of provincial governments to protect the rights defined by the bill remained unclear. The resulting uncertainty about rights within provincial and federal jurisdictions led other provincial governments to enact piecemeal legislation protecting one right at a time. Scott noted that by the 1950s even the government of Saskatchewan decided to pass Fair Employment and Fair Accommodation Practices Acts to supplement the Bill of Rights and be on firm grounds.[70]

The rejection of the Saskatchewan Bill of Rights as a model for provincial human rights legislation does not mean, however, that students of the history of human rights in Canada can afford to ignore it. The bill did not emerge fully formed from the provincial Attorney General's Office. The election of a social democratic government in the province created the opportunity for implementing measures to protect civil liberties and human rights advocated by the CCF since its establishment. Its belief that the state had a positive role in creating a more egalitarian society allowed the CCF government to pioneer in the field of human rights in Canada. Jews, who in the 1940s comprised less than 0.5 per cent of Saskatchewan's population, played a surprisingly important part in translating social democratic ideas about human rights into legislative action. As the bill's draftsman, Morris Shumiatcher deserves recognition alongside such central Canadian Jewish human rights activists as Kalmen Kaplansky, Ben Kayfetz, and Irving Himel. In collaboration with the JPRC of the western division of the CJC, Shumiatcher also led in trying to test the bill in provincial courts. Their efforts were motivated by their desire to combat not only anti-Semitism but all forms of racist and religious discrimination in Canada.

Notwithstanding the conclusion of human rights activists that the Saskatchewan Bill of Rights did not constitute the most effective way to protect human rights, the bill was an important landmark in Canadian history. It played a central role in the campaigns to combat racial and religious discrimination during the 1940s and 1950s, decades that marked a turning-point in Canadians' understanding of the rights of religious and racialized minorities. In the absence of press coverage, the general public may have lost sight of the bill, but human rights activists, especially social democrats, studied and even sought to emulate it. Although CCF attempts to pass provincial bills of

rights in British Columbia, Manitoba, and Ontario failed, the debates generated by these efforts enhanced public awareness of discrimination and the fight against it in Canada. What most human rights activists came to see as the shortcomings of this provincial bill of rights helped point the way toward fair practices acts as more effective safeguards of minority rights. The publicity afforded by discussions of provincial bills also helped to prepare the ground for the federal bill of rights in 1960 and, eventually, for amending the British North America Act by adding the national Charter of Rights and Freedoms.[71]

Author's Note: The author is especially grateful to Mrs J. Shumiatcher, Kathy Burianyk, and Chris Gebhard for permission to consult the Shumiatcher Papers at the Saskatchewan Archives Board in Regina as they were still being catalogued. Thanks are also due to Antonella Fanella of the Glenbow Archives, Janice Rosen of the Canadian Jewish Congress Archives, the anonymous referees for their suggestions, and the Humanities Research Institute of Brock University for financial assistance.

Endnotes

1   Saskatchewan, Legislative Assembly, *Debates and Proceedings* (hereafter cited as *Debates*), 19 Mar. 1947, p. 982 (J.W. Corman, MLA).

2   Saskatchewan Bill of Rights Act, 1947.

3   Walter Tarnopolsky, "The Control of Racial Discrimination," in *The Practice of Freedom: Canadian Essays on Human Rights and Fundamental Freedoms,* ed. R. St J. Macdonald and John P. Humphrey (Toronto: Butterworth's, 1979), 295.

4   Irving Abella, "Jews, Human Rights, and the Making of a New Canada," *Journal of the Canadian Historical Association* 11 (2000): 3–15; Constance Backhouse, *Colour-Coded: A Legal History of Racism in Canada, 1900–1950* (Toronto: University of Toronto Press, 1999); R. Brian Howe, "Human Rights Policy in Ontario," *Canadian Journal of Political Science* 24, no. 4 (Dec. 1991); Ross Lambertson, *Repression and Resistance: Canadian Human Rights Activists, 1930–1960* (Toronto: University of Toronto Press, 2005); Christopher MacLennan, *Toward the Charter: Canadians and the Demand for a National Bill of Rights,*

1929–1960 (Montreal and Kingston: McGill-Queen's University Press, 2003); Carmela Patrias and Ruth Frager, "This Is Our Country, These Are Our Rights," *Canadian Historical Review (CHR)* 82, no. 1 (Mar. 2001): 1–35; Herbert Sohn, "Human Rights Policy in Ontario: A Case Study" (PhD diss., University of Toronto, 1975); James W. St G. Walker, "The 'Jewish Phase' in the Movement for Racial Equality in Canada," *Canadian Ethnic Studies* 4, no. 1 (2002); and James W. St G. Walker, *"Race," Rights, and the Law in the Supreme Court of Canada* (Waterloo, ON: Wilfrid Laurier University Press, 1997).

5   "Regina Manifesto," program of the Co-operative Commonwealth Federation adopted at First National Convention, Regina, July 1933, 1.

6   File: 1944 Convention—Resolutions, vol. 13, National Conventions and Inter-provincial Conferences, 1932–60, Co-operative Commonwealth Federation Papers (hereafter cited as CCF), Library and Archives Canada (hereafter cited as LAC); "'We Are All Canadians,' Says Alistair Stewart," *Commonwealth,* 17 Apr.

1946; vol. 53, Ontario—Education, 1943–51, CCF Provinces, 1932–58, CCF.

7   MacLennan, *Toward the Charter*, 70. See also Howe, "Human Rights Policy in Ontario," 785–6, on liberal suspicion of the positive state.

8   Frank R. Scott, *What Does Labour Need in a Bill of Rights?* (summary), Dalhousie Labour-University Committee, Institute of Public Affairs, Dalhousie University, 1959, file: Year of Human Rights, 1946–9, vol. 14, Francis Reginald Scott Fonds, MG 30 D 211, LAC.

9   Angus McInnis to Douglas, 8 Apr. 1946, box 255, Tommy Douglas Papers (hereafter cited as TCD), Saskatchewan Archives Board.

10   Norman Black and Bruce York to Douglas, 3 Mar. 1945, R 33.1 LIII 878 (58), TCD.

11   *Commonwealth*, 17 Apr. 1946.

12   Minutes, CCF Trade Union Committee, Continuations Committee, 1943, folder 21, box 1, Woodsworth Memorial Collection (hereafter cited as WMC), Manuscript Collection, Thomas Fisher Rare Books Library, Toronto; and Provincial Executive meeting, 7 Jan. 1944, 9 Apr. 1944, Spadina Riding Association, 26 June 1944, WMC. See also National Conventions of 1944, 1946, and 1949, CCF.

13   Letter of congratulation, Emanuel Nowogrudsky, American representative of General Jewish Workers' Union of Poland, to David Lewis, 13 July 1944, vol. 68, Jewish Labour Committee, Sask Elections—Provincial, CCF.

14   David Lewis, *The Good Fight: Political Memoirs 1909–1958* (Toronto: Macmillan of Canada, 1981), 226.

15   "Provisional Labour Committee to Combat Racial Intolerance," press statement on the background of the Labour Committee to Combat Racial Intolerance, file 4, vol. 41, Jewish Labour Committee Papers (hereafter cited as JLC), LAC.

16   Ibid.

17   Bill Waiser, *Saskatchewan: A New History* (Calgary: Fifth House, 2005), 247–52, 332–3.

18   Lauri Barron, *Walking in Indian Moccasins: The Native Policies of Tommy Douglas and the ccf* (Vancouver: UBC Press, 1997); James M. Pitsula, "The Saskatchewan CCF Government and Treaty Indians, 1944–64," *CHR* 75, no. 1 (Mar. 1994): 21–53; and James M. Pitsula, "The CCF Government and the Formation of the Union of Saskatchewan Indians," *Prairie Forum* 19 (1994): 131–51; and Morris C. Shumiatcher, "Indian Smoke on the Western Sky," *Canadian Forum*, Mar. 1946, 283–4.

19   Douglas to Donald Ewing, 18 Dec. 1945, file: Japanese Canadians, R33.1 LIII 878 (58), TCD.

20   Corman to Douglas, 16 Jan. 1946, file: Japanese Canadians, R33.1 LIII 878 (58), TCD.

21   Fred Williams to Lewis, 10 Dec. 1943, and Mindel Sheps to Lewis, 13 July 1946, file 2: Sask: General Correspondence 1933–1958, vol. 65, CCF; W.J. Reid to Grant McNeil, MLA, 3 Jan. 1944, file: Harold Winch, 1938–1945, vol. 106, CCF.

22   Thomas Shoyama and Arthur Wakabayashi were other Japanese Canadians appointed to high-ranking civil service positions. A.W. Johnson, *Dream No Little Dreams* (Toronto: University of Toronto Press, 2004).

23   McInnis to Douglas, 8 Apr. 1946, box 255, TCD.

24   Douglas to McInnis, 3 Apr. 1946, box 137, TCD.

25   Douglas to Elizabeth Martin, 15 Jan. 1946, file: Japanese-Canadians, TCD.

26   See *Dominion-Provincial Conference [on Reconstruction] (1945): Dominion and Provincial Submissions and Plenary Conference Discussions* (Ottawa: King's Printer, 1946), 180.

27   Shumiatcher to his mother and father, 23 Apr. 1939, file 11, box 2, M8686, Abraham Shumiatcher Fonds, Glenbow Archives (hereafter cited as GSF).

28   Shumiatcher to his mother and father, 23 Apr. 1939.

29   A Coat of Many Colours: Morris Shumiatcher (tapes 76–80), 6 January 1989, Canadian Museum of Civilization Collection.

30   Shumiatcher to his mother and father, 1 Nov. 1942, file 10, box 2, GSF.

31   Minuetta to Shumiatcher, 8 June 1944, Correspondence, Miscellaneous, Shumiatcher Fonds, Saskatchewan Archives Board (hereafter cited as SSF).

32   Shumiatcher to his mother and father, 20 Jan. 1945, file 14, box 2, GSF.

33   James M. Pitsula, "The CCF Government and the Formation of the Union of Saskatchewan Indians," *Prairie Forum* 19, no. 2 (1994): 138.

34   Shumiatcher to his parents, 6 June 1940, file 10, box 2, GSF.

35   Introduction for M.A. Gray in Montreal Address on CCF, 15 Nov. 1947, CCF: MLA Gray, M.A. Winnipeg, SSF.

36   Shumiatcher to Bets, 29 May 1944, Personal Correspondence, SSF.

37   Shumiatcher to his mother and father, 28 Aug. 1944 and 3 Aug. 1944, file 14, box 2, GSF.

38   Pitsula, "CCF Government and the Formation of the Union of Saskatchewan Indians"; and Shumiatcher, "Indian Smoke on the Western Sky," 283–4.

39   A Coat of Many Colours.

40   Shumiatcher to Samuel Bronfman, 6 Oct. 1945; Saul Hayes, national executive director, CJC, to Shumiatcher, 11 Oct. 1945; M. Saalheimer to Commission on Law and Legislation, American Jewish Congress, 16 Oct. 1945, file 22, box 2, ZA 1945, CJCM. File 4: Report of Activities for Improved Human Relations of the JLC of C for the Year Ending 31 July 1947, vol. 20, MG 30 A53, Kalmen Kaplansky Fonds (hereafter cited as KK), LAC.

41   Corman to Douglas and Woodrow Lloyd, 3 Mar. 1947, file 93 (2–29), box 25, TCD; *Debates*, 4 Feb. 1947,

p. 43 (A.T. Procter, MLA); 13 Feb. 1947, p. 220 (A.T. Procter, MLA); 19 Mar. 1947, p. 994 (J.W. Corman, MLA), pp. 1001, 1003, 1006 (W.J. Patterson, leader of the opposition); and 21 Mar. 1947, pp. 1065, 1066 (P.J. Hoodge, MLA).

42   "Bill of Rights," *Star Phoenix*, 20 Mar. 1947.

43   "Doubts Expressed of Rights Bill," *Leader Post*, 22 Mar. 1947.

44   *Debates*, 4 Feb. 4, 1947, p. 42 (W.J. Patterson, leader of the opposition); 14 Feb. 1947, p. 293 (J.H. Borcklebank, MLA); 19 Mar. 1947, p. 998 (W.J. Patterson, leader of the opposition); and 21 Mar. 1947, pp. 1049B51 (A.W. Embury, MLA), 1065, 1068 (P.J. Hoodge, MLA).

45   "Rights Bill by C.C.F. Absurd Says Patterson," *Leader Post*, 5 Feb. 1947.

46   "Mr Corman Defines 'Creed,'" *Moose Jaw Times-Herald*, 1 Apr. 1947; and "Another Mistake," *Star-Phoenix*, 1 Apr. 1947.

47   "Personal Liberties Basis for Concern," *Leader Post*, 29 Nov. 1947.

48   "Fundamental Freedoms," *Leader Post*, 19 Mar. 1947; and *Debates* (19 Mar. 1947), pp. 996, 1006 (M.J. Patterson, leader of the opposition).

49   *Debates*, 13 Feb. 1947, p. 220 (A.T. Procter, MLA), 21 Mar. 1947, p. 1068 (P.J. Hoodge, MLA).

50   *Debates*, 21 Mar. 1947, p. 1062 (D.M. Lazorko, MLA), 21 Mar. 1947, p. 1053 (D.Z. Daniels, MLA).

51   *Debates*, 19 Mar. 1947, p. 991 (J.L. Corman, MLA).

52   Ibid., p. 1091.

53   Ibid., pp. 991–2.

54   *Debates*, 21 Mar. 1947, p. 1047 (W.S. Lloyd, MLA).

55   *Debates*, 21 Mar. 1947, p. 1047 (W.S. Lloyd, MLA); and 26 Mar. 1947, p. 1093 (J.W. Corman, MLA).

56   *Debates*, 21 Mar. 1947, p. 1063 (D.M. Lazorko, MLA); and Shumiatcher to M.A. Gray, 14 Apr. 1947, file: CCF MLA Gray, SSF.

57   "The Saskatchewan Bill of Rights Act," *Information and Comment*, Mar. 1949.

58   David Orlikow, "Civil Rights Bill, Manitoban's Viewpoint," *Commonwealth*, 2 Apr. 1947; *Debates*, 9 Mar. 1947, p. 983 (J.W. Corman, MLA); Corman to Clifford A. Scotton, Cooperative Press Association, 7 Sept. 1955, file: Racial Discrimination, vol. 179, CCF.

59   The Saskatchewan government's publicity materials from the late 1940s confirm this impression.

60   Paltiel to Shumiatcher, 2 May 1951 and passim, 10-1(2) Discrimination, SSF.

61   Statement of Dr M.E., Regina, 2 Aug. 1950, 10-1(2) Discrimination, SSF.

62   Rosalynd Gold, "Occupational Selection and Adjustment in the Jewish Group in Montreal with Special Reference to the Medical Profession" (MA thesis, McGill University, 1943); file 75: and Dental College, reel 1, Correspondence 1947, JPRC, CJC Central Region, MG 8 S, Ontario Jewish Archives.

63   Statement of Dr M.E.; Paltiel to Shumiatcher, 15 Mar. 1951; Shumiatcher to Paltiel, 19 Mar. 1951; and Shumiatcher to Victor Samuels, 15 Nov. 1951, 10-1(2) Discrimination, SSF.

64   Paltiel to Shumiatcher, 2 May 1951, "Discrimination," 10-1(2), SSF.

65   Shumiatcher to Douglas, 28 Aug. 1947; Shumiatcher to Corman, 25 Sept. 1947, XXXVIII (464) (44a-1-3) Prosecutions under the Bill of Rights, R 33.2, TCD.

66   Gordon Milling to Lorne Ingle, 16 Sept. 1955, file: Racial Discrimination, vol. 179, CCF.

67   Kaplansky to Ingle, 2 Sept. 1955; Milling to Ingle, 12 and 16 Sept. 1955; Sid Blum, executive secretary, JLC, Toronto, to Ingle, 20 Sept. 1955, file: Racial Discrimination, vol. 179, CCF; Ken Bryden to Bea Woods, CCF National Office, 4 Sept 1953, file: Civil Liberties, 1940–1953, vol. 147, CCF; Paltiel to Shumiatcher, 2 May 1951; and Shumiatcher to Paltiel, 5 May 1951, 10-1(2) Discrimination, SSF.

68   Milling to Ingle, 16 Sept. 1955; and Blum to Ingle, 20 Sept. 1955, file: Racial Discrimination, vol. 179, CCF.

69   Kaplansky to Ingle, 2 Sept. 1955; and Milling to Ingle, 12 and 16 Sept. 1955, file: Racial Discrimination, vol. 179, CCF.

70   Frank Scott, *The Canadian Constitution and Human Rights* (Toronto: CBC Publications Branch, 1959), especially 45ff. See Kaplansky to Ingle, 2 Sept. 1955, file: Racial Discrimination, vol. 179, CCF, on the intentions of the Saskatchewan government.

71   Douglas to J.G. Diefenbaker, prime minister of Canada, 19 Jan. 1959, XXIII 764 (23–31), TCD. See also Donna Greschner, "The Purpose of Canadian Equality Rights," *Review of Constitutional Studies* 6, no. 2 (2002): 291–323.

CHAPTER 11

Rights in the 1960s and 1970s

◎ 11.1: GENERATIONS AND THE TRANSFORMATION OF SOCIAL MOVEMENTS IN POSTWAR CANADA

Dominique Clément

Claude Forget resigned as president of the Ligue des droits de l'homme (LDH) in Montreal in 1969. It was not a happy parting. Forget accused the LDH of failing to accomplish anything substantial since its founding in 1963. The LDH, according to Forget, was composed of dilettantes and elites who had never been victimized themselves; it was an "anachronism failing to function properly."[1] With limited funds and a handful of dedicated volunteers, the LDH was capable of only a few minor accomplishments. A decade later, however, as the Liberal minister of social affairs in Quebec, Forget would find himself clashing with a very different LDH. A revolution of sorts had taken place within the confines of Quebec's leading human rights organization. An association dedicated to the preservation of civil and political rights, with a restricted membership employing elite tactics for social change, had been transformed into a grassroots organization dedicated to social, economic, and cultural rights with a mandate to promote a "société de participation."

It would be difficult to understate the remarkable transformation in Canada's social movement landscape in the few decades following the end of the Second World War. At the very least, the surging participation of people in various social movements remains, to this day, a historically unique phenomenon. Perhaps more fundamental, however, was the transformation in social movement dynamics. New strategies for social change, innovations in organization, demographic change, and a host of new grievances defined this era of social activism. "The social movements of the 1960s," says Miriam Smith, "were successful in placing new issues on the agenda of both polity and society and reflected a number of important sociological changes in family structure, the decline of both Protestant and Catholic church influence (especially in Quebec), increasing female labour force participation, the expansion of higher education, the increasingly multicultural and multiracial character of Canadian society, and the gradual shift to post-industrialism capitalism."[2]

Historians, particularly in Canada, have yet to make a significant contribution to the study of contemporary social movements. This is unfortunate because historians are ideally situated to offer a broad, long-term empirical analysis of the dynamics of these movements.

Several critical developments after the Second World War represented a rupture with social movements of the past. The transformations that occurred during this period were especially pronounced within the human rights movement, and the Ligue des droits de l'homme is a useful point of departure for the discussion of these developments. Some of the issues examined here include changing demographics, notably the impact of youth and French Canadians on social movements; the emergence of an increasingly wealthy and educated middle class; new visions or ideologies for social change; and the impact of state funding on mobilization. A confluence of social, political, and economic factors during this period, of which the emergence of a large cohort of urban, middle-class youth (the "baby boomers") was one, combined to inaugurate a new era for social movements.

Social Movement Organizations

Time magazine declared the Man of the Year for 1966 to be "The Younger Generation": "Never have the young been so assertive or so articulate, so well educated or so worldly. Predictably, they are a highly independent breed, and—to adult eyes—their independence has made them highly unpredictable. This is not just a new generation, but a new kind of generation."[3] What, precisely, defined this new generation, and what kind of impact it was going to have, the magazine's editors could not say, but they were convinced that its effects could not be ignored.

There is no doubt that a period of fervent social movement activism unfolded after the Second World War and that youth participated in these movements in large numbers. One area, in particular, in which youth played an important role was the proliferation of social movement organizations (SMOs). Whereas a social movement is "a set of opinions and beliefs in a population representing preferences for changing some elements of the social structure or reward distribution, or both, of a society," a social movement organization is "a complex, or formal, organization that identifies its goals with the preferences

of a social movement and attempts to implement these goals."[4] . . .

SMOs were a nexus for mobilizing resources and expressing grievances arising from a social movement. . . . Obviously, SMOs existed before the 1960s and 1970s, but the structural conditions of this period, from the booming economy to new educational opportunities, facilitated the emergence of an unprecedented number.[5]

The proliferation of SMOs in Canada in the sixties and seventies was astounding. The student movement and the New Left peaked in the 1960s; the number of women's groups in British Columbia increased from two in 1969 to over 100 in 1974; the first gay rights organizations were formed in Vancouver and Toronto, and a national association was instigated in 1975; and the founding of Greenpeace in Vancouver in 1971 symbolized the birth of the modern environmental movement.[6] The federal government's ban on Aboriginal political organizing for land claims, instituted in 1927, was removed in 1951, and within a decade the Aboriginal rights movement began to flourish. Four national Aboriginal associations and 33 provincial organizations were born in the 1960s; the first Aboriginal friendship centre opened its doors in Winnipeg in 1959, and others soon appeared in every major city in the country.[7] African-Canadian SMOs spread across the country, while advocates for children's rights, prisoners' rights, animal rights, peace, poverty, and official languages organized in unprecedented numbers. By the mid-1980s, the federal Secretary of State was providing funding to over 3,500 SMOs.[8]

The number of rights associations such as the Ligue des droits de l'homme also expanded during this period. Rights associations are self-identified "civil liberties" or "human rights" associations that do not claim to speak on behalf of a specific constituency but rather claim to defend the rights of all citizens (for example, the Canadian Civil Liberties Association or the Saskatchewan Human Rights Association). By the mid-1970s more than 40 new rights associations were active in Canada.[9]

Youth and childhood, as Jean-Philippe Warren notes in his book *Une douce anarchie: Les années 68 au Québec*, were entering a new phase in the 1960s. More than half the population of North America were under 25 years old in 1960. Adulthood was increasingly delayed due, in part, to new educational opportunities: education no longer ended abruptly for most middle-class Canadians after primary school; secondary school became mandatory; and people stampeded to enrol in colleges and universities.[10] In this context, youth played an important role in the expansion of SMOs. Youth spearheaded the student movement with the formation of the Combined University Campaign for Nuclear Disarmament, the Student Union for Peace Action, the Company of Young Canadians, and the Union général des étudiants québécois (UGEQ).[11] A group of young women in Vancouver and Toronto, disgusted at the rampant sexism among student radicals, formed the first women's liberation groups in Canada.[12] Many of the first gay and lesbian groups epitomized the generational gap.[13] Becki Ross notes in her history of the Lesbian Organization of Toronto that members of lesbian SMOs "were primarily students, they held part-time 'shit jobs,' they worked for state-funded feminist projects, or they started up lesbian-run small businesses."[14] One of the most successful organizations representing African Canadians, the Black United Front, was established in the late 1960s by a collection of black youth in Nova Scotia.[15] Meanwhile, rights associations became a mainstay of the Canadian social movement sector thanks, in part, to the enthusiasm of young activists. Norman Whalen and Walter Thompson, for example, were both fresh out of law school in the early seventies when they joined (and later became presidents of) the Nova Scotia Civil Liberties Association and the Newfoundland-Labrador Human Rights Association (NLHRA) respectively.[16] Another group of mostly young left-wing nationalists called the Waffle organized a dangerous, but ultimately unsuccessful, challenge to the established leadership of the New Democratic Party in 1969. In Quebec, political movements including the Parti québécois and the Front d'action politique benefited from the participation of youth in their ranks.[17] The latter contested municipal elections in Montreal in

1970, the same year as the Front de libération du Québec provoked a national crisis when its members kidnapped a British diplomat and a Quebec cabinet minister.[18] The terrorists' numbers were small, but the organization's "influence, particularly through their writing, was especially strong among youth."[19]

Still, only a minority of young people participated in social movements at this time. A large percentage "of sixties youth remained apolitical or opposed to the radicalism that was so associated with their generation."[20] To accept that the majority of youth were not activists, however, is not to vitiate their collective impact on social movements. Many people supported social movements by adhering to the movement's basic principles in ways that affected their everyday lives (and the lives of others). A minority of activists could also deeply affect the lived experience of the wider community. . . .

The surging participation of youth in social movements acted as an important catalyst during this period, but youth alone were not responsible for the proliferation of SMOs. Paul Tennant reminds us in his study of Aboriginals in Canada that, as early as 1927, one of the leading spokesmen for Aboriginals in Canada, Peter Kelly, "expressed the hope that a future generation would one day take up the land claim were his generation to fail. The graduates of the sixties became the leaders of that future generation."[21] Many of these young graduates, such as Philip Paul, Don Moses, and Rose Charlie, would become prominent leaders in the Aboriginal rights movement, but they also worked alongside veteran activists, including Joseph Gosnell, George Manuel, and Frank Calder.[22] Judy Rebick describes the sixties as a period of youthful rebellion, while pointing out that, despite the slogan "Never trust anyone over 30," young feminists found a great deal in common with feminists who were pioneers in the anti-war movement of the 1950s.[23] Rocky Jones and other young black radicals founded the Black United Front to develop a more militant course of action for African Canadians, but Jones worked with Gus Wedderburn and others in the more established Nova Scotia Association for the Advancement of Black People.[24] Wedderburn, Anderson, Manuel, and others fought tirelessly in the 1950s to set the groundwork for the work of future SMOs, and they continued to play a critical role in shaping the activism of these movements.

In addition to demographics, the expansion of post-secondary education contributed to the explosion of SMOs. Between 1963 and 1968, university enrolment in Canada increased more than it had over the previous 50 years; dozens of new institutions were born, hundreds of faculty were hired, tens of thousands of students swelled the ranks of undergraduate programs, and capital expenditures on universities across the country rose from $100 million in 1955 to over $1.5 billion by the end of the sixties.[25] This new cohort of professionals (academics, lawyers, doctors, social workers, journalists), old and young, played a central role in guiding SMOs. Their education provided them with useful skills for leading an advocacy group, such as researching, writing, organizing, public speaking, and fundraising. An elite cohort of young, educated Aboriginals in the sixties, for example, created new SMOs and encouraged Aboriginal activists to focus their resources on litigation, lobbying, and using the media.[26] The preponderance of professionals in SMOs was enhanced by the rising power of experts in contemporary debates on issues such as abortion or human rights. A feature of modern movements is that they depend on expert opinion: "Analyzing the interplay of causes, costs, consequences, and options requires extensive knowledge of esoteric subjects, unavailable to even relatively well-educated laymen. In modern societies experts play a role in defining facts and issues for many movements, from tax redistribution to the impact of pornography on individual behaviour."[27]

A third factor contributing to the proliferation of SMOs during this period was affluence and the expanding middle class. From 1962 to 1972, the annual growth rate in Canada never dipped below 4 per cent, unemployment was less than 4 per cent in 1965, and more than 145,000 new

jobs were created for people under 25 years old between 1964 and 1967.[28] Educational attainment and economic success led larger numbers of people from the burgeoning middle class to participate in voluntary associations and political activities. Mayer Zald and John McCarthy note that, in the sixties, the "American population greatly expanded its rate of participation in sociopolitical activities," and William Carroll asserts that the sixties were "the climax of a period of social movement activism in Canada."[29] Affluence creates discretionary income that can support social movements. Participation did not necessarily entail working directly with SMOs; people often participated in SMOs simply through membership dues and donations. In the United States, "educational attainment and economic position both correlate positively with sociopolitical participation; therefore, the more America becomes a middle-class society, the higher the societal rate of participation in the sociopolitical concerns."[30] The expansion of the middle class had a direct impact on social movements.

A fourth factor . . . linked to the economic boom was the emergence of new funding opportunities. SMOs could thrive without developing a large membership base, as resources were increasingly available through foundations, churches, and governments, which, since the 1960s, have provided more funding for SMOs than ever before.[31] New technologies also contributed to the proliferation of SMOs. The first Canadian television stations emerged in 1952; by the mid-1950s, more than half of Ontario households had television sets.[32] Television brought police violence in Georgia and riots in Gastown to the homes of millions of Americans and Canadians, whose support for a movement no longer depended on personal experience and immediate situational context.[33] In this way, the media helped SMOs attract larger numbers of constituent members (people who provide funding but do not participate directly in the group's activities) without having to mobilize a grassroots base. Many SMOs placed a priority on public education campaigns, or on tools such as the media and mass mailings, to spread their message and mobilize large numbers of constituent members. As a result, many "professional" SMOs had limited contact with their membership and were led by full-time staff whose central objective was to ensure the group's survival.

The conditions that facilitated the mobilization of social movements and the proliferation of SMOs did not emerge spontaneously in the 1960s. The predominance of television in North American homes was well established by the 1950s. Economic prosperity began in 1946 and lasted until the global economic recession of the mid-1970s. The sixties would become a watershed for social movement mobilization; yet activists in the 1960s built on the successes of their predecessors.

Generations in History

Writing in the 1960s and 1970s, Kenneth Keniston and Louis Feuer conceived of youth protest as a generational challenge. . . . [34] Keniston, a former Rhodes scholar and Yale professor, explained that youth protest was a manifestation of generational conflict: not necessarily a rejection of parental values, but a demand for something new. Like all revolutions, the boomers built upon older values and visions. . . .

. . . To use generation as an analytical concept is to recognize that a community of people who were all born within the same short span of years shared a common historical and cultural experience that collectively shaped their lives (for example, similar schools, common family structures, comparable economic opportunities, exposure to ideas about patriotism and politics). . . .

The demographic bulge led by the boomers was bound to have a profound impact on all aspects of Canadian society, but, as we will see below, the transformation of social movements was a result of youth and older activists working together. As Keniston suggested in 1966, youth built upon established values and visions for social change. Youth were therefore the catalysts for a transformation in the mobilization of social movements and among the leading participants in this new era of activism.

Generations of Social Movements

The first rights associations in Canada emerged in the 1930s and were thus led by a generation of activists who had collectively experienced the Great Depression, the Second World War, and the height of the Cold War. Women had only recently gained the vote in Quebec; employers and the state openly discriminated against racial minorities; Japanese Canadians were disenfranchised and deported; Jehovah's Witnesses in Quebec were vilified and harassed by the police; and communists were constant targets of repression. Quebec's infamous Padlock Act, a vaguely worded statute designed to stamp out "subversive" activities, had been condemned by civil libertarians since its inception in 1937.[35] The autocratic premier Maurice Duplessis used the law to torment suspected communists, harass Jehovah's Witnesses, and suppress radical trade unionists.

In a way, the Padlock Act was the birth mother of the country's first fledgling rights associations. Civil liberties associations, under the banner of the Canadian Civil Liberties Union (CCLU), emerged in the 1930s in Vancouver, Winnipeg, Ottawa, Montreal, and Toronto largely in response to the Padlock Act.[36] The Toronto branch was renamed the Civil Liberties Association of Toronto in 1940 and later became the Association for Civil Liberties under the leadership of Toronto lawyer Irving Himel. These rights associations had a short lifespan. The branches of the CCLU dissolved in a handful of years. Professor Arthur Lower created a new association in Winnipeg, and Frank Scott supported the formation of a civil liberties group in Montreal in the mid-1940s; both organizations lasted barely a decade. A few groups were created in Ottawa, Montreal, and Toronto in the wake of the Gouzenko Affair (1946), but they were defunct by the late 1950s.[37]

Frank Scott, the celebrated civil liberties lawyer and dean of McGill Law School, personified the first generation of civil liberties activists.[38] He was a white male with a university education who lived in a metropolitan area and enjoyed close ties to the political establishment. Few religious or racial minorities (except, notably, Jews in Toronto) were active within civil liberties associations, whose ranks were dominated by professors, journalists, lawyers, and labour leaders.[39] Senator Cairine Wilson (Ottawa) and Margaret Spaulding (Toronto) were among the few women who participated in rights associations before the 1960s.[40]

Early rights associations, including groups based in Montreal, were also dominated by English Canadians. The absence of French Canadians is difficult to explain. Ross Lambertson quotes Frank Scott, who suggested in the 1950s that liberalism was a scarce commodity in French Canada. Eugene Forsey bemoaned the quasi-fascist elements in Quebec in the 1950s that discouraged critics of the state.[41] It was perhaps indicative of the obstacles facing French Canadians that when the francophone representative of the Civil Rights Union attempted to present his brief to a parliamentary committee on human rights in 1950, he was coldly rebuked and told that the committee only worked in English.[42] Rights associations were also leading advocates for a national bill of rights at a time when many French-Canadian political leaders actively opposed it. In a letter to Irving Himel in June 1950, Senator Arthur Roebuck spoke of the divisions between English and French Canadian senators on this issue; the latter hesitated to support a bill of rights that could limit provincial powers.[43] These factors contributed to the weak presence of French Canadians among rights associations.

These early rights associations shared several other notable qualities. First, state funding was non-existent. Rights associations operated on shoestring budgets and depended on volunteer work, individual donations, or the sponsorship of wealthy patrons. Secondly, ideological divisions plagued early rights associations. This was a period characterized by bitter divisions among communists and social democrats. In Toronto, the antipathy between social democrats (and liberals) and communists was strong enough to require the formation of two separate organizations (the Association for Civil Liberties and the communist-led Civil Rights Union). The Civil Liberties Association of Winnipeg refused to allow known communists to join, and the Ottawa Civil Liberties Association disbanded largely as a result of ideological conflicts among its members.[44] Ideological divisions contributed to the failure to form a national organization. An attempt to create a national civil liberties association in Ottawa in 1946 has been characterized by Frank Clarke as a "rancorous affair."[45]

Rights associations mobilized around issues unique to this period. Antidiscrimination legislation did not exist in the 1940s, and rights associations, particularly in Toronto, would play a key role in lobbying for the first anti-discrimination laws and the 1960 federal Bill of Rights. Activists wrote letters to politicians, organized rallies in large cities, mobilized thousands of people to sign petitions, published articles and opinion columns in newspapers and popular magazines such as *Saturday Night*, hosted conferences and public seminars, and presented extensively researched briefs to government officials. When the federal government suspended habeas corpus in 1946 to detain more than a dozen suspected communist spies, civil liberties groups were among the few organizations to speak out against the government's actions.[46] In the same year, rights associations allied with Japanese Canadians and others to combat the federal government's attempts to deport British citizens of Japanese origin back to Japan.[47] Racism, anti-communism, and war played a formative role in shaping the activities of these groups.

The first generation of rights associations was defunct by the late 1950s, and the beginning of a second generation of rights associations emerged in 1962, when the British Columbia Civil Liberties Association (BCCLA) was created in Vancouver to defend Doukhobors from state harassment.[48] Soon after, in London, Ontario, another civil liberties association coalesced around revelations that the local police had arrested 10 people for shoplifting near Christmas and kept them in jail as an example to other potential shoplifters.[49] Human rights groups were established in St John's, Saskatoon, Edmonton, and 10 other cities in the wake of the countrywide celebrations for the anniversary of the Universal Declaration of Human Rights in 1968.[50] More than 40 rights associations, either self-identified civil liberties or human rights associations, were created between 1962 and 1975 (at least one in each province).[51]

Rights associations born after 1962 were deeply affected by the work of the first civil liberties associations. The limitations of the first anti-discrimination statutes and the 1960 federal Bill of Rights, for instance, inspired rights associations to lobby for expansive human rights codes and a constitutionally entrenched bill of rights.[52] Every jurisdiction in Canada was protected by a human rights code by 1977, and in 1982 the Charter of Rights and Freedoms was entrenched in the Constitution.

Frank Scott, a key figure in the CCLU who participated in the creation of the Ligue des droits de l'homme in 1963, bridged the two generations of rights associations. The LDH emerged in the midst of a period of significant social change in Quebec, a transition rooted in developments predating the 1960s. Some of the more notable developments after the war, including the Asbestos strike of 1949 and the secularization of labour unions in the 1950s, the decline of clerical influence since the 1930s, women's successful campaign for the right to vote in 1941, and the creation of Hydro-Québec in 1944, set the stage for the Quiet Revolution.[53] During the Quiet Revolution, the educational system was modernized and secularized; the role of the church was challenged in labour unions, schools, and other sectors of Quebec society; and the state began to expand forcefully its role in the economy. French Canadians aggressively challenged their marginalization in Quebec and Canada, and many participated in social movements. As in the rest of the country, social movements in Quebec entered a new age in the 1960s. Hundreds of SMOs mobilized people in the province around a wide range of grievances, from self-determination for Quebec to rights for women and students.[54]

The LDH quickly became one of the most prominent SMOs in the province. Among the leading figures in the LDH in the 1960s were Frank Scott, Pierre Trudeau, Jean-Charles Harvey, René Hurtubise, Jacques Hébert, Thérèse Casgrain, J.Z. Léon Patenaud, Alban Flamand, and Claude Forget.[55] Most of the founders were established journalists, lawyers, or professors who had experienced first-hand the repressive regime of Maurice Duplessis. Casgrain played a key role in securing, in 1940, women's right to vote in Quebec; both Scott and Trudeau faced numerous obstacles in their careers as university professors because of their political allegiances; Jean-Charles Harvey was fired as editor-in-chief of Le Soleil in 1934 for his controversial book Les demi-civilisés; and Jacques Hébert was charged with sedition for his social and political views. The LDH's founders restricted their activities to lobbying policymakers and working with municipal, provincial, and federal authorities to implement new policies or reform old ones.

Soon after Claude Forget accused the LDH of being an anachronism failing to function properly, Scott and the old guard found themselves besieged from within. The demographics of the organization were changing rapidly by the early 1970s. The association's leadership was slowly overtaken by a new cohort of activists, including Léo Cormier, Raymond Boyer, Simonne Monet-Chartrand, and Bernard Mergler. These new leaders had strong ties to other social movements and were critical of the LDH's elite tactics. At the same time, a young group of activists, including Alain Arsenault, Jean-Claude Bernheim, Normand Caron, Pierre Jasmin, and Jean-Louis Roy, joined the executive council. Maurice Champagne, a college professor born in the 1930s who had recently completed a PhD in France before joining the organization in 1971, would soon become a key figure in the transformation of the LDH.[56]

Many of the LDH's new members were drawn from other social movements in Quebec and, in particular, around Montreal. The city's importance to the social, economic, and political life of the province ensured that it would become a major centre for the mobilization of social movements. . . .

Montreal's vibrant social movement landscape was a valuable resource for the LDH. The association participated in dozens of coalitions throughout the 1970s. For example, the LDH organized a common front of SMOs in 1975 to protect nursery schools from government budget cuts; the coalition brought together such diverse groups as SOS Garderie, Association pour la défense des droits sociaux, The Confédération des syndicats nationaux (CSN), Centrale de l'enseignement du Quebec, Fédération des travailleurs du Québec, Ligue des femmes, and the Parti québécois.[57] The LDH had especially strong ties to the major provincial labour federations. Cormier, who was president of the LDH from 1973 to 1977, had worked for labour unions in Montreal for many years. He also had ties with the Parti québécois, as did other new members of the LDH, including Alain Arsenault and Simonne Monet-Chartrand.[58] In addition, many of the LDH's activists had participated in social movements for students, women, Aboriginal peoples, prisoners, and other groups. Bernard Landry was a student leader at the Université de Montréal in the mid-1960s and worked for the LDH after he graduated; he would soon become a key figure in the Parti québécois. Another former Montreal student leader, Jean Doré, joined the LDH in the 1970s and had close ties to the Parti québécois and the Montreal Citizens Movement. To facilitate the mobilization of activists around issues such as prisoners', Aboriginals', and women's rights, the association created a series of "offices," which were given extensive autonomy within the LDH and mobilized activists from a variety of social movements.[59] The ferment of the period, coupled with the influx of new activists, would have a significant impact on the activism of the LDH.

Founders of the LDH in the 1960s defined rights as civil and political rights. Article 1 of the association's original constitution in 1963 referred to individuals' rights to speech, assembly, association, religion, and due process.[60]

This conception of rights was consistent with the approach embraced by previous civil liberties associations. Early rights associations primarily defined rights in terms of negative freedom (freedom from unjust interference by the state).[61] Champagne and the new cohort of activists, however, introduced a revolutionary manifesto in 1972, calling upon the LDH to adapt to the changes occurring within Quebec society and to consider the unique problems facing the poor, women, elderly, youth, and ethnic minorities.[62] Free speech or due process was no longer sufficient; economic, social, and cultural rights were given equal, if not greater, priority to civil and political rights.[63] Instead of concerning themselves with individual rights, they aimed to achieve equality by improving the social conditions in which those rights were exercised. The contrast was most evident in the LDH's campaign for a provincial bill of rights. In the 1960s, the LDH's proposal for a provincial bill of rights did not include, for example, provisions for language rights.[64] In contrast, the LDH embraced a new policy on language rights, including, among other things, a demand for unilingual education in French in Quebec.[65] Champagne's LDH placed a priority on collective rights: "Une charte des droits de l'homme au Québec qui serait fondée sur un respect inconditionnel de droits individuels, au détriment des droits collectifs, constitueraient en ce domaine comme en d'autres, une base injuste, voir immorale."[66] . . .

Scott and many of the old guard quickly abandoned the LDH, unable to accept this new orientation. . . .

The LDH's new orientation was partly a result of new members joining the organization. According to Jean-Claude Bernheim, who worked for the LDH throughout most of the 1970s, many of the figures who joined the organization during this period had close links to the independence movement and supported the new positions on language rights and self-determination.[67] Pierre Cloutier and others with close ties with the Parti Québécois also formed a national security committee within the LDH to protest illegal RCMP activities in Quebec directed against the independence movement.[68] Scott, Hébert, Casgrain, and many others who founded the LDH would never have countenanced such policies. Many of the LDH's new members during this transition were boomers, but others, such as Mergler and Cormier, had been born before the war and had been active for many years within a variety of social movements. The organization therefore benefited from the influx of both young and established activists.

The LDH's new ideology was also a response to social and political developments in Quebec. This was the time of the Front de libération du Québec, the McGill française movement, the rise of the independence movement, and national debates about language and national unity. Many of the leading SMOs in the province had embraced Quebecois nationalism, including UGEQ, the Fédération des femmes du Québec, Front d'action politique, and CSN, among others. As well, the nationalist movement was only one of many influences on the LDH.[69] The LDH's demands for extensive social and economic reform were hardly unusual in a province that boasted, by the 1970s, "the most combative, militant and radical [labour movement] in Canada."[70] One of the province's leading labour federations, for instance, the CSN, had adopted explicitly socialist positions on the economy. UGEQ, from which a few of the LDH's future leaders would emerge, had also embraced radical positions on the economy and social policy.[71]

Many of these issues were unique to Quebec. Still, developments in Quebec, as noted earlier, mirrored trends across the country. The proliferation of social movements was a national and international phenomenon. True, movements specific to Quebec undoubtedly informed the LDH's new philosophy, but it would be too reductionist to attribute this shift solely to the situation in the province. It should not be forgotten that the LDH emerged within the context of an expanding human rights movement in Canada and at a time when many social movements were embracing new ideological frames. The New Left challenged

the ideological strictures of Scott's generation and the bureaucracy associated with the labour movement. Within the student movement, "ideological strain destroyed more than one New Left organization."[72] Instead of joining long-established women's rights groups, many young women filled the ranks of women's liberationist organizations and explicitly rejected the reform-oriented strategies of established women's groups.[73] Gays and lesbians, Aboriginals, African Canadians, and a host of other movements also struggled to unite diverse interests into a cohesive movement.[74] As Howard Ramos points out, the "divergence among traditional and elected leaders and between local and national interests, urban and rural, and radical and mainstream groups within the Aboriginal movement, as well as the differing legal statuses of Aboriginal peoples, defined the post–White Paper period and remained the case into the 1980s."[75] Among gay rights advocates, liberationist militancy on issues such as pornography and removing the age of consent "grated on assimilationist, equality-seeking advocates, who saw them as impediments to securing legislative reform."[76]

The ideological strains within the LDH also divided rights associations across the country. Should pornography be protected as free speech? Civil liberties associations said yes; human rights associations said no. These divisions were a defining feature of the country's first national rights association formed in 1971: the Canadian Federation of Civil Liberties and Human Rights Associations.[77] Organizations such as the British Columbia Civil Liberties Association and the Canadian Civil Liberties Association (CCLA) defined rights in terms of civil and political rights. In contrast, human rights associations asserted the belief that individuals had a right to economic security and that people could not exercise their political and civil rights without sufficient resources.[78] The LDH successfully lobbied the Quebec government to include a section on economic and social rights in the 1975 Quebec Charter of Human Rights and Freedoms.[79] No other human rights code in Canada contained an explicit reference to economic and social rights.

The presence of French Canadians in the LDH represented another break with the past. Virtually absent from the first generation, by the seventies French Canadians led one of the most dynamic rights associations in the country. The LDH became unilingually French in 1972.[80] . . . The LDH was also one of the founding members of the Canadian Federation of Civil Liberties and Human Rights Associations and was the second-largest rights association in Canada.[81] The work of the LDH outside Quebec included campaigns to protect refugees, eliminate capital punishment, and reform legislation dealing with immigration, privacy, and national security. It hosted the first meeting in North America of the Fédération international des droits de l'homme in 1982.[82] . . .

The influence of French Canadians among rights associations was consistent with developments across the social movement spectrum. Every francophone student association left the Canadian Union of Students in the 1960s to join the newly formed UGEQ; the Fédération des femmes du Québec was formed as an umbrella association for feminists in Quebec in 1966; and the FTQ successfully fought for greater autonomy within the Canadian Labour Congress.[83] In virtually every social movement sector, French Canadians were playing a central role within Quebec and on the national stage.

Another key shift in the dynamics of the LDH was the infusion of state funding. There was some hesitation within the ranks of the membership surrounding financial support from governments. Only a few years earlier the association had explicitly rejected state funding. Still, at the 1971 annual general meeting, the membership accepted their leaders' argument that, after nearly 10 years of working on a shoestring budget, the organization desperately needed a larger source of funding.[84] Many other SMOs in Canada followed a similar path. The federal government provided extensive funding to a wide array of SMOs beginning in the late 1960s. Federal funding for rights associations

was sufficiently pervasive that it is not an exaggeration to suggest that the state essentially bankrolled an entire network of SMOs, a trend that reversed in the 1980s when funding was increasingly cut back. The seventies were therefore a historically unique period in terms of state funding for SMOs.[85] . . .

The impact of state funding cannot be overstated. The LDH's founders had initially refused to accept state funding. As a result, the administrative council struggled to find a place to gather; meetings would take place in Casgrain's home or Hébert's publishing house. Hiring staff was impossible, and the lack of funding made it difficult to initiate legal challenges or other activities. The need for additional resources was made evident during the October Crisis in 1970, when the organization had to scramble to find funds to help individuals arrested under the War Measures Act.[86] . . . The LDH routinely accepted substantial government grants (provincial and federal) every year after 1971. . . . Membership fees barely constituted 10 per cent of the organization's revenue.[87] The LDH was a typical professional SMO in that state funding allowed it to expand its activities without having to mobilize a large number of members.

Once again, the experience of the LDH was a microcosm of developments occurring throughout the country. For most rights associations, state funding accounted for 80 to 90 per cent of their budgets.[88] With the rare exception of groups such as the Canadian Civil Liberties Association, which opposed state funding in principle, virtually every rights association received funding from the state.[89] . . .

SMOs representing women, Aboriginal peoples, and ethnic, racial, and linguistic minorities, to name a few, received state funding in the seventies.[90] . . . Organizations as diverse as the National Action Committee on the Status of Women, the Black United Front, the Multicultural Association Council of Saskatchewan, the Fédération des francophones hors Québec, and the Just Society Movement received generous financing by the state.[91] In each case, the long-term survival of the organization depended on state funding.

Conclusion

State funding, ideology, education, wealth, technology, and demographics represent only some of the factors distinguishing the two generations of rights associations. The radicalism of the sixties and seventies produced new strategies for change, new grievances to mobilize social movements, and innovations in organization and communication. To be fair, a study of SMOs can never fully capture the ferment of the period. With the proliferation of rape crisis centres, gay pride parades, recycling campaigns, civil disobedience, anti-poverty demonstrations, women's bookstores, transition houses, and myriad other forms of protest, SMOs represented only a small part of the social movement landscape. Moreover, although the proliferation of SMOs was truly impressive, in truth most people preferred to stay home and watch television. The largest rights association in Canada, the Canadian Civil Liberties Association, had fewer than 3,000 members. In his famous book *Bowling Alone*, Robert Putnam links the decline in civic participation to the boomers (and television), a development that was likely facilitated by the abundance of professional SMOs that placed a low priority on mass mobilization.[92]

Yet, in any given year, at least 15,000 to 20,000 individuals were members of one of the dozens of rights associations in Canada.[93] This rate of participation was a significant change from the elite associations created by Scott and others before the 1960s. True, grassroots social movements were hardly unique to this period. What had changed, however, was the demographics of social movements, the new issues that inspired activists, the availability of new technologies, the

unprecedented wealth that fuelled mobilization, and the provision of extensive state funding to support the creation of SMOs. These developments had a profound impact on the dynamics of social movement mobilization and organization.

Youth played an important role in these developments, but youth alone were not responsible for this transformation. Many of the more notable figures in the early human rights movement, such as Frank Scott and Kalmen Kaplansky, continued to play key roles in the movement.[94] After Scott and Hébert left the LDH, other veteran activists, including Boyer, Mergler, and Cormier, replaced them. Doug Owram acknowledges in his study of the English-Canadian student movement that "many of the best-known radicals of the decade were pre-boomers."[95] . . .

The period in which the boomers reached adulthood was a time when social movements underwent a significant transformation. Perhaps it would be more accurate to suggest that a confluence of factors during this period, of which the postwar demographic bulge was one, facilitated the proliferation and transformation of SMOs on an unprecedented scale. The combination of a demographic wave and structural changes transformed social movements. In essence, the boomers were the catalysts, and in some cases the participants, in a historically unique phenomenon.

Author's Note: The author thanks Valerie Korinek, Eric Sager, Bettina Bradbury, and the anonymous readers for their comments on this paper. To continue exploring the history of social movements and human rights in Canada, please visit www.HistoryOfRights.com.

Endnotes

1   Université du Québec à Montréal [hereafter UQAM], Service des archives et de gestion des documents [hereafter SAGD], Fond Ligue des droits et libertés [hereafter LDL], 24P1/5, Minutes of the Administrative Council, 13 March 1969.

2   Miriam Smith, *A Civil Society? Collective Actors in Canadian Political Life* (Peterborough, ON: Broadview Press, 2005), 70.

3   *Time*, 7 January 1966.

4   Mayer N. Zald and John D. McCarthy, "Resource Mobilization and Social Movements: A Partial Theory," in Mayer N. Zald and John D. McCarthy, eds, *Social Movements in an Organizational Society* (New Brunswick, NJ: Transaction Publishers, 1987), 20. An SMO is not an interest group. Miriam Smith notes, "[I]nterest groups are often distinguished from

social movements in that social movements seek to transform social and political values or seek sweeping political change, while interest groups are more narrowly focused on obtaining selective benefits from the state" (*A Civil Society?*, 11).

5   "[W]e do not believe that the existence of professional social movements is a new phenomenon; such an organizational form has existed in the past. It is the widespread nature of the phenomenon that characterizes the modern era." Mayer N. Zald, "The Trend of Social Movements in America," in Louis Kriesberg and Bronislaw Misztal, eds, *Research in Social Movements: Social Movements as a Factor of Change in the Contemporary World*, vol. 10 (Greenwich: Jai Press, 1988), 375. "Many have pointed to the large-scale changes such as the economic booms taking place in many Western countries, shifts in capitalism based on technological advances, and the dramatic expansion of higher education, which helped to nourish a youth culture (Suzanne Staggenborg, *Social Movements* [Toronto: Oxford University Press, 2007], 44).

6   For an overview of SMOs during this period, refer to Dominique Clément, *Canada's Rights Revolution: Social Movements and Social Change, 1937–1982* (Vancouver: UBC Press, 2008), 29–33.

7   Howard Ramos argues that the 1960s was a watershed for the Aboriginal rights movement. State funding, new political opportunities, and the emergence of a pan-Aboriginal identity facilitated Aboriginal mobilization. Moreover, "formally organized contention, representing a broad range of Aboriginal interests, was the exception rather than the norm during the 1950s." Howard Ramos, "What Causes Canadian Aboriginal Protest? Examining Resources, Opportunities and Identity, 1951–2000," *Canadian Journal of Sociology* 31, no. 2 (2006): 211–39, and "Aboriginal Protest" in Staggenborg, ed., *Social Movements*, 59.

8   Leslie Pal, *Interests of State: The Politics of Language, Multiculturalism, and Feminism in Canada* (Montreal and Kingston: McGill-Queen's University Press, 1993), 14.

9   Clément, *Canada's Rights Revolution.*

10   Jean-Philippe Warren, *Une douce anarchie: Les années 68 au Québec* (Montreal: Boréal, 2008), 26.

11   These are only a few of the many student organizations formed during this period. In Quebec, for instance, alongside the UGEQ was the Mouvement étudiant québécois, Jeunesse révolutionnaire québécois, Committee for an Independent Socialist Quebec, Patriotes québécois, and Intellectuels et ouvriers patriotes du Québec (Warren, *Une double anarchie*, 231).

12   *The Peak* 9, no. 11 (3 July 1968). As Naomi Black suggests, women's liberation "brought into Canadian feminism for the first time a large infusion of younger women, students or ex-students." Naomi Black, "The Canadian Women's Movement: The Second Wave,"

in Sandra Burt, Lorraine Code, and Lindsay Dorney, eds, *Changing Patterns: Women in Canada* (Toronto: McClelland & Stewart, 1993), 83.

13   Becki Ross describes the membership of the Lesbian Organization of Toronto as "small friendship circles of largely young, white, middle-class lesbian feminists." Becki Ross, *The House That Jill Built: A Lesbian Nation in Formation* (Toronto: University of Toronto Press, 1995), 54.

14   Becki Ross, "A Lesbian Politics of Erotic Decolonization," in Veronica Strong-Boag, Sherrill E. Grace, and Avigail Eisenberg, eds, *Painting the Maple: Essays on Race, Gender, and the Construction of Canada* (Vancouver: UBC Press, 1998), 198. "The majority were suspicious of 'human rights' organizing within gay liberation that targeted policy reform at the level of municipal, provincial, and federal governments; they argued that these reforms would solely benefit economically advantaged gay men and long-term, monogamous coupling" (199).

15   Dorothy Emma Moore, "Multiculturalism: Ideology or Social Reality?" (PhD dissertation, Boston University, 1980), 309–11.

16   For an overview of the human rights movement in Canada, refer to Ross Lambertson, *Repression and Resistance: Canadian Human Rights Activists, 1930–1960* (Toronto: University of Toronto Press, 2005); and Clément, *Canada's Rights Revolution.*

17   "Sur les 30 000 membres du PQ, un parti fondé en pleine grève général des cégeps en octobre 1968, la part des jeunes est immense. Une pléiade de comités d'action péquistes pénètre dans les établissements d'enseignement. Des centres de recherche, d'information et de documentation sont établis avec une rapidité peu commune. Le travail d'animation est colossal. Fondation récente oblige, des militants étudiants (Claude Charron, Louis Harel, Pierre-Paul Roy, Jean Doré, Gilles Duceppe, Réal Valiquette) se trouvent élevés à des hautes postes de direction ou d'animation au sien du parti. Des éditorialistes de la presse étudiante écrivent des discours pour les candidats souverainistes; d'anciens membres des AGE font du porte-à-parole dans les quartiers ouvriers; des organisateurs d'octobre 1968 élaborent des strategies électorales" (Warren, *Une douce anarchie*, 227–30).

18   Dominique Clément, "The October Crisis of 1970: Human Rights Abuses under the War Measures Act," *Journal of Canadian Studies* 42, no. 2 (2008): 160–86.

19   Judy Rebick, *Ten Thousand Roses: The Making of a Feminist Revolution* (Toronto: Penguin Canada, 2005), 8. Jean-Philippe Warren also discusses the relationship between young students and the Front de libération du Québec (*Une douce anarchie*, 218–26).

20   Doug Owram, *Born at the Right Time: A History of the Baby Boom Generation* (Toronto: University of Toronto Press, 1996), 160. Jean-Philippe Warren also argues that, in the context of the Quebec student

movement, only a minority of youth were militants (and many students were apolitical in the early 1960s) (*Une douce anarchie*, 13, 50, 76).

21   Paul Tennant, *Aboriginal Peoples and Politics: The Indian Land Question in British Columbia, 1849–1989* (Vancouver: UBC Press, 1990), 141.

22   Ibid., 152.

23   Rebick, *Ten Thousand Roses*, 13, 20.

24   Moore, "Multiculturalism," 310–11, 96–401.

25   Owram, *Born at the Right Time*, 180–2.

26   "The change in tactics came with the rise of a young Aboriginal elite who had been educated in the dominant school system because of forced residential schooling" (Ramos, "Aboriginal Protest," 62).

27   Mayer Zald and John D. McCarthy, "The Future of Social Movements," in Zald and McCarthy, eds, *Social Movements in an Organizational Society*, 323.

28   Owram, *Born at the Right Time*, 171–2.

29   Zald, "The Trend of Social Movements in America," 338; and William K. Carroll, ed., *Organizing Dissent: Contemporary Social Movements in Theory and in Practice*, 2nd edn (Toronto: Garamond Press, 1997), 4.

30   Zald, "The Trend of Social Movements in America," 342.

31   Ibid.; Zald and McCarthy, "The Future of Social Movements," 29–31.

32   Owram, *Born at the Right Time*, 88–90.

33   Zald and McCarthy, "Resource Mobilization and Social Movements," 25–38.

34   Kenneth Keniston, *Youth and Dissent: The Rise of a New Opposition* (New York: Harcourt Brace Jovanovich, 1971); and Lewis Feuer, *The Conflict of Generations: The Character and Significance of Student Movements* (New York: Basic Books, 1969).

35   The Padlock Act (*An Act to Protect the Province against Communist Propaganda*), passed in 1937, did not define "subversives." Under the Act, the attorney general (Duplessis) could padlock the premises of any building to prevent "subversive" activity. The law was used against unionists, Jews, Jehovah's Witnesses, communists, and people in the political left in general. Victims could only appeal to the attorney general.

36   For a history of the first generation of rights associations, refer to Dominique Clément, "Spies, Lies and a Commission, 1946–8: A Case Study in the Mobilization of the Canadian Civil Liberties Movement," *Left History* 7, no. 2 (2000): 53–78; and Lambertson, *Repression and Resistance*.

37   The federal government used the War Measures Act in 1946 to suspend civil liberties and detain a handful of suspected Soviet spies incommunicado for weeks. Igor Gouzenko was the Russian cipher clerk who defected and brought evidence of a Soviet spy ring operating in Canada. The Gouzenko Affair sparked an intense public debate about the danger of state abuse of fundamental freedoms. For further information on the Gouzenko Affair and early rights associations, refer to Clément, "Spies, Lies and a Commission."

38   Frank Scott was one of the country's leading constitutional experts. He played a key role in several famous cases in the 1950s dealing with civil liberties, including the Supreme Court of Canada's decision to strike down the Padlock Act.

39   Ross Lambertson provides extensive background information on many of the individuals who organized early rights associations in *Repression and Resistance*.

40   Ibid., 164.

41   Ibid., 48.

42   Canada, *Special Committee on Human Rights and Fundamental Freedoms* (Ottawa: Queen's Printer, 1950).

43   Library and Archives Canada [hereafter LAC], Arthur Roebuck Papers, MG 32 C68, vol. 1, file 23, Arthur Roebuck to Irving Himel, 28 June 1950.

44   Clément, "Spies, Lies and a Commission."

45   C.S. Jackson of the Civil Rights Union (Toronto) called for a broad-based organization to include organized labour, while J.P. Erichsen-Brown of the Ottawa Civil Liberties Association did not consider communists legitimate civil libertarians. Frank K. Clarke, "Debilitating Divisions: The Civil Liberties Movement in Early Cold War Canada, 1946–8," in Gary Kinsman, ed., *Whose National Security? Surveillance and the Creation of Enemies in Canada* (Toronto: Between the Lines, 2000), 177.

46   Clément, "Spies, Lies and a Commission."

47   Stephanie D. Bangarth, "'We are not asking you to open wide the gates for Chinese immigration': The Committee for the Repeal of the Chinese Immigration Act and Early Human Rights Activism in Canada," *Canadian Historical Review* 84, no. 3 (2003): 395–422.

48   Dominique Clément, "An Exercise in Futility? Regionalism, State Funding and Ideology as Obstacles to the Formation of a National Social Movement Organization in Canada," *BC Studies*, no. 146 (Summer 2005): 63–91.

49   *Liberties* 2, no. 1 (September 1969).

50   A Canadian Commission for the International Year for Human Rights was organized in 1967 by a group of prominent Canadians who had been active in the human rights movement (funded by the Secretary of State). The commission established provincial human rights committees to coordinate efforts to celebrate the anniversary. Several of the committees evolved into independent advocacy groups, and a few, including the NLHRA, are still active today. Canadian Commission, *International Year for Human Rights 1968 in Canada: Report of the Proceedings, National Conference on Human Rights and Activities of the Canadian Commission* (1969); Dominique Clément, "Searching for Rights in the Age of Activism: The Newfoundland-Labrador Human Rights Association, 1968–1982," *Newfoundland and Labrador Studies* 19, no. 2 (2003).

51 Maurice Miron, *A Canadian Organization for Human Rights: Report of a Canada-Wide Survey* (Ottawa: Canada Welfare Council, 1970).

52 For a full history of the second generation of rights associations, refer to Clément, *Canada's Rights Revolution*.

53 For an overview of the roots of the Quiet Revolution, refer to John Dickinson and Brian Young, *A Short History of Quebec* (Montreal and Kingston: McGill-Queen's University Press, 2000), chaps 8–9.

54 Jean-Guy Vaillancourt captures the scope of this phenomenon in the introduction to his article "Deux nouveaux mouvements sociaux québécois: Le Mouvement pour la paix et le Mouvement vert," in Gérard Daigle and Guy Rocher, eds, *Le Québec en jeu: Comprendre les grands défis* (Montreal: Presses de l'Université de Montréal, 1992), 4–5.

55 For a full list of the LDH's leadership from 1964 to 1975, see Lucie Laurin, *Des luttes et des droits: Antécédents et histoire de la Ligue des droits de l'homme de 1936–1975* (Montreal: Éditions du Meridien, 1985), appendix.

56 *Le Devoir*, 12 November 1998.

57 *Le Jour*, 27 June 1975.

58 *Le Devoir* hinted in one editorial that a nuclear group within the Ligue was composed of ardent separatists (14 October 1972).

59 The LDH archives at UQAM contain entire files on the committees for women, prisoners, and Aboriginals. See, for instance, files 24P6h/2 (constitution for group on Aboriginal issues); 24P7b/3 (summary of activities for group on women); and 24P1/11 (structure of the Office des droits des détenus). The prisoners' rights group was, by far, the most active.

60 LAC, Frank Scott Papers, MG 30, D211, constitution of the Ligue des droits de l'homme, vol. 46, reel 1235.

61 Lambertson, *Repression and Resistance*.

62 Ligue des droits de l'homme, *Les droits de l'homme dans la société actuelle*, 27 September 1972.

63 Civil liberties associations defined rights in terms of civil and political rights, whereas human rights associations also embraced economic, social, and cultural rights. Civil and political rights restrict state action and provide the basic "rules" for governing a liberal democratic state (negative freedom); economic, social, and cultural rights require positive state action and impose on governments to provide, for instance, adequate levels of education or health care (positive freedom).

64 Jacques-Yvan Morin, "Une Charte des droits de l'homme pour le Quebec," *McGill Law Journal* 9, no. 4 (1963).

65 The link between collective rights and language rights was further elaborated in a position paper adopted by the Ligue in 1973: "De même, les droits linguistiques pour les Québécois de langue française seront des droits collectifs qui ont une importance telle qu'ils peuvent justifier pleinement, à ce moment de notre histoire, des mesures qui auraient pour effet de créer des obligations particuliè res aux individus, notamment dans les limites qu'il faut apporter au choix de la langue d'enseignement pour les parents et les jeunes" (UQAM, SAGD, LDL, 24P1/32, *Rapport annuel de la Ligue*, 1973–4.

66 UQAM, SAGD, LDL, 24P1/32, "Le rôle de la Ligue et son orientation sociale et politique," 1974.

67 Jean-Claude Bernheim, interview with author, 26 June 2005.

68 The link between the Ligue's national security committee was raised in a 1984 internal memorandum produced for the administrative council. It was also confirmed by Jean-Claude Bernheim (ibid.; and UQAM, SAGD, LDL, 24P9f/4, "Mémoire au conseil d'administration sur l'état de la Ligue," 5 April 1984.

69 According to Lucie Laurin, Maurice Champagne believed that the Ligue could offer a more radical and assertive position on language rights because, unlike the Parti québécois, the Ligue was not beholden to the electorate (*Des luttes et des droits*, 117–18).

70 Bryan Palmer, *Working Class Experience: Rethinking the History of Canadian Labour, 1800–1991* (Toronto: McClelland & Stewart, 1992), 362.

71 Warren, *Une douce anarchie*, 42.

72 Owram, *Born at the Right Time*, 231.

73 *Women Unite! An Anthology of the Canadian Women's Movement* (Toronto: Canadian Women's Educational Press, 1972), 9.

74 Nancy Adamson, *Feminist Organizing for Change: The Contemporary Women's Movement in Canada* (Toronto: University of Toronto Press, 1988); and Tom Warner, *Never Going Back: A History of Queer Activism in Canada* (Toronto: University of Toronto Press, 2002).

75 Ramos, "Aboriginal Protest," 63.

76 Warner, *Never Going Back*, 131.

77 Clément, "An Exercise in Futility?"

78 Clément, *Canada's Rights Revolution*.

79 Charter of Human Rights and Freedoms, Revised Statutes of Quebec 1975, c.C–12.

80 UQAM, SAGD, LDL, 24P6g/1, "Les Québécois ont le droit de survivre—Position de la Ligue sur les droits linguistiques au Québec," 26 May 1974; and UQAM, SAGD, LDL, 24P6q/1, "La négation du droit a l'autodétermination dans la campagne électorale—Déclaration spéciale du Conseil d'administration de la Ligue des droits le l'homme," 13 October 1972.

81 The following newsletter provides a breakdown of membership numbers for rights associations across Canada in the 1970s: Rights and Freedoms, no. 21, March 1976, and no. 25, March 1977.

82 Lucie Laurin provides a brief institutional history of the Ligue until 1975 in *Des luttes et des droits*.

83 Palmer, *Working Class Experience*, 362.

84   UQAM, SAGD, LDL, 24P1/29, Minutes of the annual general meeting, 26 April 1971.

85   For studies on state funding for social movements in Canada during this period, refer to Clément, *Canada's Rights Revolution*; and Pal, *Interests of State*.

86   The LDH's response to the October Crisis is chronicled in Clément, "The October Crisis of 1970."

87   UQAM, SAGD, LDL, 24P1/32, Minutes of the annual general meeting, 22 February 1974.

88   UQAM, SAGD, LDL, 24P5/12, Financial Statements of the LDH, 31 December 1973; 31 December 1974; 31 December 1975.

89   The CCLA opposed state funding for numerous reasons. Many of the CCLA's leading figures, including Eamon Park, Alan Borovoy, and Harry Arthurs, believed that state funding created a perception of bias in favour of the state; others claimed that it discouraged bold and imaginative leadership. A full discussion of the CCLA's position on state funding is available in Clément, "An Exercise in Futility?"

90   For a case study of how state funding could threaten the independence of an SMO, refer to Sharon D. Stone and Joanne Doucette, "Organizing the Marginalized: The Disabled Women's Network," in Frank Cunningham, Sue Findlay, Marlene Kada *et al.*, eds, *Social Movements/Social Change: The Politics of Practice and Organizing* (Toronto: Between the Lines, 1988).

91   Except for Leslie Pal's study and my own work on rights associations, there is very little work on the history of state funding for advocacy groups in Canada. Some historians, however, have engaged with this issue as part of a larger study; see Tennant, *Aboriginal Peoples and Politics*, chaps 12–13; Margaret Hillyard Little, "Militant Mothers Fight Poverty: The Just Society Movement, 1968–1971," *Labour/Le Travail* 59 (2007): 179–98; and Ramos, "What Causes Canadian Aboriginal Protest?"

92   Robert Putnam, *Bowling Alone: The Collapse and Revival of American Community* (New York: Simon & Shuster, 2000), chap. 9. Staggenborg also suggests that "when movements rely mainly on paid staff along with financial contributions from 'paper members,' participation from large masses of people is less critical" (*Social Movements*, 30).

93   Clément, *Canada's Rights Revolution*.

94   For a history of Kaplansky's role in the human rights movement, refer to Ross Lambertson, "The Dresden Story: Racism, Human Rights, and the Jewish Labour Committee of Canada," *Labour/Le Travail* 47 (Spring 2001): 43–82.

95   Owram, *Born at the Right Time*, 160.

◎ 11.2: THE RECOGNITION OF INSTITUTIONAL RACISM IN ONTARIO: PUBLIC AND PRIVATE ENQUIRIES INTO TORONTO'S "RACE CRISIS," 1975–1982

Małgorzata Kieryło

Canadians heralded the 1970s with cautious optimism; somehow, Canadians had weathered the turbulent 1960s. To commemorate the new decade, the T. Eaton Company commissioned a full-page advertisement in the *Globe and Mail* to evaluate the "issues," "triumphs," and "lessons" of the decade past. Eaton's assessed the 1960s as an era of youth activism, pollution, space travel, war, population growth, and discrimination. The ad projected that all of these issues would continue to be challenges except for discrimination. Discrimination, Eaton's argued, was an "age-old ill" that would become obsolete because it was practised by individuals who based their beliefs on a "hysterical kind of fear." These irrational individuals, however, had social utility, as they forced humanity "to look deep into our own consciousness and rid ourselves of any trace of this same irrational fear we may find." Eaton's projected that discrimination would fade into oblivion because Canadians had learned that discrimination was "morally wrong, cruel, and worst of all, a senseless waste of human potential."[1]

The projections made by Eaton's were erroneous. In fact, the 1970s witnessed unprecedented racial violence against Canada's people of colour. Most racial attacks occurred in Metropolitan Toronto—one of Canada's most populous and diverse cities. The violence targeted new immigrants from decolonizing nations who arrived in Canada following the adoption of the "points system" in 1967—a system that attempted to attract skilled workers and business immigrants.[2] Racial violence seemed out of character for Canada's social order. Canadians were tolerant, progressive, colour-blind, and full of goodwill. This mythology of racelessness dominated the national narrative and was affirmed by Prime Minister Pierre Trudeau when he announced Canada's commitment to multiculturalism in 1971, arguing that cultural pluralism was the very essence of Canadian identity. The myth of racial harmony was also supported by prevailing conceptualizations of racism. Existing human rights legislation, for example, deemed racism as incidental and aberrant; those who were irrational and had misdirected frustration and aggression were blamed for expressions of prejudice. Legislation, therefore, was intended to protect citizens from pathological individuals who practised discrimination.[3]

During the 1970s, racial violence on the streets of Toronto challenged this static conceptualization of racism. Consistent reports of racial slurs, racist graffiti, and physical violence against people of colour resulted in the perception by government officials, people of colour, and the media that Toronto's "race relations" were strained and were reaching unprecedented proportions.[4] This perceived crisis in race relations concerned most Torontonians, as it went against Canadians' self-perception as a tolerant society.

Many viewed overt racism as incidental; media agencies and municipal, provincial, and federal officials, for example, often argued that racial attacks were perpetrated by unbalanced youths who were outside the perimeters of citizenship. These individuals were conceptualized as outside the norm, as they exhibited intolerance, hate, and prejudice—attributes that officials argued were outside the essence of Canadian identity. The media and government officials also blamed increasing overt racism on social forces, such as unemployment,

inflation, and emerging debates about the future of Canada's immigration policy.[5] Many people of colour and several rights organizations agreed—social forces affected levels of prejudice. However, several of these organizations and individuals believed that racial violence was symptomatic of institutional racism, a system of inequality that reproduced itself because it was rooted in the policies, procedures, and culture of Canada's public and private institutions.

Many Canadians, however, saw the concept of institutional racism as a peripheral, if not, American peculiarity. It was Stokely Carmichael, a Black Nationalist and leader of the Black Panther Party, who coined the term during the 1960s. For Carmichael, institutional racism meant the systemic denial of equal opportunity that resulted in high unemployment, low wages, inadequate housing, and low social status.[6] In Canada, the mythology of racelessness managed the emerging discourses of institutional racism. When organizations and individuals argued that racism was inherent in Canadian institutions, they were met with denials from state officials, who often used the rhetoric of multiculturalism to argue that claims of racism were absurd. However, the perceived sudden increase in racial violence during the 1970s played a key role in challenging the notion of a raceless Canada, and human rights activists, community-development organizations, and visible minority[7] groups formed loosely based coalitions and utilized the discourse of rights to press for state action against racial violence. These groups, however, did not always agree on the nature of racism in Canadian society, and as a result, they attributed different meanings to racial violence. The Committee against Racism, for example, conceptualized overt violence as symptomatic of defective individuals who practised discrimination. Others, such as the Urban Alliance on Race Relations, argued that overt violence reflected the systemic and institutionalized devaluation of people of colour in Canadian society.

All groups, however, expressed apprehension about deteriorating ethnic relations in Toronto.

This perceived race crisis produced anti-racism protests that resulted in private and public enquiries that attempted to explain Toronto's deteriorating race relations. These enquiries played a fundamental role in redefining the nature of racism in Canadian society and ultimately challenged existing conceptualizations of citizenship. An analysis of the enquires

reveals that overt violence was ascribed multiple meanings, as various individuals and organizations interpreted racial attacks through various lenses. For example, government-sponsored enquiries blamed increasing racial violence on the rapid influx of visible minorities and focused on individual acts of violence against people of colour. These reports conceptualized racism as a disease, as they blamed "sick" individuals or extremist groups

INSTITUTIONAL RACISM

As noted above, the term "institutional racism" was coined by Stokely Carmichael, a prominent Black Power activist and civil rights leader in the United States in the 1960s. Institutional racism is the result of the structure or operation of social institutions (such as government agencies, schools, private business) that leads to inequitable, discriminatory, or negative impacts for racial or ethnic groups. The concept developed from the recognition that not all racism or the resulting discrimination faced by racial groups can be explained by prejudice or direct and intentional inequitable treatment. The policies or procedures of institutions, such as government, can lead to inequitable or oppressive treatment or inequitable access to goods, services, or opportunities (such as in employment, higher education, or health care). Institutional factors have also been applied to explain the discrimination and inequality faced by other disadvantaged social groups, such as women, the disabled, and religious minorities.

The recognition that racism was essentially embedded in the social and economic structure of society led those committed to civil rights to recognize and advocate a need for measures beyond the anti-discrimination laws that were often the focus of early civil rights advocacy. Traditional understandings of racism focused on personal prejudice as the cause and thus on laws prohibiting intentional discriminatory treatment as well as on public education. The concept of institutional racism led to the development of measures, such as employment equity programs, that called for "quotas" or preferential treatment in the hiring of targeted minorities based on the fact that these groups already operated from a disadvantage because of their relative absence in certain occupations or sectors and the long-term impacts of inequitable opportunity.

Institutional racism has been a subject of debate particularly in the case of police services, in Canada as well as other countries. Racial profiling, defined as an action or a decision by police taken on the basis of racial stereotypes or assumptions, has led to significant controversy. Police have been charged with differential treatment when responding to calls or engaging in search programs (such as RIDE programs) depending on the race of the people involved or whether the neighbourhoods are lower income or dominated by specific racial groups. For example, young black men have charged that they are much more likely than whites to be pulled over during routine traffic patrols. In response to these charges, Canadian police forces have implemented a number of programs, such as "sensitivity" training and recruitment of officers from racial or other groups so that the police better represent the cultural and demographic composition of the people they serve.

for increased racial hostility. As race relations continued to deteriorate, state-sponsored studies began to examine other causes for the increase in racial violence; in many reports, unemployment, inflation, and urban sprawl were blamed. Enquiries commissioned by visible minorities, community-development organizations, and human rights activists, however, blamed increased racial tensions on institutional racism. These enquiries were key to the formation of a counter-narrative that challenged the persistent denial of structural racism as they exposed common problems that transcended individual experience. The conclusions of these independent enquiries were not taken seriously by the provincial and federal governments. It was further probing and sensitivity to race relations in subsequent enquiries that confirmed that racism was caused not only by personal prejudice but also by Canadian institutions.

The Shooting of Michael Habbib

Attention to racial problems in Toronto began in 1974 when both the *Globe and Mail* and the *Toronto Star* featured cases of police brutality against visible minorities.[8] Reports of police brutality led to a municipal enquiry and later a royal commission on police practices in Toronto.[9]

Police brutality was only one aspect of growing racial tensions in Toronto. Throughout the spring months of 1974 a Toronto Sikh Temple was desecrated several times.[10] In June, two black musicians were attacked during the filming of a television program by members of the Western Guard, a white supremacist organization that emerged in Ontario in 1972.[11] It was the fatal shooting of Michael Habbib in 1975, however, that sent shockwaves throughout the city. The 15-year-old victim was walking across a Toronto parking lot when a white man approached him and shot him in the face at close range. Habbib's violent and senseless death was interpreted in a variety of ways. Some believed that his death was a random incident perpetrated

by a "twisted person."[12] For Toronto's racialized minorities, the case was indicative of a trend that was emerging in Toronto's neighbourhoods. Toronto's black and South Asian residents believed that racial violence could lead to "overt conflict." Some argued that the lack of protection against overt violence was indicative of "the passive majority of Canadians to racism."[13] Such allegations were denied by state agents. Member of Parliament (MP) John Diefenbaker argued that such accusations went against the "reputation of Canada for respecting the equality of all, regardless of colour."[14] Similarly, Ontario premier Bill Davis argued that the "vast majority of Ontario citizens" were accepting of every "race, colour or creed."[15]

Habbib's tragic death spurred on a larger debate about race relations in Toronto. Much of the public debate focused on deciphering why race relations were disintegrating. Reverend Gregory Baum, professor of theological studies at St Michael's College, argued that racism was being expressed because of "fear, insecurity, and a lack of leadership by [the] government." Others held that increased racism was due to the emergence of right-wing organizations. Reverend Bruce McLeod, for example, former United Church of Canada moderator and a member of the Committee against Racism, argued that increased racial tensions were caused by white supremacists. He publicly asked the extremists to "wake up" from their delusions.[16] Rabbi W. Gunther Plaut of Holy Blossom Temple agreed—he believed that racism was propagated by "subterranean groups" who were trying to save "white values."[17]

Various ethnic and rights organizations, including the Task Force against Racial Injustice and Political Repression, the East Indian Defence Committee, the Scarborough Black Students Association, and the Black Liaison Committee, disagreed, believing instead that racism was far more pervasive. Following Habbib's funeral these groups organized several marches to protest state indifference to racism.[18] Toronto's racialized groups also expressed their views in letters to the editor, many of which made claims to citizenship and emphasized the myth of multiculturalism as public policy.[19]

The Wilson Head and Walter Pitman Enquiries

It was in this highly tense context that various institutions began to commission social science studies to gauge the changing nature of ethnic relations in Toronto. It was clear that multiculturalism programs and existing human rights policies were unable to address the growing racism in one of Canada's most diverse cities. The Ontario Human Rights Commission, with its mandate to protect individuals from discrimination in employment, housing, and public services, was the first to assess the nature of discrimination in Toronto. The commission approached Wilson Head, the director of research and planning for the Metro Social Planning Council and associate professor of social work at York University, to conduct a study for public education purposes.

Head's study, the results of which were published in 1975 in the book *The Black Presence in the Canadian Mosaic: A Study of the Perception and the Practice of Discrimination against Blacks in Metropolitan Toronto*, sought to determine the causes of increased racial tensions in Toronto by examining the attitudes, perceptions, and opinions expressed by black and white respondents to a questionnaire.[20] The survey results revealed that many blacks believed that discrimination existed in the areas of employment, housing, and education. The study demonstrated that blacks had a harder time getting promotions, but it noted that discrimination in housing was decreasing because "liberal attitudes" made people more willing to accommodate people of colour. With respect to education, the study revealed that some teachers channelled students into vocational rather than academic work because of the perception that blacks were slow learners. Respondents also criticized the police for stereotyping all blacks as criminals and accused the Metropolitan Toronto

Police of harassment and name-calling. In spite of evidence of institutional discrimination, Head argued that racial tensions were on the rise because of a few "racist groups." Specifically, he expressed concerns over the activities of the Western Guard Party.[21] A Toronto newspaper praised the report and asserted that racial harmony was possible in the city. Certainly there was evidence of discrimination, but "prejudice and racial hatred [was] not as virulent as may be found in most American cities."[22]

These assertions were soon challenged by increasing complaints of police brutality against people of colour in Toronto. Racial violence was also increasing. Subway stations, parks, public housing complexes, school playgrounds, and streets were areas where people of colour suffered harassment and physical attacks. One particular story that gripped Toronto headlines was that of Shamshudin Kanji, a 48-year-old immigrant from Tanzania. Kanji was on his way home from a religious service when several youths attacked him, called him a "Paki," and pushed him off the subway platform, crippling his knees. After Kanji spent four months in a Toronto hospital, doctors determined that he would never walk again.[23]

Like Michael Habbib's death, the violent assault of Shamshudin Kanji was interpreted in a variety of ways. The *Toronto Star* argued that the assault occurred because the attackers were under the influence of alcohol.[24] The newspaper emphasized that Canadians were generally tolerant and full of benevolence. It was those who were unstable and sick with the disease of prejudice that practised racism.[25] Toronto Transit Commission (TTC) chair Gordon Hurlburt concurred with these assertions and assured the Toronto public that subways were safe and that Kanji's assault was "an isolated incident."[26] Toronto's people of colour saw the incident through another lens; many argued that Kanji's assault reflected a much bigger problem—that racism was caused by ingrained social stereotypes that were reproduced in Canadian institutions.[27]

Shamshudin Kanji's assault, as some officials suggested, was not an isolated incident. Throughout 1976 and 1977, racial attacks continued. A week after Kanji was attacked, an East Indian woman was taunted and punched on a subway platform.[28] In December 1976, three South Asian men were beaten by three white men at a subway station.[29] In another incident, a 61-year-old Torontonian intervened when he saw some men harassing South Asians in a subway car. He was hassled and thrown onto a subway platform.[30] In another case, a West Indian man was called a "Paki" and attacked by white men in a subway car. The victim was knocked to the ground and kicked while other transit riders watched. The victim believed that "things were going to get worse" for dark-skinned people.[31]

Following these series of attacks, Canadian periodicals began to probe the causes of racial tensions. In late 1976, an article in *Weekend Magazine* maintained that the increase in racial violence was caused by the perception that too many non-whites were entering the country. In light of growing tensions, the article argued that the federal government had to curb immigration.[32] Rising racial tensions were also examined by *Maclean's* magazine. In fact, the magazine dedicated its February 1977 issue to the growing racism in Canada, specifically Toronto. One story featured a Sikh family whose members endured overt racial violence at school, in their neighbourhood, and on Toronto's subways. After residing in Canada for eight years, the family decided to move back to India.[33] Another more extensive story probed the causes of the increase in racial tensions; it concurred with Wilson Head's earlier study and argued that most of the perpetrators of racial attacks were "thugs and hoodlums," some of whom belonged to white power organizations.[34]

Racial tensions in Toronto also received international media coverage. In early 1977, the increased incidents of racial violence were examined by NBC's *Weekend*—an American television program—which argued that Toronto was a "time bomb of future racial strife." The 20-minute special blamed the deterioration of race relations in Toronto on the influx of visible minorities and

charged that overt acts of violence were being perpetrated by members of the Western Guard Party.[35] The report was significant in that it challenged the perception that Canadians were tolerant. As a result, its assertions were disputed by the media and government officials. One Toronto newspaper called the show "a horrible example of sensational journalism . . . [which] provided a very warped view of Toronto."[36] Toronto's mayor, David Crombie, denounced the NBC program, calling it "irresponsible journalism."[37] Ron Basford, the minister of justice, believed that the vast majority of Canadians found racism "despicable, distasteful, not wanted and not needed."[38] However, visible minorities disagreed. Jagdish Bhadauria of the Canadian Council for Racial Harmony, for example, called the NBC show "absolutely true" and argued that the "race crisis" was far worse than the NBC portrayal. The same sentiment was expressed by Ranvir Sharda, editor of the *India Digest*, who argued that racism was increasing "day by day."[39]

In spite of official reassurances that Canadians were tolerant, acts of violence against visible minorities continued. Victims reported that they felt unsafe in public places and did not feel protected by the law.[40] As a result of these accusations and the general concern over racism in Toronto, Metro chair Paul Godfrey established the Task Force on Human Relations in early 1977. Godfrey appointed Walter Pitman, president of Toronto's Ryerson Polytechnic Institute, to conduct a study on racism in Toronto.[41] The purpose of the study was to assess "racism in the minds of Metro Toronto's citizens." After several months of study, Pitman's report, entitled *Now Is Not Too Late*, concluded that racial attacks were both violent and progressive. To address the rising racial tensions, Pitman submitted 41 recommendations, many of which were pragmatic; for example, he called for increased safety measures on subways and argued that Metro Council should condemn racism as a matter of public policy.[42]

Pitman's report, however, focused on the Metropolitan Toronto Police. Several recommendations, 18 of the 41 to be exact, pertained to the police. The main recommendations dealt with the recruitment, selection, orientation, and training of police officers. Pitman argued that to their improve relations with Toronto's people of colour, police needed training in "cross-cultural understanding." Moreover, he believed that to weed out racists from the police force, the police department should perform psychological tests on police applicants. The report also suggested that the Metro Police Force should hire applicants from visible minorities. To achieve this, Pitman suggested that the police force drop its height and weight requirements "to accommodate members of visible minorities whose physical size does not normally meet these requirements" and implement affirmative action.[43]

Pitman's report also addressed the rise in racial tensions in Toronto. It argued that the massive immigration of visible minorities to Toronto had caused a "cultural shock" for white Canadians. Torontonians, Pitman believed, were not ready for the "shift in the racial mix of Toronto's population." He also blamed Canada's waning economy for the rise in racial tensions. Since most recent immigrants were well educated and financially secure when they entered Canada, unemployed Canadians often resented their success. Unlike Wilson Head's earlier study, Pitman's did not blame racist groups such as the Western Guard Party for increased racial violence in Metropolitan Toronto. Instead, the report presented a "scenario of a racial attack" in which the typical racist was described as a young white unemployed male with an aggressive predisposition, little education, weak family relationships, and problems with alcohol or drug use. Pitman agreed with Head that individuals perpetrated racism, but he believed that racism was far more widespread than Head had argued: racists were simply unemployed youths who "act[ed] out their passions."[44] Those who fit the criteria of Pitman's racial composite could potentially take part in acts of racial violence. Pitman's conclusions made headline news in Toronto because he revealed that racism was far more prevalent than most assumed. Headlines such as "All Minorities Hit by City's Racism, Pitman Suggests," "Metro's Blacks and Asians

Live in Constant Fear of Racial Violence, Pitman Report Says," and "We All Must Learn to Be More Tolerant, Pitman Stresses" challenged the perception that Toronto was "a non-violent, loving community."[45]

Other Voices Recognize Institutional Racism

Besides local interest in addressing racism and discrimination, various non-governmental organizations also became involved in looking into the causes of increased racial tensions in Toronto. In 1977, the Canadian Labour Congress (CLC) acquired the assistance of Daniel Hill, former director and chair of the Ontario Human Rights Commission, to produce a study on human rights. The CLC, with its long history of agitation for human rights and protective legislation, co-sponsored the study with several dozen non-governmental organizations that supported human rights.[46] In the report, entitled *Human Rights in Canada: A Focus on Racism,* Daniel Hill argued that racism was not new to Canada and that Canadians neither believed in the "cultural pluralism" that Trudeau espoused in 1971 nor translated it into practice. Canadians, Hill argued, had to re-examine their "complacency and confront the clear evidence of racism throughout Canada." According to Hill, overt acts of discrimination reflected a much wider problem; he argued that institutions, not individuals, were "perpetuating racism."[47]

South Asian organizations also expressed their concern with increased racial tensions in Ontario. In 1977, Bhausaheb Ubale, a South Asian economist, was approached by the Indian Immigrant Aid Services Association to prepare a draft on racial violence. The report, entitled *Equal Opportunity and Public Policy: A Report on Concerns of the South Asian Canadian Community Regarding Their Place in the Canadian Mosaic,* was submitted to the attorney general in 1977. In the report, Ubale demonstrated that South Asians lived in fear and were subject to physical attacks in public places. Like Daniel Hill, Ubale argued that racism was

Archives of Ontario, I0014673

Daniel Hill, commissioned by the Canadian Labour Congress, was one of several authors to argue that institutional racism underlay the racial violence and tensions evident in Canadian cities like Toronto in the 1970s.

not a new phenomenon in Canada. A brief look at the history of racialized minorities in Canada demonstrated this. Ubale asserted that racial violence reflected the attitudes of the general population, who were generally apathetic towards race issues. This apathy and racial hostility were reproduced in Canadian institutions. He proved this by examining police discrimination and unequal opportunity in employment and education.[48]

Although Ubale's extensive report provided evidence of institutional racism, his assertions were ignored by the provincial government. In a published statement entitled *Forward Together: A Statement of the Position of the Government of Ontario on the Issues Raised in the Ubale Report on the Concerns of the South Asian Community,* Premier Bill Davis expressed surprise and outrage that racism managed "to manifest itself in

Ontario." Davis argued that the province would fight racial violence with criminal law and promised to counter racial discrimination with human rights legislation and "educative initiatives." However, the province's statement failed to respond to evidence of institutional racism. In fact, Davis blamed the "racist minority" for increased racial tensions and asserted that "callous [and] cruel" individuals perpetrated racism.[49]

This narrow conceptualization of racism was also expressed in the media. Several articles in *Canada and the World*, for example, argued that individuals were at fault for increased racial tensions. According to one article racial attacks were perpetrated by "drunken youths."[50] An article entitled "People Cause Discrimination" suggested that racists were often white men who were fervent nationalists. Racism, the article suggested, could be fought with laws that would regulate behaviour.[51] This sentiment was also espoused by Ontario's attorney general, who believed that it was the responsibility of each individual to eradicate "the disease of discrimination."[52]

The Frances Henry Report

Since government officials held that the "racism problem" was caused by individuals, they looked for solutions that would defeat personal prejudice. In early 1978, the federal Department of the Secretary of State asked Frances Henry, a York University anthropologist, to examine personal racism in Toronto. The goal of the study was to determine what sorts of people held prejudicial and hostile feelings against people of colour. Henry's resulting report, *The Dynamics of Racism in Toronto*, reached the dramatic and surprising conclusion that racism was a widespread phenomenon. Using a random sample of 617 white Torontonians, the study demonstrated the prevalence of hostility against immigrants. The survey results indicated that older, unemployed, and fervently religious people with little education espoused the most racist views. With respect to the psychological aspects of racism, Henry argued that people with "rigid, inflexible and authoritarian" personalities were the most likely to hold racist views. The report made the astonishing assertion that over half of the population exhibited these traits.[53] Not surprisingly, it generated considerable discussion in the media. The *Globe and Mail*, for example, found it surprising that half of Torontonians were racist.[54] While earlier state-funded studies had blamed a small faction of society for the spreading of racial tensions, Henry's study shifted the racism debate by emphasizing that racism was a widespread phenomenon; it continued to blame individuals for racist acts, but it also offered evidence that racism penetrated into the wider society.

Police relations with visible minorities in Toronto, however, suggested that racism functioned on a systemic level. Visible minorities remained excluded from the police force, and relations between Toronto's people of colour and the force were acrimonious. East Indians, for example, complained that when they reported racial incidents to the police, their complaints were often ignored. Toronto's blacks reported being hassled by police officers during routine checks, but the police force maintained that racism was not a problem.[55]

Relations between police and the black community deteriorated significantly in August 1978 when a black man was gunned down by a police officer at a local disco. The circumstances of the shooting were questioned. The constable who shot the young man argued that he had done so in self-defence, while the Toronto black community argued that it was a clear case of racism. Protests were held at Toronto City Hall, where 100 demonstrators accused the police force of harassment and police brutality. Under pressure to demonstrate public accountability, the city established an inquest to determine whether the killing was race related,[56] but when the inquest was remanded, further protests were sparked. In November 1978, 2,000 South Asians and blacks united and marched from Toronto City Hall to the provincial legislative buildings to protest the lack of police and government action against racial attacks and evident police brutality. Signs and slogans such as "Toronto Police, Dead Body"

and "Toronto Police, Shame, Shame!" expressed the loss of faith in the public institution that was responsible for ensuring public safety.[57] When the results of the inquest were finally tabled, it exonerated the police officer and argued that the killing was not racially motivated.[58]

Police relations with ethnic minorities deteriorated even further in 1979. That summer, Albert Johnson, a Jamaican immigrant, was gunned down in his own home. Toronto police apprehended Johnson in the kitchen and shot him in the chest. Police officers involved in the case stated that they were investigating a citizen's complaint into a disturbance and argued that Johnson's behaviour caused the shooting.[59] Neighbours, however, denied filing a complaint. In spite of a well-documented list of police shootings in the *Toronto Star*, the police chief denied allegations of police brutality.[60] A few weeks after the Johnson shooting, 32 organizations organized a large march in downtown Toronto to protest the shooting. Two thousand demonstrators gathered and chanted "We want revenge" and "Murderer."[61]

The Cardinal Carter and Wilson Head Enquiries

With police accountability under scrutiny, the chair of the Council of Metropolitan Toronto asked Cardinal Gerard Emmett Carter, archbishop of Toronto, to be a conciliator between the Metropolitan Toronto Police Commission and black and South Asian Torontonians. In 1979 Carter produced a study entitled *Report to the Civil Authorities of Metropolitan Toronto and Its Citizens*. With evidence of police ill-treatment of visible minorities, Carter concluded that racism in the police force existed "beyond a doubt." Although his report revealed institutional racism within the police department, Carter hesitated to put the blame on the force as a whole. Instead, he asserted that racism existed in each individual and that "it would be impossible to imagine that some of our racism would not spill over into those in authority over the enforcement of law." While Carter's report did not name institutional racism *per se*, his recommendations focused on institutional changes to quell the visible minorities' complaints against the police: he recommended the establishment of an independent body to investigate complaints and called for periodic training of police officers in "race relations."[62]

The Carter Report did prompt immediate action from the police commission. The chief of police issued a "Declaration of Concern and Intent" that stated that police officers had to "avoid bias and prejudice and the appearance of it in all of [their] activities, public and private."[63] Some were sceptical of such initiatives. The Urban Alliance on Race Relations, for example, which had been established in 1975 by individuals concerned with human rights, argued that these measures were examples of "lip service."[64]

The lack of a clear and concrete policy to combat evidence of systemic discrimination in policing prompted the Urban Alliance to fund an enquiry into racism. In 1980 the organization sponsored and distributed a study entitled *Adaptation of Immigrants in Metro Toronto: Perceptions of Ethnic and Racial Discrimination*. The study was written by the organization's chair, Wilson Head. In contrast to Head's earlier study, this enquiry focused on institutional rather than individual racism. It examined discrimination in employment, housing, media, and public services and concluded that institutional racism was a major problem. Since structural racism was the kind "most stubbornly resistant to positive change," the study called for education and the elimination of institutional racism through equal opportunity programs and affirmative action.[65]

Head's study was released at an opportune time: racial incidents were once again increasing. A *Globe and Mail* feature on racism expressed this concern in a subheading: "First come the taunts and the insults. Then the broken windows and slashed tires. Then the fights begin, and the racial tension flares again in Toronto."[66] Similarly, the *Toronto Star* ran a series of articles on racism in Toronto, fearing that racial violence was "the wave of tomorrow."[67]

Besides reporting on cases of racial violence, the media also examined systemic racism. Articles in newspapers and periodicals highlighted the fact that racial incidents were not mere aberrations. For example, a story in *Chatelaine* magazine examined racism in a Hamilton school and discussed the plight of the Gill family, who moved to Hamilton from India in 1975 and purchased a variety store. The Gills provided examples of police indifference to racial violence and systemic racism in Canada's schools. The story concluded with the observation that many visible minorities were disillusioned with Canada's "so-called liberties and rights."[68] Similarly, the author of a story featured in *Maclean's* argued that evidence of employment discrimination suggested that Canada was "back-peddling" on human rights issues.[69] Another more extensive article in *Maclean's* declared that "Canadians have ingrained racism that we choose to pretend is not there." The article criticized Canadians for denouncing race relations in the United States without examining evidence of institutional racism in their own country.[70]

Situation Reports

In light of these exposés of racism, the Ontario government expanded personnel and funding for the Ontario Human Rights Commission and introduced a bill to strengthen the Ontario Human Rights Code.[71] The reaction by the federal government was equally proactive. In early 1982 Jim Fleming, minister of state for multiculturalism, announced the "National Programme to Combat Racism." As a part of the program, Fleming commissioned situation reports in 11 cities across Canada (Vancouver, Williams Lake [BC], Calgary, Regina, Winnipeg, Windsor, Toronto, Ottawa, Montreal, Halifax, and Saint John). The purpose of these reports was to gain insight into race relations and problems facing racialized minorities across Canada. Written by academics from each city, the reports discussed overt and institutionalized racism and were completed in 1982.

The most extensive situation report came from Toronto, where racial violence was most widespread. The report blamed overt racism on the declining economy, the activities of the Western Guard Party, and the arrival of non-white immigrants. Unlike previous state-funded enquiries into race relations, the situation report argued that institutional racism fuelled these hostile attitudes. The media, for example, often communicated that being Canadian meant being white. Employment discrimination was also evident, as people of colour experienced lower wages and less job security despite high levels of education.[72] Other situation reports arrived at the same conclusion: visible minorities were blocked from structural integration. All the reports called for an expansion of positive coverage of visible minorities in the media and advised the government to initiate an affirmative action program. Their message was clear: institutional racism resulted in second-class citizenship.

Conclusion

The recognition of structural discrimination was a gradual and contested process. The government's slow acknowledgment that systemic racism was embedded in Canadian institutions coincided with an unyielding articulation by government officials at all levels that Canada was a multicultural and tolerant nation. It was only with the rise in racially motivated violence in 1970s Toronto that Canadians began to examine the causes of the "sudden" appearance of racism. The perceived race crisis resulted in various public and private enquiries whose purpose was to explain the increased racial tensions.

In the course of this attempt to explain the "race crisis," a more chronic problem of structural racism was revealed. Initial public enquiries, for example, reflected the general perception that only a few Canadians were responsible for the increase in racial violence. The studies of both Wilson Head and Walter Pitman described institutional racism, but neither suggested that institutional racism was the main cause of racism. Both studies maintained that individuals were responsible for racism in society, and Head argued that extremist groups like the Western Guard Party contributed to the overall increase in racial tensions. Furthermore, in their discussion of racism in various institutions, neither Head nor Pitman blamed the institutions

themselves but individuals within those institutions. Moreover, Pitman's recommendation that police applicants should perform psychological tests demonstrated the belief that only a few individuals within the police force were racist.

In contrast, private enquiries were the first to emphasize that racial violence was caused by the inequalities rooted in Canadian institutions. Both Bhausaheb Ubale's and Daniel Hill's enquiries revealed that structural racism existed at all levels of government, in educational institutions, and in places of employment. However, the evidence of institutional racism was largely ignored by government officials, who focused on the individual acts of violence reported by Canadian newspapers. Since officials continued to define the "problem" of race relations as one caused by individuals, they looked for solutions that would effectively curb individual prejudice. With this goal, the federal government sponsored Frances Henry's study. The findings suggested that the majority of Torontonians were racist. This conclusion went against earlier state-sponsored studies that blamed extremists for increased racial tensions and contributed to the shift in race relations policy by demonstrating that racism was a widespread phenomenon.

Following Henry's study, the continuing criticisms of police practices led to the establishment of a municipally sponsored study on police practices in Toronto. The study, written by Cardinal Carter, recommended institutional changes within Toronto's police force. A more extensive study, sponsored by the Urban Alliance on Race Relations, reinforced the conclusions of earlier studies that discrimination existed in employment, housing, and education. These two studies prompted the media to examine systemic racism more thoroughly and brought the issue of institutional discrimination into the public discourse.

From these continuing studies of structural discrimination there emerged a new understanding of the "problem" of "race relations" in Ontario. Because this new definition emphasized systemic discrimination, officials responded with systemic solutions to the problem. In Ontario, more funding was provided for programs that promoted multiculturalism, and provincial officials announced that the Ontario Human Rights Code would be revised to give visible minorities special protection against systemic exclusion. A public complaints investigation bureau was also established where members of the public could file complaints against police officers.[73] On the federal level, the government commissioned a large study to address structural inequalities in Canadian society; the report led to the passage of employment equity legislation.[74] However, these policy initiatives have not, as social scientists have demonstrated, resulted in a deep transformation of the Canadian state.[75]

Endnotes

1   "It's 1970. Let's Take a Look," *Globe and Mail*, 1 January 1970, 36.

2   Ninette Kelley and M. Trebilcock, *Making of a Mosaic: A History of Canadian Immigration Policy* (Toronto: University of Toronto Press, 2010), 358–61.

3   See Racial Discrimination Act, Statutes of Ontario 1944, c. 51; Fair Employment Practices Act, Statutes of Ontario 1951, c. 24; Fair Accommodation Practices Act, Statutes of Ontario 1954, c. 28; Ontario Human Rights Code, Statutes of Ontario 1961–2, c. 93; and Bill C-3: *An Act to Amend the Criminal Code*, 28th Parliament, 2nd session, 1970 (Ottawa: Queen's Printer, 1970).

4   "'We didn't come here to be abused,' He Says," *Toronto Star*, 11 January 1977, C05; "Metro's Sikhs Fear Race Riots," *Toronto Star*, 29 August 1977, A1; "Riots Feared: Sikhs Demand Police Action on Race Attacks," *Toronto Star*, 29 August 1977, C1; and "Schools in North York Face Racism 'Crisis' Trustee Group Warned," *Toronto Star*, 19 April 1978, A04.

5   "Stagflation" was a key feature of Canada's economy during the 1970s and early 1980s. Economic growth slowed and inflation rates rose significantly. The slow economic growth was reflected in unemployment rates—5.5 per cent in 1974, 6.9 per cent in 1975, and 11 per cent in 1982. See Kenneth Norrie, Douglas Owram, and J.C. Herbert Emery, *A History of the Canadian Economy* (Scarborough, ON: Nelson Thomson, 2002), 402–13. With respect to immigration debates, in 1975 the federal government released the Green Paper on Immigration, which argued that Canada's labour force would grow too quickly and that immigration would eventually pose a challenge to the economy. See Canada, Department of Manpower and Immigration, *Highlights from the Green Paper on Immigration and Population* (1975), 7, 11.

6   Stokely Carmichael and Charles V. Hamilton, *Black Power: The Politics of Liberation in America* (New York: Random House, 1967).

7   The term "visible minority" is used in this article as it was commonly used during the 1970s to describe racialized individuals. However, the use of "visible minority" as a category is problematic, as it assumes that whiteness is the standard. The classification of "visible minority" continues to be used by the Canadian government, specifically Statistics Canada, to describe people who are neither white nor Aboriginal.

8   "Boy Says 2 Policemen 'So Awful, So Mean' during Drug Search," *Toronto Star*, 5 April 1974, B1; "Some Metro Policemen Are Accused of Brutality," *Toronto Star*, 20 April 1974, A10; and "On a Democratic Police," editorial, *Globe and Mail*, 18 April 1974, 6.

9   "Godfrey Wants Inquiry into Way Police Investigate Police," *Toronto Star*, 16 May 1974, A1; and "Judge Named to Head Police Brutality Probe," *Toronto Star*, 24 October 1974, 1.

10   "Vandals Deface Sikh Temple, Police Set Up Surveillance," *Toronto Star* 29 May 1974, B01.

11   "Nazi-Saluting Brownshirt Stop CITY-TV Show," *Toronto Star*, 17 June 1974, D06. The party's predecessor, the Edmund Burke Society, was established in 1967. The far-right organization changed its name to the Western Guard Party in 1972 and adopted an overtly racist platform. See Stanley, R. Barrett, "White Supremacists and Neo-Fascists: Laboratories for the Analysis of Racism in Wider Society," *Canadian Ethnic Studies* 16, no. 1 (1984): 1–15.

12   "Youth Shot to Death, Police Wound Suspect," *Toronto Star*, 7 May 1975, A01; and "'A True Friend, One Of Us' Classmates Salute Dead Boy," *Toronto Star*, 8 May 1975, A03.

13   "Racism? Is Metro Turning Sour?," *Toronto Star*, 10 May 1975, A01.

14   Canada, House of Commons, *Debates*, 13th Parliament, 1st Session, 1975, vol. VI, 22 May 1975 (Ottawa: Queen's Printer, 1975), 6002.

15   Ontario, Legislature of Ontario, *Debates*, 29th Legislature, 5th Session, 1975, 12 May 1975 (Toronto: Queen's Printer Parliament Buildings, 1975), 1734.

16   "Racism in Metro 'Terrible Disease' 300 Told at Rally for Slain Youth," *Toronto Star*, 15 May 1975, A03.

17   "An Elegy for Us," *Globe and Mail*, 15 May 1975, 43.

18   "500 High School Students Join Activists In Racism Protest," *Globe and Mail*, 16 May 1975, 05; and "Black Speaker Demands 'End to Racism,'" *Toronto Star*, 26 May 1975, C01.

19   "Toronto Turning Sour for Some Time States Resident of African Descent," *Toronto Star*, 23 May 1975, B05; "Some Police Hate Blacks, Jamaican Says," *Toronto Star*, 12 May 1975, A03; and "Pakistanis Contribute to Progress," *Toronto Star*, 29 May 1975, B5.

20   Wilson Head, *The Black Presence in the Canadian Mosaic: A Study of the Perception and the Practice of Discrimination against Blacks in Metropolitan Toronto, submitted to the Ontario Human Rights Commission* (Toronto: Ontario Human Rights Commission, 1975).

21   Ibid., 60, 1, 22.

22   "Polite Racism Pervades Life in Metro, Blacks Say," *Toronto Star*, 27 September 1975, B05.

23   "Man Is Shoved on to Tracks, Breaks His Legs," *Globe and Mail*, 5 January 1976, 1; and "Mr. Kanji Is a Fellow Human Being, 'Streets Must Remain Safe,' Two Jailed for Subway Attack," *Toronto Star*, 5 December 1976, B01.

24   "Nobody Seems to Care: Young Say Drink Is Fun, Easy to Get," *Toronto Star*, 5 January 1976, A01, A04.

25   "Dozens Offer Police Help to Find Subway Attacker," *Toronto Star*, 6 January 1976, A01, A04.

26   "Drunks Beat Subway Rider Legs Broken," *Toronto Star*, 5 January 1976, A01, A04.

27   "Minority Groups Must Be Protected," Letter to the Editor, *Toronto Star*, 13 January 1976, B05; and "Racial Violence Plaguing Nation," Letter to the Editor, *Toronto Star*, 13 January 1976, B05.

28   "Subway Crowd Ignored Pleas Woman Says after Racial Attack," *Toronto Star*, 12 January 1976, C01.

29   "Racist Attack on Subway Reported by 3 Cousins," *Globe and Mail*, 12 January 1977, 5.

30   "TTC Investigating Actions of Crew in Subway Assault," *Globe and Mail*, 4 January 1977, 1–2; and "TTC Crew Kept Train Moving Despite Racial Attack," *Globe and Mail*, 5 January 1977, 1.

31   "New Year's Race Beating Left Witnesses Stunned," *Globe and Mail*, 8 January 1977: 2; "Guyanese Man Beaten, Kicked at Subway Station in Week's 3rd Race Attack," *Globe and Mail*, 8 January 1977, 1–2.

32   Doug Collins, "Fear and Loathing in the Canadian Mosaic," *Weekend Magazine*, 11 September 1976, 8–10.

33   Hubert De Santana, "Score One for the Racists: This Family Is Going Home," *Maclean's*, 7 February 1977, 19.

34   Angela Ferrante, "Racism? You Can't Argue with the Facts," *Maclean's*, 7 February 1977, 18, 20, 21.

35   "Black Editor Criticizes NBC View of Toronto Racism," *Globe and Mail*, 3 January 1977, 1, 2.

36   "Toronto the Bad? No, NBC the Entertainer," *Globe and Mail*, 3 January 1977, 15.

37   Ferrante, "Racism?," 18.

38   Canada, House of Commons, *Debates*, 13th Parliament, 2nd Session, 1976–7, vol. III, 17 February 1977 (Ottawa: Queen's Printer, 1977), 3146.

39   "NBC View of Toronto as Racial Time Bomb Called True," *Globe and Mail*, 13 January 1977, 3.

40   Walter Pitman, *Now Is Not Too Late: A Report Submitted to the Council of Metropolitan Toronto* (Toronto: Task Force on Human Relations, 1977), 48.

41   "Racism: The Fight Starts with Facts," *Globe and Mail*, 14 January 1977, 6; and "Pitman Appointed to Direct Racism Inquiry," *Globe and Mail*, 12 January 1977, 5.

42   Pitman, *Now Is Not Too Late*, 26, 1.

43   Ibid., 2, 4. Police officers had to be at least 5'8" and 150 pounds.

44   Ibid., 38, 200, 51–92, 32.

45   "All Minorities Hit by City's Racism, Pitman Suggests," *Globe and Mail*, 10 November 1977, 5; "Metro's Blacks and Asians Live in Constant Fear of Racial Violence, Pitman Report Says," *Globe and Mail*, 29 November 1977, 3; and "We All Must Learn to Be More Tolerant, Pitman Stresses," *Globe and Mail*, 29 November 1977, 3.

46   Daniel G. Hill, *Human Rights in Canada: A Focus on Racism* (Ottawa: Canadian Labour Congress, 1977).

47   Ibid., 42, 15.

48   Bhausaheb Ubale, "Equal Opportunity and Public Policy: A Report on Concerns of the South Asian Canadian Community Regarding Their Place in the Canadian Mosaic" (draft copy submitted to the Attorney General of Ontario by the South Asian Canadian Community, 1977), 161–74.

49   Government of Ontario, *Forward Together: A Statement of the Position of the Government of Ontario on the Issues Raised in the Ubale Report on the Concerns of the South Asian Community* (1978), 1.

50   Charles. A. White, "New Victims of an Old Sickness," *Canada and the World*, April 1977, 6–7.

51   Frederick Johnstone, "People Cause Discrimination," *Canada and the World*, December 1977, 12–13. The same sentiment was expressed in Errol Townshend, "Smugness May Be the Worst Enemy," *Canada and the World*, December 1977, 20–1.

52   Ontario, Legislature of Ontario, *Debates*, 31st Legislature, 2nd Session, 1978, 20 June 1978 (Toronto: Legislature of the Province of Ontario, 1978), 3705.

53   Frances Henry, *The Dynamics of Racism in Toronto: Research Report* (Ottawa: Department of the Secretary of State of Canada, 1978), 3–94.

54   "Half of Torontonians Racist, Study Says," *Globe and Mail*, 28 February 1978, 3.

55 "Givens Is Lambasted at Hearing on Racism for 'Patronizing' Talk," *Globe and Mail*, 18 January 1978, 4.

56 "Minorities Urge Police Be Disarmed," *Toronto Star*, 2 October 1978, A3.

57 John Huot, "Fight-back against Racism," *Canadian Dimension*, December 1978, 2–5.

58 "Inquest on Evans Fair Court Rules," *Toronto Star*, 20 December 1978, A1.

59 "Police Gun Down Father of Four Waving Lawn Tool," *Toronto Star*, 27 August 1979, A1, A3.

60 "11 Shootings in Past Year," *Toronto Star*, 27 August 1979, A3; and "Angry Metro Police Chief Denies Racist Charges," *Toronto Star*, 1 September 1979, A1.

61 "2000 Protest Johnson Killing," *Toronto Star*, 2 September 1979, A3.

62 Gerard Emmett Carter, *Report to the Civil Authorities of Metropolitan Toronto and Its Citizens* (Toronto, 1979), 5, 16, 20, 9, 11, 17, 20, 24. The existing complaints department was under the jurisdiction and administration of the Metropolitan Toronto Police Department.

63 Urban Alliance on Race Relations, "A Statement of Concerns and Recommendations Regarding Human Rights in Ontario" (brief submitted to the Government of Ontario, November 1980), 14.

64 Ibid., 30.

65 Ibid., 128.

66 David Lancashire, "Racism," *Globe and Mail*, 31 May 1980, 10.

67 "Racial Violence: Wave of Tomorrow?," *Toronto Star*, 7 January 1980, A7; and "Riots, Sit-ins Things of the Past as Protest Comes of Age," *Toronto Star*, 26 December 1979, A10.

68 Val Ross, "Anatomy of a Racist Incident," *Chatelaine*, March 1979, 51–3, 68–9, 72, 74, 76–8.

69 Eleanor Wachtel, "The True North Semi-Free (the erosion of the civil rights codes)," *Maclean's*, 11 February 1980, 41.

70 Terence Macartney-Filgate, "Warming Up the Melting Pot (Racial Attitudes in Canada)," *Maclean's*, 10 May 1982, 10.

71 Ontario, Legislature of Ontario, *Debates*, 31st Legislature, 4th Session, 1980, 6 May 1980, 9 December 1980 (Toronto: Legislature of the Province of Ontario, 1979), 1505, 5096.

72 Canada, Secretary of State, Multiculturalism Directorate, *Race Relations in Metropolitan Toronto: A Situation Report* (1982), 5–6, 38, 67, 84.

73 Ontario, Statutes of the Province of Ontario, *An Act to revise and extend Protection of Human Rights in Ontario* (Toronto: Queen's Printer for Ontario, 1981), 249; and Ontario, Statutes of the Province of Ontario, *An Act for the establishment and conduct of a Project in the Municipality of Metropolitan Toronto to improve methods of processing Complaints by members of the Public against Police Officers on the Metropolitan Police Force* (Toronto: Queen's Printer for Ontario, 1981), 177.

74 Canada, House of Commons, Special Committee on Participation of Visible Minorities in Canadian Society, *Equality Now! Minutes of Proceedings and Evidence of the Special Committee on Participation of Visible Minorities in Canadian Society* (Ottawa: Queen's Printer, 1984).

75 See, for example, Frances Henry and Carol Tator, *Racial Profiling in Canada: Challenging the Myth of 'a Few Bad Apples'* (Toronto: University of Toronto Press, 2006); B. Singh Bolaria and Sean P. Hier, eds, *Race and Racism in 21st Century Canada: Continuity, Complexity, and Change* (Peterborough, ON: Broadview Press, 2007); and Vic Satzewich, *Racism in Canada* (Don Mills: Oxford University Press, 2011).

CHAPTER 12

The Charter Revolution

12.1: RIGHTEOUS LITIGATION: AN EXAMINATION OF CHRISTIAN CONSERVATIVE INTEREST GROUP LITIGATION BEFORE THE APPELLATE COURTS OF CANADA, 1982–2009

Chance A. Minnett Watchel and Matthew Hennigar

Introduction

As a result of the adoption of the Canadian Charter of Rights and Freedoms (henceforth simply "the Charter") in 1982 and the subsequent move by Canadian courts to take on more political and policy-making roles, "interest group use of litigation as a political tactic has flourished."[1] The literature regarding interest group litigation under the Charter has been criticized for some time now, however, for failing to reflect accurately who is using rights-based litigation. This is most notably the case with critics of Morton and Knopff's[2] "Court Party Thesis" (CPT), such as Hein[3] and Young and Everitt,[4] who challenge the CPT—which takes a negative view of interest groups who use the courts to advance policy goals—for overstating the activity of post-materialist leftist groups while downplaying litigation by business and ideologically conservative groups. In-depth studies of interest group litigation, including those sympathetic to the group's cause, have tended to focus on left-leaning "equality-seeking" groups and movements, such as the feminist organization LEAF (Women's

Legal Education and Action Fund)[5] and pro-LGBT (lesbian, gay, bisexual, or transgender) groups.[6]

This article focuses on a group that has been almost ignored to date,[7] despite the fact that some of its members can be regarded as "repeat players" in court: social conservatives and, even more specifically, Christian conservatives.[8] Considerable attention has been paid to the rise of the "New Right" in Canada[9] and abroad,[10] which developed as a counter-movement to the more egalitarian, secular, and post-materialist culture shift of the 1960s and 1970s identified most notably by Inglehart.[11] This important work has been primarily concerned with developments in public opinion, party politics, and elections, but has largely ignored the *legal* mobilization that has occurred within the rightist/traditionalist counter-movement, especially in the Canadian context.[12] Legal mobilization has been important for groups in this counter-movement, as the post-materialist left has pursued its goals through litigation (as well as traditional lobbying and grass-roots activism, to be sure), which often uses rights documents that enshrine the latter's values, as in the case of the Charter of Rights and Freedoms. In short, if Christian conservatives wished to challenge the claims of feminists and the LGBT movement, they needed to develop the capacity to engage in rights-based litigation. As such, the legal mobilization of Christian conservatives is further evidence of the "judicialization of politics"[13] in the Charter era.

What follows is a case study of the litigation efforts, and success rate, of Canada's most frequent conservative Christian litigant, the Evangelical Fellowship of Canada (EFC), a national association of Protestants representing approximately 77 ministry organizations, 40 affiliated denominations, 35 educational institutions, 5 observer groups, and almost 1,000 local congregations.[14] Our findings reveal that the EFC is, as expected, involved in reactive litigation against Charter claims by leftist equality-seekers, and that they are not very successful in that role, perhaps not surprisingly since they are swimming against the left-egalitarian current in public opinion and the related values that are enshrined in the Charter itself. However, more surprisingly, we also find that the EFC is engaged in more proactive litigation to protect religious

JUDICIAL "EMPOWERMENT" OR ACTIVISM

The term "judicial empowerment" refers to the expanded power of the courts in Canada to review laws or policies and strike them down as a result of the enactment of the Constitution Act in 1982, including the Charter of Rights and Freedoms. Before 1982, the Canadian courts did have the power of judicial interpretation, but it was mainly relegated to questions of federalism, in particular to determining whether a power was under federal or provincial jurisdiction. The enactment of the Constitution in 1982 expanded the powers of the courts (they were "empowered") to review laws and policies as a result of two factors. First, the Constitution Act included the Charter, thereby giving Canadians constitutional protection of their rights and freedoms. Second, the Constitution Act specifically states in section 52(1) that "any law that is inconsistent with the provisions of the Constitution is, to the extent of the inconsistency, of no force or effect." In addition, section 24(1) of the Charter states that "anyone whose rights or freedoms, as guaranteed by this Charter, have been infringed or denied may apply to a court of competent jurisdiction to obtain such remedy as the court considers appropriate and just in the circumstances." As a result, the courts have become the site of rights-based activism particularly by distinct collectivities who have used the judiciary to challenge laws and policies deemed to disadvantage, harm, or violate the equality rights of sectors of Canadian society.

Judicial empowerment has led to significant debate since 1982. Proponents view this enhanced judicial role in law-making as a positive force, as the courts are seen as an important force for protecting the rights of citizens. In essence, the courts provide an additional institution to which citizens can appeal and through which the parliamentary system can be held accountable. Conversely, opponents perceive this judicial role as negative, arguing that the role of law-making in a democratic society rests with the members of Parliament who are the elected representatives of the people. This argument is particularly pertinent in Canada where justices are appointed rather than elected. Opponents also argue that the provisions of the Charter are vague and do not provide a clear basis for interpreting the complex questions under review. Hence they assert that court decisions often reflect the ideological position of one component of society but do not necessarily encompass or represent the social values or concerns of other groups. Nonetheless, the impact of judicial activism since the Charter's adoption has led to a significant elaboration and embrace of the ideology of rights and freedoms as a defining characteristic of Canada.

freedom (and not just as a defence against equality-seekers), albeit with limited success.

Methodology

We used the following case selection criteria to permit a systematic study of EFC litigation: the case must be an appeal court ruling; the EFC participates in the case as an intervenor; and the case is decided between 1982 and 2009. Appellate court rulings are used because trial court decisions are not consistently reported and have no precedential value, and in cases where there have been multiple appeals up the judicial hierarchy (for example, the Ontario Court of Appeal and then the Supreme Court of Canada), only the highest court's ruling is included, since this avoids double-counting and the outcome in the higher court is the binding one.

Following Morton and Allen's study of feminist litigation in Canada, this paper examines multiple dimensions of success: in the immediate dispute, in law, and in policy. As Morton and Allen point out, "[T]he most obvious aspect of success is the outcome of the dispute: does the litigant . . . win [his or her] case?"[15] The second dimension—law—refers to the precedent created through legal interpretation—namely, was the legal interpretation preferred by the litigant adopted by the court? Interest groups may have no interest in the actual dispute at hand. Instead, their interest often lies in achieving "favorable jurisprudence" which can be used to achieve future policy goals.[16] Moreover, a litigant may "win" the dispute, but for the "wrong" legal reasons from their perspective. The final dimension of success—policy—can often be the most important; as Morton and Allen observe, "A victory at the levels of dispute and law will usually have marginal value for an interest group if it does not include the sought-after judicial remedy ordering policy change."[17] If the objective of the litigation is to challenge the validity or constitutionality of a policy, the alteration (nullification, severance, or extension)[18] by the courts of the impugned policy (or its subsequent repeal by legislative means) achieves the group's policy goal.

Morton and Allen differentiate between the different forms of litigation on the basis of the group's position relative to the policy status quo (PSQ). Groups can be either proactive or reactive: proactive groups are "offensive," challenging existing laws and policies, while reactive groups litigate in an attempt to defend legislation that has been challenged. For both offensive and defensive cases, there are two outcomes: a win and a loss. This results in four possible outcomes: offensive win, defensive win, offensive loss, and defensive loss. Offensive wins result in a change to the challenged policy status quo that will not be easily dislodged by subsequent legislative action. Defensive wins occur when a group successfully intervenes to maintain the existing policy status quo. Offensive losses result in wasted resources, but there is no change in the policy status quo, while a defensive loss results in both wasted resources and an unwanted change in the policy status quo. As we will see below, the EFC has, not surprisingly, focused on defensive litigation, but has also undertaken offensive litigation in support of religious freedom claims.

The EFC in Court: Overview and Statistical Findings

The annotation used in the coding of our results is, for the sake of consistency, identical to that used by Morton and Allen in their examination of feminists before the court. Table 12.1 presents the total coding for all cases, regardless of policy issue, province, or court. Cases are arranged alphabetically in the first column and are italicized when the case results in a change in the policy status quo. The second column indicates whether the EFC's intervention in the case is offensive (Of) or defensive (De) vis-à-vis the policy status quo. The third column, the policy status quo (PSQ), is a measurement of the policy *outcome* relative to the intervening group's position. Here, a positive result (+) is coded when the group engages successfully in offensive litigation, and a negative score (−) is coded when the intervenor unsuccessfully

TABLE 12.1 | EFC Success as Intervenor, by Case, 1982–2009

Case and Court	Of/De	PSQ	Dispute	Law	Policy	Average	Charter	Issue
A.A v. B.B. (OCA)	De	–	0	0	0	0	N	Gay rights
Adler (SCC)	Of	0	0	0	0	0	Y	Religious freedom/ Religious equality
Amselem (SCC)	Of	+	1	1	1	1	Y	Religious freedom
Barbeau (BCCA)	De	–	0	0	0	0	Y	Gay rights
Borowski (SCC)	Of	0	0	n/a	0	0	Y	Abortion/ Fetal rights
Chamberlain (SCC)	De	–	0	0	0	0	N	Gay rights/ Religious freedom
Dobson (SCC)	De	n/a	0	0	n/a	0	N	Abortion/ Fetal rights
Egan (SCC)	De	0	1	0	1	0.67	Y	Gay rights
Halpern (OCA)	De	–	0	0	0	0	Y	Gay rights
Harvard College (SCC)	De	0	1	n/a	1	1	N	Patenting lifeforms
Hutterian Brethren (SCC)	Of	0	0	0	0	0	Y	Religious freedom
Lafontaine (SCC)	Of	0	0.5	0	0	0.25	Y	Religious freedom
Latimer (SCC)	De	0	1	1	1	1	Y	Euthanasia
M v. H (SCC)	De	–	0	0	0	0	Y	Gay rights
McRae (FCA)	u/c	u/c	u/c	u/c	u/c	u/c	N	Tax law
Mossop (SCC)	De	0	1	0.5	1	0.83	Y	Gay rights
Owens (SKCA)	Of	+	1	n/a	1	1	N	Expression/Religious Freedom/Gay rights
Rodriguez (SCC)	De	0	1	1	1	1	Y	Assisted suicide
Rosenberg (OCA)	u/c	u/c	u/c	u/c	u/c	u/c	Y	Gay rights
Sharpe (SCC)	De	–	1	0	0.5	0.5	Y	Obscenity/Expression
Spratt (BCCA)	Of	0	0	0	0	0	Y	Expression/Abortion/ Fetal rights
Trinity Western (SCC)	De	0	1	1	1	1	N	Religious freedom/ Gay rights
Winnipeg CFS (SCC)	Of	0	0	n/a	0	0	N	Abortion/ Fetal rights
Vriend (SCC)	De	–	0	0	0	0	Y	Gay rights
	Of=8	+=2	Wins=9	Wins=4	Wins=8	Wins=8		
	De=14	0=12	Loss=13	Loss=14	Loss=12	Loss=14		
	u/c=2	–=7	n/a=0	n/a=4	n/a=2	u/c=2		
		n/a=1	u/c=2	u/c=2	u/c=2			
		u/c=2						

Note: Cases with italicized names above resulted in a change to the policy status quo (PSQ).

defends the PSQ. A "no change" (0) is coded for two different situations: a defensive win and offensive loss, as both result in no change to the policy status quo. The fourth, fifth, and sixth columns (Dispute, Law, and Policy) are all coded in the same manner. A win in any of these three columns is coded as a 1, a loss as a 0. In the event of a partial win/loss or an ambiguous result, we, like Morton and Allen, entered a code of 0.5. In a number of non-Charter cases, not applicable (n/a) is coded in the Law column because, as Morton and Allen note, "they do not create new constitutional precedents that carry over into other policy fields,"[19] and the group is simply not interested in these aspects of the case (the Policy coding in *Lafontaine*), or the courts do not address the issue (the Law coding in *Borowski*). The seventh and final column represents the average of these three, which Morton and Allen refer to as a "blended score." This blended score provides a more holistic and accurate evaluation of a group's success before the court in place of the comparatively simple success by dispute measure, and, like Morton and Allen, we require a score of 0.67 (that is, a "win" on two of the three measures) to be achieved before we would consider the overall outcome a success. Finally, cases that appear as "u/c" are uncoded because we could not obtain the factum submitted by the EFC and there was no other way (such as media sources) to ascertain the group's arguments in the case.

Our selection criteria yielded 24 cases involving the EFC. As expected, the majority (14) of their interventions were defensive, but they participated offensively in 8 cases—that is, a third of the time—with another 2 uncoded owing to insufficient information. Two-thirds of the EFC's cases have been Charter disputes,[20] with 6 of these offensive, 9 defensive, and 1 uncoded. The proportions were similar in the 8 non-Charter cases, with 2 offensive, 5 defensive, and 1 uncoded. A significant number of the cases in which the EFC intervened—11 in total—were cases brought about by gays and lesbians, making those the most numerous of the EFC's interventions. Other cases that

received a significant amount of attention were those involving freedom of religion and abortion and fetal rights.

On no dimension that we examined was the EFC more successful than unsuccessful. The dimension in which they came the closest was the policy dimension in non-Charter disputes, in which they had 3 coded wins and 3 losses. This is, however, subject to re-examination because of our inability to obtain the submitted facta (legal written arguments) for two cases: *McRae v. the Queen* (1997), which was heard before the Federal Court of Appeal; and *Rosenberg v. Canada* (1995), which was heard before the Ontario Court of Appeal. In both of these cases, the Evangelical Fellowship was granted leave to intervene. However, owing to the lack of case facta, these cases are coded as "uncoded" (u/c). Overall, the EFC fared much worse in Charter cases than in non-Charter cases, which perhaps reflects the fact that the group's values are at odds with those enshrined in the Charter (or at least with those in the Court's Charter jurisprudence); for example, 4 of the EFC's losses in this category involved the equality rights of gays and lesbians, which have been quite consistently protected by the Supreme Court of Canada since *Egan* in 1995. In non-Charter cases, the Evangelical Fellowship was successful in 3 of its 7 codable interventions (43 per cent). In Charter cases, however, its success rate dropped to approximately 33 per cent.

With respect to the PSQ, the EFC won in only 2 of its 8 offensive cases, *Amselem* and *Owens*. *Amselem* was thus the only successful attempt to change the PSQ using the Charter of 6 attempts by the EFC. *Owens*, which concerned a challenge to a statutory human rights code, was one of only 2 offensive non-Charter cases. The EFC has fared better defensively, intervening successfully in support of the PSQ in 7 of 14 cases, with 5 of 9 against Charter challenges, and 2 of 5 in non-Charter cases. More details about the EFC's arguments in these cases are presented later in this article.

In terms of individual courts, Table 12.1 also demonstrates that the Evangelical Fellowship is most active at the Supreme Court level, which is understandable for a group that intervenes strategically—that is, that seeks to influence the law at the highest level with the least expenditure of resources. Put differently, a win in the highest court is ultimately the most important. The EFC has only participated in five appellate courts: the British Columbia Court of Appeal (BCCA), the Saskatchewan Court of Appeal (SKCA), the Ontario Court of Appeal (OCA), the Federal Court of Appeal (FCA), and the Supreme Court of Canada (SCC). A full 15 of the EFC's 24 cases (63 per cent) have been before the Supreme Court. Of these 15, 7 (47 per cent) were victories according to the initial blended score. This was reduced to 6 (40 per cent) after we take into account the recoding of *Egan*. At the Ontario Court of Appeal, the group has participated in 3 (13 per cent) cases, none of which were successful endeavours. The British Columbia Court of Appeal heard 2 cases (8 per cent) in which the EFC participated, both of which were losses. The EFC participated in *McRae* before the Federal Court of Appeal, which remains uncoded. The final case, *Owens*, representing approximately 4 per cent of the total number of cases participated in, was heard before the Saskatchewan Court of Appeal.

Having demonstrated that the Evangelical Fellowship does not fare particularly well in its court interventions, we now undertake a systematic examination and evaluation of the arguments put forth by the group in the facta presented to the courts. In doing so, we uncover the legal and political agenda that we cannot simply infer by identifying the cases in which the EFC intervenes. While the reasons interested third parties may seek to intervene in a case are sometimes evident because of the nature of the case, there are instances in which the purpose of intervention is much less clear.[21] In the next section, we examine cases by policy area. We begin by presenting data showing which cases engage these specific policy areas, and then proceed with our examination of cases in which the EFC was successful, beginning with cases involving homosexuality, then freedom of religion and expression, and finally sanctity-of-life issues.

Analysis of EFC Arguments

One might assume that the EFC, as a religious advocacy group, would focus on cases related to the maintenance or promotion of an evangelical Christian way of life. While that is the case, the majority of the EFC's interventions have not been in cases where the Charter's section 2(a) freedom of religion and conscience is claimed. As illustrated by Table 12.1, only 3 of the 24 total cases involve an active section 2(a) claim by the plaintiff. The EFC, while often engaging in cases that are not explicitly religious in nature, intervenes in cases that could potentially affect the religious freedoms of Canadians, most notably cases concerning homosexuality and gay rights (11 of 24 cases), of which 7 deal with section 15 equality rights.[22] The remaining cases, which deal with the issues of abortion, the sanctity of life, and free expression, have not garnered as much attention as have cases involving the rights of gays and lesbians.

The following analysis furthers our attempt to determine how successful the EFC has been in its litigation efforts. Our coded results alone are sufficient to demonstrate that the group either did or did not get what it wanted from the courts in terms of outcome. However, raw statistical data do not indicate whether the factum submitted to the courts had any influence on the justices' final decision; that is, the outcome may be what the EFC had hoped for, but judges may have arrived at that decision for very different reasons than those outlined in the factum.

Here, we analyze the eight cases in which the EFC achieved a "successful" score in our coding, that is, those with a total average of 0.67 or above; here, we need not include judgments that produced unfavourable outcomes for the group, since we already know that the courts did not share or accept the EFC's arguments in those cases. An analysis of the degree to which the EFC's facta arguments in apparently successful cases were reflected in the courts' decisions will demonstrate the degree to which those courts agreed with the EFC's position. We analyze these cases by issue area, and where there are multiple cases involving the same issue, we do so in chronological order.

Profile of Cases

Sexual Orientation

Prior to the Supreme Court's decision in *Egan v. Canada* (1995) to extend Charter equality rights protection to sexual orientation, the Evangelical Fellowship participated in only one case involving homosexuality: *Canada v. Mossop* (1993). In *Mossop*, a federal employee challenged the exclusion of same-sex couples in his union's collective agreement after he was informed that he was ineligible to take bereavement leave to attend the funeral of his long-time partner's father. Mossop's claim was that this was discrimination on the basis of "family status," which is prohibited by the Canadian Human Rights Act. In its submission, the EFC drew a conceptual distinction between "relationships" and legal "status," and argued that the former does not automatically entail the latter. Moreover, the EFC maintained that the term "family" had never included same-sex partners[23] and that the applicant had made no challenge on Charter grounds,[24] and thus Mossop's claim must fail. While not entirely endorsing the EFC's argument, the SCC narrowly (4–3) upheld the law on the grounds that in the absence of a Charter challenge, the court could not ignore Parliament's clear intention to exclude same-sex couples. The concurring opinions of Justices La Forest and Iacobucci, along with that of Lamer and Sopinka, acknowledged and echoed the EFC's position on family status and same-sex couples. La Forest and Iacobucci, specifically, stated that they "do not think [same-sex relationships included in the term 'family' have] yet reached that status in the ordinary use of language."[25]

Egan represents a turning point in the Supreme Court's approach to gay rights and is at once both a success and an even greater failure for conservative Christian groups. While the majority of the Supreme Court justices accepted that there is no economic disadvantage suffered by gays and lesbians because of their exclusion from the OAS (Old Age Security) spousal supplement,[26] a position the EFC advocated,[27] they did not adopt the group's firm opposition to the extension of section 15 to sexual minorities.[28] The resulting nine-judge decision

declaring sexual orientation an analogously protected ground under section 15(1) of the Charter, while representing only one of the three dimensions of success, ultimately proved to be critically important for future gay rights cases. This declaration went far beyond the proposed remedy sought by the EFC, which offered three suggestions for remedy: "(i) redefining spouse with the broad and very significant ramifications discussed herein; (ii) creating another non-spousal benefit category; or (iii) by making a declaration of unconstitutionality with a temporary suspension to permit Parliament to redraft the legislation."[29]

Homosexuality and Collision with "Other" Rights: Expression and Religion

The EFC has been involved in a number of additional cases that entailed a clash between equality for gays and lesbians and the expressive and religious freedom of conservative Christians, but with more success than in the cases described above. The EFC successfully intervened on behalf of faith-based Trinity Western University (TWU), which sought to assume complete control of its teacher-training program.[30] TWU wanted to ensure that its teachers entered the profession with a Christian world view, one that included the belief that homosexuality was a "biblically condemned" activity. The British Columbia College of Teachers (BCCT) attempted to block TWU's plan, fearing that it would produce teachers who would act in a discriminatory fashion once in the profession. It was for this reason that students enrolled in the teaching program at TWU were required to take an additional year at Simon Fraser University (SFU), where they were made to sign agreements to the effect that they would refrain entirely from expressing the TWU's beliefs about homosexuality. Although conflicting Charter rights claims were not explicitly raised in this case, the Supreme Court and the intervenors identified the potential conflict between equality interests and the religious freedom of a private institution.[31] In an 8–1 decision, the Supreme Court declared that the BCCT had acted unfairly towards Trinity Western, because there was no evidence to support the conclusion that graduates of the university would discriminate against homosexual students. The students' freedom to hold a specific belief, the majority argued, did not mean they would act on it.

The EFC also intervened successfully in *Owens v. Saskatchewan (Human Rights Commission)* (2005), in which the Saskatchewan Human Rights Tribunal made an appeal regarding a decision on a hate speech complaint. Owens, a devout Christian, had expressed his objection to an upcoming gay pride parade by placing in a local newspaper an advertisement that included multiple Bible passages condemning homosexuality. Three individuals lodged a complaint with the Human Rights Tribunal, alleging that the advertisements were offensive and exposed them to hatred, which is prohibited under section 14(1)(b) of the Saskatchewan Human Rights Code. Owens was found liable during the initial tribunal hearing, and this was upheld at the Court of Queen's Bench. The EFC, as a part of the Canadian Religious Freedom Alliance, intervened to argue that there were dangers in equating biblical messages with hate speech[32] and that rights protecting homosexuals were subject to reasonable limits, like any other right.[33] The Saskatchewan Court of Appeal overturned the tribunal and lower court, finding that the advertisements did not subject gay men to violence but were merely expressions of the sincerely held religious belief that it is homosexual behaviour that is sinful and morally wrong, not sexual identity.[34] Had the court declared against the simple recitation of biblical passages that oppose particular lifestyles and moral wrongs, the EFC and their allies argued, it would essentially render the Bible—the most popular book in human history—nothing more than hate speech.

Religious Freedom/Religious Equality

As one might expect, the EFC has intervened in several cases focusing on freedom of religion, although not exclusively on behalf of Christians. Only in one, however, has it been successful. In *Syndicat Northcrest v. Amselem* (2004), the EFC supported the right of four Orthodox Jewish residents to set up "biblically mandated" *succahs* on their balcony in spite of building regulations forbidding such structures.[35] The EFC argued that religious freedom, which is protected under the Quebec Charter, includes all religious manifestations and cannot be restricted, and it went on to show that the history of persecution suffered by the Jewish people in Quebec is a reason why state inquiry into religious practices and determination of the validity of religious practices should be avoided.[36] Its position is echoed in the judgment. The Supreme Court agreed that the Orthodox Jews' religious rights had been severely and unreasonably infringed—that the right of Amselem to exercise his sincerely held religious belief, even if he was not in the majority in holding it, had not simply been limited but had been entirely denied.[37]

Sanctity of Life after Birth Cases

There are two kinds of "life" cases in which the EFC involves itself: pre- and post-birth. Of these two, the EFC has undoubtedly seen more success in the second category, having been unable to convince the courts to extend Charter protections to the unborn. Two of these post-birth life cases involve euthanasia, one regarding assisted suicide and the other "mercy killing." In *Rodriguez v. British Columbia* (1993), a woman suffering from degenerative amyotrophic lateral sclerosis (ALS) sought to have section 241(b) of the Criminal Code, which prohibits assisted suicide, overturned as a violation of her section 7, 12, and 15 Charter rights. It was Sue Rodriguez's wish that she could continue to live as long as she enjoyed her life, but once past this point she could seek to have a physician assist her in committing suicide, as she would be physically unable to do so alone (suicide is, itself, legal). The Catholic Conference of Catholic Bishops (CCCB) and the EFC pointed to the life-affirming principles of the Charter and repeated the argument made in *Borowski* that the Supreme Court should assign interpretive weight to the recognition of the supremacy of God in the Charter's preamble. As the biblical commandments condemn murder, the EFC and the CCCB posited that the criminal prohibition on assisting an individual with suicide must necessarily stay in place, as "physician-assisted suicide is a euphemism for a killing arranged by a physician so that the act will be accorded an element of societal approval."[38] They further argued that as we are created in the image of God and are social by design, precluding such an action from taking place actually benefits the community as a whole. Assisting individuals in ending their life is inherently a social interaction—it cannot be considered a private action, according to the EFC. Because of this, the EFC argued, the law must "be evaluated in light of how it helps or hinders the common good, not whether it promotes one person's self-interest."[39] The same reasoning regarding the supremacy of God and the inherent wrongness of taking a life is brought up in *R. v. Latimer* (2001), in which a 12-year-old girl with cerebral palsy was killed by her father on what he considered compassionate grounds. Mr Latimer appealed his conviction on the grounds that, given the circumstances, the 10-year minimum sentence he received for second-degree murder was cruel and unusual under section 12 of the Charter; indeed, his jury at trial had recommended that he serve only one year before being eligible for parole. The EFC, the Christian Medical and Dental Society (CMDS), the Catholic Group for Health, Justice and Life, and Physicians for Life intervened in an attempt to ensure that the dignity of a disabled person is not treated as lesser than that of a non-disabled person. The Court did not find a "right to die with dignity" clause within the Charter (nor did it find discrimination against the disabled) in Sue Rodriguez's case and rejected both Latimer's Charter claim and the trial jury's sentencing recommendation. In neither of these cases, however, did the Court adopt the divine creation justification put forth by the EFC and its allies.

The last of the "life" cases in which the EFC participated, *Harvard College v. Canada (Commissioner of Patents)* (2002), is not a case involving euthanasia or assisted suicide but it is nonetheless a case involving the sanctity and dignity of life. Harvard College applied for a patent for what are termed "oncomice," genetically altered mice implanted with oncogenes while still at the one-cell stage for the purposes of cancer research. In their submission, the EFC and the Canadian Council of Churches cautioned the courts against establishing a precedent that could eventually lead to the patenting of human beings. The college had attempted to reduce the oncomice and the process for creating them to simple chemical and genetic codes. Under this classification, the oncomice could be considered "compositions of matter"[40] and inventions and would be subject to the Patent Act. The Evangelical Fellowship argued that to grant ownership of an altered, higher life form divorces the patent holder from any moral responsibility to care for the life form, and this could lead to objectification and a morally "problematic shift in humans' perception of the natural world" entrusted to them by God.[41] In a 5–4 split decision, a majority of the Supreme Court justices found that higher life forms are not included in section 2 of the Patent Act, as they are not considered under the terms "manufacture" or "composition of matter." Again, the Court does not seem to accept the justification that life forms cannot be patented simply because they are of divine origin.

As we can see in examining the decisions in these cases and the facta provided by the EFC, we still cannot definitively determine if this group has been successful in influencing the courts. We can certainly see agreement between the EFC and the courts in certain cases, such as *Amselem* and *Mossop*. *Owens*, perhaps, is the case in which this is most exemplified, with the Saskatchewan Court of Appeal echoing the intervenor factum on the dangers of equating biblical passages to hate speech. In no case, however, have any of the courts embraced the divine creator justification put forth by the EFC as a reason for adopting or refusing to adopt specific policies.

Conclusion

When we first undertook this study, we had two main goals. The first was to acquire a more thorough understanding of the Evangelical Fellowship of Canada's legal agenda. Given the EFC's status as the most active conservative Christian litigator, such an agenda would assist us in understanding the broader legal goals of the conservative Christian movement. For the EFC, the correct outcome in many cases is one predicated on the affirmation of God and of biblical principles. As a primarily reactive group, the EFC does not typically seek to reshape "defective social institutions and systems."[42] Rather, its goal before the courts is the preservation and cementing of existing societal institutions or the imposition of religious values they deem necessary for the maintenance of a proper and ultimately morally responsible society. This is certainly a far cry from the goals of more liberal social engineers who seek to overturn existing institutions, and it highlights the fact that the EFC is part of a counter-mobilization against such groups; in cases where the EFC intervenes defensively, calls for restraint and deferral to elected legislatures almost always comprise the group's final remarks. Thus, the EFC engages with the courts more out of defensive necessity than anything else. That said, it may litigate offensively at times, such as in *Adler*, *Amselem*, *Borowski*, *Lafontaine*, and *Owens*. But these "offensive" interventions are qualitatively different from those of groups like LEAF and Egale Canada, which seek to better conditions for their members, but usually not by denying benefits or protection to those outside their respective communities. In contrast, the EFC seeks to restore the former PSQ (which benefited its membership), typically by removing benefits and protections for other groups, such as gays and lesbians.

Our second goal was to add empirical data to the study of conservative interest group litigation in Canada. Groups on the ideological right have been and continue to be under-studied despite their presence in various policy battles before the courts. The trend of focusing on those groups who often win, or on those groups who have already been targeted for study, limits the field and can lead to skewed conclusions. Ideologically liberal left-leaning groups have certainly empowered and given legitimacy to the Canadian courts' exercise of judicial review as a form of policy-making, but so too have conservative groups opted to make use of the courts to further their own agendas, including by challenging existing policies. While they may use the same methods as the groups they oppose ideologically, Christian conservatives do so for very different reasons. They do not seek to empower or legitimize the unelected judiciary, but rather to return Canada to what it was before contemporary rights discourse became popular; ironically, however, they are forced to use the new post-Charter institutional configuration to achieve their policy goals. Future research in the area of interest group litigation should expand beyond the members of the "Court Party," to consider conservative groups besides the EFC and how they are navigating the Charter era.

Endnotes

1   F.L. Morton and Avril Allen, "Feminists and the Courts: Measuring Success in Interest Group Litigation in Canada," *Canadian Journal of Political Science* 34, no. 1: 1.

2   F.L. Morton and Rainer Knopff, *The Charter Revolution and the Court Party* (Peterborough, ON: Broadview Press, 2000).

3   Gregory Hein, "Interest Group Litigation and Canadian Democracy," in *Judicial Power and Canadian Democracy*, edited by Paul Howe and Peter H. Russell (Montreal and Kingston: McGill-Queen's University Press, 2000).

4   Lisa Young and Joanna Everitt, *Advocacy Groups* (Vancouver: UBC Press, 2004).

5   See Sherene Razack, *Canadian Feminism and the Law: The Women's Legal Education and Action*

Fund and the Pursuit of Equality (Toronto: Second Story Press, 1991); Christopher P. Manfredi, *Feminist Activism in the Supreme Court: Legal Mobilization and the Women's Legal Education and Action Fund* (Vancouver: UBC Press, 2004); Lori Hausegger, "The Effectiveness of Interest Group Litigation: An Assessment of LEAF's Participation in Supreme Court Cases (MA thesis, University of Calgary, 1994); and Morton and Allen, "Feminists and the Courts."

6   See Didi Herman, *Rites of Passage: Struggles for Gay and Lesbian Legal Equality* (Toronto: University of Toronto Press, 1994); Miriam Smith, *Lesbian and Gay Rights in Canada: Social Movements and Equality Seeking, 1971–1995* (Toronto: University of Toronto Press, 1999); and Miriam Smith, *Political Institutions*

and Lesbian and Gay Rights in the United States and Canada (New York: Routledge, 2008).

7   But see Jeremy Clarke, "Social Conservatives in Court: A Reassessment of Canadian and U.S. Experience" (MA thesis, University of Calgary, 2003), for one existing piece on the subject.

8   Marc Galanter, "Why the 'Haves' Come out Ahead: Speculation on the Limits of Legal Change," Law & Society Review 9:95–160.

9   See David Laycock, The New Right and Democracy in Canada: Understanding Reform and the Canadian Alliance (Don Mills, ON: Oxford University Press, 2002); Tom Flanagan, Waiting for the Wave: The Reform Party and the Conservative Movement, 2nd edn (Montreal and Kingston: McGill-Queen's University Press, 2009); and Elisabeth Gidengil, Matthew Hennigar, André Blais, and Neil Nevitte, "Explaining the Gender Gap in Support for the New Right: The Case of Canada," Comparative Political Studies 38, no. 10 (2005): 1171–95.

10   See Piero Ignazi, "The Silent Counter-revolution: Hypotheses on the Emergence of Extreme Rightwing Parties in Europe," European Journal of Political Research 22 (1992): 3–34; and Pippa Norris, The Rise of the Radical Right: Voters and Parties in the Electoral Market (New York: Cambridge University Press, 2005).

11   See Robert Inglehart, Silent Revolution: Changing Values and Political Styles among Western Publics (Princeton: Princeton University Press, 1977); Robert Inglehart, Culture Shift in Advanced Industrial Society (Princeton: Princeton University Press, 1990); Robert Inglehart, Modernization and Postmodernization: Cultural, Economic and Political Change in 43 Societies (Princeton: Princeton University Press, 1997); and Paul R. Abramson and Robert Inglehart, Value Change in Global Perspective (Ann Arbor: University of Michigan Press, 1995).

12   We must note that there is excellent work on litigation involving Anabaptist sects (Esau 2008) and the crucial role of Jehovah's Witnesses in establishing judicial and legal recognition of civil rights in Canada (Kaplan 1989; Botting 1993), but these groups are distinct from the right-wing counter-movement discussed above.

13   C. Neal Tate and Torbjorn Vallinder, eds, The Global Expansion of Judicial Power (New York: New York University Press, 1995).

14   The Evangelical Fellowship of Canada, "Affiliates," www.evangelicalfellowship.ca/page.aspx?pid=296. A complete list of the ministries, denominations, educational institutions, and observer groups can be found at the above address.

15   Morton and Allen, "Feminists and the Courts," 65.

16   Morton and Allen cite Andrews v. Law Society of British Columbia (1989) as an example. The purpose of LEAF's intervention "was to encourage justices to adopt a set of interpretive rules that would enhance the policy leverage of section 15 for future feminist claims" (2001, 65).

17   Ibid., 67.

18   Nullification occurs when the impugned law is struck down entirely. Severance involves the court excising only the offending portion of the legislation, perhaps only a word. Extension (or "reading in"), as it implies, occurs when the Court extends the benefits or protection of the law to a class of individuals not originally included.

19   Ibid., 69.

20   It is worth noting that in one of the non-Charter cases, A.A. v. B.B., a potential Charter conflict is brought up on appeal but is not considered by the Court.

21   Morton and Allen point to the intervention of LEAF in Andrews v. Law Society of British Columbia as an example of this. The plaintiff in Andrews was male and the case itself did not engage a feminist issue. Instead, the factum submitted by LEAF urged justices to narrow the eligibility for section 15 claims to "historically disadvantaged groups," to broaden the scope to include discriminatory purpose and effect, and to shift the burden of proof from plaintiff to government. See footnote in Feminists and the Courts, 65.

22   While only 6 of the 11 cases involving homosexuality include section 15 claims, a total of 9 cases deal with section 15. The other section 15 cases are Rodriguez v. British Columbia, Adler v. Ontario, and Borowski v. Canada (Attorney General).

23   W.I.C. Binnie and Jenny P. Stephenson, Focus on the Family, the Salvation Army, REAL Women, the Evangelical Fellowship of Canada, and the Pentecostal Assemblies of Canada factum in Canada (Attorney General) v. Mossop. Supreme Court of Canada File No. 22145, at pages 4–8.

24   Ibid., at page 9.

25   Canada (Attorney General) v. Mossop, [1993] 1 S.C.R. 554, para. 60.

26   Gay and lesbian couples are, according to Justice Sopinka, actually better off because they are not eligible for the spousal supplement. Traditionally, the spousal supplement, which was lower, was meant to supplement the partner who had sacrificed employment in favour of staying home and rearing children. This was, typically, the wife. In a homosexual relationship, this gendered family dynamic disappears, as neither is entirely reliant on the other. Because homosexuals were excluded from the term "spouse," both would be eligible for the full OAS benefit. Economically, they were thus better off than a heterosexual couple.

27   Peter R. Jervis and Iain T. Benson, The Inter-Faith Coalition on Marriage and the Family factum in Egan v. Canada, [1995] 2 S.C.R. 513, at pages 4–6.

28   Ibid., at pages 12–14.

29   Ibid., at page 20.

30 *Trinity Western University v. British Columbia College of Teachers*, 2001 SCC 31, [2001] 1 S.C.R. 772.

31 David M. Brown and Adrian C. Lang, The Evangelical Fellowship of Canada factum in *Trinity Western v. BCCT*, 2001 SCC 31, [2001] 1 S.C.R. 772, at page 8; and *Trinity Western University v. British Columbia College of Teachers*, para. 29.

32 Thomas A. Schuck, The Canadian Religious Freedom Alliance factum in *Owens v. Saskatchewan (Human Rights Commission)*, 2006 SKCA 41, at pages 16–17.

33 Ibid., at page 4.

34 *Owens v. Saskatchewan (Human Rights Commission)*, 2006 SKCA 41, para. 82.

35 A *succah* (or *sukkah*) is a small, enclosed temporary hut used during the annual nine-day Jewish religious festival of Succot. It symbolizes and commemorates when God provided sustenance to the Hebrews while they were in the wilderness during the exodus from slavery in Egypt.

36 Gerald D. Chippeur and Dale Wm. Fedorchuk, The Evangelical Fellowship of Canada and the Seventh-Day Adventist Church in Canada factum in *Syndicat Northcrest v. Amselem*, 2004 SCC 47, [2004] 2 S.C.R. 551, at pages 5–9.

37 *Syndicat Northcrest v. Amselem*, 2004 SCC 47, [2004] 2 S.C.R. 551, para. 74.

38 Robert M. Nelson, The Canadian Conference of Catholic Bishops and the Evangelical Fellowship of Canada factum in *Rodriguez v. British Columbia (Attorney General)*, [1993] 3 S.C.R. 519, at page 8.

39 Ibid., at page 14.

40 William J. Sammon, The Canadian Council of Churches and the Evangelical Fellowship of Canada factum in *Harvard College v. Canada (Commissioner of Patents)*, 2002 SCC 76, [2002] 4 S.C.R. 45, at page 6.

41 Ibid., at page 9.

42 Morton and Knopff, *The Charter Revolution*, 74.

References

Abramson, Paul R., and Robert Inglehart. *Value Change in Global Perspective*. Ann Arbor: University of Michigan Press, 1995.

Botting, Gary. *Fundamental Freedoms And Jehovah's Witnesses*. Calgary: University of Calgary Press, 1993.

Brodie, Ian. *Friends of the Court: The Privileging of Interest Group Litigants in Canada*. Albany, NY: State University of New York Press, 2002.

Clarke, Jeremy. "Social Conservatives in Court: A Reassessment of Canadian and U.S. Experience." MA thesis, University of Calgary, 2003.

Esau, Alvin. "Living by Different Law: Legal Pluralism, Freedom of Religion, and Illiberal Religious Groups." In Richard Moon, ed. *Law and Religious Pluralism in Canada*. Vancouver: UBC Press, 2008.

———. "The Staying Power of the Legislative Status Quo: Collective Choice in Canada's Parliament after Morgentaler." *Canadian Journal of Political Science* 30, no. 1 (1997): 31–53.

Flanagan Tom. *Waiting for the Wave: The Reform Party and the Conservative Movement*. 2nd edn. Montreal and Kingston: McGill-Queen's University Press, 2009.

Galanter, Marc. "Why the 'Haves' Come out Ahead: Speculation on the Limits of Legal Change." *Law & Society Review* 9 (1974): 95–106.

Gidengil, Elisabeth, Matthew Hennigar, André Blais, and Neil Nevitte. "Explaining the Gender Gap in Support for the New Right: The Case of Canada." *Comparative Political Studies* 38, no. 10 (2005): 1171–95.

Hausegger, Lori. "The Effectiveness of Interest Group Litigation: An Assessment of LEAF's Participation in Supreme Court Cases." MA thesis, University of Calgary, 1994.

Hein, Gregory. "Interest Group Litigation and Canadian Democracy." In Paul Howe and Peter H. Russell, eds. *Judicial Power and Canadian Democracy*. Montreal and Kingston: McGill-Queen's University Press, 2000.

Herman, Didi. *Rights of Passage: Struggles for Gay and Lesbian Legal Equality*. Toronto: University of Toronto Press, 1994.

Ignazi, Piero. "The Silent Counter-Revolution: Hypotheses on the Emergence of Extreme Rightwing Parties in Europe." *European Journal of Political Research* 22 (1992): 3–34.

Inglehart, Robert. *Silent Revolution: Changing Values and Political Styles among Western Publics*. Princeton, NJ: Princeton University Press, 1977.

———. *Culture Shift in Advanced Industrial Society*. Princeton, NJ: Princeton University Press, 1990.

———. *Modernization and Postmodernization: Cultural, Economic and Political Change in 43 Societies*. Princeton, NJ: Princeton University Press, 1997.

Kaplan, William. *State and Salvation: The Jehovah's Witnesses and Their Fight for Civil Rights*. Toronto: University of Toronto Press, 1989.

Kelly, James B. *Governing with the Charter: Legislative and Judicial Activism and Framers' Intent*. Vancouver: UBC Press, 2005.

Laycock, David. *The New Right and Democracy in Canada: Understanding Reform and the Canadian Alliance*. Don Mills, ON: Oxford University Press, 2002.

Leishman, Rory. *Against Judicial Activism: The Decline of Freedom and Democracy in Canada*. Montreal and Kingston: McGill-Queen's University Press, 2006.

Mandel, Michael. *The Charter of Rights and the Legalization of Politics in Canada*. 2nd edn. Toronto: Thompson Educational Publishing, 1994.

Manfredi, Christopher P. *Feminist Activism in the Supreme Court: Legal Mobilization and the Women's Legal Education and Action Fund*. Vancouver: UBC Press, 2004.

Morton, F.L., and Avril Allen. "Feminists and the Courts: Measuring Success in Interest Group Litigation in Canada." *Canadian Journal of Political Science* 34, no. 1 (2001): 55–84.

Morton, F.L., and Rainer Knopff. *The Charter Revolution and the Court Party*. Peterborough, ON: Broadview Press, 2000.

Norris, Pippa. *The Rise of the Radical Right*. New York: Cambridge University Press, 2005.

Petter, Andrew. "Canada's Charter Flight: Soaring Backwards into the Future." *Journal of Law and Society* 16, no. 2 (1989): 151–65.

Razack, Sherene. *Canadian Feminism and the Law: The Women's Legal Education and Action Fund and the Pursuit of Equality*. Toronto: Second Story Press, 1991.

Sigurdson, Richard. "Left- and Right-Wing Charterphobia in Canada: A Critique of the Critics." *International Journal of Canadian Studies* 7–8 (1993): 95–117.

Smith, Miriam. *Lesbian and Gay Rights in Canada: Social Movements and Equality Seeking, 1971–1995*. Toronto: University of Toronto Press, 1999.

———. "Social Movements and Judicial Empowerment: Courts, Public Policy, and Lesbian and Gay Organizing in Canada." *Policy and Society* 33, no. 2 (2005): 327–53.

———. *Political Institutions and Lesbian and Gay Rights in the United States and Canada*. New York: Routledge, 2008.

Tate, C. Neal., and Torbjorn Vallinder, eds. *The Global Expansion of Judicial Power*. New York: New York University Press, 1995.

Young, Lisa, and Joanna Everitt. *Advocacy Groups*. Vancouver: UBC Press, 2004.

Cases and Facta

A.A. v. B.B., 2007 ON C.A. 2
Staley, Robert W., and Ranjan K. Agarwal. Factum of the Alliance for Marriage and Family (intervenor). Court of Appeal File No. C39998.

Adler v. Ontario, [1996] 3 S.C.R. 609
Jervis, Peter R. Factum for the Ontario Multi-Faith Coalition for Equity in Education (intervenor). Court File No. 24347.

Alberta v. Hutterian Brethren of Wilson Colony, 2009 SCC 37, [2009] 2 S.C.R. 567
Gibson, Charles M., and Albertos Polizogopoulos. Factum for the Evangelical Fellowship of Canada and Christian Legal Fellowship (intervenors). Court File No. n/a.

Barbeau v. British Columbia, 2003 BCCA 406
Benson, Iain T. Factum for the Interfaith Coalition on Marriage (intervenor). Court of Appeal File No. CA029048.

Borowski v. Canada (Attorney General), [1989] 1 S.C.R. 342
Thomson, Claude R., and Robert W. Staley. Factum for the Interfaith Coalition on the Rights and Wellbeing of Women and Children (intervenors). Court File No. 20411.

Canada (Attorney General) v. Mossop, [1993] 1 S.C.R. 554
Binnie, W.I.C., and Jenny P. Stephenson. Factum for Focus on the Family, the Salvation Army, REAL Women, the Evangelical Fellowship of Canada, and the Pentecostal Assemblies of Canada (intervenors). Court File No. 22145.

Chamberlain v. Surrey School District No. 36, 2002 SCC 86, [2002] 4 S.C.R. 710
Cowper, D. Geoffrey, and Cindy Silver. Factum for the Evangelical Fellowship of Canada, the Archdiocese of Vancouver, the Catholic Civil Rights League, and the Canadian Alliance for Social Justice and Family Values Association (intervenors). Court File No. 28654.

Congrégation des témoins de Jéhovah de St-Jérôme-Lafontaine v. Lafontaine (Village), 2004 SCC 48, [2004] 2 S.C.R. 650
Chipeur, Gerald D., and Dale Wm. Fedorchuk. Factum for the Evangelical Fellowship of Canada and the Seventh-Day Adventist Church in Canada (intervenors). Court File No. 29507.

Dobson (Litigation Guardian of) v. Dobson, [1999] 2 S.C.R. 753
Brown, David M. Factum for the Evangelical Fellowship of Canada (intervenor). Court File No. 26152.

Egan v. Canada, [1995] 2 S.C.R. 513
Jervis, Peter R., and Iain T. Benson. Factum for the Inter-Faith Coalition on Marriage and the Family (intervenors). Court File No. 23636.

Halpern v. Canada (Attorney General), 2003 26403 (ON C.A.)
Jervis, Peter R., Jasmine T. Akbarali, and Bradley W. Miller. Factum for the Interfaith Coalition on Marriage and Family (intervenors). Court File No. C-39172.

Harvard College v. Canada (Commissioner of Patents), 2002 SCC 76, [2002] 4 S.C.R. 45
Sammon, William J. Factum for the Canadian Council of Churches and the Evangelical Fellowship of Canada (intervenors). Court File No. 28155.

M. v. H., [1999] 2 S.C.R. 3
Jervis, Peter R., Michael Meredith, and Danielle Shaw. Factum for the Interfaith-Coalition, the Evangelical fellowship of Canada, the Ontario Council of Sikhs, the Islamic Society of North America and Focus on the Family (intervenors). Court File No. 25838.

McRae v. Canada, 1997 CanLII 4844 (F.C.A.)

Owens v. Saskatchewan (Human Rights Commission), 2006 SKCA 41
Schuck, Thomas A. Factum for the Canadian Religious Freedom Alliance (intervenors). Court of Appeal File No. 678 of 2005.

R. v. Latimer, 2001 SCC 1, [2001] 1 S.C.R. 3
Brown, David M., and Adrian C. Lang. Factum for the Evangelical Fellowship of Canada, the Christian Medical and Dental Society and Physicians for Life (intervenors). Court File No. 26980.

R. v. Morgentaler, [1988] 1 S.C.R. 30

R. v. Sharpe, 2001 SCC 2, [2001] 1 S.C.R. 45
Staley, Robert W., and Meredith Hayward. Factum for the Evangelical Fellowship of Canada

and Focus on the Family (intervenors). Court File No. 27376.

R. v. Spratt, 2004 BCCA 367
Owen, Julie L. Factum for the Canadian Religious Freedom Alliance (intervenors). Court of Appeal File No. CA29830.

Rodriguez v. British Columbia (Attorney General), [1993] 3 S.C.R. 519
Nelson, Robert M. Factum for the Canadian Conference of Catholic Bishops and the Evangelical Fellowship of Canada (intervenors). Court File No. 23476.

Rosenberg v. Canada (Attorney General), 1998 3243 (ON C.A.)

Syndicat Northcrest v. Amselem, 2004 SCC 47, [2004] 2 S.C.R. 551
Chipeur, Gerald D., and Dale Wm. Fedorchuk. Factum for the Evangelical Fellowship of Canada and the Seventh-Day Adventist Church in Canada (intervenors). Court File No. 29252.

Trinity Western University v. British Columbia College of Teachers, 2001 SCC 31, [2001] 1 S.C.R. 772
Brown, David M., and Adrian C. Lang. Factum for the Evangelical Fellowship of Canada (intervenor). Court File No. 27168.

Vriend v. Alberta, [1998] 1 S.C.R. 493
Fenerty, Milnert, Gerald D. Chipeur, Heather L. Treacy, and Andrea E. Manning. Factum for the Evangelical Christian Fellowship (intervenors). Court File No. 25285.

Winnipeg Child and Family Services (Northwest Area) v. G. (D.F.), [1997] 3 S.C.R. 925
Brown, David M. Factum for the Evangelical Fellowship of Canada and the Christian Medical and Dental Society (intervenors). Court File No. 25508.

◎ 12.2: SOCIAL MOVEMENTS AND JUDICIAL EMPOWERMENT: COURTS, PUBLIC POLICY, AND LESBIAN AND GAY ORGANIZING IN CANADA

Miriam Smith

Public attitudes towards homosexuality have been transformed over the last generation throughout the Anglo-American democracies and beyond. The rise of the lesbian and gay movement from the early 1970s challenged the existing structure of public policy on issues ranging from the recognition of same-sex relationships, adoption, and parenting rights to the regulation of queer sexuality. Same-sex marriage is the latest chapter in an ongoing process of recognition of lesbian and gay rights. Yet there is substantial cross-national variation in the recognition of lesbian and gay rights, even among similar systems such as Canada, the

United States, and Britain. This article presents a case study of lesbian and gay organizing and public policy change in Canada, a country at the forefront in lesbian and gay rights recognition. I argue that Canada provides such extensive recognition of lesbian and gay citizens because of the impact of judicial empowerment on social movement politics and public policy in the lesbian and gay area. In Canada, the entrenchment of a constitutional bill of rights in 1982 intersected with the rise of the modern lesbian and gay movement. Shaped by the process of judicial empowerment, the emerging lesbian and gay movement was drawn into the process of litigation and into a rights-based legalized politics that is not found to the same extent in other countries. In turn, the legalized networks of lesbian and gay activism were successful in pushing the courts towards the recognition of rights claims.

Canada's human rights protections for lesbian and gay citizens are among the most extensive in the world. . . .

Why does Canadian public policy on lesbian and gay rights recognition differ so markedly from that of other similar systems such as the United States and Britain? This article suggests that policy change in Canada must be read in the light of the extensive political-institutional changes entailed in the process of judicial empowerment beginning in 1982. The constitutional entrenchment of the Canadian Charter of Rights and Freedoms (Charter) gave the courts a new political importance in Canada. Before the Charter, judicial review was largely confined to enforcing the division of powers between levels of government in the federal system. On the rare occasions in which courts considered individual rights, such issues were decided in terms of constitutional and political debates over federalism. In contrast, in the wake of the Charter, the Supreme Court of Canada—the country's highest court—has adjudicated important public policy issues such as the rights of accused criminals and prisoners, tobacco advertising, DNA collection and use, language rights, corporate "freedoms,"

gun control, abortion, sexual assault laws, pornography, and lesbian and gay rights. In one generation, the Supreme Court of Canada has become central to Canadian political life, and Canadians have increasingly become accustomed to American-style debates over judicial activism.[1] This makes Canada another case in the growth of global judicial empowerment, that is, the enhancement of the role of the judiciary in the political system and the extension of the jurisdiction of courts and legal adjudication into new areas of public policy.[2]

Strong courts alone, however, are not enough to produce human rights protections for vulnerable minority groups. The US case shows that strong courts are not always friendly to lesbian and gay rights claims. . . . In Canada, the process of legal mobilization in the lesbian and gay rights case was critically shaped by the *timing* of judicial empowerment, relative to the emergence of the post-Stonewall lesbian and gay movement.

In the first section of the article, I explore the case of lesbian and gay organizing in comparative perspective in order to emphasize the ways in which the role of courts relative to social movement organizing in the lesbian and gay area differs across similar systems such as the United States and Britain. In the middle sections, I present the study of the Canadian lesbian and gay rights movement before and after the Charter, demonstrating how a movement that, like the US movement today,[3] was reluctant to use law as a political strategy has become dominated by legal mobilization. The case study was conducted using qualitative research methods, including interviewing lesbian and gay activists, lawyers, and litigants and surveying the lesbian, gay, and mainstream press as well as the major lesbian and gay rights legal cases.[4] The analysis shows how the entrenchment of the Charter opened up new political opportunities for litigation by the Canadian lesbian and gay rights movement—litigation that, in turn, translated into concrete policy gains for lesbian and gay equality. The legal mobilization of the lesbian and gay movement pushed the envelope of public policy on equality rights, anti-discrimination, relationship recognizing, and same-sex marriage. In the conclusion, I place the case study in the wider context of comparative research on courts and human rights. Many of the key debates on courts and social change have centred on the impact of courts on the actual implementation of public policy.[5] This case study demonstrates the impact of rights-based litigation on the evolution of public policy in the lesbian and gay area; however, it also emphasizes the ways in which judicial empowerment moulds the process of social movement mobilization. While litigation has produced positive results for the lesbian and gay movement in Canada, such results have been achieved via the creation of legalized forms of social movement politics.

Comparative Considerations

. . . [I]n the 20 years since the entrenchment of the Charter, rights claims have taken on a symbolic potency in Canadian society. The process of political mobilization around the courts and the decisions of the Supreme Court of Canada have established the discursive construction of "equality-seeking," "equality rights," and "Charter values," all of which are increasingly seen as tied to national identity for English-speaking Canadians. Although francophone Quebecers may not name such values as "Canadian," they are no less supportive of the rights claims of lesbians and gay men (more so, in most public opinion studies, than English-speaking Canadians). Like Canada's Medicare system, gay rights and same-sex marriage have become wedded to Canada's claims of distinctiveness, especially its distinctiveness compared to the United States. This is true even for Canadians who *oppose* same-sex marriage.[6] . . .

Explaining how similar systems such as Britain, Canada, and the United States have arrived at different policies and practices on human rights requires an approach that goes beyond public opinion analysis. In Britain, Canada, and the United States, attitudes towards homosexuality have changed over the last generation; yet, both the structure of social movement

organizing and public policy outcomes in these countries are substantially different. Public opinion polls have reported a wide range of results on same-sex marriage in Canada and the United States, ranging from a low of 28 per cent support for same-sex marriage in Canada outside Quebec (putting English-speaking Canada behind the United States in support for same-sex marriage) to a national high of 54 per cent.[7] US opinion has ranged as high as 50 per cent in support of same-sex marriage, depending on the wording of the question.[8] Yet, while Canada is legalizing same-sex marriage, the United States is banning it. Canadian human rights policies in the lesbian and gay sector are at the extreme of lesbian and gay rights *recognition*, while US policies are at the extreme of lesbian and gay rights *denial*, when similar systems are compared. To take another point of comparison, the Christian evangelical movement is an important political actor in both Canada and the United States, while politically non-existent in Britain. Yet, Canada, with a well-organized and politically active evangelical movement in its western provinces and one of its major federal political parties, is far ahead of Britain in lesbian and gay rights recognition, although Britain has no politically significant evangelical movement. Public opinion and religiosity are important contextual factors, but they cannot account for the wide-ranging cross-national policy variation in lesbian and gay rights recognition.

Policy differences on lesbian and gay rights are rapidly accelerating in the first decades of the new millennium. Neither Britain nor the United States has taken the extensive measures in recognition of lesbian and gay equality that have been taken in Canada. . . .

The social movement politics surrounding lesbian and gay rights also differs cross-nationally. Canada's lesbian and gay movement is entirely focused on litigation at the national level; in contrast, in the US case, lesbian and gay groups have undertaken a broad range of political strategies. Litigation funds are only one of the organizational types found in the US lesbian and gay movement.[9] This reflects the timing of judicial empowerment in the United States compared to Canada. In the US, courts were empowered prior to the rise of modern social movements, and they have blocked lesbian and gay rights at least as often as they have supported them. In contrast, judicial empowerment in Canada has been a product of the post-sixties universe of social movement politics. Both the content and politics of the Charter have reflected the impact of historical timing on the process of legal mobilization. Until very recently, litigation has been a marginal strategy in British lesbian and gay rights organizing. Litigation is not even mentioned as a political strategy by major lesbian and gay groups such as Stonewall and Outrage in their self-descriptions, despite the increasing importance of courts for human rights in Britain.[10] In the next 20 years, courts and legally focused politics will play a more important role in British queer organizing. As the process of judicial empowerment occurs in Britain (through the 1998 Human Rights Act, the proposed supreme court, and the impact of European Union courts), existing British social movement organizations in the lesbian and gay area will become drawn into the legally centred human rights template. . . .

The Canadian Lesbian and Gay Rights Movement: The Politics of Rights before the Charter

In order to evaluate the effects of the entrenchment of the Charter on the evolution of lesbian and gay politics, this section presents a picture of the character of the lesbian and gay movement in the period before the Charter. The rise of the modern lesbian and gay rights movement in Canada can be traced to the 1960s, when small homophile groups were established. These groups and their allies helped to create the climate for legal change, which occurred in 1969 when the Liberal government of Pierre Trudeau decriminalized homosexual acts between consenting adults as part of a sweeping reform of Canada's divorce and family law. These amendments were modelled on changes made in Britain during the same period and rested on the concept

of the right to privacy, summarized by Trudeau in his statement that "the state has no business in the bedrooms of the nation."[11]

Cross-nationally, early gay liberation organizing tended to focus on the same set of issues in Western countries: legalization of homosexual behaviour; an end to state regulation and repression of lesbian and gay life; and the passage and enforcement of anti-discrimination measures, most importantly in the area of employment.[12] Yet, although gay liberation groups made demands in these areas, many activists were convinced that changes in public policy would be very slow to come and that such changes would not necessarily materially change the lives of lesbian and gay people. Qualitative research on the Canadian gay liberation movement of the seventies—including interviews with movement leaders and activists and explorations of the relatively extensive lesbian and gay community newspapers and media of the period—indicates that most gay liberation activists did not believe that legal and public policy changes were very likely to occur.[13] Rather, the "publicly expressed demands" of the movement were aimed at contesting the stigma surrounding lesbian and gay culture and community life. The movement's contestation of the stigma of homosexuality was aimed not only at straight people but also at lesbian and gay people themselves.[14] In order for the movement to succeed, it needed to have members and political support from the lesbian and gay community. The publicly expressed claims of the movement, then, were aimed not only at influencing policy debates but also at creating, reinforcing, and politically mobilizing the lesbian and gay community. Therefore, the public statements and expressions of the activist leadership of the movement were strategically framed to build the movement as well as to influence society and public policy.

Litigation as a political strategy played an important role within this framework. Activist leaders of the period believed that the "civil rights strategy," as they called it in reference to the rights claims and political strategies of the US civil rights movement, was a means to the

Jearld Moldenhauer. Used with permission.

The first large-scale gay rights demonstration in Canada took place on Parliament Hill in Ottawa, on 28 August 1971.

fulfilment of the ideology of gay liberation.[15] Rights claims were political resources, used to politicize grievances and to create a sense of political identity.[16] Although the legal opportunity for lesbian and gay rights claims prior to the Charter was not very promising, gay liberation activists in the three major cities of movement activism—Montreal, Toronto, and Vancouver—pursued litigation as a political strategy during the seventies. A Toronto gay liberation group supported a racing steward, John Damien, who had been fired from his job for being gay.[17] In the case known as *Gay Tide*, the first gay rights challenge ever put before the Supreme Court of Canada, a Vancouver gay liberation group unsuccessfully contested a Vancouver newspaper's refusal to publish an ad for the group's newspaper.[18] In Montreal, a gay liberation group challenged a school's refusal to rent meeting space to the group. This litigation, undertaken in a context in which there were few legal resources for the defence of lesbian and gay rights, was used to raise consciousness and to create lesbian and gay organizations such as the Canadian Lesbian and Gay Rights Coalition, which took on the role of representing the lesbian and gay community in federal politics, the first time this had occurred.[19]

The civil rights strategy was not successful in changing public policy, however. With the exception of Quebec,[20] neither the provinces nor the federal government sought to include sexual orientation as a prohibited ground of discrimination in human rights legislation during the pre-Charter period.[21] State regulation and repression of lesbian and (especially) gay sexuality continued unabated during this period, with a series of raids on gay bathhouses in 1981 and a host of obscenity charges being laid against the gay liberation newspaper *The Body Politic*.[22]

This was the context in which the process of judicial empowerment occurred. . . .

The Politics of Rights after the Charter, 1985–1993

In the initial phase of judicial empowerment, during the first three years of the Charter, from 1982 to 1985, the lesbian and gay rights movement was strongly focused on AIDS organizing.[23] The effects of the Charter appeared gradually and incrementally over a long time period, finally accelerating with moves towards relationship recognition and same-sex marriage in the late nineties and early 2000s.

The first effects of the Charter were felt in the establishment of informal legal networks surrounding the Charter. Lawyers, especially young lesbian and gay lawyers, were in the vanguard of the move to deploy the Charter on behalf of lesbian and gay rights.[24] Lawyers networked through a series of legal conferences in the early nineties as well as through their organizations such as the Canadian Bar Association, the National Association of Women and the Law, and the Women's Legal Education and Action Fund. Over time, this network has been formalized into the Sexual Orientation and Gender Identity Conference of the Canadian Bar Association. Many of the lawyers who have represented litigants in sexual orientation litigation were closely involved in building these networks.[25] Lawyers were the initial "meaning makers" of the Charter in the lesbian and gay area. They were the first to see the opportunity provided by the Charter

and to think through the possibilities of Charter litigation and judicial empowerment for lesbian and gay citizens.

A second effect occurred during the process of implementing the Charter. As part of the coming into force of the equality rights section of the new Charter in 1985, the Progressive Conservative government of Brian Mulroney appointed a parliamentary committee to consider the implications of these provisions. The parliamentary committee hearings drew a large number of submissions from local lesbian and gay groups[26] and galvanized a group of lawyers and trade union activists to form an Ottawa-based group that would keep up the pressure on the federal government with regard to lesbian and gay equality rights.[27] The Equality Writes Ad Hoc Committee was formed to conduct a letter-writing campaign, to network with other human rights groups, and to lobby MPs and the Mulroney government on its response to the parliamentary committee report.[28] In the wake of some small successes in wrenching policy promises from the Mulroney government, the Equality Writes Ad-Hoc Committee transformed itself into Egale[29] at its first meeting in May 1986.[30]

In this way, through the process of the parliamentary committee hearings, the implementation of the Charter sparked the establishment of a pan-Canadian lesbian and gay litigation and advocacy group and marked the formal beginnings of Charter-centred political activism by gay and lesbian groups. These first effects of the Charter—the establishment of formal legal networks and the establishment of Egale—were closely linked, as it was mainly the members of the legal network who founded Egale.

The establishment of Egale further reinforced the institutional and policy effects of judicial empowerment in the lesbian and gay area because of the nature of Egale as an organization. From the beginning, there were important differences between the gay and lesbian organizations of the seventies, which had explicitly sought to use litigation to politicize lesbians and gays and to build the lesbian and gay communities as a social movement, and Egale, which sought equality rights as ends in themselves. While the early gay and lesbian groups were rooted in part in the youth counterculture of the period, Egale was based on the emerging middle-class communities of visible ("out") lesbians and gays who potentially stood to benefit from the recognition of lesbian and gay relationships in law. Its leadership, especially in its early period, was provided mainly, although not exclusively, by white male professionals, especially lawyers and trade unionists from Ottawa's powerful public sector unions.[31] . . .

Therefore, not only did institutional change produce new social movement organizations and informal legal networks, it also produced a certain *type* of social movement politics, namely one in which human rights recognition, codified in law, was defined as an end in itself rather than as a rights template for the tactical mobilization of a social movement.

In the wake of these new forms of social movement organization, from 1985 to 1993, several important cases began to generate legal pressure for relationship recognition and for the inclusion of sexual orientation in section 15 of the Charter and in federal human rights legislation. . . . Two of the key cases in the late eighties and early nineties were *Veysey*[32] and *Haig & Birch*.[33] In these two cases, courts ruled that the exclusion of sexual orientation from federal human rights legislation violated the rights guarantees of the Charter.[34] Because of these decisions, it was widely understood in the legal community that sexual orientation had been "read into" the Charter of Rights and into federal human rights legislation through court decisions, despite the lack of a formal federal legislative amendment and despite the lack of a ruling from the Supreme Court of Canada. The Canadian Human Rights Commission, the enforcer of the federal human rights code, was itself a strong supporter of the inclusion of sexual orientation within its ambit and immediately recognized the implications of the *Veysey* and *Haig & Birch* decisions by accepting over 200 complaints based on sexual orientation after 1992.[35] This change enabled lesbian and gay rights claimants to challenge discriminatory laws in federal jurisdiction. Throughout these cases,

intervenor coalitions between equality-seeking groups in the women's movement, ethnocultural communities, and Egale constituted a new form of group politics in advocacy litigation.[36]

The *Egan*[37] case was a turning point in lesbian and gay litigation. In this case, the Court ruled that sexual orientation was included within the ambit of the equality rights clause of the Charter. At the time of this landmark case in 1995, there had been 14 cases concerning sexual orientation under the Charter.[38] Of these 14 cases, the majority were brought by those who had either been lesbian and gay activists before bringing their cases or who became activists as a result of their cases.[39] Cases concerning the inclusion of sexual orientation as a prohibited ground of discrimination in the federal human rights act—*Veysey* and *Haig & Birch*—had been successful, while cases concerning relationship recognition had not. . . .

The initial effects of the Charter, then, included the establishment of informal legal networks, the founding of a new litigation group with a positivist, rights-based legal ideology, and a growing set of Charter litigants drawn from the grassroots of lesbian and gay activism. During this initial phase, the policy effects of the Charter on lesbian and gay rights were relatively limited. This was to change in the second phase, after 1993.

The Politics of Rights after the Charter, 1993–2003

The second phase of judicial empowerment may be dated from the election of a series of majority Liberal governments starting in 1993. During the mid-nineties, Egale was reorganized and strengthened, and the pace of favourable court decisions on lesbian and gay rights issues accelerated. At the national level, the movement was dominated by Egale, and in turn Egale began to play an important role in the process of Charter litigation, strengthening the hand of Charter litigants in the lesbian and gay area by providing legal resources and third-party intervention. In turn, as courts increasingly ruled in favour of lesbian and gay rights, the movement was provided with enhanced policy resources.

Throughout this 10-year period, partisan politics on the lesbian and gay issue can be read as a stalemate between supporters and opponents. The election of the Liberals signalled some openness to lesbian and gay rights claims. As the party that had brought Canada the Charter, the Liberals prided themselves on their commitment to human rights, thereby providing a lever for lesbian and gay activists to hold the government accountable for its actions. The 1993 election also signalled the transition from a three-party Parliament to a five-party Parliament with the fracturing of the Progressive Conservative Party and the rise of the western right-wing/populist Reform Party (later Canadian Alliance) and the Quebec-based nationalist Bloc québécois.[40] Reform in particular was a consistent opponent of lesbian and gay rights claims and was backed by evangelical Christian supporters from western Canada. The Bloc was largely supportive, although the issue was peripheral for the party. Within the Liberal caucus, there was some opposition to lesbian and gay rights from a small group of pro-family MPs. Liberal governments were highly sensitive to the opposition to lesbian and gay rights from within their own party and from the right-wing Reform/Canadian Alliance party.

In this sense, the Liberal government would have stalemated on the issue and ignored it had it not been for the impact of judicial empowerment. Court rulings provided the lesbian and gay movement with the policy resources to force policy change on reluctant legislators. The establishment of legal networks and the formation and strengthening of Egale increasingly assisted litigants in bringing successful Charter challenges. Judicial empowerment served the interests of legislators who were sensitive to the relatively strong opposition to lesbian and gay rights and who had a strong voice in Parliament in the Reform Party[41] and, to a lesser extent, within the Liberal caucus. The government preferred to deflect pressure from lesbian and gay rights opponents by shifting responsibility for the issue to the courts. At the same time, the government continued the Trudeau-era policy of supporting litigation for disadvantaged groups in the equality rights and language rights areas. Lawyers working in favour of lesbian and gay rights, as well as Egale itself as an organization, undertook legal research funded by these programs.[42] Thus, while the government was reluctant to legislate in favour of lesbian and gay rights unless forced into it by the courts, its policies continued to provide part of the support structure for lesbian and gay rights litigation.[43] . . .

The most important aspect of Egale's role was in intervening in lesbian and gay rights cases before the court and undertaking its own litigation in select cases. Although Egale attempted to direct the course of litigation towards particular issues and away from others, given the nature of the Charter and the nature of the support structure for litigation it was impossible for Egale to control the litigation agenda. Individual Charter litigants came forward with challenges, paying out of their own pockets for their cases and obtaining support from trade unions or from the *pro bono* contributions of lesbian and gay lawyers and their straight allies.[44] In deciding the direction of litigation, Egale was often pushed by the individual litigants, who at times undertook Charter challenges without any contact with Egale. For example, same-sex marriage was an issue that Egale had declined to pursue in the late nineties for fear that the case would be lost in the Supreme Court of Canada;[45] however, the issue was placed back on the litigation agenda by a same-sex couple who filed a case in Quebec.[46] Yet, throughout the series of breakthrough Charter decisions and attendant legislative changes, Egale was the main representative voice of the lesbian and gay communities. The proactive role of Egale channelled, legitimated, and gave voice to lesbian and gay rights claims—not only to the courts but also to the federal government and the public.

Over this period, a series of key decisions expanded the definition of discrimination from the individual to the same-sex couple. Table 12.2 outlines these cases. Starting with the *Egan* decision in 1995, there are 11 major decisions that raise sexual orientation as a constitutional issue under section 15 of the Charter,

TABLE 12.2 | Select Cases in Lesbian and Gay Rights in Canada, 1995–2003

Case	Venue and Year	Litigant Activists?	Egale's Role	Issue	Legal Outcome	Policy Consequences
Egan & Nesbitt v. Canada	Supreme Court of Canada, 1995	Yes	Intervenor	Same-sex spousal support under federal Old Age Security	Unsuccessful, but the Court recognized that sexual orientation was analogous to the other grounds of discrimination in the equality rights provision of the Charter	Sexual orientation is considered to be included de facto in the Charter, thus opening the way for other Charter challenges on sexual orientation.
Re K. & B.	Ontario Provincial Court, 1995	No	None	Constitutionality of opposite-sex definition of spouse in provincial adoption legislation	Successful.	Despite the fact that this decision was legally binding in Ontario only, some other provinces began to change their adoption rules in its wake.
Rosenberg v. Canada	Supreme Court of Canada, 1998	No	Intervenor	Constitutionality of opposite-sex definition of spouse in federal tax code for the purpose of registering an employer pension plan	Successful. Employers and workers could receive tax benefits in private employer pension plans even if the plans offered pension benefits to same-sex couples.	This was an important case, indicating that same-sex relationship recognition in federal and provincial legislation would likely be constitutionally required under the Charter. Note the change in the Court's direction from *Egan*.
Vriend v. Alberta	Supreme Court of Canada, 1998	No	Intervenor	Alberta's refusal to include sexual orientation in its human rights legislation	Successful. Provincial human rights legislation must provide for complaints based on sexual orientation discrimination.	The Alberta government chooses not to use the notwithstanding clause to circumvent the Court's decision. Thus, sexual orientation is "read in" or included in Alberta's human rights legislation.

(Continued)

TABLE 12.2 | (Continued)

Case	Venue and Year	Litigant Activists?	Egale's Role	Issue	Legal Outcome	Policy Consequences
M v. H	Supreme Court of Canada, 1999	No	Intervenor	Spousal support on breakup of a long-term lesbian relationship	"M" is successful. Support awarded.	Comprehensive legislation on relationship recognition, federally (2000) and in most provinces
Little Sisters Book and Art Emporium v. Canada	Supreme Court of Canada, 2000	Yes	Intervenor	Constitutionality of Canada Customs' actions in stopping the Little Sisters bookstore's imports of lesbian and gay materials at the US border	The burden of proof is on Canada Customs to show that the materials are "obscene." Canada Customs' right to stop "obscene" materials is upheld.	A draw. Little Sisters, as well as lesbian and gay bookstores in Toronto, Montreal, and Ottawa continues to have its imports seized by Canada Customs.
Barbeau et al. v. British Columbia [57]	British Columbia Supreme Court, 2001	No/Yes	Litigant	Constitutionality of common law bar on same-sex marriage	Unsuccessful. Appealed (see *Barbeau* 2002, below).	The first court to rule on same-sex marriage. The decision does not have a big impact because of the weakness of the constitutional arguments provided in the judgment.
Halpern v. Canada	Ontario Divisional Court, 12 July 2002	No	Intervenor	Constitutionality of common law bar on same-sex marriage	Successful. The common law bar is unconstitutional. Appealed (see *Halpern*, 2003, below)	The first court to rule in favour of same-sex marriage
Hendricks v. Quebec	Superior Court of Quebec, 6 Sept. 2002	Yes	None	Constitutionality of legislative and civil code ban on same-sex marriage	Successful. The bans are unconstitutional. Remedy suspended for two years. Under appeal	The second case in favour of same-sex marriage builds further policy pressure on federal government.

TABLE 12.2 | (Continued)

Case	Venue and Year	Litigant Activists?	Egale's Role	Issue	Legal Outcome	Policy Consequences
Chamberlain v. Surrey School Board	Supreme Court of Canada, Dec. 2002	Yes	Intervenor	The banning of books depicting same-sex families from the elementary school classroom in Surrey, BC	Successful. The book ban is un-constitutional.	The school board voted to continue the ban on the original books, but voted to allow two other books that depict same-sex relationships. A major setback for the evangelical movement in British Columbia.
Barbeau et al. v. British Columbia	British Columbia Court of Appeal, 1 May 2003	No/Yes	Litigant	Constitutionality of common law bar on same-sex marriage	Successful. The common law bar is unconstitutional. Remedy is suspended until July 2004. Outdated by subsequent request by *Barbeau et al.*	The third court to agree with same-sex marriage, overturning a lower British Columbia court ruling against same-sex marriage. Adds to policy pressure for action from federal government.
Halpern et al. v. Canada	Ontario Court of Appeal, 10 June 2003	No/Yes	Intervenor	Constitutionality of common law bar on same-sex marriage. Appeal from *Barbeau et al.* 2001.	Successful. The remedy is to take effect immediately. The litigants' marriages (which took place in 2001) are to be immediately recognized by the province. Unlike the other successful decisions, the Court did not give the provincial government time to devise a legislative solution.	On 18 June 2003, the federal government announced it would not appeal the Ontario decision and would draft legislation recognizing same-sex marriage. The legislation would be referred to the Supreme Court of Canada and then put to a free vote in the legislature.

TABLE 12.2 (Continued)

Case	Venue and Year	Litigant Activists?	Egale's Role	Issue	Legal Outcome	Policy Consequences
Barbeau et al. v. British Columbia	British Columbia Court of Appeal, July 2003	No/Yes	Litigant	Constitutionality of common law bar on same-sex marriage	Request for immediate lifting of British Columbia suspension in light of Ontario remedy	Suspension lifted on 8 July 2003. Marriage licences issued for same-sex couples in British Columbia.

Source: Canadian law reports.
Note: Litigant information is drawn from interviews conducted by the author or from publicly available information about litigants' identities.

based on Canadian law reports. They show the progression from the Supreme Court's clear recognition of sexual orientation as a prohibited ground of discrimination under the Charter in the *Egan* decision of 1995 through the trio of decisions on same-sex marriage in Quebec, British Columbia, and Ontario in 2002–4. Two of the 11 cases—*Egan* and *Vriend*[47]—concern the constitutional question of including sexual orientation as a prohibited ground of discrimination in the Charter itself and in human rights legislation. Six of the cases (including *Egan* again) deal with issues of same-sex relationship recognition, including adoption, pensions, spousal support upon relationship breakdown, and legal marriage. Three of the cases concern education and culture: the banning of books in a British Columbia school district (*Surrey*),[48] the certification of teacher-training programs (*Trinity Western*),[49] and the seizure of lesbian and gay reading material by Canada Customs (*Little Sisters*).[50] Egale was an active intervenor in 9 of the 11 cases and the litigant in one case. Thus, of the 11 cases, Egale was actively involved as an intervenor or litigant in all but one. In *Hendricks*,[51] Egale was informally involved and close communication occurred at the later stages of the case between the legal team and the pan-Canadian lesbian and gay legal network. This marks a substantial increase from the earlier period of Charter litigation in which Egale was involved in only 5 of 14 Charter cases.

An examination of the policy evolution represented by these cases shows that Charter jurisprudence has moved from discrimination against individuals to discrimination against same-sex couples. In *Egan*, the Supreme Court of Canada ruled that sexual orientation was analogous to the other grounds of discrimination enumerated in section 15 of the Charter and that hence it was included *de facto* or "read in" to the Charter, thus confirming the implications of the earlier judgments in *Haig & Birch* and *Veysey*. In response to this, the Liberals came under increasing pressure to amend the Canadian Human Rights Act, the legislation covering private discrimination in federal jurisdiction, to include sexual orientation, a change that had already been informally included because of the *Haig & Birch* judgment. Led by Egale, the lesbian and gay legal networks, and the Canadian Human Rights Commission itself, the Liberals acted to amend the Act in 1996. . . .

The more dramatic policy changes concerned the question of same-sex relationship recognition as an extension of anti-discrimination law. The evolution of policy in this area began with the *Egan* decision on same-sex spousal support under the federal Old Age Security pension legislation. This case failed but subsequent cases succeeded, including *Rosenberg* on the constitutionality of the exclusion of same-sex couples from the federal Income Tax Act, and most important, *M v. H*,[52] in which spousal support was awarded on the breakup of a lesbian relationship. Organizing, intervention, and advocacy created political pressures on the court and on the government's reaction to court decisions. Egale, along with trade union and other allies, were closely involved in *Egan*, *Rosenberg*,[53] and *M v. H.* The legal networks that had formed in the mid-nineties contributed the lawyers who represented the parties (including intervenors) in these cases, and Egale kept up the pressure on the federal government to amend federal laws in anticipation of and in reaction to Charter decisions.[54] . . .

As the legal direction from the Supreme Court in the wake of *M v. H* seemed clear, the federal government forestalled this omnibus case by passing the Modernization of Benefits and Obligations Act (2000). This legislation extended the benefits and obligations of common law status to same-sex couples, amending 69 federal laws and regulations affecting spousal benefits and obligations. . . . The bill equated same-sex and opposite-sex common law partners as equal in benefits and obligations to married couples, while maintaining a separate status in law for married and non-married couples.[55] . . . The Charter decisions also shaped public policy at the provincial level, as most provinces, including the three most populous provinces of Ontario, Quebec, and British Columbia, moved to forestall litigation by amending their own legislation in reaction to these rulings.

Throughout the period from 1995 to 2002, changes in public policy had occurred on the assumption that same-sex couples would not be accorded the right to legal marriage. Yet the potential for a challenge to opposite-sex marriage laws arose almost immediately in the wake of the *M v. H* decisions. The Supreme Court of Canada had accepted that same-sex relationships were worthy of legal protection and support and that they were no different from common law heterosexual relationships, which are relatively well protected in Canadian law. . . . But, *M v. H* changed the legal calculus, and even before Egale could organize marriage claimants, litigants came forward from Quebec and British Columbia. . . . Two sets of British Columbia

litigants (whose cases were joined), two sets of Ontario litigants . . . , and the Quebec couple (Hendricks-Laboeuf) came before British Columbia, Ontario, and Quebec courts. These cases resulted in legal successes in the three provinces, most notably in Ontario on 10 June 2003 when the Ontario Court of Appeal not only ruled that barring same-sex marriage was unconstitutional but made its decision immediately effective. . . . Given that same-sex marriages were occurring . . . , the federal government, which had begun parliamentary committee hearings on the issue of same-sex marriage in late 2002, decided to undertake another omnibus response to the courts, promising legislation that would legalize same-sex marriage across Canada, subject to a constitutional reference from the Supreme Court of Canada in late 2003 or early 2004.[56]

By the late nineties and the first years of the new millennium, the Charter had remade Canadian public policy on lesbian and gay rights in general and same-sex relationships in particular. The survey of the movement before and after the Charter demonstrates that the place of legally based rights-claiming within the overall ideology and frame of the lesbian and gay movement had changed fundamentally. Where once rights-claiming through litigation had been seen as means to the end of building the gay liberation movement and of fundamentally challenging heteronormative social codes, in the post-Charter period law and litigation were increasingly taken literally as the measure of political and social change. The desire for human rights recognition was no longer placed in the broader context of social and political inequality but rather was defined solely as a question of law and public policy change.

This shift in the ideological framing of the human rights issue can be plausibly linked to the entrenchment of the Charter, which is broadly seen as having given a new legalized rights consciousness to English-Canadian political culture. With regard to the effects of the Charter on the mobilizing structure of the movement, it is clear that over a 25-year period the organization of the lesbian and gay movement was transformed from locally based urban groups into a pan-Canadian legal network, dominated by lawyers and by one litigation and advocacy organization—Egale. The emergence of a national advocacy group so strongly focused on litigation and legal strategies and in which informal legal networks play such a critical role would not have occurred without the Charter. Without courts, the most likely route of change in the Canadian political system would have been through organizing within the political parties in order to influence one of the (potentially) governing parties, federally and provincially, or a broader-based lobbying and grassroots mobilization effort connecting local organization to provincial and federal organizing. Yet, as lesbian and gay organizing was focused on the courts, other forms of organizing did not occur. . . .

Conclusions

Over a 20-year period, judicial empowerment in Canada has encouraged and reinforced a certain type of social movement politics, one that is dedicated to liberal rights-claiming using litigation as its greatest strategic asset. The enhanced role of the courts in the political system as a result of the entrenchment of the Charter intersected with the rise of the lesbian and gay movement. In the subsequent time period, successful lesbian and gay rights claims before the courts and rapidly, radically changing public policies on sexual orientation

pushed the movement towards an ever-deepening material, organizational, strategic, and symbolic commitment to litigation as the means and measure of the changed status of lesbian and gay people in society. This had the effect of centring human rights as the dominant frame and ideology of the movement at the expense of the liberatory goals of the original gay liberation and lesbian feminist movements, of generating a mobilizing structure for lesbian and gay organizing that privileges legal networks and litigation-dominated organizations such as Egale, and of furnishing the movement with policy resources through legal victory. Without the mobilizing structure for litigation and without the pattern of legal victory under the Charter, elected politicians would have avoided the hot button of gay rights. The impact of judicial empowerment thus has been to force lesbian and gay rights onto the political agenda in a way that defines the issue as falling within the ambit of Charter-protected human rights, rights that are increasingly sacrosanct in Canadian political culture. . . .

Author's Note: Research was funded by the Social Sciences and Humanities Research Council of Canada. An earlier version of this article was presented at the American Political Science Association, 2003. I thank Michael Orsini, David Rayside, and the editors of *Politics & Society* for helpful comments.

Endnotes

1   Janet Hiebert, *Charter Conflicts: What Is Parliament's Role?* (Montreal and Kingston: McGill-Queen's University Press, 2002).

2   Ran Hirschl, "The Struggle for Hegemony: Understanding Judicial Empowerment through Constitutionalization in Culturally Divided Polities," *Stanford Journal of International Law* 73 (2000): 93–118; and Neal C. Tate, "Why the Expansion of Judicial Power?," in C. Neal Tate and Torbjörn Vallinder, eds, *The Global Expansion of Judicial Power* (New York: New York University Press, 1995), 1–32.

3   Rebecca Mae Salokar, "Beyond Gay Rights Litigation: Using a Systemic Strategy to Effect Political Change in the United States," in Mark Blasius, ed., *Sexual Identities, Queer Politics* (Princeton, NJ: Princeton University Press, 2001), 256–85. The US Supreme Court ruling in *Lawrence v. Texas* (2003) on the constitutionality of sodomy laws may lead to some reassessment of the role of litigation in the US lesbian and gay rights movement.

4   Lesbian and gay activists and lawyers were identified through reading the lesbian and gay media and through their public participation in the main

organizations of the movement or as lawyers in Charter cases involving lesbian and gay issues, as well as by using the "snowball" method. Two rounds of semi-structured interviews were conducted in 1995–6 and 2001–2. A small number of federal government policy-makers were interviewed as well in 1995–6. Over 50 interviews were conducted over the two rounds, and particular insights from interviews are identified by source in the references. All of the interview subjects, except for one federal policy-maker, gave permission for their words to be quoted and their identity to be revealed.

5 For example, Gerald Rosenberg, *The Hollow Hope: Can Courts Bring about Social Change?* (Chicago: University of Chicago Press, 1991); and Michael McCann, *Rights at Work: Pay Equity Reform and the Politics of Legal Mobilization* (Chicago: University of Chicago Press, 1994).

6 Michael Adams, *Fire and Ice: The United States, Canada and the Myth of Converging Values* (Toronto: Penguin Canada, 2003).

7 Patrick Fournier, André Blais, Joanna Everitt, Elisabeth Gidengil and Neil Nevitte, "How the Liberals Lost Quebec," *Globe and Mail*, 21 July 2004, A15; and Ipsos Reid, "Slim Majority (54%) Support Same Sex Marriage," www.ipsos-reid.com (13 June 2003).

8 Paul D. Brewer, "The Shifting Foundations of Public Opinion about Gay Rights," *Journal of Politics* 65, no. 4 (2003): 1208–20.

9 Craig A. Rimmerman, *From Identity to Politics: The Lesbian and Gay Movement in the United States* (Philadelphia: Temple University Press, 2002); and Patricia A. Cain, *Rainbow Rights: The Role of Lawyers and Courts in the Lesbian and Gay Civil Rights Movement* (Boulder, CO: Westview, 2000), 12–22.

10 Alkarim Jivani, *It's Not Unusual: A History of Lesbian and Gay Britain in the Twentieth Century* (Bloomington: Indiana University Press, 1997).

11 Cited in Tom Warner, *Never Going Back: A History of Queer Activism in Canada* (Toronto: University of Toronto Press, 2002), 44.

12 Barry D. Adam, *The Rise of a Gay and Lesbian Movement*, rev. edn (Boston: Twayne, 1995); and David Rayside, *On the Fringe: Lesbians and Gays in Politics* (Ithaca, NY: Cornell University Press, 1998).

13 Miriam Smith, *Lesbian and Gay Rights in Canada: Social Movements and Equality-Seeking, 1971–1995* (Toronto: University of Toronto Press, 1999).

14 Don Hann (gay liberation activist), personal interview (Vancouver, 1996); Chris Bearchell (gay liberation

activist), personal interview (British Columbia, 1996); and Tom Warner (gay liberation activist), personal interview (Toronto, 1996).

15 Ken Popert, "Gay Rights Now!," *The Body Politic*, 19 (August, 1975): 16; and Brian Waite, "Strategy for Gay Liberation," *The Body Politic* 3 (May 1972): 4.

16 Stuart A. Scheingold, *The Politics of Rights: Lawyers, Public Policy, and Political Change*, 2nd edn (Ann Arbor: University of Michigan Press, 2004), 131–45.

17 Warner, *Never Going Back*, 144–9.

18 W.W. Black, "Gay Alliance Toward Equality v. *Vancouver Sun*," *Osgoode Hall Law Journal* 17 (1979), 15–31; and J. Richstone and J. Stuart Russell, "Shutting the Gate: Gay Civil Rights in the Supreme Court of Canada," *McGill Law Journal*, 97: 1 (1981), 92–117.

19 Warner, *Never Going Back*, 154–60.

20 Ross Higgins, *De la clandestiné à l'affirmation: Pour une histoire de la communauté gaie montréalaise* (Montreal: Comeau & Nadeau, 1999).

21 Didi Herman, *Rights of Passage: Struggles for Lesbian and Gay Legal Equality* (Toronto: University of Toronto Press, 1994), 1–34.

22 Ed Jackson and Stan Persky, *Flaunting It! A Decade of Journalism from the Body Politic* (Vancouver and Toronto: New Star Books and Pink Triangle Press, 1982); and Tim McCaskell, "The Bath Raids and Gay Politics," in Frank Cunningham *et al.*, eds, *Social Movements, Social Change: The Politics and Practice of Organizing* (Toronto: Between the Lines, 1982), 54–72.

23 David Rayside and Evert Lindquist, "AIDS Activism and the State in Canada," *Studies in Political Economy* 39 (1992): 37–76.

24 Barbara Findlay (lawyer), personal interview (Vancouver, 1996).

25 Douglas Elliott (lawyer), personal interview (Toronto, 2002); and Ken Smith (lawyer), personal interview (Ottawa, 2001); Findlay interview.

26 Blair Johnston, "Equality Hearings Delayed," *Goinfo* (Ottawa) 79 (July/August 1985): 1.

27 Roger Roome, "Parliamentary Committee Recommends Equal Rights for Gays and Lesbians," *Goinfo* 82 (November 1985): 3.

28 *Goinfo* 85 (March 1986): 6.

29 Egale's original name was Equality for Gays and Lesbians Everywhere/Égalité pour les gais et les lesbiennes. The acronym EGALE means "equality" in French. In 2001, Egale changed its name from the long form to simply Egale Canada Inc. Egale also has a spinoff group called Egale Canada Human Rights Trust, which conducts human rights education work.

The latter has charitable status in Canadian tax laws and limits its political activities accordingly.

30   "Tory Government Will Offer Gays Protection," *Goinfo* 86 (April 1986): 2; and Christine Jean-François, "New Gay Rights Group Pushing for Government Action," *Goinfo* 90 (September 1986): 1.

31   Diane Kilby (Egale and trade union activist), personal interview (Ottawa, 1996); and LeBlanc interview.

32   *Correctional Services of Canada v. Veysey* (1990), 109 N.R. 300.

33   *Haig & Birch v. Canada* (1992), 9 O.R. (3d) 495, 94 D.L.R. (4th) 1, 16 C.H.R.R. D/226, 57 O.A.C. 272, 10 C.R.R. (2d) 287.

34   Geoffrey York, "Ottawa Accepts Court Ruling on Gay Rights," *Globe and Mail*, 1 October 1992, A10.

35   Nitya Iyer, "Categorical Denials: Equality Rights and the Shaping of Social Identity," *Queen's Law Journal* 19, no. 1 (Fall 1993): 179–207; Douglas Sanders, "Constructing Lesbian and Gay Rights," *Canadian Journal of Law and Society* 9, no. 2 (Fall 1994): 350–79; and Karn Patrick, "Spousal Benefits," *Capital Xtra* 37 (20 September 1994): 7.

36   Avvy Go and John Fisher, *Working Together across Our Differences: A Discussion Paper on Coalition-Building, Participatory Litigation and Strategic Litigation* (Ottawa: Court Challenges Program, 1998).

37   *Egan & Nesbitt v. Canada* (1995), 124 D.L.R. (4th) 609 SCC.

38   Deborah McIntosh, "Court Cases in Which Sexual Orientation Arguments under Section 15 of the Charter Were Raised," in Smith, *Lesbian and Gay Rights*, 157–63.

39   This is based on personal interviews with some of the litigants and on publicly available information about their activist careers.

40   R.K. Carty, William Cross, and Lisa Young, *Rebuilding Canadian Party Politics* (Vancouver: UBC Press, 2000), 32–65.

41   The western-based right-wing/populist Reform Party was renamed the Canadian Alliance in 2000. Officially, the party's name was Canadian Reform Conservative Alliance, but in everyday practice, the party used the name Canadian Alliance. In 2003, the party merged with the Progressive Conservative Party to form the Conservative Party of Canada.

42   Egale, *Annual Report* (Ottawa, 1998), 1–2.

43   On the support structure for litigation in Canada, see Charles Epp, *The Rights Revolution: Lawyers, Activists, and Supreme Courts in Comparative Perspective* (Chicago: University of Chicago Press, 1998), 178–220.

44   Elliott interview; Murray Cook and Peter Warren (litigants and activists), personal telephone interview (2001); and John Sinopoli, "To Court, to Court," *Xtra!*, 1 November 2001, 3.

45   Fisher interview.

46   Michael Hendricks, "Still Over the Rainbow?" *Montreal Mirror* 19: 7 (August 1, 2003), www.montrealmirror.com/meat/diverscite_5.html.

47   *Vriend v. Alberta*, [1998] 1 S.C.R. 493.

48   *Chamberlain v. Surrey School Board No. 26*, 2002 SCC 86, File No. 28654.

49   *Trinity Western University v. British Columbia College of Teachers*, [2001] S.C.J. No. 32.

50   *Little Sisters Book and Art Emporium v. Canada (Minister of Justice)*, 2000 SCC 69, File No. 26858.

51   *Hendricks v. Québec (Attorney General)*, [2002] J.Q. No. 3816.

52   *M v. H*, [1999] S.C.J. No. 23.

53   *Rosenberg v. Canada (Attorney General)*, [1998] 38 O.R. (3d) 577.

54   Fisher interview; and Elliott interview.

55   Egale, "Omnibus Federal Law Recognizes Same-Sex Couples," *InfoEGALE* (Ottawa), Summer 2000, 1.

56   Kim Luman, "Ottawa Backs Gay Marriage," *Globe and Mail*, 18 June 2003, A1.

57   *Halpern v. Canada* (A.G.) (2002), 60 O.R. (3d) 321 (Div. Ct.); *Barbeau v. British Columbia* (A.G.), 2003 BCCA 406; Re K. & B. (1995) 125 D.L.R. (4th) 653; and *M. v. H.* [1999] 2 S.C.R. 3. *Barbeau* and *Halpern* appear multiple times in the table in order to show the detailed progress of the "marriage cases" through the various levels of litigation and the policy interactions among the various decisions. However, in the discussion of case totals in the text, *Barbeau* and *Halpern* are each counted once each. This standardizes the method of counting the cases across the board, as the other cases have been listed by their Supreme Court appearances and not by their lower court rulings.

PART IV

Suggested Readings

Bangarth, Stephanie. *Voices Raised in Protest: Defending North American Citizens of Japanese Ancestry, 1942–49.* Vancouver: UBC Press, 2008.

Clément, Dominique. *Canada's Rights Revolution: Social Movements and Social Change, 1937–82.* Vancouver: UBC Press, 2008.

Kelly, James B., and Christopher Manfredi, eds. *Contested Constitutionalism: Reflections on the Canadian Charter of Rights and Freedoms.* Vancouver: UBC Press, 2009.

Thompson, Andrew S. *In Defence of Principles: NGOs and Human Rights in Canada.* Vancouver: UBC Press, 2010.

Walker, James W. St G. *"Race," Rights and the Law in the Supreme Court of Canada.* Waterloo, ON: Wilfrid Laurier Press, 1997.

Key Terms

anti-Semitism
civil rights
cultural pluralism
familism
feminist

human rights
humanist
liberalism
liberation (-ist)
New Left

Questions for Consideration

1. Why did the first significant human rights law originate in Saskatchewan in 1947?

2. Why did the Women's Bureau and other human rights advocates struggle with the idea of women's inequality and how was this idea addressed through legislation?

3. What were the main reasons for the development of a culture in support of rights and equality (and social movements in support of rights and equality) in the years from 1945 to the present?

4. Why have rights movements targeted the state to achieve their goals? What are the limitations of a state-oriented, legal approach (through anti-discrimination or human rights laws) to rights achievement?

5. What were the major changes to social movement politics and human rights groups after the Second World War and why?

6. What was the impact of youth on social movements during the 1960s and 1970s?

7. Examine the different explanations for the rising racial violence in Toronto in the 1970s.

8. In what ways has the Charter and judicial review empowered social groups traditionally outside of the political mainstream to achieve their policy demands?

9. Examine the impact of the Charter on the organization, method, and ideology of gay and lesbian rights.

10. In what types of litigation have conservative Christians engaged and why? What are their arguments and goals?

Relevant Websites

Canada's Human Rights History
www.historyofrights.com/introduction.html

Canadian Human Rights Commission—Publications
and Human Rights History
www.chrc-ccdp.ca/eng/content/publications
www.chrc-ccdp.ca/en/index.asp

Charter of Rights and Freedoms
http://laws-lois.justice.gc.ca/eng/Const/page-15
.html#h-39

Cooperative Commonwealth Federation—Encyclopedia
of Saskatchewan
www.esask.uregina.ca/entry/co-operative_
commonwealth_federation_ccf.html

Egale Canada Human Rights Trust
https://egale.ca/category/publications/

National Council of Women of Canada
www.ncwc.ca/index.html

Status of Women Canada
www.swc-cfc.gc.ca

Supreme Court of Canada—Judgments
www.scc-csc.gc.ca/decisions/index-eng.asp

University of Saskatchewan—Diefenbaker Canada
Centre (The Canadian Bill of Rights)
www.usask.ca/diefenbaker/galleries/virtual_
exhibit/bill_of_rights/index.php

PART V

Changing Values and Norms

continued

1971	Peace-Athabasca Delta Project Group created to assess the Peace Dam's impact	**1988**	Supreme Court rules that abortion law violates the Charter and law is overturned
1972	United Nations Conference on the Human Environment	**1992**	United Nations Conference on Environment and Development and the Rio Declaration
1972	Federal government tightens rules for applying for landed immigrant status	**1998**	Kyoto Accord is signed to decrease green house emissions
1975	Department of the Environment created in New Brunswick and replaces the Water Authority	**2000**	British Columbia issues an advisory about consuming fish poisoned by mercury because of dams
1980s	Environmental justice movement emerges	**2011**	Government announces Canada will withdraw from Kyoto Accord
1985	Reform of the Divorce Act provides "no-fault" divorce		

Introduction

It is not surprising, given the extent of change in postwar Canada, that the norms, values, and attitudes of Canadians evolved in important and fundamental ways. Some attitudinal and ideological changes have been described in other chapters of this book, such as new ideas about cultural diversity, human rights, and social justice; related to these were fundamental changes in the norms and values guiding other important areas of Canadian life.

One significant attitudinal change in the postwar years was a growing awareness of and concern for environmental impacts arising from human activity. Environmental concern and activism to protect "nature" were not entirely new to the post-1945 period; in the late nineteenth and early twentieth centuries, there emerged a small Canadian movement concerned about the degradation and depletion of forested areas and animal populations. Composed mainly of upper middles-class professionals and hunting and fishing organizations, the movement succeeded in securing conservation measures, such as licences for recreational hunting and the establishment of the first national and provincial parks. This "first wave" of environmentalism diminished by the First World War. The years following the Second World War, however, saw not only a resurgence of environmental concern but also environmental activism; moreover, concern became much more prevalent among average Canadians and the focus expanded significantly beyond conservation and/or preservation of nature to a much broader concept of humans' interaction with nature and their impact on ecosystems and the planet as a whole. The environmental movement expanded significantly in the 1960s (much like the expansion of membership in the human rights movement) as did its focus.

Examples of subfields in environmentalism today include ecology, conservation, and environmental justice. In chapter 13, Mark McLaughlin shows how greater awareness and concern about pollution in the St John River led to the creation in 1958 of a government water resource management body in New Brunswick with regulatory powers to address water pollution issues. Yet, despite public concern and widespread evidence of the degradation of the river, economic priorities ultimately clashed with environmental need. The governmental Water Authority ultimately had mixed success. While it did facilitate the development of municipal sewage treatment facilities, substantially decreasing the amount of raw sewage going into the river, the Water Authority had negligible impacts on industrial pollution. Concerned about negative economic impacts on the important pulp and paper industry, the Water Authority failed to impose regulations for fear of hindering economic growth. From a different perspective, Tina Loo examines the environmental and social impacts of the 1968 construction of a massive dam on the Peace River in northern British Columbia. From an environmental justice point of view, Loo seeks to reveal the unequal environmental impacts on the people who experienced the environmental changes, primarily Aboriginal groups who lived and secured a livelihood within the area. According to Loo, for many of these people, environmental change meant "dependence, isolation, alienation, and illness."

In both the environmental and human rights movements, activism increased significantly in the late 1960s owing to the influx of youth (baby boomers) into these movements. The youth of the 1960s not only strengthened many of the movements but also brought a strong critique of many of the institutions, values, and norms of Canadian society. While 1960s youth did not necessarily develop the concepts and ideas surrounding change in the 1960s, their strongly voiced critique and culture of resistance certainly facilitated many of the changes that would follow. One example of youth's participation in resistance is shown in Matthew Roth's article in chapter 14 on the Toronto Anti-Draft Programme (TADP) that provided aid and support to American war resisters entering Canada. Despite a pervasive Cold War mentality, many young Canadians rejected the assertion that US military involvement in Vietnam was necessary to contain communism, positing that American action was imperialistic and denied Vietnam's right to self-determination. The anti-war movement, located primarily in the New Left, joined the American movement to encourage young American men of military age to resist the draft. Yet, as Roth reveals, the TADP services and advice to these resisters changed over time, in part due to growing uncertainty (and some opposition) over whether these young Americans should come to Canada. Christabelle Sethna's article in chapter 14 reveals another aspect of youth's critique of values in the case of student demand for access to birth control. Made available by prescription in 1961, the birth control pill facilitated the "sexual revolution," allowing single, young women to engage increasingly in sexual relations for purposes of pleasure rather than pregnancy. At the University of Toronto, female students sought prescriptions for the pill from Health Services but were denied, as the service counselled abstinence and restraint for women who were not married. This refusal led to action by both male and female students, with the latter demanding access to the pill regardless of marital status. As Sethna notes, these students utilized a range of arguments, including the right of women to control their own sexuality and the demand that students have input into university policy and governance.

One of the most dramatic changes in values and norms in postwar society were those related to gender and the rights and responsibilities of women and men within the family. The rise in women's labour force participation, the demand for women's equality in all spheres of life, the increase in education levels, and the greater availability of white-collar occupations for women led to a gradual acceptance of women's employment outside the home and in occupations traditionally deemed male. Within the family, as well, postwar society saw a gradual shift to more involvement by men in parenting their children and performing domestic chores. Yet the extent to which absolute gender equality has been achieved in work and family life is debatable. In chapter 15, Barbara Freeman examines this question by examining the experiences of women newspaper journalists from 1945 to 1975. Significant equality gains were made, particularly in the movement of women from the "women's pages" to positions of "hard news" journalism from the mid-1960s to the late 1970s. Yet, as Freeman argues, women journalists continued to face "more subtle forms of discrimination" and the need to balance work with family or home life. Robert Rutherdale focuses on the changing concept of fatherhood and how it relates to the ideas of masculinity from the late 1940s to the 1960s. In particular, he addresses the fear expressed in postwar literature that men, including fathers, faced a crisis of masculinity. Rutherdale argues that fathers did not experience a crisis of masculinity in their attempts to parent their children. Instead, he finds that fathers utilized three types of male parenting, all related to the masculine concept of "responsible family manhood."

CHAPTER **13**

The Environment

⊚ 13.1: "As Thick as Molasses": Water Pollution Regulation in New Brunswick, 1947–1975

Mark J. McLaughlin

On 1 April 1968, Fred A. McCain, Progressive Conservative representative for Carleton County, stood up in the New Brunswick Legislative Assembly and exclaimed, "I don't know whether anybody in this House has ever tried to go down the St John River in a boat from our area, but unless you did, I don't think you could appreciate the stench and the amount of pollution, floating and dissolved, that is actually in that stream." He explained that he "knew that it was bad, because I lived beside it and smelled it, but until I actually got in a boat and went down that stream, I had absolutely no conception of the amount of pollution. In places the whole stream was as thick as molasses."[1]

The descriptive portrait painted by McCain was an effective way to convey the sad state of some of New Brunswick's waterways in the mid-twentieth century, but attempting to guide a boat through a river with the consistency of molasses also serves as the perfect metaphor to illustrate the pace of water pollution regulation in the province. In many respects, New Brunswick was a leader in water resource management in the 1950s and 1960s, and yet the provincial government did not make significant progress in dealing with the largest source of water pollution in the province, pulp

and paper manufacturing, until the 1970s. With an estimated value of $175 million at the end of the 1950s, three-quarters of which was attributed to the pulp and paper industry, forestry was the largest economic sector in the province and the figurative "molasses" in the metaphor mentioned above.[2] The importance of forestry to the provincial economy positioned the New Brunswick government in the middle of a classic encounter between economic considerations and environmental concerns by the mid-twentieth century. New Brunswickers, like most Canadians, expected more from the state in the years after the Second World War, including better management of the province's waterways, particularly by the end of the 1960s when awareness of the environmental repercussions of "modern" lifestyles had reached an all-time high. The New Brunswick government responded to public concerns about pollution with a technocratic approach to water resource management, creating the New Brunswick Water Authority in 1958 and assigning to it the regulatory powers to enforce the various provisions of the New Brunswick Water Act when it was passed in 1961. The supposed objectivity of the Authority's management approach was eventually shattered by the politics of pulp and paper in New Brunswick; thus it did not meet the environmental expectations of the province's residents. Amidst growing frustrations with the Water Authority, the provincial government gradually disbanded the organization in the early 1970s and reassigned its regulatory duties to a newly created Department of the Environment in 1975.

Prior to the Second World War, there was relatively little systematic regulation pertaining to water pollution in Canada and even less enforcement. The British North America (BNA) Act of 1867, the document that founded Canada as a federalist state, accorded the provinces jurisdiction over lands and resources, including nearly all water resources, but granted the federal government jurisdiction over ocean-based and anadromous fisheries and international and navigable rivers.[3] While the Act designated most aspects of resource management and environmental regulation as provincial responsibilities, the majority of pre-1950s regulatory activities on issues of water quality were conducted under federal legislation. The Fisheries Act of 1868 prohibited the discharge of "deleterious substances" into waters containing fish, and the federal government, in conjunction with provincial officials when freshwater fish species were involved, intermittently regulated sources of water pollution that negatively affected fish populations. However, this limited regulatory activity was often ineffective. The federal and provincial governments adhered to laissez-faire economic orthodoxy in the late nineteenth and early twentieth centuries, ensuring that economic considerations usually trumped environmental concerns.[4] The federal government, for example, passed a series of "sawdust acts" in the late nineteenth century to limit the effects of sawmill waste on fish and the navigability of rivers. Nonetheless, fearing the devastating economic consequences of such legislation to the lumber industry, federal officials frequently exempted sawmills from water pollution regulations.[5]

Provincial government involvement in the regulation of water pollution increased significantly by the mid-1950s. After the lean years of the Great Depression and several years of rationing during the Second World War, the average Canadian citizen entered the postwar period with an expectation of overall improvement in the quality of life. Moreover, government planning of the wartime economy and high levels of wartime employment demonstrated that state intervention could have a positive impact on the lives of individual citizens.[6] Increased acceptance of state intervention among the general public coincided with the maturation of a technocratic approach to resource management in Canada. Progressive conservation ideals "were extended . . . [across the country in the beginning of the twentieth century] . . . by a growing cadre of bureaucrats and experts committed to eliminating the wasteful exploitation of resources by promoting the wise and rational use of nature's bounty." By the 1940s and 1950s, provincial resource managers believed strongly in the supposed objectivity and "capacity of technology, science and management to order and improve" natural environments.[7] In the case of water resource management, chemists and sanitation engineers developed what they referred to as "stream sanitation" in the first half of the twentieth century. Stream sanitation theory conceptualized bodies of water as finite resources that had to be managed wisely for the sake of future generations, and it provided the means to quantify water pollution damage through standardized measurements such as "biochemical oxygen demand" (BOD), a measure of the amount of oxygen used by micro-organisms to decompose organic wastes in water, and theoretical concepts such as "assimilative capacity," the ability of a body of water to receive wastes without harmful effects on humans and wildlife.[8] Stream sanitation theory allowed provincial officials to respond to some public concerns about water pollution. In New Brunswick, for example, Chief Medical Officer J.A. Melanson noted in 1946 that for quite some time there had been increasing demands for the Department of Health to focus on issues such as "water supplies, milk and food control, sewerage disposal, environmental sanitation and plumbing." Consequently, department employee Alwyn J. Cameron, who attended Harvard University's sanitation engineering program in the mid-1940s, was appointed New Brunswick's first provincial sanitation engineer on 1 August 1947.[9]

ENVIRONMENTAL MOVEMENT

The "modern" environmental movement can be described as having three waves or stages over the course of the twentieth century to the present. These stages are not exclusive or completely differentiated from one another in terms of ideology, objectives, and time period; nonetheless, they reveal the evolution of environmentalism.

The modern environmental movement began in the late 1880s primarily as a result of economic motives. Pressured mainly by a small group within the political and economic elite, governments began to create the first national and provincial parks as fish, game, and wilderness reserves for the purposes of tourism and recreation. While revenue generation was the main priority in this early conservation movement, conservation of the natural environment was fuelled by the anti-modernist mindset of many of the Anglo-Canadian elite, who idealized the lifestyle, values, and characteristics of the pre-industrial past. This anti-modernism created the demand for wilderness experiences in such forms as vacationing at the lavish hotel in Banff National Park or canoeing, hunting, or fishing tours. This first wave of environmental conservation had evolved by the interwar years to include the primary goal of preserving or conserving wilderness and wildlife. Additional parks, bird and game preserves, and hunting/fishing regulations and licensing were created to protect and preserve the natural environment and the wildlife of the country.

The second wave of environmentalism, beginning in the 1960s, expanded this focus on conservation to include concern over the dire effects of human activities on the environment—most notably the issue of pollution and its negative impacts on wildlife and the natural environment. In 1969, the organization Pollution Probe was created at the University of Toronto. One of its first actions was to analyze and publicize the negative effects of phosphates in laundry detergents on the Great Lakes and other waterways. Its focus expanded subsequently to include air pollution issues and the harmful effects of pesticides. Similarly, in 1971, Green Peace was formed in Vancouver, initially to protest nuclear testing, but soon to draw attention to the environmental impacts of nuclear weapons and nuclear power.

By the 1980s, the environmental movement moved into a third phase, characterized by the further expansion of the issues of concern and the number of organizations involved. The range of organizations and objectives of modern environmentalism include issues such as the promotion of organic farming and energy conservation and the need to reduce greenhouse gases. In fact, climate change has become a primary issue of the third wave. As a result, a further characteristic of this period is a move towards creating measures to coordinate the activities of environmental groups and activists, nationally and internationally, in part because of the need to strengthen their influence on governments and in part because of the recognition that many environmental issues, such as climate change, can only be dealt with on a multinational level. Modern environmentalism has also increasingly integrated environmental issues with social justice issues. Environmental justice groups seek to publicize and address the fact that some human groups experience the impacts of environmental harm more than others.

It did not take long for the provincial sanitation engineer's attention to turn to the question of water pollution in New Brunswick. As early as 1948, Cameron reported that the provincial government had no policy on stream sanitation, and he strongly recommended the establishment of a "stream control commission" to study the matter of New Brunswick's polluted waterways.[10] In a paper presented at the thirty-seventh annual meeting of the Canadian

Public Health Association in Halifax in June 1949, Cameron warned of the possible ill effects of water pollution from industrial and municipal sources on the health of New Brunswickers and on the long-term viability of industries such as agriculture, tourism, and the fisheries. He decried in particular the fact that the "beautiful" St John River "serves as a sewer throughout its entire length along the western boundary of New Brunswick," and he renewed his call for a provincial commission to study the problem of stream pollution.[11] By the early 1950s, Cameron called for the provincial government to form a "water control board" that would recommend legislation to curb additional pollution from industrial development and municipal sewage disposal.[12]

The largest sources of water pollution in New Brunswick for most of the twentieth century were pulp and paper mills. The contraction of the province's lumber industry in the 1920s and the successive rise of the pulp and paper industry by 1930 marked an important transition in the industrial sources of water pollution in the province. A total of seven pulp mills and pulp and paper mill complexes, or integrated mills, were built in New Brunswick from 1920 to 1960.[13] The various mills utilized chemical (sulphite or kraft), mechanical (physical grinding), or chemi-mechanical pulping processes to separate the plant fibres used to make paper from the polymers that bind the fibres together and other plant materials not used to make paper.[14] The oldest mills in the province were chemical or chemi-mechanical sulphite mills that used tens of thousands of litres of water per tonne of manufactured pulp, which was discharged back into surrounding waterways. While the harmful effects of mill effluents were generally considered undesirable, economic factors often eclipsed any environmental concerns that might have arisen with the arrival of a pulp and paper mill to a town or city. The Industrial Inquiry Commission on the Pulp and Paper Industry in New Brunswick noted in the early 1970s that throughout the province's history "[pulp and paper] [m]ills have been built and encouraged by all elements in the community seeking jobs, profits and the prosperity which has traditionally been associated with this industry."

Accordingly, "[n]o thought was given to the effect upon the environment" and "[c]ommunities learned to live with the characteristic odours and rivers appeared to be inexhaustible resources."[15]

Some problems associated with pulp and paper mill effluents were reported in New Brunswick as early as the mid-1930s. In 1936, for example, fishermen in the Bathurst area complained to the Fisheries Research Board of Canada (FRB) that pollution from Bathurst Power and Paper's mill had altered fish channels in the town's harbour. Fishermen also described the occurrence of fish kills and the accumulation of "green-sludge" and wood waste in their nets, and some even claimed that "acid discharge" from the mill had prematurely degraded their nets. The FRB dispatched R.H. M'Gonigle, a fish biologist, to investigate the allegations in November 1936, and he found no evidence of harm to fish or undue damage to nets. M'Gonigle returned to Bathurst in November 1940 after additional complaints were lodged about water pollution from the mill, and he also conducted tests near the mills in Dalhousie, Atholville, and Edmundston-Madawaska after additional complaints about damage to the fisheries in those areas. M'Gonigle reported passable ranges of acidity, alkalinity, and salinity and acceptable oxygen values at all locations, but he could not complete his surveys of the effects of mill pollution on fish because of the lateness of the year.[16] A.H. Leim, another fish biologist, continued M'Gonigle's investigations in September 1941 and the summer of 1942. Leim detailed that there were high levels of algal pollution in the waters near the mills, that there was a significant "wood debris nuisance," and that "[c]onditions at Bathurst and Atholville were undoubtedly close to the danger point," but he concluded that there was "no serious situation" under existing conditions. Leim's conclusions were based on the fact that it appeared that no "fishes of particular value" were harmed by the mill effluents. Federal scientists were mostly concerned with determining whether water pollution from the mills damaged local populations of economically valuable fish.[17] As long as the regional fishing economy was not greatly affected, the federal government considered some levels of water pollution tolerable.

The New Brunswick government first moved to regulate water pollution in the mid-1950s. In March 1956, Hugh John Flemming's Progressive Conservative government (1952–60), prompted by Provincial Sanitation Engineer Cameron's recommendations and general concerns about increasing levels of water pollution in the province, created the Water Resources and Pollution Control Board (WRPCB). The nine-member board had a mandate to investigate the sources of water pollution in New Brunswick; the effects of pollution on public health, fish, wildlife, agriculture, recreation, and electric power development; and the "best present and future uses" of the province's waterways.[18] The WRPCB met on three occasions in 1956 and delivered a report to the provincial government by the end of that year. In the report, board members noted that bodies of water in New Brunswick near areas that were used for agriculture or were inhabited by people were "more or less polluted or contaminated" and that "[t]his is a matter of general knowledge and requires no proof," while the main sources of water pollution were identified as "sanitary sewage, storm water and industrial waste." The most important recommendation in the WRPCB's report was that a "water resources authority [be formed] . . . to further investigate the use and abuse of water in this Province and to recommend appropriate action to the Provincial Government."[19] The WRPCB continued to examine the question of water pollution in New Brunswick throughout 1957, and the board further recommended a program of water sample collection and testing in various parts of the province to determine the true sources of pollution and to provide an accurate reflection of the severity of the problem.[20]

In response to the WRPCB's report and studies, Flemming's administration created the New Brunswick Water Authority in April 1958. An amendment to the act that created the WRPCB authorized the provincial government to make regulations for the control and allocation of water resources and the prevention of water pollution in New Brunswick, and the Water Authority was mandated to enforce regulations and to "perform such other duties as may be assigned to it."[21] Initially located within the Department of Lands and Mines, jurisdiction over the Authority passed to the Department of Municipal Affairs in April 1959 and then reverted to the Department of Natural Resources, formerly Lands and Mines, in late 1967.[22] In addition, the provincial government appointed John S. Bates, a chemical engineer in the Canadian pulp and paper industry since the 1920s and former chairman of the New Brunswick Forest Development Commission, as the first chairman of the Water Authority. Antoine J. Lacroix, also a former member of the Forest Development Commission, was selected for the position of vice-chairman, and the third member, Edward W. Hagerman, was an associate professor of mechanical engineering at the University of New Brunswick, a former Fredericton city councillor, and an expert on issues of water resource management. Edward S. Fellows, a forester and long-time provincial government employee, was the Authority's executive secretary.[23]

The Water Authority spent much of its first three years gathering information about water pollution in New Brunswick. Bates commissioned James F. MacLaren Associates, sanitation engineering consultants with offices in Saint John and Toronto, to conduct water sample surveys of the province's main waterways and coastal areas. Interim reports by MacLaren Associates, completed in August 1958 and January 1959, confirmed quantitatively previous qualitative observations that the vast majority of pollution in the province's waters came from industrial enterprises of various sorts and municipal sewage. Industrial sources of pollution included starch plants on the St John River and mining operations in Bathurst; however, the most polluted waterways were those areas near or downriver from one of New Brunswick's seven pulp and paper mills. In the St John River, for example, pollution levels were highest downriver from the Fraser Companies integrated mill in Edmundston-Madawaska. Wastes from the mill had largely depleted oxygen levels (deadly to fish) in the section of the river from Edmundston to the Grand Falls dam, while the portion of the river from Edmundston to Perth-Andover, a distance of approximately 100 kilometres, could not be used as a source of domestic water supply without waste water treatment. In other cases, wastes from Fraser's pulp mill in Chatham earned the Miramichi River the title of "the only heavily polluted watercourse on the East Coast of the Province," and the Restigouche River and Bathurst area were so polluted by the pulp and paper mills on the province's northern coast that MacLaren Associates recommended that "bathing should not be allowed in the areas studied."[24]

In early 1961, Louis J. Robichaud's Liberal government (1960–70) increased the Water Authority's regulatory powers when it passed the New Brunswick Water Act. Based largely on information gathered by the Authority, the legislation clearly defined what was to be considered "water pollution" in New Brunswick, assigned the Authority "jurisdiction and control over the use, allocation and pollution of all surface, ground and shore waters, along with approval of alterations to the natural features of waterways," and reconstituted the WRPCB as an advisory board to the Authority. Moreover, the Water Authority was given means to enforce the province's new anti-pollution regulations. Individuals or municipalities failing to comply with any provisions in the Water Act could receive a maximum fine of $100 per day (or, in the case of individuals, a maximum of six months' imprisonment), whereas corporations could receive a penalty as high as $500 per day.[25]

The Water Authority's most significant contribution to water resource management in New Brunswick was its work to curb municipal sources of pollution. The Water Act stated that municipalities could no longer dump untreated wastes into waterways after 1961, so Authority officials worked with municipal governments to coordinate the construction of sewage works across the province throughout the 1960s. The Act also authorized the minister of the department responsible for the Water Authority to provide various forms of financial and technical aid to municipalities.[26] In terms of financial assistance, the New Brunswick government's financing program, once combined with federal incentives, could cover up to 55 per cent of the capital charges on a municipal sewage treatment facility, an amount J.G. Lockhart, a Water Authority official in the late 1960s, referred to as "the highest financial assistance [to municipalities] of any province in Canada." The Authority's efforts to curb municipal sewage were quite successful. Only one New Brunswick community (Shediac) treated its wastes in 1956, whereas 29 communities treated their sewage to some degree in 1968 and numerous others were in the process of conducting sewage engineering studies.[27] Due to concerns about pollution buildup in the head ponds of hydroelectric dams, many of these new treatment facilities were installed in municipalities along the St John River. By the 1970s, levels of coliform bacteria (fecal matter, *E. coli*) had been reduced dramatically in all reaches of the New Brunswick portion of the St John River, with reductions of up to 90 per cent from 1960s levels in many areas.[28]

The Water Authority was far less successful at regulating industrial sources of water pollution. There were three main reasons for this limited regulatory activity. The first was the decentralized nature of the organization. In the late 1950s and early 1960s, John Bates conceptualized the Authority as a "coordinating group to enlist the active and widespread cooperation of all concerned [about water pollution] throughout the province and beyond its boundaries." Instead of "centraliz[ing] its activities" or proposing to "design, construct, or operate any large projects of water supply or pollution control," the Water Authority followed a semi-interventionist approach to water resource management.[29] This allowed private industry to continue to pollute unabated for most of the 1960s.

The second reason for the limited regulation of industry was that the Authority was more concerned about the effects of pollution on inland waters than on coastal marine waters. While maintaining that marine pollution would need to be regulated in the long term, Authority officials contended that oceanic waters would dilute industrial and municipal wastes enough so as to cause limited damage to surrounding environments. In other words, they believed that marine waters had more assimilative capacity than rivers, streams, or lakes. There was supposedly "less leeway" with inland bodies of water, because they could not dilute as much pollution and were used by municipalities as sources of potable water.[30] Consequently, the Water Authority paid little regulatory attention to industrial enterprises on or very close to the coasts for much of the 1960s. For example, of the seven pulp and paper mills built in New Brunswick prior to 1960, five were located on or very near the coasts (in Atholville, Dalhousie, Bathurst, Saint John, and St George), while the other two mills, Fraser's integrated mill in Edmundston-Madawaska and kraft pulp mill in Newcastle, were located on freshwater.[31]

The final reason was that Authority officials did not want to hinder economic growth with what they considered to be overly strict regulations. Authority officials, most of whom had deep ties to the forestry sector, were particularly concerned about the possible effects of water pollution regulations on the operational costs of the pre-1960 pulp and paper mills. They believed that a distinction had to be made between regulating water pollution from "existing industries" and regulating water pollution from "future industries" or extensions of existing mills. As John Bates explained in an address in October 1958, many established industrial operations had been started when water pollution was not a serious concern and when there was not "the benefit of modern technique to choose equipment which would reprocess their effluents." It was "reasonable," in Bates's opinion, to expect new mills or factories to meet current pollution control standards, but it was difficult to expect the same of older enterprises because of "considerable capital cost."[32] After the passage of the Water Act in 1961, all mills built thereafter or in the process of being built had to incorporate pollution controls "equivalent to the best modern practice of the industry." However, it was still considered "uneconomic" in the early 1960s for the older pulp and paper mills, especially the sulphite

pulp mills, to utilize existing pollution control technologies. Due to the decentralized nature of the organization, Authority officials entered lengthy negotiations with the pulp and paper companies that had mills in New Brunswick prior to 1960 "in an attempt to find solutions to these serious pollution problems."[33]

As the Water Authority stalled on the issue of industrial pollution, the federal government became more interested in water resource management in New Brunswick. In the late 1950s and 1960s, federal involvement in provincial jurisdictions of resource management increased significantly through a series of regional economic development programs. The goal of these programs, such as the Atlantic Development Board (ADB), formed in 1962, was the economic uplift and modernization of regions across the country considered "poor."[34] In New Brunswick, the economic development project that fixed federal attention on issues of water quality was the building of hydroelectric dams on the St John River. Starting in the mid-1950s, the St John River had been at the centre of the provincial government's "power for industry" economic growth strategy. The New Brunswick Electric Power Commission (NBEPC) constructed hydroelectric dams at the mouth of a St John River tributary, the Tobique River, in 1953 and at Beechwood, a community located approximately 55 kilometres downriver from the Grand Falls dam, in 1958.[35] In March 1959, the federal and New Brunswick governments formed the Saint John River Board to explore further development of the waterway, including other potential sites for hydroelectric dams; John Bates, as chairman of the Water Authority, was one of two provincial representatives. The board's 1960 report, which was not made public until 1964, "made the economic and technical case for a large dam on the New Brunswick side of the St. John River," and it determined that the Mactaquac area above Fredericton was the best location. The report also examined the impact of a large hydroelectric dam on "other water uses" of the river, although it "tended to downplay potential negative impacts." By the early 1960s, the NBEPC and provincial government officials had expanded plans for the project from one large dam to a multi-purpose development scheme for the whole Mactaquac region, a change designed in large part to make the project eligible for federal regional economic development funds. Proponents of the Mactaquac project were eventually able to secure $20 million from the ADB for the construction of the dam.[36]

The federal government was mainly concerned about the potential effects of a hydroelectric dam in the Mactaquac area on fish populations and human health. In 1959 and 1960, Fisheries Research Board of Canada scientist John B. Sprague conducted water quality tests for the federal government along the full length of the New Brunswick portion of the St John River. Sprague determined that Fraser's pulp mill in Edmundston was easily the largest source of pollution on the river, while the various hydroelectric dams simply compounded the problem for fish. The dams' head ponds often acted as collection points for pollution, creating conditions ripe for deoxygenation, and during times of very low river flow, "water passed only through the turbines, and aeration [of oxygen with the water] was negligible." Sprague concluded that another dam in Mactaquac, "by reducing aeration during critical times of low flow, [would] lead to further degradation of water quality unless the heavy load of pollution is lessened."[37] Furthermore, the Public Health Engineering Division of the Department of National Health and Welfare conducted a six-week water quality study of the St John River in the summer of 1960, the most comprehensive study of the river up to that time. Predictably, the most polluted section of the river extended from Fraser's pulp mill in Edmundston to the Grand Falls dam, which was "practically depleted of oxygen" and had "a false river bottom" or large "sludge deposit." The authors also found "a zone of gross pollution" below each community, but it appeared that the river was "capable of assimilating sewage wastes in the volume currently contributed." They concluded that the "natural self-purification" capacity of the river had been exceeded and that increased

levels of pollutants would "result in complete degradation of long stretches of the river, to the detriment of a multiple-use principle and beneficial use by the public."[38]

The possibility of another hydroelectric dam on the St John River contributed to a growing public awareness in New Brunswick, as elsewhere, of water pollution and other environmental issues associated with economic development. This postwar growth in environmental awareness emerged from progressive era conservation and preservation ideas and coincided with the development of ecology as a distinct scientific discipline after 1950. In addition, by the 1960s, a series of environmental issues at the local, national, and international levels, from radioactive fallout to deforestation, had focused the public's attention on the negative effects of humans' interaction with the natural world.[39] The NBEPC made public its intentions to build a dam in Mactaquac, which would have an 80-kilometre-long head pond, in January 1964. Opposition to the dam soon developed. The main group opposed to the dam was the Association for the Preservation and Development of the Saint John River in Its Natural State (APDSJR), formed during the winter of 1964. Using letters to the editor, advertisements, public meetings, and petitions, the APDSJR "brought together New Brunswickers who were opposed to Mactaquac for a variety of reasons." The association's focus on the river's "natural state" extended to concerns about water pollution. In a brief to the provincial cabinet in late 1964, members of the APDSJR devoted more than one-fifth of their presentation to the potentially negative effects of accumulated pollution in the dam's head pond on human health and the river's fish populations. They cited heavily from John Sprague's study, which had been published a few months prior, to point out that Mactaquac's proposed head pond would severely reduce the river's ability to assimilate waste due to water stagnation, and the resultant decreased levels of oxygen in the river would be extremely deadly to fish.[40]

Under pressure from the federal government and the general public, the Water Authority launched a comprehensive pollution abatement

The Fraser Companies' pulp mill in Edmundston, New Brunswick, c. 1950s. The mill's location adjacent to the St John River provided Fraser with a convenient "sink" for mill effluents.

program for the upper portion of the St John River valley in 1964. The Authority spent the rest of the 1960s coordinating the construction of sewage treatment facilities in almost a dozen of the larger municipalities located along the river and negotiating pollution control agreements with industrial polluters, such as McCain's food-processing plant in Florenceville, the second largest source of industrial pollution on the river.[41] As a key component of the pollution abatement program, Water Authority officials approached the Atlantic Development Board in April 1964 for $1 million to help established industrial operations in the St John River valley offset the costs of installing pollution control technologies. After a similar brief presented by the Nova Scotia Water Authority in September 1964, the ADB created a $2-million fund "as an incentive for abatement

of industrial pollution on freshwater stretches of Atlantic rivers."[42] Members of the Authority also persuaded the NBEPC to set up a $400,000 fund to cover 20 per cent of the pollution treatment costs to industry along the St John River (up to a maximum grant of $150,000 per project), and the federal government provided businesses with "a two-year write-off period for taxation purposes on treatment works."[43] Potentially, the leading beneficiary of all this government aid was the largest industrial polluter on the river, Fraser's integrated mill in Edmundston-Madawaska.

In its attempts to regulate industrial sources of pollution, the Water Authority encountered much resistance from the pulp and paper industry, a trend best exemplified by the Authority's negotiations with Fraser as part of the St John River pollution abatement program. By late

1966, the Authority had already been in negotiations with Fraser officials for eight years to reduce the Edmundston pulp mill's BOD measurement, which had a "population equivalent" of at least 1.7 million people, by approximately 75 per cent.[44] After a meeting with Premier Robichaud in December 1966, Fraser president P.L. Hovey wrote to the premier in January 1967 to give his company's position on the St John River pollution abatement program. He asserted that Fraser was committed "to mak[ing] improvements in its effluent," but the company could not agree to "a program or time schedule that is unrealistic or beyond its financial capacity." Hovey argued that "unreasonable" pollution control measures would make it extremely difficult for Fraser to remain competitive in the global paper market. His company preferred a time schedule of ten years, or at least a minimum of three years, for the realization of its pollution control program, which Hovey estimated would cost approximately $15 million to implement. Stating that the "desired prompt upgrading of the river for fish culture and recreational use is in the public interest" and that available government aid was insufficient, Hovey took the position that the federal and provincial governments and Fraser should each pay one-third of the pollution abatement costs.[45] Continued negotiations between the Water Authority, the federal government, and Fraser resulted in a general agreement by October 1968: the Authority pledged $2.8 million in pollution abatement aid, the ADB offered $1 million, and the NBEPC confirmed a grant of $150,000.[46]

By 1970, the Water Authority had achieved few successes in its attempts to regulate water pollution emanating from pulp and paper mills. Authority officials had negotiated pollution abatement agreements with only one of the companies that had mills in New Brunswick prior to the passage of the Water Act in 1961.[47] Even these agreements with Fraser did little to reduce significantly the environmental impact of mill effluents until the early 1970s, as the company relied on an experimental chemical pulping process, known as the "Fraser process," in the second half of the 1960s.[48] Fraser had a

difficult time perfecting the effluent treatment system associated with the new process, and after several extensions to the pollution abatement agreements, the company abandoned the experimental process and installed biological treatment facilities at both the Edmundston and Newcastle mills in the first half of the 1970s. Meanwhile, of the four mills built in New Brunswick after 1961, the Water Authority had a pollution abatement agreement with only one of them by 1970. The majority of the newer mills, including those erected in Nelson, Saint John, and St George, were on or near the coast, so members of the Authority largely ignored those mills for most of the 1960s and turned their attention to the newer mill on the St John River, St Anne Pulp and Paper's kraft mill in Nackawic.[49] Owing to the mill's close proximity to the Mactaquac head pond (the dam started operating in 1968), Water Authority officials "indicated [in early 1967] that not only primary and secondary but also tertiary treatment will be required at this very critical location." However, when the mill went into operation in 1970, it did not come close to meeting any of the Water Authority's pollution control criteria, although the Authority never fined St Anne-Nackawic under the Water Act.[50]

By the end of the 1960s, the Water Authority's limited regulation of industrial sources of pollution was the source of much criticism in New Brunswick. Premier Robichaud's administration expanded and modernized the Authority's technical and administrative branches during its reorganization of government services in the late 1960s, which included the agency's transfer to the Department of Natural Resources in 1967; but these reforms were not enough to appease the Water Authority's critics.[51] It was within this context of dissatisfaction and frustration that Fred McCain told the New Brunswick Legislative Assembly in 1968 that the water of the St John River was "as thick as molasses." Members of the Progressive Conservative opposition demanded to know why so little had been done to clean up pollution in the province's waterways, even though a large amount of taxpayers' money had been devoted to such schemes as the

St John River pollution abatement program.[52] In addition, in the summer of 1969, the lead story of the first issue of the *Mysterious East*, an alternative news magazine published in Fredericton, was an exposé on the problem of water pollution in Canada, with a particular focus on the situation in New Brunswick. Part of the article presented an analysis of the Water Act, listed the various major polluters in the province, and then asked the question, "Why haven't the polluting industries been prosecuted under the Water Act?" The most likely answer, according to the article's author, was that "the provincial government values the friendship of industry over the concerns of conservation."[53] Furthermore, John Sprague, the FRB scientist, was one of the founding directors of the province's first environmental organization, the Conservation Council of New Brunswick, officially founded in October 1969.[54] As co-chairman of the council's "water committee," Sprague teamed up with the Saint John *Telegraph Journal*, the province's largest newspaper, in May 1970 to publish a series of four high-profile reports on water pollution in New Brunswick. The newspaper's editor explained that "this series of articles is to tell the people of the province what they must know." The first article, titled "Water Act Has Teeth—Why Isn't It Used?," questioned the limited regulatory action in New Brunswick and urged the Water Authority to use the Water Act to end the problem of water pollution. It also pointed to the fact that "industry contributes 66 times more pollution than the 50,000 people in the upper St John River valley." The subsequent articles examined the case of the St John River ("The Noble River: Long Sections Are Dirty, Smelly, Virtually Fishless"), the various sources of industrial pollution in the province, including all of the pulp and paper mills, and the larger ecological impacts of water pollution.[55]

Faced with mounting scepticism about the effectiveness of the Water Authority, the New Brunswick government made significant reforms to the province's water pollution regulatory process in the first half of the 1970s. A prime motivator for these changes, besides general frustration with the Authority, was the federal government's increasing interest in the issue of water quality. In the summer of 1970, the federal government passed the Canada Water Act, which provided for a federal role in the general management of the country's inland waterways. One of the act's four parts authorized the federal government to negotiate agreements with individual provinces for the establishment of cooperative studies of the comprehensive water resource management of a given area. The federal and New Brunswick governments subsequently created the Saint John River Basin Board in June 1970. The board conducted a series of studies in the early 1970s on the long-term management of the St John River, and it presented its final report in April 1975.[56] Heightened federal involvement in the issue of water pollution regulation, combined with pressure from the Official Opposition and the public, prompted Minister of Natural Resources William R. Duffie to give notice to all of the pulp and paper companies in the province in early 1970 that they had to install primary treatment systems by the end of 1971. Duffie also informed the companies that secondary treatment had to be installed at "certain mills at least as soon as they are enlarged or the pulping process changed."[57] This direct edict at long last compelled the province's pulp and paper companies to begin to reduce the amounts of pollution emanating from their mills. Most of the companies had installed or were in the process of installing effluent treatment systems by the mid-1970s.[58] Additionally, following their electoral victory in New Brunswick in October 1970, Richard Hatfield's Progressive Conservatives, highly critical of the Water Authority while in opposition during the 1960s, moved the Authority from the Department of Natural Resources to a newly created environmental division in the Department of Fisheries in early 1971, and most of its regulatory powers were reassigned to various division branches. In 1975, the New Brunswick government created a separate Department of the Environment, which focused primarily on issues of water resource management for the remainder of the 1970s. At that point, the Water Authority was phased out of existence.[59]

The New Brunswick Water Authority had a mixed legacy. Its creation in the late 1950s reflected both changing public values and the triumph of a technocratic approach to resource management in Canada. In the case of municipal sewage, the approach was quite successful. The Water Authority negotiated the installation of sewage treatment systems throughout the province in the 1960s, reducing coliform bacteria in parts of the St John River by up to 90 per cent. Authority officials were far less successful at regulating industrial sources of pollution. Technocratic resource management, with its focus on "objective" science and technology, ran headlong into the political realities of pulp and paper in New Brunswick. In a small province with few industries, the pulp and paper industry had a lot of political influence, and Water Authority officials, many of whom had deep ties to the forestry sector, particularly during the organization's earliest years, bowed to this influence for much the 1960s. As a result, the Water Authority did not meet the regulatory needs of the province's residents, having failed to objectively regulate pollution emanating from pulp and paper mills. Hydroelectric development on the St John River had focused federal and public attention on the issue of water quality by the mid-1960s, which put pressure on the Authority to do more about industrial pollution. But the damage was done. Cynicism about the effectiveness of the Authority peaked by 1970, prompting the New Brunswick government to phase it out of existence over the next several years. Once the Water Authority's regulatory powers had been reassigned to a centralized Department of the Environment in 1975, the problem of water pollution was dealt with much more effectively. The water quality of the St John River, for example, improved markedly after the late 1970s.[60] While still not perfect, the regulatory process surrounding water pollution in New Brunswick at least moved faster than a boat through a river of molasses after 1975.

Author's Note: The author would like to thank everyone at the Network in Canadian History and Environment's EH+ writing workshop at McMaster University (29 April 2011) for their helpful comments, Jason Hall and Bill Parenteau for their edits, and the Social Sciences and Humanities Research Council of Canada, which supported this research through a Canada Graduate Scholarship. Finally, a big thank you to Catherine Briggs for all her work as editor.

Endnotes

1   New Brunswick, *Synoptic Report* (Fredericton, 1968), 577.

2   New Brunswick, *Annual Report of the Department of Lands and Mines* (Fredericton, 1958), 9.

3   Canada, *A Consolidation of the Constitution Acts, 1867 to 1982* (Ottawa: Department of Justice, 1998), 26–32; and Matthew D. Evenden, *Fish versus Power: An Environmental History of the Fraser River* (Cambridge, UK: Cambridge University Press, 2004), 8–9.

4   Arn M. Keeling, "Charting Marine Pollution Science: Oceanography on Canada's Pacific Coast, 1938–1970," *Journal of Historical Geography* 33, no. 2 (2007): 408–18.

5   Gilbert Allardyce, "'The Vexed Question of Sawdust': River Pollution in Nineteenth-Century New Brunswick," in Chad Gaffield and Pam Gaffield, eds, *Consuming Canada: Readings in Environmental History* (Toronto: Copp Clark, 1995), 119–30; and R. Peter Gillis, "Rivers of Sawdust: The Battle over Industrial Pollution in Canada, 1865–1903," *Journal of Canadian Studies* 21, no. 1 (1986): 84–103.

6   Margaret Conrad and Alvin Finkel, *Canada: A National History*, 2nd edn (Toronto: Pearson Longman, 2007); Sean Kennedy, *The Shock of War: Civilian Experiences, 1937–1945* (Toronto: University of Toronto Press, 2011); and Peter S. McInnis, *Harnessing Labour Confrontation: Shaping the Postwar Settlement in Canada, 1943–1950* (Toronto: University of Toronto Press, 2002).

7   Graeme Wynn, "Foreword: This Is More Difficult Than We Thought," in Dean Bavington, *Managed Annihilation: An Unnatural History of the Newfoundland Cod Collapse* (Vancouver: UBC Press, 2010), xi–xxiii.

8   Jamie Benidickson, *The Culture of Flushing: A Social and Legal History of Sewage* (Vancouver: UBC Press, 2007); Keeling, "Urban Waste Sinks as a Natural

Resource: The Case of the Fraser River," *Urban History Review* 34, no. 1 (2005): 58–70; and Joel A. Tarr, *The Search for the Ultimate Sink: Urban Pollution in Historical Perspective* (Akron, OH: University of Akron Press, 1996).

9   New Brunswick, *Annual Report of the Department of Health* (Fredericton, 1946), 10; and *Annual Report of DH* (Fredericton, 1947), 12.

10 New Brunswick, *Annual Report of DH* (Fredericton, 1948), 54.

11 Alwyn J. Cameron, "Opportunities for a Program of Stream Sanitation in New Brunswick," *Canadian Journal of Public Health* 72, no. 4 (1950): 164–6.

12 Cameron to Chief Medical Officer, 17 February 1953, Records of the Office of Hugh John Flemming (Flemming Papers), RS 415, file E2f4, Provincial Archives of New Brunswick (PANB).

13 Bill Parenteau, "The Woods Transformed: The Emergence of the Pulp and Paper Industry in New Brunswick, 1918–1931," *Acadiensis* 22, no. 1 (1992): 5–43; and New Brunswick, *Annual Report of DLM* (Fredericton: 1949), 13–14.

14 Christopher J. Biermann, *Essentials of Pulping and Papermaking* (San Diego: Academic Press, 1993), 32–40.

15 Industrial Inquiry Commission on the Pulp and Paper Industry in New Brunswick, *Final Report of the Industrial Inquiry Commission on the Pulp and Paper Industry in New Brunswick* (Fredericton: Government of New Brunswick, 1972), I38–9.

16 R.H. M'Gonigle, *Report of an Investigation of Alleged Pollution from Certain Pulp Mills in Northern New Brunswick* (St Andrews: Fisheries Research Board of Canada, 1940).

17 A.H. Leim, *Report of Investigation of Pollution from Pulp Mills in Northern New Brunswick, September 1941* (St Andrews: Fisheries Research Board of Canada, 1952) and *Report on Pulp Mill Pollution Investigations in the Bay of Chaleur in 1942* (St Andrews: Fisheries Research Board of Canada, 1952).

18 New Brunswick, *New Brunswick Acts* (Fredericton, 1956), 46–7.

19 Water Resources and Pollution Control Board, *The Report of the Water Resources and Pollution Control Board* (1956); Records of the Deputy Minister of Natural Resources (DMNR), RS 106, file 34/1, PANB; and John S. Bates, "The New Brunswick Water Authority," presentation to the American Water Works Association, Canadian Section, Maritime Branch, Fredericton, NB, 2 October 1958, Flemming Papers, RS 415, file F2d1, PANB.

20 Hugh John Flemming to Bates, 20 September 1957, including attached memo from Bates to Flemming, DMNR, RS 106, file F2d1, PANB.

21 New Brunswick, *New Brunswick Acts* (Fredericton, 1958), 66–7.

22 New Brunswick, *Annual Report of DLM* (Fredericton, 1959), 127; *Annual Report of the Department of Municipal Affairs* (Fredericton, 1960), 22; and *Annual Report of the Department of Natural Resources* (Fredericton, 1968), 6–7, 134.

23 New Brunswick, *Annual Report of DLM* (Fredericton, 1959), 127; and Bates, *By the Way, 1888–1983* (Hantsport, NS: Lancelot Press, 1983), 77.

24 MacLaren Associates, *An Interim Report to the New Brunswick Water Authority on Preliminary Survey of Pollution in the Saint John River's Watershed* (1958) and *An Interim Report to the New Brunswick Water Authority on Preliminary Survey of Pollution in the North Shore and East Coast Areas of New Brunswick* (1959), Flemming Papers, RS 415, file F2d2, PANB.

25 New Brunswick, *Annual Report of DMA* (Fredericton, 1964), 40; and *New Brunswick Acts* (Fredericton, 1960–1), 98–104.

26 New Brunswick, *New Brunswick Acts* (Fredericton, 1960–1), 100.

27 J.G. Lockhart, untitled presentation to the Woodstock Rotary Club, 20 November 1967, 5–8; and J.G. Lockhart, *Water Pollution Control in the Province of New Brunswick* (1968), DMNR, RS 106, file 34/7, PANB; and R.C. Ballance, *Report on Condition of Sewage Treatment Facilities in New Brunswick* (Fredericton: New Brunswick Water Authority, 1963).

28 Scott D. Kidd, R. Allen Curry, and Kelly R. Munkittrick, eds, *The Saint John River: A State of the Environment Report* (Fredericton: Canadian Rivers Institute, 2011), 87– 8.

29 Bates, "The New Brunswick Water Authority," 2–3.

30 Bates, *Water Supply and Pollution in New Brunswick and the Other Atlantic Provinces* (1960), 2–5, Flemming Papers, RS 415, file F2d2, PANB; and New Brunswick, *Annual Report of DMA* (Fredericton: 1962), 27.

31 Industrial Inquiry Commission, Final Report of the Industrial Inquiry Commission, III4–16.

32 Bates, "The New Brunswick Water Authority."

33 New Brunswick, *Annual Report of DMA* (Fredericton, 1963), 30–1; and *Annual Report of DMA* (Fredericton, 1964), 36–7.

34 James Bickerton, *Nova Scotia, Ottawa, and the Politics of Regional Development* (Toronto: University of Toronto Press, 1990); and Donald J. Savoie, *Visiting Grandchildren: Economic Development in the Maritimes* (Toronto: University of Toronto Press, 2006).

35 James L. Kenny and Andrew Secord, "Public Power for Industry: A Re-examination of the New Brunswick Case, 1940–1960," *Acadiensis* 30, no. 2 (2001): 84–108.

36 James L. Kenny and Andrew Secord, "Engineering Modernity: Hydroelectric Development in New Brunswick, 1945–1970," *Acadiensis* 39, no. 1 (2010): 3–26.

37 J.B. Sprague, *Chemical Surveys of the Saint John River, Tributaries, Impoundments, and Estuary in*

1959 and 1960 (St Andrews: Fisheries Research Board of Canada, 1964).

38   Canada, *Survey Report, Effects of Pollution, Saint John River, New Brunswick and Maine, 1960* (Ottawa: Department of National Health and Welfare, Public Health Engineering Division, 1960).

39   Mark J. McLaughlin, "Green Shoots: Aerial Insecticide Spraying and the Growth of Environmental Consciousness in New Brunswick, 1952–1973," *Acadiensis* 40, no. 1 (2011): 3–23; and Donald Worster, *Nature's Economy: A History of Ecological Ideas*, 2nd edn (Cambridge: Cambridge University Press, 1994), 342–87.

40   Kenny and Secord, "Engineering Modernity," 13, 18–20; and the Association for the Preservation and Development of the St John River in Its Natural State, *Brief Presented to Premier Louis J. Robichaud and Members of the Cabinet* (1964), Records of the Office of Premier Louis J. Robichaud (Robichaud Papers), RS 416, 1964, file 227, PANB.

41   Lockhart, untitled presentation, 10–11; and New Brunswick, *Annual Report of DNR* (Fredericton, 1968), 138.

42   Nova Scotia Water Authority, *Brief to the Atlantic Development Board Requesting Financial Assistance for the Abatement of Pollution on Rivers of the Atlantic Provinces* (1964), Robichaud Papers, RS 416, 1964, file 101, PANB; and New Brunswick, *Annual Report of DMA* (Fredericton, 1966), 25.

43   Lockhart, Water Pollution Control, 11.

44   Bates to Louis J. Robichaud, 22 July 1966, Robichaud Papers, RS 416, 1967, file 173, PANB.

45   P.L. Hovey to Robichaud, 14 January 1967, Robichaud Papers, RS 416, 1966, file 151, PANB.

46   New Brunswick, *Annual Report of dnr* (Fredericton, 1969), 123; and William Duffie to Jack Davis, 21 June 1968, Davis to Duffie, 20 December 1968, and Duffie to Davis, 11 March 1969, DMNR, RS 106, file 224g3, PANB.

47   New Brunswick, *Annual Report of DNR* (Fredericton, 1970), 84.

48   New Brunswick, *Annual Report of DMA* (Fredericton, 1964), 36–7; and Lockhart, untitled presentation.

49   New Brunswick, *Annual Report of DNR* (Fredericton, 1970), 84; and Industrial Inquiry Commission, *Final Report of the Industrial Inquiry Commission*, III4–16

50   Minutes of a Joint Meeting of the New Brunswick Water Authority and Its Advisory Board, 25 April 1967, p. 5, DMNR, RS 106, file 34/8, PANB; and Industrial Inquiry Commission, *Final Report of the Industrial Inquiry Commission*, III14–15 and VII18.

51   New Brunswick, *Annual Report of dnr* (Fredericton, 1968), 5–7, 130–6; and Della M.M. Stanley, *Louis Robichaud: A Decade of Power* (Halifax: Nimbus Publishing, 1984).

52   New Brunswick, *Synoptic Report* (Fredericton, 1968), 574–8.

53   *Mysterious East* (Fredericton), Summer 1964.

54   Audio recording of the CCNB founding meeting, 18 October 1969, Fredericton, NB, recording in the CCNB's possession, Conserver House, Fredericton, NB; and McLaughlin, "Green Shoots."

55   *Telegraph Journal* (Saint John), 20–3 May 1970.

56   Canada–New Brunswick Saint John River Basin Board, *The Final Report of the Saint John River Basin Board* (Fredericton, 1975), 1–6; and Canada, *The Canada Water Act Annual Report* (Ottawa, 1973–4), 1–11.

57   New Brunswick, *Annual Report of DNR* (Fredericton, 1970), 84.

58   New Brunswick, *Annual Report of the Department of Fisheries and Environment* (Fredericton, 1972), 42; *Annual Report of DFE* (Fredericton, 1973), 57; *Annual Report of DFE* (Fredericton, 1974), 53–5; and *Annual Report of the Department of the Environment* (Fredericton, 1975), 9–10.

59   New Brunswick, *Annual Report of DFE* (Fredericton, 1972), 46–7; *Annual Report of DE* (Fredericton, 1975); and McLaughlin, "Green Shoots."

60   Kidd, Curry, and Munkittrick, *The Saint John River*, 77–93.

◎ 13.2: Disturbing the Peace: Environmental Change and the Scales of Justice on a Northern River

Tina Loo

In law, "disturbing the peace" is an offence against the public order provided by the state. But the phrase evokes much more than its black letter definition. It resonates with the raucous sounds of urban revelry: shouting, pounding feet, sirens, and slamming doors.

Although the Peace of this essay is a river in northern British Columbia, disturbing it also disrupted an established order, albeit a human ecological one.[1] That disruption was also a matter of the senses. In 1968, the provincial government dammed the Peace to generate hydroelectricity, setting into motion a series of environmental and social changes (see Map 13.1). While scientists gauged this transformation in terms of cubic metres per second of water flow, percentages of vegetation change, and parts per million of sediment, the peoples of the Peace experienced it much more directly, seeing, hearing, smelling, feeling, and tasting the changes in the land. Important itself, understanding the sensual dimensions of change is the key to understanding the differing scales at which environmental transformation was apprehended. More broadly, it is the key to understanding the dynamics of environmental politics and the possibilities for environmental justice.

The current global debate over climate change has now made the connections between environment and politics apparent to us all, but scholars have been exploring them for some time. In the last 20 years, researchers, mainly in the United States, have charted the environmental effects of urbanization and industrialization, and in the process argued that the risks associated with these changes were borne unequally.[2]

Poor people tend to live in poor environments. Why? Because they lack access to political power and hence are not in the position to influence decision-making about the location of dumps, for instance, or sewage outflows.[3] Terms such as "environmental racism" and "environmental inequality" are used to describe and explain why people on the social, economic, and political margins by virtue of race, class, and gender live in marginal environments.[4] The social is the spatial.

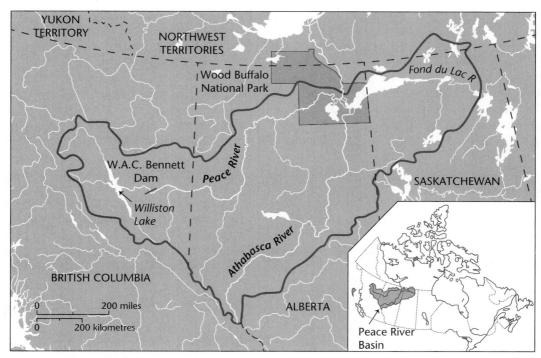

Map 13.1 The Peace River Basin

Map by Eric Leinberger

A new kind of politics arose from the toxic landscapes of American cities. The "environmental justice movement" emerged in the 1980s and was aimed at calling attention to and rectifying the unequal distribution of environmental risks "where we live, work and play," both in the United States and around the world.[5] In so doing, the movement challenged the traditional focus of North American environmentalism, pushing it beyond what to some was its elitist, white, and middle-class preoccupations with resource conservation and wilderness preservation.[6]

Proponents of environmental justice argue that solutions to environmental problems have to address underlying social, economic, and political inequities (and vice versa).[7] Eradicating poverty and pollution had to go hand in hand. Drawing on the rhetoric and strategies of the US Civil Rights movement, environmental justice activists have worked for distributive and procedural justice, often framing their claims as human rights—the right to clean air and water, to living in an environment free of toxins.[8] Rights and rights discourse have become powerful tools in the global pursuit of environmental and social equity.

Many of the principles of environmental justice were enshrined in the Rio Declaration issued by the United Nations Conference on Environment and Development in 1992. Among other things, Rio asserted that environmental protection was an "integral part of the development process" and that "the eradication of poverty . . . [was] an indispensable requirement for sustainable development."[9] Two years later, in 1994, the Clinton administration took steps to implement the principles of environmental justice. It issued an executive order requiring every US federal agency "to make achieving environmental justice part of its mission."[10] In its wake, several American states and some cities have passed similar legislation.[11]

In Canada, the best-known examples of environmental inequality involve Aboriginal peoples. For instance, the mercury poisoning at Grassy Narrows in Ontario in the 1960s and 1970s and the water problems that currently afflict many Aboriginal reserves across the country have commanded national attention.[12] Despite this, however, environmental justice has not become "institutionalized" in Canadian government policy as it has in the United States.[13]

While researchers in both Canada and the United States have been good at identifying instances of inequality and explaining their causes, they have not been as effective in using such episodes to understand what, conceptually, is involved in rectifying environmental and social inequalities. That is what this story of the Peace River aims to do.

Initially, the literature on environmental justice focused on identifying examples of the unequal distribution of environmental harms and explaining them. Scholars and activists argued about whether such inequalities were the result of intentional discrimination and whether that discrimination was a manifestation of racism or of class divisions. Subsequent work complicated the picture, embracing more sophisticated analyses of race and class that focused less on describing unequal outcomes and more on the complex process of creating environmental inequality.[14]

At the same time, another group of researchers began questioning the extent and nature of the problem. Was environmental injustice really a national or a regional problem? Was it really the product of racism or poverty? Or was the siting of environmental hazards simply the outcome of a series of rational economic choices on the part of those involved?[15]

Apart from the particular empirical results, this second body of work raised important general questions about the correct scale at which to measure environmental injustice. Should it be the city, neighbourhood, census tract, or zip code? This is a complicated methodological and technical question, and one with political significance. Depending on the scale of analysis, injustice can appear and disappear; its nature can change, and with it the possible and appropriate remedies.

As these scholars searched for the proper scales at which to measure environmental injustice, others, mainly in political geography, asked whether the scales that were the subject of debate really existed. Working from the insights provided by research in the social construction of space, they problematized the concept of scale itself.[16] In their view, scales are not given but are constituted by capitalism and serve its ends.[17] Moreover, the socially constructed nature of scale is most visible in the struggle between capital and labour.

Different groups of people have different interests in framing problems—that is, in determining the scale at which a particular issue is perceived and dealt with. How is it, scholars ask, that certain events come to be labelled as being of "global" significance while others are deemed "national" or "regional" or "local"?[18]

To be successful, social movements must frame issues in ways that can mobilize sympathies and, more importantly, resources at a variety of scales, from the ground up. For instance, by characterizing the location of hazardous waste sites in neighbourhoods that were predominantly African American as "environmental racism," grassroots activists were able to avail themselves of the powerful rhetoric and strategies of civil rights in seeking redress.[19] This kind of "scale jumping" is what transforms "their problem" into "our problem"— and gets results.[20]

Rather than examining how inequalities were created or how people mobilized against them, I explore what was entailed in rectifying environmental and social inequalities, in actually doing justice to a river and its peoples. The impact of damming the Peace River is important for what it reveals of the different ways in which people envisaged and experienced environmental transformation. On the Peace, the two were related: doing environmental justice was very much a matter of grappling with the different scales at which environmental change was thought about, lived, and addressed. Solutions framed at one scale could not resolve the problems experienced at another.

This argument builds on the literature dealing with the social construction of scale, but takes it in two different directions. First, it emphasizes the importance of time in defining the scales of inequality. Because geographers

have written many of the most stimulating and important analyses of scale, it is perhaps not surprising that scale is defined largely in spatial terms. But what happened on the Peace River reveals that different temporal, as well as spatial, framings animated the struggle for environmental justice. Second, without disputing the power of capitalism to constitute scale, in the context of the Peace River, other influences were more apparent. Ideology, science and technology, and the experience of living with the river constructed the scales at which the environment, environmental change, and inequality were perceived.

Visions

For much of the twentieth century, and particularly after the Second World War, high modernism was influential in constituting a particular view of nature.[21] In Canada, nowhere is this more apparent than in British Columbia. Long before most historians were thinking about the relationship between environment and politics, British Columbia premier W.A.C. Bennett was establishing a political career based on a particular vision of the environment and environmental transformation. Some time after he was elected in 1952, Bennett went on a tour of northern British Columbia. He asked his driver to pull over at a highway viewpoint where he could look out over the Peace River valley. Seeing him, a passing trapper asked, "Mister, what are you staring at?" Bennett apparently pointed down at the valley and answered with a question of his own: "Look down there. What do you see?"

"I see a small, winding, muddy river."

"Well, my friend," said the premier, "I see dams. And I see power. And I see development. I see roads, highways, bridges, and growing communities. I see cities—prosperous cities with schools, hospitals, and universities. I see beautiful homes with housewives baking bread."[22]

Bennett, like Canadian prime minister John Diefenbaker, had his own "northern vision."[23] In it, British Columbia would become a prosperous modern industrial society by exploiting its natural resources. Hydroelectricity would transform the province, shifting power away from the southern coast to the central interior. In the overblown rhetoric of the time, each of the communities in the Prince George area was a "potential Pittsburgh," part of a "new Canadian Ruhr."[24] Like Canadian premiers who would follow him, Bennett also believed that his province's energy resources would give it political leverage in its dealings with Ottawa, shifting the balance of power in Confederation. In short, for Bennett the Peace was a river of destiny.

To realize that destiny, Bennett's government formed a partnership with private enterprise, with a man whose ambitions were equal to the scale of the premier's vision. That man was Axel Wenner-Gren, the Swedish vacuum cleaner salesman who had gone on to head Electrolux and consort with persons rich, famous, and, occasionally, fascistic. While his alleged Nazi associations were enough to get him blacklisted by the governments of Great Britain, the United States, and Canada, they did not prevent others from dealing with him.[25] In 1956, the Bennett government granted Wenner-Gren resource rights to one-tenth of the province. Approximately 130,000 square kilometres in size, "Swedish Columbia," as it was dubbed by its detractors, was an area equivalent to the British Isles. In return for this fiefdom, Wenner-Gren agreed to complete surveys of the area and come up with a comprehensive plan for developing its hydroelectric, forestry, and mineral resources by 1959.[26]

The possibilities of a nature transformed by expertise were seductive enough to transcend political ideologies. When the Wenner-Gren group faltered, Bennett's Social Credit government—believers in a small state—nationalized electricity generation, creating the British Columbia Hydro and Power Authority (BC Hydro) in 1961 to complete the Peace project. The enthusiasm for big dams and for megaprojects in general was not limited to Canadian politicians and bureaucrats, but was broadly shared globally and locally. Around the world, regimes across the political spectrum engaged in dam-building, often with the support

and enthusiasm of ordinary people. In 1965 alone, 50,000 people flocked to Portage Mountain, where the Bennett Dam, as it was dubbed, was being built. In all, Hydro welcomed over 500,000 visitors during the course of construction, from 1961 to 1968.[27] This was a time when environments undergoing transformation were celebrated—a particular moment in the environmental history of North America conveyed by an aesthetic that American historian David Nye has labelled the "technological sublime."[28] These landscapes also were distinguished by a particular scale.

When Axel Wenner-Gren and W.A.C. Bennett looked at British Columbia's "environment" they saw it schematically: their bird's-eye view flattened and simplified it. Rivers were reduced to elevations and megawatt-hours, highlighting the connections among them and the relationship between their development and that of other resources.[29] A river like the Peace was part of a system—not an ecosystem, but a nervous system, one belonging to an industrial giant just waiting to be jolted into action with the help of experts. It was left to the engineers to execute the grand plan for development; they were the midwives of a high modernist vision that rendered British Columbia's environment a space of flows—flows of energy, capital, and power—that respected few boundaries but at the same time enhanced the province's clout.

Effects

Perhaps the most surprising thing about the Peace project and the W.A.C. Bennett Dam was the extent to which the vision was realized. While Wenner-Gren's plans for "heated polar cities" and a monorail connecting British Columbia to the Yukon fell by the wayside, power from the Peace did shift the economic geography of the province from the coast to the central interior. In 1964, the prospect of available power led BC Forest Products to announce it would spend $60 million building a "forestry complex" in the region. The result was the "instant town" of Mackenzie, where a number of pulp mills and sawmills, as well as various logging operations,

The Canadian Press/Jonathan Hayward

Named after former BC premier Bill Bennett, the W.A.C. Bennett Dam, 19 April 2010.

were centred, providing employment for thousands, both directly and indirectly.[30] . . .

Of course, damming the Peace was not without environmental and social costs. In the immediate vicinity of the dam and reservoir, the problems were caused by too much water. The Bennett Dam turned parts of three rivers—the Finlay, Parsnip, and the Peace—into a huge lake: the Williston Reservoir runs 250 kilometres north-south and another 150 kilometres east-west (see Map 13.2). Its creation destroyed habitat, changed the immediate climate of the area, and compromised biodiversity. In addition to flooding 350,000 acres of forested land and drowning countless animals, the reservoir blocked the east-west migration of the now endangered mountain caribou across the Rocky Mountain Trench.[31]

The same waters that prevented the mountain caribou from migrating also forced some of the human residents of the trench to move. Some 40 or 50 members of the Tsay Keh Dene

First Nation, Sekani peoples then known as the Ingenika, were relocated to new reserves when it became clear that their settlements and traplines near Fort Grahame and Finlay Forks would be inundated by the reservoir's waters.[32] The Ingenika were not the only human residents of the trench who lost their lands, however. In all, approximately 100 non-Aboriginal people and some 14,000 acres of land as well as mineral and timber rights were also at risk. The $1.7 million the BC Hydro paid to acquire all the properties and associated rights facilitated the construction of the dam, but did little to settle the issue.[33]

Those who were able to stay where they lived experienced a change in the weather. While it is widely accepted that large bodies of standing water like reservoirs have general climatic effects, the exact nature and extent of those effects for Williston Lake are largely unknown. But for those who lived in the area, they were clear. The most common complaint was how

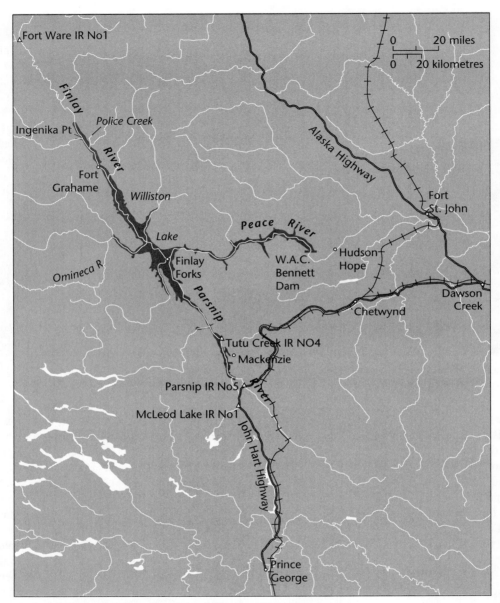

Map 13.2 Extent of Flooding Caused by the Bennett Dam

Adapted by Eric Leinberger from Peace River Power Development Company, Limited, and BC and BB Power Consultants, Limited, *Peace River Hydro-Electric Project*, vol. 1 (Vancouver: BC and BB Power Consultants, Limited, 1959); and Brian G. Blackman, *Fisheries Resources of the Williston Reservoir Twenty Years after the Impoundment* (Prince George: BC Hydro and Peace-Williston Fish and Wildlife Compensation Program, 2001).

much windier it seemed.[34] That was bad enough, but for Jed Woolley the change in climate also compromised his ability to make a living. He demanded that BC Hydro compensate the area's farmers for the increased cold and humidity that prevented their grain, legumes, and seeds from drying properly.[35] Ed Summers, who ran cattle on the Tompkins farm, experienced the humidity in the form of a heavy fog that rolled over his land in the fall.[36] While some dam supporters dismissed Woolley's and Summers's claims, there is scientific evidence to back their anecdotal observations, which suggested that temperatures fell and humidity increased in the area surrounding the reservoir.[37]

If change was in the air, it was also in the waters of Williston Lake. The lacustrine environment of the reservoir supported different kinds and numbers of fish than had the riverine habitat it replaced.[38] Arctic grayling, mountain whitefish, and rainbow trout populations declined, while other species thrived, among them lake whitefish (which came to comprise half the fish population in the reservoir), dolly varden, kokanee, lake trout, ling, and peamouth chub.[39] Writing in 1989, BC Hydro vice-president C.W.J. Boatman lauded the changes, noting that "[i]n total numbers . . . there are likely more fish in the basin today than prior to reservoir formation . . . due to a major increase in aquatic habitat."[40]

Despite their increased numbers, the fish population was not entirely healthy. By the time Boatman wrote, bull trout in the reservoir possessed levels of mercury that exceeded Health Canada guidelines, and by 2000 levels were high enough for British Columbia to issue a Fish Consumption Advisory for bull trout and dolly varden.[41] Released as a result of the decomposition of the trees and vegetable matter on the reservoir floor, mercury enters the food chain when it is absorbed by small organisms like plankton and algae and becomes concentrated in the tissues of larger ones. Because bull trout are at the top of the lake's food chain, the bioaccumulation of mercury in their tissue is highest.[42]

The Peace River flows from west to east, and then north, emptying into the Arctic Ocean. Downstream, in Alberta and the Northwest Territories, the environmental and social problems caused by the dam were due to a lack of water. When the river was dammed and the reservoir began to fill (1968–71), the impact on the area known as the Peace-Athabasca Delta became the focus of immediate attention, largely because of its ecological significance (see Map 13.3). Designated by the Ramsar Convention as a wetland of international

importance, and part of Wood Buffalo National Park, the Peace-Athabasca Delta is one of the most biodiverse northern environments in Canada, home to more than 530 species of vegetation and vertebrates.[43] It is also a crucial staging ground for migratory birds from all four of North America's flyways. Approximately 400,000 birds use the delta on their way to the Mackenzie River lowlands and the Arctic in the spring, while more than 1 million stop there in fall during their migration south. In addition, the delta's undisturbed grass and sedge meadows are among the largest in the world and provide range for one of the largest free-roaming herds of bison.[44]

After the Bennett Dam was completed, water flows on the Peace decreased 15 to 70 per cent, depending where on the river measurements were taken.[45] Reduced flow meant that the river's channels were not scoured to the same extent: water quality was compromised, as sediments and toxins were left to accumulate rather than being flushed out. As well, water levels in the delta's lakes and "perched basins" (elevated bodies of water replenished by periodic flooding) fell, and over time some disappeared all together.[46] The rejuvenating floods that had come every two or three years stopped. Since the mid-1970s there has only been one.[47] The delta was drying out. By the time the Williston reservoir was full in 1971, the water cover had been reduced by 38 per cent, and by 1989, wetlands and wet marshes had declined by 47 per cent.[48] As lake and basin levels fell, willows and sedge colonized the areas of the delta left exposed by the receding water.

These changes in water level and vegetation had further effects on fish and wildlife. There were fewer channels for walleye to reach their spawning grounds and for juvenile fish to reach important nursery areas. If they got there, there was often less food available for them, further compromising their survival.[49] In terms of wildlife, the delta's muskrat, migratory bird, and moose populations were threatened by the loss of wetland habitat. By 1996, for instance, muskrat had declined 89 to 95 per cent from their pre-dam levels, a loss that had a severe impact on the Aboriginal peoples who relied on them.[50] . . .

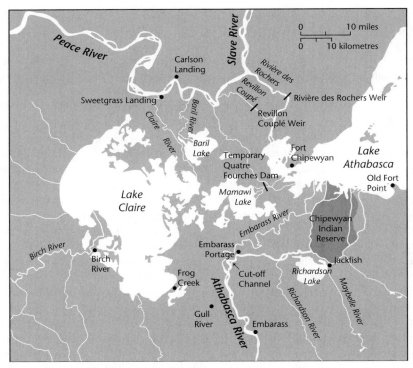

Map 13.3 The Peace-Athabasca Delta

Adapted by Eric Leinberger from Stuart Adams and Associates, *Fort Chipewyan Way of Life Study: An Assessment of Impacts of the W.A.C. Bennett Dam on the People of Fort Chipewyan and the Peace-Athabasca Delta and Suggestions for Action* (Vancouver: Stuart Adams and Associates, 1998).

In making sense of the environmental changes that occurred in the wake of the Bennett Dam, scientists saw the river as a system, as Axel Wenner-Gren and the premier did—but an ecosystem, not a hydraulic one, made of related parts. Hydrology, ecology, and technology shaped the scales at which scientists assessed the river. The aerial photography and LANDSAT images that allowed them to assess changes in vegetation cover in the Peace-Athabasca Delta meant that they literally had a bird's-eye view. However, unlike that of Wenner-Gren and Bennett, the scope of the scientists' vision was augmented by its high resolution: in addition to being able to see the delta as a whole and track changes in its appearance, for instance, they were also able to discern shifts in sediment or toxins at the level of parts per million and changes in the river flows in cubic metres per second—that is, at

micro-scales that were beyond humans' ability to discern unassisted by technology.

Experiences

Enumerating the effects of damming the Peace—the changes in habitat, climate, and biodiversity—conveys the nature and extent of environmental transformation, but it does not capture how people experienced it, how they apprehended these changes, and what they meant. It was the meaning of change and the human scale at which it was experienced that was fundamental to understanding the possibilities and challenges of practising environmental justice.

For the thousands of people employed in the pulp and paper industry, environmental change meant jobs—economic opportunity. For millions of industrial and residential consumers, it meant cheap electricity. And by virtue of the favourable terms of the Columbia River Treaty made possible by the Peace development, it meant revenue for the provincial treasury from the sale of downstream benefits to the United States ($254.4 million in cash). But for a minority of people, many of whom were Aboriginal, environmental change meant dependence, isolation, alienation, and illness. When the peoples of the Peace lost their farms and traplines, they lost more than the land that fed them; they lost their autonomy.

The holdings around Hudson's Hope and in the vicinity of the Williston reservoir were sufficiently productive to provide sustenance for many families, both Aboriginal and white. Elizabeth Beattie and her husband had come to Hudson's Hope before the First World War, establishing a thousand-acre farm in the Peace Valley, a place where they could "grow anything. . . . It was more or less a vegetable valley." The $28,000 she got from BC Hydro for the family property was enough to buy her a house in town, but little more. The Beattie boys could not re-establish themselves on the land and went to work for wages, Jim for the Department of Highways and his brother for an outfitter.[51]

Full-time waged work supported the Beatties and other displaced white settlers, but it was either unavailable to Aboriginal peoples, or not wanted by them. For the Athabasca Chipewyan, a living delta with its large population of muskrat was, according to elder Victorine Mercredi, "like having money in the bank."[52] But soon after the Bennett Dam was completed, the bank failed, and welfare payments to both the Ingenika and the residents of the Peace-Athabasca Delta increased.

In Fort Chipewyan (the main community in the delta), the average yearly per capita income declined by a third between 1965 and 1970. In the same period, the amount of federal social assistance rose 80 per cent, while that provided by the province increased 300 per cent.[53] It was a trend that dismayed Ingenika like Albert Poole, who worried about the enervating effects of welfare. "[N]owadays most everybody gets social assistance," he remarked in 1989. The young

people at Ingenika Point have "nothing at all to do. . . . We visit. Watch TV. Lots of TV. Lots of videos."[54]

If environmental change meant dependence, it also meant isolation, between generations and communities. Not only could welfare have debilitating effects, but it also cut young people off from their traditions. With social assistance, fewer young people were interested in spending time in the bush with their relations.[55]

The loss of connection with the past was compounded by the physical isolation of Aboriginal communities that came as a result of damming the Peace. Prior to 1968, the Ingenika had lived in Finlay Forks or in one of three reserve settlements, Fort Ware, Fort Grahame, or McLeod Lake, all former Hudson's Bay Company posts where many Ingenika families had traded furs for generations. The dam flooded Fort Grahame and Finlay Forks and turned the river into a large, dangerous, and unnavigable lake. For most boats, the waters of the reservoir were too rough and unpredictable to be travelled safely. Those who tried encountered unexpected winds, large waves, and hundreds of thousands of acres of debris—trees that had been cut but not removed before the reservoir was filled.[56] For all intents and purposes, the waters of Williston Lake separated the Ingenika at Fort Ware from relatives and friends at McLeod Lake and at the new reserves at Tutu Creek and on the Parsnip River (see Map 13.2). In 1977, BC Hydro's own consultant argued that the isolation imposed by the reservoir had "radically altered" Ingenika society and culture and was at least partially responsible for the "high incidence of social disorganization" that characterized some of their communities.[57]

Around Fort Chipewyan, the drying of the delta meant economic isolation. For almost two centuries, a staples economy had connected the northern community to the world. Established in 1788, Fort Chipewyan was one of the major centres of the fur trade and an important base for European exploration of the Canadian North and West. Although the trade began to decline in the late nineteenth century, trapping remained a central part of the region's economy in the postwar period, employing more than 60 per cent of the male labour force.[58] While the Bennett Dam did not the cause the decline of trapping, its ecological effects dealt a serious blow to the economic viability of the industry, causing it to fall off somewhat more steeply there than in other comparable parts of Canada.[59] The fate of Fort Chipewyan was the fate of other northern resource towns; in the postwar period, it became a society in search of a commercial economy.[60]

Isolation was just one aspect of a broader sense of alienation provoked by environmental change. Those changes were perceived through the body as much as the mind. The environmental history of the Peace was a history of the senses: the sounds of the bush, the colour of ice, the shape of the river.[61] For Hudson's Hope resident Earl Pollon, dynamite and earth movers signalled the ear-splitting arrival of modernity.[62] While Pollon complained about the noise, downstream Josephine Mercredi worried about the quiet. Changes to the river's flow and ice formation meant that there were no longer the same spectacular ice jams in the spring that were so important to flooding and replenishing the delta. The land signalled its thirst with silence: "Today you go on Reserve [201], you look, you listen for the sounds of birds, waterfowl, ducks, geese. You don't hear anything anymore."[63]

The dissonance of environmental change was not just aural, but visual. Because the water released from the Williston reservoir in the winter was warmer than the water in the Peace, ice formed later in the river, and instead of freezing into the usual flat pans, the cover was thicker and rougher, especially on the middle portions of the Peace.[64] It looked different. "Back in the 50s when the river broke up in the spring, the river ice that came down . . . was solid blue ice that broke up in big chunks," recalled Margaret Marcel in 1996. "But after the Bennett dam was built . . . you don't see the big thick blue ice. . . . Today all you see is small little chunks of ice."[65]

Changes to the river's water and ice regime changed its morphology. Lowered flows meant more sediment remained in the river. Sand and silt built up, narrowing the river at many points and creating sandbars, small islands, and wider shorelines, which were slowly colonized by vegetation.[66] As new physical features appeared in the river and along its banks, old familiar ones disappeared. Islands became hills.[67] Lakes vanished under willow and sedge. "Today, I don't know where that lake is," said puzzled trapper Daniel Marcel of Big Egg, one of the delta's large perched basins. Nevertheless, every day during trapping season he went out looking, knowing it was "for almost nothing."[68]

Daniel Marcel had faith that his efforts might someday be rewarded, that the lake and the muskrat would come back. But such rituals of environmental belief were almost impossible in desecrated landscapes. Upstream, the dam had killed the river, despoiling places of spiritual as well as material significance. A bush pilot recalled one particularly distressing moment for the Ingenika. "A piece of land had broken off and slid into the lake," explained A.C. Geddes. "It was where their graveyard was, and there were coffins, some whole and some all broken up, bones and bodies strewn all down the bank." It was a scene from a northern hell: dead bodies in a dead river already choked with the corpses of trees. The Ingenika knew this was no natural disaster. When Geddes landed to see if he could help, they rushed up to him. "'Are you the government? Indian Affairs?' 'No.' 'Our ancestors are angry.'"[69] . . .

In addition to dependence, isolation, and alienation, the peoples of the Peace experienced environmental change as illness. The current high level of cancer among Fort Chipewyan residents might be attributable to the accumulation of toxins in the delta's waters, something facilitated by the reduced flows resulting from the Bennett Dam.[70] But cancer is only the most recent example of the affliction of environmental change.

Upstream, dust storms seemed to be the cause of many of the ailments that troubled those living around the Williston reservoir. Dust made it hard to breathe—especially if you were very old or very young—and irritated the skin and eyes.[71] "The sand gets in your eyes, ears, everything," complained Jean Isaac. "And . . . our people have a lot of skin sicknesses that comes out in little welts and different ways." . . . [72]

After the dam was constructed and the Ingenika were dispossessed of their traplines, alcoholism emerged as a major social problem on the new reserves—so much so that many Ingenika abandoned the reserves for the bush in 1971.[73] To BC Hydro and the Department of Indian Affairs, this was inexplicable behaviour. The reserves at Tutu Creek and Parsnip River had, after all, been chosen by the Ingenika and met their requirements for access to jobs and services.[74] For the Ingenika, the move was the only sensible thing they could do; it was an act of community self-preservation. Jean Isaac left because she "didn't want to stay near the bars [at Mackenzie]."[75] Chief Seymour Isaac agreed. Moving to the Parsnip reserve "was a big mistake," he told the Department of Indian Affairs in 1975: "[I]t's too close to town and [there are] too many people coming in and out with booze."[76] . . .

The ways in which the peoples of the Peace experienced environmental change point to the meanings attached to the land and the material and emotional work that the places that had been lost had performed. Land and water were dignity and security. They were connection—across space, time, and people—and they were wellness. Those meanings were embedded in places as expansive as a delta and as intimate as a garden plot, a trapline, or the very bodies of the individuals who worked and played in them.

Challenges

Doing right by this river and its peoples would require solutions that addressed the depth, extent, and embeddedness of their sense of wrong. It was a challenging task, and the difficulties that accompanied it reveal that "the politics of environmental justice pivot around defining the scales of inequity."[77] On the Peace River, the struggle for environmental justice was rooted in the different scales at which people experienced changes in the land and at which others tried to deal with them. Because the scale of human experience was incommensurate with the scale of management, achieving environmentally just solutions remained elusive.

Shortly after the Bennett Dam was completed, a group of scientists working at the University of Alberta and for various federal agencies challenged the government to act. They focused their concern on the delta, which they considered a "Canadian resource" meriting national attention.[78] Their pressure led to the creation of a number of intergovernmental task forces beginning in 1971. The Peace-Athabasca Delta Project Group reported its findings and recommendations in 1973 and was followed by an implementation committee (1987) and a series of technical studies (1996). Their aim was to understand the river's hydrology, assess the dam's impact, and offer solutions to deal with the low water levels. Ultimately, their task was nothing less than "restoring the role of water to the delta."[79] In the 1970s, that meant building control structures on the smaller rivers and channels that flowed out of the delta to prevent water from leaving—or at least to slow it down (see Map 13.3 for locations of control structures). In other words, it meant building more dams. Retaining water would keep the delta from drying out and prevent habitat degradation. These engineering solutions were, at best, only partly successful in hydrological and biological terms.[80] In terms of restoring the social and economic role of water to the delta, however, these engineering solutions fell far short.

The failure of the task force to formulate solutions that addressed the social as well as the environmental impacts of the Bennett Dam was due to the different scales at which the problem in the delta was perceived. The solutions implemented by the Peace-Athabasca Delta Project Group were framed at a systemic level. They conceptualized the Peace as a hydrological system in which water moved up and down in the reservoir, and from west to east and north, through a large geographic area.

In contrast, a different spatial framing characterized how the peoples of the Peace saw the river and assessed its transformation. Rather than a hydrological system, they understood it as an intimate geography of belonging. Riverbanks, garden plots, lakes, and traplines were prominent features in personal maps of attachment that located them in relation to one another and connected them to their past, present, and future. Yet these features were invisible at the scale and resolution that characterized the way politicians and scientists envisioned the environment and environmental change.

While the spatial dimensions of scale have been explored in discussions of environmental justice, the temporal dimensions of scale have not. Yet time also distinguished how the peoples of the Peace and the members of the project group saw the problem to be solved. Nowhere was this clearer than in an exchange between the band councils for Athabasca Chipewyan and Mikisew Cree and the project group. Invited to comment on plans to build control structures in the delta to retain water, the bands had this to say: "The Government people say that the proposed dam will make things the way they always were on the Delta. This would be good . . . But many people who remember the low water years wish the dam could make the Delta even better." The bands went on to ask for an all-weather road, improvements to the airport, better schools, help with starting a quarry, and jobs in tar sands development.[81]

The Peace-Athabasca Delta Project Group and the government were flummoxed. What did airports have to do with the delta's problems? Everything, as it turned out. But the connection between airports and water was only visible if one stood where the Athabasca Chipewyan and Mikisew Cree did and shared their temporal horizons. The project group did not.

Scientists and Aboriginal peoples worked from different timelines, from different notions about when history started. The project group wanted to return water levels in the delta to their "natural" ones—that is, to what they had been before the Bennett Dam was constructed in 1968. But from the perspective of the Aboriginal peoples in the delta, 1968 was an almost arbitrary date; certainly, the state of human affairs in the delta before 1968 left much to be desired. The Bennett Dam might have contributed to

their problems—and for that matter to those upstream in British Columbia—but from the bands' standpoint, the damage caused by the dam merged almost seamlessly into the larger impacts of centuries of colonization and structural changes in the economy that rendered many northern communities poor.[82]

Different configurations of space and time thus lay at the heart of the struggle for environmental justice in the delta. The framing that Aboriginal peoples gave the water problem combined a limited spatial scale (a lake or the reserve) with an expansive temporal one (the history of colonialism). The way the project group framed the problem was just the opposite: its scientists used an expansive spatial scale (the watershed) with a limited temporal one (after 1968). These different configurations made the solutions offered by each group incomprehensible to the other, and because of this, the proposed solutions themselves became sources of conflict. . . .

If nothing else, these differing concepts of change (and potential solutions) should leave us with an appreciation of how different temporal and spatial scales shaped how environmental change on the Peace was perceived and how those scales themselves were constituted by ideology, experience, and science. The high modernism of Axel Wenner-Gren and W.A.C. Bennett produced a simplified futurescape that highlighted the economic potential of the environment, reducing rivers to flows of power, and celebrated large-scale, state-sponsored environmental change. In contrast, the experience of living, working, and playing on the Peace produced a more intimate and textured historical geography, one that rooted people to place and located them in time. Many of those roots were damaged—drowned or desiccated—by the dam, with destabilizing effects. Distinct from both, scientists' assessments of the impact of damming the Peace were shaped by developments in hydrology and ecology, and changed from ones that emphasized the dam's negative effects to others that presented them as negligible.

The importance of scale in constituting environmental change suggests that we need to broaden our thinking about environmental justice, moving beyond questions of the distribution of risk and procedural fairness. In framing solutions, we must grapple with multiple scales: not just the large-scale space of flows and the small-scale space of places, but with deep time and human time—with when history starts and where history happens.

Author's Note: Research funding for this article was provided by the Office of the Dean of Arts, University of British Columbia. Karen Routledge provided research assistance. Thanks to the editors of this special issue, Matthew Evenden and Alan MacEachern, for their comments on earlier drafts, as well as to Robert McDonald, H.V. Nelles, Elizabeth Piper, Meg Stanley, and John Stubbs.

Endnotes

1   In fact, damming the Peace was illegal, a contravention of the Navigable Waters Protection Act. The government of British Columbia appears to have known this before the dam was constructed; certainly the Canadian federal government considered the structure illegal—but chose not to act. That part of the story is, however, beyond the scope of this essay. For an introduction, see James Howell, "The Portage Mountain Hydro-Electric Project [the W.A.C. Bennett Dam]," in *Northern Transitions*, vol. 1: *Northern Resource and Land Use Policy Study*, ed. Everett B. Peterson and Janet B. Wright (Ottawa: Canadian Arctic Resources Committee, 1978), 34–7.

2   Early key studies include Robert D. Bullard, "Solid Waste Sites and the Black Houston Community," *Sociological Inquiry* 53 (1983): 273–88; United States General Accounting Office, *Siting of Hazardous Waste Landfills and Their Correlation with Racial and Economic Status of Surrounding Communities* (Washington, DC: United States General Accounting Office, 1983); and United Church of Christ, *Toxic Waste Sites and Race in the United States: A National Report on the Racial and Socio- economic Characteristics with Hazardous Waste Sites* (New York: United Church of Christ Commission for Racial Justice, 1987).

3   Julian Agyeman, Robert Bullard, and Bob Evans give what they call the "traditional" definition of environmental injustice: it is a situation in which "people of color are forced, through their lack of access to decision-making and policy-making processes, to live with a disproportionate share of environmental 'bads'—and thus to suffer the related public health problems and quality of life burdens." They go on to note that "[e]nvironmental justice activists claim that the 'path-of-least-resistance' nature of locational choices within our economy functions to the detriment of people of colour, and, moreover, this disproportionate burden is an intentional result." Julian Agyeman, Robert D. Bullard, and Bob Evans, "Exploring the Nexus: Bringing Together Sustainability, Environmental Justice and Equity," *Space and Polity* 6 (2002): 81–2.

4   There is a debate in the literature about whether environmental injustice is primarily an outcome of racism or poverty. For Robert D. Bullard it is "a race thing, not a poverty thing." Andrew Hurley disagrees, exploring how industrial capitalism exploited the divisions of race and class to its benefit, in the process producing different kinds of environmental inequalities. See Robert D. Bullard, "Environmental Justice for All," in his *Unequal Protection: Environmental Justice and Communities of Color* (San Francisco: Sierra Club Books, 1994), 5–6; and Andrew Hurley, *Environmental Inequalities: Class, Race, and Industrial Pollution in Gary, Indiana, 1945–1980* (Chapel Hill: University of North Carolina Press, 1995). Laura Pulido tries to get beyond the race versus class debate, arguing for a more complex view of racism. See her essay "A Critical Review of the Methodology of Environmental Racism Research," *Antipode* 28 (1996): 142–59.

5   Patrick Novotny, *Where We Live, Work and Play: The Environmental Justice Movement and the Struggle for a New Environmentalism* (Westport, CT: Praeger, 2000). For a review of environmental inequality outside the United States, see Francis O. Adeola, "Cross-National Environmental Injustice and Human Rights Issues: A Review of Evidence in the Developing World," *American Behavioral Scientist* 43 (2000): 686–706.

6   For a discussion of how traditional environmentalism marginalized and oppressed certain groups of people, see, for instance, Karl Jacoby, *Crimes against Nature: Squatters, Poachers, Thieves, and the Hidden History of American Conservation* (Berkeley and Los Angeles: University of California Press, 2001); and Mark David Spence, *Dispossessing the Wilderness: Indian Removal and the Making of the National Parks* (New York: Oxford University Press, 1999).

7   The "Principles of Environmental Justice" were defined at the First National People of Color Environmental Leadership Summit in 1991. See www.ejnet.org/ej/principles.html.

8   On the connections between the US civil rights movement and the environmental justice movement, see Eileen Maura McGurty, "From NIMBY to Civil Rights: The Origins of the Environmental Justice Movement," *Environmental History* 2 (1997): 301–23; Stephen Sandweiss, "The Social Construction of Environmental Justice," in *Environmental Injustices, Political Struggles: Race, Class, and the Environment*, ed. David E. Camacho (Durham, NC: Duke University Press, 1998), 31–57; and Robert D. Bullard and G. S. Johnson, "Environmental Justice: Grassroots Activism and Its Impact on Public Policy," *Journal of Social Issues* 56 (2000): 555–78. Other scholars make the case that what we now call "environmental justice" activism predated the civil rights movement and was a part of race, gender, and class inequities in North America and elsewhere. See Dorceta E. Taylor, "American Environmentalism: The Role of Race, Class, and Gender in Shaping Activism, 1820–1995," *Race, Gender, and Class* 5 (1997): 16–62. Laura Pulido frames her study of the Southwest as an examination of subaltern struggles for environmental justice. See her *Environmentalism and Economic Justice: Two Chicano Struggles in the Southwest* (Tucson: University of Arizona Press, 1996).

9   www.unep.org/Documents.multilingual/Default.asp?DocumentID=78&ArticleID=116 3.

10   www.epa.gov/compliance/resources/policies/ej/exec_order_12898.pdf.

11   Evan J. Ringquist, "Environmental Justice: Normative Concerns and Empirical Evidence," in *Environmental Policy in the 1990s: Reform or Reaction?*, 3rd edn, ed. Norman J. Vig and Michael E. Kraft (Washington, DC: CQ Press, 1997), 247–8.

12   Anastasia M. Shkilnyk, *A Poison Stronger Than Love: The Destruction of an Ojibwa Community* (New Haven, CT: Yale University Press, 1983). In addition, the toxic effects of the tar ponds on the residents of Sydney, Nova Scotia, have attracted attention. See Maude Barlow and Elizabeth May, *Frederick Street: Life and Death on Canada's Love Canal* (Toronto: HarperCollins, 2000).

13   The term is Ryan Holifield's and it describes the situation in the United States: "Defining Environmental Justice and Environmental Racism," *Urban Geography* 22 (2001): 79.

14   See, for example, Hurley, *Environmental Inequalities*; Pulido, *Environmentalism and Economic Justice*; Laura Pulido, "Rethinking Environmental Racism: White Privilege and Urban Development in Southern California," *Annals of the Association of American Geographers* 90 (2000): 12–40; and David N. Pellow, "Environmental Inequality Formation: Toward a Theory of Environmental Justice," *American Behavioral Scientist* 43 (2000): 581–601.

15   On various explanations for environmental inequity in the global context, see Adeola, "Cross-National Environmental Injustice and Human Rights Issues," 690ff. For the United States, see Robert W. Williams, "Environmental Injustice in America and Its Politics of Scale," *Political Geography* 18 (1999): 49–73. For a critique of the central argument of environmental justice—namely that environmental harms are distributed unequally and that those on the social margins bear the burden of them—see William Bowen, "An Analytical Review of Environmental Justice Research: What Do We Really Know?," *Environmental Management* 29 (2002): 3–15.

16   George Towers, "Applying the Political Geography of Scale: Grassroots Strategies and Environmental Justice," *Professional Geographer* 52 (2000): 25. He notes that the work of Edward Soja and Henri Lefebvre was particularly important in shaping inquiry into the social construction of space.

17   For an overview, see Williams, "Environmental Injustice in America and Its Politics of Scale." On scale and capitalism, see Neil Smith, *Uneven Development: Nature, Capital, and the Production of Space*, 2nd edn (Oxford: Basil Blackwell, 1990).

18   Andrew Herod and Melissa W. Wright, "Placing Scale: An Introduction," in *Geographies of Power: Placing Scale*, ed. Andrew Herod and Melissa W. Wright (Oxford: Blackwell Publishing, 2002), 2ff.

19   For an overview and a specific example, see Hilda E. Kurtz, "The Politics of Environmental Justice as the Politics of Scale: St James Parish, Louisiana, and the Shintech Siting Controversy," in *Geographies of Power: Placing Scale*, ed. Herod and Wright, 249–73.

20   "Scale-jumping" is discussed in Herod and Wright, "Placing Scale," 4, 10–11; and Towers, "Applying the Political Geography of Scale," 27.

21   On high modernity, see James C. Scott, *Seeing Like a State: How Certain Schemes to Improve the Human Condition Have Failed* (New Haven, CT: Yale University Press, 1998).

22   Cited in David J. Mitchell, *W.A.C. Bennett and the Rise of British Columbia* (Vancouver: Douglas & McIntyre, 1983), 255.

23   John Diefenbaker was prime minister between 1957 and 1963. In the election campaigns of 1957 and 1958 he articulated his "northern vision," a plan for national economic development based on exploiting the resources of Canada's North.

24   Jack Scott, "Jack Scott Visits Wenner-Grenland," *Vancouver Sun*, 1957, 1, VPL Clippings File: "Dams-BC-Peace River to 1957"; and "A Great Project for the North," *Province* (Vancouver), 10 October 1957, 6.

25   Memorandum for the Deputy Custodian Re: Mr. Castleden's question with respect to the placing

of Mr. Axel Wenner-Gren's name on the list of specified persons, 3 April 1957, Canada, Custodian of Enemy Property, "Wenner-Gren, Axel," Library and Archives Canada [LAC], RG 117, series A-3, vol. 2060, file 6251.

26   "Here is the text on Wenner-Gren," *Vancouver Sun*, 1957. VPL Clippings file Dams-BC Peace River to 1957. Stuart Keate, "Axel in Wonderland," *Saturday Night*, 13 April 1957, 50, in Canada, Canadian National Railways. "British Columbia-Wenner-Gren Development." LAC, RG 30, Series V-A-9-j, volume 14440.

27   "Peace Project Gears Up for Spring Thaw," *Vancouver Times*, 15 March 1965, in VPL Clippings File: "Dams-BC-Peace River-1964-1967; and Gordon M. Shrum, foreword to Bruce Ramsay and Dan Murray, *Big Dam Country: A Pictorial Record of the Development of Peace River Country* (Fort St John: Dan Murray, 1969), n.p.

28   David E. Nye, *American Technological Sublime* (Cambridge, MA: MIT Press, 1994).

29   The Peace was dammed to promote the exploitation of forestry and mining resources. But it was also dammed because it was not a salmon river; its waters were impounded so that those of the Fraser, which supported another valuable resource (salmon), would not be. As Matthew D. Evenden argues, the government of British Columbia made choices between fish and power. See his *Fish versus Power: An Environmental History of the Fraser River* (Cambridge, UK, and New York: Cambridge University Press, 2004).

30   Greg Halseth and Lana Sullivan, *Building Community in an Instant Town: Geography of Mackenzie and Tumbler Ridge, British Columbia* (Prince George: University of Northern British Columbia Press, 2002), 30–4; and Patricia Marchak, *Green Gold: The Forest Industry in British Columbia* (Vancouver: UBC Press, 1983), 306–11.

31   The figure for acres flooded is from Douglas Baker, Jane Young, and J.M. Arocena, "An Integrated Approach to Reservoir Management: The Williston Reservoir Case Study," *Environmental Management* 25 (2000): 567. There is no count of how many animals were drowned. However, there are anecdotal accounts, like that of bush pilot Pen Powell. "The things I saw I wish I could forget," he recalled. "I and a friend were flying one day around the highth [*sic*] of the disaster . . . and saw a large herd of moose that were trapped on a piece of high ground by floating debris and pulled over trees. We counted well over one hundred moose in about a ten-acre area, the next day we came back over the same area and it was completely covered with water and lots of dead moose floating among the debris." See Powell to Matheson, 30 May 1989, 3, Shirlee Smith Matheson Fonds, University of Calgary Archives [UCA] Acc. 685/00.16, box 43, file 4. The reservoir's impact on mountain caribou is from Scott Simpson, "A Dam

Never Forgotten: Trouble on the Peace," *Vancouver Sun*, 8 July 2004, F3.

32   While 40 to 50 families were moved to new reserves, all of the approximately 200 members of the band were affected by the flooding. See Mary Christina Koyl, "Cultural Chasm: A 1960s Hydro Development and the Tsay Keh Dene Community of Northern British Columbia" (M.A. thesis, University of Victoria, 1993), 69.

33   Boatman to Matheson, 15 May 1989, 4, Shirlee Smith Matheson Fonds, UCA Acc. 685/00.16, box 43, file 4. Boatman noted there were five expropriations related to the project, "most of them necessary to overcome problems transferring title."

34   See, for example, interview with Jean Issac, Ingenika Point, 16 April 1989, 5, Shirlee Smith Matheson Fonds, UCA Acc. 685/00.16, box 44, file 3. Scientific research corroborates this observation. See D.G. Schaefer, *Climatological Impacts of Peace River Regulation and a Review of the Possible Effects of Climatic Change on Agriculture in the Area* (Victoria: BC Hydro and Power Authority, 1976), 51.

35   John Sawatsky, "Explainers Meet Opposition," *Vancouver Sun*, 14 February 1974, VPL Clippings File: "Dams-BC-Peace River-1970-74."

36   Nat Cole, "'You Hate to See the Beauty of Peace River Disturbed,'" *Vancouver Sun*, 10 October 1970, 12, VPL Clippings File: "Dams-BC-Peace River-1970-74."

37   A study done for BC Hydro noted that the effects of the reservoir were limited to the area immediately surrounding it. While temperatures fell by a few degrees, no discernible difference in humidity was detected. However, studies did indicate an increase in fog in the fall months. See Schaefer, *Climatological Impacts of Peace River Regulation*, 50–4.

38   The general pattern was as follows: tremendous increases in fish populations in first few years after the flood, followed by decline, and then stabilization. The shift in species composition was due to fluctuating water levels that destroyed shorelines that had supported aquatic plants and insect populations important to riverine species. The average annual drawdown in the Williston reservoir between 1972 and 1987 was 16.8 metres, more than enough to create "a basically abiotic littoral zone." Brian G. Blackman, *Fisheries Resources of the Williston Reservoir Twenty Years after Impoundment* (Prince George, BC: BC Hydro Peace/Williston Fish and Wildlife Compensation Program, 1992), vi, 1.

39   Ibid., 19ff.

40   Boatman to Matheson, 15 May 1989, 3, Shirlee Smith Matheson Fonds, UCA Acc. 685/00.16, box 43, file 4.

41   Brian G. Blackman, *Peace-Williston Compensation Program Summary of Activities, 1988–1997* (Prince George, BC: Peace-Williston Compensation Program, 2001), 5; Mary Ellen Wood and Luke Trip, *Examining*

Fish Consumption Advisories Related to Mercury Contamination in Canada (Hull, QC: Environment Canada, n.d.), 7, at www.ec.gc.ca/MERCURY/EN/efca.cfm.

42   British Columbia, Ministry of Environment, *State of Environment Reporting*, at www.env.gov.bc.ca/soerpt/993contaminants/trout.html.

43   "Submission to the ICC Inquiry—Specific Claim—Athabasca Chipewyan First Nation by D.W. Schindler (summary expert opinion), November 1996": Canada, Indian Claims Commission, *Athabasca Chipewyan First Nation Inquiry—W.A.C. Bennett Dam and Damage to I.R. 201*, ICC Exhibit 17, 2.

44   www.mb.ec.gc.ca/nature/whp/ramsar/df02s06.en.html. Also see Peace-Athabasca Delta Project Group, *The Peace-Athabasca Delta: A Canadian Resource* (Edmonton: Peace-Athabasca Delta Project Group, 1972), 24–36.

45   Northern River Basins Study Board, *Northern River Basins Study Report to the Ministers* (Edmonton: Northern River Basins Study, 1996), 62–3.

46   While the reservoir filled, mean peak summer water levels in Lake Athabasca fell from a pre-dam level of 209.95 metres to 209.10 metres. After 1972, the mean peak summer water level in the lake was somewhat higher, but still well below the pre-dam level, at 209.55 metres. See D.R. Jaques, *Vegetation Habitat Types of the Peace-Athabasca Delta, 1976–1989* (North Vancouver: Ecosat Geobotanical Surveys, 1990), 7, 14.

47   David Schindler, "The Effects of Climate Warming and Cumulative Human Activity on Canada's Freshwater in the 21st Century," in *Water and the Future of Life on Earth*, ed. Patricia Gallaugher and Laurie Wood (Burnaby, BC: Simon Fraser University Continuing Studies in Science, 2002), 2–6, at www.sfu.ca/cstudies/science/ resources/1276879869.pdf.

48   Ibid., Major Findings, Section 3.5, Flow Regulation-Effects on the Peace-Athabasca Delta; and Submission to the ICC Inquiry—Specific Claim—Athabasca Chipewyan First Nation by D.W. Schindler (summary expert opinion), November 1996, 2: Canada, Indian Claims Commission, *Athabasca Chipewyan First Nation—W.A.C. Bennett Dam and Damage to I.R. 201*, Exhibit 17. By early in the twenty-first century, Schindler estimated that 78 to 85 per cent of wetlands and wet marshes would be lost. On the loss of food for fish and wildlife, see Jeffrey E. Green, *A Preliminary Assessment of the Effects of the W.A.C. Bennett Dam on the Athabasca River Delta and the Athabasca Chipewyan Band: An Information Document by the Athabasca Chipewyan Band to the Department of Justice and the Office of Native Claims* (Vancouver: Delta Management Group, Ltd., 1992), 23: Canada, Indian Claims Commission, *Athabasca Chipewyan First Nation W.A.C. Bennett Dam and Damage to I.R. 201*, ICC Exhibit 1A, tab 1.

49   Green, *A Preliminary Assessment of the Effects of the W.A.C. Bennett Dam*, 23: Canada, Indian Claims Commission, *Athabasca Chipewyan First Nation–W.A.C. Bennett Dam and Damage to I.R. 201*, ICC Exhibit 1A, tab 1.

50   Submission to the ICC Inquiry—Specific Claim—Athabasca Chipewyan First Nation by D.W. Schindler, 3.

51   Earl K. Pollon and Shirlee Smith Matheson, *This Was Our Valley* (Calgary: Detselig, 1989), 212–13.

52   Canada, Indian Claims Commission, *Athabasca Chipewyan First Nation Inquiry: W.A.C. Bennett Dam and Damage to Indian Reserve 201* (Ottawa: Indian Claims Commission, March 1998), 24.

53   Note that the average yearly per capita income in Alberta in 1970 was $2,400. Montcrieff, Montgomery & Associates, Ltd., *Draft Report to the Socio-Economic Sub Committee of the Peace-Athabasca Project* (Edmonton: Montcrieff, Montgomery & Associates, Ltd., 13 December 1971), 53–54. Alberta. Department of Environment, Peace-Athabasca Delta Study Task Force. Provincial Archives of Alberta [PAA], GR 1988.0422, box 1, file "Socio-Economic Sub-Committee."

54   Interview with Albert Poole, 16 April 1989, 3, Shirlee Smith Matheson Fonds, UCA Acc. 685/00.16, box 44, file 3.

55   Ibid. Also see Green, *A Preliminary Assessment of the Effects of the W.A.C. Bennett Dam*, 30.

56   On the failure to clear the Williston Reservoir of timber, see Marchak, *Green Gold*, 308–9. The sight of the Ingenika trying to travel the lake haunted A.C. Geddes of Hudson's Hope, who worked for a time clearing debris. "They would try to go across the lake in their old riverboat[s], . . . the debris . . . knocking the props off. . . . They're stranded out there on the water and trying to build a little fire on those mats [of timber]" while they waited for the logs to shift and give them a way out. Interview with A.C. Geddes, 14 May 1989, 7, Shirlee Smith Matheson Fonds, UCA Acc. 685/00.16, box 44, file 3.

57   Veit-Draft Report, 22 March 1977, 2, 5: Canada, Department of Indian Affairs, LAC, RG 10, file 985/19-4-609.

58   Montcrieff, Montgomery & Associates, Ltd., *Draft Report*, 26: Alberta, Department of Environment, Peace-Athabasca Delta Study Task Force, PAA, GR 1988.0422, box 1, file "Socio-Economic Sub-Committee."

59   Stuart Adams and Associates, *Fort Chipewyan Way of Life Study: An Assessment of Impacts of the W.A.C. Bennett Dam on the People of Fort Chipewyan and the Peace- Athabasca Delta and Suggestions for Action* (Vancouver: Stuart Adams and Associates, 1998), 161.

60   This theme is pursued in a different context in Cole Harris, "Industry and the Good Life around Idaho

Peak," *Canadian Historical Review* 66 (1985): 315–43.

61   On this approach, see Joy Parr, "Notes for a More Sensuous History of Twentieth- Century Canada: The Timely, the Tacit, and the Material Body," *Canadian Historical Review* 82 (2001): 720–45; Linda Nash, "The Changing Experience of Nature: Encounters with a Northwest River," *Journal of American History* 86 (2000): 1600–29; and Christopher Sellers, "Thoreau's Body: Towards an Embodied Environmental History," *Environmental History* 4 (October 1999): 486–515.

62   Pollon expressed himself in verse: "God! How I hate it! Yes, hate it! / I wish this dam project in hell! / With all this rumble and racket / I'd sooner hear harness and bell." Pollon and Matheson, *This Was Our Valley*, 183.

63   Canada, Indian Claims Commission, *Athabasca Chipewyan First Nation Inquiry*, 75.

64   Northern River Basins Study, *Final Report*, Major Findings, Section 3.5: Flow Regulation-Ice Formation.

65   Testimony of Margaret Marcel, ICC Transcript, 10 October 1996, 60–1: Canada, Indian Claims Commission, *Athabasca Chipewyan First Nation Inquiry*, ICC Exhibit 15.

66   Northern River Basins Study, *Final Report* (Ottawa: Northern Rivwwer Basins Study, 1996), section 3.5, www3.gov.ab.ca/env/water/nrbs/index.html.

67   Testimony of Josephine Mercredi, ICC Transcript, 10 October 1996, 53: Canada, Indian Claims Commission, *Athabasca Chipewyan First Nation Inquiry*, ICC Exhibit 15.

68   Ibid., 74.

69   Interview with A.C. Geddes, 14 May 1989, 8: Shirlee Smith Matheson Fonds, UCA Acc. 685/00.16, box 44, file 3.

70   Patrick Brethour, "Why Is Cancer Sweeping Tiny Fort Chipewyan?," *Globe and Mail*, 23 May 2006.

71   Baker, Young, and Arocena, "An Integrated Approach to Reservoir Management," 573.

72   Interview with Jean Issac, Ingenika Point, 16 April 1989, 5: Shirlee Smith Matheson Fonds, UCA Acc. 685/00.16, box 44, file 3.

73   *Veit-Draft Report*, 22 March 1977, 4: Canada, Department of Indian Affairs, Relocation of Indians-Ingenika Band, LAC, RG 10, Acc. V-1994-95/559, box 1, file 985/19-4-609.

74   Report on Ingenika Band of Indians in Occupation of Crown Lands at Ingenika River, 19 February 1974, 2: ibid.

75   Interview with Jean Isaac, Ingenika Point, 16 April 1989, 5: Shirlee Smith Matheson Fonds, UCA Acc. 685/00.16, box 44, file 3.

76   Isaac to Rhymer, 18 September 1975, 1: LAC, RG 10, file 985/19-4-609.

77   Williams, "Environmental Injustice in America and Its Politics of Scale," 49.

78   Peace-Athabasca Delta Project Group, *The Peace-Athabasca Delta*. The title page has the inscription: "This is remote country. This is beautiful country. This is rich country. This is what Canada is all about."

79   Peace-Athabasca Delta Technical Studies, *Peace-Athabasca Delta Technical Studies—Final Report 1996* (Fort Chipewyan: Peace-Athabasca Delta Technical Studies, 1996), 1–2. The other reports are Peace-Athabasca Project Group, *The Peace-Athabasca Delta Project Technical Report: A Report on Low Water Levels and Their Effects on the Peace-Athabasca Delta* (Edmonton: Peace-Athabasca Delta Project Group, 1973); and Peace-Athabasca Delta Implementation Committee, *Peace-Athabasca Delta Water Management Works Evaluation: Final Report* (Governments of Canada, Alberta, and Saskatchewan: Peace-Athabasca Delta Implementation Committee, April 1987). At the same time the technical studies were underway, a larger intergovernmental research initiative also investigated the Peace River. See Northern River Basins Study, *Final Report*.

80   Peace-Athabasca Delta Implementation Committee, *Peace-Athabasca Delta Water Management Works Evaluation: Final Report*, v.

81   Submission to the Environment Conservation Authority by the Athabasca Cree and Chipewyan Bands, Fort Chipewyan, Alberta, 3: Alberta, Department of Environment, Peace-Athabasca Delta Study Task Force Files, PAA, GR 1988.0422, box 2, file: Peace Athabasca Hearings 1973.

82   Their perspective is shared by indigenous peoples in the United States and around the world. In *Defending Mother Earth*, Jack Weaver argues that "Natives view the environmental depredations being visited upon them as merely one more manifestation of colonialism that has attacked their lives for over five hundred years. Ecojustice, therefore, cannot be discussed apart from that racism and colonialism." Cited in Paul C. Rosier, "Fond Memories and Bitter Struggles: Concerted Resistance to Environmental Injustices in Postwar Native America," in *Echoes from the Poisoned Well: Global Memories of Environmental Injustice*, ed. Sylvia Hood Washington, Paul C. Rosier, and Heather Goodall (Lanham, MD: Lexington Books, 2006), 36. Writing about the situation of indigenous peoples around the world, Heather Goodall argues that "[h]istory is central to questions of how those indigenous people have understood environmental injustice because . . . [p]ower in colonies has been exercised through control over space and environment." See her "Indigenous Peoples, Colonialism, and Memories of Environmental Injustice," in ibid., 74.

CHAPTER 14

Youth and Resistance

◎ 14.1: "How to Walk Safely in Immigration's Minefield": The Toronto Anti-Draft Programme and the Changing Needs of American War Resisters in Canada during the Vietnam War

Matthew Roth

No narrative of the "sixties" in the United States is complete without a focus on the anti–Vietnam War protests that were commonplace throughout the era. Yet it is often overlooked that similar protests were also prevalent in Canada, especially on university campuses across the country.

At first glance, it may seem odd that the Vietnam War was, in the words of one Canadian historian, the "most important rallying-point for protest throughout the decade" for Canadian youth.[1] After all, Canada's armed forces were not sent to Vietnam. Yet the point becomes clearer when one considers the myriad of ways in which Canada was involved in the Vietnam War. Along with a general moral outrage towards American involvement in Southeast Asia, many in the Canadian anti–Vietnam War movement objected to Canadian industries' implicit connections to the American war effort, including their manufacture of napalm destined for Vietnam. They also questioned how neutral Canada really was in its role in the International Control Commission. "From the beginning," one writer has commented, "the concern of the Canadian anti-war movement was *to make the*

connection between Canadian citizenship and the suffering of victims of war."[2]

The focus of this article is on another significant way in which Canada was directly linked to the war—in becoming the home and refuge for tens of thousands of young Americans who resisted both their country's draft laws and military involvement in Vietnam by coming to Canada. While many Canadians are aware that a large number of American "draft dodgers" arrived in Canada during the Vietnam War, not many know how they got here or who helped them once they arrived. The Toronto Anti-Draft Programme (TADP) gained a reputation as one of the most important organizations providing aid and support to war resisters in Canada. Its history reveals the pivotal role it played in this nation's war resistance movement. Despite the invaluable aid it furnished to countless resisters, the process of immigrating to Canada remained, at best, daunting for the young individuals who made the journey north from the United States because of their ideological and moral opposition to the Vietnam War. Still, as this article will show, TADP evolved over time, adapting its strategies and altering its services to meet the changing needs of American war resisters in Canada.

As with the other options available to those who resisted the draft and war, the decision to leave the United States for another nation was rarely an easy one. Leaving one's friends and family behind for a foreign land was an intimidating prospect for many. Nevertheless, a large number of Americans opted to do just that and headed north of the border to Canada. Between 1965 and 1974, approximately 50,000 young Americans came to Canada in response to the Vietnam War, but the exact number is hard to determine.[3] Although women were not eligible for the draft, they came in even greater numbers than men, as companions and on their own. In fact, these young men and women constituted "the largest politically motivated" exodus of Americans to Canada since the American Revolution.[4]

For the many who chose to resist the war by coming to Canada during the Vietnam era, the transition was made easier by aid organizations in Canada. The Toronto Anti-Draft Programme, the

NEW LEFT MOVEMENT AND SUPA

The New Left was a 1960s movement comprising mainly young people, with a high membership particularly in the universities. Existent in Canada, it was also prominent in other western countries such as the United States and Britain. The name "New Left" revealed both its similarity to the ideals of the "old" left of socialist and Marxist politics of the pre-1945 period but also a deviation from many of the ideals and practices of the old left. Both were movements of the left, having an ideology centred on and critical of capitalism as the basis of social and economic inequality. However, the New Left viewed the socialist/Marxist theories of the old left as inadequate because of their singular focus on class and thus on socio-economic inequality. As well, the New Left rejected the structure and organization of old left groups and political parties, which they viewed as authoritarian and hierarchical. The New Left advocated for more open political structures, both in party organization and governance, calling for practices such as participatory democracy. Expanding their concern beyond class/labour inequality and national issues, the New Left focused on issues like the imperialism of the Western world, the Vietnam War, support for decolonization and self-determination in the "Third World," and nuclear disarmament. Nationally, New Left groups embraced many of the issues of the social movement politics of the era, including separatism in Quebec, sexual equality, and environmentalism.

The Student Union for Peace Action (SUPA) was one group within the larger movement of the New Left. Its origins were actually within an anti-nuclear movement that began in the late 1950s in the universities. SUPA developed and strengthened through the 1960s owing to the increase of young middle-class baby boomers in Canadian universities committed to and involved in social movement politics. Concerned with the above issues, SUPA members engaged in many causes, such as support programs for American draft resisters as part of their opposition to American involvement in Vietnam. SUPA also advocated for a greater student voice in university governance, policies, and services.

The New Left declined through the 1970s for a number of reasons, including disillusionment resulting from the events of the October Crisis. Its decline was also a product of one of its inherent characteristics; its rejection of both a traditional organizational structure and a distinct program and policy focus led to the fragmentation of its component parts and membership. Nonetheless many of its members and causes would continue in the social movement politics of the decades after the 1960s.

largest of the many groups aiding resisters in Canada, estimated that "in 1969 alone they dealt with 20,000 young U.S. men interested in coming to Canada."[5] The Toronto Anti-Draft Programme did not spontaneously arise to meet the needs of resisters, as its origins were in the Canadian New Left student movement. It arose out of the Student Union for Peace Action (SUPA), an organization that was founded in 1964 and began to aid resisters in 1966.[6] SUPA played a central role in the New Left in Canada and "pressed the issue of Canadian responsibility towards and complicity in the Vietnam war."[7] TADP split from SUPA and moved into an office of its own at 2279 Yonge Street in the fall of 1967 after SUPA decided to stop supporting immigration to Canada as a way of opposing the draft.[8] Over TADP's history, many individuals entered and left the organization. Various members of TADP appeared as spokespeople for the organization in newspaper articles; the majority of them were young American war resisters.

Mark Satin was a central figure during the transitional phase between SUPA and TADP, as he co-founded TADP. Satin was raised in Minnesota and spent most of his high school years in Texas; by the time he arrived in Toronto in 1967, he already had a long history of activism despite his young age, including a stint in the American New Left/anti-war organization Students for a Democratic Society.[9] The war in Vietnam led to Satin's disillusionment with the American system as it did for so many others of his generation: "The war . . . made a lot of things clear to me. There were so many hypocrisies about it, and you got to see that your government was not the greatest and most honest in the world like you were brought up to believe."[10]

Satin's opposition to the war left him with few alternatives, most of which he found unacceptable. "As a CO I would have been serving the war machine in a non-combatant way—the only thing I wouldn't be doing was pulling the trigger," he said. "Jail was out because the U.S. makes no distinction between political prisoners and murderers, drug addicts and rapists. As far as my friends would know, I would be in jail as a criminal."[11] After receiving a copy of SUPA's

Escape from Freedom or 'I didn't raise my boy to be a Canadian,' Satin decided to immigrate to Canada, yet he admitted he had little knowledge of the country and thought it had "log cabins and igloos in the middle of town."[12] After arriving in Canada, Satin felt that he had made the right decision. "I feel as though a great weight has been lifted from my shoulders. It's colder here, but you feel warm because you know you're not trying to kill people," he said.[13] During his time at TADP, Satin made a great contribution to the resistance movement with a document he co-wrote and edited titled *Manual for Draft-Age Immigrants to Canada.*

The publication of TADP's *Manual for Draft-Age Immigrants to Canada* was an important factor in explaining why so many war resisters ended up in Canada. The second edition of the *Manual* was a comprehensive document that

Laura Jones/Baldwin Street Gallery.

Copies of the *Manual for Draft-Age Immigrants to Canada* being assembled in Toronto, 1967.

covered many aspects of immigrating to Canada, outlining the various ways to apply for visitor, student, and landed-immigrant status. Any question a prospective resister could have had about the immigration process was answered, whether it concerned who was prohibited from entry, how to apply for citizenship, or even whether a dog, cat, or a variety of other pets could be brought across the border. The *Manual* was also exhaustive in its attempt to familiarize individuals with life in Canada.

The impact of the *Manual* on the migration northwards was immense. From 1968 to 1971, six different editions of the *Manual* were published.[14] Sixty-five thousand copies had been printed by the time of its fifth edition in 1970.[15] It will never be known where all the *Manuals* ended up, but a record of the bulk sale orders kept by TADP shows that they were distributed far and wide. Copies were sent all over the United States to other counselling services, anti-war and peace organizations, private individuals, and universities. New York and California received their fair share, but orders were also placed from states like Tennessee, North Dakota, and Hawaii—not the first places that come to mind as hotbeds of anti-war activism in the United States during this era.[16]

Countless resisters have mentioned the role that the *Manual* played in their decision to leave the United States for Canada. In his study of resisters, John Hagan notes that more than a third of his sample had read the *Manual* before leaving the United States, while almost another quarter obtained a copy upon arrival in Canada.[17] Kenneth Emerick's study finds that at least a third of the draft resisters he interviewed had access to the *Manual*, which he refers to as "an invaluable guide."[18] Joseph Jones points out that the number of copies pressed "offers an uncanny numerical correspondence to the target audience who actually came to Canada."[19]

Historian David S. Churchill refers to the *Manual* as "the bible for resisters who wanted to make the move north."[20] The *Manual* went beyond providing facts; as Churchill has written, it "was a way in which aid groups, expatriates and Canadian activists prefigured Toronto as cultural and political space." He contends that "an image of Toronto emerged, one that was inclusive, politically progressive, anti-imperialist and counter-cultural."[21] Indeed, all of Canada was presented as an inviting place to live. As another author has put it, "If a resister had any doubts about going to Canada before he read the book, he seldom had any after finishing it."[22]

The optimistic portrayal of Canada is evident throughout early editions of the *Manual*. An entry in the preface of the second edition—written by an employment counsellor with the Department of Manpower and Immigration who, the editor notes, was writing as a private citizen—advised readers that although many Canadians felt their government was not perfect, "they are also aware that Canada may well be the most functioning democracy in the world." The author of the entry also suggested that discrimination was "more subdued" than in the United States and made it known that most Canadian companies would hire resisters.[23] The author of the introduction to the *Manual* also reminded potential resisters that Canada was not the "end of the world": "You do not leave civilization behind when you cross the border. (In fact, many Canadians would claim that you enter it.)"[24]

The employment, living conditions, and housing situations for resisters were other aspects of Canada that the *Manual* presented in a favourable light. Canada was also shown to be both socially tolerant and culturally advanced. Any resisters who came to Canada would be following the tradition of a long line of American dissenters, which included Loyalists and African Americans. The resisters, it was written, would be welcomed as well and would receive a generally sympathetic reception from Canadian citizens, media, churches, and even the Royal Canadian Mounted Police, which "seems to like young Americans."[25] Historian J.M.S. Careless, the author of the section on culture in the *Manual*, highlighted the diversity of Canadian culture: "Marshall McLuhan, the electron microscope, Banting and Best's discovery of insulin, ice hockey and the Calgary Stampede"—all of which revealed that Canada was "no barren wilderness to live in."[26]

Mark Satin stated that his reason for writing the *Manual* was the increasing amount of correspondence "requesting information." The *Manual* was not, as he reiterated in the press at the time of its publication, meant to entice resisters to immigrate to Canada. Satin was adamant that TADP did not "advertise immigration" and denied that the organization's literature "encourages people to immigrate."[27] "All our pamphlet does," remarked Satin, "is try to remind them they have a choice and, if they decide to leave, how they can do it."[28] However, it was also reported that Satin admitted that the *Manual* would increase the number of resisters who came to Canada because he was confident there were many people who wanted to, but did not have the know-how.[29]

To be sure, some negatives were presented, most notably in the introduction, which noted that coming to Canada usually meant cutting oneself off from friends and family and that resisters might not be able to return to the United States legally. "Immigration," warned the *Manual*, "is not the best choice for everyone."[30] Another voice of caution in the preface to the *Manual* came from a lawyer who warned resisters that not all Canadians would be welcoming.[31] Weighing the option of immigrating to Canada was ultimately left up to the individual, and the *Manual*'s introduction suggested that making this decision was the hardest part: "The toughest problem a draft resister faces is not how to immigrate but whether he really wants to. And only you can answer that. For yourself. That's what Nuremberg was all about."[32]

Nevertheless, the picture that emerged in the pages of the *Manual* was that Canada had much to offer and that there was little to discourage resisters from immigrating. Canada and Canadian society were presented as considerably more attractive alternatives than the other choices facing a young man of draft age who opposed the war, given the domestic and foreign problems America was experiencing. "We have not tried to sell you on Canada . . . ," noted the author of

the introduction, "but the truth is that Canada is a nice place to be."[33]

The shift in the Canadian government's policy towards resisters between 1966 and 1969 is examined in John Hagan's *Northern Passage*. Hagan examines how an initially unwritten policy that was averse to resisters evolved into a liberalized policy that did not discriminate against them. He also notes that the Canadian government's declaration of May 1969 that both draft *and* military resisters "would be admitted to Canada without regard to their military status" led to a dramatic increase in the number of resisters who came to Canada. As word of the "open-door" policy spread, "the number of draft-age males entering Canada as landed immigrants each month tripled between April and August of 1969."[34] As noted above, resisters who read a copy of the *Manual* during this period would not have found much to dissuade them from coming.

TADP could have not foreseen the tremendous changes that would occur in the years that followed. By the time the sixth and final edition of the *Manual* was published in 1971, its tone and contents had changed markedly.[35] In this edition, TADP highlighted two major reasons why resisters should carefully weigh their options. First, the situation in the United States had changed drastically in the preceding years, as many young men could now avoid military service more easily. TADP stressed the importance of obtaining "competent draft counseling" in the United States; the organization "estimated that at least 75% of draft age men should be eligible for deferments or exemptions, provided that they receive good draft counseling."[36] Second, employment prospects for resisters were unfavourable. Along with the high rate of unemployment, resisters faced two additional problems finding jobs in Canada according to the *Manual*: first, up to 60–80 per cent of all Canadian businesses were controlled by American interests that were "increasingly . . . refusing to hire Americans of draft age,"[37] and second, a "backlash" against the American domination of the economy combined with a "sense of national pride" in some sectors of the economy had led to a "reluctance [on the part] of Canadians to hire immigrants while so many Canadians [were] out of work" and to hiring policies favouring "only people of Canadian origin."[38]

The terminology used here—"backlash" and "sense of national pride"—also points to another reason that TADP changed its position during this time period. TADP was continually forming its policy within the context of larger debates about Canadian nationalism and anti-war activism in the United States. The role of American war resisters in Canada was a hotly contested issue among the Canadian New Left and the general public, as well as within the American anti-war movement. Even individual war resisters differed over questions of assimilation and whether to oppose the war as new Canadians or as Americans-in-exile. Others questioned whether war resisters should be in Canada at all.[39] These debates were also part of the larger concerns of many Canadians about the increasing "Americanization" of the Canadian economy and culture and "the search for a distinctive Canadian voice at a time of tremendous change and conflict."[40]

The frequent turnover of staff at TADP—Satin was out of the organization by 1968—meant that dominant personalities and their respective positions on these issues heavily influenced the organization at different periods throughout its history. The day-to-day operational records of TADP left many unanswered questions about what was happening behind the scenes; internal conflicts among staff and supporters over standpoints are not evident.[41] However, Churchill has argued that by the late 1960s, TADP "began to articulate a strong nationalist stance."[42]

Although the final edition of the *Manual* still held that the decision about whether or not to come to Canada ultimately rested with the individual, it was now clear that the organization had become reluctant to advertise Canada as a welcome refuge. While the *Manual* still offered plenty of information about immigration, it no longer included many of the chapters that in the early editions had highlighted the positives about Canada, and it implied that resisters should only come to Canada as a last resort.

Arguably the biggest change that led to the new standpoint was a consequence of a change in the type of resisters who were making their way to Canada. Those who came to Canada should not be viewed as a homogeneous group, as they came from a wide variety of backgrounds and differed in class, race, and gender among other things. As Katie McGovern from TADP notes, there was no "typical" resister.[43] Yet, as McGovern and many others have noted, one important distinction was between draft resisters and military resisters.

The distinction between draft and military resisters is critical in understanding TADP's shift in outlook. The first resisters who came to Canada were primarily those who were resisting the draft. Typically, these draft resisters, or "draft dodgers," as they were usually called, were middle class and college or university educated. As the war progressed, military resisters, or "deserters," as they were often referred to, arrived in greater numbers. They were generally less educated and from working-class backgrounds.[44] Some military resisters who came to Canada had already served in Vietnam before deciding to resist by refusing any future participation.[45]

During the winter of 1969 and spring of 1970, more military resisters came to Canada than draft resisters.[46] The Canadian government's policy was not the only reason greater numbers of military resisters were heading north, however. The development of the anti-war GI movement in the United States in 1968 was another critical factor, as many individuals in the military became aware of Canada as an option during these years.[47] As TADP's Bill Spira noted, typical draft resisters encountered the anti-war movement in college, whereas average military resisters usually did not encounter the movement until they were in the armed forces. This observation and the large number of military resisters arriving at TADP's office led Spira to quip, "I guess you might say then that the army is our biggest recruiter."[48]

During this same period, draft resisters stopped coming to Canada in large numbers. The decrease in the number of draft resisters was the result of several factors, including changes in

American draft laws.[49] Certain events in Canada also led to the decrease. The October Crisis in 1970 and the resulting use of the War Measures Act, which suspended civil liberties, gave some potential resisters pause as they questioned how much freedom they would find north of the border.[50]

While TADP had focused on immigration counselling and finding employment and housing for resisters in its initial years, and continued to do so throughout its existence, the large number of military resisters who arrived in 1969 and 1970 had a great impact on the services the organization provided. Whereas middle-class draft resisters had little trouble becoming landed immigrants and obtaining jobs, most military resisters found these tasks and the transition to life in Canada more difficult. Military resisters often left the United States in haste and commonly arrived in Canada with few possessions or assets.[51]

In April 1970, TADP's Naomi Wall appeared in Toronto before the Government Committee on Youth to stress the serious problems faced by recently arrived resisters—the majority of whom were military resisters. She explained that they were having trouble finding employment and getting landed-immigrant status and were not eligible for government assistance. Since many were "afraid to ask 'establishment' agencies . . . for help because it would define them as undesirable candidates for immigration," they had few places or people to turn to. Wall pointed out the hypocrisy of the government in allowing resisters to enter Canada but doing nothing for them once they arrived. She also informed the committee that in the previous two months, two American resisters had committed suicide.[52]

Both Hagan and Churchill have identified how the increasing numbers of military resisters in Canada led TADP to believe that its scarce resources should be given to those who needed its help the most.[53] It is important to note that this shift in focus had practical implications for TADP, as the needs of military resisters arriving in Canada led the organization to turn towards priority counselling. By the time the sixth and final edition of the *Manual* was published, TADP felt that priority counselling was the most vital service it provided.[54] Priority counselling involved advising those who needed it most, and those most in need were usually draft resisters whose date of induction had passed and, especially, military resisters; neither group could return to the United States without fear of reprisal. TADP felt that the individual resister's need was determined in part by the options available to that individual.[55]

Helping resisters explore their options and avoid unnecessarily drastic measures was another important aspect of priority counselling. After an individual contacted TADP, a counsellor would explain that Canada was not the only option and present alternatives.[56] A potential immigrant was also made aware of the seriousness of the decision, as resisters often arrived without having received any counselling (or inaccurate counselling) in the United States.[57] Caution was especially taken with resisters who could legally return to the United States, as these individuals had the option of going back and either waiting for their circumstances to improve or earning money before immigrating to Canada.[58] They were advised to try to obtain deferments or conscientious objector status and to appeal court decisions. These activities would not only buy time but also employ legal means to create a backlog in the United States' Selective Service System.[59]

The cautious tone of the final edition of the *Manual* was also evident in TADP's supplement to the *Manual*, which focused on Sweden. Like Canada, Sweden had been a refuge for resisters, since they could not be extradited for "draft related offenses."[60] By 1972, many resisters wanted to leave Sweden and wondered if Canada would be a suitable alternative. In response, TADP began to look into the rules and regulations to see if it was possible for Americans in Sweden to come to Canada.[61]

In August 1972, the "Sweden Supplement: Immigrating to Canada from Sweden" was released by TADP. The eight-page document provided information on immigrating to Canada from Sweden. It began with a bleak overview of the current economic situation in Canada and the "bitter reality" of unemployment. TADP observed that the "corporate head offices in New York close Canadian subsidiaries long before they close their U.S. plants": "From those wonderful people who brought you Vietnam, you get Canadian unemployment."[62] Things were even worse for immigrants, as the immigration department had "instituted a number of unwritten unofficial policies" that conspired to keep immigrants out of Canada and to "keep Canadian jobs for Canadians."[63]

Despite the dire situation, TADP provided detailed immigration procedures for those who nevertheless wanted to or needed to come to Canada. As well, TADP pointed out that among the advantages of leaving Sweden for Canada were Canada's cultural similarity to the United States, its friendly populace, and its low crime rate, which rarely went beyond stolen hubcaps. Yet TADP was quick to remind readers that Canada was no utopia. The suspension of civil liberties that occurred after the government invoked the War Measures Act in 1970 led TADP to warn that Canada could "be just as repressive as the U.S."[64]

The increasingly cautious approach evident in TADP literature did not translate into less commitment to providing assistance to resisters. TADP continued to help out those in need of support and once again demonstrated an ability to adapt to changing circumstances. To facilitate people who wanted to return to the United States, TADP studied military law and became involved in draft and military counselling. Draft counselling was given to individuals who had left the United States and had problems with their draft boards. TADP helped many who had draft-related problems by looking into their cases and attempting to resolve issues. Discharge counselling involved helping an individual obtain a discharge from the military. Over time, this became the most requested service TADP offered.[65] TADP even noticed that an increasing number of military resisters who had no intention of immigrating to Canada travelled to their office because "they have heard that we can help get them discharges."[66]

TADP was also called into action when the Canadian government unexpectedly changed the rules of immigration on 3 November 1972. It was no longer possible for any immigrant to apply for landed-immigrant status at the border or from within Canada.[67] The decision was detrimental to American resisters, as the only other ways left to apply were either at a Canadian embassy or consulate in the United States, where the wait time was generally three to six months, or by mailing an application to Canada; both scenarios had little chance of success.[68] The change was also a serious issue for resisters who had not yet obtained landed-immigrant status but were already in Canada, as they were "unlanded, unable to work, [and] unable to return to the US."[69]

In response, TADP began organizing "a nation-wide pressure campaign."[70] In a letter to a contact in Winnipeg, Dick Brown, one of the leading figures in the organization in the early 1970s and a resister himself, suggested that help should be sought from anyone.[71] Only a month after the border had closed, Brown wrote in another letter that TADP had "tapped every inside source in Ottawa which would listen."[72]

The reply to a letter from a resister in Sweden during the spring of 1973 illustrates how hopeless the situation had become in Canada. The man had inquired about immigrating to Canada and was told that there were only two ways to apply for landed-immigrant status from Sweden at this point, and neither was encouraging. One was to apply through the Canadian embassy in Sweden and try to earn enough "points," but Dick Brown explained why it was unlikely that his application would be successful. The alternative, Brown pointed out, was virtually pointless unless the man had divine powers: "[One] method would be to mail your application straight into the Immigration Department in Ottawa and pray; problem is unless you happen to be Jesus Christ your prayers won't be answered." Brown reassured the man that TADP had "been looking like you wouldn't believe for a loophole," but had not found one so far. He nevertheless hoped that the information would be more helpful than the Canadian officials had recently been: "That's as direct information as we have for your questions. Hope it's of some help, the government certainly hasn't been here." What is also interesting is that Brown mentions that he was including a copy of the "Sweden Supplement" with the letter, but that it was already out of date. Considering that it had been published only nine months earlier, one can get a sense of how fast immigration laws could and were changing.[73]

Although the situation would not improve for American resisters who still wanted to come to Canada, it did get better for those who were in Canada but not yet landed immigrants. Once again it is evident that TADP was able to respond to the changing needs of resisters. During the summer of 1973, the Department of Manpower and Immigration introduced legislation to help immigrants who were in Canada become landed. One of the reasons the government did this was to clear up the backlog of cases before the Immigration Appeal Board.[74] The bill offered any immigrant in Canada who had been in the country since 30 November 1972 a period of 60 days to come forward and apply for landed-immigrant status under relaxed requirements. The minister of manpower and immigration stressed that this would be the "last opportunity" to "gain permanent residence while in the country," and any illegal immigrant who did not register in the 60-day time period could be "deported without appeal."[75] It was estimated that there were 5,000 to 20,000 American war resisters not yet landed in Canada and 150,000 to 200,000 immigrants in total who were in this position.[76]

The government's Adjustment of Status Program offered Canadian aid organizations a chance to help resisters who were not landed in Canada; yet it also presented a great challenge—how could they reach all the potential candidates within a short time period and also convince them that it was an opportunity? Nine aid groups in Canada, with the support of churches in Canada and the United States, joined together through the Canadian Coalition of War Resisters and attempted to solve the problem by launching a

"National Immigration Program." The program hoped to achieve two goals: first, to inform war resisters of the government initiative, and second, to advise resisters to "contact one of our aid centers to receive accurate information and assistance on how to apply for and obtain landed immigrant status."[77] The coalition, which TADP was a part of, was coordinated by aid groups in Montreal and Winnipeg and also included groups in Vancouver, Regina, Ottawa, Halifax, Calgary, and Edmonton.[78]

The coalition launched a major publicity campaign to get the word out during the period between 15 August and 15 October 1973. The group had a bus carry the message across Canada for two months in an attempt to reach as many people as possible. The bus was multicoloured and had "Last chance for landed immigrant status" painted on its side.[79] A number of radio spots and one television commercial were also produced featuring popular folk singers.[80] TADP made sure that the spots were on stations throughout southern Ontario.[81] TADP also sent a representative around the province to spread the news.[82]

A final way that TADP responded to the challenge was to release a 13-page document titled "Sixty Days of Grace: Your Last Chance" to help resisters understand the issue. Throughout the document, TADP stressed the ease of obtaining landed-immigrant status through the government's program. For those who met the criteria, it was "absurdly simple": the government was "virtually giving away landed immigrant status" to those who could obtain employment or a job offer and prove that he or she had been in Canada continuously since 30 November 1972.[83] The government would also overlook the usual requirements; it did not matter if you had entered Canada unlawfully, worked illegally, entered Canada with a false passport, or had stayed in Canada after being issued a deportation order. The "points system" was in effect being set aside.[84]

Although TADP stressed that it was an easy process, it also noted that many rules and regulations were not clear. TADP's document helped resisters understand the finer details of the government's program. The document also walked resisters through the actual registration process. "[T]o make sure all goes well," "you must know the traps and pitfalls along the way and how to avoid them." TADP suggested that the information would show resisters "how to walk safely in immigration's minefield."[85] For example, it advised that the best time to apply for landed-immigrant status was when the government office was busy, as "the officer simply won't have the time to hassle anyone."[86]

Only about 3,000 resisters became landed during the Adjustment of Status Program in Canada, despite the efforts of TADP and other aid groups. This was fewer than they had anticipated. Many felt that 60 days had not been a long enough time to make everyone aware of the program.[87]

Around the time of the Adjustment of Status Program, it was becoming clear to TADP that Canada would no longer be welcoming resisters. According to TADP's "Immigration Fact Sheet," which was released in August 1973 in place of a new edition of the *Manual* owing to "a lack of funds," the "golden age of easy immigration to Canada" was "now a page in history." With few exceptions, war resisters could apply for landed-immigrant status only from within the United States, which was not a viable option for most of them.[88] Although some resisters still crossed the border seeking refuge, they did so less frequently.

From 1972 onwards, many groups, including TADP, increasingly turned their attention to the issue of amnesty for resisters who wanted to return to the United States; this matter would dominate the final years of the organization's existence. By 1974, TADP's operations were winding down, but it still received several telephone calls each month from military resisters interested in immigrating and draft resisters wanting to know if they could safely return to the United States.[89] The response to a letter written in 1975 demonstrates how TADP continued to offer support and advice on immigration even after the fall

of Saigon. A resister wrote TADP from England, explaining that he had left the United States and "never settled anywhere." His passport was due to expire. He had decided that if worst came to worst, he would fly to Canada, but he wondered if he would be allowed to live and work in Canada.[90] TADP informed the resister that Canada would "probably be [his] best bet," but reminded the individual that "visitors can only remain here for three months at the most, cannot work and are grilled at the airport to insure that the visitor will not remain here and 'take jobs from Canadians.'" The individual was advised to immigrate legally before his passport expired, was told about the points system, and was informed that a job offer was critical. Although the organization no longer had the "facilities to look for jobs," the resister was told that TADP would "see what we can come up with."[91]

The support that TADP offered in this letter points to one final reason organizations such as TADP were essential. The emotional support they gave their clients was one of their most vital services. As one author has written, the aid organizations in Canada both "calmed newcomers" and "provided the basis for first friendships in the new nation."[92] Resisters did not seek out "official" agencies for assistance because they wanted, as Dick Brown noted during the 60-day pardon period, to "turn to non-government groups to find out from a non-government person what is really going on."[93] When resisters came to Canada, they wanted to talk to someone who understood their needs, but also understood what they were resisting and why they were doing so. It made sense, therefore, to seek out others like themselves. After all, many of the counsellors at TADP were resisters who had made the same decision earlier.

Understanding how TADP and American war resisters in Canada fit into the larger Canadian and American anti-war movements is somewhat problematic. The relationship was clearly complicated. The Canadian movement was influenced by its American counterpart, yet was also distinct, as it focused on issues that centred on

Canada's role in the war.[94] The presence of so many American war resisters in Canada undoubtedly changed the very nature of the Canadian anti-war movement. The extent to which they did so is not entirely clear. Individuals like Mark Satin complicate the issue. As seen above, he was involved in the American and Canadian New Left student organizations—the main focus of both being on Vietnam—before co-founding TADP. Although it is imperative to explore the differences between the anti-war movements of both countries, it may be worthwhile to question the traditional nationalistic conceptions of social movements, since continually dividing the Vietnam anti-war movement into separate Canadian and American segments may occasionally involve a false dichotomy. After all, Satin was not alone among resisters who both figuratively and actually crossed borders and boundaries; it is worth remembering that all anti-war activists, regardless of the country they were in, shared the ultimate goal of ending the war in Vietnam.

In summary, although TADP always reminded war resisters that the final decision was their own, the tone of the *Manual for Draft-Age Immigrants to Canada* undoubtedly influenced their decision. The *Manual* was distributed far and wide in the United States, and early editions portrayed Canada as a haven for resisters and did little to dissuade them from coming to Canada. By its final edition, however, the approach was much more cautious. It highlighted the difficulty resisters might have finding employment in Canada and also reasoned that there was little need for most people to leave the United States because of the increased ease in resisting the war at home through deferments and exemptions. The change in outlook had practical implications when TADP began practising "priority counselling."

The more cautious tone in the organization's literature indicates that Canada was going through transitions of its own. American war resisters were caught up in larger trends and debates affecting the country, which included a newfound Canadian nationalism and changing immigration policies. The history of American war resisters in Canada reminds us of the important changes occurring in Canada during the time period.

Despite a change in approach, the Toronto Anti-Draft Programme continued to play an essential role in the war resister movement in Canada. As the needs of war resisters changed, TADP developed strategies to respond to those changes. For almost every challenge that resisters faced in their new land, TADP was able to help. Before individuals even reached Canada, the *Manual for Draft-Age Immigrants to Canada* explained what they should do when they got there. Once they arrived, the organization helped them become landed immigrants and find employment and housing. As more and more military resisters came to Canada, TADP became expert on military law and prioritized those whose needs were the most pressing. When resisters in Sweden wanted to come to Canada, TADP learned about Swedish and Canadian immigration regulations. Whenever the Canadian government unexpectedly changed the immigration regulations, resisters could count on TADP to interpret the bureaucratic jargon and explain the new rules in language they could understand. When the new laws favoured resisters, such as the Adjustment of Status Program, TADP was able to get the word out to those who were unaware of such changes or did not trust the government.

Through it all, the organization was a consistent source of accurate information and continued to provide support when others had ceased to do so. TADP and other aid organizations were not, as some seem to suggest, peripheral to the lives of American war resisters in Canada.[95] The process of immigrating to Canada posed significant difficulties, and the Toronto Anti-Draft Programme was there to ease the transition for those who resisted the war by moving north of the US border.

Note: This article is based on and extracted from a larger study. See Matthew Roth, "Crossing Borders: The Toronto Anti-Draft Programme and the Canadian Anti-Vietnam War Movement" (MA thesis, University of Waterloo, 2008).

Endnotes

1   Doug Owram, *Born at the Right Time: A History of the Baby-Boom Generation* (Toronto: University of Toronto Press, 1996), 219.

2   Myrna Kostash, *Long Way from Home: The Story of the Sixties Generation in Canada* (Toronto: James Lorimer, 1980), 45.

3   John Hagan, *Northern Passage: American Vietnam War Resisters in Canada* (Cambridge: Harvard University Press, 2001), 3. The exact number of resisters is highly contentious. For an in-depth analysis, see Joseph Jones, *Contending Statistics: The Numbers for U.S. Vietnam War Resisters in Canada* (Vancouver: Quarter Sheaf, 2005).

4   Hagan, *Northern Passage*, 3.

5   Michael Keating, "The War Evaders in Canada: Many Will Stay, but Many Want to Go Back," *Globe and Mail*, 18 September 1974, 3. *ProQuest*.

6   Renée Kasinsky, *Refugees from Militarism: Draft-Age Americans in Canada* (New Brunswick, NJ: Transaction Books, 1976), 96.

7   Kostash, *Long Way from Home*, 47.

8   Joseph Jones, "The House of Anansi's Singular Bestseller," *Canadian Notes & Queries* 61 (2002): 19.

9   Hagan, *Northern Passage*, 75; Kasinsky, *Refugees from Militarism*, 98; and Roger Neville Williams, *The New Exiles: American War Resisters in Canada* (New York: Liveright, 1971), 62–4.

10 Dan Wakefield, *Supernation at Peace and War* (Boston: Atlantic-Little, Brown, 1968), 11.

11 Williams, *New Exiles*, 62–3.

12 Hagan, *Northern Passage*, 75; and Harry Rosenthal, "Canada Increasingly Draft Dodgers' Haven: No One Knows How Many Americans Have Crossed Border but Number Grows Daily," *Los Angeles Times*, 2 June 1968, H19. *ProQuest*.

13 Jules Witcover, *The Year the Dream Died: Revisiting 1968 in America* (New York: Warner, 1997), 6.

14 Jones, "House of Anansi's," 19.

15 Kasinsky, *Refugees from Militarism*, 86.

16 "Bulk Order Record," box 2, Pocock (Jack) Memorial Collection (MS COLL 331) in the Thomas Fisher Rare Book Library at the University of Toronto (hereafter cited as Pocock, U of T).

17 Hagan, *Northern Passage*, 77–78.

18 Kenneth Fred Emerick, *War Resisters Canada: The World of the American Military-Political Refugee* (Knox, PA: Free Press, 1972), 101.

19 Jones, "House of Anansi's," 19.

20 David Churchill, "When Home Became Away: American Expatriates and New Social Movements in Toronto, 1965–1977" (PhD diss., University of Chicago, 2001), 159, *ProQuest*.

21 Ibid., 191.

22 Williams, *New Exiles*, 67.

23 Mark Satin, ed., *Manual for Draft-Age Immigrants to Canada*, 2nd ed. (Toronto: Toronto Anti-Draft Programme/House of Anansi, 1968), 1–2.

24 Ibid., 5.

25 Ibid., 79–80.

26 Ibid., 60.

27 "They Can't Come Home Again," *Hartford Courant*, 3 June 1968, 17. *ProQuest*.

28 Barry Craig, "5,000 Manuals Published Here for U.S. Draft-Dodgers," *Globe and Mail*, 12 February 1968, 5. *ProQuest*.

29 Ibid.

30 Satin, ed., *Manual for Draft-Age Immigrants*, 5–6.

31 Ibid., 1.

32 Ibid., 6.

33 Ibid., 5.

34 Hagan, *Northern Passage*, 34–5.

35 Jones, "House of Anansi's," 19.

36 Toronto Anti-Draft Programme, ed., *Manual for Draft-Age Immigrants to Canada*, 6th edn (Toronto: Toronto Anti-Draft Programme, 1971), 16.

37 Ibid., 15.

38 Ibid.

39 For further discussion on these issues, see Churchill, "When Home Became Away"; Hagan, *Northern Passage*; and Kasinsky, *Refugees from Militarism*.

40 Dimitry Anastakis, ed., *The Sixties: Passion, Politics, and Style* (Montreal: McGill-Queen's University Press, 2008), 7.

41 The main source of primary materials used in this paper was the day-to-day files of the Toronto Anti-Draft Programme.

42 Churchill, "When Home Became Away," 251.

43 "American Draft Dodgers Defended by Pacifist," box 17, Pocock, U of T.

44 "TADP," n.d., box 13, folder 9, Pocock, U of T. It should be noted that TADP also found that by 1969 draft resisters who came to Canada were increasingly less educated and from working-class backgrounds.

45 Williams, *New Exiles*, 267.

46 Ibid., 324.

47 Kasinsky, *Refugees from Militarism*, 15.

48 "Anti-draft Center Thrives in Canada," *Hartford Courant*, 1 April 1970, 34. *ProQuest*.

49 Williams, *New Exiles*, 324.

50 Kasinsky, *Refugees from Militarism*, 139.

51 Emerick, *War Resisters Canada*, 102–3.

52 Ross H. Munro, "Some U.S. Draft-Dodgers Turning to Crime, Even Suicide, Toronto Woman Tells Committee," *Globe and Mail*, 24 April 1970, 1. *ProQuest*.

53 Hagan, *Northern Passage*, 102; and Churchill, "When Home Became Away," 251. See Williams, *New Exiles*, for further discussion on the change in policy in 1970.

54   TADP, ed., *Manual for Draft-Age Immigrants*, 7.

55   Ibid., 9.

56   "TADP," n.d., box 13, folder 7, Pocock, U of T.

57   "TADP," n.d., box 13, folder 9, Pocock, U of T.

58   Ibid.

59   Greg J. Robertson, "Snags Develop in Changing America's Deserters to Canadian Citizens," *Hartford-Courant*, 11 August 1970, 4. *ProQuest*.

60   James Dickerson, *North to Canada: Men and Women against the Vietnam War* (Westport, CT: Praeger, 1999), 2.

61   Dick Brown to Herb, 1 August 1972, box 19, Pocock, U of T.

62   TADP, "Sweden Supplement," August 1972, box 19, Pocock, U of T, 1.

63   TADP, "Sweden Supplement," 1.

64   Ibid.

65   "TADP," n.d., box 13, Folder 7, Pocock, U of T.

66   "CCC Newsletter to Aid Centres," 19 July 1971, box 21, Pocock, U of T.

67   Hagan, *Northern Passage*, 148.

68   Dick Brown to Stan, 8 December 1972, box 13, Pocock, U of T.

69   TADP, "Brief for Bloor Street United Church," June 1973, box 13, Pocock, U of T.

70   Dick Brown to Stan, 8 December 1972, box 13, Pocock, U of T.

71   Brown to Brothers and Sisters, 17 November 1972, box 13, folder 1, Pocock, U of T.

72   Brown to Stan, 8 December 1972, box 13, Pocock, U of T.

73   Brown to Parker, 16 April 1973, box 19, Pocock, U of T.

74   Canada, Office of the Minister, Department of Manpower and Immigration, "For Release," 18 June 1973, box 14, Pocock, U of T.

75   Canada, Office of the Minister, Department of Manpower and Immigration, "For Release," 14 August 1973, box 14, Pocock, U of T.

76   Hagan, *Northern Passage*, 151; and Zimmerman to Friends, n.d., box 14, Pocock, U of T.

77   "News Release," 31 July 1973, box 14, Pocock, U of T.

78   Ibid.

79   "Bus Carries Immigration Message," n.d., box 14, Pocock, U of T.

80   Rich Killmer, Tim Maloney, and Dave Deauchene, "Memo," 9 August 1973, box 14, Pocock, U of T.

81   Brown, "Notice to All Counsellors," 6 September 1973, box 14, Pocock, U of T.

82   TADP, "Report on Finding People," n.d., box 14, Pocock, U of T.

83   TADP, "Sixty Days of Grace: Your Last Chance," 1973, box 14, Pocock, U of T, 1.

84   Ibid., 2.

85   Ibid., 8.

86   Ibid., 9.

87   Kasinsky, *Refugees from Militarism*, 203–4, 295.

88   TADP, "Immigration Fact Sheet," August 1973, box 13, Pocock, U of T, 1.

89   Keating, "War Evaders in Canada," 3.

90   Letter to TADP, 1975, box 1, Pocock, U of T.

91   Letter from TADP, 25 July 1975, box 1, Pocock, U of T.

92   David S. Surrey, *Choice of Conscience: Vietnam Era Military and Draft Resisters in Canada* (New York: Praeger, 1982), 141.

93   Brown to Ian and Bruce, 26 September 1973, box 14, Pocock, U of T.

94   Hagan, *Northern Passage*, 68.

95   See, for example, Frank Kusch, *All American Boys: Draft Dodgers in Canada from the Vietnam War* (Westport, CT: Praeger, 2001).

◎ 14.2: THE UNIVERSITY OF TORONTO HEALTH SERVICE, ORAL CONTRACEPTION, AND STUDENT DEMAND FOR BIRTH CONTROL, 1960–1970

Christabelle Sethna

The birth control pill is routinely associated with the so-called sexual revolution of the 1960s. Yet this case study of the impact of the pill on the University of Toronto reveals that young, single, white, middle-class women students were not always able to access this prescription contraceptive at the campus Health Service. The refusal or reluctance of the Health Service to prescribe the pill to single women students resulted in heightened male and female student pressure on the Health Service to do so. The development of and changes to the Health Service's policy on the provision of oral contraceptives to single women students reflected the often contradictory moral, legal, and administrative positionalities of that service. The result was a complex dynamic marked by conflict and collusion.

On 15 February 1967, the *Varsity*, the main student newspaper for the University of Toronto (U of T), published an angry letter from undergraduate student Jim Sayers. A furious Sayers denounced Dr George E. Wodehouse, director of the campus Health Service, for prescribing "celibacy and avoidance" instead of the birth control pill to single women students. "I wish the members of the otherwise inadequate Health Service would keep their personal convictions from interfering with the function of the Service," Sayers frothed, "[t]o Dr. Wodehouse, and to those who may have a knife at his back, I say . . . give the pill to those who *want* it, and see if the sky falls down. I'm sure it won't." Taking a final swipe, he demanded: "how long will a pluralist campus tolerate such a naive, neo Puritan, self-righteous, not to mention totalitarian attitude?"[1]

In the 1960s, a so-called sexual revolution that sanctioned premarital sex for young, white, single, middle-class women coincided with the introduction of the birth control pill, thereby motivating campus Health Services to consider the provision of the pill to unmarried female students.[2] Unfortunately, published accounts that trace the impact of oral contraceptives on campus are sparse and often cursory. . . .

In this preliminary case study of the U of T, I chart the on-campus struggle that the university's Health Service and the student population waged over the pill. I argue that the refusal or reluctance of the Health Service to prescribe the pill to single women students resulted in heightened student pressure on the Health Service to do so. The development of and changes to the Health Service's policy on the provision of oral contraceptives to single women students reflected the often contradictory moral, legal, and administrative positions of that service. Students, both male and female, tapped into shifting and interconnected political discourses that ranged from student power to population control to

women's liberation in order to liberalize the Health Service's policy on pill prescriptions. However, Health Service personnel, individual students, and various student factions were not always at odds with each other. Rather, their interaction can be characterized more correctly as one of conflict, collusion, and co-optation.

The U of T Health Service

Initially, the main concern of the Health Service, established in 1906, was to keep the student body free from exposure to infectious diseases like tuberculosis. As the student population swelled with returning servicemen after the end of the Second World War, the Health Service expanded rapidly. Despite cramped conditions, it came to include separate facilities for men and women, a clinical consulting service, a psychiatric service, an athletic injury service, and an infirmary. It even offered a screening program for parasitic infections and tropical diseases for students travelling to and from Afro-Asian countries. An Advisory Committee to the Health Service, chaired by the dean of the Faculty of Medicine, was composed of senior representatives from various departments within the Faculty of Medicine, as well as the chairman and the president of the university, ex officio. The Advisory Committee met annually but the Health Service director met more frequently with the dean of the Faculty of Medicine in regard to the Health Service. Wodehouse became Health Service director in 1950 and retired in 1984. Dr Frances Stewart, a physician employed at the Health Service before the war, was the Health Service's assistant director and the head of the Women's Division between 1946 and 1976. Both Wodehouse and Stewart had served in the armed forces during the war, making them a generation older than the student clientele of the 1960s.[3]

During this decade the enrolment of male and female students in universities increased considerably.[4] With this demographic surge, the Health Service experienced a 20 per cent rise in total utilization and a 24 per cent jump in its office consultations. Wodehouse was quick to assert that the statistics did not indicate that more students were unwell. Rather, they reflected two trends. The first was students' growing acceptance of the Health Service as their primary health care option. The second was, as he put it, "student interest in sex education and contraceptive education and prescription."[5] The word "prescription" was a master stroke of linguistic subtlety. It allowed the ever-discrete Wodehouse to refer indirectly to heightened student demands that the Health Service prescribe oral contraceptives to single women students. Tuberculosis had obviously taken a back seat.

Sex and Birth Control in Canada

Scholars have shown that before the 1940s, heterosexual courtship among white, middle-class youths was a competitive system that encouraged individuals to date different partners. After 1945, in keeping with the Cold War quest for national security, dating patterns changed.[6] Couples went steady, dating one individual regularly, often until marriage. Despite the widespread acknowledgment of necking and petting activity in steady relationships, young women were required, however, to safeguard their virginity.[7] However, unintended pregnancies increased after 1945 in single women younger than 20 years of age. A drop in the mean age of menarche and in marriage rates after 1951 for females aged 15 to 19 contributed to this trend.[8]

Early in the 1960s the term "sexual revolution" was used to indicate the "suspected impact" of the birth control pill on the sexual behaviour of female students in institutions of higher education.[9] Whether premarital sexual behaviour in young, white, middle-class women actually changed significantly during the decade remains the subject of debate.[10] . . . Canadians claimed to have detected a "massive increase" in single females reporting sexual intercourse, especially in the anglophone, urban university population.[11] . . . Additional research showed that because of the direct relationship between coital experience and age, a sizeable proportion of males and females would have intercourse

for the first time while at university.[12] Surveys of this group's sexual activity revealed that approximately 28 per cent of males and females engaged in heavy petting on dates. Of the males, 22 per cent admitted to having had sexual intercourse, while nearly 15 per cent of females did. However, 15 per cent of females and almost the same percentage of males admitted not having any knowledge of contraceptives. Sex education in schools was spotty. A 1964 survey showed not one of 55 urban school systems taught family life education as a separate subject. For 35 of the respondents, sex education was included in subjects like home economics and social sciences. Contraception was rarely discussed as a topic. It was not surprising that by the mid-sixties, one-third of the 26,000 unwed mothers in Canada were reported to be teenagers.[13]

Youths' ignorance of contraception was fuelled by the fact that birth control was illegal in Canada. From the late nineteenth century onward, the Criminal Code prohibited abortion as well as the sale, advertisement, and dissemination of contraception. A few birth control clinics influenced by the eugenics movement dispensed contraceptives to poor married women from the 1920s on. The courts determined in the 1930s that birth control was permissible if in the public good. Nevertheless, in the early 1960s, a Toronto pharmacist was convicted of selling condoms through the mail. Canada's birth control laws also had a negative effect on the country's performance at the United Nations. Canadian delegates could not officially support UN family planning initiatives abroad because birth control was still illegal at home.[14] Abortion, whether self-induced or performed by medical or non-medical personnel, remained an underground secret practice. Between 1962 and 1966, abortion was the main cause of maternal deaths in some provinces, such as Ontario.[15]

The federal government approved the oral contraceptive pill on a doctor's prescription in 1961. The pill, which offered nearly 100 per cent protection against conception, had the potential to free married *and* single women from unintended pregnancy. . . . However, oral contraception was earmarked for married women, or for women engaged to be married, for their family planning goals.[16]

When it came to prescribing the pill to single women, physicians, in general, were torn by moral and legal considerations. Some refused to prescribe the pill because they were against premarital sex or because they were afraid of being viewed as promoting sexual promiscuity. Others were concerned that they could face criminal suits for dispensing contraceptives. The treatment of minors who fell below provincial age limits for consent to medical care was another legal grey area. It was speculated that without parental notification, the gynaecological examination often required for a pill prescription and the pill prescription itself could lead technically to charges of battery or to contributing to the delinquency of a minor.[17] It was not surprising, therefore, that young women were often reluctant to approach a family physician to discuss their contraceptive needs for fear of being rejected.[18]

The U of T Health Service Policy on Contraceptive Prescription

. . . There was no doubt, however, that the moral and legal considerations of prescribing the pill to single women were compounded for university Health Services. Some Health Service doctors dismissed student requests for contraception, complaining that they required "counselling and mental discipline," not "more permissiveness in the form of the 'pill.'"[19] Nevertheless, many doctors at Health Services, especially those who held faculty appointments, felt compromised by the possibility of public exposure.[20]

Universities, in their role of guardian, *in loco parentis*, feared the negative reaction of parents and government officials.[21] Moreover, Health Services were confused over their function in relation to a sexually active student population.[22] Few of the university Health Services polled in 1965 were willing to provide single women students with the pill. A survey of 323 Canadian and American institutional members of the American College Health Association (ACHA) revealed that more than 55 per cent of the respondents did not

prescribe the pill for contraceptive purposes. Those campus Health Services that refused to prescribe the pill took the position that contraception was not their responsibility. Those campus Health Services that did, suggested, in a manner that anticipated pro-choice statements regarding abortion, that pill prescriptions were a private matter between physician and patient. In total, 44 per cent of the respondents prescribed the pill for married students but 76 per cent reported that they would not prescribe the pill to any unmarried student. . . . [23]

On 14 September 1965, Wodehouse, an active ACHA Council member, informed the Advisory Committee to the Health Service that there had been "widespread agitation by students in other centers for the provision of sex education, contraceptive information and education and contraceptive prescription." In the United States, scandals concerning campus Health Services that had surreptitiously prescribed the pill to unmarried students were mushrooming in the popular and student press.[24] Wodehouse warned that a similar situation was "imminent" at the U of T.[25] There was little reason to suspect otherwise. Given the direction of New Left politics, U of T students were already working to change the structure of society via direct action, individual human development, and participatory democracy. Sexual experimentation was viewed as an important part of the generational rebellion against the old order.[26] Students charged that the university itself was a hypocritical institution that took moral positions on students' drinking, drug taking, and sexual activity while enjoying immoral relationships with industries that promoted war, racism, and weapons production.[27] However, many politically active students believed that political change was impossible because the *in loco parentis* role of universities had infantilized students. It was only a matter of time until some students could claim that the same authoritarianism had also blocked their access to the pill. Student Marvin Ross expressed the tenor of the times when he commented that students were not to be treated as infants "to be suckled by Simcoe Hall." U of T students, he noted, were adults. They grew up very quickly when they realized that "not all middle class boys and girls should and do remain celibate until they are married."[28] . . .

To stave off possible criticism of the Health Service from students while balancing the concerns of Health Service staff, university administrators, government officials, and parents, the Advisory Committee took two important steps. First, it invited two students from the student government—the Students' Administrative Council (SAC)—to sit as representatives, and Robin Ross, U of T registrar, director of student services, and the person responsible for the Health Service's budget, to sit as a new member. The invitation to the two students may have reflected the Advisory Council's responsiveness to student demands for student participation on university bodies. However, it is more likely that the invitation signalled the Advisory Committee's pragmatic desire to co-opt student concerns. . . .

Second, the Advisory Committee hammered out a formal Health Service policy on contraceptive prescriptions. Its members agreed that although Health Service staff could assist with educating students about birth control,

> it would be an improper and unfitting policy at this time for the [Health] Service to provide indiscriminate contraceptive prescription. While it was recognized that contraceptive prescription will always remain a matter of individual medical judgement and decision, in general, at the University, such prescription should be limited at present to married students and to those students in their period of premarital counselling.[29]

Wodehouse would later claim that the policy was deliberately "indecisive" so as to permit physicians to meet some of the contraceptive needs of single women students.[30] Ever discrete, he reported to the U of T president that although the Health Service continued to limit pill prescriptions to students who were married or engaged, "it seems likely that at least a number of other patients will continue to present themselves who will require individual medical judgement in the advice given."[31] The policy's loophole phrase—"contraceptive prescription must always remain a matter of individual medical judgement and decision"—hinted at the autonomy of Health Service doctors. Yet the physicians themselves were unsure of their position. Dr David Smith, from the Men's Division of the Health Service, remembers prescribing the pill to any female student who happened to see him: "George [Wodehouse] had to be very careful. There were some terrible fuddy duddies at the University. But when kids came in, we gave it [the pill] to them." However, Dr Ruth Davis in the Women's Division tells a different story: "We wouldn't have prescribed the pill if it were illegal. George [Wodehouse] was very careful about the law."[32]

Student Pressure on the Health Service

Despite its best intentions, the Advisory Committee failed to prevent student agitation for birth control. On the one hand, the Advisory Committee's attempt at juggling the needs of students in regard to the other constituencies involved was nothing short of Herculean. On the other hand, student frustration with their respective Health Services was at a boil across Canada. . . .

One of the earliest examples of student demands for birth control services occurred at U of T's University College Literary and Athletic Society. Known colloquially as "The Lit," the society was founded in 1854. It was the oldest student union in Canada and publisher of the first issue of the *Varsity*, the U of T's main student newspaper, in 1880. At a December 1965 meeting, Lit president Daniel Cooper proposed a bold motion to set up a student birth control program:

> Since the Society considers the existing laws on birth control are unsuitable, and desires their ultimate change to suit present conditions, and since we believe that steps toward sex education should be taken, be it therefore moved that University College Literary

and Athletic Society sponsor a programme of lectures and seminars on sex education and birth control; that the Lit try to secure the support of the University Health Service and the college administration for such a programme; that after such a programme is held, the Lit assess the success of the programme and consider taking further steps.[33]

Lit members were aware that what they were proposing was illegal under the Canadian Criminal Code. That's why the motion asked for the support of the college administration and the Health Service. The Health Service, the students understood correctly, was technically breaking the law because it was already dispensing birth control information and devices to engaged and married students. The motion passed, but with heated discussion. Several members wanted the Lit to force a test case of the law. They proposed sending a married student to the Health Service to get birth control information and then demand that the Health Service be prosecuted. Others objected, claiming that a test case would only compromise whatever birth control services the Health Service was already providing.[34] The Lit's next step was to seek SAC endorsement for their birth control program. . . . The motion, however, failed at SAC.

Although SAC did not initially stand behind the Lit's birth control program, support for the issue was growing. Up until the mid-1960s, SAC had functioned as a student government intent on providing students with social, cultural, and communications services. Still, early indications of SAC's radicalization were apparent. In 1959, because of an incident of racial discrimination at a women's sorority, SAC sponsored a lecture on "The Problem of Race Relations."[35] A few years later, SAC president Jordan G. Sullivan cited Bissell's address to student leaders on campus—"you are deeply conscious of yourselves as citizens going into a world where you will be asked to share greater and greater responsibility"—to introduce some changes in direction.[36] SAC was becoming more independent. It was sponsoring model parliaments, decrying

discrimination in student housing, and debating Canada's involvement in the nuclear arms race. During the 1965–6 academic year, the council "began to deal with the political issues that would dominate its discussions and activities throughout the ensuing decade."[37]

The two major issues on the table were the financing of higher education and student participation in university government. On the first point, SAC sided with the Canadian Union of Students (CUS) to call for the elimination of tuition fees. On the second point, SAC insisted that because the student "is a mature individual capable of governing himself [*sic*]," students should have an equal say with faculty in the governing of the university.[38] The lack of this recognition on the part of the university administration had given rise to the demands for student power. Student power, according to a SAC brief to the Commission on University Government (CUG), was seeking to give students equality and respect; to assume a degree of control in shaping their lives; to participate in decision-making; to establish a sense of community; and to make major changes to the university, education, and relationships with others.[39]

The newly elected SAC leaders made the same appeal in regard to access to contraceptives. One of the first actions Tom Faulkner, the incoming SAC president, took in the spring of 1966 was to sketch out new areas of responsibility SAC could assume under his tenure. Faulkner suggested that SAC "must always be trying to do more for the student." Therefore, he proposed that the Education Commission, one of SAC's committees, must continue to promote its drama workshops, political affairs, and a music program. But it could also investigate organizing seminars on studying, note taking, exam preparation, and birth control and sex education.[40] Faulkner's wish list for the Education Commission indicated the casualness with which seminars on birth control and sex education could be added to commonplace student concerns. It also spoke to the influence of other student groups that supported birth control and that expected SAC to take a leading role in the matter. The Student Democratic Union

(SDU) developed an extensive action program for SAC. It included increased student aid, lower food prices, book discounts, greater student participation in university government, better course evaluation methods, and the provision of birth control information. "Since personal moral behaviour is the responsibility of the individual and not the state or the university," the program read, "the SDU will support the individual's right to birth control information. The SDU will ask the Health Service to make birth control information available to all who request it, and in the event that the Health Service fails to assume this responsibility, the SAC will undertake it."[41]

. . .

The *Varsity* Weighs In

Shortly after the Second World War, the *Varsity* carried numerous stories about the need for a mental health clinic on campus that pressured the Health Service Advisory Committee to do its bit.[42] Two decades later, this student newspaper became SAC's powerful ally in promoting students' access to birth control services. U of T students were first apprised of the pill's wonders in a *Varsity* article reprinted from the *Dalhousie Review* and published in the spring of 1965. Authored by Tony Bond, the piece was illustrated with a photo of oral contraceptives and captioned enticingly: "These little pills make by far the best method of contraception." Bond did not criticize university Health Services but rather Canada's archaic birth control laws. Despite the illegality of contraceptives, the pill was available. Abortions had merely gone underground. At the United Nations, Canada was forced to sit "like a Presbyterian prude" because it could not participate in debates about birth control. The situation was especially serious because of the possibility of a Third World population explosion.[43] . . .

Over the next few years, the *Varsity* carried several reports, debates, articles, and letters about birth control. Abortion was the most contentious topic, generating fiercely opposing views. When Paul Macrae, a third-year sociology student,

opined that the illegality of abortion was harmful to women, another student responded that Macrae's article was the product of a "confused mind." Reporting on other university Health Services from near and far was another major preoccupation. *Varsity* readers learned, for example, that the head of the Health Service at the University of Western Ontario had denied prescribing birth control pills to single women students and that Berkeley University students in the United States had voted 4–1 in favour of the distribution of pills by their campus Health Service.[44]

In early 1967 the newspaper published a lengthy interview with a young, single, pill-taking student identified only as "Carol." On the one hand, her anonymity gave the lie to the decade's stereotype of sexual openness. On the other, it permitted her to be very forthcoming. Consequently, this interview was one of the few instances in which the opinion of a female student on oral contraception was highlighted so centrally in the *Varsity*. Carol recounted that when her girlfriend became pregnant, she was forced into a shotgun marriage. Carol was determined not to meet the same fate. She and her boyfriend were having a "meaningful relationship" that necessarily included sexual intercourse. However, she did not want to get pregnant. She wanted a career but did not want to deny herself sex even if it did not lead to marriage. "I don't believe in the Doris Day movie world where the girl doesn't have any sex urges," Carol was quoted as saying. She insisted that it was more moral "to take the pills with no illusions, than to take chances believing in the chaste Doris Day world. You take the pills so your life, and the lives of a child and other people, won't be ruined." Carol said she did not go to the U of T Health Service because she was told that its doctors did not prescribe pills unless girls could prove they were getting married. It was unclear how she obtained this information. She decided to phone Planned Parenthood to get the name of a doctor who provided her with the pill. "I think this is an evasion of responsibility on the part of the Health Service," Carol concluded. Alongside Carol's interview was a quote from Wodehouse centred in a square box. It contained the very words that led an enraged Sayers to write to the *Varsity*:

> For single girls . . . we feel that celibacy and avoidance is proper. We are, however, willing to provide information about the mechanics and emotional aspects of sex to any girl who asks us. If an unmarried girl is determined to get pills, and can show me what she is doing . . . we will put her in touch with a reputable doctor. That is the least we can do.[45]

The contrast between the young, single female student and the veteran male Health Service director was sharp and unmistakable. Carol appeared realistic, responsible, and adult. Wodehouse seemed ancient, inadequate, and out of touch. At face value, Carol's testimony reflected the shift in the sexual mores that sanctioned premarital sex. At a deeper level, it signalled her desire for a sex life *and* a career. Both needs can be read as indicators of a burgeoning women's liberation consciousness. They may also be viewed as aspirations peculiar to a white, middle-class sense of entitlement to personal and professional fulfilment that an unintended pregnancy could potentially destroy. Precisely because campus Health Services were stingy with pill prescriptions, Carol and her peers began flooding family planning clinics that had originally been established to dispense contraceptives to poor married women. As state-funded medical insurance became more accessible, this clientele gravitated toward private physician care, only to be replaced at family planning clinics by a population of ambitious and goal-directed single women university students requiring pills, not platitudes.[46]

Ambition and goal-directedness were characteristic of five other pill-popping single women students subsequently profiled in the *Varsity*. . . .[47]

The interviews offered proof that premarital heterosexual intercourse was a fact of life on the U of T campus. They also indicated that the pill was the contraceptive preferred most often by single women students because it offered them a clean solution to the "mess" of an unintended pregnancy. Whether involved with one steady partner or with several men, single women students were willing to seek out contraceptive protection with or without the assistance of the Health Service to safeguard their personal and professional gains. . . .

For its own part, SAC barrelled ahead, approving the formation of a birth control program committee to coordinate seminars at women's residences and to distribute information from local Planned Parenthood groups that contained the names of doctors who would supply contraceptives. Allowing that SAC had long been known for its "lethargy," the *Varsity* praised SAC's efforts as "encouraging."[48] The birth control program was a direct indictment of the Health Service. Faulkner acknowledged that the distribution of birth control information was technically illegal. But he asserted that the Health Service was reluctant to "give such information to anyone but married women."[49] . . . Faulkner ended up on the hot seat. Shortly after SAC approved of the birth control committee's activities, Ontario attorney general Arthur Wishart threatened to investigate. Faulkner reacted with defiance. He was quoted in the *Varsity* as saying: "[T]here is a remote chance that I could go to jail over this, but it is very remote, and I'm prepared to risk it."[50]

Precisely because of the publicity the *Varsity* continued to give the birth control issue, Wodehouse furnished Jack Sword, acting president of the University of Toronto, with a copy of a letter he had sent to George Tatham, dean of students at Glendon College, York University. Wodehouse asserted that other than the Heath Service policy, there was no official university statement on birth control. "I feel it might be helpful," he wrote, therefore, to Sword, "if you had this at hand."[51] Wodehouse acknowledged that the policy may be seen as indecisive, or as interfering with parental responsibilities. He revealed that the Health Service was torn between its obligations to the patient, its position within the university, and its "strong reservations about the propriety" of prescribing contraceptives to single women, especially if under age 21 and a ward of their families. He acknowledged that the Health Service held regular discussion groups with groups of women students in the women's residences on sex education and family life education. Health Service doctors also allowed engaged students to start taking the pill anywhere from two to five months before their wedding date. And when the examining physician found unmarried patients to be "stable, well-informed and clear in their intentions," as was almost always the case, they could be referred to a gynaecologist or to the Toronto General Hospital where they would receive contraceptive advice and care. Using the vocabulary of infectious diseases, he asserted that many single, pill-seeking patients had already established a sexual relationship with a man they planned to marry and to whom they had been sexually "exposed" for several months before their Health Service visit. Under such circumstances, he would prefer as a parent to know that students were "getting adequate help in avoiding pregnancy and its complications."[52] . . .

For both students and doctors at the Health Service, the issue of abortion was impossible to avoid. Faulkner identified himself as a virgin and therefore, the "most sexually naive point man" for birth control. Yet he later claimed he was motivated to push ahead with the SAC student birth control program because of accounts of illegal abortion. He had heard that young U of T women were becoming pregnant and "scraping themselves with coat hangers."[53] Wodehouse's annual report to the university president for 1967–8 admitted as much. Wodehouse acknowledged that there was a rash of unplanned pregnancies on campus. In some cases, the student's pregnancy led to marriage, in a few others to abortion. The Health Service refused to refer students seeking abortions to unauthorized abortionists. Because of the strict interpretation of an existing law that permitted abortion only in the case of a danger to a woman's life, 60 to 70 per cent of the Health Service's referrals were successful.[54] Wodehouse openly expressed his frustration at two situations—when pregnant students would not or could not marry, and when, unable to access the therapeutic termination of a pregnancy in a local hospital, pregnant students went ahead with an illegal abortion in other cities.[55] . . .

Widening the Loophole on Pill Prescriptions

In response to the abortion issue, the Advisory Committee decided on 7 March 1968 to widen the loophole in the Health Service's policy on prescription contraceptives. With Faulkner now sitting as one of the student representatives, the Advisory Committee reaffirmed the need for the Health Service policy and its loophole. This time, however, the members agreed that "some circumstances arising in increasing numbers might justify a broadening of this phrase." The language was discrete. But there was no mistaking the intention. The loophole now made room for Health Service physicians to prescribe the pill on the spot to single students in the hope of preventing unplanned pregnancies and subsequent illegal abortions. Perhaps to reassure nervous administrators, colleagues, and parents, and to stem a possible flood of single students seeking the pill, the Advisory Committee confirmed that the Health Service would not prescribe "on demand." Such a practice "would not constitute good or adequate treatment of the individual." Importantly, signalling its cooperation with SAC, the committee also advised that the Health Service and Faulkner could explore the development of a sex education program for students.[56]

The Health Service's more liberal public stance on pill prescriptions had a direct impact on student visits. Over the 1968–9 academic year, the Women's Division of the Health Service reported that its gynaecological service had increased "by leaps and bounds." A total of 29 cases had to be referred for obstetrical and gynaecological consultation, representing the third highest number of consultations after psychiatric and surgical cases.[57] The shift on pill prescriptions had undoubtedly occurred because of student pressure. It may also have been motivated by the belief that the reform of the country's birth control legislation was at hand. Indeed, in 1969 Parliament passed a bill intended to take effect in August that decriminalized contraception and liberalized abortion. By this time, many Canadians had experienced a major change of opinion in regard to contraception. In 1952, 48 per cent of Canadians polled said the practice of birth control was not morally wrong. By 1965, that number registered at 66 per cent.[58] . . .

For Canadians, abortion remained a more contentious issue than contraception. In the mid-sixties, a majority of Canadians surveyed agreed that the legal reasons for an abortion—to save a woman's life—should include the preservation of a woman's mental and physical health.[59] The new law technically took these additional concerns into account. But the conditions under which a legal abortion was now permissible after 1969 proved extremely restrictive. Legal abortions were permitted only if a woman had a referral from her doctor to a hospital's therapeutic abortion committee (TAC). The TAC, consisting of three or more doctors (the doctor who referred the woman for an abortion could not sit on the TAC), had to rule that an abortion was necessary to preserve the woman's health. Hospitals were not obligated to strike TACs. Nowhere was there a consistent definition of what constituted health. Moreover, doctors could refuse to perform abortions; many remained divided over the morality of the procedure.[60] As a result, the new law did not stop illegal abortion. Performed by medical and non-medical personnel or self-induced, illegal abortions were estimated at 100,000 a year.[61] Discontent over a law that neither prevented illegal abortions nor decreased maternal deaths from botched abortions led women involved in a nascent women's liberation movement to organize around the repeal of the abortion law.[62]

One consequence of the growth of the women's liberation movement meant that the issue of access to contraception and abortion came increasingly under the purview of feminist politics on campus. A newly founded group, called the Women's Liberation Movement (WLM), took action. In the summer of 1969, it set up a Birth Control Centre at U of T. Approximately 20 people a day came in to look at various contraceptive devices and pamphlets on birth control. The main source of information on birth control that the WLM distributed was the *Birth Control Handbook*.[63] Concerned with the problem of illegal abortion, a student birth control committee struck by the McGill Student Council published the *Handbook* in 1968.[64] It provided details on a wide range of birth control devices and methods. In the case of an unwanted pregnancy, it also endorsed abortion performed by competent, medically trained doctors. The *Handbook* supported the right of all sexually active women, regardless of their class, marital status, or age, to reproductive freedom. The editors also denounced the population-growth lobby, arguing that American imperialism and racism, not overpopulation, were the real cause of poverty in the Third World.[65] . . .

Harriet Kideckel, a U of T graduate who worked at the centre, was concerned with the plight of poor students. She predicted that by the time the spring exams were over approximately 100 students would be pregnant and seeking abortions. Middle-class students could afford to raise the money to travel to the United States to have an abortion. But poor students could not. Their student loans and summer earnings would not be able to cover the costs. Kideckel blamed the Health Service for making it difficult for a single woman to obtain the pill.[66] Despite Kideckel's claims, the Criminal Code reforms emboldened the Health Service to provide students with on-the-spot pill prescriptions and much more—so much so that those students who were still under their parents' medical insurance plan were not billed for certain services. The Health Service was concerned that parents would become aware of the sexually related nature of the problems for which their children were being treated.[67]

Contraception and Abortion

For the Health Service, the post-1969 period was full of ironies, large and small. The publication of Barbara Seaman's best-selling book, *The Doctor's Case against the Pill* (1969), generated widespread concern about the pill's negative side effects. Seaman provided frightening medical evidence that showed the pill was linked to both fatal and nonfatal complications.[68] The ensuing furore over her findings led to Senate hearings in the United States in early 1970. The Canadian Medical Association (CMA) responded quickly, urging that the pill should not be withdrawn. Rather, it advised that each doctor had to weigh carefully the benefits of virtually 100 per cent effective contraception against possible side effects for each patient. For example, the pill was not to be recommended to those with a history of diabetes or thrombosis.[69]

News of the pill's negative side effects forced Wodehouse into a difficult position. As Health Service director, he had taken student heat for a Health Service policy that, on the surface, had restricted pill prescriptions to students who were married or engaged. He now found himself defending the pill's safety while, simultaneously, rationalizing the Health Service's decision to prescribe oral contraceptives to his student clientele, whether married or single. Wodehouse turned to the *Varsity*, the very same newspaper that had denounced the Health Service for its timidity regarding pill prescriptions, to outline his defence of the oral contraceptive. Using the CMA statement as a guide, Wodehouse announced that the Health Service would prescribe the pill to any student who requested it. However, she first had to pass a thorough medical examination. Any patient who did not would be advised about other contraceptive methods. In effect, the Health Service's criterion for pill prescriptions was no longer the patient's moral suitability as designated by her marital status but her physiological fitness based on the outcome of her medical examination.[70]

The Health Service co-sponsored with SAC and the Department of Obstetrics and Gynaecology a series of evening educational sessions for students on the subjects of sexuality and reproduction, featuring experts from groups like Planned Parenthood. The Women's Division of the Health Service recorded large jumps in patient visits. Increasing numbers of students were coming in already pregnant. During the 1970–1 academic year, 165 students came to the Health Service suspecting pregnancy. All of them had had unprotected sexual intercourse. A total of 65 were pregnant.[71] In the autumn of 1971, the Advisory Committee made a decision to formally review and update the Health Service policy on contraceptive prescription that had been formulated six years previously. The new policy reflected the difficult reality the Advisory Committee was now facing. In comparison, the dilemma surrounding pill prescriptions paled.

In an all-out effort to reduce unwanted pregnancy, the Health Service would offer "every facility within its power" to provide sex education, contraceptive prescription, and, where indicated, assistance in the termination of pregnancy. Never using the word "abortion," the new policy included two caveats. It stated plainly that the termination of pregnancy was "a most undesirable and inadequate" method of birth control and "no substitute for adequate contraception." Moreover, if the termination of pregnancy ran counter to the examining physician's "religious and moral convictions," the physician would inform the patient and refer her to another doctor who did not hold the same views. Fearing controversy, the chair of U of T's Department of Obstetrics and Gynaecology urged that any public discussion of the new policy stress the importance of education and contraception over abortion.[72] . . .

This preliminary case study demonstrates that during the so-called sexual revolution of the 1960s, the pill was not readily available to young, white, single women. Despite their privileges of race and class, many of these women had difficulty getting access to the pill on the U of T campus because of the refusal or reluctance of the university's Health Service to prescribe it. While U of T students and the Health Service staff occasionally worked together for student access to birth control services, male and female student pressure on the Health Service was a significant factor in promoting single women students' access to the pill. The relationship of male and female students to the Health Service was grounded in student expectations of sexual freedom unmarred by the threat of an unwanted pregnancy and was also coloured by the Health Service's attempts to negotiate those expectations within the moral, legal, and administrative restrictions at U of T. The result was a complex dynamic marked by conflict and collusion. . . .

Author's Note: I thank Steve Hewitt, Mary Bird, Harold Averill, Mary Auxi Guiao, Charles Levi, and Jane Wodehouse for their assistance. Steven Maynard and two anonymous reviewers for *Historical Studies in Education* (*HSE*) provided insightful commentary. I am grateful to the Faculty of Education, University of Ottawa, and to the Social Sciences and Humanities Research Council of Canada for funds provided to hire research assistants Amélie Chrétien, Adinne Schwartz, and Corrie Level. Versions of this paper have been presented at the annual meeting of the Canadian Historical Association, University of Toronto, Toronto, 27–9 May 2002, and at the International Federation for Research on Women's History, Queen's University, Belfast, Ireland, 11–14 August 2003.

Endnotes

1   Jim Sayers, "Give the Pill to Those Who Want It," *Varsity*, 15 February 1967, 4.

2   F.K. Harding, "The College Unmarried Population Explosion," *Journal of School Health* 35, no. 10 (December 1965): 450–7; Willard Dalrymple, "A Doctor Speaks of College Students and Sex," *Journal of the American College Health Association* (*JACHA*) 15, no. 3 (February 1967): 279–86; Emanuel Klein, "The Need for Family Planning as a Student Health Service," *JACHA* 16, no. 1 (October 1967): 95–8; Ethel M. Nash, "The College Physician's Role in Sex Education," *JACHA* 15: Supplement (May 1967): 66–71; "Contraceptives for Students: An Invitational Symposium," *Journal of Reproductive Medicine* 4, no. 2 (February 1970): 9–18.

3   University of Toronto Archives (UTA), A83-0036, box 34, file: University Health Service (UHS), "University Health Service: University of Toronto," pp. 1–27, June 1976, and Health Service Records, "Minutes of the Advisory Committee to the University Health Service," 14 September 1965, p. 1. Existing records of the Health Service are meagre; the most rewarding primary sources are the minutes of the Advisory Committee. Both Wodehouse and Stewart are now deceased. Neither, to my knowledge, left private papers on deposit.

4   Dominion Bureau of Statistics, *Education in Canada: A Statistical Review for the Period 1960–61 to 1970–71* (Ottawa: Statistics Canada, 1973), 58.

5   G.E. Wodehouse, "The Director of the University Health Service," University of Toronto, *President's Report 1965–1966*, 218.

6   Elaine Tyler May, *Homeward Bound: American Families in the Cold War Era* (New York: Basic Books, 1988).

7   See Beth L. Bailey, *From Front Porch to Back Seat: Courtship in Twentieth-Century America* (Baltimore and London: The Johns Hopkins University Press, 1989 [1988]).

8   Christabelle Sethna, "'WE WANT FACTS NOT MORALS!' Unwanted Pregnancy, the Toronto Women's Caucus and Sex Education," in *Ontario Since Confederation: A Reader*, ed. Edgar-André Montigny and Lori Chambers (Toronto: University of Toronto Press, 2000), 410.

9   David Allyn, *Make Love, Not War: The Sexual Revolution: An Unfettered History* (New York: Routledge, 2001), 4.

10 For a summary of various arguments for and against the periodization of the sexual revolution of the 1960s, see Alan Petigny, "Illegitimacy, Postwar Psychology, and the Reperiodization of the Sexual Revolution," *Journal of Social History* 38, no. 1 (Fall 2004): 63–80. See also Ira L. Reiss, *The Social Context of Premarital Sexual Experience* (New York: Holt, Rinehart and Winston, 1967).

11 Charles W. Hobart, "Sexual Permissiveness in Young English and French Canadians," *Journal of Marriage and the Family* 34, no. 2 (May 1972): 302; and W.E. Mann, "Canadian Trends in Premarital Behaviour: Some Preliminary Studies of Youth in High School and University," *Bulletin: The Council for Social Service*, December 1967, 1–63.

12 F. Michael Barrett, "Sexual Experience, Birth Control Usage, and Sex Education of Unmarried Canadian University Students: Changes between 1968 and 1978," *Archives of Sexual Behavior* 9, no. 5 (1980): 385.

13 William Edward Mann, *Canadian Trends in Premarital Behaviour: Some Preliminary Studies of Youth in High School and University* (Toronto: Council for Social Service, 1967), 24–9; Elise Jones *et al.*, *Teenage Pregnancy in Industrialized Countries* (New Haven and London: Yale University Press, 1986), 82; Canadian Education Association, *The Present Status of Sex Education in Canadian Schools*, Report No. 2, September 1964; and Sethna, "'WE WANT FACTS NOT MORALS!,'" 410.

14   Angus McLaren and Arlene Tigar McLaren, *The Bedroom and the State: The Changing Practices and Politics of Contraception and Abortion in Canada, 1880–1997*, 2nd edn (Toronto: Oxford University Press, 1997).

15   Robin F. Badgley, Marion Powell, and Denyse Fortin Caron, *Report of the Committee on the Operation of the Abortion Law* (Ottawa: Minister of Supply and Services, 1977), 66.

16   Christabelle Sethna, "A Bitter Pill," in *Canada: Confederation to the Present*, ed. Bob Hesketh and Chris Hackett (Edmonton: Chinook Multimedia, Inc., 2001); http://chinookmultimedia.com/poccd/registered/web_papers/case_studies5.php.

17   See Martin G. Wolfish, "Birth Control Counselling in an Adolescent Clinic," *Canadian Medical Association Journal* 105, no. 7 (9 October 1971): 750; Walton Prescott, "A College Health Service *Should Not* Dispense Birth Control Devices and Medications," *JACHA* 16, no. 3 (February 1968): 240–3; and Henri Major, *Notes on the Law of Birth Planning in Canada* (Ottawa: Canadian Advisory Council on the Status of Women, 1975), 5–7.

18   Paul Sachdev, "Canadian Research in Family Planning: Its Implications for Social Work," in *Family Planning and Social Work* (Ottawa: Ministry of National Health and Welfare, 1976), 544–5.

19   Prescott, "A College Health Service *Should Not*," 241, 242.

20   Maurice M. Osborne, Jr, "A College Health Service *Should* Dispense Birth Control Information, Services and Medications," *JACHA* 16, no. 3 (February 1968): 235–50.

21   Owram, *Born at the Right Time*, 268.

22   Library and Archives Canada (LAC), RG 33, series 89, "A Report Prepared for the Royal Commission on the Status of Women on Behalf of the Council of Associations of University Student Personnel Services," Brief 426, August 1968, p. 17. My thanks to Tanya Middlebro for help with this reference.

23   "Dispensing of Birth Control Information, Devices and Medications in College Health Services: A Panel Discussion: Report of the Committee on Ethical and Professional Relationships," *JACHA* 16, no. 3 (February 1968): 233–5. See also LAC, "A Report Prepared," 17.

24   Allyn, *Make Love, Not War*, 38–9.

25   University Health Service, Minutes of the Advisory Committee to the University Health Service, 14 September 1965, p. 3.

26   Beth Bailey, *Sex in the Heartland* (Cambridge, MA, and London, UK: Harvard University Press, 1999), 157.

27   UTA, A1000-1984, A84-1046, Brief by D.J. McCulloch, Advisory Bureau, University of Toronto, July 1968, pp. 3-4. See also Owram, *Born at the Right Time*, 216–47; and Martin Friedland, *The University of Toronto: A History* (Toronto: University of Toronto Press, 2002), 526–42.

28   Marvin Ross, "Students Are Treated Like Children," *Varsity*, 2 November 1966, 5.

29   UHS, Minutes of the Advisory Committee to the University Health Service, 14 September 1965, p. 3. See also Wodehouse, *President's Report, 1965–1966*, 218.

30   UTA, A75-0021, Box 103, File: Health Services, letter to J.H. Sword from G.E Wodehouse, 6 October 1967, and letter to George Tatham from G.E. Wodehouse, 6 October 1967.

31   G.E. Wodehouse, "The Director of the University Health Service," *President's Report, 1966–1967*, 236.

32   Personal telephone interview with Dr David Smith, 9 May 2002, and with Dr Ruth Davis, 16 May 2002.

33   Student Administrative Council (SAC), SAC Statutes, 1966–1967, p. 4.

34   Volkmar Richter, "Lit plans sex lectures," *Varsity*, 8 December 1965, 1.

35   E.A. Macdonald, "The General Secretary-Treasurer of the Students' Administrative Council," *President's Report, 1960*, 138.

36   Jordan G. Sullivan, "The President of the Students' Administrative Council," *President's Report, 1965–1966*, 170.

37   SAC, S. K., Untitled document on the history of SAC, 1975?, p. 18.

38   UTA, A84-0019, Box 061, File: SAC University Government Commission, 1968–1969, "SAC Brief to the Commission on University Government," 10.

39   Ibid., 6.

40   UTA, A84-001, Box 061, File: SAC, University Government Commission 1967–1968, "Dear Council Member," by Tom Faulkner, 9 March 1966.

41   UTA, A84-0019, Box 061, File: SAC University Government Commission 1967–1968, Student Democratic Union, "A Programme of Action for the Students' Administrative Council," 1967?, p. 2.

42   UHS, Minutes of the Advisory Committee to the University Health Service, 11 April 1946, p. 5.

43   Tony Bond, "Conception and Birth: Birth Control . . . a factual survey . . . Abortion," *Varsity: Review*, 12 March 1965, 1. My thanks to Catherine Gidney for this reference.

44   "Western Denies Birth Control Charges," *Varsity*, 13 January 1967, 21, and "Berkeley Votes 4 to 1 for the Pill," *Varsity*, 16 January 1967, 15.

45   "Birth Control Pills Lead to Sexual Responsibility: Co-Ed," *Varsity*, 6 February 1967, 6–7.

46   Kathleen Belanger and Eleanor J. Bradley, "Two Groups of University Student Women: Sexual Activity and the Use of Contraception," *JACHA* 19, no. 5 (June 1971): 307–12; and Marion G. Powell, "Changing Profile of a Family Planning Clinic," in *Family Planning in Canada: A Source Book*, ed. Ben Schlesinger (Toronto: University of Toronto Press, 1974), 196–8.

47   "The Pill: Five Who Do," *Varsity*, 17 March 1967, 7.

48   "Page Four: Of Birth Control, Draft Dodgers and Hippies," *Varsity*, 22 September 1967, 4.

49   SAC, Second General Meeting of the Students' Administrative Council, 20 September 1967, p. 11.

50   "SAC draws government attention by backing birth control committee," *Varsity*, 22 September 1967, 1.

51   UTA, A75-0021, Box 103, File: Health Services, letter to J.H. Sword from G.E. Wodehouse, 6 October 1967.

52   Ibid., Health Services, letter to Professor George Tatham from G.E. Wodehouse, 6 October 1967.

53   Personal telephone interview with Tom Faulkner, 13 April 2002.

54   Agi Lukacs, "Health Service Cuts Abortion Red Tape," *Varsity*, 3 February 1971, 3.

55   G.E. Wodehouse, "The Director of the University Health Service," *President's Report 1967–1968*, 150.

56   UHS, Minutes of the Advisory Committee to the University Health Service, 7 March 1968, pp. 1–2.

57   UHS, F.H. Stewart, "Women's Division: Annual Report," 20 May 1969.

58   Canadian Institute of Public Opinion, "An Increasing Number of People Favour Birth Control," 13 February 1965.

59   Canadian Institute of Public Opinion, "Canucks Want More Extended Reasons for Legal Abortion," 11 September 1965.

60   Gerald Waring, "Report from Ottawa," *Canadian Medical Association Journal* (*CMAJ*) 98, no. 8 (28 February 1968): 419.

61   Cope W. Schwenger, "Abortion in Canada as a Public Health Problem and as a Community Health Measure," *Canadian Journal of Public Health* (*CJPH*) 64, no. 3 (May/June 1973): 223–9. For further information, see Badgley, Caron, and Powell, *Report of the Committee*; and Janine Brodie, Shelley A.M. Gavigan, and Jane Jenson, *The Politics of Abortion* (Toronto: Oxford University Press, 1992), 36–43.

62   Eleanor Wright Pelerine, *Abortion in Canada* (Toronto: New Press, 1972).

63   "Birth Control Spreading," *Varsity*, 22 September 1969, 12.

64   McGill Student Union, Box 28, Minutes, November 1967–June 1968, 18 January 1968, pp. 2349–50.

65   Donna Cherniak, Allan Feingold, and the Students' Society of McGill University, eds, *Birth Control Handbook* (Montreal: Journal Offset Inc., August 1970 [1968]).

66   Harriet Kideckel, "Abortion Now a Fact of Life . . . If You're Rich," *Varsity*, 2 October 1970, 3.

67   UHS, G.E. Wodehouse, "Advisory Committee to the University Health Service Director's Interim Report," 20 October 1971, p. 2.

68   Barbara Seaman, *The Doctors' Case against the Pill: 25th Anniversary Edition* (1969; Alameda, California: Hunter House, 1996).

69   "The Pill: Thousands of Canadian Women Have Been Needlessly Upset," *CMAJ* 102, no. 3 (14 February 1970): 227.

70   G.E. Wodehouse, "Health Service Director Warns Students about Pill," *Varsity*, 11 February 1970, 5.

71   G.E. Wodehouse, "The Director of the University Health Service," *President's Report 1970–1971*, 159.

72   UHS, Minutes of the Advisory Committee to the University Health Service, 10 November 1971, 1.

CHAPTER 15

Gender, Work, and Family

◎ 15.1: BREAKING OUT OF THE GLASS CAGE: WOMEN NEWSPAPER JOURNALISTS IN CANADA, 1945–1975

Barbara Freeman

Introduction

The three decades following the Second World War were ones of great transition for Canadian women in almost every political, economic, and social aspect of their lives. The personal and professional experiences of female newspaper journalists illustrate how much the world of paid work changed, especially for middle-class women in predominantly male, white-collar occupations. Sequestered away on the women's pages, where they had to write about fashions, housekeeping, and child care, female reporters slowly began to aspire to more exciting assignments beside their male colleagues in the newsrooms. It took them 30 years to accomplish that goal as a generational cohort rather than as a handful of individuals, an occupational shift that roughly paralleled that of other women professionals.

This article will emphasize the gender segregation that originally relegated most female journalists to the domestic sphere of the women's pages; the overt and subtle gender biases they faced; their attempts to win equal pay, respect, and recognition from senior editors and management; and how they brought public attention to the many inequities that all Canadian

women faced. Their experiences suggest that while women journalists slowly began to win the respect of their male colleagues, they continued to face sex discrimination, including management resistance to equal pay and promotions, until they learned to fight back.[1]

A Brief History of Women in Newspaper Journalism

Women first started working in journalism in the late nineteenth century when the owners of the daily newspapers decided to attract more readers and advertisers by dividing their publications into news, business, sports, and women's sections. They hired female writers to write mainly about domestic advice, recipes, fashion notes, and celebrity news, segregating them in offices away from the general newsroom where the men were engaged in covering politics, business, crime, and sports. In other words, life on any newspaper was a reflection of the way middle-class men and women lived in Canadian society at the time, with women playing the supporting roles to the men's more worldly pursuits, and gender segregation the norm. The women's pages, however, gave female journalists the opportunity to discuss some of the issues that their readers were quite concerned about, such their need for legal rights. After most Canadian women won the right to vote, during and just after the First World War (1914–18), women's page writers focused most of their efforts on society notes, fashion, homemaking, and child-raising while still recording the activities of the various women's political and professional associations and clubs. Only a handful of exceptional women managed to break away from the women's pages to cover general news or specialty areas.[2]

Much of Canadian women's struggle for equal rights up until the Second World War (1939–45) and afterwards had to do with overcoming ingrained prejudices about proper gender roles. These attitudes stressed women's femininity, domestic skills, and biological ability to bear children over their other capabilities, especially in relation to men, who learned to prize their masculinity and their capacity to provide for their wives and children.[3] In reality, not all families fit that pattern, but the laws that governed work and family life took it as the norm, which meant that men were paid a "family" wage and women paid a lesser, "living wage," even if they worked just as hard as the men or had to support their families as well.[4] Women's organizations still occupied themselves politically in a variety of ways into the 1950s, 1960s, and 1970s, lobbying for changes in the many laws that discriminated against women in the workforce and at home.[5]

Female journalists stood out from most women in Canada's paid labour force because they did not fit the usual profile. In 1941, there were about 3,400 male journalists and authors working in all forms of print media and just over 700 female ones, a ratio of 83 to 17 per cent. Both sexes were predominantly of British or other European descent, a demographic that held true for decades afterwards. Most of the men were over the age of 35 and married, while the majority of female journalists were of the same age but single, representing an anomaly among the women in the Canadian workforce, most of whom were also single but younger—that is, under 35 years of age. At the time, women made up about 20 per cent of the paid labour force and only one in 25 was married. The prevailing wisdom was that a career and motherhood did not mix; a woman could

have one or the other, but not both, at least not at the same time. The predominance of single, mature female journalists suggested that they considered full-time newspaper work demanding enough without having to care for a husband and children, although it was also common for them to leave staff positions and do freelance writing from home once they had children.

During the Second World War, when men left their jobs to enlist in the military, more Canadian women, regardless of marital status, entered the workforce to replace them; many of these women became very involved in volunteer work or joined the armed forces in non-combat support roles.[6] Some newspaperwomen took over the reporting and editing positions their male colleagues once held, while others took leaves of absence from journalism to work with the government agencies that dealt with home-front concerns. Most of them remained on the women's pages, however, unless they had lost their jobs because of newsprint shortages during the war.[7]

After the war ended, the Canadian government, using legislation and propaganda, told women that they should leave the workplace to make room for the returning soldiers and concentrate on providing them with a warm and comforting home life and children. The result was a return to a middle-class cultural bias firmly in favour of female domesticity, preferably in the suburbs. But a number of other women, having developed a new self-confidence and a certain amount of financial independence, found it difficult to lose their jobs. Women who were separated, divorced, widowed, or married to disabled soldiers had to support their families, while "career girls" wanted the right to use their talents in jobs that engaged them regardless of their marital status.[8] As the Second World War was ending, the outspoken president of the Canadian Women's Press Club, Dora Dibney, declared in its publication, *The Newspacket*, that all women should have the right to work outside the home, a position a number of the members supported. Others felt that women with salaried husbands should not compete with single journalists who had no other source of income. Dibney also pointed out that the traditional practice of segregating newswomen had had a detrimental effect during the war, when the men were at the front. Newspapers could have hired more females to replace them, she argued, "If women had been given a chance to learn the tricks of the trade and not been shunted off to one side."[9] The low regard for women's work in general affected female journalists' rates of pay as well as their ability to expand their professional horizons. Almost all of the newspaperwomen wrote for the women's pages, working just over 45 hours a week and making $22.30 per week, whereas the men worked slightly over 48 hours and made $39.59 per week, nearly twice as much.[10] Not surprisingly, during and after the war, a number of Canadian Women's Press Club members became involved in promoting the Newspaper Guild, an American union that had been trying to organize journalists and other newspaper personnel in Canada since the Depression, a decade earlier. The guild was not successful until 1949, when it unionized the *Toronto Star*. The press club members went on public record as supporters of equal pay for equal work, demanding an end to the wide pay gaps between men and women that fluctuated according to the newspapers concerned.[11]

THE GLASS CEILING

The term "glass ceiling" refers to the barriers to advancement in the labour force faced by women, barriers that block their promotion to higher-level positions or to certain types of jobs. It is debated as to who first used the term, but it has been used extensively since the 1980s to denote this form of inequity despite the substantive gains made by women since the "second wave" of the women's movement. It is a "ceiling," as it denotes a barrier to upward mobility in career advancement, and it is made of "glass," because women can aspire to and see the higher-level positions they cannot achieve. Thus, it is related to the problem of occupational segregation by which women remain relegated to lower-level jobs/positions in certain sectors of the labour force or remain segregated in positions or occupations deemed "female" (and conversely omitted from those deemed "male"). Thus, Barbara Freeman in this article has coined the term "glass cage" to refer to the limits placed on the career opportunities for women journalists. In this case, the glass confined them to certain "female" areas of journalism, the women's or lifestyle pages, and blocked them from moving to other areas, such as news.

The recognition of a glass ceiling in the 1980s was part of the conceptualization of more indirect and complex institutional and systemic factors creating barriers to equality for women as well as for other minorities, such as racial/ethnic groups and gays and lesbians. Thus, the glass ceiling has been theorized as being caused by a range of factors, including those based in gender roles and gender ideology. For one, the fact that women bear children and also continue to assume much greater responsibility for family and household labour than males is believed to reduce the ability of women to devote themselves fully to career advancement or to pick careers that will balance well with family responsibilities. This factor combines with labour force and employer policies that still do not allow for an effective "work-home balance." As well, gender ideology still ascribes different traits or qualities (physical, psychological, intellectual) to men and women. For women, such ideology is seen as contributing to the glass ceiling. For example, the concept that women ascribe more to consensual forms of decision-making as opposed to authoritarian methods may impede the promotion of women to senior management positions in large, private corporations but not necessarily to directorships in the human or social services owing to the differences in organizational structure and human resources operation between these two sectors.

Attitudes, however, are slow to evolve and so are workplaces, with or without unions. Most of Dibney's generation found that the only postwar newspaper openings available to them were back on the women's pages, and the same was true for the younger journalists. Male editors and news reporters did not consider the female staff working on the women's pages real reporters because they were producing what was considered soft news about women and their concerns rather than the hard news of politics, business, crime, and the police beat. Generally, news managers thought women were too sensitive, vulnerable, or simply not tough-minded enough to handle, for example, the terrible carnage of traffic accidents or the distressing details of rape trials.[12] Although, again, there were some exceptions,[13] the common pattern of female journalists writing for women and their male colleagues writing for men continued on many newspapers well into the 1960s, with the sexes often segregated in two different work areas. Management at many newspapers segregated the women's departments from the main newsroom by walls that were either solid or inset with windows, like a glass cage, reinforcing the gender biases that divided them.[14]

Within the Glass Cage: Writing for the Women's Pages

Judy Creighton began working as a journalist for the *Times* in Victoria, BC, in the late 1950s when she was an 18-year-old high school graduate. She remembers that the editorial content of the traditional women's pages culturally "reflected exactly what was going on . . . the (house with a) picket fence" postwar ideal of suburban home and family. She quickly realized that she had a lot to learn about writing for newspapers and went through a gruelling apprenticeship. She vividly recalls the "very, very harsh and very, very difficult" women's page editor, Elizabeth Forbes, summarily throwing her stories into the wastepaper basket, "and they just went by like paper airplanes . . . until I finally got it." Forbes, who always wore a hat and gloves, the approved attire for respectable "ladies" at the time, insisted that

the three young women who worked for her were similarly dressed.

Forbes's emphasis on their appearance and decorum reflected the strong sense of class that permeated the *Times* women's pages, with prominent women taking pride of place in its coverage of their professional and service club gatherings, as well as society balls and other events. Creighton's usual assignment was to write up these social notes as well as the engagement and wedding announcements that reflected the romantic and cultural importance of these life passages to the young women, their families, and friends.

At that point in her young life, however, Creighton was content just to be working on the *Times*'s women's page. "I was so happy to be in the newspaper business, at least I thought I was in the newspaper business . . . that I didn't care what I was doing," she recalls.

She next took a job at the *Daily Colonist* in Victoria, which was fortuitous because she had married and soon became pregnant. Once her condition became obvious, she was kept inside editing copy, as "they would not send me out on the street. . . . I could not be representing the newspaper in that state." Aside from the fact that pregnancy signalled that a woman was sexually active, a personally private matter even for married women then, there was also a social bias against expectant women and young mothers working for pay. In any case, few daycare centres existed, reliable housekeepers were hard to find, and middle-class mores branded any woman who had someone else care for her children a maternal failure, Creighton recalls. "People frowned on it . . . it was just not done."[15]

Thanks to an unusually accommodating management, she was able to bring her infant into the office while she was nursing her, which was a novelty for the sports reporters, who liked to play with the child. But once the baby began to walk, Creighton had to quit her job and return home. There, she wrote freelance articles for various publications, a common strategy for new mothers among journalists, until her second child was born two years later and she returned to the *Times*. Over the next few years, she and her husband, who was a chartered accountant, juggled their job schedules and a series of housekeepers to accommodate their children's needs, moving, as his career advanced, from Victoria to London, Ontario, in 1967. At one point, her husband cared for their children at night while Creighton, who was "bored silly" at home, worked part-time at the *London Free Press* as an assistant editor. Encouraged by a few of her more progressive friends, she soon accepted a full-time position in its women's department "even though by this time, it was becoming a ghetto. I really didn't want to be in the women's department but that's where I was."[16]

Creighton's decision to go back to full-time work reflected a pattern that was becoming more common in Canadian society as a whole by the 1960s. Changes in the cost of living, the availability of more consumer goods, and a desire to be able to pay for higher education for their children and better health care for their families meant that two incomes were better than one. Mothers were better able to work for pay, either full-time or part-time, once their children were in school all day.[17] There were also women like Creighton who really needed the stimulation of a career and began returning to the workforce when their children were still quite young if they could find and afford reliable help. By the early 1960s, the proportion of married women in the workforce had reached one in five females.[18] Not everyone, including male news managers, approved of having mothers in the workforce, but there was a growing public acceptance of their presence and of women in predominantly male occupations as well.[19]

It was taking time, however, for government and industry leaders to catch up to public opinion and start treating women in the workforce, especially those who were wives and mothers, fairly. Middle-class women in Canada and elsewhere began to question their legal and social status in society, and their professional, business, and service clubs began lobbying the government for changes in the law on the grounds that "simple justice" for women was their human right. In Ottawa, the minority Liberal government of Prime Minister Lester Pearson appointed the Royal Commission on the Status of Women, which, in 1968, held public hearings across Canada. Chairwoman Florence Bird and her commissioners heard many complaints. There were hardly any women in prominent positions in politics or the professions; there were few effective laws requiring equal pay for the same work; a husband could claim all the family assets if his marriage broke up; police considered wife-battering a private, domestic affair; advertising and disseminating the birth control pill and other devices was still technically illegal, except to married women with a doctor's prescription; abortion was also illegal except when the mother's life was in danger; and publicly funded daycare was virtually non-existent.[20]

The commission received over 400 formal briefs, hundreds of letters, and comments from audience members who spoke up from the floor at the hearings. Even a few women journalists got involved, complaining that neither management nor their union, the Newspaper Guild, did much to help them gain equality on the job or access to the more prestigious news beats. They explained that some of their bosses, even at the unionized newspapers, justified lower salaries for women's page reporters by claiming that they did not do the same work as the men in the newsrooms. Others received equal pay with their male colleagues according to their journalistic experience, but not promotions.[21]

Two years later, the Bird Commission handed the federal government 167 recommendations that would help Canadian women attain "equal opportunity" with men through changes in the labour laws and workplace practices, and other innovations. The report cited 1968 federal statistics that showed that Canadian men earned $6,779 annually, while women earned $3,984; in other words, more than two decades after the Second World War, men were still earning almost twice as much as women. The commission said employers routinely ignored the equal pay laws that did exist and underpaid women in female-dominated occupations.[22] The news media, mostly female reporters, covered the hearings and the recommendations extensively, giving Canadian women a loud, collective voice.[23] Clearly, change was in the air, and women activists of different political stripes pressured the government to implement the commission's recommendations.

At that point, the women's movement was becoming more diverse in its political outlook. While liberal feminists wanted to bring about changes within the current political and economic system, a new generation of socialist and radical feminists believed it was necessary to overthrow capitalism, patriarchy, or both. These members of the grassroots "women's liberation movement," often dismissively referred to as "women's libbers," were also in the vanguard of change, but treated with more suspicion and derision because of their politics, even though many of their essential goals were the same as those of the more established women's groups.[24]

Most of the newspaperwomen who covered the Bird Commission and the women's movement were liberal feminists or at least found the issues worthy of attention, but a number of the men in their newsrooms openly sneered at any attempt to improve women's status. At the *London Free Press*, some of Judy Creighton's colleagues scrawled caustic remarks about women's equality on the pertinent news articles and stuck them on the wall. Both female veterans and newcomers shared her experiences of newsroom prejudice, some of them reacting angrily to sexist comments and actions from the more conservative male editors and reporters. At the National Press Club in Ottawa, the men voted by a narrow margin in January 1970 to continue its male-only membership policy, until gender equality advocates of both sexes organized a very effective political and media campaign that forced them to reverse their decision.[25] Five years later, the Toronto Men's Press Club changed its own male-only policy, and its name, and elected Creighton as its first female director and, later, first female president. Before she moved to the *Toronto Star*, however, her marriage broke up and she took at job at the *Victoria Colonist* as the editor of its new "Lifestyles" pages.[26]

From Women's to Lifestyles Pages: Women's Rights in the News

The Lifestyles page was an innovation—a response to growing criticism from inside and outside the newspaper industry that the traditional women's page format of social notes and clubwomen's news was an anachronism, especially given the changes in modern women's lives. At the same time, the journalists were writing more about social issues, documenting the gender biases females of all ages routinely encountered everywhere. Whether these segments of the newspaper were still referred to as the "women's page," "lifestyles," or the "family section," they increasingly stressed women's equality issues over their social and homemaking lives. At some newspapers, there was no longer a physical wall between the men and the women, and stories about women's rights more often made the news section of the paper.[27] While there was always the risk that those stories would fall through the cracks and Lifestyles would revert to the older women's page format,[28] historically, these sections have always been the first to carry news of equality rights and that was still true in the 1970s.[29]

There were lots of interesting news stories to write concerning the struggle for women's rights and the organizations involved, such as the newly formed National Action Committee on the Status of Women, which attempted to work with disparate women's groups under one political umbrella.[30] Regardless of their personal politics, all journalists were expected to be objective; that is, they were not to express their own views unless they were writing an editorial or an opinion column, and they should not become activists themselves, although sometimes that rule was quietly broken.[31] At the same time, the newswomen knew that gender discrimination affected their own careers and personal lives and those of their counterparts in other white-collar fields shared with men, such as medicine, architecture, and the law. Women in female-dominated professions, such as nursing and social work, were waging their own battles for recognition as well, while the struggles of working-class, immigrant, and Aboriginal women were ongoing.[32]

The extent to which newspaperwomen could write about women's issues largely depended on what their own editors considered interesting and suitable material for their readers. In 1973, Creighton moved on from the *Colonist* to the family section of the liberal and progressive *Toronto Star*, where she found plentiful opportunities to write about women's concerns and broader social issues. She wrote stories, for example, about the ongoing need for birth control and abortion counselling and the marital property legislation that still discriminated against wives.[33]

In 1975, she moved to the Canadian Press (CP) news agency in Toronto, a cooperative wire service that gathered and disseminated news stories to its 100 member newspapers across the country.[34] As its "family editor," Creighton felt like she was "bashing my head against a stone wall" when it came to covering women's political issues in her daily news digest. One day, she recalls, she got into a heated telephone debate with a resistant news editor in Ottawa who considered the stories she was offering him "fluff." She retorted, "I don't call child abuse fluff, I don't call women battering fluff, and I don't call rape fluff, and that's what we're covering here." And he said, "Oh, we can do that on the general (news) side," and I said, "But those trials don't get covered because you think it's non-news." And he said, "Well it's not as important as Parliament." She continued trying to get these stories out on the wire anyway. Later in her career, she went on to specialize in senior citizens' issues and Canada's culinary scene.[35]

Rocking the Boat: Women Journalists Fight for Equal Pay

Even as they were writing about the equal rights of Canadian women, the female journalists of the 1960s and 1970s were aware that they themselves still suffered discrimination on the job. Twenty-five years after the Canadian Women's Press Club endorsed the principle of equal pay, women journalists and their supporters finally organized themselves effectively enough to make it happen, realizing that, like other women in the workforce, they needed the support of their employers, their professional associations, and their unions. The Canadian Newspaper Guild, then an affiliate of its American counterpart, represented the journalists at a number of newspapers across Canada, but certainly not all of them. One of the keys to equal pay and opportunities for women who did belong to the guild was the willingness, or not, of their local branch to support them, and of their management to adhere to the agreements.

Eleanor Dunn became a union activist because she wanted to fight discrimination at the *Ottawa Citizen*, where the Newspaper Guild local, she recalled, did not do much to help the women writing in what was referred to as "the social department." In March of 1968, she accepted the offer of a job there as the assistant women's editor with regular daytime hours, so she could be at home with her journalist husband and five children at nights and on weekends and still hire a housekeeper. She was also hoping her new position would be "a foot in the door" that would lead to a job in the *Citizen* newsroom, which traditionally had only one female reporter at a time. She felt she was well qualified. She had taken journalism courses at Carleton University and had run two weekly newspapers with a business partner.

Dunn recalls that the young male journalists at the *Citizen* generally supported the newswomen's aspirations but many of the older men, who had started their own careers as "copy boy" errand-runners after high school graduation, did not. They openly resented the new generation of university-educated young people, especially the women, who were starting their own careers in junior reporting positions. Dunn was publicly critical of the local guild for not fighting for all its female members, and she complained to the Bird Commission during one of its hearings and, later, to the Special Senate Committee on Mass Media (1970), which explored the effects of corporate ownership concentration on journalistic quality.[36] She also decided to do something herself to change gender discrimination at the *Citizen* and strategized with her female colleagues. She realized that some of them thought they had no time to get involved in union politics after hours, and perhaps male distain in some quarters discouraged them from doing so. "They liked to complain about it, but they didn't want to sort of rock the boat or get involved," she recalled, but she persuaded them that their situation was not going to improve if they did not take action themselves. "Well, I had the ladies in the social department all organized and we all went to a meeting. Of course, guild meetings are always poorly attended so if you can get five or six people to go and vote as a block you can accomplish a number of things." The women received unexpected support from the men in the circulation department, who wanted the same pay as news reporters and were hoping the women would back them in return. A few of the more liberal-minded men on the editorial and reporting staff were also on the women's side. At the next round of bargaining with management, the guild fought for and won equal pay for its female members. Moreover, the Newspaper Guild across the country was so aggressive that by the mid-1970s, salary rates had jumped to $311 per week for a reporter with five years experience.[37] In the meantime, Dunn became secretary of the Ottawa Newspaper Guild, a feminized position that she pragmatically treated as a stepping-stone to the presidency, a position she held for five years. Later, she became the union's first women's rights coordinator for North America and then an international vice-president. In the interim, Dunn and other staffers persuaded the *Citizen*'s management to shift its women's page content from the traditional social and homemaking articles to a Lifestyles format that focused more on women's issues. She attained her goal of a reporting job in the *Citizen* newsroom and often wrote analysis and commentary as well. She later went on to other jobs in TV news, a hotel workers' union, and public relations at a hospital.

Dunn believes that the women journalists of the 1960s and 1970s were not only instrumental in persuading their own newspapers to treat them fairly, but helped bring about changes in the labour law and workplace practices, such as equal pay, by writing articles about discrimination against women. At the same time, newspaper managers began to realize that women journalists represented an untapped pool of newsroom talent, and it was to the companies' advantage to hire them and pay them fairly. "Once we started moving on the equal pay thing, it became like a snowball and it just got bigger and bigger and bigger, and all the unionized papers in Canada changed their pay structure to ensure that everybody got paid the same." She added, "We'll never go back to what it was pre-1968. Those days are gone forever."[38]

Gender Shift in the Newsroom: Women on the News Beats

The mid-1960s to 1970s marked a period when women as a generational cohort started gaining acceptance in newspaper newsrooms on an equal basis with men. By 1975, there were 2,450 journalists on daily newspapers in Canada, of which 21 per cent or 515 were women, an increase of only 4 per cent in the male-female ratio over 1945. Most of these women worked on small urban dailies and still dominated the "soft news" beats designated for women reporters, as they did on the big city papers. The bigger the newspaper, the less chance they had of covering the more senior and predominantly male specialties of politics and business. By that time, however, both sexes were covering local news beats, indicating that newswomen were making some progress as a group.[39]

Rosemary Speirs was one of the young women at the forefront of that change, as she never worked on the women's pages in the first place. In 1963, she applied for a summer job in the Canadian Press newsroom in Toronto. The bureau chief, John Dauphinee, listened as she explained that, at 17, she had written a newspaper column for teenagers for the *Toronto Telegram* and had more recently been working on the *Varsity*, the campus newspaper at the University of Toronto, where she was studying for a master's degree. He replied, "Well that all sounds great, but I must tell you frankly, that we don't hire little girls." Speirs, who was 22, rose from her seat and retorted, "I am not a little girl!" He laughed, but then he gave her a job covering general news. "I guess he wanted to see if I was going to be able to handle it if he plunged me into a newsroom with 50 men." She was told later by a colleague that the male journalists staged a brief walkout in protest at having a woman in their midst, but Dauphinee told them they had to accept his hiring decision.[40] Speirs met a similarly indignant reaction from her newsroom colleagues when she took a job at CP in Montreal the following year. The day she took her place on the editing desk in the newsroom, the men made their objections known to her boss, Bill Stewart, who "told them that women in his bureau were part of the changing nature of the news business."[41] Despite some of her colleagues' initial attempts to discourage her from becoming a reporter, she "loved it and decided that's what I wanted to do." At least, she recalled, they were direct about their resentment, but she knew she had the backing of a supportive management. To her mind, it was easier to deal with blatant prejudice because she could be just as open about fighting back. "It's not as enervating as systemic discrimination that's built in but never spoken about. Maybe it's much more frustrating to just feel you're never advancing and to always be told, 'Don't be silly. Your sex has nothing to do with it.' That's much harder."

On the other hand, she soon learned that news managers were beginning to realize that they had a vested interest in hiring smart and capable young women for newsroom work, because female labour was cheaper. At the time, CP was not unionized, which meant the wire service could pay her less than men with equivalent education and professional experience. One day, Speirs recalled, she heard her editor, Bill Stewart, talking on the phone to another newsroom manager:

> [He was] saying that what he had learned through hiring me was that he could have a better-educated, better-quality reporter, cheaper, than he could for an equivalent male, and that male newspaper managers would be very smart to start looking at young women as a resource. He was selling it. And I remember feeling a little funny about it. . . . And I think he did persuade quite a few people that it worked. You could take a woman and throw her on the regular news run and not be sorry that you'd done it.

Stewart supported her professionally, nonetheless. "I remember him kindly. I remember quite a few men kindly and the system not at all kindly."[42]

As a journalist, Speirs specialized in an area that really interested her, organized labour, which had a strong presence in Canadian society. Although she came from a middle-class family, Speirs grew up and went to school in Scarborough, Ontario, then a predominantly working-class town.[43] She saw her CP assignment to travel with the Bird Commission across the country in 1968 as an opportunity to explore the various forms of discrimination Canadian women, including herself, were still facing.[44]

At the time of the commission hearings, she was studying part-time for a PhD in labour history, despite the still common academic prejudice against graduate female students she had encountered along the way.[45] She loved working at CP, where she had covered many industrial relations stories as a general news reporter, so she was "very hurt and upset" when a formal, newly created labour beat went to a young man without nearly her experience and qualifications. CP management turned down her application, she recalled, "on the grounds that it would be difficult for a woman to cover the labour beat"; that businessmen in particular "would not be impressed, or confide in a young woman." Actually, she had no trouble connecting with her male news sources in order to pick up news tips, she recalls. "They were delighted to talk to me." Going to a pub or bar with one's sources for interview purposes "was important to the labour beat then. And I think they found it more pleasant to drink with me than with some of the male labour beat reporters. I would never have used that [her looks] as a means of getting a story or anything else," she laughs, " but I don't think it hurt that I was in my early twenties and redheaded."[46]

After the news agency overlooked her for the new labour beat, Speirs was ready to move on to the *Toronto Star*, whose managers had been impressed with her CP stories and offered her a job. "The *Star* was far from perfect but a better employer for women than probably any other news operation at that time." Her editor-in-chief, Martin Goodman, treated everyone equally, a number of reporters and columnists of both sexes were supportive of equal rights for women, and the

Rosemary Speirs, pictured here in 1993 when she was the *Toronto Star*'s Parliament Hill bureau chief in Ottawa.

women's liberation movement "was rolling along, so I think of this as not a bad period, actually."[47]

At the *Star*, Speirs continued to specialize in labour issues for several years, incorporating articles about women in the workforce force. "I'm always conscious of women's issues. I think it's the job of any reporter to report on half the population."[48] In 1975, for example, she wrote a story about a brief from the Ontario Federation of Labour, which represented the province's 800 trade unions, to the provincial government that said over one million women in the workforce were being greatly underpaid, compared with men. The Ontario labour law stipulated that women be paid equally if they were doing exactly the same work as men, but it did not cover predominantly female occupations, such as secretarial work, retail sales, and nursing in relation to men who were doing comparable jobs but were being paid more.[49]

She also worked at Queen's Park, where she could not help but notice the lack of women in Ontario politics. Every day, she looked down from the Press Gallery onto a "sea of men" on the floor of the legislature, "making decisions which negatively affected women." On one of her first days there, a number of the male MLAs jeered at a young female politician, Sheila Copps, telling her to "go back to the kitchen." Speirs later witnessed Copps and other female politicians enduring even worse sexist insults as MPs on Parliament Hill, which she later covered for the *Globe and Mail* and the *Toronto Star*. Growing tired of the many ways women were openly and covertly discouraged from gaining public office, the journalist eventually put her personal feminist politics into action by co-founding the "Committee of '94," which evolved into "Equal Voice," both of them non-partisan organizations dedicated to involving more women in electoral politics.[50]

Conclusion

The 30 years after the end of the Second World War was a time of slow but steady change for women in newspaper journalism, as it was for all women in the paid workforce. While there were many reasons for the transition, including the evolving economic needs of Canadian families and shifts in social attitudes concerning gender roles, those changes would not have occurred if Canadian women had not fought for them. They became involved in the struggle for equal rights in their workplaces, in their unions and professional associations, and in the women's movement itself. By the 1970s, Canadian men had finally begun to accept the idea that they should accept women working beside them as equals without jeering at them or preventing them in more subtle ways from getting the salaries and promotions they deserved.

The newspaper world of that time provides a snapshot of the challenges women faced in one particular white-collar occupation. Journalists like Judy Creighton, who were once restricted to writing for the very traditional women's pages, insisted on covering women's many economic and political concerns, including equality rights, on the Lifestyles

pages during the late 1960s and early 1970s. Newspaper Guild activists such as Eleanor Dunn fought for equal pay and fair treatment in their own newsrooms, while making their own journalistic transition from the women's page, to Lifestyles, to the newsroom. In the meantime, newsroom pioneers such as Rosemary Speirs experienced both blatant prejudice and mixed support from male news managers and colleagues while carving out their own reporting specialties, such as industrial relations and politics. The women's progress did not mean an end to the so-called glass ceiling, the systemic discrimination that still prevented many female journalists from obtaining specialized news assignments, senior editorships, and management positions.[51] Nevertheless, they established women's equality rights in the newsroom and demonstrated their ability to succeed as well, thereby contributing to the growing public acceptance of women in Canada's workforce.

Endnotes

1   This article is based on oral history interviews, journalism articles, biographies, the records of professional media professional organizations, and other historical sources on women in the Canadian print media. Women in radio and television faced similar employment circumstances, but government broadcast regulations stressing gender equity, which did not apply to the print media, gave them more support after the 1970s. Both the men and the women who wrote for magazines tended to sell their work freelance and those who were given staff positions were usually male, except at *Chatelaine*, Canada's sole women's magazine during most of the 1940s to the 1970s. See G.J. Robinson, *Gender, Journalism and Equity: Canadian, US and European Perspectives* (Crestkill, NJ: Hampton Press, 2005); Valerie J. Korinek, *Roughing It in the Suburbs: Reading Chatelaine Magazine in the Fifties and Sixties* (Toronto: University of Toronto Press, 2000).

2   Marjory Lang, *Women Who Made the News: Female Journalists in Canada 1880–1945* (Montreal and Kingston: McGill-Queen's University Press, 1999), chaps. 8 and 9; and Gail Cuthbert Brandt, Naomi Black, Paula Bourne, and Magda Fahrni, *Canadian Women: A History*, 3rd edn (Toronto: Nelson Education Ltd, 2011), chap. 7.

3   Pat Armstrong and Hugh Armstrong, *The Double Ghetto: Canadian Women and Their Segregated Work*, updated 3rd edn (Toronto: Oxford University Press, 2009), chaps. 4 and 5.

4   Alice Kessler-Harris, *A Woman's Wage: Historical Meanings and Social Consequences* (Lexington: University Press of Kentucky, Blazer Lecture Series, 1990).

5   Joan Sangster, "Women's Activism and the State," in Sharon Anne Cook, Lorna R. McLean and Kate O'Rourke, eds, *Framing Our Past: Canadian Women's History in the Twentieth Century* (Montreal and Kingston: McGill-Queen's University Press, 2001), 201–11.

6   Lang, *Women Who Made the News*, 6, 15–20; Brandt *et al.*, *Canadian Women*, 315–25.

7   Lang, *Women Who Made the News*, 95–8.

8   Jennifer A. Stephen, "Balancing Equality for the Post-War Woman: Demobilizing Canada's Women Workers After World War Two," *Atlantis* 32, no. 1 (2007): 122–32; Brandt *et al.*, *Canadian Women*, 323–9, 354–61. See also Veronica Strong-Boag, "Canada's Wage-Earning Wives and the Construction of the Middle-Class, 1945–1960," *Journal of Canadian Studies* 29, no. 3 (1994), 5–25.

9   Dibney's emphasis as cited in Lang, *Women Who Made the News*, 98, 126–30.

10   Canada Census 1941 figures cited in Lang, *Women Who Made the News*, 19.

11   Lang, *Women Who Made the News*, 101–4; and Catherine McKercher, *Newsworkers Unite—Labor, Convergence, and North American Newspapers* (Lanham, MD: Rowan and Littlefield, 2002), 108.

12   Rosemary Speirs interviewed by the author, 15 December 1992 and 17 November 2011; Barbara M. Freeman, "Flash Your Feminist Bloomers," in Marguerite Andersen, ed., *Feminist Journeys/Voies feminists* (Ottawa: Feminist History Society, 2010), 137–42.

13   Simma Holt, *Memoirs of a Loose Cannon* (Hamilton, ON: Seraphim Editions, 2008), chap. 10; and Marjorie Nichols with Jane O'Hara, *Mark My Words: The Memoirs of a Very Political Reporter* (Vancouver and Toronto: Douglas & McIntyre, 1992).

14   Sheila Arnopolous interviewed by the author, 4 April 1996; and Maggie Siggins interviewed by the author, 26 August 1995.

15   Judy Creighton interviewed by the author, 17 August 1995; and Brandt *et al.*, *Canadian Women*, 365.

16   Creighton interview.

17   Brandt *et al.*, *Canadian Women*, 325–9.

18   Ibid., 325.

19   Barbara M. Freeman, *The Satellite Sex: The Media and Women's Issues in English Canada, 1966–1971* (Kitchener-Waterloo, ON: Wilfrid Laurier University Press, 2001), 68; and Monica Boyd, "Canadian Attitudes toward Women: Thirty Years of Change" (Ottawa: Labour Canada, Women's Bureau, 1984), 10–22.

20   Freeman, *The Satellite Sex*, chap. 1.

21   Ibid., 55–6; and, regarding the many letters Canadian women sent to the commission on labour issues, see Joan Sangster, "Invoking Experience as Evidence," *Canadian Historical Review* 92, no. 1 (2011): 135–61.

22   *Report of the Royal Commission on the Status of Women* (Ottawa: Information Canada, 1970), 66–80.

23   Freeman, *The Satellite Sex*, chap. 9.

24   Jacquetta Newman and Linda A. White, *Women, Politics and Public Policy* (Toronto: Oxford University Press, 2006), chap. 4.

25   Creighton interview; Siggins interview; Eleanor Dunn interviewed by the author, 8 July 1994; Holt, *Memoirs*, chap. 11; and Freeman, *The Satellite Sex*, chaps 2, 9.

26   "Woman Elected Director of Press Club," *Globe and Mail*, 10 February 1975, 5; "Woman Heads Club," *Toronto Star*, 11 February 1979, A4; and Creighton interview.

27   Siggins interview.

28   Creighton interview.

29   Dustin Harp, "Newspapers' Transition from Women's to Style Pages: What Were They Thinking?," *Journalism* 7, no. 2 (2006): 197–216.

30   Brandt *et al.*, *Canadian Women*, 530–43.

31   Barbara M. Freeman, *Beyond Bylines—Media Workers and Women's Rights in Canada* (Waterloo, ON: Wilfrid Laurier University Press, 2011), chap. 5.

32   Deborah Gorham, "No Longer an Invisible Minority: Women Physicians and Medical Practice in Late Twentieth-Century North America," in Dianne Dodd and Deborah Gorham, eds, *Caring and Curing: Historical Perspectives on Women and Healing in Canada* (Ottawa: University of Ottawa Press, 1994), 183–211; Joan Grierson and the For the Record Committee, eds, *For the Record: The First Women in Canadian Architecture* (Toronto: Dundurn Press, 2008); Joan Brockman, *Gender in the Legal Profession: Fitting or Breaking the Mould* (Vancouver: UBC Press, 2001); Therese Jennissen and Colleen Lundy, *One Hundred Years of Social Work: A History of the Profession in English Canada, 1900–2000* (Waterloo, ON: Wilfrid Laurier University Press, 2011); Kathryn McPherson, *Bedside Matters: The Transformation of Canadian Nursing 1900–1990* (Toronto: Oxford University Press, 1996); Joan Sangster, *Transforming Labour: Women and Work in Post-war Canada* (Toronto: University of Toronto Press, 2010); and Armstrong and Armstrong, *The Double Ghetto*, chap. 2.

33   In 1969, the federal government made birth control legal for all and abortion acceptable if a hospital committee of three doctors agreed the woman's life or health was directly at stake. Jane Jensen in Janine Brodie, Shelley A.M. Gavigan, and Jane Jensen, *The Politics of Abortion* (Toronto: Oxford University Press, 1992), chap. 2; Judy Creighton, "Nurse Offers Abortion Counseling," *Toronto Star*, 3 November 1973, D1; and Creighton, "Wife Lost Share of Land Wants Laws Changed," *Toronto Star*, 20 February 1974, E2.

34   Canadian Press. *CP Style Book: A Guide for Writers and Filing Editors* (Toronto: Canadian Press, 1974).

35   Creighton interview; Creighton, "Breast Cancer Spurs Co-Author of Slow-Cooke Book to Adopt Healthier Lifestyle," *Brandon Sun*, www.brandonsun.com/entertainment/breaking-news/breast-cancer-spurs-co-author-of-slow-cooker-book-to-adopt-healthier-lifestyle-139858013.html?thx=y, online 28 February 2012.

36   Dunn interview; and Freeman, *The Satellite Sex*, 53–5.

37   Dun interview; "Guild Votes Tomorrow on *Star*'s Final Offer," *Toronto Star*, 29 May, A3. The Ottawa guild's financial records went missing in the 1970s, and a local guild history does not reconstruct comparative gender differences in pay during the time Dunn was at the *Citizen*. Author Daniel Drolet claims, however, that it was "perfectly acceptable" to pay

women less than men. In 1969, the starting rate for a novice *Citizen* reporter was $102.71 a week. Daniel Drolet, "A History of the Ottawa Newspaper Guild," www.ottawanewsguild.ca/website/?page_id=522, 2007, online 17 February 2012. In contrast, in 1968, apprentice summer reporter Anne Roberts made the non-union starting rate of $85 a week at CP's Edmonton bureau but quickly earned a raise to $95. Freeman, *Beyond Bylines*, chap. 5, n21, 268.

38 Dunn interview.
39 Robinson, *Gender, Journalism and Equity*, 35–42.
40 Speirs interview, 1992; and Speirs email communication with the author, 16 February 2012.
41 Bill Stewart, who worked at CP for 45 years and was the Montreal bureau chief while Speirs was there, did not remember this incident but declared that he would not have tolerated such a protest. William Stewart interviewed by the author, 27 August 1995.
42 Speirs email. Bill Stewart did not remember this incident and insisted that CP would not have paid women less, but he was not entirely clear about the timeframe for his assertion. He also admitted that he was "still hostile to the guild," but would not elaborate. Stewart interview, 2011. The Canadian Wire Services Guild, a branch of the Newspaper Guild, unionized Canadian Press employees in September 1975, but a year later, management and the union were still arguing over the terms of the contract. Speirs interview; and Ed Finn, "Resumption of Rotating Strikes Predicted by Unionist," *Toronto Daily Star*, 13 September 1976, B10.
43 Speirs interview, 2011.
44 Speirs interview, 1992; Rosemary Speirs, "Equal Pay Laws Often Ignored Report Says," *Toronto Daily Star*, 7 December 1970, 4; and Freeman, *The Satellite Sex*, chap. 4.
45 Speirs interview, 2011; and Ann Rochon Ford, *A Path Not Strewn with Roses: One Hundred Years of Women at the University of Toronto, 1884–1994* (Toronto: University of Toronto Press, 1985).
46 Speirs interview, 2011.
47 Ibid.
48 Speirs interview, 1992.
49 Rosemary Speirs, "Women Denied $1 Billion in Pay Labor Body Says," *Toronto Star*, 21 May 1974, A3.
50 Speirs interview, 2011; Rosemary Speirs's speech to the Ontario legislative interns at Queen's Park, 2 March 2004. Equal Voice, www.equalvoice.ca/, online 16 February 2012; and Linda Trimble and Jane Arscott, *Still Counting: Women in Politics across Canada* (Toronto: University of Toronto Press, 2003).
51 Robinson, *Gender, Journalism and Equity*, chap. 5; Susan Korah, "Creating Gender Equity in the Newsroom: A Front Page Challenge for the Southam Task Force on Women's Opportunities," Master of Journalism thesis, Carleton University, 2001.

◎ 15.2: THREE FACES OF FATHERHOOD AS A MASCULINE CATEGORY: TYRANTS, TEACHERS, AND WORKAHOLICS AS "RESPONSIBLE FAMILY MEN" DURING CANADA'S BABY BOOM

Robert Rutherdale

. . . My work on family manhood in English-speaking Canada in the 1945 to 1975 period—a specific masculinity—sees fathers as gendered beings as a consequence of how their own life stories took shape through formative influences that marked their classed, ethnic, and generational life paths. How their biographies intersect with the periods and places they were rooted in as they grew up, matured, and became fathers concerns me more than simply drawing isolated examples of fatherhood practices from diverse source material. Oral history and autobiographical life writing can serve as particularly revealing sources for this. From intimate family relations to their public roles in work and local community-based leisure, fathers' varied masculinities emerge in identifiable categories—as "faces of fatherhoods"—but only as outcomes of their parenthood that were relationally constructed over the life course. Fathers exercised their responsibilities through a variety of potential behaviours connected to their basic functions of provider and parent. Fatherhood's many potential *faces*, as John Demos suggested shortly before work on the subject began its fruitful escalation, are a useful way to conceptualize and categorize their masculinity as family men.[1] Below, I consider fathers in this period as tyrants, as teachers, and as workaholics: again, faces of fatherhood that appear as intersecting outcomes evident in the life stories of fathers, in the cases below, as part of a generation of fatherhood in English Canada.

That the many gendered faces of fatherhood, as providers, nurturers, guides, and models of manhood for their children, negative and positive, cannot be seen as outcomes entirely of their own making may seem obvious. But I raise this, in part, because this was something surprisingly absent from the teller's perspectives in many of the life stories I collected in my oral historical fieldwork.[2] Conceptually, my approach explicitly attempts to focus on connections evident between the autobiographical elements of a life story and the broader social forces, situations, and relationships within which interview subjects invariably attempt to place themselves. . . .

To cite a recurring masculinity in the gendered texts of memory, I refer here to the myth of the "self-made" man. This narrative figment emerged repeatedly in my interviews when the fathers who raised children in the postwar decades (all grandfathers and some great-grandfathers today) also spoke of their individual roads to self-sufficiency—how they "made it" after the Second World War. In many ways, of course, many did "succeed" as consistent providers, as reliable parents, and as active citizens in the wider society. As John Tosh points out in his influential earlier work, it is in the home, at work, and in relation to other men that fathers have made their appearances in history.[3] Their masculinities as fathers, again, are relational. But, using life stories, what *types* of fatherhood, what categories of specific masculinities, emerged during the baby boom years? My concern is with how anglophone Canadian men, either Canadian-born or newcomers, who grew up in the late 1920s and 1930s and matured during the war years constructed their fatherhoods in the era that followed—of the baby boom, of the Cold War ethos, of increased consumerism, of contexts rarely rehearsed with any broad force in the preceding interwar and wartime periods. My focus here is on fathers' relationships with their children during this period, an era of the so-called generation gap of the 1960s. What connections can be drawn between masculinity, fatherhood, and responsible manhood? Within their family relations, how did fathers express their masculinity as their children grew up in the 1950s and matured themselves in the 1960s and early 1970s?

Masculinity Crisis?

We should begin by noting that both masculinity and fatherhood were often seen in the 1950s, as the baby boom intensified, as entering a period of crisis.[4] As James Gilbert points out in reference to this salient masculinity panic that spilled back and forth across the Canada-US border in the 1950s, economic, bureaucratic, and institutional forces were blamed for eroding the "traditionally" assertive, "self-directed" masculinities of men in "former times." These, too, were little more than mythical figments. Within this new mid-century discourse, personnel departments in large corporations, along with mass culture, suburbanization, and consumerism, were often blamed for the crises men were to have faced as authentic beings. So were the popular middle-class prescriptions for family "togetherness," along with the tranquilizing "good citizenship" and "group dynamics" men were said to be encouraged to foster in their own behaviours. In the course of developing such narratives, women became a primary target. The "increasing feminization of culture," Gilbert notes, as a part of postwar normalization was said to be threatening modern men *as men*, as essentialized masculine beings.[5] As part of a broader masculinity crisis, family men—with fathers in the middle at mid-century—were said to be losing their paternal authority, undergoing extreme instabilities despite the obvious signs of material progress. They were no longer "heads" of their own households.

. . . My research points in different directions. Some "lost" family men can indeed be found, but not within a crisis of masculinity. Family men appeared in my oral histories and life writing to be raising children as they themselves matured, though they seldom admitted or perceived changes in their fundamental self-concepts. What they did try to exercise, successfully or not, was masculine power and control as male parents attempting to achieve "responsible family manhood," a social category of masculinity that recognizes a father's formal powers defined by both the state and social sanction. Informally, and in the flow of daily life, this category can often leave open the question of how responsible fatherhood is exercised. Wielding power and control over one's offspring or child dependents can mean many things.

Father as Tyrant

Tyrannical fatherhood is approached here as a parenting practice that reflects a boldly assertive, sometimes cruel, masculinity. While sons and daughters may resist this model as they grow up, negotiation is displaced by the imperative that children follow a tightly controlled, overtly patriarchal "father-rule" script in the stories of fatherhood that emerge. Sons and daughters and other children under their care must conform to the fathers' demands.

The first two examples here come from contexts that may appear unusual at first for discovering the tyrannical fatherhood masculinity. Across Canada during the baby boom period, from the late 1940s to the mid-1960s, fathers increasingly were called upon to serve their local communities as parents who helped guide the recreation of their own children and their peers, particularly in growing towns and cities where rapid family formation rates produced a high demand for male volunteers. While few fathers in such settings emerged as full-blown tyrants, this could be a site of such encounters, especially when the strain of parenting one's own children and those of others came into potential conflict. Coaching and scouting leadership roles could introduce this in terms of fathering sons and their teammates and fellow scouts. Fathers *in loco parentis* often found themselves transmitting principles observed at home to groups of boys drawn from local communities, and a pattern of fatherhood in the home might spill over to the type of father that appeared in the public hockey rink, scout hall, or other venue of children and youth recreation. Such sites could even heighten the tyrannical face of fatherhood.

In Prince George, British Columbia, Roy Gibson remembered his community service most distinctly this way as a scoutmaster. His leadership philosophy seemed influenced by a Depression-scarred childhood. Both as a father and a scoutmaster, Gibson felt that self-reliance, more than anything, had to be instilled in boys. He remembered hoping that his hard lessons might serve as their best example. "You were in a corral," he said of his childhood, "and within that corral certain things had to be done and that was all there was to it. Whether you liked it or not, you did it. Now that's—my years with the Scouting movement—this is what I put across to the boys."

His three sons all joined Scouts. He claimed to show no favouritism, but more significantly he suggested close parallels between the values he espoused as a parent and those he upheld as a scoutmaster. When asked in a general way what good fatherhood was all about, Gibson replied:

> Teaching the kids to paddle their own canoe. . . . If you can't take care of yourself nobody else is going to. And yet, they're teaching in the schools, and this I found very difficult to counter in Scouting—I was teaching one set of values and they would see another set. And they couldn't make up their minds as to who was right. And it was the older group of boys, basically after they left my group—where they went in Venturers— where you'd see it finally, where the boy made up his mind. And he fell off the fence one way or another. And, if they fell off on my side of the fence, OK, they're still around the community. They're members of the community—some of the others are in jail![6]

Sam Taylor's life story unfolded partly through a difficult relationship with his own father . . . growing up in the Depression in Prince George, British Columbia. He recalled an alcoholic father, an abusive father, and a father who ultimately deserted Sam and his family in the middle of Canada's Depression years. One telling instance of his father's tyranny was recalled as follows:

> I can remember running all the way home from that school up here all the way downtown to tell my father that I stood second in the class of 40 kids. I never stood second, up that high. And this one girl beat me because she was the school inspector's daughter and got teaching at home and so on. But I stood second. And that big idiot stood there and said, "What the hell good is that, standing second? If can't stand first, don't stand anything." I expected a dime, or a reward, or a kind word. And then he walks away. I never worked in school after that. He took it out of me—in grade five! At 11 years of age, or 10 I think it was at the time. He knocked it right out of me, right there.

Taylor, who fathered six sons, struggled with his upbringing when his turn came to parent boys at that age in the 1950s and early 1960s. He remembered, through a narrative he considered pivotal in influencing his parenting thereafter, a moment of tyrannical community-based fatherhood when coaching one of his boys in bantam hockey in the early 1960s. He had been acting, as he admitted, as an autocrat behind the bench who stretched any reasonable limit. Finally, the pleading face and beseeching words of one of the boys playing alongside his son reminded him of a fathering face he was ashamed had become, to some degree, his own: "I'm trying to do what you say, coach," the lad looked up to say, "but I'm just an 11-year-old boy." And yet, in summing up his notion of what a father should be in essence, Taylor stated: "A father first of all has to be a leader. Somebody has to be a leader. If the woman is a leader, the other men laugh at the father, don't they? . . . 'Oh hell, you know who wears the pants in the family,' y'know."[7] Noting the potential censure of other men, other fathers perhaps, the face of father as tyrant appeared in Sam Taylor's invocation of what a family man had to become in his masculine conduct. He confessed to seeing, at his worst, his father's face in his own behaviour. Taylor also claimed he had fought against it, and even won over it in the end.

Tyrannical fathers, of course, have appeared in many guises in history. Their manifestation in the 1960s, however, could sometimes appear as a period-specific feature, but was always more than that when the life story of the father as a whole was considered. . . .

. . . For some fathers, the potential conflict of the sexual revolution, parenting, and a sense of fundamental values as a family man could inspire a tyrannical face.

David Benson of Prince George showed this in expressing the "right way" to bring children up—the search for responsible family manhood in the face of perceived changes that were seen as threatening to a father's sense of basic "family values." Here, we see an authoritarian face of fatherhood in the 1960s . . . that moved, more commonly in many fathers, toward an "either/or" system of discipline, a black-and-white moral code. The "right way" to grow up during the sexual revolution seemed clear to Benson as a father of boys in this period. As he put it,

> We always had a problem, y'know, after the flower children days, and so forth—the "freedom of sex." Sex freedom and, y'know, sleep with anything you want and whenever you can and whatever. This wasn't in our generation and it wasn't in our bringing up, eh? And trying to instil that in our sons, y'know, when they're in their prime, y'know. My influence on them was that: "Hey mister—be careful who you take out," y'know. "If she's good enough to take her to bed you'd better be thinking about marrying her—because that's the way it is done and that's the right way." So that, that's the thing that raised my family, and how I was raised.[8]

Benson, as the last example here, sat somewhere on the edge of tyrant and teacher . . . Attitudes toward sexuality and maturation during Canada's sexual revolution pushed many fathers to be more authoritarian in their control of their daughters' sexuality than in their control of that of their sons, reflecting the double standard in sexual relations of the 1950s that was challenged on so many fronts from the early 1960s onwards. What . . . Doug Owram approached as the disappearance by the late 1960s and early 1970s (particularly on college campuses) of the "cult of virginity," which unmarried daughters in the 1950s had endured, may have challenged a paternal authority that was, in fact, seldom exercised by fathers teaching sons about sex.[9] Clear examples of fathers teaching their sons about sex are relatively rare in the primary evidence. The following case thus provides a somewhat unique and useful illustration of the "responsible" father as teacher rather than tyrant. The role is gendered. The masculinity of a moderate paternal figure displaces the fiercely controlling patriarch.

Father as Teacher

Everett Barclay and his son, Linwood, were part of a nuclear family of four that included Linwood's mother and an older brother. Linwood recounts many influences in his life, but none more significant than his father. His sensitive portrait of father as teacher, delivered here as a tender story set squarely in the sexual revolution, serves as a reminder that fatherhood's relational aspect often takes shape through the eyes of an adolescent dependent: "Dad and I were alone in our new improved, 60-foot-long house trailer," Linwood recalled, speaking of his life as a teenager when his parents ran a trailer park campsite in Ontario cottage country in the late 1960s. He remembered his father

> asking me how I liked this girl from high school I was seeing at the time, and I said I liked her quite a bit. He said he didn't want to intrude on my privacy or anything like that by demanding that I tell him what exactly this girl and I might be up to, but he said there were some things I should know, even though I was only fifteen, and just because he was going to tell me these things didn't mean he was promoting anything, if I got his drift. It was just that I should be informed, he said.

He got a pencil and paper and proceeded to sketch out the basics of condom use. Given

that he was a trained artist, his drawing, while not exactly *Gray's Anatomy*, was clear enough for the purposes of this lesson. "You have to wear one of those," he said, "and it has to be on right. All the way on. You get what I'm saying?"

I nodded. I didn't know what to say, so I said nothing. I couldn't recall Dad being this direct before, or quite this honest about what went on between the sexes. I felt uncomfortable, but at the time very close to him. That was due to the fact that this was not the kind of talk Mom would ever have with me.

As though he'd been reading my mind, when he finished the lesson he looked worriedly at his drawing. "I guess we'd better get rid of this before your mother sees it," he said. "She'll say, "Everett, what's *this*?'" And we both laughed as he tore the paper into small bits, crumpled them up, and stuffed them deep into the garbage. He was wise to destroy the evidence.[10]

To the memories of a boy who later wrote poignantly about a father he missed so much after he passed away (Linwood's father died of cancer two years later) many such accounts could be added. Fathers, hardly in crisis about who they were as men, often simply went about their daily lives as fathers who taught through example, as role models, or, occasionally, in direct interaction with their children.

This often came about if fathers as providers were observed by their children. David Zieroth grew up on a family farm in Manitoba in the 1950s. His close contact with a providing father, which his agricultural upbringing necessitated, was in this case fondly remembered. Perhaps to emphasize this fact, Zieroth chose a present-tense narration: "I love my father, and he loves me," began one passage describing a father who

> shows me how to handle a machine, or we bend our heads over a tool, and, and he talks to me, and sometimes we laugh about something I don't understand. He tells me

what to do, and I do it. I'm eager to help because I believe it will gain entry to my father. . . . I can tell my father is looking at me from the distance of the forty-five years he's already put under his belt when I'm born, the last of his four kids. . . . After lunch, before he goes back to his work, he lies on the couch in the living room to snooze for fifteen minutes, not really sleeping, eyes closed, doing some private calculation that restores him.[11]

Zieroth recalled trying to get as deeply as possible into the mindset of his father, especially when he worked. Most telling was Zieroth's yearning to know everything that his father appeared to know about the world around them: "I would like to follow him into his dreams, to see him the way he sees himself. Since I can't, I stay close to him, go where he goes."[12] Zieroth suggested that his father became a young boy's guide to the world of work partly because they lived on a farm, but fundamentally because his role as a manful provider and teacher melded with the masculine role modelling that held a special appeal for young Zieroth. . . .

The last illustration here introduces a case in which play rather than work shaped the masculinity of father as teacher. It also serves, again through the role of ice hockey coach, as a contrast to Sam Taylor's illustration above. Mike Zuke grew up in Sault Ste Marie, a steel mill city located in northern Ontario, during the Second World War. His father had worked in the mill, and he became a postal worker. He married after the war and parented two daughters and three sons, all baby boomers. He also acquired considerable local notoriety as a community-based parent through sports, namely ice hockey, a favourite pastime among male youth throughout the city's history. He coached, established a huge and well-provisioned backyard hockey rink that became a local landmark, and was a teacher of hockey to boys all his life. . . .

Zuke Sr grew up playing and loving hockey, stealing away free time to watch senior hockey games, a community entertainment mainstay. . . .[13] He never gave up his enthusiasm for the game, especially as a father and teacher of both his own sons and of many others. Zuke's backyard rink began even before he and his wife, June, had children: "The year after we were married, we went to a city skating rink," he recalled. "There were about four hockey games going on and pucks whizzing all over the place. We skated for about twenty minutes and left. As I'm walking back, I looked at all the land I had and said, why can't we have our own rink? I started one the next day."

For Zuke, preparing the surface and first flooding became a 44-year ritual that grew to embrace the local neighbourhoods at a time of expanding family formation in the Sault, as elsewhere, with plenty of local children filling the streets, schools, parks, and arenas. Zuke's enthusiasm for the game and for teaching it as a hockey coach gradually became a popular part of the city's social history. "There has only been one complaint issued from a tranquil neighbourhood regarding Zuke's winter amusement park," Zuke mentioned in a story that came back to his role as teacher of the sport and community-based father: "We had an old couple across the street," he said, pointing to the house as he recalled a chance event that he claimed had made him an even better teacher of the game. "The guy used to get up for work at five in the morning. Late at night in twenty below weather, you could hear the puck hitting the boards for miles. His wife called over and asked us to keep the noise down. So I decided to use a ball. It was the best thing that ever happened. I read a book by the Russian coach Tarasov twenty-five years later. He said the best way to develop shooting accuracy is with a ball. I thought, Holy geez, we've been doing it all along."[14]

The enthusiasm Mike Zuke, as a father, had for his rink clearly revived the boy within the man, a strong sentimental attachment to the joy of movement, play, and identity with team sporting excellence. "When kids would come over to play I'd join in," Zuke was to have declared as he laughed with a "hooked nose," as Cuthbert describes, "rearranged by at least one high stick": "I'd call my son Michael and say, 'Come on, let's play.' He'd say, 'I can't until I finish my homework.' Usually, it's the parent telling the kid to do his homework."[15] When Zuke's backyard rink responsibilities increased as his children grew up, his sense of himself as a teacher of hockey came into focus throughout the city. He coached Bantam (11–12 years) and Junior (14–18 years) hockey, always as an amateur who loved the game and all that it could teach. And no doubt backyard rink fathers elsewhere in Canada, holding with freezing hands a garden hose in nighttime darkness when the temperatures are often best for flooding, shared Zuke's sense in that era that winter recreation was going to be good for their sons and their sons' friends.

As creator of a father and son encounter at a time, in the 1960s and early 1970s, when girls' recreational hockey had yet to find its fair place in Canada, Zuke provided scope for the masculine face of father as recreational coach and teacher of the sport. . . . Of course, father-as-teacher in many cases had little to do with formal education. In each case, no doubt, fathers acted to assist children to grow up, mature, and prepare for their lives ahead. Preparing their children, sons especially, for their lives ahead as paid workers was something they often did in the postwar economy as role models rather than active parents.

Father as Workaholic

In many interviews, fathers underscored as their biggest single regret the time spent working when, in retrospect, they feel today they should have been at home with their families. It seems too common, has nothing to do with the crisis of masculinity feared to have swept the modern world after the Second World War, and stands now, arguably, as a significant lament of a generation of family men. Their efforts to be good providers and "responsible fathers" could lead down the wrong path, even if they did not realize where they were heading at the time. Moreover, for some fathers, even volunteer public service, at nights and weekends too, could become a regret. As one father, Roy Phillips, put it:

As a father I was not too good with the kids. Because I was too involved [in community service work]. Sometimes when I'd come home from work, they'd say, "Daddy, are you going to play with us tonight?" I'd say, "Nope, sorry kids—teaching St John's Ambulance tonight." Or "Sorry kids, no, I'm going to armouries tonight." Or "Sorry kids there's a church meeting, tonight." I've eaten my *heart* out over that. Because I missed so much time with those kids when I *should* have been—sitting with them, y'know. Bigshot. Gotta be, gotta be part of the community. That's a *painful* thing when you realize "What the *hell* did you do it for?" Yeah, you spent time, you made friends. You had fun. Matter of fact, in the army you gotta a bit of money. You got two bills, payday twice a year, sorta thing. And there was a good social life there too.[16]

But that came with costs recognized only in hindsight.

With respect to paid work, the responsibility of earning became a time constraint without limits in the gendered family regime, especially in cases where the father was the sole breadwinner. His provider role eclipsed his parenting and spousal roles. But at the time he may, in fact, have felt that his work schedule reflected his willingness to assume *more* responsibility for his family, not less. He was doing the right thing. He was exercising his masculine privileges as a father with a keen eye to financial security and his family's well-being over the long run.

But, for many fathers, the long run never ran out. "Do I have regrets?" former national evangelist, provincial politician, one-time actor, novelist, inventor, advertiser, and journalist Charles Templeton asked himself in the early 1980s. Templeton had worked most of his life in Toronto in a career in public life that began at age 17 with an illustration for a political cartoon page in the depths of Canada's Great Depression. Templeton parented five children, two from his second wife's first marriage, but later admitted after they had left home: "I have often been so immersed in what I am doing that I have neglected friendships, even my family."[17] His son, Brad, born toward the end of Canada's baby boom in 1960, nonetheless recalled his father with considerable fondness. Brad Templeton remembered a time when his father actually worked out of the home. But not, at least so it appears, to spend more time with his family. As Brad Templeton related, when his father "took on the role of morning newscaster he arranged to be able to do the news from a room built at the back of our garage. This gave him time to try more independent pursuits, namely writing and inventing."[18] It might be said that Templeton Sr was an ideal role model for the postwar "Renaissance man" of his generation in English Canada who travelled across the country to pursue his many avocations and paid professions. But he was also, by his own admission, an erstwhile workaholic. His business hours and waking hours, as he described them in terms that modelled assertive masculinity in the workforce, he saw as one and the same. On his success he wrote: "If I have been successful in what I have done it has usually been because all my energies have gone into the work at hand. I knew nothing about 'hours of business'—for me they have been all my waking hours."[19]

Of course, countless fathers may regret, and with cause, time spent at work. The pervasiveness of this lament should prompt historians of this particular masculine trait in fathers at work to contextualize it within both the career course and the life course of any individual father's history as a father. This particular face of fatherhood, in other words, appears in fathers who may have overworked at one point in their career but learned to adapt to parenting demands within their respective family as a gendered and classed regime. Family lives had long life courses, and while some fathers may have grown accustomed to, even comfortable with, the masculine face of father as workaholic, it was not always worn by family men as a sign of their drive for success.

The following illustration introduces this potential ambiguity in the judgments made by a father in the postwar period facing considerable stress and conflict between his home life, challenged by a daughter with cystic fibrosis, and

his demanding career in the lumber business, a family business in his case that thrived in southern Ontario during the 1960s as suburbs grew.

This portrait of a lumber firm owner and father from Brantford, Ontario, Doug Summerhayes, comes through the memoir of his daughter, Heather. She recalled a father distracted by the dual demands of parenting a chronically ill child and running his business. Her sister would have died during her childhood without intensive, ongoing treatment at home and in hospital. Doug Summerhayes dealt with this and with his daily demands at the office, at the lumberyard, and on the road. His daughter writes of a father who loved her, yet forgot she was even there from time to time: "[M]y father was indeed sad, profoundly sad," she recalled of him during a period in their family's past when the local paper, the *Brantford Expositor*, ran stories like "Saddened Father Tells Cystic Fibrosis Story."

Perhaps as compensatory behaviour, Doug Summerhayes seemed to bury himself in his work: "He distanced himself from sorrow with activity," his daughter remembered. "He was always on the telephone or on the fly. Out the door, in the car, off to the lumberyard. Late for a meeting, gone to make a speech, rushing to the airport. Even when he was home he was distracted." . . .

Two incidents, from this period, remained marked in his daughter's memories. The first was when he took her to the lumberyard at Tillsonburg and told her to wait in the car: "'I'll be just few minutes,' he promised." As she described, "Two hours later, when I wandered into the showroom complaining that I had to pee, he looked at me stunned, and asked me where the hell I'd come from." The next was more dramatic: "A few months later, on a cold January afternoon, he forgot to pick me up from my ballet lessons at the YWCA. I waited and waited, watching the shadows lengthen outside the lobby window." After calling home and his office and with "no dimes left to take the bus" she decided to walk: "I slipped and stumbled down the glistening sidewalk in the freezing twilight, hatless, bootless, without mittens, wearing only my coat, ballet slippers, and leotard." Then, she saw her father race past in the car:

> Frantic, I yelled and waved. He made a U-turn in the middle of the hill and sped back where I stood. I clambered into his car, all snotty and frosted red. We did not know whether to laugh or cry. He handed me his big linen hankie so I could blow my nose. "You forgot me," I exploded in tears. "Aw, come here," he said chuckling, folding me up in his long arms and pulling me to his chest. "Why, Daddy?" I wept into his overcoat. "What made you forget?" "I don't know." His arms fell away from me. He removed his glasses and pinched his nose between his eyes. He sighed deeply. "I guess I've just got a lot on my mind lately."[20] . . .

Father as workaholic does not imply an addiction to work, but rather a chosen work life that has an impact on absences at home—a masculine drive for power in the public sphere through work. Self-employed fathers, professionals, and politicians were among those in this period . . . who took pride in their hard work, often measuring this by the sacrifice they had to make at home. But working-class fathers, too, working shifts, at distant work sites from their homes, or moving from job to job to make ends meet, also often had little choice but to place work demands before those of family. These illustrations do not suggest a crisis in masculinity. They do not recount the experiences of men and perceptions of children who felt their masculinity as fathers was under attack. Some fathers may, in retrospect, have come to wish they could have spent more time home as involved parents, but perhaps only through a kind of life myth provided by memory. Lévi-Strauss argued that myths can "provide a logical model capable of overcoming an apparent contradiction."[21] In this case, a "time away" myth, when expressed by the fathers themselves, can reflect the dual sense of power and achievement as masculine agent some fathers feel when looking back at their accomplishments as men, but not when looking back at their accomplishments as fathers. Their "greatest

single regret" becomes a mythical lamentation, a life myth rehearsed in memories of family life, used to overcome the logical contradiction of not being home to parent. Masculine power in the public sphere was, and is in memory, the *preferred* category of manhood for fathers who moan and groan in old age that they wish they could turn back the clock and return to spend more time with children who have long since grown up. Fathers did not face a crisis over their masculinity as providers. For fathers, wearing the workaholic face either periodically or constantly in their working lives could be a chosen, if not preferred, avenue of time expenditure. In labour markets that discriminated against women and in gendered family regimes that privileged male breadwinning, masculine power, and privilege were often exercised by fathers through this face, father as workaholic. Ironically, it was often worn at the time—when Canada's postwar generation of children were growing up—as a face of responsible family manhood.

Conclusion

At one extreme, being responsible could translate into authoritarian fatherhoods that verged on the tyrannical. Indeed some of the "lost" men in the examples above did not succeed in their masculine search for effective male parenting, but not because their masculinity had eroded. They did not know how best to apply male assertiveness as fathers either with their children or in acting *in loco parentis*. In many cases of tyrannical fatherhood, if anything served to influence how this dysfunctional category of masculinity was expressed, it was how these men had grown up themselves, how particular models of fatherhood and parenting had taken shape for them when they were boys and youths in the interwar period.

For many fathers, too, work demands were satisfied to pursue what was considered to be *responsible* fatherhood. During part of these fathers' careers, employment gains led to workaholic patterns that some may have been able to correct, but that others failed to address throughout their working lives. But this was not a disruption of masculine assertiveness in shaping the provider's role. Rather, it was a question of balance, or lack thereof. Fulfilling the drive for security was a sign of a father's masculinity, not its erosion. Laments for this were often expressed in hindsight and represented undoubtedly, for some, their biggest single regret when they looked back on their own lives. . . .

Between the tyrants and the workaholics fell many fathers who nurtured, who taught their children whatever they thought was important in a non-authoritarian manner, or who became in their children's eyes good role models as teachers of how to live and how to grow up. These family and fatherhood histories, again, did not signify a masculinity crisis; quite the reverse. In such cases, masculine role modelling as seen in the face of father as teacher demonstrated a category of masculinity that suited the activity or problem at hand in guiding children toward some recreational pursuit or new level of understanding. For purposes of historical interpretation, fatherhood histories emerged in this period through types of male parenting connected to men's efforts to

be responsible parents, good or bad, successful or not. . . . As a category of masculinity, responsible family manhood can offer a useful analytical spectrum. At one extreme, some fathers emerged in the postwar decades as tyrants through their relationships with their children. In a more positive light and within their intimate relations at home, others emerged as male parents who were, in fact, not in crisis at all, either as fathers or as role models. Still others did seem, as the prescriptive literature warned, unable to rectify very real, even destructive, tensions between their provider and parenting functions. Work could become a hazardous yet empowering form of escape in workaholic patterns that some fathers later came to regret. But even this face of fatherhood was not a failed category of masculinity so much as a misapplied one that foiled efforts to be an effective, involved parent. Being on the job too much took its place among the less successful aspects of male parenting in the flow of daily experiences for many fathers.

These categories—tyrant, teacher, and workaholic—were constructed over the family's life course through relationships with spouses and children. . . .

Endnotes

1   See John Demos, "The Changing Faces of Fatherhood," in idem, *Past, Present, and Personal: The Family and Life Course in American History* (Oxford, 1986), 41–67.

2   As noted in the conclusion of the paper, approximately 120 life stories, as memoirs, autobiographies, and biographies, and 30 oral history interviews (fathers and other family members) have been assessed in the larger project from which this is drawn. In a variety of Canadian locales (located in Nova Scotia, Ontario, Saskatchewan, and British Columbia), life story interviews were conducted in English and followed the ethics guidelines of the Social Sciences and Humanities Research Council of Canada. I have also incorporated life writing rooted in the memories of family experience in the 1945–75 period from Newfoundland to British Columbia: approximately 120 memoirs and autobiographies from the perspectives of daughters, sons, wives and mothers, and husbands and fathers.

3   See John Tosh, "What Should Historians Do with Masculinity: Reflections on Nineteenth-Century Britain," in idem, *Manliness and Masculinities in Nineteenth-Century Britain: Essays on Gender, Empire, and Family* (Harlow, UK, 2005), 29–56.

4   Canada's baby boom was concentrated in the 1949 to 1961 period. See Doug Owram, *Born at the Right Time: A History of the Baby Boom Generation* (Toronto, 1996), especially chap. 1.

5   James Gilbert, *Men in the Middle: Searching for Masculinity in the 1950s* (Chicago, 2005), 217.

6   Roy Gibson interview, Prince George, BC, 22 March 1995 (pseudonyms are used in all references to interview subjects).

7   Sam Taylor interview, Prince George, BC, 15 March 1995.

8   David Benson interview, Prince George, BC, 4 April 1995.

9   See Owram, *Born at the Right Time*, especially chap. 10. See also Christabelle Sethna, "'Chastity

Outmoded!' The *Ubyssey*, Sex, and the Single Girl, 1960–70," in Magda Fahni and Robert Rutherdale, *Creating Postwar Canada: Community, Diversity, and Dissent, 1945–1975* (Vancouver, 2008), 289–314.

10 Linwood Barclay, *Last Resort: Coming of Age in Cottage Country* (Toronto, 2000), 101–2.

11 David Zieroth, *The Education of Mr. Whippoorwill: A Country Boyhood* (Toronto, 2002), 7–8.

12 Ibid., 10.

13 Chris Cuthbert and Scott Russell, *The Rink: Stories from Hockey's Home Towns* (Toronto, 1997), 259.

14 Ibid., 258. Anatoly Tarasov has been called the father of Soviet hockey. For over two decades Tarasov was the head coach of the Moscow Red Army Team.

He also coached Olympic and world championship teams representing the USSR. Tarasov wrote over 20 books about hockey.

15 Cuthbert and Russell, *The Rink*, 259.

16 Bill Thompson interview, Sault Ste Marie, ON, 11 May 2004.

17 Charles Templeton, *Charles Templeton: An Anecdotal Memoir* (Toronto, 1983), 348.

18 Brad Templeton's memories of his father are found on his webpage. See "Charles Templeton (1915–2001)," www.templetons.com/brad/cbt.html.

19 Templeton, *Charles Templeton*, 348–9.

20 Ibid., 97–9.

21 Claude Lévi Strauss, *Structural Anthropology* (London, 1958), 229.

PART V

Suggested Readings

Barrington, Dean. *Managed Annihilation: An Unnatural History of the Newfoundland Cod Collapse.* Vancouver: UBC Press, 2010.

Dummitt, Christopher. *The Manly Modern: Masculinity in Postwar Canada.* Vancouver: UBC Press, 2007.

Loo, Tina. *States of Nature: Conserving Canada's Wildlife in the Twentieth Century.* Vancouver: UBC Press, 2006.

Martel, Marcel. *Not This Time: Canadians, Public Policy, and the Marijuana Question, 1961–1975.* Toronto: University of Toronto Press, 2006.

Owram, Doug. *Born at the Right Time: A History of the Baby Boom Generation.* Toronto: University of Toronto Press, 1997.

Palmer, Bryan D. *Canada's 1960s: The Ironies of Identity in a Rebellious Era.* Toronto: University of Toronto Press, 2009.

Key Terms

conservation
counter-culture
ecosystem
hydrological
in loco parentis

"laissez-faire" economics
modernism
patriarchy
technocratic

Questions for Consideration

1. What is meant by a "technocratic" approach to pollution and how might it be used in developing solutions to pollution or environmental problems?

2. Examine the tension between economic development and social and environmental needs/demands.

3. What factors led to increased awareness and action to address the environmental impacts of human action in the years after 1945?

4. What is meant by "environmental justice" and how is this concept related to the changes experienced by the people impacted by the Peace River dam?

5. How and why did the content of the TADP manual for American draft resisters change?

6. What factors led to the critique of social values (such as those surrounding sexuality) and to the mobilization of 1960s youth?

7. What changes in values and beliefs among young people led to the demand for birth control?

8. In what ways has gender ideology changed over the postwar years and in what ways has it not changed?

9. What was the "crisis of masculinity" in the period from 1945 to the 1960s and is it an accurate description of the experiences of postwar fathers?

Relevant Websites

Canadian Dimension—"Canada 1960s"
http://canadiandimension.com/articles/2482

Government of Canada. Environment Canada
www.ec.gc.ca/default.asp?lang=En&n=FD9B0E51-1

Green Emerge—Articles on Environmental Movement
www.greenemerge.com/Canada.html

Greenpeace—Publications
www.greenpeace.org/canada/en/
documents-and-links/

PBS—"People and Events: The Pill and the Sexual Revolution"

www.pbs.org/wgbh/amex/pill/peopleevents/e_revolution.html

Statistics Canada—"Fifty Years of Families in Canada, 1961–2011"
www12.statcan.gc.ca/census-recensement/2011/as-sa/98-312-x/98-312-x2011003_1-eng.cfm

University of British Columbia Library—Vietnam War Resisters in Canada
www.library.ubc.ca/jones/amcan.html

Vanier Institute of the Family
www.vanierinstitute.ca/home_page

Conclusion

The two primary themes of this book are change and challenge. Since 1945, there is no doubt that Canada and Canadians have experienced fundamental change, politically, economically, and socially; this change has transformed and redefined the nation such that the Canada that exists today bears little resemblance to the nation that emerged from the Second World War. Yet challenges also defined these years, challenges that caused uncertainty, division, and conflict, many of which are ongoing. Thus, many of the changes and challenges of the postwar years continue to evolve, presenting both uncertainty and intrigue about the future.

To examine these dominant themes of change and challenge, the book is divided into five parts: national identity and nationalism; federalism, liberalism, and regionalism; Canada and the world; the rights revolution; and changing values and norms. While all of these themes are important in an examination of Canada's development since 1945, they incorporate additional significant themes that overlap with the chapter divisions. Thus, in this conclusion to the collection, the interconnections between the themes and sections of the book and the additional themes and issues will be discussed so that we might more fully understand the development of Canada since 1945.

Related to the development of the welfare state discussed in Part II is the greater security and opportunity—and thus the significant improvement in the standard of living and lifestyles—experienced by "average" Canadians after the Second World War, a theme only indirectly examined in this book. While the creation of the welfare state generated debate over federalism and government intervention into the lives of Canadians, the welfare state was also a product of the demand for greater socio-economic security and equity. Premised on the liberal concept of "social citizenship" and furthered by the promise of a "just society," legislation in the areas of health, education, and welfare, combined with other reforms, such as the implementation of health and safety standards for workers, improved the overall conditions and economic security of Canadians. The labour movement, strengthened by government-protected collective bargaining and the development of public-sector unions by the 1960s, as examined in the first reading in chapter 6, furthered this improvement and diminished the stark class divisions that had existed prior to the Second World War. The change in lifestyles also related to improvements in gender equality and the rights and labour force participation of women, topics examined in Part IV and, partially, Part V. This important theme fits within the rights revolution theme of Part IV, as economic equality and social justice were important components of the equality and rights movements, particularly given the connections between socialists and labour and the civil rights movements that Carmela Patrias reveals in the second reading in chapter 10.

Another important theme of the book that overlaps several sections is the long-standing question of national unity. The instability occasioned by the ongoing (and growing?) regionalism and uncertainty surrounding the nature of federalism, as well as by the potential weakening of the social union brought on by decentralization of power and neo-liberalism, must be understood in terms of the distinctive ethnocultural nationalisms of Quebec and the First Nations, examined in Part I. With both Quebec and the First Nations deemed as nations within a nation, the nationalist concepts and political demands of both of them seriously undermine the concept of Canada as a nation in the traditional geo-political sense. Many would argue that the political self-governance and geographic concepts of territory held by both groups, if achieved, would undermine the unity of the nation. Other aspects of identity explored in Part I have been perceived as destabilizing forces for national unity. The multicultural diversity of Canada, brought about by both official policies and the demands for rights and equality furthered by the rights revolution, has made building national unity on the basis of a common identity an impossibility. Many argue that our celebration of diversity ultimately precludes the development of common characteristics that define us as "Canadian." The Charter of Rights and Freedoms, often viewed as the paramount achievement of Canada's rights revolution and in itself a form of nation-building as it made the Constitution purely "Canadian," nonetheless greatly exacerbated the tension between Quebec and the rest of Canada and furthered the reality of a decentralized federation by empowering the judiciary over Parliament and expanding provincial powers.

Yet, ironically, many of the factors that potentially destabilize the union also contribute to the tenuous sense of identity held by Canadians, and thus the theme of national identity explored in Part I overlaps and includes issues and themes explored in other parts of the book. Multiculturalism, both in the growing ethnic and cultural diversity of Canadians and as an official policy of promoting and protecting cultural diversity, has increasingly come to identify Canada since the 1960s. While certainly related to the equality and rights movements outlined in Part IV, multiculturalism and the culture of rights and equality—most clearly symbolized by the Charter—have increasingly combined to create a civic identity for Canadians based on the principles of diversity, tolerance, and equality. Diversity informs Canadian identity in other ways as well. The diversities of regions, geographies, and regional identities and cultures, as much as they polarize the country, have also come to symbolize a distinctly Canadian (as opposed to American) nature.

While the wilderness, climate, and vastness of Canada have long been characteristics of identity in Canadian literature and art, different expressions of this "wilderness" identity can be noted since 1945, particularly in the notion of Canada as an Arctic nation, creating a small but notable reason for Canada's concern for Arctic sovereignty, and in the environmental movement and its growing popularity and advocacy among Canadians. Regional identities have been envisioned as part of Canada's distinctiveness; examples include the popularity of maritime music and the sitcom *Corner Gas*, which is situated in the slow-moving town of Dog River, Saskatchewan. Overall, as is evident in the article on Canadian culture in chapter 3, expressions of a distinct Canadian identity permeate much of Canada's cultural forms and find some resonance among Canadians, regardless of the extent to which cultural protection has helped Can-Con survive.

Questions of national identity also correlate with the foreign policy and relations issues examined in Part III. A prominent theme in several of the articles is the extent to which Canada has directed its actions in the interest of securing international peace and of protecting human rights and well-being (rather than being constrained by alliance politics). This question relates to an important component of national identity that has developed since 1945—Canada as a "peacekeeper" and a country motivated by humanitarianism in its international relations. Canada's peacekeeper image developed from its prominent role in United Nations peacekeeping initiatives since 1945 and, of course, from Lester B. Pearson's use of peacekeeping to resolve the Suez Crisis in 1956. The extent to which Canada has defended the rights and needs of peoples in other troubled regions of the world is more contentious but certainly relates to the culture of rights and equality that informs a significant part of Canadian identity. Canada's success in this role has also depended on its involvement in the larger international community and on the actions of non-governmental organizations that have sought to ensure the well-being and human rights of people throughout the world. The influence of international organizations and groups on Canadian ideas and policies is noted in a number of articles in the rights revolution section but would benefit from greater investigation.

The theme of Canadian sovereignty within international relations—in particular Canada's ability to act independently of US leadership in world affairs—correlates with several other themes or issues explored in the book and in the historical scholarship on this period. Stephen Azzi's article in chapter 9 points to one important debate since 1945—the implications of the substantial integration, and thus "dependence," of Canada's economy into the US economy since 1945. The implications for Canadian government control over national economic policies have become even more pressing with the trade liberalization and globalization that have accelerated since the 1980s (as examined partially in chapter 6). While many scholars note the economic benefits for economic growth occasioned by globalization and by the development of an integrated North American economy, debate continues as to whether Canada has become too dependent on access to the US economy and whether such dependence could influence Canadian foreign policy decisions, the motivation being to avoid alienating US favour. While this issue is evident in Part III, the implications for Canadian sovereignty in policy-making go beyond trade or foreign policy to encompass such related components as environmental policy.

The environmental movement, examined in Part V, is an international force, much like the human rights movement, and environmental issues are increasingly becoming of global concern, as evident in the debates surrounding the Kyoto Accord. Global environmental issues—like global warming—require international cooperation and raise the question as to whether Canada can become a leader or will fail to act responsibly as defined by the environmental movement owing to its determination to avoid alienating the United States. More directly, the Canadian environmental movement's goal of achieving or improving environmental standards within the country is potentially compromised if such standards do not exist in the United States or other countries with which Canada conducts business, since a significantly higher cost would accrue to Canadian business in meeting environmental regulations. Similarly, social and labour standards, such as those developed to ensure the just society, could be affected by international trade agreements or by the question of Canadian business competitiveness in a globalized trade environment. Finally, questions of sovereignty, economic development, and environmentalism all come together in the important issue of Canada's sovereignty in the Arctic, as seen in chapter 9, further revealing the interconnections between the different sections of the book.

Among the most important themes structuring this book are the developments in human rights and equality since 1945. This is the subject of Part IV, and the overlap of rights and equality issues and movements with other major themes and sections of this book is evident from the above discussion. The achievements and controversies surrounding human rights and equality relate to issues of the welfare state and "social citizenship" and to the role of government in creating a just society. They have also been shown to relate to multiculturalism and to be an aspect of the Canadian identity, while also being a theme that goes beyond Canada's national boundaries to influence aspects of Canada's international relations and policy. In addition, the issues surrounding Quebec and the First Nations also fall under the major theme of the rights revolution. While the political goals and national ideologies of Quebec and the First Nations influence important themes of postwar history, such as federalism, regionalism, and national unity, they could be argued to be a natural outcome of the concept of rights and equality that has been evolving since the end of the Second World War. Since 1945, the rights ideology has expanded as more potential reasons for discrimination have found recognition, and thus the groups and collective minorities deserving of protection have also enlarged. As noted, early human rights organizations fought primarily against racial and religious discrimination; in successive decades, sex, sexual orientation, disability, and age, among other criteria, came to be recognized as the basis for rights activism. Similarly, the concept of what constitutes a "right" and how this right can be protected and social equality promoted have also expanded. The recognition that inequality and discrimination can be perpetuated in complex, systemic, and institutional ways has similarly made it clear that social justice may require more complex solutions than the implementation of public education campaigns or anti-discrimination laws. Thus, the Quebecois and the First Nations may possess rights specific to their historical circumstances and separate from those of other groups; cultural distinctiveness may require the expansion of the concept of rights to include some form of political and territorial self-governance, a right that currently appears to conflict with ideas about a shared national interest. This relates to another issue or debate surrounding the rights revolution. The protection of individual or group rights can conflict with the rights of others in society or with the larger social well-being. An evident example is the extension of legal marriage to gay and lesbian couples. While seemingly a straightforward measure to address discrimination against same-sex couples, the redefinition of marriage in 2005 potentially violated the rights of religious groups from whom the traditional definition of marriage as a union between a man and a woman originated. While this conflict appears to have been resolved, with individual religions being allowed to decide on their own strictures whether to accept same-sex marriage, the example does reveal the complexity and conflict that permeate the goal of building a society premised on rights and equality for all.

The rights movements point to an additional important theme and that is the impact of the baby boom generation. As noted in the Introduction, the history of the postwar years has been indelibly shaped by this generation, born between 1945 and 1965, because of its large size. The needs, demands, and actions of this group as they moved through the various stages of the life cycle have directly shaped social, political, and economic policy and issues. As discussed in Part IV, the baby boomers strengthened the different rights movements, their participation transforming them into mainstream movements and giving greater credence to the ideas and critiques put forward. Similarly, Part V reveals the impact of the youthful baby boomers in challenging the social and political values of Canada. Both of these examples point to the impact of this cohort during the late 1960s and early

1970s as they became teenagers and young adults and took leading roles in the activism of these tumultuous decades. This large group, however, indirectly influenced a number of other events and issues of this time period. The welfare state—more specifically the expansion of health, education, and welfare—was in part a natural outcome of the demand on society to meet the needs of this large cohort. Along with addressing the societal desire for greater economic security and social justice and thus for a better life for these young people than that of previous generations, the Canadian society enacted social policies, such as expanded educational facilities and programs, to accommodate the large number of young people moving through the system. The combination of these factors propelled the baby boomers into social activism but specifically led young baby-boomer women to challenge traditional gender ideologies, achieve increasingly higher levels of education, and become permanent members of the labour force. While many of the social and ideological changes and challenges would have occurred regardless, as the baby boomers were not the only agents of change, nonetheless their demographic strength influenced the speed and direction of change. Today, the baby boomers continue to influence, most notably in social policy debates concerning the rising cost and questionable sustainability of medicare as the boomers enter their senior years. Their influence on governmental policy is also evident in the fact that the baby boomers are members of government.

Finally, the changes to values and norms examined in Part V interconnect with several other issues and themes, some examined in this book and some not. As noted in the discussion above, the desire for greater economic security, equality of opportunity, and a just society influenced social movements, political ideologies and policies, and issues of identity and national unity. Such goals were the product of changes in social values and norms as Canadians rejected older traditional norms surrounding issues of morality, gender, family, race, and class. The rejection of inequitable power and gender roles within the family fuelled significant changes, such as the movement of women into the labour force and a greater role for fathers in parenting, even if total equality in the public and private spheres was not achieved immediately. The liberalization of values exemplified by a rejection of the moral belief that sex should only occur within marriage similarly was related to the growing individualism and secularism of society and the rejection of moral codes previously utilized to subjugate women, minorities, and the poor. An example of this trend not included in the book is the debate surrounding liquor laws. Provincial liquor laws underwent significant liberalization after 1960 as a result of the rejection of the older temperance idea that alcohol use was a deviant behaviour vested in the lower orders of society—immigrants, working-class males, and prostitutes—and thus socially harmful. Postwar society, however, increasingly viewed alcohol use as an acceptable leisure activity, with the choice to consume a private one, as long as the behaviour did not extend to social harm, such as through drunk driving. The emphasis on individualism and individual rights meant that behaviours and values that did not cause larger social harm were viewed as matters that should be left to individual choice and not regulated. This spurred an overall greater tolerance of diversity, the ethnocultural diversity and multiculturalism noted above, but also the growing diversity of gender roles and the variability of family forms and types of conjugal unions seen in Canadian families since the 1960s. Clearly, while substantial change has occurred in social values and norms and in lifestyles, particularly in the areas of gender and family, challenges remain, as significant debate and concern continue to surround the question of whether these changes in moral values, gender roles, and family life constitute a natural progression or a fundamental destabilization of society.

This question of "progress" versus "breakdown" leads to a final point about the nature of an examination of the years from 1945 to the present. It has been emphasized in the chapters of this book that these were years of substantial and fundamental change in a relatively short historical time of just over 65 years. It has also been emphasized that many of the changes are still underway and thus represent challenges yet to be resolved and outcomes that are uncertain. The question of whether changes to family and gender constitute progress or social instability is an example of this theme of challenge (and uncertainty). Issues such as national unity, identity, the rights of the First Nations, the place of Quebec within Confederation, the future of the welfare state, the implications of trade liberalization, and many of the other themes raised in this book all point to the benefits that can be derived by studying the history of modern Canada. The benefits arise from gaining an understanding of how and why Canada has changed so markedly and how it has come to be the nation it is today, but they also arise, perhaps, from being given a better means for grappling with the challenges still before us.

Glossary

anti-Semitism Prejudice and/or hatred toward Jews

Auto Pact 1965 trade agreement between Canada and the United States that removed tariffs on autos and auto parts, creating North American free trade for the auto industry

Bill of Rights 1960 federal statute prohibiting discrimination on the basis of race, colour, national origin, religion, and sex

civil rights The personal rights held by an individual resulting from his or her citizenship within a nation

colonialism The practice of acquiring control over another territory and its people, usually characterized by exploitation of its resources and inequitable treatment of its people

conservation Movement or action to preserve and protect the natural environment and wildlife

counter-culture A protest movement of youth in the 1960s and 1970s against the values and norms of their parents

cultural pluralism A society in which minority groups maintain their unique cultural identities and respect for cultural diversity is encouraged

decolonization The transition from colonial status to political independence; the dismantlement of the imperial empires held by European powers, such as Britain, after the Second World War

ecosystem A system of interaction among organisms and the physical environment

ecumenical Promoting, or relating to, unity among the world's Christian churches

evangelization To preach the tenets of a religion usually with the objective of conversion

familism Social system in which the interests and needs of the family take precedence over those of the individual; ideology that promotes family values and interests as the basis of social stability

feminism Ideology promoting equal political, economic, and social rights for women

Fordist System of production based on mass production and production efficiency and the payment of decent wages to workers to allow for mass consumption

governance The act or method of governing

humanism Philosophy that focuses on the nature and value of human beings and seeks rational explanations for human concerns rather than religious ones

human rights The fundamental rights and freedoms that belong to all individuals as human beings

hydrology The study of the distribution and effects of water on the earth's surface and in its atmosphere

"imagined community" Concept developed by Benedict Anderson of a nation as a socially constructed community, existing because its members believe ("imagine") it to be

imperialism The extension of control of one state or people over others, usually by territorial acquisition or political and economic dominance

in loco parentis A legal term that refers to a person who assumes parental rights and responsibilities for a child

internationalism The ideal or practice of encouraging cooperation among nations, usually in the interest of peace, security, or a common good

Keynesian economics Economic theory that argues for greater state intervention in the economy to encourage economic well-being through contra-cyclical spending and wealth redistribution programs

"laissez-faire" Theory in which government should not interfere in the economy or private sector (through regulations, tariffs, taxes, etc.)

liberalism Political philosophy that argues for social progress through representative, parliamentary government that promotes freedom of the individual and civil and political liberties

liberation(ist) A movement or an ideology directed towards achieving equal rights and opportunity for a minority or disadvantaged group

modernism Ideological movement that rejected the nineteenth-century concept that humans were above nature, arguing human interconnection and dependence upon nature

multilateral Participation by multiple nations in an organization, an agreement, or a common cause

multiversality The idea that identities and differences among people are multiple and incorporate factors beyond ethnicity or national origin and that there are differences and divisions of identity within minority communities because of the multiple social universes that inform identity

neo-liberal Political and economic philosophy that argues that direct governmental intervention in the economy be limited so as to facilitate greater marketplace control

New Left Political movement of the 1960s that advocated social and economic equality among groups and nations and was critical of capitalism, imperialism, and traditional parliamentary governing systems

non-alignment A foreign policy choice to reject alliance or membership with another nation or bloc of nations; neutrality

October Crisis A series of events in 1970 triggered by the kidnapping of James Cross, British trade commissioner, and Pierre Laporte, minister of labour and immigration, by the Front de libération du Québec

"opt-out" Refers to provisions that allow a provincial government to choose not to participate in a social program but still to receive money allotted for the program from the federal government

patriarchy A system of society in which men hold power over women, in government, in the economy, and in the family

provincialism To focus on the interests of a province or locality rather than on those of the larger nation

racialized The social construction of racial identities or interpretations

social conservatism An ideology that promotes adherence to traditional or past social values, particularly with relation to morality, family, and sexuality

Social Credit A political philosophy and party that calls for expansion, rather than redistribution, of the money supply in order to increase consumer spending and therefore overall social well-being

social democratic A political philosophy that advocates for greater social and economic equality through democratic political practices and policy measures that balance socialism with capitalism, including (but not exclusive to) a comprehensive welfare state and government regulation or ownership of major economic sectors

social security A broad term encompassing any government program directed towards promoting the social and economic well-being of citizens

technocratic Relating to a theory or system of government in which science and technology are the basis for decision-making

transnational Extending beyond national boundaries or involving several nations

universality Refers to social security measures that are inclusive or apply to all citizens regardless of socio-economic position

Western alienation Refers to the discontent of the western provinces resulting from the belief that their interests are neglected by the federal government in its spending and national policies, generally in favour of central Canada (Quebec and Ontario)

Credits

Grateful acknowledgment is made for permission to use the following material:

Azzi, Stephen. "Foreign Investment and the Paradox of Economic Nationalism," in Norman Hillmer & Adam Chapnick, eds, *Canadas of the Mind. The Making and Unmaking of Canadian Nationalisms in the Twentieth Century* (Montreal & Kingston: McGill-Queen's University Press, 2007, 63–88.

Behiels, Michael D. "Mulroney and a Nationalist Quebec: Key to Political Realignment in Canada?" In *Transforming the Nation: Canada and Brian Mulroney*. Montreal & Kingston: McGill-Queen's University Press, 2007.

Blake, Raymond. "Intergovernmental Relations Trumps Social Policy Change: Trudeau, Constitutionalism, and Family Allowances," *Journal of the Canadian Historical Association*, 2007, 18(1): 207–39.

Brouwer, Ruth Compton. "When Missions Became Development: Ironies of 'NGOization' in Mainstream Canadian Churches in the 1960s," *Canadian Historical Review*, 2010, 91(4): 661–93. Reprinted with permission from University of Toronto Press (www.utpjournals.com).

Clément, Dominique. "Generations and the Transformation of Social Movements in Postwar Canada," *Histoire Sociale/Social History*, 2009, 42, 84: 361–87.

Finkel, Alvin. "Alberta Social Credit and the Second National Policy," in Robert Wardhaugh, ed., *Toward Defining the Prairies: Region, Culture and History*. Winnipeg: University of Manitoba Press, 2001: 29–50.

Goldfield, Michael and Bryan D. Palmer. "Canada's Workers Movement: Uneven Developments," *Labour/Le Travail*, 59 (Spring 2007), 149–77. Reprinted by permission of the publisher.

Hayday, Matthew. "Fireworks, Folk-dancing and Fostering a National Identity: The Politics of Canada Day," *Canadian Historical Review*, 2010, 91(2): 287–314. Reprinted with permission from University of Toronto Press (www.utpjournals.com).

Loo, Tina. "Disturbing the Peace: Environmental Change and the Scales of Justice on a Northern River," *Environmental History*, 2007, 12(4): 895–919.

Newhouse, David. "Aboriginal Identities and the New Indian Problem," in Norman Hillmer & Adam Chapnick, eds. *Canadas of the Mind. The Making and Unmaking of Canadian Nationalisms in the Twentieth Century*. Montreal & Kingston: McGill-Queen's University Press, 2007: 287–99.

Patrias, Carmela. "Socialists, Jews, and the 1947 Saskatchewan Bill of Rights," *Canadian Historical Review*, 2006, 87 (2): 265–92. Reprinted with permission from University of Toronto Press (www.utpjournals.com).

Preston, Andrew. "Balancing War and Peace: Canadian Foreign Policy and the Vietnam War, 1961–1965," *Diplomatic History*, 2003, 27(1): 73–111.

Purdy, Sean. "'It was Tough on Everybody': Low-Income Families and Housing Hardship in Post–World War II Toronto," *Journal of Social History*, 2002, 37(2): 457–82.

Rutherdale, Robert. "Three Faces of Fatherhood as a Masculine Category: Tyrants, Teachers, and Workaholics as 'Responsible Family Men' during Canada's Baby Boom" in *What is Masculinity?* Edited by John H. Arnold and Sean Brady. Basingstoke, United Kingdom: Palgrave Macmillan, 2011: 323–48.

Sethna, Christabelle. "The University of Toronto Health Service, Oral Contraception and Student Demand for Birth Control, 1960–70," *Historical Studies in Education*, 2005, 17(2): 265–92.

Smith, Miriam. "Social Movements and Judicial Empowerment: Courts, Public Policy, and Lesbian and Gay Organizing in Canada," *Politics and Society*, 2005, 33 (2): 327–53.